The Pros Talk
Microsoft® Visual FoxPro™ 3

PINNACLE PUBLISHING SPECIAL REPORTS

Strategic Issues for Developers

Edited by Whil Hentzen

Pinnacle Publishing, Inc.

Microsoft·Press

PUBLISHED BY
Microsoft Press
A Division of Microsoft Corporation
One Microsoft Way
Redmond, Washington 98052-6399

Library of Congress Cataloging-in-Publication Data

The pros talk Microsoft Visual FoxPro 3 / Pinnacle Publishing, Inc. ;
   Doug Hennig ... [et al.].
      p. cm.
    Includes index.
    ISBN 1-57231-233-5
    1. Visual FoxPro for Windows.   2. Database management.
3. Client/server computing.   I. Hennig, Doug.   II. Pinnacle
Publishing, Inc.
QA76.9.D3D779   1996
005.75'65--dc20   95-53870
                                                       CIP

Printed and bound in the United States of America.

1 2 3 4 5 6 7 8 9   RM-T   1 0 9 8 7 6

Distributed to the book trade in Canada by Macmillan of Canada, a division of Canada Publishing Corporation.

A CIP catalogue record for this book is available from the British Library.

Microsoft Press books are available through booksellers and distributors worldwide. For further information about international editions, contact your local Microsoft Corporation office. Or contact Microsoft Press International directly at fax (206) 936-7329.

The reports in this book were originally published as four separate volumes in the Special Report series by Pinnacle Publishing, Inc., Kent, WA.

Pinnacle Director of Ancillary Products: Brent P. Smith

Book development, production, and coordination by
Laing Communications Inc.

Editorial Coordination: Christine Laing, Lori Ljubicich, Emily Smith
Design and Production: Sandra Harner

For Microsoft Press

Acquisitions Editor: David Clark
Project Editor: Laura Sackerman

Pinnacle Publishing, Inc. & Microsoft Press

Pinnacle Publishing (www.pinpub.com), located in Kent, Washington, is a leading provider of technical newsletters, special reports, CD-ROMs, and add-in software for developers and power users throughout the world. Pinnacle publishes technically excellent information products for developers using Microsoft FoxPro, Microsoft Access, and Microsoft Visual Basic, as well as Microsoft Visual C++ and Microsoft SQL Server.

Microsoft Press (www.microsoft.com/mspress/) is the publishing division of Microsoft Corporation. As the official publisher of information about Microsoft products and services, Microsoft Press is dedicated to providing the highest quality computer books and multimedia training and reference tools that make using Microsoft software easier, more enjoyable, and more productive.

Contents

Welcome to *The Pros Talk Microsoft Visual FoxPro 3*

FoxPro has evolved significantly since the early versions of FoxBase+ in the mid-1980s. Back then, we pushed the envelope of advanced programming techniques by having validation clauses called within a user-input field on the screen. FoxPro version 2 left many programmers gasping for breath as Fox morphed from a procedural language to an event-driven, design-surface-based programming environment.

While a large time investment was necessary to learn FoxPro 2 well enough to fully exploit its power, those who spent the time found they could create applications that were inconceivable before version 2. Indeed, I know of one FoxPro application that manages more than 128 gigabytes (that's GB, not MB) of data, another that does real-time data collection from oceangoing ships worldwide via satellite, and a third that was used to update the U.S. joint chiefs of staff about logistical requirements during Operation Desert Storm.

Now the standard has been raised yet again. With Visual FoxPro, you can develop remarkably robust desktop, LAN/WAN, and client/server applications. The native data dictionary, the native client/server connectivity, the ability to switch transparently between local and remote databases, the new user-interface design tools, and the first fully object-oriented functionality in an Xbase database product—these functions make Visual FoxPro the tool of choice for state-of-the-art, high-performance, low-maintenance database applications. Again, this power comes at a price—the learning curve is steeper than the one you encountered with FoxPro 2.x.

However, the effort definitely is worth it. Over the last six months I've had the opportunity (and the misfortune) to see a number of Visual FoxPro applications written by individuals who hadn't invested time in the learning curve. I found that if the results of the application were anywhere near complete, they left a great deal to be desired. The programmers cherry-picked Visual FoxPro features, ending up with hodgepodge applications that looked as if they were assembled by multiple programmers who weren't allowed to talk to each other.

These programmers often couldn't get functions to work correctly and resorted to quick fixes and kludges that made reliability questionable and maintainability impossible. More often than not, the language was blamed for having shortcomings or holes. In truth, the problems were caused by the programmers' lack of familiarity and understanding.

This scenario, which is being played out repeatedly in businesses worldwide, is this book's *raison d'etre*. The four authors who have collaborated here are highly skilled developers who have specialized in their subject areas. Nowhere will you find a more comprehensive drill-down on the four features that set Visual FoxPro apart from the competition: the data dictionary, client-server functionality, the Form Designer and native controls, and object-oriented programming concepts and use. Note that we have not tried to cover every one of Visual FoxPro's features and functions; there are plenty of information sources for other aspects of Visual FoxPro. Instead, we have focused—in detail—on these four areas because using them can really give you a competitive edge with Visual FoxPro.

You'll find these four reports so densely packed with information that your head will spin before you get through a single reading. Don't let this worry you. We recommend that you plan to read this book several times. With each review, you are likely to find new nuggets that didn't make sense or seem relevant during an earlier pass. If you have comments about the book in general, please contact me via CompuServe at 70651,2270; if you have specific technical questions about one of the sections, please contact that author directly via CompuServe. Doug Hennig can be reached on CompuServe at 75156,2326; Steve Sawyer can be reached at 75730,455; Robert Green is at 76104,2514; and Dave Frankenbach can be contacted at 72147,2635. You also are welcome to contact any of us in section 2, Publications, of CompuServe's FoxUser forum.

Whil Hentzen
Milwaukee, WI
November, 1995

REPORT 1

Visual FoxPro Data Dictionary

Doug Hennig

Introduction

I've been programming personal computers since 1978. I started with a Commodore PET, then moved through Apple][+ and Macintosh, ending up with IBM compatibles. I've been programming professionally since 1982. The problem with being in this industry for that long is that you become jaded after a while. It seems as if, regardless of the glitz, hype, and hard-driving rock music played at product introductions, each new software package is more of the same stuff we've seen for years. It's been a long time since a piece of software really excited me and fired up my imagination. Then along came Microsoft Visual FoxPro.

Before getting into that, let me briefly introduce myself. No, I'm not that long-haired hippie magician you might remember from the seventies (although he's a Canadian too). I'm a guy who writes programs for a living. I've probably written more than a hundred applications of varying sizes over the years for many clients in different industries. I like to think I've learned, from painful experience, what it takes to successfully develop an application that meets a client's needs.

I started using dBASE II about a year after it was released, then switched to FoxBASE+ in 1988 when I realized that dBASE IV (which had just been released) was totally insufficient. I've used Microsoft FoxPro since it was released because it gives the right combination of things I feel are important for developing business applications:

• A well-documented and accessible DBF file structure.

- An easily learned and understood programming language (although it suffers from what some people call "dBloat," the tendency for the language to become larger and more functionally redundant as a result of efforts toward backward compatibility).
- Power tools like the Screen and Report Builders that make hand-coding screens and reports a thing of the past.
- A powerful development environment including a Command window that allows me to try things interactively, a Project Manager that ties all the pieces that make up an application together and build an APP or EXE for me, and wonderful Debug and Trace windows that have almost made debugging applications fun.

In 1992, four long-time colleagues and I started Stonefield Systems Group Inc. Although our business is primarily custom application development for government and small and medium-sized businesses, Stonefield also markets several FoxPro add-on products that I've developed, including *Stonefield Data Dictionary*, an active data dictionary for FoxPro, and *Stonefield AppMaker*, an application development framework.

In writing this report, I made a few assumptions about you:

- You're familiar with database design concepts. I'm not going to define terms such as normalization or referential integrity. If you don't know what they mean, go find out, then come back. I'll be right here waiting.
- You're not into books that present a lot of fluff. This report is meaty. I present ideas in a "things they don't tell you but you need to know" approach, and cover practical issues—not just how, but also why and when.
- You appreciate a conversational, as opposed to a rigid formal ("stuffy" in my opinion), style of writing. Let's face it: this report isn't about spies or international intrigue, it's about computers.

Introduction to the Data Dictionary

Visual FoxPro 3 is the latest version of what many believe is the best Xbase development tool available. However, calling Visual FoxPro a new version of FoxPro is like calling a 1996 Corvette an upgrade of a Ford Pinto. Sure, they'll both get you from point A to point B, but in a Corvette you'll get there faster, in more comfort, and have a lot more fun along the way.

Visual FoxPro is much more than just a new version of a great tool; it's more like a whole new product. There are many new tools and features, such as:

- Object orientation. It puts Visual FoxPro in a whole new class of development tools.
- Client/server access (via ODBC) built into the language.
- New power tools such as the Form Designer, Class Designer, Database Designer, Table Designer, and View Designer, not to mention wizards and builders to speed up creation and maintenance of application objects.
- New Form controls such as grids, PageFrames (tabbed Forms), real toolbars (not just a bunch of buttons in a window), and OLE controls (better than the VBXs Microsoft Visual Basic programmers have used for years).
- The ability to easily change almost anything (such as which fields are displayed and what pictures are used for them) while an application is running, not just at design time,
- A new event model that says good-bye to foundation READ.

- New data types such as integers and double-precision numbers.
- Support for null values.
- Built-in data buffering.
- Transaction processing.
- And, the subject of this report, a data dictionary.

Are you overwhelmed yet? If not, fire up Visual FoxPro. After an hour playing with the sample application and control samples that come with the product, you will be. You'd better be prepared to spend some time learning all of these new features.

What Is a Data Dictionary?

FoxPro has always provided the developer with wonderful tools (sometimes called *design surfaces*) to make development faster and easier: the Screen Builder, the Project Manager, the Report Builder, and so forth. However, until now FoxPro has always lacked a data dictionary.

A data dictionary is a repository of information about databases. It provides a way to manage all of the data elements that make up an application. It typically includes information about features such as file names, field names, types, sizes, and index expressions.

You might wonder why a data dictionary is important when FoxPro already provides the Display Structure command to determine DBF structures. Here are several reasons:

- File definitions keep the minimum amount of information about a field (the name, type, and size). There is no place in the file structure to record other information such as the purpose of a field or validation information. Index file definitions keep only the index expression and index or tag name, not information about whether or not the index is the primary key for the file. Relations are not stored at all, so the developer must program them by hand every time they're needed.
- Because field names are only 10 characters long and don't allow spaces, developers must often resort to using cryptic field names such as COMP_NUM for company number and LAST_UP for date of last update. Users certainly won't know what these names mean, and even developers can forget after a while.
- File definitions are stored in the Header of the file itself. People who have experienced a power outage or had a file server crash while they were doing data entry know that file Headers can become corrupted, potentially destroying the only definition for the file structure. Also, when files

are installed for the first time, developers must either ship an empty copy of the file or write a program by hand to create the file.

- When a file structure changes, it's possible that indexes will need to be rebuilt or new indexes will need to be created. This is a manual process using FoxPro's built-in commands.

- The complexity of an application with even a relatively small number of files and fields can quickly overwhelm a developer who must rely on memory to keep track of which field belongs in which file, and each file's use.

By providing a complete description of the data elements in an application, a good data dictionary provides you with the necessary information to rebuild DBF files and indexes, track field definitions and purposes, and identify design flaws before they become maintenance nightmares.

Data-Driven Applications

Extending the concept of the data dictionary leads to the idea of *data-driven* applications. The term data-driven means that the application works from the data rather than the other way around. Data-driven routines use the data dictionary as their source of information about how to do their job, instead of the user having to hard-code the necessary tasks.

Many utilities like the one shown have been written to reindex the files in an application. For example:

```
use COMPANY
index on COMP_NUM    tag COMP_NUM
index on upper(COMPANY)tag COMPANY
index on upper(LAST_NAME) tag CONTACT
use INVOICES
index on INV_NUM     tag INV_NUM
```

There are two problems with this approach.

- If you add or remove a file from the application or change a tag, you must remember to change the reindex utility. Otherwise, you could have a maintenance headache the next time the user reindexes the files.

- You have to custom write a similar program for every application you write.

With a data dictionary, you could write a simple routine that uses the data dictionary to determine which files to reindex and how to reindex them.

Think of the data dictionary as the engine that drives the application. When you make a change to the data dictionary, any data-driven module will automatically adjust to the data definitions. No more hand writing or modifying database maintenance routines!

Using data-driven techniques provides you with benefits that include the following:

- Reduced development time. Why reinvent the wheel? Once written, data-driven routines can be included in every application you develop without modification. You simply add them to the project, call them from somewhere (a menu, a Form, or a program), and forget about them.

- Reduced maintenance effort. When you change the data dictionary, many aspects of a data-driven application automatically adjust *without programming*. To continue the reindexing example previously mentioned, when you add a new tag to an index you don't need to worry about whether the tag was created at the client site. Simply have the client choose the *Recreate Indexes* function (or something similar) from the menu.

Using a data dictionary and data-driven techniques can reduce development time and maintenance efforts in numerous applications.

You might wonder whether a data-driven routine is slower than a hard-coded routine. The answer is yes, the application will run a little more slowly, but the increased flexibility will more than offset this cost. When data-driven routines are used for batch processes such as reindexing or updating files, the overhead cost is small compared with the amount of time spent executing the process. Even when the routines are called during data entry, the overhead is minimal because the data dictionary files generally contain a small number of records and use tags on the most frequently sought expressions. On the types of machines Microsoft recommends for use with FoxPro, the effect is hardly noticeable.

What This Report Will Cover

Now that you're hungry to learn more about Visual FoxPro's data dictionary, you should know what this report does and does not cover:

- Naturally, it will cover the data dictionary built into Visual FoxPro. The report will look at all the good stuff, point out some warts, and talk about workarounds. (Some of the concepts previously mentioned, such as reindexing files from information in the data dictionary, aren't actually possible using the Visual FoxPro data dictionary as it comes out of the box.)

- The report will not cover everything you need to know about programming. Although the syntax of some commands and functions is examined in detail, this report is not intended to replace the Visual FoxPro manuals or online help files. Rather, it supplements them.

- The report will cover a few concepts (such as data buffering) that aren't specifically under the topic of the data dictionary but are related to the subject, are very important to know, are not covered in other reports in this book, and are *cool*!

- The report will not cover things that haven't changed from Microsoft FoxPro 2.x (such as Index On and Pack), except where new features affect these commands. For example, Append Blank still adds a new record, but it may cause an insert trigger to fire and may insert fields with default values or nulls.

- The report will not provide a detailed discussion of Visual FoxPro's datasessions or DataEnvironments. Although they'll be mentioned, they won't be discussed in any detail because they're covered in Steve Sawyer's report on the Form Designer.

Conventions

The following conventions are used in this report:

- The long-standing Xbase convention is to use uppercase letters for keywords and lowercase letters for assigned names (variables, tables, field names, and so forth). My personal convention is just the opposite: lowercase for Visual FoxPro keywords and uppercase for assigned names. For example:

```
create table EMPLOYEE ;
   (EMP_ID C(10), ;
   FIRST_NAME C(10), ;
   LAST_NAME C(15), ;
   primary key EMP_ID tag EMP_ID)
```

I find this much easier to read because (in my opinion) assigned names stand out better. Whichever method you use, I think we'll both find the Visual FoxPro world changing us somewhat. Objects and properties usually are entered in mixed case (such as This.ControlSource) in other languages, and this convention seems to be moving into Visual FoxPro.

Just to be really off-base, I use single quotes for character strings instead of the more common double quotes (simply because you don't need to press *Shift* to get a single quote).

- Words in angle brackets within commands are meant to be replaced by a name of some type. For example, Create Database <Name> means type something like Create Database MYDATA or Create Database COMPANY. Don't type the angle brackets.
- This report takes an exploratory approach. The idea is to try out concepts as you encounter them to reinforce what you've just learned. Most of the examples will work, but some deliberately won't so that you can learn from that, too.

These examples will be introduced in "Time to Play!" boxes.

Time to Play!

These boxes will contain commands you can enter or menu functions you can choose to perform specific actions such as creating tables or trying out triggers.

Some of these examples use databases and tables created in preceding examples. If you don't have time to complete certain examples, you'll find most of the sample tables and code on the enclosed CD. The "Time to Play!" box will indicate what files are required and where to find them.

2 | Databases

The heart of Visual FoxPro's data dictionary is the *database container*, or DBC. This section will explore the DBC—how it's implemented, what it contains, and how to work with it—and will provide some practical examples to follow.

"New" Terminology

The Xbase world has always been a little different from the rest of the database community in regard to the terms it uses for a number of concepts.

In relational database systems, data is stored in two-dimensional structures called *tables*. In Xbase, these things are called *databases*. This leads to things like the DBF (Database File) extension used for a file containing data and the Close Databases command that closes such a file. Unfortunately, database means something different to other (non-Xbase) database people. To them it means the set of all the data for an application, a system, or even an entire business. To users of relational databases, tables consist of *rows* and *columns*. In Xbase lingo, these are referred to as *records* and *fields*.

Now Visual FoxPro is bringing Xbase users into sync with the rest of the database community. The files where data is stored are now called tables. A database is now considered to be a set of tables rather than just one file. Records and rows tend to be used interchangeably in Visual FoxPro, as do fields and columns. This terminology shift is necessary for several reasons:

- Microsoft is positioning Visual FoxPro as more than just a tool for desktop database applications. The company sees it as a front end for client/server applications. More than one person has referred to Visual FoxPro as a "PowerBuilder killer." Whether this comes to fruition or not, Visual FoxPro certainly has what it takes to develop robust client/server applications. In order to be taken seriously in this realm, Microsoft had to ensure that FoxPro developers could avoid the schizophrenic mix of terminology that has been present so far.

- As SQL becomes more entrenched in FoxPro, developers are tending to concentrate more on sets of data and less on individual tables and records. In Xbase, there wasn't really a common term for a set of tables.

This shift in terminology doesn't just affect how you communicate with other developers. Several commands have changed context as a result. For example, the Close Databases command no longer closes all open tables. Instead, it closes the current database and all of its tables. Other open databases and their tables are left open. A new Close Tables command closes only the tables for the current database, leaving the database itself open with other databases and their tables.

Don't worry if you occasionally catch yourself saying database when you mean table. It'll take a while for old-time Xbasers to completely make the switch in their minds and hearts.

How Visual FoxPro Implements Databases

Visual FoxPro implements databases in a different manner than Microsoft's other database products. In Microsoft Access, for example, all of the data is contained in the database, which is a single file with an MDB extension. Tables and the data they contain are stored in different sections of the database.

Visual FoxPro, by comparison, keeps data in individual files with each table as a separate file with the familiar DBF extension. The database is stored in a *database container*, a file with a DBC extension. As you might guess, a DBC file is actually a Visual FoxPro table (the associated index and memo files have DCX and DCT extensions, respectively). Like other tables, a Visual FoxPro table can be opened, browsed, and edited.

The DBC file doesn't contain any of the data in the tables, nor does it contain the tables themselves. Instead, it contains information about the tables. For example, the DBC contains the name of each table in the database, along with the name of each field and index that make up each table.

The Visual FoxPro database includes information about

- Tables
- Fields
- Indexes
- Relationships between tables (called *persistent relationships*)
- Information (called *connections*) describing how to access remote data sources such as Microsoft SQL Server tables
- *Cursors* (or *views*) created from local tables, remote tables, or a combination of each using a SQL command

Interestingly, the Visual FoxPro database doesn't contain information stored in the Header of the DBF and CDX files. In other words, you won't find the type and size of each field, nor will you find the index expression for each tag. This type of information is called *metadata*, or data about data. Metadata is important for two reasons:

- Knowing the metadata for a table (name, type, size of each field) is crucial to creating the table.
- The metadata for each index (index expression, filter expression, and ascending and descending setting) is necessary for creating a table's tags.

The reason the DBC doesn't contain this structural information is that the DBC is considered to be an extension to the DBF and CDX rather than a source of metadata. It provides additional information about tables and their indexes that, until Visual FoxPro, was hard-coded in programs and screens (or perhaps in a third-party data dictionary or one you created yourself). This additional information includes the following:

- A table's location
- Record-level validation rules and error messages
- Field-level validation rules and error messages
- The name of the index uniquely identifying each record in a table (the *primary* key)
- Relationships between tables
- Referential integrity rules (for example, what to do with child records when the user tries to delete a parent record)

Should You Use a Database or Not?

Before you go any further, you should know that the fact that Visual FoxPro supports databases doesn't mean that you're required to use them. You can continue to use tables that aren't part of a database (called *free tables*) just as you did in FoxPro 2.x.

However, there are some very good reasons for using databases instead of free tables:

- You can define *long names* for tables and fields. Long names can be up to 128 characters long, although they can still contain only letters, numbers, and underscores. This means you can refer to a table by the name THIS_IS_MY_CUSTOMER_TABLE, and have a field within this table called THIS_IS_A_REALLY_LONG_NAME. Long names allow you to get away from cryptic names such as GLLYBUD and use more descriptive names such as GL_LAST_YEAR_BUDGET. Visual FoxPro uses long names instead of "real" names in many places such as browse column headers and the values returned by Field() and Afields().

- You can store comments for fields and tables describing their purpose, the modules that maintain them, the date of the most recent update, or any other important information.

- Databases act as guardians of your data. Although you can program data integrity rules so that your application's users can enter only valid data, that doesn't deal with users who open a table using Visual FoxPro and browse it. With free tables, you have no control over what happens to the data under those conditions. With a database, however, you can define default values for fields (automatically entered when new records are created), field-level validation, record-level validation, and even referential integrity handlers to ensure that parent records can't be deleted if any child records exist. This code can and should be stored within the database itself (as a *stored procedure*) so that anything accessing the data (programs or users in interactive mode) must follow your rules.

- Visual FoxPro now supports transaction processing so that you can ensure that either all of the updates that compose a "transaction" are properly completed or none of them are. For example, an automated teller application might allow you to transfer money from one account to another. You wouldn't be very happy if the program crashed after taking money out of one account but before it could deposit it into the other. Visual FoxPro allows you to start a transaction by using the Begin Transaction command. Only when everything went well would your program issue an End Transaction to actually write out the updates to the tables. If something went wrong during the processing, or if the program crashed, no updates at all would be written out. However—and here's the punch line—transaction processing works only with tables in a database.

For all these advantages, there's really only one drawback: for reasons that will be addressed later, a table can belong only to a single database. Thus, a database must be shared by all applications needing access to the tables contained in the database. As a result, there may be times in a Visual FoxPro application when using free tables would make more sense than using a database. If your application needs to share tables with older applications (such as FoxPro 2.x or dBASE), you'll have to forego the advantages a database provides.

Your First Database

OK, enough theory—it's time to get to the good stuff!

There are two ways you can create a database: visually and programmatically. To create a database visually, do one of the following:

- Select New from the File pad. In the dialog box that appears, choose Database, then click New File.
- If the Visual FoxPro Standard toolbar is displayed, click the New button. The New dialog box will appear again.
- If you want to create a database and add it to a project, open the project in the Project Manager and select the Databases object. (To see the Databases object, either click the Data tab, or, from the All tab, expand the Data object in the list.) Then click the New button or choose New File from the Project pad in the menu bar.

In all of these cases, Visual FoxPro prompts you for a name and location for the database using the standard Create dialog box. After specifying a name and location, Visual FoxPro automatically issues a Modify Database command. (Its function will be discussed shortly.)

To create a database programmatically, type Create Database <Name> in the command window. The <Name> parameter can include a path if you don't want the database to be created in the current directory. If you forget to specify the name, Visual FoxPro will display a dialog box so you can enter one.

After entering the command, it will not look as if anything has happened. The only difference you'll see is that the Database drop-down list on the Standard toolbar now contains the name of your database. To actually see something, you need to modify the database using the Modify Database command.

Time to Play!

Using either of the two methods described previously, create and modify a database named SCRATCH. For example, type the following:

```
create database SCRATCH
modify database
```

Notice the Database Designer window (described in the next part) is empty. This is because you haven't defined any tables in the database.

To follow along in the next section, you may want to open one of the sample databases included on the source code disc that accompanies this book. To do so, type the following:

```
open database COMPANY
modify database
```

The Database Designer

The Modify Database command brings up the Database Designer, Visual FoxPro's visual tool for maintaining databases. As you can see in Figure 2-1, the Database Designer shows all the tables contained in the DBC graphically.

Figure 2-1.

The Database Designer window

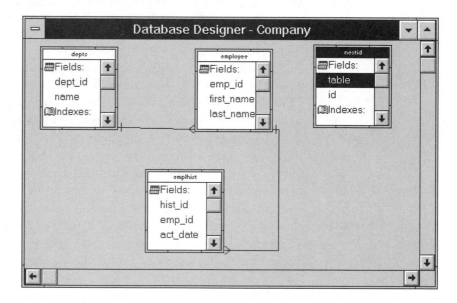

The Database Designer contains a number of elements.

- The title of the Database Designer window shows the name of the database being modified. In Figure 2-1, the database COMPANY is being modified.

- Each table is shown as a small window within the Database Designer window. The half-height title of each window contains the name of the table. As with any child window, these windows can be moved within the Database Designer window. You may need to scroll the Database Designer window to see all of the tables.

- Each table window contains the list of fields and indexes that make up that table. (Fields and Indexes are preceded by icons to make them stand out among the other names.) You can scroll a table window up and down to see all of the field and index names.

- The selected table window has a highlighted title. In Figure 2-1, NEXTID is the selected table.

- Some tables have lines connecting them. These lines represent *persistent relationships*, which will be explored a bit later. One nice feature of the Database Designer is that, as you move a table window that has relationship lines to other windows, those lines adjust automatically. This means you can rearrange tables to minimize crossing or overlapping lines.

Manipulating Database Objects

As with almost everything else in Visual FoxPro, there are several ways you can manipulate objects in the Database Designer.

- When the Database Designer window is on top, a Database pad appears in the menu bar. This menu offers functions that add or remove tables, create a new tables, and so forth.

- You can display the Database Designer toolbar by choosing Toolbars from the View pad and checking Database Designer. The Database Designer toolbar appears as it is shown in Figure 2-2.

  Manipulating toolbars will not be described here. If you've never done fun things like docking a toolbar, please read the Visual FoxPro documentation to see what you're missing.

Figure 2-2.

The Database Designer toolbar

The Database Designer toolbar has many of the functions that appear under the Database pad. To see what each button does, move the mouse pointer over it but don't click the mouse button. After a moment, a *ToolTip* (a tiny yellow box displaying the purpose of the button) will be displayed for the button.

ToolTips are a wonderful user interface enhancement. They make it unnecessary to have icons with text in them to explain what they do. The great thing about them in Visual FoxPro is that *you can define them for your objects in your own forms.* Please see Steve Sawyer's report on the Form Designer for information on how to create ToolTips.

• If you haven't already discovered it, Visual FoxPro has implemented *shortcut menus* as a speedy way of manipulating many types of objects. The shortcut menu is brought up by clicking the right mouse button when the mouse pointer is positioned over an object. For example, position the mouse pointer over a table window and click the right mouse button. A menu of functions for the table comes up beside the mouse pointer. To execute one of these functions, just select it from the menu.

To see how menus appear for different objects, move the mouse pointer so that it's still inside the Database Designer window but is not positioned over any table or relationship line. Then click the right mouse button. Notice the menu that comes up is different from the one for tables.

The following functions are available in the Database Designer. (The letters in parentheses after the function name indicate where the function can be found: M for in the Visual FoxPro menu under the Database pad, T for Database Designer toolbar, D for database shortcut menu, and S for table shortcut menu.)

• *New Table* (M, T, D). This creates a new table and adds it to the database. Selecting this function brings up a dialog box in which you enter the name of the table and the location you choose for it. After specifying the name and location, the Table Designer appears so that you can define the fields and indexes that make up your table. The next section discusses tables, indexes, and the Table Designer in detail.

• *Add Table* (M, T, D). This adds an existing table to the database. When you select this function, Visual FoxPro displays a dialog box for you to select which table you want to add. The selected table is added to the database and appears as a table window in the Database Designer. See the discussion on adding tables later in this section for the consequences of adding a table to a database.

• *New Remote View* and *New Local View* (M, T, D). These functions allow you to define remote and local views. Views are discussed in Section 7.

- *Modify* (M, T, S). This brings up the Table Designer so you can modify the structure of the selected table. This function is available only when a table is selected.
- *Browse* (M, T, S). This brings up a browse window for the selected table. This function is available only when a table is selected.
- *Remove* (M, T, S). This function appears as Delete in the table shortcut menu and is available only when a table is selected. It allows you to remove the selected table from the database, and to choose whether or not to delete it from disk as well. The dialog box shown in Figure 2-3 appears when this function is selected.

Figure 2-3.

The Remove (or Delete) Table dialog box

If you select *Remove*, the table is removed from the database, but is not physically deleted from the disk. Selecting Delete both removes it from the database and deletes it along with any associated FPT and CDX files. See the discussion on removing tables later in this section for the consequences of removing a table from a database.

- *Rebuild Table Indexes* (M). This function, which is available only when a table is selected, re-creates the indexes for the selected table.
- *Remove Deleted Records* (M). As you may be aware, deleted records aren't physically removed from the table until you use the Pack command. This function performs the same task as Pack.
- *Edit Relationship* (M). This function, which is available only when you've clicked a relationship line, can also be chosen by double-clicking the line. See Section 6 for details on working with persistent relationships.
- *Referential Integrity* (M, D). This function brings up the Referential Integrity Builder. The builder, which is discussed in detail in Section 6, allows you to define what happens to a child table when records are inserted or parent records are deleted or updated.

- *Edit Stored Procedures* (M, T, D). This function opens an editing window for the procedures stored in the database. See Section 6 for information on stored procedures.
- *Cleanup Database* (M). Visual FoxPro implements a database as a table. As with other tables, deleted records (caused by modifying table structures or removing tables from the database) aren't physically removed from the table until you use the Pack Database command. Cleanup Database packs the DBC and its associated DCT memo file.
- *Collapse* and *Expand* (S). These functions help you deal with a cluttered Database Designer window. To minimize a table window to just its title, select Collapse. Expand returns it to its former size. You can also adjust the table window size by dragging its borders.
- *Collapse All* and *Expand All* (D). These functions expand or collapse all table windows at one time.

Maintaining Databases Programmatically

The Database Designer allows you to manipulate a database visually. However, there may be times when you want to work with a database programmatically. This is especially important if you need to maintain a database from within a program. This discussion covers the commands Visual FoxPro provides to maintain databases.

Opening a Database

A database must be open before you can maintain it. The Open Database command is used for this purpose. This command has the following syntax:

```
open database
   [<Name> | ?]
   [exclusive | shared]
   [noupdate]
   [validate]
```

You'll notice that many of the arguments are similar to those in the Use command. This makes sense because the DBC is a table. Now look at the arguments individually.

```
<Name>
```

This argument specifies the name of the database to open; a DBC extension is automatically used if it isn't specified. If you don't specify the name or if you enter ?, the Open dialog box will be displayed so you can select which database to open.

```
exclusive | shared
```

These arguments open the database in either exclusive or shared mode. Opening a database exclusively is like opening a table exclusively: other users cannot open it. If a database isn't open exclusively, you won't be able to make any changes to the database or any of its contents. (For example, you won't be able to modify any table structures.) If you don't specify either of these keywords, Visual FoxPro uses the setting of Open Exclusive in the Data page of the Options dialog box in the Tools pad to determine how the database is opened.

- If Open Exclusive is checked and saved as the default setting, the database is opened exclusively.
- If Open Exclusive is not checked and that setting is saved as the default, the database is opened in shared mode.

The Isexclusive() function allows you to determine how a database was opened. Isexclusive(<Database>, 2) returns .T. if the specified database was opened exclusively.

```
noupdate
```

If the Noupdate argument is specified, the database is opened as read-only.

```
validate
```

The Validate argument causes Visual FoxPro to validate the database as it's opened. See the discussion in this section on validating databases for a description of what this process does.

Opening a database doesn't automatically open the tables within it; you still have to include a Use statement for each table to open it. However, because the database contains a reference to the location of the table, you don't have to specify a path in the Use command. The next section will cover a generic routine that opens all of the tables contained in a database.

If a table included in a database is opened but the database isn't already open, Visual FoxPro will automatically open the database. However, the database won't be the current database. (See the "Selecting a Database" discussion in this section for instructions on how to make it the current one.) This is similar to the Use <Table> in 0 command, which opens a table but doesn't make it the current table. Closing the table doesn't automatically close the database.

Adding Tables

The Add Table command adds an existing table to the selected database. (The Create Table command, which creates a new table

Closing a Database

The Close Databases command does one of several things.

- If there's a current database, this command closes it and all open tables contained in the database. Other databases, their tables, and free tables aren't affected.
- If there isn't a current database, the command closes all free tables and selects workarea 1.
- If you use Close Databases All, all open databases, their tables, and all free tables will be closed. (This is the same action provided by the FoxPro 2.x version of this command.)

Which Databases Are Open?

Because you can open several databases at once, Visual FoxPro provides a few functions to determine which databases are open, whether a particular database is open, and the name of the current database.

The Dbc() function returns the name and path of the current database, or an empty string if no database is selected.

The Dbused(<Name>) function returns .T. if the specified database is open.

The Adatabases() function stores the names and locations of all open databases into a two-dimensional array. The first dimension contains the database name while the second contains the path. If Adatabases() returns 0, no databases are open and the array will not be created (or updated if it already existed). As a result, you should always check the result of Adatabases() before trying to process the array.

The Adatabases(<ArrayName>) function is one of many commands that allows you to write generic code. Because it tells you the name and location of each open database, you don't have to hard-code that information into routines. For example, the following generic function called CLOSEDAT will close all databases and their tables but leave all free tables open.

CLOSEDAT.PRG

```
local lnDATA, laDATA[1], lnI
lnDATA = adatabases(laDATA)
for lnI = 1 to lnDATA
   set database to laDATA[lnI, 1]
   close database
next lnI
return .T.
```

The program CLOSEDAT.PRG is included on the source code disc only. You may have noticed the command Local in this code. Visual FoxPro now allows you to define truly local variables, ones that cannot be seen by higher calling routines or by routines called by this one. A new Lparameters command does something similar for parameters. See the Visual FoxPro documentation for more information on these commands and variable scoping in general.

Time to Play!

Now you can check out a few of the commands and functions that have just been covered. Try the following. (This example assumes you've installed Visual FoxPro in a directory called Visual FoxPro and that you've installed the sample data that comes with it.)

```
open database \VISUAL FOXPRO\SAMPLES\DATA\TESTDATA
? dbc()          && displays C:\VISUAL FOXPRO\SAMPLES\DATA\TESTDATA
open database \VISUAL FOXPRO\SAMPLES\MAINSAMP\DATA\TASTRADE
? dbc()          && displays C:\VISUAL
   FOXPRO\SAMPLES\MAINSAMP\DATA\TASTRADE
set database to TESTDATA
? dbc()          && displays C:\VISUAL FOXPRO\SAMPLES\DATA\TESTDATA
? dbused('TASTRADE')          && displays .T.
lnDATA = adatabases(laDATA)
? lnDATA                       && displays 2
display memory like laDATA     && displays the following:

   LADATA Pub A
     ( 1, 1) C "TASTRADE"
     ( 1, 2) C "C:\VISUAL
   FOXPRO\SAMPLES\MAINSAMP\DATA\TASTRADE.DBC"
     ( 2, 1) C "TESTDATA"
     ( 2, 2) C "C:\VISUAL FOXPRO\SAMPLES\DATA\TESTDATA.DBC"

close database
? dbc()                        && displays an empty string
? dbused('TESTDATA')           && displays .F.
? adatabases(laDATA)           && displays 1
```

Getting Information About the Database

The Display Database and List Database commands display information about the selected database including tables, fields, indexes, relations, connections, and views. (List outputs continuously while Display pauses every screen.) By default output goes to the screen, but you can specify To Printer (include the Prompt keyword to display a Print dialog box first) or To File <Filename>. If you use either of these options, use Noconsole to suppress output to the screen.

Here's the output from List Database with \VISUAL FOXPRO\SAMPLES\DATA\TESTDATA.DBC as the selected database. (Only two tables are shown and some fields have been removed for brevity.)

```
Database Name:          TESTDATA
Database Path:          c:\visual
    foxpro\samples\data\testdata.dbc
Database Version:       10
Table       customer
            *Path               customer.dbf
            *PrimaryKey       cust_id
            Field     cust_id
            Field     company
            Field     contact
            Field     postalcode
            Field     country
            Index     cust_id
                      *Unique            TRUE
            Index     company
                      *Unique            FALSE
            Index     contact
                      *Unique            FALSE
            Index     postalcode
                      *Unique            FALSE
Table       orditems
            *Path               orditems.dbf
            Field     line_no
            Field     order_id
            Field     product_id
            Index     order_id
                      *Unique            FALSE
            Index     product_id
                      *Unique            FALSE
            Relation  order_id
                      *RelatedTable      orders
                      *RelatedTag        order_id
                      *RelatedChild      order_id
            Relation  product_id
                      *RelatedTable      products
                      *RelatedTag        product_id
                      *RelatedChild      product_id
```

There's an indispensable pair of functions that obtain or set values about different objects in a database: Dbgetprop() and Dbsetprop(). These functions will be featured several times in this report, each time in terms of the specific objects being discussed. Since this section concentrates on databases, they'll be discussed from that perspective.

There's not a lot of information you can obtain about a database itself using Dbgetprop(). This function is called as follows:

```
dbgetprop(<Name>, 'Database', <Property>)
```

In this function, <Name> should be replaced with the name of the database from which you obtain information, and <Property> should be replaced with "Comment" to get the database comment, or with "Version" for the database version number. (That number is based on the version of Visual FoxPro you are running.) This will be used to determine if a database has the structure for an older version of Visual FoxPro and needs to be automatically converted to the current format.

With Dbsetprop(), you can only update the "Comment" property for databases. This function is called as follows:

```
dbsetprop(<Alias.FieldName>, 'Database', 'Comment', <Value>)
```

As you can see, these two routines don't help you much with databases. However they really shine when used with other objects like tables, fields, connections, and views. You'll see these routines in action in later sections.

Another function that obtains information from a database is Indbc(). This function will tell you whether or not a particular object is included in a database. It's called using the following syntax:

```
indbc(<ObjectName>, <Type>)
```

In this function, <ObjectName> is the name of the object while <Type> is one of the following object types: Connection, Field, Index, Table, or View. If the specified object is included in the current database, Indbc() returns .T.

Adbobjects() is a function that fills an array with the names of objects of a certain type from the current database. It's called with the following syntax:

```
adbobjects(<ArrayName>, <Type>)
```

In this function, <ArrayName> should be replaced by the name of the array into which the names will be placed and <Type> should be replaced with one of these object types: Table, Relation, Connection, or View. The function returns the number of objects found. The structure of the array depends on what type is specified. When Table, Connection, and View are specified, the names of the objects (or long names in the case of tables) will be contained in a one-dimensional array. In the case of Relation, the array will have one row per relation and the following columns:

Column	Contents
1	The name of the child table
2	The name of the parent table
3	The name of the tag used for the child table
4	The name of the tag used for the parent table
5	Referential integrity rules (see the structure on the DBC later in this section for the format of these rules)

Deleting a Database

Although it's a rare occurrence, a time may come when you need to delete a database. While you might think you can simply erase the DBC, DCT, and DCX files, doing that will cause a problem. Because a table's Header indicates that it is included in a database, the table can't be opened unless that database is already open or can be found. If the database files have been erased, you won't be able to open any of the tables that were referenced in the database. (This section's discussion of fixing database problems provides a solution to this problem.) The Delete Database command is a better way to get rid of a database because it automatically frees the tables in the database before erasing it.

This command has the following syntax:

```
delete database <Name> | ?
   [deletetables]
```

In this case, <Name> is the name of the database to be deleted. Entering ? displays the Open dialog box from which you can choose the database. The database must be closed when this is attempted or you'll get an error. If you include the Deletetables keyword, Visual FoxPro will delete all the tables (including their associated CDX and FPT files) in the database as well.

Packing a Database

The Pack Database command does programmatically what the Cleanup Database function under the Database pad does: it packs the DBC and its associated DCT memo file. The database must be open exclusively, and none of its tables can be open.

Detecting and Fixing Database Problems

Databases contain links to tables by paths and file names. Changing file names or moving tables or databases to different directories breaks these links. For example, if STAFF is a table in the TIMEBILL database, the following commands result in the dialog box shown in Figure 2-4.

```
rename STAFF.DBF to EMP.DBF
rename STAFF.CDX to EMP.CDX
open database TIMEBILL
use EMP
```

Figure 2-4.

The dialog box resulting from renaming a table behind the database's back

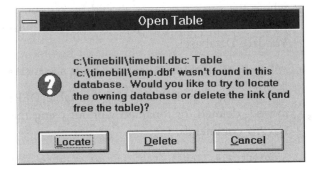

Selecting Delete from the dialog box in Figure 2-4 will mark the DBF's Header as a free table. Choosing Locate will allow you to select a different database, but because no database contains the new table name, you will continue to get this dialog box until you select either Delete or Cancel. If you choose Delete, you should also remove the table from the database, which still has a reference to the table under its former path and name.

To resolve a broken link programmatically, do the following:

- Mark the table's Header as a free table with the Free Table <NewTableName> command. The table cannot be open during this process.
- Open or select the database and remove the table's reference from it using Remove Table <OldTableName>.

You can check for problems with broken links in the current database by using the Validate Database command. This command ensures that the database contains the proper locations of tables and indexes, and that the database has a record for each field and tag in each table. You must open the database exclusively to use this command.

```
Structure for table:        C:\VFP\SAMPLES\DATA\TESTDATA.DBC
Number of data records:     115
Date of last update:        02/26/96
Memo file block size:       64
 Code Page:                 1252
   Field   Field Name    Type              Width   Dec    Index    Collate    Nulls
       1    OBJECTID      Integer               4                              No
       2    PARENTID      Integer               4                              No
       3    OBJECTTYPE    Character            10           Asc      Machine   No
       4    OBJECTNAME    Character           128           Asc      Machine   No
       5    PROPERTY      Memo (Binary)         4                              No
       6    CODE          Memo (Binary)         4                              No
       7    RIINFO        Character             6                              No
       8    USER          Memo                  4                              No
** Total **                                    164
```

Several things in the DBC structure might seem strange to you, including the Integer and Memo (Binary) field types and the fact that Memo fields use 4 bytes instead of the usual 10. These oddities will be covered in the next section when new data types are discussed. DBCs have the following indexes:

```
Index tag: OBJECTNAME Collate: Machine Key: STR(PARENTID)+OBJECTTYPE+LOWER(OBJECTNAME)
   For: .NOT.DELETED()
Index tag: OBJECTTYPE Collate: Machine Key: STR(PARENTID)+OBJECTTYPE
   For: .NOT.DELETED()
```

DBCs contain the following fields:

- *OBJECTID.* This is the ID for the object in the current record. OBJECTID is a sequential number and always equals Recno() for the record. Each table, field, index, relation, connection, and view is stored in a separate record.

- *PARENTID.* This matches the OBJECTID of this object's parent record. For example, each field and each index in a table have the table's OBJECTID value as their PARENTID values.

- *OBJECTTYPE.* This field shows the object's type. See the table at the end of this list for the various object types.

- *OBJECTNAME.* This field contains the name of the object, stored in lowercase. For tables and fields, this field contains the long name rather than the actual name.

- *PROPERTY.* This field contains property information about the object. See Section 10 for a detailed description of the properties for each object type and how those properties are stored in the PROPERTY field.

- *CODE*. This field contains code built into the database, called *stored procedures*. Stored procedures are discussed in Section 6.
- *RIINFO*. Referential integrity information for relation records is listed in this field. Each character in the field represents a rule: the first character is for updates, the second is for deletes, and the third is for inserts. The remainder are for future use. In each position, C means cascade, R means restrict, and a space means ignore. Thus CCR means cascade updates, cascade deletes, and restrict inserts. This information is discussed in Section 6.
- *USER*. Microsoft has thoughtfully provided a field where you can add your own information. This field is not maintained by Visual FoxPro, and you can store anything you choose there. See Section 8 for a discussion of extending the Visual FoxPro data dictionary.

Here are the contents of a sample DBC, showing the various object types:

OBJECTID	PARENTID	OBJECTTYPE	OBJECTNAME	PROPERTY	RIINFO	CODE
1	1	Database	Database	\<properties>		
2	1	Database	TransactionLog			
3	1	Database	StoredProceduresSource			\<code>
4	1	Database	StoredProceduresObject			\<compiled code>
5	1	Table	customer	\<properties>		
6	5	Field	cust_id	\<properties>		
7	5	Index	cust_id	\<properties>		
8	5	Relation	cust_id	\<properties>	\<RI info>	
9	1	Connection	myconnection	\<properties>		
10	1	View	clientsales	\<properties>		
11	10	Field	sum_order_amt	\<properties>		

Looking at this DBC, you'll notice several things.

- The first four records are automatically inserted into the DBC when it's created. The first record is a description of the database itself. The second record describes the log for transactions as they are issued. The third and fourth records contain the source and object code, respectively, for stored procedures.
- The other records in the DBC were automatically created as tables, relationships, connections, and views were added to the database.
- Records 2, 3, and 4 have a PARENTID of 1, meaning they are child records of the database itself. This is also true for all tables, connections, and views.

- The field and index records (records 6 and 7) have a PARENTID of 5. This indicates that they belong to the CUSTOMER table, which has an OBJECTID of 5. The field in record 11 has a PARENTID of 10, meaning it belongs to the CLIENTSALES view in record 10.
- Fields can be associated with either tables or views. For example, the field in record 6 belongs to the CUSTOMER table while the field in record 11 belongs to the CLIENTSALES view.
- Relationship records have the PARENTID of the child table (or the "many" table in a one-to-many relationship). The relationship name is the name of the tag used for the child table.

If you have used the command Set Deleted Off, you may notice many deleted records in the DBC, especially if you have edited table structures since the last time you packed the database. When you edit a table structure, Visual FoxPro deletes any existing field records for the table and re-creates them all. As a result, the DBC can get quite bloated with deleted records with time.

When you pack a database, Visual FoxPro renumbers all OBJECTID fields so that they match the record number. This means it must also adjust any references to the OBJECTID in the PARENTID of any related records.

Other Database Tidbits

There are a few remaining database-related points that don't fall under any in the previous categories.

- The Data and Remote Data pages in the Options dialog box under the Tools pad affect database and table design tools. These pages are discussed in Section 11.
- This report doesn't cover the topic of datasessions. (See Steve Sawyer's report on the Form Designer for a discussion of datasessions.) However, if you are familiar with them, you're probably aware that tables are scoped to private sessions. This means that a table open in one private session isn't necessarily open in another.
- Databases, on the other hand, aren't scoped in this way. Opening a database in one session makes it open in all sessions, including the default one. An internal counter stored for each database increases as new sessions open the same database, usually as a Form is run. Once all of the sessions close the database, it will be closed. You won't get an error if you open a database that's already open as long as you use Set Exclusive Off. The Adatabases()

function will see all open databases regardless of which tables are opened in a private session.

- The description displayed in the Project Manager for databases, tables, and fields actually contains the comments for those objects stored in the database. Changes made in the Project Manager are written back to the database.

- Don't mess with the information stored in PROPERTY. For example, you may be tempted to change the location of a table by finding its record in the DBC and editing its path in PROPERTY. Unless you're careful, this type of change can cause an invalid record in the database. (For example, Validate Database will give an error message.) If you're interested in knowing more about how information in PROPERTY is formatted so that you *can* change it safely, see Section 10.

3 | Tables and Indexes

Visual FoxPro provides you with a lot of new features affecting tables and indexes, including new data types, null support, table and field level validation, and triggers. This section will discuss the changes that have been made to tables and indexes in Visual FoxPro.

Some of the new properties associated with tables have changed the Header structure of DBF files. For example, a new object has been added to table Headers to allow null values. Other new properties such as table and field level validation rules are stored in the database. You'll remember from the previous section that Visual FoxPro ensures that these rules are enforced by requiring the database to be open when the table is open. If you don't open the database, Visual FoxPro will do it for you. The name and path of the DBC is added to the DBF Header so that you know which database the table is contained in. This is called the *backlink*. A consequence of this backlink is that each table can belong to only one database.

As a result of these changes to the DBF Header, tables created in Visual FoxPro (or tables that were created in FoxPro 2.x but had their structure changed in Visual FoxPro) cannot be opened in applications that aren't aware of the new structure. In FoxPro 2.x, for example, you'll get the infamous "Not a table/DBF" error message if you try to open a Visual FoxPro table. This means that you cannot take advantage of the new features Visual FoxPro provides in any tables that must be accessed either by older versions of FoxPro or other applications.

For more on the structure of the DBF Header and how it differs between Visual FoxPro and FoxPro 2.x, see Section 9.

New Data Types

Visual FoxPro also supports several new data types, each of which will be discussed here as it relates to data. For information on the functions specific to these data types, please refer to the Visual FoxPro documentation.

Binary Character and Memo Fields

FoxPro 2.5a introduced support for international features such as automatic code page translation of Character and Memo fields. (See the Visual FoxPro documentation for a description of code pages and other international features.) Automatic translation works well for fields containing ASCII text, but it can cause data corruption in fields containing non-ASCII values such as encrypted passwords, character-based keys, copies of word processing documents, or bitmap files. To prevent problems with such fields, you can use the Set Nocptrans command immediately after opening a table to specify which fields should *not* be automatically translated. The main problem with this approach is that Set Nocptrans must be specifically issued by the application or by the user if the table is opened interactively. If a table structure changes, you must change all routines using this command to reflect those changes. Failure to use this command can result in data corruption.

Fortunately, Visual FoxPro provides a better means of specifying that certain fields contain non-ASCII data and are therefore not subject to automatic translation. Two new data types, binary versions of Character and Memo fields, provide this ability. Because these data types are defined directly in the table structure, there's no danger of forgetting to specify which fields should not be translated when a table is opened. In Visual FoxPro, you should use only Set Nocptrans to access older tables.

Currency Fields

Currency fields were designed to overcome the limitations of Numeric fields. Normal Numeric fields are physically stored in a table as the digits that make up the number. This leads to a number of considerations:

- The field must be sized according to the largest number it will contain. For example, you would specify a 5-digit field

sets it to 1. As you can see, some numbers produce unexpected results.

However, Set Blocksize To 0 results in a 1-byte block size. This means that a 1-byte memo will take 9 bytes (8 for the Header plus 1 for the information), a 2-byte memo takes 10 bytes, and so forth. The 64-byte memo mentioned earlier takes up 72 bytes in the FPT, not 128 as it did when the block size was 64.

Assuming the last byte of every memo spills over into the next block (which is then mostly empty), the amount of wasted space in an FPT file is (Set('BLOCKSIZE') - 1) * Reccount() bytes. For a 100,000-record table with a block size of 64, there could be 6,300,000 bytes of wasted space. With a block size of 1, wasted space is eliminated because each memo takes only the space it needs. In some admittedly non-scientific testing, there was no performance difference between a 64-byte block size and 1-byte block size, so there doesn't appear to be a downside to using a 1-byte block size.

Null Fields and Values

Visual FoxPro provides support for null fields and values. Null is a value, not a data type. Although it is not a zero or a blank value, a null represents the absence of data. It's simplest to think of a null value as meaning "I don't know what the value is." Fields and memory variables of any type can contain a null value. For example, a Character field and Numeric memory variable can both be null.

In many designs, null and blank or zero may be synonymous. However, nulls are not involved in mathematical operations such as averaging, while zeros are. For example, say that you are a teacher using the following table of students' marks for various exams:

Student	Exam #	Mark
Allan	1	25
Bobby	1	90
Beth	1	95
Joe	1	75
Karen	1	62
Allan	2	0
Bobby	2	
Beth	2	93
Joe	2	79
Karen	2	72

Notice that Allan didn't answer a single question in exam #2, so he received a 0. Bobby, on the other hand, was sick that day and didn't receive any grade for this test. What's Bobby's average? In systems without null support (such as FoxPro 2.x), his average would be (90 + 0)/2 or 45. When nulls are supported, the second test mark doesn't count (because it doesn't represent data), making his average 90.

Time to Play!

Because null means "I don't know," nulls don't get along well with their peers. Anything added to or subtracted from a null value is null. To see this for yourself, try the following. (If you don't feel like typing all this, run TESTNULL.PRG supplied on the source code disc.)

TESTNULL.PRG

```
X = .NULL.              && to assign null to a value, use .NULL.
? X and .T.             && displays .NULL.
? .NULL. + 0            && displays .NULL.
? X + 0                 && operator/operand mismatch; hmm, why is
                           that?
? type('X')             && displays "L"; that's because X wasn't
                           originally assigned a "real value",
                           therefore, like other variables declared
                           PUBLIC, it's initialized as a Logical
                           variable. What if we declare a variable
                           type first?
X = ''
? type('X')             && displays "C", as expected
X = .NULL.
? type('X')             && displays "C"; the type hasn't changed,
                           only the value
? X + 'TEST'            && displays .NULL.
? empty(X)              && displays .F.; null is not the same as
                           empty
? isblank(X)            && also displays .F.
? X = .NULL.            && displays .NULL.; hmm, isn't something
                           that's null equal to something else
                           that's null? Let's try a more direct
                           approach
? .NULL. = .NULL.       && displays .NULL. ?!?
? isnull(X)             && Displays .T.
Y = 10                  && Assign Y a numeric value
? nvl(5, Y)             && Displays 5
? nvl(X, Y)             && Displays 10
```

These results make sense if you remember that null means "I don't know." After all, the answer to the question "Does something I don't know equal something else I don't know" is "I don't know."

Because you can't determine if a value is null by comparing it to .NULL., Visual FoxPro has provided the Isnull() function. Isnull(<value>) returns .T. if the value is null and .F. if not.

Fields in a table will not store a null value unless they are defined to accept null values. A new command, Set Null, determines how null values are supported by the Create, Create Table, Alter Table, and SQL Insert commands. The default setting is Set Null Off, which means you must specifically check the NULL column in the Table Designer or use the Null clause when using the Create Table or Alter Table command to allow a field to accept null values. Also, any fields not specifically named in the SQL Insert command will have blank values inserted instead of null values. With Set Null On, fields you add in the Table Designer have NULL checked automatically and fields automatically accept null values unless you use the Not Null clause in the Create Table or Alter Table commands. (You can uncheck NULL if you choose.) In addition, any fields supporting null values but not specifically named in the SQL Insert command will insert null values rather than blank values.

There are a few other tidbits about nulls that will be helpful.

- A null value can be placed in a field in a browse or edit window by pressing Ctrl+0 (Ctrl+zero).
- Nulls sort before anything else, so an index on a field containing nulls will have all the null values at the top of the index order.
- A trappable error (error #1581) will occur if you try to put a null value in a field (using Replace) that doesn't accept null values.
- Aggregate functions such as sum and count ignore null values in fields, as do SQL Select aggregate functions such as Sum() and Count().
- Code such as "if X > Y" won't work if either variable contains a null value. You might have to use something like "If Not Isnull(X) And Not Isnull(Y) And X > Y."
- The new Nvl() function helps in situations where it's possible an expression will be null but you don't want to do anything with a null. This function has the following syntax:

```
nvl(<Expression 1>, <Expression 2>)
```

If <Expression 1> is null, the function returns <Expression 2>; otherwise, it returns <Expression 1>. For example, say you're printing mailing labels from a table in which the postal or zip code may contain nulls. Because postal workers could get confused if they see .NULL. on the label, you might want to use the expression Nvl(POSTAL_CODE, Space(Len(POST_CODE))), which will print the postal or zip code if it's filled in or a blank space if it's null.

- Copy Structure Extended has a new column, FIELD_NULL, that indicates whether or not the specified field will accept null values. Similarly, Afields() has a new column to indicate if fields support nulls.

Because they must be treated specially, nulls can kind of be a pain, so it's best to use them in tables only when your applications need them. For most applications, using zero or blank to indicate no data is adequate. For example, you probably don't need null support in a postal or zip code field. To most people, a blank field would indicate that the postal or zip code isn't known. However, if you need to distinguish between records that don't have a postal or zip code and those that do but it isn't known, you'll need this field to accept null values.

Table Designer

The Table Designer is Visual FoxPro's new visual tool for maintaining the structure of tables. Visual FoxPro provides several ways to bring up the Table Designer:

- To create a table, select New from the File pad. In the dialog box that appears, choose Table, then click New File.
- If the Visual FoxPro Standard toolbar is displayed, you can create a table by clicking the New button; the New dialog box appears.
- You can add or modify a table in a database or a free table from the Project Manager. Consult the Visual FoxPro documentation for instructions.
- From the Database Designer, you can create a new table or modify an existing one; see Section 2 for a description of how to do this.
- You can modify a table from the View window, which can be brought up from the Window pad by clicking the View button in the Standard toolbar, or by typing Set in the Command window. After you've selected the table, click the Properties button, and choose Modify.
- From the Command window, you can type Create <Table> to create a table or Modify Structure to modify the selected table.

For a free table, one that is not part of a database, the Table Designer appears as shown in Figure 3-1.

a name aren't enough to make it unique, Visual FoxPro will add a number in the final character to make it unique. For example, the field names THIS_IS_A_VERY_LONG_NAME and THIS_IS_A_VERY_LONG_NAME_TOO are actually stored in the table as THIS_IS_A1 and THIS_IS_A2.

Validation Rules and Text

In Visual FoxPro you can define field validation rules and the text to display if the validation fails. This ability is one of the two most powerful features of Visual FoxPro's data dictionary. The other, support for the table-level validation rules and triggers, will be discussed later in this section. By defining data validation rules that are enforced at the engine level, you prevent invalid data from getting into your tables, whether it be by users typing in a browse or a program that neglected to do proper data checking. In fact, it means you can separate the tasks of database design and user interface design. Forms don't have to "know" how to validate the data; they just have to respond to errors the database returns when trying to store incorrect data.

Now look at some simple examples of validation rules (more complex ones come later). Suppose you don't want a customer name to be left blank. Using Not Empty(CustomerName) as the validation rule in conjunction with appropriate validation text would prevent that.

To ensure that the customer's state or province can be found in a table of valid states and provinces, you could use Seek(StateProv, 'STATES'). However, there's a problem with this. If the STATES table isn't open, you'll get an error message. In that case, you might want to use a user-defined function (UDF). For example, you could use VALSTATE('StateProv') as the validation expression and create the following function:

```
function VALSTATE
lparameters lcFIELD
local llUSED, llRETURN_CODE
llUSED = used('STATES')
if not llUSED
   use STATES in 0
endif not llUSED
llRETURN_CODE = seek(lcFIELD, 'STATES', 'STATE')
if not llUSED
   use in STATES
endif not llUSED
return llRETURN_CODE
```

Notice the new third parameter in the Seek() function: it indicates which tag to use for the search so you don't have to save the former order, set it to the desired one, and then set it back later. That saves about a half-dozen lines of code in this routine alone.

To bring up Visual FoxPro's Expression Builder to enter the validation rule or text, click the button with the ellipsis (...) beside the textbox.

Be careful when you define validation rules. An improperly defined rule could mean that you can't enter any data or could cause an error to occur at an inopportune time. For example, using something like Not Empty(CustomerName) will cause a problem: you can't add records in a browse window because doing so creates a record with blank fields. This causes the validation rule to fire, giving an error and preventing the record from being added. Unlike the VALID clause of a FoxPro 2.x screen or the :V clause you put on a field in a browse, Visual FoxPro validation rules are executed automatically. The point of a validation rule is to *prevent invalid data from getting into your table.* This means that if you said the field can't be blank, it can't be blank under any circumstances. However, using buffering allows you to add records in a browse window because the validation rules aren't evaluated until you try to move to another record. Buffering will be discussed in detail in Section 5.

Like a validation rule, a validation text expression can be any valid expression, even a UDF. Often, the expression will be an error string to display, in which case you enter the text surrounded with quotation marks the way you would any character string. If you don't specify validation text, the message "Field <FieldName> validation rule is violated" will be displayed. Leaving the validation text blank is a bad idea because this is too cryptic to be useful to the user (and even sounds vaguely rude). However, you should note the validation text is displayed only when the validation rule is violated by changes made interactively, such as using a browse window or typing in a field in a Form. Unless you have an error trap set, violations in program code still trigger the "Field <FieldName> validation rule is violated" message.

> ***Important Safety Tip:*** If you often enter aliases in objects like validation rules and index expressions, this is a good time to break that habit. The current version of Visual FoxPro doesn't automatically update aliases in things like validation rules and index expressions when you rename a table, so you'll be stuck with invalid validation rules and index expressions until you manually edit all of them out. If you use the Expression Builder, you'll want to uncheck Always Add Alias in the Expression Builder Options dialog box so it doesn't automatically add the alias to fields you select.

Default Value

The default value is the value that'll be entered into a field when a record is added interactively (in a browse, for example) or programmatically (with Append Blank or when the SQL Insert command is used and a value for the field isn't specified). The default can be any expression, including a UDF, as long as it evaluates to the same type as the field. Date() is one default value you can use in many tables for Date_Record_Added fields.

Probably the most useful default value is an automatically incrementing value. This is useful for all kinds of fields including invoice numbers, voucher numbers, or any field that's the primary key of its table. To set it up you'll need a control table containing the next value to assign a particular field in a particular table. Say, for example, that the table NEXTID has a structure like the following:

```
Structure for table:        C:\TOOLS\DDBOOK\SAMPLES\NEXTID.DBF
Number of data records:     3
Date of last update:        02/02/96
  Code Page:                1252
```

Field	Field Name	Type	Width	Dec	Index	Collate	Nulls
1	TABLE	Character	10		Asc	Machine	No
2	ID	Integer	4				No
** Total **			15				

TABLE contains the name of the table, while ID is the next available value for that table. The tag on TABLE allows you to search for the record for the table you need to obtain a value for.

Here's a UDF called NEXT_ID. This routine is passed a table name, and finds the appropriate record in NEXTID.DBF. If the record doesn't exist, it creates a record for the table. It then increments ID to get the next available value, and returns that new value. If this routine can't increment ID because the record is locked by someone else, it returns .NULL. The program NEXT_ID.PRG is supplied on the source code disc.

NEXT_ID.PRG

```
lparameters lcTABLE
local lnCURR_SEL, llUSED, lnCURR_REPR, lnKEY

* Save the current work area, open the NEXTID table (if
* necessary), and find the desired table. If it doesn't exist,
* create a record for it.

lnCURR_SEL = select()
llUSED     = used('NEXTID')
if llUSED
   select NEXTID
   set order to TABLE
else
   select 0
   use NEXTID order TABLE
endif llUSED
seek upper(lcTABLE)
if not found()
   insert into NEXTID values (lcTABLE, 0)
endif not found()

* Increment the next available ID.

lnCURR_REPR = set('REPROCESS')
set reprocess to 10 seconds
if rlock()
   replace ID with ID + 1
   lnKEY = ID
   unlock
else
   lnKEY = 0 && Force it to numeric before setting to .NULL.
   lnKEY = .NULL.
endif rlock()

* Cleanup and return.

set reprocess to lnCURR_REPR
if not llUSED
   use
endif not llUSED
select (lnCURR_SEL)
return lnKEY
```

The final task is to use this UDF in the default value for any fields that need an automatically assigned value. For the EMP_ID field of the EMPLOYEE table, the default expression would be NEXT_ID('employee').

> ### Time to Play!
>
> Now take a look at the COMPANY database included for this report on the source code disc. It includes the NEXTID table described earlier in this section under "Default Value," and a table called EMPLOYEE.
>
> ```
> open database COMPANY exclusive
> use EMPLOYEE
> modify structure
> ```
>
> Notice that the default value for the EMP_ID field uses the NEXT_ID function provided previously. To see how it works, open a browse window for the table and add a few records. The shortcut key has been changed to Ctrl+Y from FoxPro 2.x's Ctrl+N, which now follows the Microsoft Windows standard and triggers the New() function in the File pad. Notice that the EMP_ID field of each new record gets the next available value. Open the NEXTID table and see where these values are coming from.

Another useful purpose for a field's default value is to prevent a validation rule error from occurring at an inopportune time. As you saw earlier, using a validation rule such as Not Empty(CustomerName) can prevent you from adding new records interactively. By specifying a default value for the field, you avoid this problem.

Captions

The field long name really isn't suitable for consideration as a full-text description of a field to present to a user because it can't have any spaces in it. The caption for a field is much better suited to this role. The caption is automatically used as the column Header in a browse window, and can be obtained from the database at any time using the Dbgetprop() function. In an example of this function that will appear later, you'll define a pop-up list of fields for a table that shows the caption for each field instead of the field name.

Comments

This is a Memo field in which you can enter any comment you choose about the field including its purpose, and examples of contents.

Table Properties

There are several properties available for tables in the Table Designer: long names; comments; validation rules and text; and insert, delete, and update triggers.

Long Names

As you'll remember from the previous section, a table long name can be up to 128 characters and can be used to refer to the table in place of the file name. For example, even though a table's file name may be EMPDATA.DBF, you can use the syntax shown to open the table by its long name.

```
use Employee_Data_File
```

Comments

Comments are Memo fields where you can enter any comments you choose about the table including its purpose, programs, or modules that maintain it.

Validation Rules and Text

As you saw earlier, you can define field-level validation rules that are evaluated when a field's value changes. Similarly, you can define table-level validation rules that are evaluated when Visual FoxPro tries to write an edited record to the table—for example, when the record pointer is moved or the table is closed. Table validation can be used to handle rules that field validation can't. Here are two examples:

- Dependencies between fields. For example, you can leave either field A or field B blank, but not both. You wouldn't want to put this type of validation at the field level because you'd have to use the validation rule for each field to test if both fields are empty. If the rule fails, it forces the user to enter something in the last field they were in, regardless of whether that is the one that should be changed.
- Updating other tables. To improve performance, you may have totaled information from detail records stored in summary records. For example, you might store an invoice total that comes from records in an invoice detail table in the invoice master table. This update can be done as the table validation for the detail table.

Time to Play!

This example will show when validation rules are evaluated. First you need to create a program called SHOWRULE.PRG using the following code (or use the copy supplied on the source code disc):

```
lparameters lcFIELD
wait window 'Evaluating rule for ' + lcFIELD
return .T.
```

Next, create a database (or open an existing one) and create a table called SHOWRULE within it using the following structure. (If you don't want to create this table, use the copy supplied on the source code disc.)

```
Name      Type        Len     Validation
FIELD1    Character   10      SHOWRULE('Field 1')
FIELD2    Character   10      SHOWRULE('Field 2')
```

Enter SHOWRULE('Table') as the table validation rule. Save this table and respond "No" to the Input Records Now? dialog box.

Then browse the table, add a new record, and notice that a window shows the validations for each field and for the table being executed. Enter anything into FIELD1 and press Tab. Notice that the window that appears is showing the field validation rule is being executed. Enter something into FIELD2 and press Tab. Again, the window appears as the validation for FIELD2 is executed. Add another record. A window comes up showing Visual FoxPro is evaluating the table validation rule. This makes sense because it has to do the table validation for the record you're leaving. Enter something into both fields for record #2. Add a new record, and press the up arrow key to move back up through records 2 and 1. Notice that no window appears since no data is being changed.

Close the edit window and modify the structure of the table. Add FIELD3 with a validation rule of SHOWRULE('Field 3'). When you save this change, notice that you get a window indicating the table validation rule is being executed for each record in the table.

Now browse the table, move to FIELD3 for the first record, type something, and press the down arrow key to move to the next record. You'll see the validation for FIELD3 firing (because you're trying to exit that field), then the table validation will appear. The validation for FIELD1 and FIELD2 don't fire because you didn't change them.

Be careful when you define table validation rules. As you saw in the last "Time to Play!" exercise, the table validation rule is evaluated for each record when table structure changes are saved. If you specify a UDF and the program to execute can't be found or if the validation rule fails for even a single record, the structure changes aren't saved. Also, even if the individual field validations succeed, an improperly defined table rule could mean that you can't save a record.

As with field validation text, table validation text is displayed only when the validation rule is violated by changes made interactively, such as in a browse window or by typing in a field in a Form.

Triggers

Triggers are lines of code that are executed in response to an event. Visual FoxPro supports three table events: inserting, updating, and deleting records. For example, when a record is added to a table (using Append Blank or SQL Insert), an insert event occurs. If a trigger for the event has been defined, the trigger fires.

Because triggers are complex subjects, they are covered on their own in Section 6.

Keys and Indexes

Note that some database management systems have different meanings for the terms key and index. Because there is no distinction between them in Visual FoxPro, these terms are used interchangeably in this report.

As you saw earlier, the Table Designer includes an Index tab that allows you to define both fields and indexes for a table at the same time. Except for a change to the user interface, the only difference between the way Visual FoxPro and FoxPro 2.x deal with indexes is that with Visual FoxPro you can now define an *index type* for each tag. For free tables, there are three types of indexes.

- Regular. This index type is like the indexes in earlier versions of FoxPro. They are compact tags stored in a structural CDX file, a CDX file with the same name as the DBF that is opened automatically with the table.

- Unique. Although this index type has been available as far back as FoxBASE+, it is still probably one of the most confusing issues in the FoxPro world. When they first encounter them, many people (especially those with exposure to other database systems) think that when a record is added to a table, a unique index will cause FoxPro to give an error and prevent the addition if the key value is duplicated. In reality no error is given, and only the first occurrence of a duplicate key value is included in the index. Duplicate records may exist in the table, but only the first one is "visible" when the table's order is set to that index.

In the past you created a unique index by using Set Unique On before creating the index or by using the Unique keyword for the Index On command. With Visual FoxPro, now you can do it visually by selecting unique as the index type.

To make matters even more confusing, the Create Table and Alter Table commands now support the SQL standard Unique keyword to create indexes that truly prevent duplicate values, called *candidate* indexes, instead of unique indexes. Thus, "unique" has two different meanings depending on whether you define a table using the Table Designer or programmatically.

If unique indexes simply hide duplicate records instead of preventing them, it's difficult to find a good use for them. Different people might come up with different reasons, but one case occurs when you need duplicate values for a certain field in a table but under certain conditions you want to see only unique values. For example, you can have a security table with several records for each user, each specifying a module in the application and what the user's rights are for that module. Before FoxPro 2.0's introduction of the SQL Select statement, you had to create a unique index on the user name to create a list of all users defined in the application. That way it listed each user only once. Now with the Select command's Distinct and Order By clauses, this method is really useful only if you have very large tables and don't want to affect performance by using Select each time you need the unique list.

As a result, unique indexes should be used only in the rarest of situations.

- Candidate. This is your first new index type! As mentioned earlier, a candidate index is one that will allow neither null nor duplicate values. You'll see why this type of index is called "candidate" in a moment.

  As most developers are aware, it's very important that every record has a value to uniquely identify it. Although there are many theoretical reasons for this, one practical reason is that you must uniquely identify a record to know if you have the correct one. For example, you might have a table of employees and decide to use the employee's social security number (SSN) as the primary key. If you have a table containing events for each employee (hiring, reviews, promotions, training, and so forth), that table would be related to the employee table by SSN. However, suppose you have a foreign employee who doesn't have an SSN. Leaving SSN blank would be fine—the events records would also have a blank SSN so they can find the appropriate employee—until you hire the second person without an SSN.

For this reason, you need to use something that can uniquely identify each record. That means the attribute (a single field or combination of fields) cannot be duplicated or blank. It might be something like an employee ID code assigned by the user or a sequential value assigned by the system (as you saw in the discussion of default values for fields). If it's a value assigned by the user, before Visual FoxPro you'd have to ensure that the value isn't blank or a duplicate using code like the following:

```
if empty(M.ORDER_ID)
   wait window "Please don't leave the order # blank."
else
   set order to ORDER_ID
   lnRECNO = recno()
   seek M.ORDER_ID
   if found() and (glADD_MODE or recno() <> lnRECNO)
      wait window 'This order # already exists.'
   endif found() ...
   go lnRECNO
endif empty(M.ORDER_ID)
```

Now here's the good news: all you need to do to implement duplicate checking in Visual FoxPro is to define a candidate index on the ORDER_ID field. If the user tries to enter a duplicate order number when adding or editing a record, FoxPro will generate an error (error #1884) that your application can trap. Candidate indexes will allow a blank value, but only in one record because any other record with a blank value would be a duplicate. However, using a table or field validation rule can prevent this.

Because null values mean "I don't know," they aren't allowed in any field used for a candidate index. Visual FoxPro won't give you an error if you define a candidate index on a field that supports nulls, but it will if you try to enter a null value into the field.

Think about how much time this will save you writing duplicate checking code for every table in your system!

For tables included in a database, another index type is available: *primary*. A primary index is essentially a candidate index (automatically preventing null and duplicate key values). The difference is that while you can define as many candidate indexes as you like, a table can have only one primary key. The distinction between primary and candidate keys is mainly for relationships, which you'll see in more detail in the next section when relationships are discussed.

Because the database holds the name of the tag that's a table's primary key, Visual FoxPro automatically changes the index type to candidate when you remove the table from the database. The name "candidate" was chosen because it will also refuse duplicate or null values (and thus uniquely identifies a record). Such an index is a "candidate" to be the primary key, but another, more suitable candidate was chosen instead.

Except for free tables (which can't have a primary key), why would you need to use a candidate index if you have a primary key? You'll see an example later when the use of another type of key, a *surrogate key*, is discussed.

You'll also encounter a *foreign key*. A foreign key isn't really an attribute of the table it's in; it's simply a way to tie it to another table. Between related tables the linking field is normally the primary key of one table and a foreign key in the related table. For example, suppose you have two tables: CUSTOMER, a table of customers; and CATEGORY, a table of customer categories (such as regular, major, and dead-beat). CUSTOMER has a field called CUSTCAT that relates to the CODE field in the CATEGORY table. An index on CODE is the primary key for CATEGORY, because it uniquely identifies a category record. An index on CUSTCAT is called a foreign key because the code value in this field serves only to link CUSTOMER to the proper record in CATEGORY.

Although you can define a foreign key using the Create Table and Alter Table commands, you can't select it as an index type from the Table Designer. This is because, from a structural point of view, a foreign key is just another kind of index. Foreign keys will appear again in the next section on relationships.

Time to Play!

Now look at how primary and candidate keys provide automatic null and duplicate key detection. To do this, you'll create a table to contain the names of NFL football players. First, because you can't define a primary key for free tables, create a database called SPORTS. Then add a table called PLAYER to the database with the following fields:

```
ID        Character     4
LNAME     Character     15
FNAME     Character     10
```

Create a primary index with a tag name of ID and an expression of ID. Save this table and respond "No" to the Input Records Now? dialog box. If you don't feel like creating the database and table, use the copies supplied on the source code disc.

Continued on next page

Browse this table and add the following records:

```
Record #      ID       LNAME        FNAME
1             0000     Montana      Joe
2             0001     Rice         Jerry
3             0000     Green        Mean Joe
```

When you try to enter record 3, you should get a "Uniqueness of index ID violated" error. The table works just as you hoped, providing duplicate checking without code!

Now leave the ID blank and add another new record by pressing Ctrl+Y. Oops, you get the same error message. Because Mean Joe Green has a blank ID (which is valid because it's not null), you can't add another record with the same ID. Appending a blank record would do just that.

Well, Mean Joe hasn't played football in a while, so click in the DELETED column to delete his record, then add the new one. You get the same error, so you should check to see if Deleted is set off so Visual FoxPro can still "see" Mean Joe's record. Bring up the Command window, type Set Deleted On, and click back in the browse window. Mean Joe's record disappears, so add that new record again. Once again, you get the error.

As you can see from this example, a blank key value is considered to be valid, but, like any other key value, it can't be duplicated. Another thing to note is that even if you use Set Deleted On, deleted records are included in the check for duplicate values. These facts have all kinds of implications:

- Although it's poor design to allow a blank primary key, FoxPro 2.x let you get away with it since data integrity checking wasn't built into the engine. This means that you're going to have to clean up existing tables before trying to bring them into the Visual FoxPro world by defining primary or candidate keys.

- If you've allowed even a single record with a blank key value into the table, you won't be able to add a record in a browse window, even if the record has been deleted. This will occur until the table is packed.

- Even though a record's been deleted, you can't reuse its primary key value until the record's been physically removed from the table by packing. For example, a design that allows incorrect invoices to be deleted and reentered with the same invoice number will fail if the invoice number is the primary key.

- Packing tables has many potential problems: the table must be open exclusively so that no one else can access it while it's being packed, packing takes a long time and requires a lot of free disk space for large tables, and so forth. As a result many people have implemented a "record recycling" scheme. This scheme is quite ingenious: instead of adding a new record, you locate an existing deleted record, recall it, and use it as the new record. Because most tables add records more frequently than they delete them, deleted records will rarely hang around for very long. The only consideration in this scheme is how to find a deleted record quickly. One way to do this is to blank the key value when it's deleted, thus making it "float to the top" of the table in index order. This is a simple routine that you can type in and use in place of Append Blank to create a "new" record:

```
procedure NEW_REC
local lcCURR_DEL, llDONE
lcCURR_DEL = set('DELETED')
set deleted off              && so we can "see" deleted records
go top
llDONE = .F.
do while not llDONE
  do case

* If this record is deleted and we can lock it, recall it
* and we're done.

    case deleted() and rlock()
       recall
       llDONE = .T.

* If this record is deleted but we can't lock it, try the
* next one.

    case deleted()
       skip

* If this record isn't deleted, there aren't any more, so
* just add a new one.

    otherwise
       append blank
       llDONE = rlock()
  endcase
enddo while not llDONE
if lcCURR_DEL = 'ON'
  set deleted on
endif lcCURR_DEL = 'ON'
return
```

The problem with this scheme under Visual FoxPro is that it relies on the fact that all deleted records have a blank primary key placing them at the top of the table in index order. You can't do this in Visual FoxPro because only one record can have a blank key value.

Fortunately, there are solutions to this problem.

- If the primary key value is assigned by the user, you can define a validation rule of Not Empty(<FieldName>) for the field to prevent creating records with a blank key value. Because this doesn't resolve the problem of being able to add records in a browse, you can also define a default value for the field. Users will get an error if they don't change the key value from its default and then try to add another record, but at least they can add records interactively.

- If you have a filter of Not Deleted() on the primary key, you can actually get Visual FoxPro to accept duplicate key values if the records with the duplicate values are deleted. The next "Time to Play!" shows an example of this. Be sure to note that having this filter on the primary tag doesn't take the place of having a tag on Deleted(); you'll still want one of those for Rushmore optimization. (For more information on Rushmore optimization, consult the Visual FoxPro documentation.) Also, for Rushmore to really do its thing, you'll want a tag (a regular key) on the same expression as the primary key but without a filter.

  The only problem with this scheme is that you cannot create a filter for the primary key using Create Table or Alter Table, and while there's an Index On ... For ... Candidate, there's no such command for primary indexes. Using Index on ... For ... on a primary key causes it to be changed to a regular key. Thus, the only current way to create a filter for the primary key is through the Table Designer.

- Rather than worrying about whether a primary key value might be used more than once, you can use a *surrogate key*. You actually saw an example of a surrogate key when you used the NEXT_ID() routine as the default value for a field. It's called a surrogate key because the field really doesn't represent any data about the record itself; it simply takes the place of whatever you *think* identifies a record (like CustomerName, which may have duplicates) to provide something that truly does identify the record. Because each record will have a unique sequential value as its primary key, you'll never have a duplicate value, even with deleted records.

  Some users might want to assign their own unique values to records. For example, say you have a table of customers with a category field. This field is looked up in a category table to ensure that it contains a valid value, but the users want to define their own category codes, which must be unique. The answer is to let them. You can use a surrogate key field as the primary key, and never show that

Time to Play!

Now look at how the ideas previously discussed work in a real example. Edit the Mean Joe Green record in PLAYER.DBF so it has an ID of 0002. (You may have to Set Deleted Off to see it because you deleted it in the previous exercise.) Note that if you don't do this, you'll get a validation error when trying to make the following changes to the table.

Bring up the Table Designer for PLAYER.DBF and change the ID tag so it has Not Deleted() as the filter. Change the ID field so it has Not Empty(ID) as the validation rule, and add something appropriate for the validation text (perhaps "Don't leave the ID blank!") with "9999" as the default value. Then save these changes. In the Command window, type the following:

```
set deleted off
set order to ID
browse
```

You should see only Joe Montana's and Jerry Rice's records from the previous exercise because, although Deleted is off, the ID tag has a filter so you won't see Mean Joe Green's deleted record. With the browse window still open, click in the Command window and type:

```
set order to
```

Click back in the browse window. Mean Joe's record should now appear since the filter is no longer set.

Press Ctrl+Y to add a new record. Because of the default value for ID, you won't get an error when the new record is added. (You would otherwise, since ID can't be blank.) Blank the ID value and press Tab. You should see the validation text you entered for this field.

Enter 0000 into ID, then press the up arrow key to move to the previous record. You'll get an error because Joe Montana already has 0000 as the ID. Enter 0002 into ID and press the up arrow key. This time, you can enter a duplicate key value because Mean Joe's record is deleted. You might be wondering why Visual FoxPro isn't catching the duplicate key if you can see Mean Joe's record. The reason is that duplicate key validation is done at the index level, not the table level. The index can't "see" Mean Joe's record because of the filter on Not Deleted().

Recall Mean Joe's record by clicking the delete column and notice that Visual FoxPro gives a "Uniqueness of index ID violated" error.

Working with Tables

This discussion focuses on working with tables: creating them, modifying their structures, and opening and closing them. Common operations that haven't changed from previous versions of FoxPro such as Seek, Skip, or Locate will not be discussed. Instead the discussion will concentrate on the new features that Visual FoxPro provides.

Any changes made programmatically to tables (such as Index On, Delete Tag, and Alter Table) automatically update the database just as if the changes were done in the Table Designer.

The Table Wizard

The Table Wizard is one of the wizards included in Visual FoxPro. It allows you to create tables visually with certain structures predefined. The Table Wizard is invoked when you select Wizards from under the Tools pad and choose Table, or when you choose Wizard from the New dialog box while creating a new table from a menu. The Table Wizard is shown in Figure 3-5.

Figure 3-5.

The Table Wizard

Creating a Table Programmatically

There are several ways to create a table programmatically. If you want to create a table with the exact structure of another table, you can use the Copy Structure command. You can also create a table using the Create From command, in which you specify a table describing the structure of the new table. These commands haven't changed for Visual FoxPro, so they won't be described here. See the Visual FoxPro documentation for more information.

Of more interest is the Create Table command. This command is described in the Visual FoxPro documentation as a SQL command because it's one of the commands that uses SQL syntax.

With Create Table, you can create both free tables and tables included in a database. If a database is selected, Create Table will automatically add the table to the database unless you specifically tell it not to. If no database is selected, the table will be a free table.

The syntax for Create Table is as follows:

```
create table <Table> [name <LongName>] [free]
  (<FieldName> <Type> [(<Width> [, <Decimals>])]
     [null | not null]
     [check <ValidExpr> [error <ErrorMessage>]]
     [default <DefaultExpr>]
     [primary key | unique]
     [references <ParentTable> [tag <ParentTag>]]
     [nocptrans]]
  [, <FieldName> <Type> ... ]
  [, primary key <KeyExpr> tag <TagName>]
  |, unique <KeyExpr> tag <TagName>]
  [, foreign key <KeyExpr> tag <TagName> [nodup]
       references <ParentTable> [tag <ParentTag>]]
  [, check <ValidExpr> [error <ErrorMessage>]])
  | from array <ArrayName>
```

As you can see, the Create Table command has many new options in Visual FoxPro because of the information stored in the new table structure and database container. Now take a look at the arguments for this command:

```
<Table>
```

This is the file name for the table. It must be a legal MS-DOS name and can include the path for the table. If a database is selected and you don't include the Free keyword (described shortly), you'll get an error if the table has the same name as a table already existing in the database.

```
name <LongName>
```

This allows you to specify a long name (up to 128 characters) to use in place of the file name when referring to the table. You'll get an error if <LongName> has already been used for another table in the database or if you specify a long name when no database is selected. (The long name is stored in the database.)

```
free
```

This option is used if a database is selected and you don't want the new table added to it.

```
<FieldName> <Type> [<Width> [, <Decimals>])]]
```

These represent the field name, type, width, and number of decimal places. <FieldName> can be a long name if the table will be included in a database. You'll get an error if you specify a name longer than 10 characters when a database isn't selected or when Free is specified.

<Type> is a letter that specifies the field's data type. You don't have to specify the width or number of decimals for any data types with a fixed size (such as Date fields, which always use 8 bytes). <Decimals> defaults to a value of 0 if it isn't specified for Numeric, Float, or Double fields. The following are the letters to use for each data type:

Data Type	Type	Width	Decimals
Character	C	<width>	-
Date	D	-	-
DateTime	T	-	-
Numeric	N	<width>	<decimals>
Float	F	<width>	<decimals>
Double	B	-	<decimals>
Currency	Y	-	-
Logical	L	-	-
Memo	M	-	-
General	G	-	-

```
null | not null
```

These arguments are used to override the setting of Set Null. Having Set Null Off (the default) is like specifying Not Null (does not allow null values) on every field, while Set Null On is like specifying Null (allow null values) on every field. If you don't specify either of these arguments and include the Primary Key or Unique arguments, the field will not allow null values.

```
check <ValidExpr> [error <ErrorMessage>]
```

This syntax defines a validation rule and error message for the field. <ValidExpr> is any valid Visual FoxPro expression, but often specifies a user-defined function to call. You'll get an error if you include this argument when the table isn't being added to a database.

`default <DefaultExpr>`

This defines a default value for the field. <DefaultExpr> can be any valid Visual FoxPro expression, including a user-defined function, but must be of the same data type as the field. You'll get an error if you include this argument when the table isn't being added to a database.

`primary key | unique`

These keywords specify that an index should be created on this field with a tag name matching the field name. Primary Key specifies a primary index while Unique specifies a candidate index. You'll get an error if you define more than one field using the Primary Key argument, or if you include this argument when the table isn't being added to a database.

Note that there is the potential for confusion here. This Unique keyword does *not* mean the same thing as the Unique keyword in the Index On command or the Set Unique command. Please refer to the part in this section on indexes for the distinction between candidate and unique indexes.

`references <ParentTable> [tag <ParentTag>]`

This argument creates a regular index on the field and defines a persistent relationship with another table. (Persistent relationships are discussed in the next section.) <ParentTable> is the name of the parent for the new table. If you include Tag <ParentTag>, the relationship is based on the specified tag in the parent table; otherwise the relationship is based on the parent's primary key. You'll get an error if the parent table doesn't have a primary key, if it isn't part of a database, or if you include this argument when the table being defined isn't added to a database.

`nocptrans`

This specifies that the Character or Memo field should be a binary field. See the part in this section on data types for a description of binary Character and Memo fields.

`primary key <KeyExpr> tag <TagName>`

This argument creates the primary key for the table using the specified expression and tag name. This argument is really used in only two instances: if the primary key for the table involves more than one field (such as Dtos(DATE) + STAFF) or if the index expression is not simply the field name (for example, Upper(LASTNAME)). This is because it's easier to create a primary key on a field by using the Primary Key argument for that field, and you'll get an error if you specify more than one primary key for a table. You'll also get an error if you include the argument when a table isn't being added to a database.

```
unique <KeyExpr> tag <TagName>
```

This argument creates a candidate index using the specified expression and tag name. As with primary keys, it's easiest to create a candidate index on a field by using the Unique keyword for that field, so this argument should be used when the candidate index involves more than one field or the index expression is more than just the field name by itself.

```
foreign key <KeyExpr> tag <TagName> [nodup]
   references <ParentTable> [tag <ParentTag>]
```

This argument creates a foreign key using the specified expression and tag name, and defines a persistent relationship with the specified parent table. The index created is a regular index unless Nodup is included, in which case it's a candidate index. If you include Tag <ParentTag>, the relationship is based on the specified tag in the parent table. If not, the relationship is based on the parent's primary key. You'll get an error if the parent table doesn't have a primary key, if it isn't part of a database, or if you include this argument when the table being defined isn't added to a database.

```
check <ValidExpr> [error <ErrorMessage>]
```

This defines a validation rule and error message for the table. <ValidExpr> can be any valid Visual FoxPro expression, but often it specifies a user-defined function to call. You'll get an error if you include this argument when the table isn't being added to a database.

```
from array <ArrayName>
```

Instead of including all of the arguments (such as fields, indexes, and validations) for the Create Table command, you can specify the name of an array containing the name, type, width, decimals, null support, validation rule and message, and default value for each field, as well as the validation rule and message for the table. See the part later in this section on the Afields() function for the exact structure of such an array. Note that creating a table from an array doesn't allow you to specify other information about the table, such as primary and candidate indexes or persistent relationships. That information can be added after the table has been created by using the Alter Table command.

There are a few other notes about creating tables with the Create Table command.

- You don't need to use the Select 0 command before using Create Table. The lowest available work area is automatically selected and the new table is opened exclusively in that work area.

- Although it's not recommended, you can create fields using the names of Visual FoxPro reserved words. For example, DATE and SELECT are acceptable field names. However, Create Table has a bug in the current version of Visual FoxPro: you can't create fields with the names UNIQUE, PRIMARY, FOREIGN, or CHECK (which are keywords in the command), but you can with other keywords, DEFAULT, REFERENCES, NAME, FREE, ERROR, TAG, NOCPTRANS, and NULL. Also, you can create a table with those field names using the Table Designer.

- Although long field names can be used for tables attached to a database, tag names are still limited to 10 characters. If you explicitly provide a tag name longer than 10 characters (for example, Primary Key CUSTOMER_NUMBER tag CUSTOMER_NUMBER), you'll get a "Tag name too long" error message. However, you can also get this error even if you don't explicitly provide the tag name, such as Create Table ... CUSTOMER_NUMBER primary key, ..., because this command would try to create a tag named CUSTOMER_NUMBER.

 ### *Time to Play!*

Now try some of these new options for Create Table. You'll have to manually enter this code because these tables don't exist on the source code disc.

```
close all
create table TESTNULL ;
  (FIELD1 C(10) null, ;
  FIELD2 C(10) not null)
insert into TESTNULL (FIELD1) values ('TEST')
insert into TESTNULL (FIELD2) values ('TEST')
browse
```

Notice that the first record has a blank for FIELD2, which doesn't support null values, while the second record has .NULL. in FIELD1, which does support them. Now try something else:

Continued on next page

```
create table CATEGORY ;
  (CODE C(1) primary key, ;
  NAME C(30))
```

Oops, you got an error message. Primary Key is allowed only for tables in a database, and no database is currently open. You can remedy that with the following code:

```
create database SCRATCH
create table CATEGORY ;
  (CODE C(1) primary key, ;
  NAME C(30))
```

That's better.

```
create table TESTFREE free (FIELD1 C(10))
modify database
```

Notice TESTFREE isn't included in the database. Now try a more complex example:

```
create table COMPANY ;
  (COMP_ID I primary key ;
    default NEXT_ID('COMPANY'), ;
  NAME C(30), ;
  COMPCAT C(1) references CATEGORY ;
    check seek(COMPCAT, 'CATEGORY', 'CODE'), ;
  TEST C(1), ;
  check not empty(NAME))
```

This command creates COMPANY.DBF with four fields, creates a primary key on COMP_ID, defines a default value for COMP_ID that calls NEXT_ID() to provide the next available key value, creates a regular index on COMPCAT, defines a relationship between COMPANY and CATEGORY, defines a validation rule for COMPCAT that ensures its value exists in the CATEGORY table, and defines a table validation rule. All that in just one command!

Opening a Table

Opening a database doesn't automatically open the tables in it; you still need the Use command to open each table. However, if a table included in a database is opened and the database isn't already open, Visual FoxPro will automatically open the database. Visual FoxPro opens a table using its long name as the alias.

The following generic routine called OPENDBF (included on the source code disc) can be used to open all tables in the current database:

```
local laTABLES[1], lnTABLES, lnI
lnTABLES = adbobjects(laTABLES, 'Table')
for lnI = 1 to lnTABLES
   use (laTABLES[lnI]) in 0
next lnI
```

Because the database contains a reference to the location of the table, you don't have to specify a path in the Use command. For example, if the current directory is C:\MYAPP and the selected database references G:\DATA\CUSTOMER and H:\COMMON\ACCOUNTS, you can issue just two lines to open both tables:

```
use CUSTOMER in 0
use ACCOUNTS in 0
```

However, you must be sure to specify your directory in cases where tables with the same name exist in more than one directory. For example, suppose you have a database open in the current directory, \MYAPP. The open database references a table called CUSTOMER in the \PRODDATA directory. Another table, also called CUSTOMER, exists in the current directory but is obviously not included in the open database. If you were to use the Use CUSTOMER command, the one in the current directory would *not* be opened but the one in \PRODDATA would. The only way to open the CUSTOMER table from the current directory is to explicitly state the directory: Use \MYAPP\CUSTOMER.

That brings up another point. If you're used to switching between copies of tables with the same names in different directories such as test and production data or versions of tables for different companies (commonly done with accounting systems), you might use code like the following to open the appropriate copy of the tables:

```
if lcCHOICE = 'Test Data'
   lcDIRECTORY = '\MYAPP\TEST'
else
   lcDIRECTORY = '\MYAPP\PROD'
endif lcCHOICE = 'Test Data'
use (lcDIRECTORY + 'ACCOUNTS') in 0
* open other tables too
```

However, you'll have a problem if you expect to have only one database for your application and use code like this. This is because the name and path of the table are hard-coded in the database while the name and path of the database are hard-coded in the DBF

Header. Thus, you can't have both the TEST and PROD copies of the ACCOUNTS table defined in the same database.

Before you get upset about this point, there's a simple but imperfect solution: put a copy of the DBC in each directory containing the copies of the tables. Then, your routine to open tables would look like the following:

```
if lcCHOICE = 'Test Data'
   lcDIRECTORY = '\MYAPP\TEST'
else
   lcDIRECTORY = '\MYAPP\PROD'
endif lcCHOICE = 'Test Data'
open database (lcDIRECTORY + 'MYDATA')
use ACCOUNTS in 0
* open other tables too
```

This isn't perfect because each time you make a change to the database, you must copy the DBC, DCT, and DCX files to each directory containing a copy.

Cool Tip on DataEnvironments: Although DataEnvironments in forms are beyond the scope of this report (please see Steve Sawyer's report on the Form Designer for information on DataEnvironments), the concept of variable data locations has an impact there as well. The DataEnvironment stores the name and path of the database for each table used in the form. This can be changed at runtime, allowing you to open a different copy of a table in a different directory. Simply use code similar to the following in the Load event of the form:

```
This.DataEnvironment.Cursor1.Database = lcDIRECTORY + 'MYDATA.DBC'
This.DataEnvironment.Cursor2.Database = lcDIRECTORY + 'MYDATA.DBC'
etc.
```

This changes the database for each table to the desired copy.

Because a table can only be part of one database, some problems arise when tables must be used by several different applications. For example, a general ledger (GL) accounts table would be used by accounts payable (AP) and accounts receivable (AR) applications. If you want to have separate databases for AP and AR, you must devise a method for handling the GL table they have in common. One way is to have free common tables so there are no restrictions on how many applications they can be used in. However, because free tables don't have access to many of the advantages a database provides, a better solution is to create a database of common tables. Each application could therefore open its own specific database and the common database.

To open a table in a database that's open but is not the current one, use the syntax Use <Database>!<Table>. For example:

```
open database AR
open database COMMON        && COMMON is now the current
                           && database
use ACCOUNTS in 0          && ACCOUNTS is in COMMON
use AR!CUSTOMERS in 0      && CUSTOMERS is in AR
```

Closing a Table

As you saw in the discussion about databases, the command you used to close tables in FoxPro 2.x, Close Databases, does a lot more in Visual FoxPro:

- If there's a current database, Close Databases closes it and all open tables contained in the database. Other databases, their tables, and free tables aren't affected.
- If there isn't a current database, Close Databases closes all free tables and selects work area 1.
- If you use Close Databases All, all open databases, their tables and all free tables are closed. (This is the same action provided by the FoxPro 2.x version of this command.)

A new command, Close Tables, does the following:

- If a database is selected, it closes all open tables contained in that database but leaves the database open. Free tables and tables in other databases aren't affected.
- If no databases are open, it closes all free tables.
- If you use Close Tables All, all tables (those in databases and free tables) are closed.

Deleting a Table

As you saw in the discussion of databases, you can both remove a table from a database and physically delete it by using the Remove Table command and including the Delete keyword. In fact, that is the best method for deleting tables. Other methods can leave the database invalid, forcing you to use the Validate Database command to correct the problem.

To delete a free table, use either the Erase or Delete File command to delete the DBF and associated tables (FPT and CDX if they exist). One nice feature about these commands is they don't generate an error if a file doesn't exist, so you don't have to check for the existence of an FPT or CDX; you can simply delete them. However, the file must not be in use at any workstation. It's best to use Set Safety Off unless you want the user to be asked to confirm the file deletion. Here's an example:

```
erase CUSTOMER.DBF
erase CUSTOMER.FPT
erase CUSTOMER.CDX
```

Modifying a Table's Structure

Modifying a table's structure at your own site is easy: simply type
Modify Structure, make any necessary changes, and click OK to save
the changes. However, modifying the structure of a table at a remote
site is more difficult. There were all kinds of tricks you could use in
FoxPro 2.x, such as using a SQL Select statement to create a new
table having the modified structure, or using Afields() and modifying
the contents of the array before creating a new table from it and
appending from the old table. However, none of these were much
fun to use. They required extensive planning and careful coding to
avoid messing something up.

Visual FoxPro now provides the SQL Alter Table command to
modify the structure of tables programmatically. Use this command
once and you'll never want to go back. Here's the syntax:

```
alter table <TableName>
    [add | alter [column] <FieldName>
      <Type> [(<Width> [, <Decimals>])]
      [null | not null]
      [check <ValidExpr> [error <ErrorMessage>]]
      [default <DefaultExpr>]
      [primary key | unique]
      [references <ParentTable> [tag <ParentTag>]]
      [nocptrans]]
    |
    [alter [column] <FieldName>
      [set default <DefaultExpr>]
      [set check <ValidExpr> [error <ErrorMessage>]]
      [drop default]
      [drop check]]
    |
    [drop [column] <FieldName>]
    [set check <ValidExpr> [error <ErrorMessage>]]
    [drop check]
    [add primary key <KeyExpr> tag <TagName>]
    [drop primary key]
    [add unique <KeyExpr> tag <TagName>]
    [drop unique tag <TagName>]
    [add foreign key [<KeyExpr>] tag <TagName>
        references <ParentTable> [tag <ParentTag>]]
    [drop foreign key tag <TagName> [save]]
    [rename column <OldFieldName> to <NewFieldName>]
    [novalidate]
```

Many of the arguments for Alter Table are the same as those for Create Table, so only the arguments that differ will be discussed here.

```
<TableName>
```

This is the name of the table to modify. Like the SQL Insert command, if the table isn't open when Alter Table is used, it will be automatically opened in the lowest available work area. However, the current work area will not change.

```
add [column] <FieldName>
```

This argument specifies the name of a field to add to the table. You'll get an error if a field with that name already exists. The rules applying to long field names described in Create Table also apply here.

```
alter [column] <FieldName>
```

This argument specifies the name of the existing field to modify. You'll get an error if the specified field doesn't exist.

```
set default <DefaultExpr>
```

This argument defines a default value for an existing field.

```
set check <CheckExpr> [error <ErrorMessage>]
```

This argument defines a validation rule and text for an existing field.

```
drop default
```

This statement deletes the default value for an existing field.

```
drop check
```

This statement deletes the validation rule and text for an existing field.

```
drop [column] <FieldName>
```

This argument removes the specified field from the table, and removes any information about it (such as default value and validation rule) from the database. You won't be allowed to use this argument if anything referencing the field (such as index expressions or validation rules) becomes invalid.

```
set check <ValidExpr> [error <ErrorMessage>]
```

This argument defines the table's validation rule and text.

```
drop check
```

This statement deletes the validation rule and text for the table.

```
add primary key <KeyExpr> [tag <TagName>]
```

This defines the primary key for the table. If the tag name isn't specified and <KeyExpr> is a single field, the tag is assigned the same name as the field.

```
drop primary key
```

This command deletes the primary key (not the fields the index is created on) and any persistent relationships based on it.

```
add unique <KeyExpr> [tag <TagName>]
```

This argument defines a candidate index for the table. If the tag name isn't specified and <KeyExpr> is a single field, the tag is assigned the same name as the field.

```
drop unique tag <TagName>
```

This deletes the specified candidate index and any persistent relationships based on it.

```
add foreign key <KeyExpr> tag <TagName> references
   <ParentTable> [tag <ParentTag>]
```

This argument creates an index using the specified expression and tag name, and defines a persistent relationship with the specified parent table.

```
drop foreign key tag <TagName> [save]
```

This argument removes the specified index and the persistent relationships it's involved in. If you simply want to remove the relationship and not the tag, use the Save keyword.

```
rename column <OldFieldName> to <NewFieldName>
```

This renames a field. Note that renaming a field in the table doesn't automatically rename it in index expressions, validation rules, or anywhere else you've used the name. You must make those changes manually. Alter Table won't allow you to make the desired change if a validation rule or index expression will not be valid afterwards.

```
novalidate
```

If you change a table using Alter Table so that existing data in the table violates some rules, Visual FoxPro will give an error and will not make the change. For example, if you have a table without a defined primary key, you won't be able to define a primary key on a field if that field has duplicate values. The Novalidate keyword tells Visual FoxPro to make the change anyway. Of course, you'll run into trouble as soon as you try to work with the table and Visual FoxPro tries to enforce the rules, so it's important to clean up the data as soon as possible.

There are a few things to note about the Alter Table command.

- Alter Table can be used with free tables, but you won't be able to use arguments that would affect information stored in a database. These include Default, Foreign Key, Primary Key, References, or any of the Set arguments.

- Depending on what changes were made to the table, Alter Table might update only the database and not the table itself. For example, arguments involving Default don't affect the structure of the table. In other cases, only the table Header may be affected. For example, renaming a field or changing the null support for a field doesn't affect the records in the table, so only the Header is updated. Anything affecting the data contained in the table (such as adding or removing fields or changing a field's type or width) will cause a complete rebuild of the table and may take some time, especially with large tables.

- Because Alter Table commands are program code, they can be documented, rerun, and printed out. By creating carefully documented routines using Create Table and Alter Table statements, you have the ability to define and document your tables' structures. As discussed in the previous section, you can use GENDBC.PRG to automatically generate such a schema for your databases. See Section 12 for a sample schema generated by GENDBC.

- As with the Create Table command, you must ensure that tag names don't exceed 10 characters in length to avoid getting a "Tag name too long" error.

Time to Play!

In the previous "Time to Play!" exercise, you created several tables in a database called SCRATCH. Now you can use Alter Table to change their structures:

```
open database SCRATCH exclusive
use COMPANY exclusive
list structure
alter table COMPANY ;
   add column ADDRESS C(30) ;
   add column CITY C(30) ;
   add column POSTCODE C(10) ;
   drop column TEST ;
   drop foreign key tag COMPCAT save ;
   drop check
list structure
```

Using that code you added three new fields, deleted one field, removed the relationship between COMPANY and CATEGORY (but kept the index on COMPCAT), and removed the table validation.

```
use CATEGORY exclusive
list structure
alter table CATEGORY ;
   add column TYPE C(2), ;
   rename column CODE to CATCODE
list structure
```

Here, you added a new field and renamed another.

Renaming a Table

The command Rename Table <Table1> To <Table2> changes the long name of the specified table to a new name. Because Visual FoxPro doesn't automatically update aliases in things like validation rules and index expressions when you rename a table, you'll need to manually edit any place you used the former name.

This command doesn't change the name of the DBF; you must do that from the operating system or by using the Rename command. However, changing the DBF name has a consequence: because the database contains a link to the table by path and file name, changing the file name will break that link. See the discussion of fixing database problems in Section 2 for the explanation of this problem and its solution.

Making a Table Usable in FoxPro 2.x

As previously mentioned, tables created in Visual FoxPro (or those created in FoxPro 2.x but changed structurally in Visual FoxPro) cannot be accessed in FoxPro 2.x because of changes in the DBF Header. To make a table usable in FoxPro 2.x, a new option with the Copy command can be used: Copy To <File> Type Fox2x. This command will create a new file with the specified name using a FoxPro 2.x file Header. Null values are converted to blanks; Currency, Double, and Integer fields are converted to Float fields; and DateTime fields are converted to Date fields. However, you should be aware that you might lose some data in this conversion.

Getting and Setting Database Properties

Previously you looked at the Dbgetprop() and Dbsetprop() functions from a database point of view. These functions also work with a specific table or fields in a table.

When used with tables, Dbgetprop() is called with the following syntax:

```
dbgetprop(<Alias>, 'Table', <Property>)
```

In this argument, <Alias> is the name of the table and <Property> is one of the following:

Property	Returns
Path	The path and file name
Comment	Comment
PrimaryKey	The tag name of the primary key
RuleExpression	Validation rule
RuleText	Validation text
InsertTrigger	Insert trigger
DeleteTrigger	Delete trigger
UpdateTrigger	Update trigger

When used with fields, Dbgetprop() is called as follows:

```
dbgetprop(<Alias.FieldName>, 'Field', <Property>)
```

In this argument, <Alias.FieldName> represents the field you are interested in and the table it belongs to. For example, to get information on the LAST_NAME field from CUSTOMER, you would use CUSTOMER.LAST_NAME. The argument also uses <Property> as one of the following:

Property	Returns
Caption	Field caption
Comment	Comment
DefaultValue	Default value
RuleExpression	Validation rule
RuleText	Validation text

Where Dbgetprop() is versatile, you'll find that you're rather limited in what you can change with Dbsetprop(). The Dbsetprop() function will accept only "Caption" for fields and "Comment" for fields and tables. For tables, Dbsetprop() is called as:

```
dbsetprop(<Alias>, 'Table', <Property>, <Value>)
```

For fields, dbsetprop() is called with this syntax:

```
dbsetprop(<Alias.FieldName>, 'Field', <Property>, <Value>)
```

One useful purpose for Dbgetprop() is in an error-trapping routine to display meaningful information about a field or table. As mentioned earlier, field and table validation text are displayed only when the validation rule is violated by changes made interactively, such as in a browse window or by typing in a field in a Form. Violations in program code display a generic "Validation rule is violated" message unless an error trap is set. You could have the error-trapping routine display a meaningful message once it's determined what type of error occurred, but that would duplicate what's already stored in the database. Following is a portion of an error-trapping routine that displays the proper text when a field validation rule is violated. This routine uses the new Aerror() function, which populates an array with information about the error; you'll see this function in more detail later. Here's the code:

```
...

* Put the error number in laERROR[1], the message into laERROR[2], the field
* (if applicable) into laERROR[3], and the work area # (if applicable) into
* laERROR[4].

= aerror(laERROR)
do case

* A field validation rule was violated, so get the field validation text from the
* database. Display either it or, if there isn't validation text for the field, the
* generic error message.

  case laERROR[1] = 1582
    lcTEXT = dbgetprop(alias(laERROR[4]) + '.' + laERROR[3], 'Field', ;
      'RuleText')
    = messagebox(iif(empty(lcTEXT), laERROR[2], lcTEXT)

...
```

The next routine is called GETFIELD (included on the source code disc that comes with this book). It uses Dbgetprop() to display a pop-up list of fields, but uses the field caption (hopefully something meaningful) instead of the field name:

GETFIELD.PRG

```
local lnI
define popup FIELD_POP from 0, 0 title 'Select Field'
for lnI = 1 to fcount()
   define bar lnI of FIELD_POP prompt dbgetprop(alias() + '.' + field(lnI), ;
     'Field', 'Caption')
next lnI
on selection popup FIELD_POP deactivate popup
activate popup FIELD_POP
wait window 'You selected ' + field(bar())
```

Another function, Cursorgetprop(), has a variety of uses that you'll see in later sections. However, one of its best uses for tables is returning the name of the database the table belongs to. To determine this, use Cursorgetprop('Database').

Putting a Table Structure into an Array or Table

The Afields() function existed in previous versions of FoxPro, but has changed in Visual FoxPro to give more information. It creates an array (or updates an existing one) containing the structure of a table, returning the number of fields in the table. It has the following syntax:

```
afields(<ArrayName> [, <WorkArea> | <Alias>])
```

In this argument, <ArrayName> is the array to create or update. In addition, <WorkArea> is the work area of the table, and <Alias> is its alias. If you don't specify a table with either of these, the table in the current work area will be used. The array is two-dimensional, with one row per field in the table and the columns as follows:

Column	Information
1	Field name
2	Type
3	Width
4	Decimal places
5	Null values allowed (.T. or .F.)
6	Code page translation not allowed (.F. for all field types except binary Character and Memo)
7	Field validation rule
8	Field validation text
9	Field default value
10	Table validation rule
11	Table validation text

You saw the Afields() function used in the NEW_REC() routine described earlier to recycle deleted records. Afields() was used to get the name and default value for each field.

Note that columns 10 and 11 actually contain table information instead of field information. If a table validation rule and text have been defined, this information will be placed in only the first row of the array. The remainder of the rows will have blank values in these columns.

Like Afields(), Copy Structure Extended existed in previous versions of FoxPro, but has additional fields now. This command creates a table having the following structure:

Field	Type	Contents
FIELD_NAME	C	Field name
FIELD_TYPE	C	Type
FIELD_LEN	N	Width
FIELD_DEC	N	Decimal places
FIELD_NULL	L	Null values allowed (.T. or .F.)

Continued on next page

Continued from previous page

Field	Type	Contents
FIELD_NOCP	L	Code page translation not allowed (.T. for all field types except non-binary Character and Memo; note how this differs from the equivalent column in an Afields() array)
FIELD_DEFA	M	Field default value
FIELD_RULE	M	Field validation rule
FIELD_ERR	M	Field validation text
TABLE_RULE	M	Table validation rule
TABLE_ERR	M	Table validation text

As noted with Afields(), TABLE_RULE and TABLE_ERR contain information only in the first record.

Other Functions

Sys(2029) returns a character value indicating a table type for the selected or specified table. Essentially, it's giving you the first byte in the DBF Header. Return values are as follows:

Code	Type
3	FoxPro 2.x or dBASE with no Memo fields
48	Visual FoxPro
67	dBASE IV SQL table with no Memo fields
99	dBASE IV SQL System table with a Memo field
131	FoxBASE+ and dBASE III PLUS table with a Memo field
139	dBASE IV table with a Memo field
203	dBASE IV SQL table with a Memo field
245	FoxPro 2.x with a Memo field

Primary() and Candidate() return .T. if the specified index is a primary or candidate key, respectively.

Tagcount() returns the number of tags in the specified CDX file. This is a handy function because the only way to process tags before Visual FoxPro was with a loop like the one shown.

```
lnI = 1
do while not empty(tag(lnI))
   * do something with tag(lnI)
   lnI = lnI + 1
enddo while not empty(tag(lnI))
```

Now, simply using For lnI = 1 To Tagcount() is more intuitive.

Tagno() returns the index number for the specified tag. It's handy because most index functions expect you to pass the index number rather than the tag name. For example, Key() provides the index expression for a given index, but because you know the name of a tag and not its number, you had to use code like the example shown:

```
lnI   = 1
lcKEY = ''
do while not empty(tag(lnI))
   if tag(lnI) = '<desired tag name>'
      lcKEY = key(lnI)
      exit
   else
      lnI = lnI + 1
   endif tag(lnI) = '<desired tag name>'
enddo while not empty(tag(lnI))
```

Now you can simply use Key(Tagno('<desired tag name>')). Here's a simple expression that returns the primary key expression for the current table:

```
key(tagno(dbgetprop(alias(), 'Table', 'PrimaryKey')))
```

The Display Tables and List Tables commands display the tables contained in the current database. Display Structure and List Structure commands now show which fields accept null values.

Watch Out for This!

You might have a problem if you change the structure of tables at your office then simply copy the DBC and its associated DCX and DCT files to a client's site where the tables already exist. If the table and the database container are out of sync, you won't be able to open the table. The only solution you'll have to resolve this problem is to remove the table from the database and readd it.

Without using any additional tools you or other people write, the only way to ensure that the database and tables are updated at your client's site is programming with Create Table, Alter Table, Add Table, and so forth. (Microsoft does provide the GENDBC utility described in the discussion of databases, but this is generally useful only for creating a database and its tables from scratch rather than converting the structure of an existing database.)

One Last Tip

As you saw, Visual FoxPro will automatically cause an error when field or table validation rules fail, when primary or candidate keys are not unique, or when you try to put a null value into a field that doesn't support them. However, you should know that *these errors aren't always directly trappable.* In other words, you can't use On Error to set up an error handler and always expect it to be executed when one of these conditions occurs. These errors are trappable only when the data is changed programmatically (by using the Replace command, for instance). If an error occurs in a browse or by typing data into a field in a Form, Visual FoxPro will either display the validation text or a generic error message (if there is no validation text).

The only way to handle these types of errors is to use buffering for all table changes, use Tableupdate() to write out the changes, and then determine what went wrong if Tableupdate() fails. Buffering will be covered in Section 5 so you can see exactly how this will work.

4 Relations

One shortcoming that has, until now, existed in Xbase systems is a lack of persistent relationships between tables. Unlike table structures, which are defined in the Header of the DBF file, and index structures, which are defined within the CDX file, relationships between tables are defined only in program code. You must specifically code Set Relation or SQL Select statements with join conditions to relate or join tables together.

If you haven't encountered the problem of not having relationship information defined in one place, try this exercise: look at any fairly large system someone else wrote and try to figure out which tables are related. It's an extremely time-consuming process requiring you to examine every program in the system. Yet it's an essential part of application maintenance because you must know what impact changes to the structure of one table will have on related tables. Having the structures of each table in the system without knowing the relationships between them means you have only part of the picture.

With Visual FoxPro, persistent relationships between tables can now be defined in the database. These relationships are not only useful for documentation purposes; they can also be used as default relationships between tables added to the DataEnvironment of forms and reports, and in the Query and View Designers.

Before you look at how Visual FoxPro implements relationships, spend a little time looking at relationships in general so you can understand why Visual FoxPro does what it does.

Types of Relationships

There are three types of relationships between tables:

- *One-to-many*. Every record in the "one" table has zero or more related records in the "many" table, while every record in the "many" table has *exactly* one related record in the "one" table. Often the "one" table is referred to as the parent and the "many" table as the child. This type of relationship is abbreviated as *1:M*.

  This type of relationship is sometimes confused with a one-to-one relationship because, looking at it from the child table, there's only one record that matches in the parent table. To determine the type of relationship properly, it's important to look at both sides of the relationship. A M:1 relationship is the same thing as a 1:M, but from a different viewpoint.

  A typical example is a table containing invoice information (such as invoice number, date, and customer) and a table of invoice line item information (line number, part number, cost, and so on). Each invoice has one or more line item records, but each line item record belongs to just one invoice. These tables would probably be related by the invoice number.

  Another example is a company table with a state or province code that gets looked up in a state or province table. Each company record belongs to a single state or province, but each state or province may have many companies belonging to it.

- *One-to-one*. Tables in one-to-one (*1:1*) relationships can, in some ways, be considered extensions of one another. For example, a company table may have a one-to-one related file containing additional information about the company. This type of relationship is not very common because it's simpler to combine the two tables into one. However, it may be useful if you want to conserve disk space when some fields will be filled in only for certain records. In that case, the optional fields are moved to another table and you only create a record in the related table when those fields are filled in.

- *Many-to-many*. A good example of a many-to-many (*M:M*) relationship is the one between a table of doctors and hospitals. Each doctor can provide services at any of a number of hospitals, and each hospital will have many doctors providing services. There's a difficulty in defining this type of relationship. Because you need a field in each table to find the matching record in the other table, you must decide how many hospital fields to store in the doctor table as well as how many doctor fields to store in the hospital table.

To resolve this problem, a third table is required to link the first two. The linking table will contain a foreign key for each of the related tables. In the doctor-hospital example, there would be a field for doctor ID and one for hospital ID. Each record in the linking table acts as an intersection between the two tables. Only if the linking record exists does a certain doctor practice at the specified hospital. If there are other attributes of the intersection (for example, the doctor's parking space number and office number at the specific hospital), those fields would be in the linking table.

Here's what the tables might look like:

HOSPITAL.DBF:

Hospital #	Name
001	Mercy General
002	Children's Hospital
003	Chicago Hope

DOCTORS.DBF:

Doctor #	Name
001	John Brown
002	Mary Green
003	Susan White

LINK.DBF:

Hospital #	Doctor #	Office #	Park #
001	001	123	A435
001	003	201	B453
002	002	11-38	Blue 11
002	003	9-16	Gold 75
003	001	East 45	10
003	002	East 71	102
003	003	West 15	85

In this case, there's a 1:M relationship between DOCTORS and LINK, and a 1:M relationship between HOSPITAL and LINK. When all the smoke clears, the net effect is a M:M relationship between DOCTORS and HOSPITAL.

Foreign Keys

For a relationship to exist between two tables, a field or combination of fields must exist in each table allowing you to find the matching record in the other table. Usually, the field will represent data belonging to one of the tables. For example, in the case of an invoice table and an invoice line item table, the invoice number linking the two tables is really an attribute of the invoice table (which contains information about invoices), not the line item table (which contains information about items sold). The only reason the invoice number field exists in the line item table is so you can determine which invoice the item belongs to.

The linking field between related tables is normally the primary key of one table (the table that the data belongs in). Because the field is only in the other table for linking purposes, it's referred to as a *foreign key*. A foreign key is not a type of index you can choose from the Table Designer because there's nothing special about it. You normally use a regular index for a foreign key field.

Sometimes the foreign key field may also be involved with the primary key. For example, in the invoice and invoice line item scenario, INVOICE_NUMBER is the primary key for the invoice table because there's only one record with a given invoice number. In line item, the primary key might be INVOICE_NUMBER + LINE_NUMBER because there's only one line number for each invoice. This type of index is called a *compound index* because more than one field's involved. However, you can't use the compound key for a relationship with the primary key. When Visual FoxPro compares strings with Exact set to off, it compares them up to the length of the shorter one. Thus, seeking for 1001 (invoice #1001) will find 100101 (the first line for invoice #1001). However, the relationship would work only in one direction because seeking for 100101 will not find 1001. This means that while you can define INVOICE_NUMBER + LINE_NUMBER as the primary key for the line item table to ensure that the user doesn't enter the same line twice for a given invoice, you must define another tag on INVOICE_NUMBER alone to use in the relationship with the invoice table.

Another example of this is the doctor-hospital example. HOSPITAL_NUMBER is the primary key for the hospital table and DOCTOR_NUMBER is the primary key for the doctor table. In the linking table, HOSPITAL_NUMBER and DOCTOR_NUMBER are both foreign keys for linking with their respective tables. You may also want to create the primary key for the table as either DOCTOR_NUMBER + HOSPITAL_NUMBER or HOSPITAL_NUMBER + DOCTOR_NUMBER so the user can't define the same doctor-hospital combination more than once.

Persistent Relationships Versus Temporal Relationships

Earlier it was mentioned that Xbase systems didn't have *persistent relationships*. In Visual FoxPro, relationships are called persistent because they are defined in the database, and can be used without program code whenever needed. In FoxPro 2.x, relationships were set and removed using the Set Relation command. Because they're defined only in program code and exist only until they're no longer used, these relationships can be termed *temporal*.

There's a significant philosophical difference in how temporal and persistent relationships are defined. The use of Set Relation in creating a temporal relationship is governed by the following rules:

- The table from which the relationship is set (the *source*) doesn't need a special index, nor does it require an active order.
- The table into which the relationship is set (the *target*) must have a controlling order that matches the expression used to relate the tables. For example, in order for Set Relation To ORG_ID Into ORGANIZ to work, ORGANIZ must have an order set to a tag whose key values match the ORG_ID field in the source table. There is an exception to this: if the target table doesn't have an order set, you can still set a relationship into it as long as the relation expression represents a record number for the target table.
- As the record pointer is moved in the source table, the target table uses an implicit Seek command on the relation expression to move its record pointer accordingly. If the matching record cannot be found, the target table is positioned at the end of the file.

A persistent relationship in Visual FoxPro is more like the join condition in a SQL Select than like the Set Relation command.

- There's no distinction between source and target tables.
- You define how to match records in each table by specifying which element in one table matches which element in the other table. However, while SQL Select requires that you indicate which field or expression from one table matches which field or expression in the other, persistent relationships require that you specify which tag matches another tag. This means that you must define a tag for each table and specify those tags as ways to match records in each table.
- Because you're defining how to match records between tables, the relationship can work in either direction. Either table can be the source or the target, depending on how

the relationship is needed. In the case of a query or view, there is no concept of source or target because the purpose is to create a Cursor of joined information.

During the beta cycle for Visual FoxPro, a number of people expressed concern regarding the second point. Because a tag wasn't required for the source table in FoxPro 2.x, they didn't want to have to define one in Visual FoxPro. In fact, you don't have to if you want to continue using temporal relationships in Visual FoxPro. However, to define a persistent relationship, you must define a tag for each table because those tags define the relationship.

If this troubles you, look at it this way: a persistent relationship is used to create a query or view, and it can be used to set a relationship in either direction. A tag is required on both tables to obtain the fastest performance. This isn't so strange when you consider that you need a tag on the fields or expressions involved in the join conditions to have Rushmore optimize your SQL Select. Given a child record, you need a tag for the parent table to find the matching parent record. To find the first child for a given parent, you need a tag in the child table.

You don't necessarily need to define every relationship between tables as a persistent one. Feel free to continue using temporal relationships when it makes sense for you to do so. You can use the Set Relation command just as you did in FoxPro 2.x, and can even define temporal relationships visually in the DataEnvironment of Forms and reports. For more information on setting up the DataEnvironment in Forms, see Steve Sawyer's report on the Form Designer.

Setting Persistent Relationships in the Database Designer

Now it's time to move beyond the theory into practice. Defining a relationship between two tables in the Database Designer is easy: you simply drag an index from one table to another. (If this doesn't seem intuitive, remember that persistent relationships are always defined from one index to another.) One way to do this is to scroll both tables so the indexes you want to use are visible in each table window, then drag one of the indexes to the other. Another way is to scroll only the table you will drag from until the desired index is visible, drag that index to the other table and, while continuing to hold down the mouse button, scroll the other table until the appropriate index is visible. Then drop the index you're dragging on top of it. It sounds complicated, but is actually harder to describe than it is to do.

There are some rules about where certain indexes can be dragged.

- Don't bother trying to drag a regular index; Visual FoxPro won't let you drop it anywhere.
- If you drag a candidate or primary index and drop it on a regular index, you will get a 1:M relationship.
- If you drag a candidate or primary index and drop it on a candidate or primary index, the result is a 1:1 relationship.

Because you can only drag a candidate or primary index to another index, you are always setting a relationship from the "one" (or parent) table to the other table (either "many" or "one," depending on the type of index involved).

After dropping the index onto the other table, the dialog box shown in Figure 4-1 will be displayed. You can change the index for each table if you wish. The relationship type that appears in the dialog box is based on the types of indexes chosen.

Figure 4-1.

The Edit Relationship dialog box

Relationships are shown as lines between tables. (See Figure 4-2.) One end of the line has a bar across it. This end connects to the "one" table. The other end of the line has a "fork" symbol, which connects to the "many" table. The lines are always drawn from index to index, so if the index isn't visible in the window, the line will extend from the bottom of the table.

Figure 4-2.

The Database Designer using lines to show relationships between tables

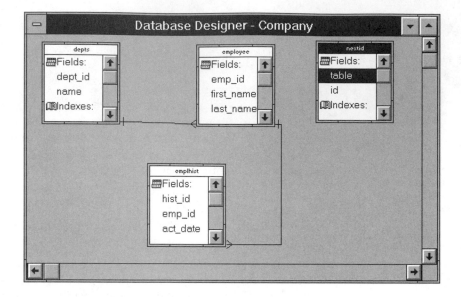

The relationship lines for a table automatically adjust position if you drag the table within the Database Designer window. This means you can create a more visually appealing layout by dragging tables to minimize the number of lines that must cross each other.

Editing or Deleting a Relationship

To edit a relationship, double-click the relationship line. Alternatively, you can click to select the line, then either click the right mouse button and select Edit Relationship from the shortcut menu, or select Edit Relationship from the Database pad. The dialog box shown in Figure 4-1 is displayed so you can edit the indexes for each table in the relationship.

To delete a relationship, click the relationship line then either press Delete or click the right mouse button and select Remove Relationship from the shortcut menu.

Defining, Editing, and Deleting Persistent Relationships Programmatically

As you saw when tables were discussed, you can specify arguments in the Create Table and Alter Table commands that define or remove persistent relationships. You can use Create Table to create a tag on the specific field and set a relationship into the specified existing parent table. (Note that this is backwards from the Database Designer, where you specify the relationship from parent into child.)

```
create table ...
   <FieldName> <Type> [(<Width> [, <Decimals>])]
   [references <ParentTable> [tag <ParentTag>]]
   ...
```

You can also use the following syntax to define the relationship after all the fields to define have been listed.

```
create table ...
   [, foreign key <KeyExpr> tag <TagName> [nodup]
      references <ParentTable> [tag <ParentTag>]]
   ...
```

To define a relationship for an existing table when you are also adding or editing a column, you can use this syntax:

```
alter table ...
   [add | alter [column] <FieldName>
   [references <ParentTable> [tag <ParentTag>]]
   ...
```

You can also use the next syntax to define the relationship without changing the table structure.

```
alter table ...
   [add foreign key [<KeyExpr>] tag <TagName>
      references <ParentTable> [tag <ParentTag>]]
   ...
```

To delete a relationship, use the syntax shown.

```
alter table ...
   [drop foreign key tag <TagName> [save]]
   ...
```

The Save keyword indicates the index should not be removed. If you don't specify it, both the relationship and the index are deleted.

Time to Play!

Now create a few tables and some relationships between them. This code is the basis for an order entry system (these tables don't exist on the source code disc):

```
create database ORDENTRY
create table CUSTOMERS ;
    (CUSTOMER_ID I default NEXT_ID('CUSTOMERS'), ;
    NAME C(30), ;
    ADDRESS C(30), ;
    CITY C(30), ;
```

Continued on next page

Continued from previous page

```
      POSTAL_CODE C(10), ;
      primary key CUSTOMER_ID tag CUST_ID)
create table PRODUCTS ;
    (PART_NUMBER I, ;
    DESCRIPTION C(30), ;
    PRICE Y, ;
    QUANTITY_ON_HAND I, ;
    primary key PART_NUMBER tag PART_NUM)
create table ORDERS ;
    (ORDER_NUMBER I default NEXT_ID('ORDERS'), ;
    ORDER_DATE D, ;
    CUSTOMER_ID I, ;
    primary key ORDER_NUMBER tag ORD_NUM, ;
    foreign key CUSTOMER_ID tag CUST_ID references CUSTOMER)
create table ORDER_DETAIL ;
    (ORDER_NUMBER I, ;
    LINE_NUMBER N(3), ;
    PART_NUMBER I, ;
    PRICE Y, ;
    QUANTITY I, ;
    primary key str(ORDER_NUMBER) + str(LINE_NUMBER, 3) ;
       tag ORDER_DET, ;
    foreign key ORDER_NUMBER tag ORD_NUM references ORDERS, ;
    foreign key PART_NUMBER tag PART_NUM references PRODUCTS)
modify database
```

Using Persistent Relationships

Now that you can define persistent relationships, you should know what to do with them.

Persistent relationships have several uses:

- They are used as the default relationships between tables added to the DataEnvironment of Forms and reports, and in the Query and View Designers. For example, if you add two related tables to the DataEnvironment of a Form, Visual FoxPro will automatically set a relationship between them based on their persistent relationship. Visual FoxPro will automatically create a SQL join condition when you add related tables to the Query Designer.

- As you'll see in Section 6, persistent relationships allow you to enforce referential integrity.

- Because they're already defined in the database, you can use them to set up relationships in places without a DataEnvironment such as program (PRG) files.

As you saw in Section 2, Adbobjects() is a function that fills an array with the names of objects of a certain type from the current database. In the case of relations, it's called with the following syntax:

```
adbobjects(<ArrayName>, 'Relation')
```

In this argument <ArrayName> is the name of the array into which the relation information is placed. The table has one row per relation and uses the following columns:

Column	Contents
1	Child table
2	Parent table
3	Child tag
4	Parent tag
5	Referential integrity rules (see Section 2 for information)

You can use this information to create a data-driven routine to set up relationships. For example, if you have a processing routine that needs to set up all relationships from a particular table, you could use the following code. (SETUPREL.PRG is included on the source code disc.)

```
lparameters lcCHILD
local laRELATIONS[1], lnRELATIONS, lnI, lcPARENT, lcEXPR

* Select the child table (open it first if necessary).

lcCHILD = upper(lcCHILD)
if used(lcCHILD)
   select (lcCHILD)
else
   select 0
   use (lcCHILD)
endif used(lcCHILD)

* Get all relationships from the database.

lnRELATIONS = adbobjects(laRELATIONS, 'Relation')
for lnI = 1 to lnRELATIONS

* We only want relationships for the child table we're
* interested in.

   if laRELATIONS[lnI, 1] = lcCHILD

* Open the parent table (if necessary) and set its order to
* that used by the relationship.

      lcPARENT = laRELATIONS[lnI, 2]
      if not used(lcPARENT)
```

Continued on next page

Continued from previous page

```
        use (lcPARENT) in 0
      endif not used(lcPARENT)
      set order to (laRELATIONS[lnI, 4]) in (lcPARENT)

  * The relationship expression to use is the index expression
  * for the child tag defined in the relationship.

      lcEXPR = key(tagno(laRELATIONS[lnI, 3]))
      set relation to &lcEXPR into (lcPARENT) additive
    endif laRELATIONS[lnI, 1] = lcCHILD
  next lnI
```

Here's an example of how this routine would be called to set up relations for the order details table before processing it:

```
do SETUPREL with 'ORDER_DETAIL'
** process the order details here
set relation to
```

Persistent relationships between tables work differently than the temporal relationships you're used to. However, defining persistent relationships is important because it allows you to use one location (the DBC) to store the complete information about your tables. This information includes their structures as well as their relationships. You get the added benefits because persistent relationships are automatically used in Forms and reports, saving you a few steps.

5 | Buffering and Transactions

One of the things you've probably picked up by now is that while you can continue to do things the "old" way, Visual FoxPro often provides you with a better way to perform the same task. For example, you saw earlier that field validation rules can now be stored in the database, so you don't have to code those rules in every module of every application that accesses the field. The techniques used to edit records in Forms can also be updated.

Here's an "old" way to write code to edit a record in a data entry screen:

- The screen has Get objects for memory variables with the same names as the table's fields (for example, M.CUST_ID and M.NAME).

- When the user positions the table to a particular record (for example, using the Next button), use the Scatter Memvar command to transfer the record to the memory variables and the Show Gets command to refresh the values shown on the screen. The user cannot edit the variables (which are either disabled or have When clauses that evaluate to .F.) because the user is currently in "view" mode.

- When the user chooses the Edit button, you can try to lock the record. If that's unsuccessful, you can display an appropriate message. If it worked, check the value of each field against its memory variable—if the two don't match, another user must have edited and saved the record since you first displayed it. In that case, display an appropriate message and use Scatter Memvar and Show Gets again, allowing the user to see the current contents of the record.

- If the fields and memory variables match, either enable the Get objects or make their When clauses evaluate to .T. so the user can edit the variables.
- When the user chooses the Save button, do some validation to ensure everything was entered according to your rules, then Gather Memvar to update the record from the memory variables and unlock the record. Disable the Get objects or make their When clauses evaluate to .F. so the user is once again in "view" mode.

Notice that in this scheme you don't do a direct Read against the record. Instead, you allow the user to edit memory variables, writing only those memory variables back to the record if everything went well. This method protects the table because it doesn't allow any data to be stored unless it passes all the rules. Also notice the record is locked while the user is editing the memory variables. This prevents another user from editing the same record at the same time. It does, however, suffer from the "out to lunch" syndrome—if the user starts the edit then goes to lunch, the record stays locked and unavailable to other users for editing.

This isn't the only way to edit records, of course. You could do the lock just before saving the record instead of when the edit mode starts. This minimizes the time the record is locked, allowing other users access to it. It has its own drawback, though. If the user edits the variables and clicks Save, what happens if some other user edited the record in the meantime? Do you overwrite their changes? Do you prevent the record from being saved? These are design issues you must handle on a case-by-case basis.

The purpose of this effort is to protect the data. If you were writing an application that only you would ever use, you'd probably make it simpler by just using Read against the fields in the record directly. That would make the screen act like the "form" equivalent of a Browse, because everything you typed would go directly into the record. However, because you can't trust those pesky users to know what they can and can't enter, you have to protect the data by building a "firewall" between the user and the table. In FoxPro 2.x, creating this firewall took a significant amount of coding.

Visual FoxPro provides a built-in firewall mechanism that gives you the best of both worlds: a direct Read against a record that only permits the data to be written after it passes all the tests. This mechanism is called *buffering*.

Buffering

Using memory variables to hold the contents of a record is like creating a buffer of data. The data is transferred from the record to the buffer by using Scatter Memvar and from the buffer to the record with Gather Memvar.

Not only can Visual FoxPro do this type of single record buffering (called *record* or *row buffering*) automatically, it also supports another type of buffering (called *table buffering*) in which multiple records are accessed through a buffer.

Record buffering is normally used when you want to access or update single records. It is common in data entry mechanisms like the one described earlier: the user can display or edit a single record in the Form. Table buffering would be the choice for updating several records at a time. A common example of this is an invoice Header-detail screen. By using table buffering for the invoice detail table, you can allow the user to edit detail lines as long as they choose, and then save or cancel all of the detail records at once.

In addition to two buffering mechanisms, there are two locking mechanisms. The first "old" way described earlier is a *pessimistic* locking scheme—the record is locked as soon as the user chooses Edit and stays locked until they choose Save. This ensures that no one else can change the record while this user is doing so, which may or may not be a good thing, depending on your application. The second "old" method described is an *optimistic* locking mechanism—the record is locked only for the brief amount of time it takes to write the record, then is immediately unlocked. This maximizes the availability of the record (also known as maximizing *concurrence*) but means you have to handle conflicts that could occur if two users edit the record at the same time. As you'll see in a moment, this is easy to do in Visual FoxPro. As a result, optimistic buffering is probably the mechanism of choice for most applications.

Because records can be automatically buffered, there's no longer a need to use the manual buffer mechanism. In other words, now you can Read directly against the fields in the record and not worry about maintaining memory variables for each one. To save the changes, you simply tell Visual FoxPro to write the buffer to the table. To cancel the changes, you tell it not to. You'll see how to do that in a moment.

Visual FoxPro implements buffering by creating a Cursor whenever a table is opened. The Cursor is used to define properties for the table. In the case of local tables, the only property for the Cursor to define is the manner that buffering is performed. Views and remote tables have additional properties you'll see in the discussion of connections and views. Those properties are set using the Cursorsetprop() function and examined with Cursorgetprop(). You'll see the use of these functions shortly.

Row buffering has an interesting implementation for appended records. As records are added to the buffer, they're assigned a negative record number. Recno() returns -1 for the first appended record, -2 for the second, and so on. You can use the Go command with a negative number to position the buffer to the appropriate appended record. This has an implication for routines handling record numbers—instead of testing for Between(lnRECNO, 1, Reccount()) to ensure lnRECNO is a valid record number, you'll now have to test for Between(lnRECNO, 1, Reccount()) or lnRECNO < 0.

You'll see an example of how all of this works in the next "Time to Play!" exercise. First, though, you'll get into the details of how you can put buffering to work.

Using Buffering

Buffering is turned off by default, so Visual FoxPro acts like FoxPro 2.x when writing updates to a table. To use buffering, you must specifically turn it on. Buffering is available for both free tables and those that are part of a database. Buffering also requires you to issue the Set Multilocks On command because its default is also off. You'll get an error message if you forget to do this. You can put MULTILOCKS = ON in your CONFIG.FPW file or use the Options function under the Tools pad to save this setting as the default.

Buffering is controlled using the Cursorsetprop('Buffering', <n>, <Alias>) function. You don't have to specify <Alias> if you're setting buffering for the current table. <n> is one of the following values depending on the buffering and locking method you wish to use:

Buffering/Locking Method	<n>
no buffering	1
record, pessimistic	2
record, optimistic	3
table, pessimistic	4
table, optimistic	5

For example, to enable optimistic record buffering, use Cursorsetprop('Buffering', 3). To determine what buffering is currently in use for a table, use Cursorgetprop('Buffering').

To enable buffering in a Form, you could specify Cursorsetprop() for each table in the Form's Load method, but the preferred approach is to set the Form's BufferMode property to either optimistic or pessimistic. (The default is "none".) The Form will then automatically use table buffering for tables bound to Grids and row buffering for all other tables. If you use a DataEnvironment for the Form, you can override the Form's BufferMode for a particular table by setting its BufferModeOverride property as desired.

While the user is editing the data in the buffered record, you have access to the value they've entered into each field, but also the former value of each field and the current value of each field (the value actually on disk). Two new functions, Oldval() and Curval(), were added for this purpose. Here's how you obtain the appropriate values:

To Get:	Use:
the value the user entered (i.e. the value in the buffer)	<fieldname> or <alias.fieldname>
the value before the user changed anything	Oldval('<fieldname>')
the current value in the record	Curval('<fieldname>')

Curval() and Oldval() can be used only with optimistic buffering.

You may be wondering how the value returned by Curval() would differ from the one returned by Oldval(). It obviously wouldn't if only a single user is running the application. However, on a network and with optimistic locking, it's possible that a second user edited the same record and saved changes after the first user started editing the record. Here's an example:

Bob brings up record #2 in CONTACTS.DBF and clicks the Edit button.

Field	Value	Oldval()	Curval()
LAST_NAME	Jones	Jones	Jones
FIRST_NAME	Bill	Bill	Bill

Bob changes the first name to Sam but doesn't immediately save the record.

Field	Value	Oldval()	Curval()
LAST_NAME	Jones	Jones	Jones
FIRST_NAME	Sam	Bill	Bill

Mary brings up record #2 in CONTACTS.DBF, clicks the Edit button, changes the first name to Eric, and saves. At Bill's machine, Curval() shows the change.

Field	Value	Oldval()	Curval()
LAST_NAME	Jones	Jones	Jones
FIRST_NAME	Sam	Bill	Eric

Notice that FIRST_NAME, Oldval('FIRST_NAME'), and Curval('FIRST_NAME') all return different values. By having access to the original value, the buffered value, and the current value for each field in a record, you can do two things.

- You can determine which fields the user changed by comparing the buffered value to the original value.
- You can detect whether other users on a network made changes to the same record after the edit had started by comparing the original value to the current value.

If you don't care about the old and current values and simply wish to detect if a field was edited by the user, you can use Getfldstate(). This new function returns a numeric value indicating if something about the current record has changed. Getfldstate() is called as follows:

```
getfldstate(<FieldName> | <FieldNumber> [, <Alias> | <WorkArea>])
```

It returns one of the following values:

Value	Description
1	No change
2	The field was edited or the deletion status of the record was changed
3	A record was appended but the field was not edited and the deletion status was not changed.
4	A record was appended and the field was edited or the deletion status of the record was changed.

Changing the deletion status means either deleting or recalling the record. Note that deleting and then immediately recalling the record will result in a value of 2 or 4 even though there's no net effect on the record.

If you don't specify an alias or work area, Getfldstate() will operate on the current table. Specifying 0 for <FieldNumber> will return the append or deletion status of the current record. If you specify -1 for <FieldNumber>, the function will return a character string with the first digit representing the table status followed by one digit for the status of each field. This is equivalent to the following code:

```
lcRETURN = str(getfldstate(0), 1)
for lnI = 1 to fcount()
   lcRETURN = lcRETURN + str(getfldstate(lnI), 1)
next lnI
return lcRETURN
```

For example, in the previous scenario where two people edited a record simultaneously, the function Getfldstate(-1) would return 112. The first digit indicates the record was not appended or deleted, the second that the first field was unchanged, and the third that the second field was changed.

Getfldstate() can be used to determine if anything in the current record has changed. For example, if you want to enable the Save and Cancel buttons only when the user actually changes something, you could use code similar to this.

```
if getfldstate(-1) = replicate('1', fcount() + 1)
   * disable the buttons, since nothing's changed
else
   * enable the buttons
endif getfldstate(-1) = replicate('1', fcount() + 1)
```

By the way, Getfldstate() has a companion function called Setfldstate(). This function has the same syntax as Getfldstate() but takes an additional parameter to note what value to set the field state to. Essentially, this function can fool Visual FoxPro into thinking a field was changed when it really wasn't. It can also make Visual FoxPro think a field wasn't changed when it really was.

Writing a Buffered Record

Now look again at the example of Bill and Mary changing the same record. When Bill clicks the Save button, how would you tell Visual FoxPro to write the buffer to the record? With record buffering, the table is updated in several instances such as when you

- Move the record pointer
- Issue a new Tableupdate() function
- Use the Rlock() function
- Try to close the table
- Change the buffer mode

However, note that the last two wouldn't normally be used when saving a record, and there's no need to manually use Rlock(). Visual FoxPro will automatically unlock the record once it's completed the update. The usual mechanism is either of the first two methods.

With table buffering, moving the record pointer and locking a record will not update the table. (The whole point of table buffering is that several records are buffered at once.) As a result, the usual way is to issue the Tableupdate() function.

Tableupdate() returns .T. if the buffer was successfully written to the record. If the record buffer was not changed (the user didn't edit any fields, add a record, or change the deleted status for the record), Tableupdate() will return .T. but actually do nothing.

Tableupdate() can take a few optional parameters:

```
tableupdate(<AllRows>, <Forced>, <Alias> | <Workarea>)
```

The first parameter indicates what records to update: .F. tells it to update only the current record, while .T. means update all records (effective only if table buffering is used). If the second parameter is .T., any changes by another user will be overwritten by the current user's changes. Unless the third parameter is specified, Tableupdate() will update the current table.

You can also cancel the changes the user made. With the memory variable approach, you use Scatter Memvar to restore the memory variables to the values stored on disk. With buffering, use the Tablerevert() function to do the same for the buffer.

Time to Play!

You can see how row and table buffering work by trying out some of the functions that support them. This exercise may appear long, but it really will take only a few minutes, and you'll see some interesting things. Enter the following code, or run BUFFER.PRG and then BUFFER2.PRG on the source code disc. BUFFER2.PRG will step through the code so you can watch the results in the Debug window.

```
set database to          && just in case a database was selected
create table TEMP ;
  (FIELD1 C(10), ;
  FIELD2 C(10))
set multilocks on              && must do or we get an error
set deleted off                && we want to see deleted records
= cursorsetprop('Buffering', 3)    && optimistic row buffering
activate window debug
```

In the Debug window, enter the following (each on its own

Continued on next page

linc) so you can see what they do under different conditions: Recno(), Getfldstate(0), Getfldstate(1), Getfldstate(-1), Reccount(), FIELD1, and Oldval('FIELD1'). Type Browse in the Command window to see what happens with the table.

Now try typing the following:

```
append blank
```

The Debug window should look like this:

```
recno()             1
getfldstate(0)      3          && appended record
getfldstate(1)      3          && non-edited field in appended
                               && record
getfldstate(-1)     "333"      && appended record and non-edited
                               && fields
reccount()          1
FIELD1              "         "
oldval('FIELD1')    .NULL.     && new record, so no old value yet
```

Now type:

```
replace FIELD1 with 'test'
```

The Debug window should show:

```
recno()             1
getfldstate(0)      3
getfldstate(1)      4          && edited field in appended record
getfldstate(-1)     "343"
reccount()          1
FIELD1              "test    "
oldval('FIELD1')    .NULL.
```

Then save the record using the following code.

```
= tableupdate()
```

The Debug window should show:

```
recno()             1
getfldstate(0)      1          && "normal" record
getfldstate(1)      1          && "normal" field
getfldstate(-1)     "111"      && "normal" record and fields
reccount()          1
FIELD1              "test    "
oldval('FIELD1')    "test    "    && oldval now = buffer
```

Now create another record in a different way:

```
scatter memvar blank
insert into TEMP from memvar
```

The Debug window should show:

```
recno()             2
getfldstate(0)      3
```

Continued on next page

Continued from previous page

```
getfldstate(1)     4      && field was sort of edited because
                          && INSERT replaced fields with memvars
getfldstate(-1)   "344"
reccount()         2
FIELD1             "       "
oldval('FIELD1')   .NULL.
```

Now save the record in a slightly different way to see how it works. Type = Rlock(). The contents of the Debug window are predictable.

Edit the record by typing replace FIELD1 with 'test'. The Debug window should show the following:

```
getfldstate(0)     1
getfldstate(1)     2      && field was edited
getfldstate(-1)   "121"
FIELD1            "test   "
oldval('FIELD1')   "       "
```

Now abandon the edit by typing = Tablerevert().

Next you can look at table buffering to see how appended records are handled. Type the following code:

```
= cursorsetprop('Buffering', 5)
append blank
```

The Debug window should show this code.

```
recno()           -1      && first appended record in table
                          && buffer
getfldstate(0)     3
getfldstate(1)     3
getfldstate(-1)   "333"
reccount()         3
FIELD1             "       "
oldval('FIELD1')   .NULL.
```

Add two more records, putting something into FIELD1:

```
append blank
append blank
replace FIELD1 with '5'
```

The Debug window should now show:

```
recno()           -3      && third appended record in table buffer
reccount()         5
```

Click the Browse window and look at how Recno() changes in the Debug window as you move up and down through the records. Move back to the last record and, in the Command window, type: = Tableupdate().

Click back in the Browse window. Notice what was record -3 is now record 3 (you can tell it was record -3 because FIELD1

Continued on next page

contains "5"). Records -1 and -2 still have negative record numbers because Tableupdate() affects only the current record. Now update the entire table:

```
= tableupdate(.T.)
```

Click back in the Browse window. All records have positive record numbers; they're now all "real" records. Add three more blank records using Append Blank. After adding the last one, the Debug window will appear as follows:

```
recno()          -3     && third appended record in table buffer
reccount()       8
```

Cancel the addition of the last record by typing = Tablerevert().

Click the Browse window. Notice record -3 doesn't appear any more, but -1 and -2 are still there. Also, Reccount() in the Debug window now says 7. You can get rid of the other two records by typing = Tablerevert(.T.).

Click the Browse window and move the record pointer to record 3 (the one with "5" in FIELD1). In the Command window, type delete and notice the changes in the Debug window:

```
getfldstate(0)     2       && deleted record
getfldstate(1)     1       && unedited field
getfldstate(-1)    "211"
```

Update the table by typing = Tableupdate(); the Debug window should now show:

```
getfldstate(0)     1       && "normal" record
getfldstate(1)     1
getfldstate(-1)    "111"
```

It looks just like a "normal" record except it's deleted. Add three more blank records using Append Blank. After adding the last one, type the following:

```
go -2
delete
= tableupdate(.T.)
```

This will move you to the second appended record, delete it, and update the entire table. Click the Browse window and notice the former record -2 is now record 7. It has also been deleted. If you want to avoid adding a deleted appended record to the table, you must use the Tablerevert() function on that record before using Tableupdate(.T.).

Handling Errors

Continuing on with the Bill and Mary example, the code that executes when Bill clicks the Save button uses the Tableupdate()

function to try to write the buffer to the record. Remember that Mary edited the record and saved her changes as Bill was editing the same record. When Bill clicks Save, Tableupdate() will return .F., meaning that his changes weren't written to disk.

This is because Visual FoxPro will not write the buffer to the record when:

- A second user changes and saves a record while the first user is editing it (as happened in this example). In such instances, Visual FoxPro automatically compares Oldval() and Curval() for each field. If it detects any differences, there will be a conflict.
- The user enters a duplicate primary or candidate key value.
- A field or table rule is violated, or a field that doesn't support null values is null.
- A trigger fails.
- Another user locks the record. This can be minimized by avoiding manually locking records with Rlock() and using the same buffer locking mechanism for a table in all Forms and programs that access it.
- Another user deletes the record.

You must decide what to do when Tableupdate() fails. Also, if your application allows the user to click the Next or Previous button while editing a record, you must handle the error that will occur when the automatic save is attempted. In both of these cases, the proper place to handle this is in an error-trapping routine.

(Interestingly, if you issue the Rlock() function attempting to update the table and the update fails for one of these reasons, Rlock() will trigger an error instead of returning .F.)

Error handling has been improved in Visual FoxPro. You can still use the old way to set an error trap, which is to use the On Error command to specify a procedure to execute when an error occurs. This error routine would typically look at Error() and Message() to determine what happened, then take the appropriate action.

Visual FoxPro now provides an automatic error-handling mechanism: the *Error* method. If an Error method exists for an object or Form, it will automatically be executed when an error occurs without you having to manually set the trap. Aerror() is a new function that helps to figure out what went wrong. When you pass it an array name, it creates or updates the array with the following elements:

Element	Type	Description
1	Numeric	The error number (same as Error()).
2	Character	The error message (same as Message()).
3	Character	The error parameter (for example, a field name) if the error has one (same as Sys(2018)) or .NULL. if not.
4	Numeric or Character	The work area in which the error occurred if appropriate, .NULL. otherwise.
5	Numeric or Character	The trigger that failed (1 for insert, 2 for update, or 3 for delete) if a trigger failed (error 1539), or .NULL. if not.
6	Numeric or Character	.NULL. (used for OLE and ODBC errors).
7	Numeric	.NULL. (used for OLE errors).

For example, Aerror(laERROR) will create or update an array called laERROR.

Here are the common errors that may occur when Visual FoxPro attempts to write the buffer to the table:

Error #	Error Message	Comment
109	Record is in use by another	
1539	Trigger failed	Check element 5 to determine which trigger failed.
1581	Field does not accept null values	Check element 3 to determine which field was involved.
1582	Field validation rule is violated	Check element 3 to determine which field was involved.
1583	Record validation rule is violated	
1585	Record has been modified by another	
1884	Uniqueness of index violated	Check element 3 to determine which tag was involved.

You can handle most of these errors in a straightforward manner by telling the users the problem and leaving them in edit mode to correct it or cancel. Although error #1585 (record has been modified by another) can be tricky, there are several ways you could handle it.

- You could tell the user that someone else modified the record, then cancel that user's edits with Tablerevert(). However, this approach will probably not be popular with users.
- You can force the update of the record using Tableupdate(.F., .T.). This causes the other user's changes to be overwritten by the current user's. The current user might be happy, but the other user probably won't be.
- You can display the changes the other user made to the record in another copy of the same Form. This is easy to do with Visual FoxPro's ability to create multiple instances of the same Form. The user can then decide whether the changes the other user made should be kept or not, then you can either use Tableupdate(.F., .T.) to force the update or Tablerevert() to cancel.
- You can begin by determining if there is a "real" conflict— did both users change the same field or not. This is probably the most sensible option. If they updated different fields, you could tell Visual FoxPro to update only the field this user changed, leaving the other user's changes intact. One example is an order processing system. One user may have edited the description of a product while another user entered an order for the product, thereby decreasing the quantity on hand. These changes aren't mutually exclusive. If you make your table update less granular by updating only the modified fields instead of the entire record, you can satisfy both users.

  This method works in a logical series of steps.

  - If you find a field where Oldval() is different than Curval(), that indicates that the field was edited by another user (user #2). If the field's buffered value is the same as Oldval(), this user (user #1) didn't change the field, so you can prevent overwriting its new value by setting the buffered value to Curval().
  - If you find a field where the buffered value is different than Oldval(), that means the field was edited by user #1. If Oldval() equals Curval(), user #2 didn't change this field, so it can be safely overwritten.
  - If you find a field where the buffered value is different than Oldval() but the same as Curval(), both users made the same change. While this may seem unlikely, it could happen if someone sent a change of address notice to a company and somehow two users updated the record at the same time. Because the changes were identical, you could safely overwrite the field.
  - If you find a field where the buffered value of a field is different than both Oldval() and Curval(), and

Oldval() and Curval() aren't identical, the two users changed the same field to different values. This is the only instance of a "real" conflict, and you must decide how to handle it.

In the case of inventory quantity on hand or account balances, one possibility is to apply the same change user #2 made to the buffered value. For example, if Oldval() is 10 and Curval() is 20, user #2 increased the amount by 10. If the buffered value is 5, user #1 is decreasing the amount by 5. The new buffered value should therefore be value + Curval() - Oldval(), or 15.

In the case of Date fields, business rules and common sense might help. For example, in a patient appointment scheduling program with a field containing the date of a patient's next visit, the earlier of the two dates is probably the correct one. If, however, it's prior to the current date, you can assume the later date is the correct one.

Other types of fields, especially Character and Memo fields, often can't be resolved without asking user #1 to make a decision about either overwriting user #2's changes or abandoning their own. Allowing user #1 to see user #2's changes can help them make this decision.

Here's some code that will do this type of conflict resolution. (This code assumes you've already determined the problem is error #1585 and the record had been modified by another user.)

```
llCONFLICT = .F.
for lnI = 1 to fcount()
   lcFIELD      = field(lnI)
   llOTHER_USER = oldval(lcFIELD)    <> curval(lcFIELD)
   llTHIS_USER  = evaluate(lcFIELD) <> oldval(lcFIELD)
   llSAME_CHANGE = evaluate(lcFIELD) == curval(lcFIELD)
   do case

* Another user edited this field but this user didn't, so
* grab the new value.

      case llOTHER_USER and not llTHIS_USER
         replace (lcFIELD) with curval(lcFIELD)

* Another user didn't edit this field, or they both made
* the same change, so we don't need to do anything.

      case not llOTHER_USER or llSAME_CHANGE

* Uh-oh, both users changed this field, but to different
* values.

      otherwise
```

Continued on next page

Continued from previous page

```
                    llCONFLICT = .T.
            endcase
        next lnI

        * If we have a conflict, handle it.

        if llCONFLICT
            lnCHOICE = messagebox('Another user also changed this ' + ;
                'record. Do you want to overwrite their changes ' + ;
                '(Yes), not overwrite but see their changes ' + ;
                '(No), or cancel your changes (Cancel)?', 3 + 16, ;
                'Problem Saving Record!')
            do case

        * Overwrite their changes.

                case lnCHOICE = 6
                    = tableupdate(.F., .T.)

        * See the changes: bring up another instance of the Form.

                case lnCHOICE = 7
                    do form MYFORM name oNAME

        * Cancel the changes.

                otherwise
                    = tablerevert()
            endcase

        * No conflict, so force the update.

        else
            = tableupdate(.F., .T.)
        endif llCONFLICT
```

Time to Play!

Take a look at the EMPLOYEES Form on the source code disc.

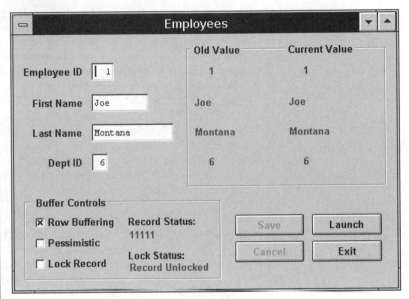

This Form has some interesting features.

- You can see the value in all three buffers (the record buffer, Oldval(), and Curval()) at once, in addition to the "record status," Getfldstate(-1).
- You can turn buffering on and off (the default is on), and choose optimistic (the default) or pessimistic locking. You can also explicitly lock the record and see the lock status.
- As you edit the record, the Save and Cancel buttons are automatically enabled. Look at the Form's Refresh method to see how this is done. This method is called from the GetFocus and LostFocus methods of every field as well as the Activate method for the Form.
- This Form allows you to simulate a multiuser situation by launching a second copy of the Form (using the Launch button). Because the Form's DataSession property is set to Private, each instance is independent and simulates a different user on a network. As there are no record navigation buttons on this Form, each instance is viewing and editing the same record.
- The Exit button asks if you want to save your changes if you edited the record but didn't save it. If this code wasn't there,

Continued on next page

Continued from previous page

closing the table would automatically cause the update to be attempted, which may not be what the user wants.

• The Form's Error method handles problems that occur when a record is saved. The conflict resolution scheme outlined earlier is used here so you can see how it works.

Run the Form. Edit the First Name and press Tab. Notice that the Record Status changes: the position representing that field becomes "2". Also, the Save and Cancel buttons become enabled. However, nothing else changes, especially Old Value and Current Value. Because optimistic row buffering is used by default, the record isn't locked and changes aren't written until you choose Save.

Click the Exit button without saving the change. It will ask if you want to save the changes or not. It calls the Click method for either the Save or Cancel button, depending on which you choose.

Run the Form again and launch another instance. Edit the First Name field in one of the Forms. Notice Record Status changes. Switch to another Form without saving in the first one. Edit the First Name and save. Notice that Old Value and Current Value change to contain the new value, and Record Status changes back to 11111.

Switch back to the first Form. Notice that while the First Name field, the field value, Old Value, and Current Value are all different, Current Value has the saved value from the other Form. Click the Save button—you'll get several messages showing what the conflict resolution routine found as it checked each field. Try changing the same field to the same value in each Form, changing different fields, and changing the same field to different values to see how each instance is handled.

Check the box for pessimistic locking in both Forms, then edit a field in one of the Forms. Notice that Record Status changes as it did with optimistic locking, but Lock Status changes to show that the record is now locked.

Again, switch to the second Form without saving in the first one. Try to type in a field. You'll immediately get an error message because the record is locked in the second Form, and, with pessimistic locking, Visual FoxPro tries to lock the record as soon as you change anything. Save in the other Form and switch back to this one again.

Turn off row buffering and then edit the First Name field. Visual FoxPro updates the record as you exit each field. You'll see Record Status and Lock Status change briefly as the record written, then they change back and Old Value and Current Value are updated.

Try out different combinations of settings: optimistic buffering on one Form and pessimistic in another; row buffering activated on one Form and deactivated on another; using the Lock button to force a record lock on one Form and edit the record (with and without buffering, with optimistic and pessimistic locking). Playing with several instances of the Form can be very useful in understanding exactly how buffering impacts multiuser record editing.

Writing a Buffered Table

As you saw earlier, Tableupdate(.T.) attempts to write all records in a table buffer to disk. As with the row buffered version, it will return .F. if it can't update a record because, among other reasons, another user changed it.

The error-trapping routine you saw earlier works well for row buffering because you're concerned with only one record at a time. However, with table buffering, you have to look at each record individually. Because you might have a mixture of modified and unmodified records in the buffer, you need to determine which records will be updated. To make matters more complicated, if Tableupdate(.T.) fails, you won't know where it failed. Some records may have been saved and there could be more than one record in conflict.

The new Getnextmodified() function will tell you exactly what you need to know: the record number for the next modified record. If it returns a value of 0, there are no more modified records in the buffer. This function accepts two parameters. The first is the record number after which to begin searching for the next modified record, and the second is the alias or work area to search in. Initially, you should pass the value 0 as the first parameter so Getnextmodified() will find the first modified record. To find the next modified record, pass the record number for the current record.

Here's an example of the earlier conflict management routine, modified to handle table buffered changes when Tableupdate(.T.) fails:

```
lnCHANGED - getnextmodified(0)
do while lnCHANGED <> 0
   go lnCHANGED
   if rlock()
     llCONFLICT = .F.
     for lnI = 1 to fcount()
        lcFIELD       = field(lnI)
        llOTHER_USER  = oldval(lcFIELD)   <> curval(lcFIELD)
        llTHIS_USER   = evaluate(lcFIELD) <> oldval(lcFIELD)
        llSAME_CHANGE = evaluate(lcFIELD) == curval(lcFIELD)
        do case

* Another user edited this field but this user didn't, so grab the new value.

        case llOTHER_USER and not llTHIS_USER
           replace (lcFIELD) with curval(lcFIELD)

* Another user didn't edit this field, or they both made the same change, so we don't
* need to do anything.
```

Continued on next page

Continued from previous page

```
              case not llOTHER_USER or llSAME_CHANGE
```

* Uh-oh, both users changed this field, but to different values.

```
              otherwise
                  llCONFLICT = .T.
          endcase
      next lnI
```

* If we have a conflict, handle it.

```
      if llCONFLICT
          lnCHOICE = messagebox('Another user also changed this ' + ;
              'record. Do you want to overwrite their changes (Yes), ' + ;
              'not overwrite but see their changes (No), or cancel ' + ;
              'your changes (Cancel)?', 3 + 16, 'Problem Saving Record!')
          do case
```

* Overwrite their changes: we don't actually need to do anything because we'll do
* them all later (this case is here only for clarity).

```
              case lnCHOICE = 6
```

* See the changes: bring up another instance of the Form.

```
              case lnCHOICE = 7
                  do form MYFORM name oNAME
```

* Cancel the changes in this record only.

```
              otherwise
                  = tablerevert()
                  unlock record lnCHANGED
          endcase
      endif llCONFLICT
```

* We couldn't lock the record, so cancel this user's changes.

```
  else
      = messagebox("Sorry, we couldn't save record #" + ltrim(str(lnCHANGED)))
      = tablerevert()
      unlock record lnCHANGED
  endif rlock()
```

* Find the next modified record and process it.

```
  lnCHANGED = getnextmodified(0)
enddo while lnCHANGED <> 0
```

* Since we reverted any changes where we found a conflict and the user wanted to
* cancel their own changes, let's force the remainder of the updates.

```
= tableupdate(.T., .T.)
```

If you attempt to close the table or change the buffering mode when a table has changes in a table buffer that haven't been written out to disk, you'll get an error (#1545): "Table buffer for alias <Alias> contains uncommitted changes."

> ***Note about* Rlock() *and* Unlock:** Notice the Unlock Record lnCHANGED in the preceding program. Unlock alone unlocks all record locks in the current or specified table, but Unlock has been enhanced to allow the unlocking of a single record. This is especially important in routines such as triggers and table buffer handlers. Rlock() also has a new twist: if you pass it a value of 0 as the record number to lock, it'll try to lock the table Header. When the table Header is locked, no other users can add records to the table.

Transactions

As you've seen, table buffering is a convenient way to buffer a number of changes to a table, then write or abandon those changes all at once. However, there's one flaw with this approach—records in the buffer can be locked or edited by another user. In such cases, Tableupdate(.T.) will return .F. and the error-trapping routine can be called. The problem is that some records have been saved and some haven't. This leaves a fairly complicated mess on your hands should you need to back out changes that have already been made.

For example, when you go to the bank to transfer money from your savings account to your checking account, the account update program reduces your savings account balance by the appropriate amount, then tries to increase your checking account balance by the same amount. The program might look something like this:

```
seek M.ACCOUNT1
replace BALANCE with BALANCE - M.AMOUNT
seek M.ACCOUNT2
replace BALANCE with BALANCE + M.AMOUNT
llSUCCESS = tableupdate(.T.)
if not llSUCCESS
   do ERROR_ROUTINE
endif not llSUCCESS
```

In the meantime, an automated check-clearing program has been processing your checking account, and has reduced its balance by the total of several checks. The program detects a conflict and decides to abandon the update by issuing Tablerevert(.T.). However, because the savings account was successfully updated, its change is no longer in the buffer and the update remains. Now the bank has an "out-of-balance" situation that will be difficult to track down, and one very angry customer when you get your bank statement at the end of the month.

Fortunately, Visual FoxPro provides a mechanism that can resolve this problem: the *transaction*. A transaction is a specific group of changes that must be either all made at once or all abandoned. A transaction is started with the Begin Transaction command. Any table changes after this command has been issued, even those made with Tableupdate(), are not written to the disk until an End Transaction command is encountered. Think of a transaction as a "buffer's buffer." The transaction is held until you determine that all changes can be made successfully and you issue an End Transaction. If the program crashes or the computer is rebooted before End Transaction is encountered, or if your program issues a Rollback command because one of the changes couldn't be made successfully, none of the changes are actually written to disk.

Now look at the bank update example, this time using a transaction as a "wrapper" for the update.

```
begin transaction
seek M.ACCOUNT1
replace BALANCE with BALANCE - M.AMOUNT
seek M.ACCOUNT2
replace BALANCE with BALANCE + M.AMOUNT
llSUCCESS = tableupdate(.T.)
if llSUCCESS
   end transaction
else
   rollback
endif llSUCCESS
```

If the first account balance was changed but the second couldn't be successfully, llSUCCESS will be .F., and the Rollback command will prevent the first change from being written to disk. If everything went well, End Transaction will write out both changes at once.

Here are some other concepts regarding transactions:

- Transactions can be used only with tables attached to databases. Free tables need not apply.
- Transactions apply to memo (FPT) and index (CDX) files as well as to the DBF.
- Commands and functions that alter the database, the table, or the table's indexes cannot be used during a transaction. For example, issuing Alter Table, Delete Tag, Index On, Tablerevert(), or Close Databases during a transaction will generate an error. See the Visual FoxPro documentation for a complete list of restricted commands.

- You can nest transactions up to five levels deep. When an inner-level transaction is completed, its changes are added to the cache of changes for the next transaction level rather than being written to disk. Only when the final End Transaction is issued are all the changes written out. You can use the Txnlevel() function to determine the current transaction level.

- Unlike other Visual FoxPro structured programming constructs (such as For/Next or Scan/Endscan), Begin Transaction, End Transaction, and Rollback don't have to be located in the same program. You could, for example, have a common routine for starting transactions and another one for ending them. Transactions should be kept as short as possible, however, as any records being updated during a transaction are completely unavailable to other users, even for reading.

- Records automatically locked by Visual FoxPro during a transaction are automatically unlocked when the transaction is complete. Any locks you set manually are not automatically unlocked; you are responsible for unlocking those records yourself. If you use Unlock during a transaction, the record actually stays locked until the transaction is done, at which time all specified records are unlocked.

- Although transactions give you as much protection as they can, it's still possible a hardware failure or server crash could occur while the information is being written to disk by the End Transaction command. This could cause data to be lost.

- Transactions apply only to local tables. Transactions for remote tables are controlled using the Sqlsetprop(), Sqlcommit(), and Sqlrollback() commands. See Robert Green's client/server report for information on transaction processing with remote tables.

Here's another look at the save routine and the error-trapping routine. (In the error routine, code in the Do While loop isn't shown since it's the same as the previous version.)

```
begin transaction
if tableupdate(.T.)
   end transaction
else
   rollback
   do ERROR_ROUTINE
endif tableupdate(.T.)

procedure ERROR_ROUTINE
```

Continued on next page

Continued from previous page

```
* Do setup stuff here, including checking what happened. If we
* found error #1585, do the following code.

lnCHANGED = getnextmodified(0)
do while lnCHANGED <> 0

...

enddo while lnCHANGED <> 0

* Since we reverted any changes where we found a conflict and
* the user wanted to cancel their own changes, let's force the
* remainder of the updates and then unlock all the records we
* manually locked.

begin transaction
if tableupdate(.T., .T.)
   end transaction
   unlock

* Some other error occurred now, so rollback the changes and
* display an  appropriate error message (you could also try to
* handle it here if you wish).

else
   = aerror(laERROR)
   rollback
   = messagebox('Error #' + ltrim(str(laERROR[1])) + ': ' +
      laERROR[2] + ' occurred while saving.')
endif tableupdate(.T., .T.)
```

Time to Play!

You can kill two birds with one stone by playing with both buffered tables and transactions while looking at the TESTTX Form on the source code disc. This Form has some interesting features.

- It presents a Grid of records from the EMPLOYEE table and uses table buffering so you can edit many records before trying to save the changes.
- As you edit the record, the Save and Cancel buttons are automatically enabled.
- This Form allows you to simulate a multiuser situation by launching a second copy of the Form (using the Launch button).
- You can explicitly lock records to see what happens in another instance of the Form when trying to save.
- The Form's Error() method handles problems as it tries to update the record. The conflict resolution scheme outlined earlier is used here so you can see how it works.

Continued on next page

Run the Form and launch a second instance. Edit several records in the first Form, then switch to the second Form without saving in the first. Edit several records, making at least two the same as records edited in the first Form. Then click the Save button.

Switch back to the first Form. Notice that any records you edited in the second Form but not this one now show the current values from the table, but the ones you edited in this Form show their edited values. Click the Save button—you'll get several messages showing what the conflict resolution routine found as it checked each field of each edited record. Try changing the same field to the same value in each Form, changing different fields, and changing the same field to different values to see how each instance is handled.

Try changing the same record in each copy of the Form, click Save in one copy, then lock the record using the Lock Record CheckBox. Try to save in the other copy of the Form.

6 | Referential Integrity, Triggers, and Stored Procedures

Maintaining data integrity is a very important issue for database developers to consider. However, so is maintaining referential integrity. Referential integrity (RI) means every child record has a matching parent. For example, if an employee table is a child of a department table, every employee must have a matching department. This means the department ID field cannot be blank, nor can it contain an invalid department ID.

One of the ways the department ID might be invalid is to allow the user to leave it blank or enter an invalid code when adding or editing an employee record. This can easily be prevented using a validation rule like the following for the field, ensuring that the department ID exists in the department table.

```
seek(DEPT_ID, 'DEPARTMENTS')
```

The department ID can also become invalid by allowing a department with employees assigned to it to be deleted, or allowing the department ID to be changed. Under such conditions, the department ID in the employee records will no longer match a valid ID in the department table, so the employee records are considered to be *orphaned*.

To prevent orphans, these events must be handled properly. When the department ID is changed, the logical thing to do is to find every record with the old ID in the employee table and change it to the new ID. This is called an *update* operation, while the action taken is a *cascade*. When the user attempts to delete a department, the application will first check if any employees have that department ID, and if so, give an error and prevent the deletion. This is called a *delete* operation and the action taken is a *restrict*. Either action can be taken with either type of operation; for example, you may decide to cascade deletes (deleting all the employees for the department being deleted) instead of restricting them.

Failure to handle RI can have all kinds of implications. A simple one is that a report showing employees and the departments they work in will have a blank department name if the employee record is orphaned. However, you can have more serious consequences as well. For example, a SQL Select statement joining two tables will fail to pick up any records from the child table if the matching parent can't be found. A report calculating total sales by customer type will ignore all invoices for which the customer cannot be found. Thus, the total at the bottom of this report will not balance with a manual totaling of the invoices. This type of problem can lead users to a severe lack of confidence in the system, which in turn may cause the system to be pulled out of production. It's not unheard of for consultants to lose clients or for programmers to lose their jobs over something that seems rather trivial at first glance.

Enforcing Referential Integrity

There are two ways to ensure RI is maintained. Some database management systems, such as Gupta's SQLBase Server, support *declarative* RI. This means that you are telling the database to handle the events automatically by defining a relationship between the two tables and setting the rules to follow for delete, update, and insert events.

FoxPro supports a different mechanism called *procedural* RI. Instead of the database engine automatically performing RI actions, procedural code is written to perform the appropriate action. While declarative RI may seem preferable, procedural RI is actually more flexible because you, not the database engine, decide exactly how the RI should be enforced.

FoxPro versions prior to Visual FoxPro supported procedural RI in only the loosest of ways: you had to write code to perform the appropriate actions and ensure the code was called whenever the event took place. This means that changes made in a browse window or in programs that didn't bother with RI issues often resulted in orphans.

Triggers

Visual FoxPro has strengthened RI support immensely by allowing you to define *triggers*. Triggers are pieces of code automatically executed when a particular event occurs. For example, if you define a function as the delete trigger for a table, Visual FoxPro calls the function (firing the trigger) whenever either a programmatic or interactive attempt is made to delete a record. If the trigger code returns .T., the record is deleted. If it returns .F., the record won't be deleted and a trappable error occurs.

Triggers are stored in databases, so they can't be defined for free tables. You can define triggers for three events for each table: inserting, updating, and deleting records. Any program or interactive session (such as a browse or a Form) causing an insert, update, or delete event to occur will cause the trigger to fire.

Triggers are typically used for referential tasks. For example, update and delete triggers are often used for parent tables to prevent orphaning child records. The insert trigger is usually used for a child table to ensure that a foreign key field matches a record in a parent table. Examples of actions taken by a delete trigger include preventing a record from being deleted if there are any child records (called a *restrict delete rule*) and deleting the child records (a *cascading delete*).

The fact that both programmatic and interactive events can cause a trigger to fire provides you with a powerful mechanism for protecting your data. Together, triggers and the other rules defined in a database help you maintain both data integrity (preventing invalid data from getting into tables) and referential integrity (preventing invalid links between tables).

Firing Triggers

The following table shows which programmatic and interactive events cause triggers to fire.

Trigger	Programmatically	Interactively
Delete	Delete SQL Delete	A record is deleted in a browse window.
Insert	Append Blank Append From Append From Array Import SQL Insert Recall	A record is added or recalled in a browse window.
Update	Gather Replace Replace From Array SQL Update	A field in a non-deleted record is edited in a browse window or a form.

Notice that the Pack command doesn't cause a trigger to fire because the delete trigger would have been fired when the records being removed from the table were marked for deletion. Interestingly, Zap doesn't cause the delete trigger to fire either. This means that if you're using triggers to help maintain referential integrity, you should use Delete All followed by Pack instead of the Zap command to delete all records, because Delete All will cause the delete trigger to fire for every record. Of course, it's not often that you'll delete every record in a table related to another table, so this may not be an important point for you.

A trigger won't necessarily fire immediately. Triggers fire after all other rules (field validation, primary and candidate index validation, and table validation), and, when table buffering is used, they don't fire until Tableupdate() is issued. The next "Time to Play!" exercise explores the order in which rules and triggers fire.

When a trigger does fire, it actually fires after the event has occurred. For example, Deleted() will return .T. in a delete trigger routine and Recno() returns a new record number (that is, Reccount() + 1) inside insert trigger code. Having the trigger return .F. is like having an "undo" for the event that caused the trigger to fire.

Triggers can be nested. In fact, they're automatically nested if necessary. If the trigger code for one table causes an event to occur in another table, that other table's trigger code will fire. For example, cascading deletes from parent to child to grandchild are automatically performed by creating delete triggers for the parent and child tables. The parent table's trigger deletes the child record, which causes the child table's trigger to fire, which in turn deletes the grandchild record.

There is a limit on what can be done in a trigger. You aren't allowed to move the record pointer, add a record, modify a record, or delete a record in the table to which the trigger belongs. This is because those actions would cause the table's insert, update, or delete trigger to fire, potentially starting an endless loop of recursive trigger firings. You can, however, add, modify, or delete a record in another table, so be careful not to write triggers than end up calling each other (trigger for table A updates a record in table B, causing table B's update trigger to fire, which updates a record in table A, causing table A's update trigger to fire, and so on). You'll get an "Illegal recursion in rule evaluation" error if you do.

If a trigger was fired from a programmatic event and fails (returning .F.), a trappable error (error #1539) occurs. The error-trapping routine can determine which table was selected and which trigger failed by using the new Aerror() function. See Section 5 on buffering and transactions for a description of this function.

If the trigger that failed was fired from a browse or Grid, the error is not trappable. In other words, even if you have On Error set to an error handling routine, the user will still get a Trigger Failed dialog box instead of your nice error message. In this dialog box, the user might be presented with choices of OK or Revert (depending on which trigger failed). Choosing OK leaves the data in the field so it can be corrected, while Revert replaces the edited data with its former values. The only way to prevent this dialog box from appearing is to trap and resolve the error within the trigger routine itself and return .T. regardless of the outcome. For example, the following delete trigger routine always returns .T., but might undo the deletion if necessary. If buffering is turned on, it uses Tablerevert() to undo the change. Otherwise it uses Recall.

```
if <condition that makes trigger fail>
   wait window 'You cannot delete this record.' nowait
   if cursorgetprop('Buffering') > 1
      = tablerevert()
   else
      recall
   endif cursorgetprop('Buffering') > 1
endif ...
```

Defining Triggers

Triggers can be defined interactively using the Table Designer. Begin by clicking the Table Properties button to display the dialog box shown in Figure 6-1.

```
 ┌─────────────────────────────────────────────────────────────┐
 │  ─          Table Properties                                  │
 ├───────────────────────────────────────────────────────────────┤
 │  Validation Rule:   [                              ]  [...]    │
 │  Validation Text:   [                              ]  [...]    │
 │  INSERT Trigger:    [ ins_empl()                   ]  [...]    │
 │  UPDATE Trigger:    [ upd_empl()                   ]  [...]    │
 │  DELETE Trigger:    [ del_empl()                   ]  [...]    │
 │  Comment:                                                      │
 │  [ The employee table contains the employees for the      ▲ ] │
 │  [ company.                                                  ] │
 │  [                                                          ▼ ] │
 │                                                                │
 │        [    OK    ]         [   Cancel   ]                     │
 └─────────────────────────────────────────────────────────────┘
```

You can define the insert, update, and delete triggers by entering
an expression (usually a call to a UDF) into the appropriate trigger.
Click the button with the ellipsis (...) if you wish to bring up the
Expression Builder to assist with entering the expression.

Triggers can also be defined programmatically using the Create
Trigger command. This command has the following syntax:

```
create trigger on <Alias>
   for delete | insert | update as <Expression>
```

In this argument, <Expression> must evaluate to a logical
expression when the trigger occurs. Here's an example of using this
command:

```
create trigger on EMPLOYEES for delete as DEL_EMPL()
```

To remove a trigger, use the Delete Trigger command.

```
delete trigger on <Alias> for delete | insert | update
```

Time to Play!

Now look at how triggers work. Begin by typing the following code, or by running the program TRIGGER.PRG, which is included on the source code disc:

```
create database SCRATCH
create table CATEGORY ;
   (CODE C(1) primary key check CODEVAL(), ;
   NAME C(30), ;
   check TABLEVAL())
create table COMPANY ;
   (NAME C(30), ;
   COMPCAT C(1) references CATEGORY check empty(COMPCAT) or ;
      seek(COMPCAT, 'CATEGORY', 'CODE'))
create trigger on CATEGORY for update as UPD_CAT()
create trigger on CATEGORY for delete as DEL_CAT()
```

The reason for creating field and table validation rules for CATEGORY is so that you can see the firing order of rules, primary key validation, and triggers. Also, Empty(COMPCAT) is in the field validation rule so you don't get an error when adding a new record in a browse window. (The Seek() function in the rest of the rule would fail because the new record has a blank COMPCAT field.)

You'll need a few programs for the rule and trigger routines for the CATEGORY table. (Note that all the programs described in this exercise exist on the source code disc if you don't feel like typing them.) First, UPD_CAT.PRG, which is called when the update trigger fires.

```
local lcOLD_CODE
lcOLD_CODE = oldval('CODE')
wait window 'In UPD_CAT: old value = ' + lcOLD_CODE + ;
   ', new value = ' + CODE
select COMPANY
set order to COMPCAT
seek lcOLD_CODE
do while found()
   replace COMPCAT with CATEGORY.CODE
   seek lcOLD_CODE
enddo while found()
select CATEGORY
return .T.
```

The purpose of this routine is to cascade the change of the CODE field in CATEGORY to the COMPCAT field in COMPANY.

The next routine is DEL_CAT.PRG, which acts as the delete trigger.

Continued on next page

```
local llRET_CODE
wait window 'In DEL_CAT'
select COMPANY
set order to COMPCAT
seek CATEGORY.CODE
llRET_CODE = not found()
select CATEGORY
return llRET_CODE
```

This routine prevents a CATEGORY record from being deleted if a COMPANY record depends upon it. This is an example of a restrict rule.

A couple of simple programs, CODEVAL.PRG and TABLEVAL.PRG, will round things out:

CODEVAL.PRG:

```
wait window 'In CODEVAL'
```

TABLEVAL.PRG:

```
wait window 'In TABLEVAL'
```

Now that the setup is out of the way, you can try a few things. First, open the Database Designer and notice a relationship line connects the two tables as expected. Modify the structure of CATEGORY and look at the field and table validation rules and the triggers. You can define this information visually or programmatically, so everything appears as expected.

Browse the CATEGORY table and press Ctrl-Y to add a new record. Notice the CODEVAL and TABLEVAL routines execute in that order, showing that field validation rules are evaluated before table validation rules. Enter "A" in the CODE field; CODEVAL executes again. Enter "Code A" in NAME and press Ctrl-Y to add a new record. TABLEVAL executes to validate the current record, then UPD_CAT executes as the update trigger fires. Thus, validation rules are evaluated before triggers fire. Enter "A" into the CODE field again, then press Ctrl-Y. You'll see CODEVAL execute, then TABLEVAL, then the message "Uniqueness of index CODE violated" is displayed since the primary key "A" already exists. Thus, you've determined rules and triggers are evaluated in the following order:

- field validation
- table validation
- primary and candidate index validation
- triggers

Enter "B" for CODE and "Code B" for NAME. Press Ctrl-W to save and close the browse; you'll see the TABLEVAL and UPD_CAT routines execute.

Now open a browse window for COMPANY. Add several records with a COMPCAT of "A" and several with "B." Try entering

Continued on next page

Continued from previous page

a value of "C"; the field validation rule will prevent you from doing so.

Select CATEGORY again and browse. Change CODE in the first record from "A" to "C" (CODEVAL will execute), and press the down arrow key. You'll see TABLEVAL execute, then UPD_CAT, and then the error message "Illegal recursion in rule evaluation" will be displayed. The error occurs because UPD_CAT tries to cascade the change of "A" to "C" by replacing COMPCAT in COMPANY with the new value. This causes the field validation rule for COMPCAT to be evaluated, which has a Seek() function to ensure the new code exists. Unfortunately, you're not allowed to move the record pointer for the table which caused the update trigger to fire.

Select COMPANY, modify its structure, and change the field validation rule for COMPCAT to Empty(COMPCAT) Or (COMPCAT = CATEGORY.CODE and not Deleted('CATEGORY')) Or Seek(COMPCAT, 'CATEGORY', 'CODE'). This avoids moving the record pointer in CATEGORY if it's already positioned on the record you're interested in and it isn't deleted.

Select CATEGORY and once again change "A" to "C." This time, no error occurs. Select COMPANY and browse. You'll notice that COMPCAT now contains "C" in all records that had "A." Referential integrity is maintained by cascading the key change.

In the browse window for CATEGORY, delete a record. You'll see CODEVAL execute, then TABLEVAL, then DEL_CAT. You'll get a "Trigger failed" error and the record won't be marked for deletion because DEL_CAT restricts the deletion if there are any records in COMPANY matching the key value to be deleted.

Stored Procedures

Triggers are further enhanced by the addition of *stored procedures* to Visual FoxPro. A stored procedure is a routine stored within the database itself. The source code is stored in the CODE field of the StoredProceduresSource record in the DBC and the compiled code is stored in the CODE field of the StoredProceduresObject record. Stored procedures are usually used for trigger code and any routines the trigger code must call.

Because the procedures are stored in a database, the database can protect itself from improper changes to the data without requiring an external program to do the work. It also means once the triggers and stored procedures are defined, the application programmer doesn't have to worry about knowing those rules or implementing them in every program that accesses the database. Another advantage is that if the rules change, they change in one place rather than in every program that accesses the database. Because the trigger code is stored in the database, and the only way to access a table is through the database, there's no way for users or programmers to circumvent the rules enforced through the triggers. This isn't exactly the same as object-orientation, but it does provide encapsulation of data and code into a database.

Stored procedures are read into memory when a database is opened, so they also perform faster than code that must be read from a disk. They are executed before routines in the active procedure file and stand-alone programs. This means that a stored procedure will be called even though there's a program with the same name on disk.

Stored procedures can be maintained from the Database Designer by choosing Edit Stored Procedures from the Database pad, clicking the right mouse button and choosing Stored Procedures from the shortcut menu, or by clicking the Edit Stored Procedures button in the Database Designer toolbar. Any of these actions will bring up an edit window containing the stored procedures for the current database.

There are several commands available to maintain stored procedures. Modify Procedures brings up an edit window with the stored procedures for the current database. Append Procedures From <File> appends the code in the specified file to the stored procedures in the current database. You can use the Overwrite keyword to overwrite the stored procedures rather than appending them. Use Copy Procedures To <File> to create a file containing the stored procedures; the optional Additive keyword adds the stored procedures to the end of an existing file. List Procedures and Display Procedures output the stored procedures in the current database to the screen, printer, or file, depending on the additional keywords supplied.

To see an example of stored procedures, open the TASTRADE database that comes with Visual FoxPro; it's located in the SAMPLES\MAINSAMP\DATA directory. Bring up the edit window for stored procedures using one of the methods described. Notice that one of the routines is called NEWID(). This routine is very much like the NEXT_ID() routine you looked at when covering field defaults in Section 3 (Tables and Indexes). It's called as the default expression for the primary key field in several tables, so it was written as a generic routine. This brings up the question of whether or not generic routines called from triggers, field or table validations, or default expressions should be stored in a stored procedure or in a traditional PRG file.

The advantage of putting such routines in the stored procedures of a database is that the database becomes a self-contained entity; it doesn't rely on outside programs for anything. However, there's a big drawback—every database using these generic routines has to duplicate the code within its stored procedures. If you discover a bug or want to enhance a generic routine, you'll have to find every database containing the routine and apply the same changes. What a maintenance headache!

A better approach is to put routines enforcing business rules specific to a database in the stored procedures for the database, and put generic, reusable code where it belongs—in library routines. The drawback to this approach is the database can't stand by itself. The library routines have to be available or the stored procedures calling them will fail. However, if you don't allow users of applications to browse tables directly from the Command window, this isn't a major concern. Also, if someone does browse a table and try to make changes, the trigger and validation routines will fail (an error trap can provide a more elegant interface than just having the program bomb) and no changes to the data will be permitted. In other words, if you can't ensure the data is valid, don't allow it to be changed.

> *Note:* If you're concerned that someone might mess with or steal the source code in your stored procedures, remember that while the DBC contains both source and compiled versions of your stored procedures, Visual FoxPro executes only the compiled version. This means that you can delete the source code version before distributing the DBC to someone and the stored procedures will still work.
>
> Of course, to avoid deleting your only copy of the source code you'll want to use a scheme something like the following:
>
> 1. Create your stored procedures in a PRG file. For testing purposes, you can Set Procedure To the PRG file.
> 2. Once everything works, move the contents of the PRG into the database's stored procedures using Append Procedures.
> 3. Force the stored procedures to be compiled using the Compile Database command.
> 4. Delete the source code version of the stored procedures by opening the database as a table, finding the record for the source code version of the stored procedures, and deleting the contents of the CODE Memo field. (See Section 1 for information on how to do all that.) Alternatively, you can use the BUILDAPP program that comes with Visual FoxPro to remove all source code from an entire application. See the Visual FoxPro documentation for information on BUILDAPP.

The Referential Integrity Builder

In the last "Time to Play!" exercise, you looked at two very simple routines to cascade primary key changes and restrict deletion of parent records if there are any child records. These routines have no provision for handling a failed update if another user locked one of the child records; they don't handle situations involving grandchild records; and they are hard-coded to use certain tag names, field names, and Seek expressions.

Hand crafting RI routines is difficult. Instead, you should use one of two approaches:

- You can write generic routines covering every possible contingency that never need to be altered, even when table structures and relationships change.
- You can automatically generate routines that are hard-coded to the current table and relationship conditions but can be regenerated when things change.

Microsoft has provided Visual FoxPro with an RI Builder taking the latter approach. To bring up the RI Builder, open the Database Designer and do one of the following:

- Bring up the Edit Relationship dialog box by double-clicking a relationship line. You can also click a line, click the right mouse button, and choose Edit Relationship from the shortcut menu. Then choose the Referential Integrity button.
- Click a relationship line, click the right mouse button, and choose Referential Integrity from the shortcut menu.
- Choose Referential Integrity from the Database pad.

The dialog box shown in Figure 6-2 will appear. Although you might have selected a particular relationship line, this dialog box displays all relationships defined in the database. There are columns for the parent and child tables and their tags, as well as columns for the rules to use for update, delete, and insert events. Tabs below the list allow you to choose a particular event and the rule to use for the relationship selected in the list. You can also click the appropriate cell in the list and choose the desired rule from the drop-down menu that appears. The update and delete events pertain to the parent table and define what should happen to the child table. The insert event is for the child table and defines whether the foreign key must match a parent record or not.

Figure 6-2.

The Referential
Integrity Builder

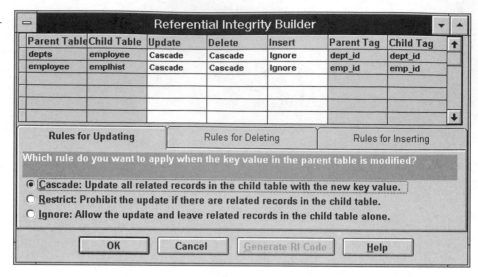

You can choose one of the following rules:

- *Restrict.* If a record exists in the child table, the parent update or delete event is not permitted. Restrict is often used in the case of a delete event, because, for example, you don't want a user to delete a customer category code if any customer records use that code. In the case of an insert event in the child table, the record cannot be added if any foreign key field contains a value that doesn't match a record in the parent table.

- *Cascade.* Every record in the child table will have the new value placed into the foreign key field (in the case of an update event) or it will be deleted (in the case of a delete event). Cascade is normally used for an update event. It's also sometimes used for the delete event. In the doctor-hospital example of the section on relations, deleting a doctor should result in the deletion of all records for that doctor in the doctor-hospital linking table. This rule is not available for an insert event, since that event affects the child table, not the parent table.

- *Ignore.* No action is taken on the child table. While this may sound like a bad choice, under rare circumstances it may be necessary to leave the child records alone. For example, in a project tracking system, you have tables of projects, activities performed for each project, and employees who perform those activities. What should happen to the activity records when an employee leaves the company? You don't want to restrict the deletion of the employee; after all, they're gone. Cascade doesn't seem right, because you still want to record the fact that the activities took place. In this case, Ignore seems like the best approach. Although the matching employee record no longer exists, at least you know the employee ID for each activity. This employee ID could be looked up in an archive of former employees if necessary. Another option, which is supported in some database systems but not in the Visual FoxPro RI Builder, is to store .NULL. in the foreign key field. .NULL. means "I don't know" and since the employee record is gone, you don't know who did the activity.

A consequence of using the ignore rule is that a SQL Select statement will ignore child records without a matching parent. You'll have to use an outer join, the discussion of which is beyond the scope of this report, to pick up those child records with an invalid foreign key.

The rules you enter in the RI Builder are stored in the RIINFO fields of the appropriate relationship records in the DBC.

After entering the rules for each relationship, click the OK button. You will be asked if you want to save your changes and generate RI code. Select Yes to do so. You will also be informed that the builder will attempt to merge generated RI code with your non-RI stored procedures. To be on the safe side, it creates a file called RISP.OLD containing any existing stored procedures for the database before it generates any code. It also uses And to combine any existing triggers for each table with its own triggers, which have names like __ri_<trigger>_<alias>().

Time to Play!

Now look at how the RI Builder works. Start by creating a database and a few tables with relationships between them, and then bring up the Database Designer. (You can also run the program RI.PRG, which is included on the source code disc.)

```
create database SCRATCH
create table CLIENTS ;
  (CLIENT_NUM I primary key, ;
  NAME C(30))
create table MANAGERS ;
  (EMP_NUM I primary key, ;
  NAME C(30))
create table PROJECTS ;
  (PROJ_NUM C(5) primary key, ;
  NAME C(30), ;
  CLIENT_NUM I references CLIENTS, ;
  EMP_NUM I references MANAGERS)
```

Continued on next page

Continued from previous page

```
insert into CLIENTS values (1, 'Microsoft Corp.')
insert into CLIENTS values (2, 'IBM')
insert into CLIENTS values (3, 'Apple')
insert into MANAGERS values (1, 'Bob Jones')
insert into MANAGERS values (2, 'Mary Green')
insert into MANAGERS values (3, 'Shirley Smith')
insert into PROJECTS values ('70-01', 'VFP Alpha', 1, 3)
insert into PROJECTS values ('70-02', 'VFP Beta', 1, 1)
insert into PROJECTS values ('71-01', 'Warp Beta', 2, 2)
insert into PROJECTS values ('72-01', 'System 7.5', 3, 2)
insert into PROJECTS values ('72-02', 'Quicktime GX', 3, 1)
modify database
```

Now bring up the RI Builder and define the following rules for the relationships:

Parent	Child	Update	Delete	Insert
CLIENTS	PROJECTS	Cascade	Cascade	Restrict
MANAGERS	PROJECTS	Cascade	Restrict	Restrict

Allow the builder to generate RI code for the database. Choose Stored Procedures from the Database pad to view the stored procedures the RI Builder generated. Modify a table, click the Table Properties button, then notice the names the RI Builder inserted for the various triggers for the table.

Bring up a browse window for PROJECTS and press Ctrl-Y to add a new record. Visual FoxPro tells you that the trigger failed. Adding a new record to PROJECTS inserts blank values into the CLIENT_NUM and EMP_NUM fields. Because you defined the insert rule as Restrict, the trigger code generated by the RI Builder won't allow you to have values in these fields that don't match records in the CLIENTS and MANAGERS tables. As a result it prevents the new record from being added.

To append records in a browse window, bring up the RI Builder again, change the insert rule to Ignore, and regenerate the RI code. In a "real" situation, you'd use buffering instead.

Now open browse windows for all three tables and arrange them so you can see all three windows at the same time. Then try the following:

- Delete Bob Jones's record in the MANAGERS window. You should get a "Trigger failed" message because records in PROJECTS are related to this record and the deletion rule for the relationship is Restrict.
- Change EMP_NUM for Mary Green from 2 to 4. You should see EMP_NUM for projects 71-01 and 72-01 change to 4 automatically. (You may have to click the PROJECTS window to refresh its information.)
- Delete the Apple Computers record in the CLIENTS window. You should see the last two projects records deleted

Continued on next page

> automatically. (Again, you may have to click the PROJECTS window first.)
>
> - Recall the Apple Computers record. The deleted projects records aren't automatically recalled. However, if you want this action to occur, you could write your own insert trigger for CLIENTS (recalling a record fires the insert trigger) to recall any deleted matching child records in PROJECTS.

Generated RI Code

If you want to see what the code generated by the RI Builder looks like, flip to Section 13. Comments have been added to the code to help explain it because it's quite dense and totally undocumented.

7 | Connections and Views

FoxPro 2.x allowed you to access client/server databases if you installed the Connectivity Kit, an add-on library from Microsoft, or some other third-party library. With Visual FoxPro, access to other databases is built in. Visual FoxPro uses Open Database Connectivity (ODBC) to allow you to connect to any database for which an ODBC driver is available. For example, Access, Oracle, Watcom, and SQL Server databases are all accessible from Visual FoxPro now. Visual FoxPro does client/server!

One of the benefits of client/server development is that network traffic is reduced because only records that match a query are sent to the workstation. Visual FoxPro provides several features to help performance with back-end databases: progressive fetching, delayed memo download, and batch updating, among others. Those features will be discussed later in this section.

Even if it exists on the same machine as Visual FoxPro, data in another database is called *remote data*. There are two aspects to accessing other databases: *connections* and *views*, both of which must exist in a database. Connections define what remote data to access and provide some options about that access, while views are simply a predefined SQL Select statement to retrieve the data.

Connections and (especially) views are such large topics that a whole book could be written on them. This section will provide an overview of the subjects, and will focus mainly on local data.

Connections will be discussed in passing. For more information on client/server databases and how connections and views tie into them, see Robert Green's client/server report in this book.

 Aha—are you thinking about flipping to the next section? Don't make the mistake of thinking that views are only for people doing client/server development. Views can either be local (using native Visual FoxPro tables) or remote (using remote data). As you'll see, a local view is a great tool for quickly developing a view of your data. Stick with it—it'll be worth it.

The View Designer

There are two ways you can create a view: visually and programmatically. You'll see how to create one programmatically later. You create a view visually using one of the following actions (all but the last require the Database Designer window to be open):

- Bring up the database shortcut menu by clicking the right mouse button while pointing to the Database Designer window, and select New Local View.
- Click the New Local View button in the Database toolbar.
- Select New Local View from under the Database pad.
- Select New from the File pad. In the dialog box that appears, choose View, then click New File.
- If the Visual FoxPro Standard toolbar is displayed, click the New button. The same New dialog box will appear.
- If you want to create a view and add it to a database in a project, open the project in the Project Manager and select the Databases object. (To see the Databases object, either click the Data tab, or from the All tab, expand the Data object in the list.) Click the + to expand it, click the + for the desired database to expand it, select Local Views, then click the New button or choose New File from the Project pad in the menu bar.

Any of these actions will bring up the View Designer shown in Figure 7-1. The View Designer consists of an area displaying the tables involved in the view and five tabbed pages of information about the view.

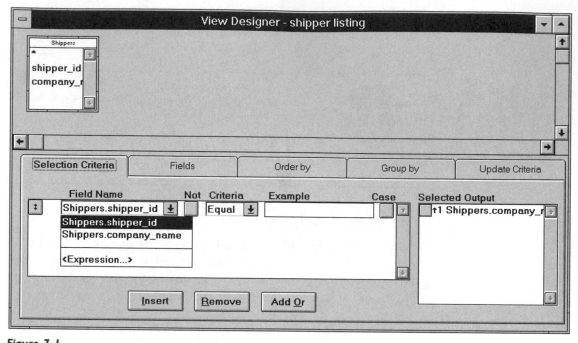

Figure 7-1.

The View Designer

Now look at a number of elements appearing in the View Designer:

- The title of the View Designer window shows the name of the view being modified. In Figure 7-1, it's "shipper listing."

- As in the Database Designer window, each of the tables in the view is shown as a small window within the View Designer window. These windows can be moved around within the View Designer window.

- A table window contains an * (representing "all fields") and the list of fields that make up the table. You can scroll a table window to see all of the field names.

- While the Database Designer shows persistent relationships between tables as lines connecting the indexes in the tables, the View Designer shows them as lines connecting fields. This makes sense because a SQL Where clause specifies a join condition as table1.field1 = table2.field2. As in the Database Designer, when you move a table window that has relationship lines to other tables, the lines adjust automatically.

- When the View Designer window is on top, a Query pad appears in the menu bar. This menu has functions to add or remove tables, select one of the five tabbed pages, and so forth.

Figure 7-2.

The View Designer toolbar

- You can display the View Designer toolbar by choosing Toolbars from the View pad and checking View Designer. The View Designer toolbar appears in Figure 7-2.

    The View Designer toolbar has many of the functions that appear under the Query pad. Each button has a ToolTip to display what it does.

- The View Designer also has a shortcut menu that is brought up using the right mouse button to click the View Designer window.

By the way, if you've had a chance to play with the new Query Designer tool in Visual FoxPro, you might notice that it's almost identical to the View Designer. The only apparent difference is the Update Criteria tab that appears in the View Designer. Views are similar to queries in the fact that they are both predefined SQL Select statements. However, there are a couple of differences:

- While queries give read-only results, views are Updatable.

- The Query Designer creates a QPR file, which is essentially a program file containing a SQL Select statement and any other statements necessary. The View Designer creates a view, which exists in a database and can be opened and accessed like a table.

The following functions are available in the View Designer. (The letters in parentheses after the function name indicate where the function can be found: M is for in the menu bar under the Query pad, T is for the View Designer Toolbar, P is for a View Designer page, and S is for the shortcut menu.)

- *Add Table* (M, T, S). This function adds a table to the view. When you select it, Visual FoxPro displays a dialog box in which you can select the table to add. The selected table is added to the view and appears as a table window in the View Designer. If the newly added table has a persistent relationship defined for any table already in the view, a join condition will automatically be created between the two tables. You can also add a table to a view by dragging it from the Database Designer window to the View Designer window.

- *Remove Table* (M, T, S). This function, which is available only when a table is selected, allows you to remove the selected table from the view.

- *Remove Join Condition* (M). This removes the selected join condition between two tables from the Selection Criteria list.

- *Selection Criteria, Output Fields, Order By, Group By,* and *Update Criteria* (M, P). These functions display the appropriate page in the View Designer.

- *View SQL* (M, T, S). View SQL displays an edit window containing the SQL Select statement executed when the view is opened.
- *Advanced Options* (M). This displays the Advanced Options dialog box.
- *View Parameters* (M). This function allows you to define a parameterized view, which will be discussed later in the section.
- *Comments* (M). Comments brings up a dialog box in which you can enter the comments for the view.
- *Run Query* (M, S). This function runs a query and displays the results in a browse window.
- *Edit Join* (T). This allows you to edit the join condition for two tables. This function can also be selected by double-clicking the lines joining two tables or by clicking the button with left and right arrowheads beside the join condition in the selection criteria list.
- *Maximize/Restore Table View* (T). This function expands or restores the table area of the View Designer.

Because a view creates a SQL Select statement, there are several Select clauses to consider. The table area reflects the From clause, and the five tabbed pages represent the other clauses.

Selection Criteria

The first page (shown in Figure 7-1) shows the selection criteria for the view, the Where clause for the SQL Select statement.

The Where clause is constructed by specifying a field or an expression, a comparison operator, and a value to compare to. The Field Name pop-up menu lists all fields from all tables included in the view. (Choosing <Expression...> from the list brings up the Expression Builder.) The Criteria pop-up menu has the following operators: equal, like, exactly like, more than, less than, is NULL, between, and in. You can select the Not button to add "not" before the condition in the Where clause. In the Example column, enter the values to compare to the field or expression. For most of the operators, you can enter a constant value (for example, "JONES" or 10) or an expression (such as another field name). No value is required (or allowed) for "is NULL." For "between," enter two values separated by commas. For "in," enter two or more values separated by commas. If you select the Case button, the Upper() function will be used for Character or Memo fields to make the query case-insensitive.

To add a new condition, enter it into the blank condition line that appears at the bottom of the list. You can insert a new condition above the selected one by pressing the Insert button. A condition can be removed by clicking Remove, or can be moved relative to the other conditions by dragging the mover arrow that appears to the left of the condition.

Individual conditions specified in the list are combined using And in the Where clause. To use Or, select the Add Or button. This will add a line with only Or in it and a new condition line below it.

Join conditions for tables appear first in the selection criteria list. These conditions are added to the list automatically as tables having persistent relationships are added to the view. You cannot edit a join condition directly in the list. Instead, double-click the line joining the two tables, click the Edit Join button in the View Designer toolbar, or click the double-headed arrow button to the left of the condition in the list. The dialog box shown in Figure 7-3 will appear.

Figure 7-3.

The Join Condition dialog box

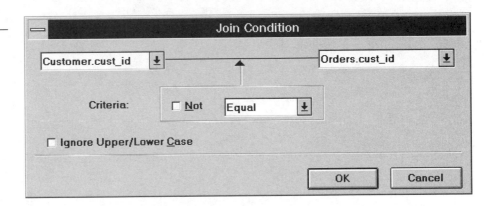

Select the fields involved in the join condition from the pop-up menu for each table, and specify the operator used to compare them (equal, like, exactly like, more than, and less than; Not can be used if necessary). Check Ignore Upper/Lower Case to add the Upper() function to each field.

You can remove the join condition by clicking the line joining the tables and selecting Remove Join Condition from under the Query pad or pressing Delete.

Fields

The second page shows the output fields for the view. This page is shown in Figure 7-4.

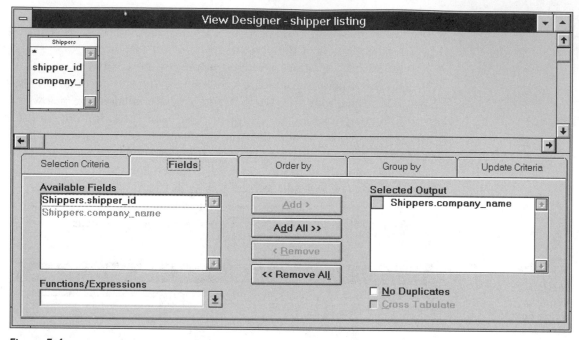

Figure 7-4.

*The Fields page of
the View Designer for
defining output fields*

The Available Fields list shows all fields from all of the tables
included in the view, while the Selected Output list contains the
fields that will be output to the result set. You can add a field to the
Selected Output list by double-clicking it in the Available Fields list,
or by selecting it in that list and choosing the Add button. The Add
All button adds all fields to the output. Fields added to the output
are disabled in the Available Fields list. Fields can be removed from
the Selected Output list by double-clicking them, or by selecting
them and choosing Remove. The Remove All button clears the
Selected Output list. You can change the order of the fields in the
Selected Output list by dragging the mover arrows that appear in
front of each field in the list.

To use one of the SQL aggregate functions, select the Functions/
Expressions ComboBox. The functions available are: Count(), Sum(),
Avg(), Min(), Max(), Count(distinct), Sum(distinct), and Avg(distinct).
After you choose one of these functions, a pop-up menu will appear
displaying all of the available fields for which the function can be
chosen. After you select which field to apply the function to, the
new expression will appear in the ComboBox. To add it to the
Selected Output list, select the Add button. If you choose, you
can also type an expression directly in the Functions/Expressions
ComboBox.

Checking the No Duplicates box adds a Distinct clause to the Select statement.

The Cross Tabulate button adds the command DO (_GENXTAB) WITH '<ViewName>' to the SQL Select statement generated by the view. This option can be checked only when you've selected exactly three fields for output to represent the X axis, the Y axis, and the value for each X-Y combination. If you check the Cross Tabulate box, the Group By and Order By fields are automatically selected while all the other options in the view are disabled. Uncheck the option if you need to edit something else in the view.

Order By Clause

The third page allows you to specify the Order By clause for the Select statement. This page is shown in Figure 7-5.

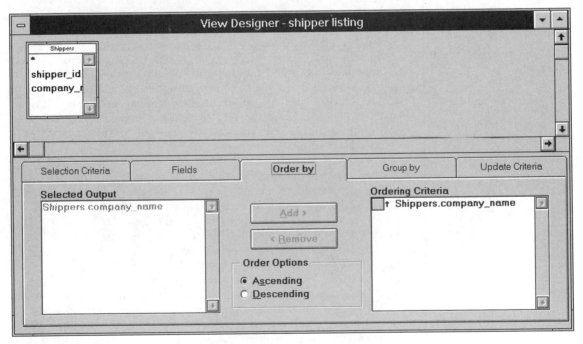

Figure 7-5.

The Order By page of the View Designer for specifying the ORDER BY clause

The Selected Output list shows the fields you've selected for output. To add one to the Ordering Criteria list, double-click it or select it and click Add. To remove a previously selected ordering criterion, double-click it in the Ordering Criteria list or select it and click Remove. By default, the result is sorted in ascending order for each field, but you can click Descending to change the sort order. You can rearrange the order of the fields in the Ordering Criteria list by dragging the mover arrows that appear in front of each field in the list.

Time to Play!

Now take a break from examining the View Designer by creating a view with what you've learned so far. The TESTDATA database that comes with Visual FoxPro includes tables for customers, orders, and products. Say, for example, that you want a list of orders by customer, and you want that list to be available on demand. Begin by opening the database.

```
open database \VISUAL FOXPRO\SAMPLES\DATA\TESTDATA exclusive
modify database
```

Create a new local view using one of the methods described earlier (clicking the right mouse button when the mouse pointer is over an open area in the Database Designer window, choosing New Local View from the shortcut menu, and then choosing New View). The View Designer window will appear with the Add Table or View dialog box prompting you to select a table for the view. Select CUSTOMER.

Because you want the view to display orders by customer, you need to add the ORDERS table to the view. Select Add Table from the shortcut menu for the View Designer and choose ORDERS. Notice that because a persistent relationship exists between CUSTOMER and ORDERS, Visual FoxPro draws a line between these two tables and adds a condition to the Selection Criteria tab based on the relationship.

Click the Fields tab and add the following fields to the view: Customer.company, Orders.order_id, Orders.order_date, and Orders.order_amt. Click the Order By tab and order the view by Customer.company and Orders.order_date.

To see the SQL Select statement generated by the view, choose View SQL from the shortcut menu. To execute the statement and open the view, choose Run Query from the shortcut menu. A browse window will display all the orders sorted by customer name. Then close the browse window.

Click Orders.order_date in the Ordering Criteria list, then select the Descending OptionButton. Run the query again and notice the orders are now displayed with the most recent one for each customer first. Close the browse window.

Save the view and name it Cust_Orders. While you could use a space between Cust and Orders, using an underline works better because you don't have to put quotes around the view name when accessing it programmatically.

Notice the view now appears in the Database Designer window as if it were a table. As you move the mouse pointer over the view and click the right mouse button, notice that Browse and Modify are enabled. Browse runs the query and Modify brings up the View Designer window for this view.

Group By Clause

The fourth page of the View Designer allows you to specify the Group By clause for the Select statement. This page is shown in Figure 7-6.

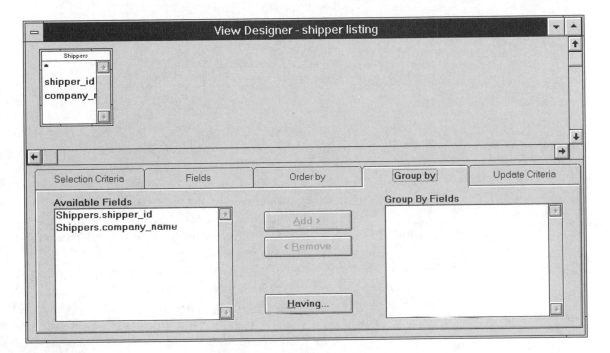

Figure 7-6.

The Group By page of the View Designer for specifying the GROUP BY clause

The Available Fields list shows all fields from all tables included in the view. To add one to the Group By Fields list, double-click it or select it and click Add. To remove a field from the Group By Fields list, double-click it, or select it and click Remove. You can rearrange the order of the fields in this list by dragging the mover arrows that appear in front of each field.

To specify a Having clause for the Select statement, click the Having button. The dialog box shown in Figure 7-7 will appear.

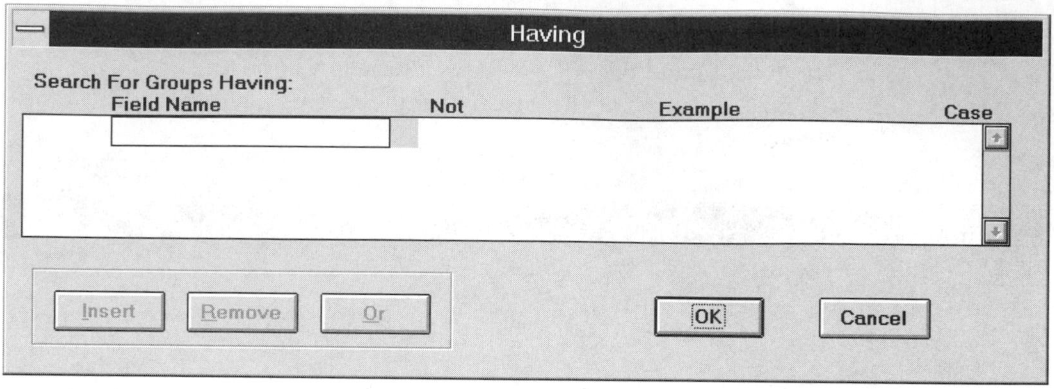

Figure 7-7.

The Having dialog box for defining the HAVING clause

The Having clause is constructed by specifying a field or an expression, a comparison operator, and a value to compare to. The Field Name drop-down menu lists the SQL aggregate functions, all fields, and <Expression>, which brings up the Expression Builder. If you select an aggregate function, you'll also have to select the field to apply the function to. The Criteria pop-up menu has the following operators: equal, like, exactly like, more than, less than, is NULL, between, and in. You can select the Not button to add "not" before the condition in the Having clause. In the Example column, enter the values to compare to the field or expression. For most of the operators, you should enter a constant value (for example, "JONES" or 10) or an expression (such as another field name). No value is required (or allowed) for "is NULL." For "between," enter two values separated by commas. For "in," enter two or more values separated by commas. If you select the Case button, the Upper() function will be used for Character or Memo fields to make the query case-insensitive.

To add a new condition, enter it into the blank condition line that appears at the bottom of the list. You can insert a new condition above the selected one by clicking the Insert button. A condition can be removed by clicking Remove, or can be moved relative to the other conditions by dragging the mover arrow that appears to the left of the condition.

Individual conditions specified in the list are combined using And in the Where clause. To use Or, select the Add Or button. This will add a line with only Or in it and a new condition line below it.

Time to Play!

The Cust_Orders view you created in the previous "Time to Play!" exercise is useful if you want to see every order by customer, but must be modified if you want to see only the total sales by customer. You can create a new view that will give you that information.

First, open the database if necessary.

```
open database \VISUAL FOXPRO\SAMPLES\DATA\TESTDATA exclusive
modify database
```

Create a new local view and add the CUSTOMER and ORDERS tables to it. Click the Fields tab and add Customer.company to the output. Click the Functions/Expressions drop-down menu arrow, choose SUM() from the list, then Orders.order_amt from the Fields pop-up menu. Click the Add button to add the expression SUM(Orders.order_amt) to the output. Click the Group By tab and group the view by Customer.company.

To see the SQL Select statement generated by the view, choose View SQL from the shortcut menu. To execute the statement and open the view, choose Run Query from the shortcut menu. A browse window will display all customers in alphabetical order with the total of all orders placed by each. Close the browse window, then save the view and name it Sales_by_Customer.

Update Criteria

In FoxPro 2.x, the results of a SQL Select statement could be sent to a read-only Cursor, which couldn't be edited, or to a table, which could be edited but not used to update the master tables without programming. In Visual FoxPro, a view can be made updatable, allowing changes made to the data in the view to update the same data in the master tables. The last page in the View Designer is used to define how changes made to the results Cursor for the view should be used to update the tables the data came from. This is shown in Figure 7-8.

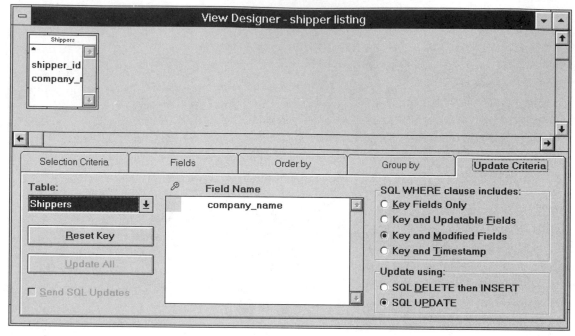

Figure 7-8.

The Update Criteria page of the View Designer for specifying how the view updates the tables it's based upon

The list of fields which appears in the middle of this page shows the output fields for the view. The Table drop-down menu determines whether fields from a particular table or fields from all tables will be shown. In the field list, you can select which fields are key fields and which are updatable. Key fields are used to uniquely identify the records in the master tables which need to be updated with changes made in the view results set. To mark a field as a key field, check the key column in front of the field name. Clicking the Reset Key button unchecks all key fields.

The column beside the key column indicates whether the field is updatable or not. You cannot make any fields from a particular table updatable until you have flagged the key field for that table. If a field isn't marked as updatable, changes can still be made to the field, but the results aren't written back to the master tables. To make all fields updatable, click the Update All button.

The SQL WHERE Clause Includes section of the page is used to determine how Visual FoxPro handles multiuser conflicts when trying to update the master tables. If a second user changed one of the records the first user did, this option determines when the update process will fail. The choices are shown in the following table.

Option	Update Fails If...
Key Fields Only	The key field in the master table has changed
Key and Updatable Fields	Any field flagged as updatable has been changed
Key and Modified Fields	Any field changed in the view result set has been changed in the master table
Key and Timestamp	A remote table has a timestamp and it's been changed in the table

The Update Using section determines what method Visual FoxPro uses to update master tables. SQL DELETE then INSERT means that the master record matching a changed record in the view is deleted using the SQL Delete command and readded with the new data using SQL Insert. If SQL UPDATE is selected, the SQL Update command is used instead. SQL UPDATE is faster because only a single SQL command is needed, but it may not work in some situations. An admittedly rare example might be if the primary key in one record was changed to a new value and the primary key in another record was changed to the former value for the first record. SQL DELETE then INSERT will always work, but it might cause delete and insert triggers to fire. This could cause unwanted side effects such as deleting all child records for a parent simply because the parent's address field was changed.

The Send SQL Updates box must be checked for the view to be updatable. It cannot be checked unless at least one field is defined as updatable, which also means a key field must be flagged.

Time to Play!

Now try creating an updatable view. Open the COMPANY database from the source code disc and create a view.

```
open database COMPANY exclusive
create sql view
```

The View Designer will come up, prompting you to choose a table. Select the table EMPLOYEE. Don't bother entering any selection criteria. In the Fields tab, add all fields to the view. In the Update Criteria tab, uncheck the updatable column for DEPT_ID; you want only LAST_NAME and FIRST_NAME to be updatable. EMP_ID should be flagged as the key field. Check the Send SQL Updates box, then save the view under the name MyView.

Continued on next page

Continued from previous page

Next do the following:

```
close tables
use MyView
set
```

Notice that both MyView and EMPLOYEE are open. Because MyView is an updatable view, EMPLOYEE must be open so the updates can occur. Open browse windows for both MyView and EMPLOYEE and adjust their window sizes and positions so you can see both browse windows simultaneously.

Edit every field in the first record of MyView, then press the down arrow key. Click in the EMPLOYEE browse window and note that only FIRST_NAME and LAST_NAME were updated as you specified.

Advanced Options

The Advanced Options function under the Query pad allows you to define connection information and to fine-tune the performance characteristics of the view. This is shown in Figure 7-9.

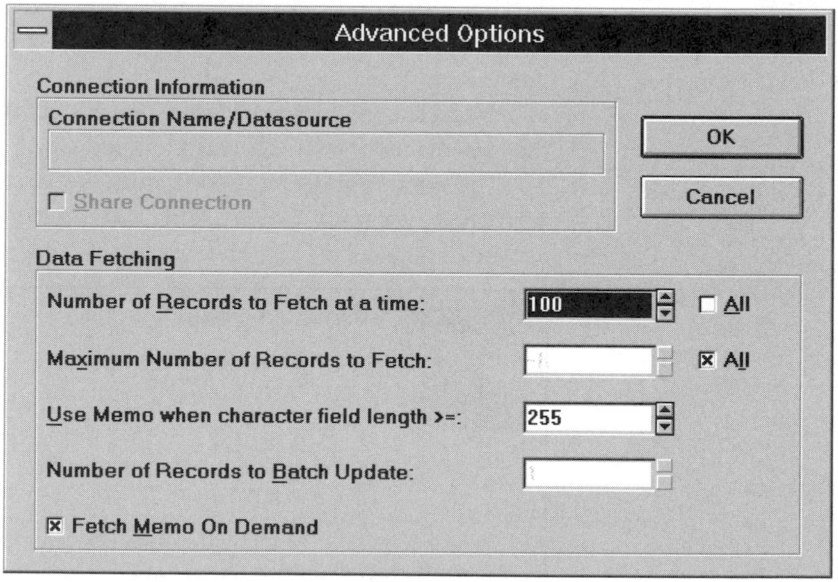

Figure 7-9.

The *Advanced Options dialog box of the View Designer*

The options in this dialog box are as follows:

- *Connection Name/Datasource.* This is the name of the connection or datasource for a remote view.

- *Share Connection.* If this option is checked, several views can use the same connection, reducing the resources required for multiple connections.

- *Number of Records to Fetch at a Time.* If the All CheckBox beside this option is checked (the value appears as -1), all records matching the view criteria will be downloaded from the back-end database before any of them can be viewed or edited. If you enter a number other than -1 (such as the default of 100), Visual FoxPro will use *progressive fetching.* That is, it will fetch the first 100 records and make them available for viewing or editing. While you are viewing the first set of records, Visual FoxPro receives the next set of 100 records in the background. This continues until all the records have been downloaded.

- *Maximum Number of Records to Fetch.* This option controls the maximum number of records that can be returned by the query. This helps limit the amount of processing required when you have a large database and a query that inadvertently returns a large number of records. The All CheckBox beside it is checked by default (the value appears as -1), meaning all records matching the view criteria will be downloaded. Uncheck All and enter a number to limit the result set size. This number must be greater than or equal to the number of records to fetch at a time.

- *Use Memo When Character Field Length >=.* This option, which defaults to 255, indicates at which size Visual FoxPro will place a string into a Memo field instead of a Character field in the result set.

- *Number of Records to Batch Update.* This option determines how updates are batched to the back-end database. With the default value set to 1, each record that is changed is sent to the database as a separate update. If the value is set to 15, 15 updates are batched and sent to the server as a single transaction.

- *Fetch Memo on Demand.* This item is checked by default, downloading Memo fields from the server only when they are required (such as when the Memo for a particular record is displayed in a Form). Uncheck this item to download all Memos for all records when the query is executed.

Creating Views Programmatically

Views can be created programmatically using the new Create SQL View command. Because views are contained in databases, a database must be selected before this command can be executed. Create SQL View has the following syntax:

```
create sql view <Name> [remote]
  [connection <ConnectionName> [share]
  |connection <DataSourceName>]
  [as <SQLselectStatement>]
```

In this argument, <Name> is the name of the view to create, and has the same rules as long names for tables. The keyword Remote indicates that remote tables are involved in the view. You can specify which connection to use when the view is opened by providing either the name of the connection or the datasource. If you include the Share keyword, the view will use a shared connection when possible. If the keyword is excluded, a unique connection that cannot be shared with other views is established when the view is opened. <SQLselectStatement> is any valid SQL Select statement. You don't specify the destination, however; the results are put into a Cursor with an alias of the view name.

 ### *Time to Play!*

Here's an interesting exercise: creating a self-referential persistent relationship and a view to handle it. Suppose that you have a staff table that contains the name of each employee and that employee's manager. Because each manager is also an employee, the result is that the manager field in the employee table points to another employee record. This is a *self-referential* relationship.

Here's some code (included in SELFREF.PRG on the source code disc) that will create such a table and the relationship to itself:

```
create database SELFREF
create table STAFF ;
  (EMP_NUM I primary key, ;
  LAST_NAME C(25), ;
  FIRST_NAME C(15), ;
  MANAGER I)
alter table STAFF ;
  add foreign key MANAGER tag MANAGER references STAFF
insert into STAFF values (1, 'Green', 'Shirley', 1)
insert into STAFF values (2, 'Smith', 'Joe', 1)
insert into STAFF values (3, 'Jones', 'Lois', 1)
```

Continued on next page

```
insert into STAFF values (4, 'Wilde', 'Oscar', 2)
browse
```

Notice that you can see the employee number for each employee's manager, but not the manager's name. For that, you would need to find the employee record whose EMP_NUM field matched the MANAGER field. A view should handle this nicely.

```
create sql view STAFF_MANAGER as;
  select STAFF.EMP_NUM, ;
       STAFF.LAST_NAME, ;
       STAFF.FIRST_NAME, ;
       padr(trim(MANAGERS.FIRST_NAME) + ' ' + ;
         MANAGERS.LAST_NAME, 41) as MANAGER;
    from STAFF, STAFF MANAGERS ;
    where STAFF.MANAGER = MANAGERS.EMP_NUM ;
    order by STAFF.LAST_NAME, STAFF.FIRST_NAME
use STAFF_MANAGER
browse
```

Notice the Use and Browse commands were used to open and browse the view just as they would a table.

The View Wizard

In addition to creating views programmatically or using the View Designer, you can also create them using the View Wizard.

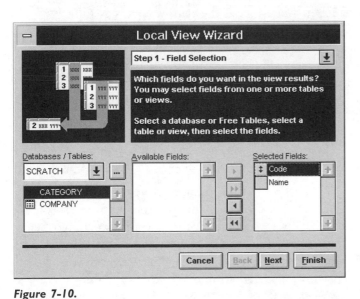

The View Wizard is one of the wizards included with Visual FoxPro. It's invoked when you select Wizards from under the Tools pad, choose Query, and then select either Local View Wizard or Remote View Wizard. It's also accessed by choosing Wizard from the New dialog box when you create a new view from a menu. The View Wizard is shown in Figure 7-10.

Working with Views

As mentioned earlier, a view acts like a table: you can open it, browse it, replace fields, report on it, and so forth.

Figure 7-10.

The View Wizard

There are several commands and functions that allow you to work with views. As you saw in the preceding exercise, Use has been updated to allow it to open views. When a view is opened, its Select statement is executed to create a result Cursor whose alias is the view name. This Cursor can then be manipulated as necessary. Two keywords have also been added to Use:

- Norequery [<DataSessionNumber>]. As with tables, views can be opened in more than one work area when necessary. Every time another copy of a view is opened, the Select statement is executed to retrieve the data. This might not be necessary and can have performance implications, especially on large remote tables. Specifying Norequery when the view is opened prevents the Select statement from being executed. Instead, the result set of an existing Cursor is used. If <DataSessionNumber> is specified, that datasession is examined for an existing Cursor. If it is not specified, all datasessions are checked. For information on datasessions, see the Visual FoxPro documentation or Steve Sawyer's report on the Form Designer in this book.
- Nodata. This keyword specifies that the view should be created without any data. This is primarily used to create a Cursor so you can determine the view's structure without having to wait for any data to be downloaded.

Two functions are important for ensuring that the view contains current information. The Requery() function reissues a view's Select statement, essentially discarding the current Cursor and creating a new one. It returns a value of 1 if the data was successfully retrieved, or a value of 0 if it was not. This function is especially useful with parameterized views, which you'll see in a moment. Refresh() gets new values for all records that haven't been updated in the view. This function is especially important before using Curval() in order to ensure the latest copy of the data is available. It has the following syntax and returns the number of records refreshed:

```
refresh([<Records> [, <Offset>]] [, <Alias> | <Workarea>])
```

In this syntax, <Records> is the number of records to refresh. You can specify a value of 0 or omit this parameter to refresh only the current record. <Offset> specifies where the refresh should begin relative to the current record. For example, a value of -10 indicates that the refresh should start ten rows earlier than the current one. Specify 0 or omit this parameter to refresh only the current record. The <Alias> or <Workarea> parameter is needed only if the view isn't in the current work area.

The Adbobjects() function can be used to determine what view and connections have been defined in the current database. It's called with the following syntax:

```
adbobjects(<ArrayName>, <Type>)
```

In this syntax, <ArrayName> is the name of a one-dimensional array into which the names are placed, while <Type> will either be "Connection" or "View." The function returns the number of objects found.

The function Used(<ViewName>) will return .T. if the specified view is open. Delete View <ViewName> removes the specified view from the database, while Modify View <ViewName> [Remote] brings up the View Designer for the specified view. You can probably figure out what Rename View <ViewName1> To <ViewName2> does. Display Views and List Views show information about the view in the current database.

 Time to Play!

Now take some time to examine Refresh() and Requery(). Two "Time to Play!" exercises ago, you created an updatable view of EMPLOYEE called MyView. Now open both the COMPANY database that comes on the source code disc and that view.

```
open database COMPANY
use MyView
```

Open browse windows for both MyView and EMPLOYEE (which was opened automatically with MyView because MyView is updatable) and adjust their window sizes and positions so you can see both browse windows simultaneously.

Edit every field in the first record of MyView, then press the down arrow key. When you click in the EMPLOYEE browse window, notice that only FIRST_NAME and LAST_NAME were updated as you specified. Next edit FIRST_NAME and LAST_NAME in a different record in EMPLOYEE. When you click back to the MyView window, notice that the edits to EMPLOYEE aren't shown.

Then refresh the view:

```
= refresh(reccount(), 1)
```

This tells Visual FoxPro to refresh all records in the view starting with the first one. Notice that the record you edited in EMPLOYEE now shows its current values in the view. Also notice that the record which has the EMP_ID you edited in the View is now marked as deleted. That's because that record can't be matched up with anything on the key field in EMPLOYEE since the key field in MyView was changed.

Continued on next page

Continued from previous page

```
= requery()
```

The MyView browse window now shows an exact copy of EMPLOYEE since you essentially discarded the Cursor and created a new one.

Parameterized Views

If you wanted to see all customer orders over $500, you could create a view something like the following:

```
open database \VISUAL FOXPRO\SAMPLES\DATA\TESTDATA exclusive
create sql view SALES_OVER_500 as ;
   select CUSTOMER.COMPANY, ;
          ORDERS.ORDER_ID, ;
          ORDERS.ORDER_DATE, ;
          ORDERS.ORDER_AMT ;
      from CUSTOMER, ORDERS ;
      where CUSTOMER.CUST_ID = ORDERS.CUST_ID and ;
          ORDERS.ORDER_AMT > 500 ;
      order by CUSTOMER.COMPANY
```

While that view works well, it's limited to orders over $500. If you wanted to see customer orders over $1,000, you'd have to create another, nearly identical view. In the long run, differing selection criteria could force you to create quite a few views.

A better approach is to use a *parameterized view*. With a parameterized view, some of the specifications in the Where clause aren't determined until runtime. To specify a parameterized view, enter a variable name preceded by a question mark where the runtime substitution should take place. For example, the view previously shown could be re-created using parameterized views.

```
create sql view SALES_OVER_SOME_VALUE as ;
   select CUSTOMER.COMPANY, ;
          ORDERS.ORDER_ID, ;
          ORDERS.ORDER_DATE, ;
          ORDERS.ORDER_AMT ;
      from CUSTOMER, ORDERS ;
      where CUSTOMER.CUST_ID = ORDERS.CUST_ID and ;
          ORDERS.ORDER_AMT > ?lnVALUE ;
      order by CUSTOMER.COMPANY
= dbsetprop('SALES_OVER_SOME_VALUE ', 'View', 'ParameterList', ;
   "lnVALUE 'N'")
```

The Dbgetprop() function is used to ensure that Visual FoxPro knows that lnVALUE should be numeric.

When this view is opened, Visual FoxPro looks for a variable called lnVALUE and uses its value for the comparison. If the variable doesn't exist, Visual FoxPro displays a dialog box asking the user for a numeric value to assign to the variable, and then uses that value.

Thus, to display orders over $500, you could use the following syntax:

```
lnVALUE = 500
use SALES_OVER_SOME_VALUE
browse
```

Then to display orders over $1,000, you could reassign the variable's value and requery the view:

```
lnVALUE = 1000
= requery()
browse
```

Parameterized views can be created visually in the View Designer by using View Parameters under the Query pad to define the name and type of each parameter variable, then entering ?<VariableName> as the value to compare a field to.

Parameterized views are especially useful for views containing only those child records that match the current parent record. An example of this would be a customer Form showing orders for the current customer in a Grid. By creating the child view as a parameterized view (for example, Where ORDERS.CUST_ID = ?CUSTOMER.CUST_ID), you simply Requery() the child view as you move through customer table to ensure that it shows the orders for the current customer.

Setting and Obtaining View and Connection Information

The Dbgetprop(), Dbsetprop(), Cursorgetprop(), and Cursorsetprop() functions allow you to determine and programmatically set options about views and connections that you can also set visually using the View Designer. Dbsetprop() and Cursorsetprop() can change many of the same properties. The difference between these functions is that Dbsetprop() changes the property in the database (making it a permanent change) while Cursorsetprop() changes the property only for the current view.

As a brief refresher, Dbgetprop() is called with the following syntax:

```
dbgetprop(<Name>, <Type>, <Property>)
```

In this argument, <Name> is the name of the object (including the view name as an alias for fields, such as customer_view.customer_name). The parameter <Type> is the type of object (Field, View, or Connection), and <Property> is the name of the property you want the value of. Dbsetprop() uses the same syntax, but includes a fourth parameter for the value to set the property to.

The following table shows the properties obtained or set for fields in a view using Dbgetprop() and Dbsetprop() with "Field" for the object type parameter. All of these properties are read and write.

Property	Description
Caption	Field caption
Comment	Comment
DataType	Data type for the field
DefaultValue	Default value
KeyField	.T. if the field is involved in an index
RuleExpression	Validation rule
RuleText	Validation text
Updatable	.T. if the field can be updated
UpdateName	Name of the field to update

The following are properties for views using "View" for the object type. Only those shown as read and write can be changed with Dbsetprop():

Property	Description	Read-Write
BatchUpdateCount	Number of update statements sent to the back-end database	Y
Comment	Comment	Y
ConnectName	Named connection used	N
FetchMemo	.T. if Memo and General fields are fetched with view results	Y
FetchSize	Number of records to fetch at a time from remote tables when progressive fetches is enabled	Y
MaxRecords	Maximum number of records to fetch	Y
ParameterList	Where clause parameters for parameterized views	Y
RuleExpression	Validation rule	Y

Continued on next page

Property	Description	Read-Write
RuleText	Validation text	Y
SendUpdates	.T. if SQL Update is used to update remote tables	Y
ShareConnection	.T. if the view can share its connection handle with other connections	Y
SourceType	View source: local or remote	N
SQL	SQL statement to execute	N
Tables	Tables involved in the view	Y
Updatable	Fields which can be updated	Y
UpdateName	Remote field names	Y
UpdateType	Update type: SQL Update or SQL Delete then Insert	Y
UseMemoSize	Size above which a field result is placed in a Memo field	Y
WhereType	What the Where clause should be comprised of for remote tables updates	Y

The following are properties for connections using "Connection" for the object type. All of them are read and write.

Property	Description
Asynchronous	.T. for an asynchronous connection
BatchMode	.T. for batch mode
Comment	Comment
ConnectString	Connection string for login
ConnectTimeout	Connection timeout in seconds
DataSource	Name of the ODBC data source
DispLogin	Determines when the ODBC login dialog box is displayed: always, never, or only if required
DispWarnings	.T. to display non-trappable warnings
IdleTimeout	Idle timeout in seconds
PacketSize	Network packet size
Password	Connection password
QueryTimeout	Query timeout in seconds

Continued on next page

Continued from previous page

Property	Description
Transactions	Determines if transaction processing is automatically or manually handled
UserID	Connection user ID
WaitTime	Time in milliseconds for Visual FoxPro to wait before checking if SQL statement has been executed

The syntax for Cursorgetprop() follows:

```
cursorgetprop(<Property>, [<Workarea> | <Alias>])
```

Cursorsetprop() adds another parameter: which value to set the property to. The following are the properties determined or set (if indicated as read and write) using these commands:

Property	Description	Read-Write
BatchUpdateCount	Number of update statements sent to the back-end database for buffered tables	Y
Buffering	Type of buffering and locking to use	Y
ConnectionHandle	Handle for connection	N
ConnectName	Named connection used	N
Database	Name of database the table or view belongs to	N
FetchMemo	.T. if Memo and General fields are fetched with view results	Y
FetchSize	Number of records to fetch at a time from remote tables when progressive fetches is enabled	Y
KeyFieldList	List of primary fields	Y
MaxRecords	Maximum number of records to fetch	Y
SendUpdates	.T. if SQL Update is used to update remote tables	Y
ShareConnection	.T. if the view can share its connection handle with other connections	Y
SourceName	Long name of view or table in a database or path and file name for free table	N
SourceType	View source: local or remote	N

Continued on next page

Property	Description	Read-Write
SQL	SQL statement to execute	N
Tables	Tables involved in the view	Y
UpdatableFieldList	Fields which can be updated	Y
UpdateNameList	Remote field names	Y
UpdateType	Update type: SQL Update or SQL Delete then Insert	Y
UseMemoSize	Size above which a field result is placed in a Memo field	Y
WhereType	What the Where clause should be comprised of for remote tables updates	Y

An example of a useful purpose for this function is Cursorgetprop('SourceType'), which returns a value of 1 for a local view, 2 for a remote view, and 3 for a table. This helps distinguish where the data resides, since a view can be opened and browsed like a table.

8 | Extending the DBC

As you've seen so far, Visual FoxPro's database allows you to extend the information stored in the DBF and CDX file Headers to contain other important repository information. However, some information is missing from the DBC that you might have expected to be there, including

- Table structural information such as field name, type, and size
- Index structural information such as index expression and filter
- Useful non-structural information such as input and output masks (pictures) for fields

There are some other limitations as well.

- Visual FoxPro provides a caption for fields which, as you saw in the section on tables, can act as a full-text description shown to the user. However, there is no similar information for tables or indexes.
- No event is triggered when a database is opened. This means that there's no ability to do things like open all or some of the tables in the database, or ask for a password and close the database if the wrong one is entered.
- Although Forms and reports have DataEnvironments, there's no built-in function to set up a relation defined in the database for a program.

Fortunately, Microsoft provided the ability to extend Visual FoxPro's database by several means.

- The DBC is a table you can manipulate even while the database is open.
- The USER field in the DBC can contain information you define.
- You can add additional fields to the DBC as required.

These extended database features mean that you can add additional information to the database to provide features Visual FoxPro doesn't have. (Note that while you can add additional fields to the DBC, adding new records is a bad idea because Visual FoxPro will consider the database to be invalid.)

There are several potential strategies for extending the DBC.

Strategy #1: Adding Information to PROPERTY

Your first thought is probably to wonder why you can't just add new information to the PROPERTY field in the DBC. Unfortunately this approach won't work. The information in this field is formatted in a specific way (see Section 10 for a description of how the information is stored) and only certain types of information are expected. Deviating from Visual FoxPro's expectations can result in a database full of errors, and possibly even cause system crashes.

Strategy #2: Adding New Fields

Because the DBC is a table, you can add new fields to it to store the additional information. The only requirement for a new field is that the field name starts with U_ so Visual FoxPro knows it's a user-defined field. For example, if you want to store an input mask for each field, you can add a Character field called U_INPUT. To flag whether a table should be opened at the start of an application, create a Logical field called U_AUTO.

While this approach sounds promising, it's less desirable than the others being discussed because you must add a new field to the DBC for each new extended property to be defined. This limits the number of properties you can add because a table can have only 255 fields. While this may sound like a lot, consider that each third party tool you might want to buy could easily add several dozen new fields to the DBC. It wouldn't be long before you'd run out of fields.

Strategy #3: Using USER

A better strategy involves putting information into the USER field in the DBC. This Memo field is·unused by Microsoft and can store any information you choose. However, it's only one field so you must figure out how to store different types of information in it.

Consider that the extended information you want to track is like the properties of an object in a Form. How does Visual FoxPro allow you to define new properties for a Form? If you open a Form as a table with Use <formname>.SCX and browse it, you'll see a field called PROPERTIES. Open this field and you'll notice that each of the properties for an object is stored on a separate line using the format shown.

```
<property name> = <value>
```

You can use a similar approach with the USER field in the DBC. As you define properties for DBC objects, you'll add a line in USER specifying the property name and its current value.

PUTDD.PRG and GETDD.PRG are two companion programs included on the source code disc that store and retrieve properties for DBC objects. (Two other supporting routines, ISPROP.PRG and GETFNAME.PRG, are also included.) These routines were designed to use a syntax similar to Dbsetprop() and Dbgetprop().

The syntax for PUTDD is:

```
PUTDD(<Name>, <Type>, <Property>, <Value>)
```

In it, <Name> is the name of the object. For indexes, fields, and relations, you should include the name of the table as an alias to the object name. For example, specify CUSTOMER.CUST_ID for the CUST_ID field of CUSTOMER.

<Type> is the type of the object. Valid types are Table, Field, Index, and Relation.

<Property> is the property to store the value for. If the property doesn't exist, PUTDD will create it.

<Value> is the value to store for the property. It can be of type Character, Numeric, Date, or Logical.

PUTDD will return .T. if it successfully stored the value for the property.

The syntax for GETDD is similar:

```
GETDD(<Name>, <Type>, <Property>)
```

GETDD returns the current value for the specified property. If either the property or the object doesn't exist, GETDD returns .NULL.

Time to Play!

Here are some examples using GETDD and PUTDD.
First, you can define a new property called AutoOpen
for certain tables and a property for indexes called
"Caption." (Like Caption for fields, it'll be something more
presentable to the user than the tag name.)

```
open database \VISUAL FOXPRO\SAMPLES\DATA\TESTDATA exclusive
= PUTDD('customer', 'Table', 'AutoOpen', .T.)
= PUTDD('orders',   'Table', 'AutoOpen', .T.)
= PUTDD('customer.cust_id', 'Index', 'Caption', 'Customer #')
= PUTDD('customer.company', 'Index', 'Caption', 'Company Name')
```

This code can be found in TESTDD.PRG on the source code
disc.

If the AutoOpen property is .T. for a particular table, you'll
open that table at the start of the application by calling the
following code. (This routine is called OPENTABS.PRG on the
source code disc.)

```
lnTABLES = adbobjects(laTABLES, 'Table')
for lnI = 1 to lnTABLES
   if nvl(GETDD(laTABLES[lnI], 'Table', 'AutoOpen'), .F.)
     use (laTABLES[lnI]) in 0
   endif nvl(GETDD(laTABLES[lnI], 'Table', 'AutoOpen'), .F.)
next lnI
```

Notice the use of Nvl() to prevent a problem with GETDD
returning .NULL. if the property doesn't exist for a particular table.

Run the following routine (SELTAG.PRG on the source code
disc) to allow you to choose the active tag for a table from the
caption rather than the tag name (although the tag name is used if
a caption hasn't been defined):

```
local lnI
define popup INDEX_POP from 0, 0 title 'Select Index'
for lnI = 1 to tagcount()
   define bar lnI of INDEX_POP prompt nvl(GETDD(alias() + '.' + ;
     tag(lnI), 'Index', 'Caption'), tag(lnI))
next lnI
on selection popup INDEX_POP deactivate popup
activate popup INDEX_POP
set order to iif(bar() = 0, order(), tag(bar()))
```

Notice the similarity of this routine to one you saw in the
section on tables that allowed the user to select a field by its
caption.

Strategy #4: Using EDC

While the strategy of using USER to contain user-defined properties
works well, there's an even better approach: Tom Rettig's Extended

Database Container (EDC) Class Library, which is part of TRUE (Tom Rettig's Utility Extensions).

Tom Rettig is well known and well respected in the Xbase (and FoxPro) world. He has spoken at many developer conferences, is the author of TRO (an application development framework product), and has written numerous books and public domain routines including the XCAT data dictionary for FoxPro 2.x. Tom has unselfishly provided EDC to the Visual FoxPro community as a public domain tool to use and abuse. If you ever have a chance to meet Tom, be sure to thank him for this and the many other contributions he has made.

EDC is a class library that, like PUTDD and GETDD, allows you to define properties for database objects and get the values of those properties. However, EDC goes beyond the two simple routines you looked at. EDC provides methods to

- Manage the database and its extended database container.
- Analyze the contents of the DBC's PROPERTY field.
- Determine if the database has been updated more recently than its extended database container.
- Measure the amount of time it takes to perform an EDC method. This allows you to determine the performance hit of using a data-driven routine compared to the less flexible and maintainable hard-coded approach.
- Provide auto-incrementing properties for many types of fields.

EDC also has complete error trapping built in.

In short, EDC provides a good foundation for the development of your own data-driven routines.

On the source code disc accompanying this book is a file called TRUE.EXE. This is a self-extracting file that contains a number of files. Files that are part of EDC include:

- EDCLIB.PRG (the EDC library program)
- TRUE.H (an INCLUDE file defining constants used by EDCLIB)
- EDC.DOC and TRUE.DOT (Word 6 for Windows document and template files describing EDC and how to use it)

See EDC.DOC if you wish to use EDC as a visual class library (VCX) rather than a PRG file.

Here's how EDC works:

- An extended database container (EDC) file is created for a database the first time the EDC is opened using EDC's lOpen method. This file is a table in the same directory with the same name as the database but with an EDC extension (you can also create a "free" EDC that isn't associated with any database). It contains at least two fields: CUNIQUEID, which contains a unique ID value linking the record to a record in the database; and MEDCOBJECT, a Memo field that holds user-defined objects that aren't part of a database.

- The USER field in the database contains a unique ID linking it to the CUNIQUEID field of a record in the EDC. This value is assigned the first time an extended property is defined for an object. Thus, each object in the database can have its own record in the EDC containing sets of extended properties.

- In addition to CUNIQUEID and MEDCOBJECT, the EDC contains one Memo field for each set of extended properties. You can have as many different sets of extended properties as you choose, up to the limit of the number of fields in a table. Each third-party vendor, for example, can have its own set of extended properties while sharing a single common structure (the EDC). The Memo field you should use is specified when the lOpen method is used to open the EDC. If the Memo field doesn't exist, EDC creates it. For example:

```
open database MYDATA
set procedure to EDCLIB additive
oEDC = createobject('EDC')
oEDC.lOpen('MYMEMO')
```

This code creates an object called oEDC based on the EDC class. If MYDATA.EDC doesn't exist when oEDC is instantiated, it will be automatically created. The call to the lOpen method tells EDC that you're going to be using the properties for this database defined in the MYMEMO field. If this field doesn't exist in MYDATA.EDC, it will be created.

- To manage more than one set of extended properties, create several objects from the EDC class. For example, the following code would manage two sets of extended properties for the same database, one stored in a Memo field called DOUG and the other in TOM:

```
open database MYDATA
oEDC1 = createobject('EDC')
oEDC2 = createobject('EDC')
oEDC1.lOpen('DOUG')
oEDC2.lOpen('TOM')
```

To create or update an extended property for a database object, use the USetProp() method. USetProp() has parameters similar to

Dbsetprop(): you pass it the name of the object, the type, the property name, and the value. The value can be Character, Currency, Date, DateTime, Logical, or Numeric. For example, to set the InputMask property of the COMPANY field in CUSTOMER.DBF, you would use the following syntax:

```
oEDC.uSetProp('customer.company', 'Field', 'InputMask', '@!')
```

The UGetProp() method, which gets an extended property's value, uses parameters similar to Dbgetprop(): the name of the object, the type, and the property name. UGetProp() returns the value of the property, or .NULL. if either the object or the property doesn't exist. Here's an example that will set the InputMask property of the Company field on the current Form to the InputMask stored as an extended property in the database:

```
Thisform.txtCompany.InputMask =
    oEDC.uGetProp('customer.company', 'Field', ;
    'InputMask')
```

With data-driven function calls like this in the Init methods of Forms, every Form will dynamically adjust when the InputMask stored in the database is changed.

To populate an array with all the extended properties of an object, pass ALL as the property name and pass an array as a fourth parameter. (It must be passed by reference by preceding the array name with @.) In this case, UGetProp() returns the number of properties found for the object. For example:

```
local laPROPERTY[1]
lnPROPS = oEDC.uGetProp('customer.company', 'Field', 'All',
    @laPROPERTY)
```

Another useful method in EDC is UIncProp(). This method increments an extended Numeric, Currency, or Date property. It can be used to assign the next available value for a table's primary key, get the next invoice number to use, and so forth. Pass UIncProp() the name of the object, the type, the property name, and, optionally, the increment value to use. (If it isn't passed, the value is incremented by one.) UIncProp() returns the next available value.

Time to Play!

Now try an example using a few of the EDC functions. Open the TESTDATA database that comes with Visual FoxPro and manage it using EDC. You'll use MYTEST as the name of the extended properties field in the EDC file. The first time you do this, EDC will create TESTDATA.EDC with a Memo field called MYTEST. Note that the following code is included in TESTEDC.PRG on the source code disc:

```
open database \VISUAL FOXPRO\SAMPLES\DATA\TESTDATA exclusive
set procedure to EDCLIB additive
oEDC = createobject('EDC')
oEDC.lOpen('MYTEST')
```

Now define properties for some objects:

```
oEDC.uSetProp('customer.cust_id', 'Field', 'NextID', 1)
? oEDC.uGetProp('customer.cust_id', 'Field', 'NextID')
? oEDC.uIncProp('customer.cust_id', 'Field', 'NextID')
? oEDC.uIncProp('customer.cust_id', 'Field', 'NextID')
oEDC.uSetProp('customer.cust_id', 'Index', 'Caption', ;
   'Customer #')
oEDC.uSetProp('customer.company', 'Index', 'Caption', ;
   'Company Name')
? oEDC.uGetProp('customer.cust_id', 'Index', 'Caption')
```

The source code disc contains a couple of sample routines to show other uses for EDC. SETUPEDC.PRG and its companion program AUTOOPEN.PRG show how to define a property called AutoOpen for tables and how to use that property to open tables that have the property set to .T. (for example, when an application starts up). To run this program use Do SETUPEDC.

TESTSEC.SCX is a Form showing how a security property can be defined for fields, and how it can be used to prevent users below a certain security level from editing or even viewing certain fields. If you run this Form (Do Form TESTSEC), you will first see a message box informing you that your security level is being set to 1 and that you can try other levels by initializing a variable called lnSECURITY before running the Form. With lnSECURITY set to 1, the Form shows only a few fields, all of which are disabled. In the Command window, type lnSECURITY = 2 and then do the Form again. This time, the Form is larger and contains more fields. The fields you could see last time are now enabled, but the new ones are disabled. Set lnSECURITY to 3 and do the Form again. Now all fields are enabled.

All the essential code that handles this is in the Init method of the Form. Take a look at the code to see how it sets the security level of some fields differently than others, how it disables or hides certain fields based on the user's security level and the level for the field, and how the Form size and the position of the button are adjusted when necessary.

EDC has many other functions as well. See the EDC.DOC file for more details.

Strategy #5: Using DBCX

At the 1995 Microsoft FoxPro Developers Conference, several third-party add-on developers announced support for a new program called Codebook Compliant. A Codebook Compliant application, or tool, is one that uses the class libraries and data dictionary extensions described in the Visual FoxPro Codebook 3.0 by Yair Alan Griver. This purpose of this program is to allow tools to work together using a common base of extensions. This means, for example, the data dictionary extensions used by FoxFire!, a report generator tool from MicroMega, are compatible with any application using the Codebook approach. This takes you a long way towards a set of "plug and play" tools that simply drop into an application and all work together.

Like EDC, DBCX is a class library that manages data dictionary extensions. However, DBCX has some fundamental differences from EDC:

- EDC is based on a table with an EDC extension containing sets of extensions, each set being in its own Memo field. DBCX, on the other hand, consists of a registry table (DBCXREG.DBF) and a separate table for each set of extensions. The registry table contains one record for each set of extensions.

- To manage more than one set of extensions in EDC, you create multiple objects from the EDC class, each managing a particular Memo field in the EDC table. Each set of DBCX extensions is managed by its own class, which is defined in the registry table. However, you don't need to create an object to manage each set of extensions because the DBCX MetaMgr class automatically creates objects contained within it that manage all of the extensions defined in the registry. Thus, a single DBCX object manages all of the extensions available.

- The properties for a particular object are stored in a Memo field in EDC with each property name and value on a separate text line. In DBCX, properties are stored in individual fields in an extension table where the name of the field is the same as the name of the property. Properties are added to EDC by adding a new text line to the Memo field. A new field must be added to the extensions table to create a new DBCX property, which has implications in a multiuser environment. This means while the number of EDC properties that can be defined is limited only by disk space, a maximum of 255 (the maximum number of fields in a Visual FoxPro table) DBCX properties can be defined for a given set of extensions. It also means while EDC property names can be up to 128 characters long, a DBCX property name must be no longer than 10 characters (the size of a field name in a free table).

- When you get a property for an object from EDC, the library routine locates the appropriate object in the DBC table, finds the matching record in the EDC table, then finds the property in the Memo field and obtains the value. Obtaining several properties for the same object means repeating these steps each time. In DBCX, the first step is to locate the appropriate object and get its unique ID value. Then, each time you need to get a property for that object, you pass the ID value to the routine, which simply accesses the appropriate field in that object's extension record. (It may already be the current record.)

- EDC uses a "sparse" method of storing properties. Each object might have a different set of properties, and only those properties for an object take up space. In DBCX each property is a separate field so properties that don't pertain to a certain object (such as the index expression property for a field) still take up space in the extension table.

- Obtaining a list of EDC properties for a particular object means parsing the Memo field for the object's properties. When the DBCX class is instantiated, a Cursor is automatically created containing every property defined in the extension set.

After reviewing this discussion of the differences between EDC and DBCX, the following conclusions can be formed:

- EDC is more flexible because properties can easily be added simply by updating a Memo field, each object can have a different set of properties if necessary, and the property name can be more descriptive without a 10-character limit.

- DBCX is faster because it pulls information directly out of fields rather than having to parse a Memo field, and it doesn't bother trying to locate an object if it's already been found.

The files that make up DBCX are

- DBCXMGR.PRG (the DBCX library program)
- DBCXREG.DBF, FPT, and CDX (the DBCX registry table)
- DBCXSPEC.DOC (a Microsoft Word 6 for Windows document describing the DBCX specifications)

- One or more sets of extensions tables (for example, CDBKMETA.DBF, FPT, and CDX) and classes that manage them (such as CDBKMGR.PRG)

Here's how DBCX works:

- Someone who wishes to create a set of data dictionary extensions creates a table to contain the extensions and a class to manage them. The table will contain an ID field as well as one field per property. The class is usually subclassed from the DBCX BaseMgr class defined in DBCXMGR.PRG, and might do nothing different from the base class than specify the name of the extensions table. They would then add a record to DBCXREG.DBF specifying the following items:
  - The name and version number of the extensions
  - The name, path, and alias of the extensions table
  - The name, path, and class library for the extensions manager
- Like EDC, the USER field in the database contains a unique ID linking it to the ID field of a record in the extensions table. This value is assigned the first time an extended property is defined for an object.
- An object is created from the DBCX MetaMgr class, using code like the following:

```
open database MYDATA
oMetaMgr = createobject('MetaMgr')
```

- In the Init method of the MetaMgr class, an object is created and added to the oMetaMgr object for each class defined in the registry table. As each manager object is created, it opens its particular extension table. The MetaMgr class then calls the DBCXGetPropList method of each manager object to put a list of the properties it supports (basically, a list of the fields in its extension table) into a Cursor. Thus, a single Cursor contains a list of every property defined by every set of extensions contained in the registry.

Getting the value of a property for a particular object is a two-step process: get the ID value for the object, then get the property for that ID value. For example, to get the InputMask property of the COMPANY field in CUSTOMER.DBF, use the syntax shown:

```
lnID = oMetaMgr.DbGetDBCKey(dbc(), 'customer.company', 'Field')
oMetaMgr.DBCXGetProp('InputMask', lnID)
```

Of course, once the ID value has been obtained, it can be used to get or set other properties. For example, you can define the InputMask for the field using this syntax:

```
oMetaMgr.DBCXSetProp('InputMask', '@!', lnID)
```

To create a new property, use the DBCXCreateProp method. This method requires the name of the property, the name of the manager object to add the property to (the manager object name is "o" plus the name of the manager class as defined in the registry), and, optionally, the property type (the default is Memo), size (the default is 10), and number of decimals (default is 0). Here are a couple of examples:

```
oMetaMgr.DBCXCreateProp('MyNewProp', 'oCdbkMgr')
oMetaMgr.DBCXCreateProp('MyTestProp', 'oCdbkMgr', 'C', 2)
```

Other methods include Show() and Print() (to display and print properties) and SetRow(), which simply moves the extension table to the record with the specified ID.

9 | File Structure Differences

This section describes the DBF structural differences between FoxPro 2.x and Visual FoxPro. As mentioned in Section 3, tables created with Visual FoxPro are not backwardly compatible with FoxPro 2.x because of the backlink area in the table Header (which exists whether a table is attached to a database or not). However, Visual FoxPro doesn't modify the Header of a 2.x table unless any of the following additions have been made:

- One or more fields support null values.
- The table used one of the new data types (Binary Character, Binary Memo, Currency, DateTime, Double, or Integer).
- The table was added to a database.

In addition to the backlink area, there are some other interesting differences in the file structures, especially if you use some of the new field types or use fields supporting null values. This section will take an exploratory approach, although you can just jump to the conclusions if you're not the adventurous type.

First, create a table in FoxPro 2.x.

```
create table TEST2X ;
  (CFIELD C(1), ;
  NFIELD N(1), ;
  LFIELD L(1), ;
  DFIELD D(8))
insert into TEST2X (CFIELD) values ('A')
```

Continued on next page

```
insert into TEST2X (NFIELD) values (1)
insert into TEST2X (LFIELD) values (.T.)
insert into TEST2X (DFIELD) values (date())
use
```

Then switch to MS-DOS and use DEBUG to examine the table.

```
C:\TEST>debug test2x.dbf
-d100
16AD:0100  03 5F 05 04 04 00 00 00-A1 00 0C 00 00 00 00 00   ._..............
16AD:0110  00 00 00 00 00 00 00 00-00 00 00 00 00 00 00 00   ................
16AD:0120  43 46 49 45 4C 44 00 00-00 00 00 43 01 00 00 00   CFIELD.....C....
16AD:0130  01 00 00 00 00 00 00 00-00 00 00 00 00 00 00 00   ................
16AD:0140  4E 46 49 45 4C 44 00 00-00 00 00 4E 02 00 00 00   NFIELD.....N....
16AD:0150  01 00 00 00 00 00 00 00-00 00 00 00 00 00 00 00   ................
16AD:0160  4C 46 49 45 4C 44 00 00-00 00 00 4C 03 00 00 00   LFIELD.....L....
16AD:0170  01 00 00 00 00 00 00 00-00 00 00 00 00 00 00 00   ................
-d
16AD:0180  44 46 49 45 4C 44 00 00-00 00 00 44 04 00 00 00   DFIELD.....D....
16AD:0190  08 00 00 00 00 00 00 00-00 00 00 00 00 00 00 00   ................
16AD:01A0  0D 20 41 20 20 20 20 20-20 20 20 20 20 20 20 31   . A            1
16AD:01B0  20 20 20 20 20 20 20 20-20 20 20 20 54 20 20 20                T
16AD:01C0  20 20 20 20 20 20 20 20-20 31 39 39 35 30 35 30            1995050
16AD:01D0  34 1A 63 B1 AD 6B 46 DF-F8 BF 69 01 00 F8 72 72   4.c..kF...i...rr
16AD:01E0  75 70 74 2C 00 BE 4A C9-4A D4 4A 7F 00 00 4D 8A   upt,..J.J.J...M.
16AD:01F0  4D 95 4D A0 4D AB 4D B6-4D C1 4D CC 4D D7 00 00   M.M.M.M.M.M.M...
-q
```

Create a table with the same structure in Visual FoxPro.

```
set null off
set database to
create table TEST30 ;
   (CFIELD C(1), ;
    NFIELD N(1), ;
    LFIELD L(1), ;
    DFIELD D(8))
insert into TEST30 (CFIELD) values ('A')
insert into TEST30 (NFIELD) values (1)
insert into TEST30 (LFIELD) values (.T.)
insert into TEST30 (DFIELD) values (date())
use
```

Again, switch to MS-DOS and use DEBUG to examine the table.

```
C:\TEST>debug test30.dbf
-d100
16AD:0100  30 5F 05 04 04 00 00 00-A8 01 0C 00 00 00 00 00   0_.............
16AD:0110  00 00 00 00 00 00 00 00-00 00 00 00 03 00 00 00   ................
16AD:0120  43 46 49 45 4C 44 00 00-00 00 00 43 01 00 00 00   CFIELD.....C....
16AD:0130  01 00 00 00 00 00 00 00-00 00 00 00 00 00 00 00   ................
16AD:0140  4E 46 49 45 4C 44 00 00-00 00 00 4E 02 00 00 00   NFIELD.....N....
16AD:0150  01 00 00 00 00 00 00 00-00 00 00 00 00 00 00 00   ................
16AD:0160  4C 46 49 45 4C 44 00 00-00 00 00 4C 03 00 00 00   LFIELD.....L....
16AD:0170  01 00 00 00 00 00 00 00-00 00 00 00 00 00 00 00   ................
-d
16AD:0180  44 46 49 45 4C 44 00 00-00 00 00 44 04 00 00 00   DFIELD.....D....
16AD:0190  08 00 00 00 00 00 00 00-00 00 00 00 00 00 00 00   ................
16AD:01A0  0D 00 00 00 00 00 00 00-00 00 00 00 00 00 00 00   ................
16AD:01B0  00 00 00 00 00 00 00 00-00 00 00 00 00 00 00 00   ................
16AD:01C0  00 00 00 00 00 00 00 00-00 00 00 00 00 00 00 00   ................
16AD:01D0  00 00 00 00 00 00 00 00-00 00 00 00 00 00 00 00   ................
16AD:01E0  00 00 00 00 00 00 00 00-00 00 00 00 00 00 00 00   ................
16AD:01F0  00 00 00 00 00 00 00 00-00 00 00 00 00 00 00 00   ................
-d
16AD:0200  00 00 00 00 00 00 00 00-00 00 00 00 00 00 00 00   ................
16AD:0210  00 00 00 00 00 00 00 00-00 00 00 00 00 00 00 00   ................
16AD:0220  00 00 00 00 00 00 00 00-00 00 00 00 00 00 00 00   ................
16AD:0230  00 00 00 00 00 00 00 00-00 00 00 00 00 00 00 00   ................
16AD:0240  00 00 00 00 00 00 00 00-00 00 00 00 00 00 00 00   ................
16AD:0250  00 00 00 00 00 00 00 00-00 00 00 00 00 00 00 00   ................
16AD:0260  00 00 00 00 00 00 00 00-00 00 00 00 00 00 00 00   ................
16AD:0270  00 00 00 00 00 00 00 00-00 00 00 00 00 00 00 00   ................
-d
16AD:0280  00 00 00 00 00 00 00 00-00 00 00 00 00 00 00 00   ................
16AD:0290  00 00 00 00 00 00 00 00-00 00 00 00 00 00 00 00   ................
16AD:02A0  00 00 00 00 00 00 00 00-20 41 20 20 20 20 20 20   ........ A
16AD:02B0  20 20 20 20 20 20 31 20-20 20 20 20 20 20 20 20         1
16AD:02C0  20 20 20 54 20 20 20 20-20 20 20 20 20 20 20 20      T
16AD:02D0  31 39 39 35 30 35 30 34-1A AF 21 CB 40 AF 21 CB   19950504..!.@.!.
16AD:02E0  40 04 22 CB 40 04 22 CB-40 2F 21 CB 40 2F 21 67   @.".@.".@/!.@/!g
16AD:02F0  44 68 20 1F 41 7D 22 D3-40 AF 21 D3 40 AF 21 D3   Dh .A}".@.!.@.!.
-q
```

Now look at the differences in the file structures. (If you aren't familiar with hexadecimal notation, don't worry; just compare the following text to the DEBUG information.)

- The first byte (byte 0), which contains an identification byte, contains 03 for TEST2X.DBF, but 30 for TEST30.DBF. This means Visual FoxPro has a new identification byte for tables. In FoxPro 2.x, this byte contains F5 if the table has an associated FPT file (that is, there's at least one Memo or General field in the table). In Visual FoxPro, this byte always contains 30, but byte 28 contains an indicator of what associated files are defined for the table. It will have the values 00 (no FPT, no CDX), 01 (there is a CDX), 02 (there is an FPT), 03 (both CDX and FPT), or 07 (this is a DBC file).

- Bytes 8 and 9, which contain a pointer to the first data record in the table, contain A1 00 for TEST2X.DBF but A8 01 for TEST30.DBF. This means the Header of the table is 263 bytes bigger in TEST30.DBF. You can verify this by using the Header() function in each version to return the size of the DBF Header. In FoxPro 2.x, this function returns 161 but in Visual FoxPro it returns 424. You'll see why in a moment.

- Byte 29 contains 03 in TEST30.DBF and 00 in TEST2X.DBF.

- The eight rows of values starting at address 0120 contain the descriptions of the four fields in the table. The line starting at address 01A0 has a 0D (end of field definition) and the contents of the first record in TEST2X.DBF. However, TEST30.DBF has 0D followed by almost seventeen rows of zeros before the first record starts. That's why the Header of TEST30.DBF is 263 bytes larger. This area contains the backlink to the database (the DBC name and relative path) the table is contained in. Because the first character following the 0D is a 00, TEST30.DBF is not contained in a database.

Now create a table whose fields support null values.

```
set null on
set database to
create table TESTNULL ;
   (CFIELD C(1), ;
    NFIELD N(1), ;
    LFIELD L(1), ;
    DFIELD D(8))
insert into TESTNULL (CFIELD) values ('A')
insert into TESTNULL (NFIELD) values (1)
insert into TESTNULL (LFIELD) values (.T.)
insert into TESTNULL (DFIELD) values (date())
use
```

Using DEBUG, the table looks like this:

```
C:\TEST>debug testnull.dbf
-d100
16AD:0100   30 5F 05 04 04 00 00 00-C8 01 0D 00 00 00 00 00   0_..............
16AD:0110   00 00 00 00 00 00 00 00-00 00 00 00 00 03 00 00   ................
16AD:0120   43 46 49 45 4C 44 00 00-00 00 00 43 01 00 00 00   CFIELD.....C....
16AD:0130   01 00 02 00 00 00 00 00-00 00 00 00 00 00 00 00   ................
16AD:0140   4E 46 49 45 4C 44 00 00-00 00 00 4E 02 00 00 00   NFIELD.....N....
16AD:0150   01 00 02 00 00 00 00 00-00 00 00 00 00 00 00 00   ................
16AD:0160   4C 46 49 45 4C 44 00 00-00 00 00 4C 03 00 00 00   LFIELD.....L....
```

Continued on next page

Continued from previous page

```
16AD:0170  01 00 02 00 00 00 00 00-00 00 00 00 00 00 00 00   ................
-d
16AD:0180  44 46 49 45 4C 44 00 00-00 00 00 44 04 00 00 00   DFIELD.....D....
16AD:0190  08 00 02 00 00 00 00 00-00 00 00 00 00 00 00 00   ................
16AD:01A0  5F 4E 75 6C 6C 46 6C 61-67 73 00 30 0C 00 00 00   _NullFlags.0....
16AD:01B0  01 00 05 00 00 00 00 00-00 00 00 00 00 00 00 00   ................
16AD:01C0  0D 00 00 00 00 00 00 00-00 00 00 00 00 00 00 00   ................
16AD:01D0  00 00 00 00 00 00 00 00-00 00 00 00 00 00 00 00   ................
16AD:01E0  00 00 00 00 00 00 00 00-00 00 00 00 00 00 00 00   ................
16AD:01F0  00 00 00 00 00 00 00 00-00 00 00 00 00 00 00 00   ................
-d
16AD:0200  00 00 00 00 00 00 00 00-00 00 00 00 00 00 00 00   ................
16AD:0210  00 00 00 00 00 00 00 00-00 00 00 00 00 00 00 00   ................
16AD:0220  00 00 00 00 00 00 00 00-00 00 00 00 00 00 00 00   ................
16AD:0230  00 00 00 00 00 00 00 00-00 00 00 00 00 00 00 00   ................
16AD:0240  00 00 00 00 00 00 00 00-00 00 00 00 00 00 00 00   ................
16AD:0250  00 00 00 00 00 00 00 00-00 00 00 00 00 00 00 00   ................
16AD:0260  00 00 00 00 00 00 00 00-00 00 00 00 00 00 00 00   ................
16AD:0270  00 00 00 00 00 00 00 00-00 00 00 00 00 00 00 00   ................
-d
16AD:0280  00 00 00 00 00 00 00 00-00 00 00 00 00 00 00 00   ................
16AD:0290  00 00 00 00 00 00 00 00-00 00 00 00 00 00 00 00   ................
16AD:02A0  00 00 00 00 00 00 00 00-00 00 00 00 00 00 00 00   ................
16AD:02B0  00 00 00 00 00 00 00 00-00 00 00 00 00 00 00 00   ................
16AD:02C0  00 00 00 00 00 00 00 00-20 41 20 20 20 20 20 20   ........ A
16AD:02D0  20 20 20 20 0E 20 20 31-20 20 20 20 20 20 20 20      .  1
16AD:02E0  20 0D 20 20 20 54 20 20-20 20 20 20 20 20 0B 20    .    T        .
16AD:02F0  20 20 20 31 39 39 35 30-35 30 34 07 1A AF 21 D3   19950504...!.
-q
```

Comparing TESTNULL.DBF and TEST30.DBF, you'll find:

- Bytes 8 and 9 (the pointer to the first data record in the table) contain A8 01 for TEST30.DBF but C8 01 for TESTNULL.DBF. This means that the Header of the table is 32 bytes bigger in TESTNULL.DBF. You'll see why in a moment.

- Bytes 10 and 11 contain the length of a record, including the "deleted" flag. Notice for TEST30.DBF, the length is 0C, which is 12 decimal. This is expected, since the length of the fields (1 + 1 + 1 + 8) plus the deleted flag (1) is 12. However, for TESTNULL.DBF, the length is 0D, which is 13 decimal. This means that there must be an extra 1-byte field stored in each record. Because each field definition takes 32 bytes, the Header is 32 bytes larger. You'll see where this extra field comes from shortly.

- The eight rows of values starting with address 0120 contain the descriptions of the four fields in the table. Notice that the third byte in the second row of each field's definition is 00 for TEST30.DBF but 02 for TESTNULL.DBF. This obviously must be the null flag for the field. This byte will contain one of five values:

Value	Contents
00	FoxPro 2.x field
02	FoxPro 2.x field that can accept null values
04	One of the new field types (Currency, DateTime, Double, Integer, Binary Character, or Binary Memo)
05	System field (not visible to user)
06	One of the new field types that can accept null values

Note that the Visual FoxPro Help topic on table structures indicates that 01 is a System field, 02 means the field can store null values, and 04 is a binary field. Although these settings look different in this table, they really aren't because these values are summed to give the actual value for a field. For example, System fields (01) will contain binary information (04) for a value of 05. All of the new field types are considered binary fields, and so have a value of 04.

- The line starting with address 01A0 has a 0D (end of field definition) and starts the backlink area in TEST30.DBF. However, TESTNULL.DBF has another field defined there. The field name is _NullFlags and it has a field type of 0, which is an invalid field type. It also has the third byte in the second row set to 05 (System field). Thus, this is not a "real" field you can see and work with, but instead is something Visual FoxPro uses internally. It has a field size of one (from the first byte on the next line), which explains why the record size of TESTNULL.DBF is one larger than TEST30.DBF. You'll see how this new field is used in a moment.

- The first record in TEST30.DBF starts at the ninth byte in the line 02A0. The 20 is a space in the deleted flag, meaning the record is not deleted. The character following that is the "A" in CFIELD. In TESTNULL.DBF, the first record starts at the ninth byte in the line 02C0. The two records are the same up to the third byte from the end of that line. At that point, an extra byte (0E) can be found in TESTNULL.DBF. This makes sense because there's an extra 1-byte _NullFlags field at the end of each record. The second record has a 0D in this position, the third a 0B, and the fourth a 07.

- Now look at the binary representation of these _NullFlags values:

0E	=	0 0 0 0 1 1 1 0
0D	=	0 0 0 0 1 1 0 1
0B	=	0 0 0 0 1 0 1 1
07	=	0 0 0 0 0 1 1 1

Looking at the bits from right to left, notice that a zero appears where a field in that position is not null. For example, 0E is the byte associated with the first record. This record has the first field filled in and the rest null. It has a 0 in the rightmost bit and values of 1 in the three bits to the left. (Because you have only four fields, you'll look only at the rightmost four bits).

This means that Visual FoxPro is using the bits in a single byte in every record to mark which of up to eight fields have null values in that record. If a table has more than eight fields, additional _NullFlags bytes are added as needed.

Feel free to try other table structures to see how they are constructed: free versus attached tables, tables containing Memo or General fields, new field types, and so forth.

10 | How Properties Are Stored in the DBC

The PROPERTY Memo field in a DBC contains properties for a database object. Each property is formatted as follows:

```
<L1> <L2> <L3> <L4> <N1> <N2> <B1> ... <Bn> <VALUE>
```

This sequence is repeated for each property within PROPERTY.

<L1> through <L4> represent the length of the entire property. This length is stored as a 4-byte binary number, with the least significant byte in <L1>. For example, a length of 15 would be stored as 15 0 0 0. (Note that this doesn't mean the digits "1 5 0 0." but instead represents Chr(15) Chr(0) Chr(0) Chr(0)). A length of 260 would be stored as 255 5 0 0.

<N1> and <N2> represent the length of the ID code for the property. This length is stored as a 2-byte binary number, with the least significant byte in <N1>. Because all current properties have an ID less than 255, these bytes normally contain 1 0.

<B1> through <Bn> are the ID codes for the property stored as a binary number of a length defined in <N1> and <N2>. Because all current properties have an ID less than 255, only 1 byte is normally used.

<VALUE> is the actual value of the property. Strings are terminated with Chr(0).

Here is a table showing the currently defined properties:

Type	Property	ID	Example Value	Example Property
Database	Comment	7	This is my comment	26 0 0 0 1 0 7 This is my comment 0
	Version	24	0010	11 0 0 0 1 0 24 0 0 1 0
Table	Path	1	dbfs\customer.dbf	25 0 0 0 1 0 1 dbfs\customer.dbf 0
	Subtype (always 1)	2	1	8 0 0 0 1 0 2 1
	Comment	7	This is my comment	26 0 0 0 1 0 7 This is my comment 0
	RuleExpression	9	Chkvalid()	18 0 0 0 1 0 9 Chkvalid() 0
	RuleText	10	"Customer validation text."	35 0 0 0 1 0 10 "Customer validation text." 0
	InsertTrigger	14	Inscust()	17 0 0 0 1 0 14 Inscust() 0
	UpdateTrigger	15	Updcust()	17 0 0 0 1 0 15 Updcust() 0
	DeleteTrigger	16	Delcust()	17 0 0 0 1 0 16 Delcust() 0
	PrimaryKey	20	Cust_id	15 0 0 0 1 0 20 Cust_id 0
Field	Comment	7	This is my comment	26 0 0 0 1 0 7 This is my comment 0
	RuleExpression	9	Chkfield()	18 0 0 0 1 0 9 Chkfield() 0
	RuleText	10	"Field validation text."	32 0 0 0 1 0 10 "Field validation text." 0
	DefaultValue	11	Date()	14 0 0 0 1 0 11 Date() 0
	Caption	56	Customer ID	19 0 0 0 1 0 56 Customer ID 0
Index	Primary/Candidate (1 = yes)	17	1	8 0 0 0 1 0 17 1
Relation	ChildTag	13	cat_code	16 0 0 0 1 0 13 cat_code 0
	ParentTable	18	category	16 0 0 0 1 0 18 category 0
	ParentTag	19	code	12 0 0 0 1 0 19 code 0
Connection	Comment	7	This is my comment	26 0 0 0 1 0 7 This is my comment 0
	DataSource	29	Excel Files	19 0 0 0 1 0 29 Excel Files 0
	Asynchronous (1 = yes)	64	1	8 0 0 0 1 0 64 1
	BatchMode	65	1	8 0 0 0 1 0 65 1
	(1 = yes)			
	ConnectString	66	MYID;mypw	17 0 0 0 1 0 66 MYID;mypw 0
	ConnectTimeout (4-digit binary value)	67	15	11 0 0 0 1 0 67 0 0 0 15

Continued on next page

Type	Property	ID	Example Value	Example Property
	DispLogin	68	1	8 0 0 0 1 0 68 1
	DispWarnings (1 = yes)	69	1	8 0 0 0 1 0 69 1
	IdleTimeout (4-digit binary value)	70	0	11 0 0 0 1 0 70 0 0 0 0
	QueryTimeout (4-digit binary value)	71	0	11 0 0 0 1 0 71 0 0 0 0
	Password	72	mypw	12 0 0 0 1 0 72 mypw 0
	Transactions (1 = yes)	73	1	8 0 0 0 1 0 73 1
	UserID	74	myuser	14 0 0 0 1 0 74 myuser 0
	WaitTime (4-digit binary value)	75	100	11 0 0 0 1 0 75 0 0 0 100
	PacketSize (4-digit binary value)	78	4096	11 0 0 0 1 0 78 0 0 16 0
View	Subtype (6 for local, 7 for remote)	2	6	8 0 0 0 1 0 2 6
	Comment	7	This is my comment	26 0 0 0 1 0 7 This is my comment 0
	RuleExpression	9	Chkvalid()	18 0 0 0 1 0 9 Chkvalid() 0
	RuleText	10	"Customer validation text."	35 0 0 0 1 0 10 "Customer validation text." 0
	ParameterList	12	cust_idxx,'C';xx_yy,'D'	31 0 0 1 0 12 cust_idxx,'C';xx_yy,'D' 0
	BatchUpdateCount	28	1	8 0 0 0 1 0 28 1
	ConnectName	32	tastrade	17 0 0 0 1 0 32 tastrade 0
	FetchMemo (1 = yes)	36	1	8 0 0 0 1 0 36 1
	FetchSize (4-digit binary value: -1 = all)	37	100	11 0 0 0 1 0 37 0 0 0 100
	MaxRecords (4-digit binary value: -1 = all)	39	-1	11 0 0 0 1 0 39 255 255 255 255
	ShareConnection (1 = yes)	40	0	8 0 0 0 1 0 40 0

Continued on next page

Continued from previous page

Type	Property	ID	Example Value	Example Property
	SourceType (1 = local, 2 = remote)	41	1	8 0 0 0 1 0 41 1
	SQL	42	SELECT Customer.company, Orders.order_id, Orders.order_date, Orders.order_amt FROM testdata!customer, testdata!orders WHERE Customer.cust_id = Orders.order_id ORDER BY Customer.company, Orders.order_date DESC	216 0 0 0 1 0 42 SELECT Customer.company, Orders.order_id, Orders.order_date, Orders.order_amt FROM testdata!customer, testdata!orders WHERE Customer.cust_id = Orders.order_id ORDER BY Customer.company, Orders.order_date DESC 0
	Tables	43	customer,orders	23 0 0 0 1 0 43 customer,orders 0
	SendUpdates (1 = yes)	44	0	8 0 0 0 1 0 44 0
	UpdateType: SQL Update (1) or SQL Delete then Insert (2)	46	1	8 0 0 0 1 0 46 1
	UseMemoSize (4-digit binary)	47	255	11 0 0 0 1 0 47 0 0 0 255
	WhereType: key fields only (1), key and updatable fields (2), key and modified fields (3), or key and timestamp (4)	48	3	8 0 0 0 1 0 48 3
Field in View	UpdateName	35	Customer.company	24 0 0 0 1 0 35 Customer.company 0
	KeyField (1 = yes)	38	0	8 0 0 0 1 0 38 0
	Updatable (1 = yes)	45	0	8 0 0 0 1 0 45 0
	DataType	77	C(40)	13 0 0 0 1 0 77 C(40) 0
			D	9 0 0 0 1 0 77 D 0
			Y NOCPTRANS	19 0 0 0 1 0 77 Y NOCPTRANS 0

With Dbgetprop() returning the value for any of these properties, you might wonder why you would want to know the structure of information storage. One reason is that most of this information is considered read-only to Dbsetprop(). You can change these things using the Table Designer, but if you need to change something at runtime, the only way to do it is to physically modify the contents of the DBC. Knowing how the information is stored allows you to do this. Take caution, however; if you improperly change the property for a record, you may make the DBC invalid.

Because it's rather tedious (and potentially dangerous if you make a mistake) to calculate the length and update the PROPERTY field correctly, a routine called PUTPROP.PRG (included on the source code disc) will do that for you. It expects the database file is open as a table (Use <database>.DBC Again) and is positioned to the correct record. You call it with two parameters: the ID # of the property to update and the value to replace it with. Here's an example:

```
use \VISUAL FOXPRO\SAMPLES\DATA\TESTDATA.DBC again
locate for OBJECTTYPE = 'Table' and OBJECTNAME = 'customer'
= PUTPROP(1, '\newdir\another\customer.dbf')
```

Now examine an example of where this might be useful. In Section 3, there was a solution to the problem of having different copies of the same tables in different directories (such as test and production data or accounting files for different companies). The solution was to have a copy of the database in each directory (because the database could contain only one copy of each table) and open the database in the appropriate directory to get at the tables in that directory. However, there's another solution: changing the path to the tables that are stored in the database. Because the path is a property of a table stored in the PROPERTY field of the table's record in the DBC, changing the path property will point the database to a different copy of the table. For example, if there was a function called CHANGEPATH that changed the path stored in the DBC, you could use code like the following:

```
* Open the test data.

lcDIRECTORY = '\TEST\'
do CHANGEPATH with 'CUSTOMER.DBF', lcDIRECTORY
use CUSTOMER

...

* Open the production data.

lcDIRECTORY = '\LIVE\'
do CHANGEPATH with 'CUSTOMER.DBF', lcDIRECTORY
use CUSTOMER
```

CHANGEPATH would call PUTPROP to change the path of the specified table in the DBC.

A drawback to this approach is that changing the path to a table in the database means that every user on the network is pointing to the same copy of the table, even though some may want to work with test data and others with production data. A solution to this is to have all tables on the network backlinked to a copy of the database on the current user's hard disk and have CHANGEPATH change only the user's local copy of the database. That way, each table thinks it belongs to only one database (such as C:\TEST\MYDATA.DBC) when in fact there are many copies of that database. There is the problem, of course, of keeping all those copies of the database updated. Nobody said this would be easy.

11 | Tools Options and Work Area Properties

Figure 11-1.

The Data page of the Tools Options dialog box

The Options function in the Tools pad has a couple of pages that affect databases and table. The first page is Data, shown in Figure 11-1.

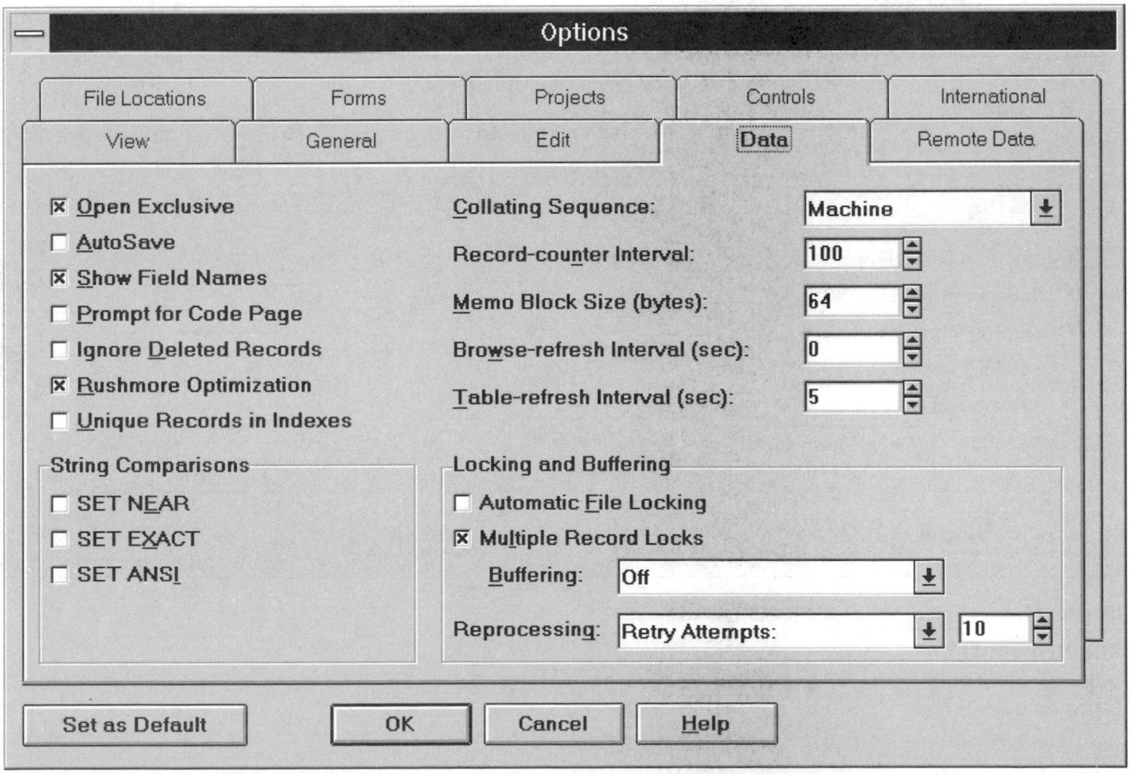

The Data page of the Tools Options dialog box

As you can probably guess, the settings in this page are really just a visual way of using various Set commands. For example, Open Exclusive does the same thing as using Set Exclusive, Browse Refresh Interval and Table Refresh Interval control the same item as Set Refresh, and checking Multiple Record Locks is the same as Set Multilocks On. The advantage of using this Options dialog box is that you can change several things at once without typing (or even knowing the proper commands and syntax), and can set them as defaults automatically used whenever you start Visual FoxPro.

The other page is Remote Data, shown in Figure 11-2. The options in this page act as the default values to use in the Advanced Options dialog box in the View Designer (the Remote View Defaults section of this page) and in the Connection Designer (the Connection Defaults section).

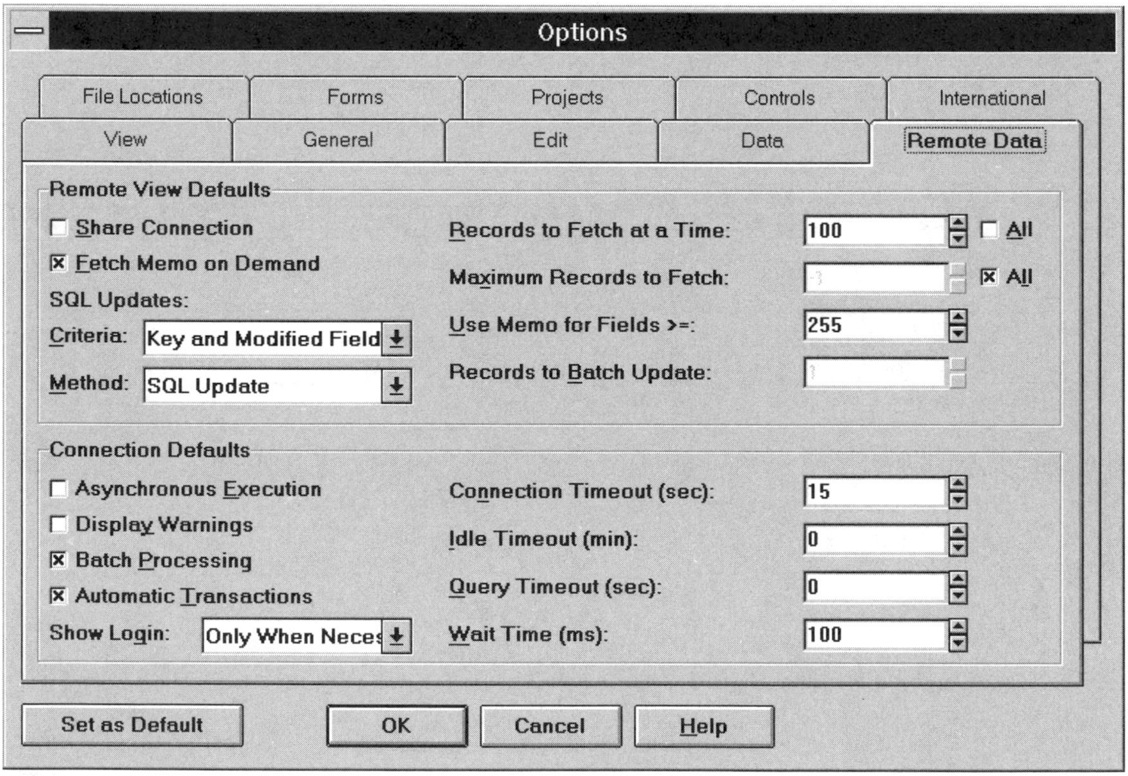

Figure 11-2.

The Remote Data
page of the Tools
Options dialog box

When the View window (not the View Designer window) is open, a Properties button is available. Also, when a browse window is open a Table pad appears in the menu bar with a Properties function under it. Choosing either of these brings up the Work Area Properties dialog box shown in Figure 11-3.

Figure 11-3.

The Work Area Properties dialog box

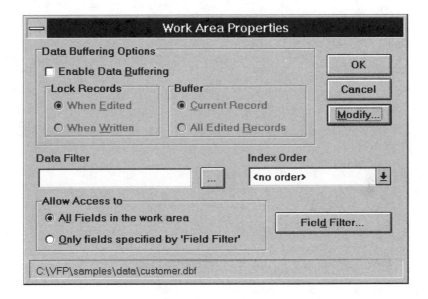

As with the Options dialog box, the settings in this dialog box allow you to visually change various settings. Changing the Data Buffering Options, for example, is like issuing Cursorsetprop('Buffering') with the appropriate value.

12 | Sample Schema Generated by GENDBC

The following file, TASTRADE.PRG, was automatically generated by running the GENDBC program described in Section 2 and specifying the TASTRADE database that comes with the Visual FoxPro sample files. This program is quite long, so it isn't included in its entirety here. Instead you'll find only those portions that help show what GENDBC does. Added comments are shown in this typeface rather than the typeface used for the code.

In addition to TASTRADE.PRG, GENDBC also creates TASTRADE.KRT, a file containing the stored procedures from TASTRADE. You won't look at that code at all, as it's used in TASTRADE.PRG in an Append Procedures statement.

```
*  ***********************************************************
*  *
*  * 05/15/95             TASTRADE.DBC              22:00:49
*  *
*  ***********************************************************
*  *
*  * Description:
*  * This program was automatically generated by GENDBC
*  * Version 1.2
*  *
*  ***********************************************************
```

Here you'll create the database, append the stored procedures, and compile the code.

```
CREATE DATABASE 'TASTRADE.DBC'

********* Procedure Re-Creation *********
IF !FILE( [C:\TEMP\TASTRADE.krt] )
    ? [Warning! No Procedure File Found!]
ELSE
    g_SetSafety = SET('SAFETY')
    SET SAFETY OFF
    APPEND PROCEDURES FROM 'C:\TEMP\TASTRADE.krt'
    COMPILE DATABASE TASTRADE.DBC
    SET SAFETY &g_SetSafety
ENDIF
```

This part creates tables using the following code: Create Table statements create the table and handle field validation; Index On creates all of the indexes; Alter Table defines primary and candidate keys; Dbsetprop() defines table and field comments and field captions; and Create Trigger statements create the triggers.

```
***** Table setup for ORDERS *****
CREATE TABLE 'ORDERS' (ORDER_ID C(6) NOT NULL DEFAULT newid(), ;
            CUSTOMER_ID C(6) NOT NULL, ;
            SHIPPER_ID C(6) NOT NULL, ;
            ORDER_NUMBER C(6) NOT NULL DEFAULT newid("order_number"), ;
            ORDER DATE D NOT NULL DEFAULT DATE(), ;
            SHIP_TO_NAME C(40) NOT NULL, ;
            SHIP_TO_ADDRESS C(60) NOT NULL, ;
            SHIP_TO_CITY C(15) NOT NULL, ;
            SHIP_TO_REGION C(15) NOT NULL, ;
            SHIP_TO_POSTAL_CODE C(10) NOT NULL, ;
            SHIP_TO_COUNTRY C(15) NOT NULL, ;
            DISCOUNT N(2, 0) NOT NULL DEFAULT 0, ;
            FREIGHT Y NOT NULL, ;
            DELIVER_BY D NOT NULL CHECK deliver_by=>order_date ;
                ERROR "Cannot be earlier than Order Date" ;
                DEFAULT DATE()+7, ;
            NOTES M NOT NULL, ;
            EMPLOYEE_ID C(6) NOT NULL DEFAULT defaultemployee())

***** Create each index for ORDERS *****
INDEX ON SHIPPER_ID TAG SHIPPER_ID
INDEX ON CUSTOMER_ID TAG CUSTOMER_I
INDEX ON EMPLOYEE_ID TAG EMPLOYEE_I
INDEX ON ORDER_NUMBER TAG ORDER_NUMB
ALTER TABLE 'ORDERS' ADD PRIMARY KEY ORDER_ID TAG ORDER_ID
ALTER TABLE 'ORDERS' ADD UNIQUE CUSTOMER_ID+ORDER_ID TAG CUST_ORD

***** Change properties (if any) for ORDERS *****
= DBSETPROP("ORDERS.ORDER_ID", "Field", "Comment", "Unique ID of this order" )
= DBSETPROP("ORDERS.CUSTOMER_ID", "Field", "Comment", ;
   "ID of customer who placed order" )
= DBSETPROP("ORDERS.SHIPPER_ID", "Field", "Comment", "Shipper ID" )
```

Continued on next page

Continued from previous page

```
= DBSETPROP("ORDERS.ORDER_NUMBER", "Field", "Comment", ;
  "Order number (automatically generated)" )
= DBSETPROP("ORDERS.ORDER_DATE", "Field", "Comment", "Order date" )
= DBSETPROP("ORDERS.SHIP_TO_NAME", "Field", "Comment", "Ship to name" )
= DBSETPROP("ORDERS.SHIP_TO_ADDRESS", "Field", "Comment", "Ship to address" )
= DBSETPROP("ORDERS.SHIP_TO_CITY", "Field", "Comment", "Ship to city" )
= DBSETPROP("ORDERS.SHIP_TO_REGION", "Field", "Comment", "Ship to region" )
= DBSETPROP("ORDERS.SHIP_TO_POSTAL_CODE", "Field", "Comment", ;
  "Ship to postal (zip) code" )
= DBSETPROP("ORDERS.SHIP_TO_COUNTRY", "Field", "Comment", "Ship to country" )
= DBSETPROP("ORDERS.DISCOUNT", "Field", "Comment", "Order discount percent" )
= DBSETPROP("ORDERS.FREIGHT", "Field", "Comment", "Total freight charges" )
= DBSETPROP("ORDERS.DELIVER_BY", "Field", "Comment", ;
  "Date order must be delivered" )
= DBSETPROP("ORDERS.NOTES", "Field", "Comment", "Miscellaneous notes" )
= DBSETPROP("ORDERS.EMPLOYEE_ID", "Field", "Comment", "Employee ID" )
= DBSETPROP("ORDERS", "Table", "Comment", "Order Information")
CREATE TRIGGER ON 'ORDERS' FOR DELETE AS __ri_delete_orders()
CREATE TRIGGER ON 'ORDERS' FOR INSERT AS __ri_insert_orders()
CREATE TRIGGER ON 'ORDERS' FOR UPDATE AS __ri_update_orders()
ALTER TABLE 'ORDERS' SET CHECK valorder()
```

This part creates views with the following elements. Create SQL View statements create the view and Dbsetprop() defines view and field properties.

```
**************** View setup for SALES SUMMARY ***************

CREATE SQL VIEW "SALES SUMMARY" ;
  AS SELECT STR(YEAR(Orders.order_date), 4) + STR(MONTH(Orders.order_date), ;
  2),  SUM(Order_line_items.unit_price) AS sum_unit_price ;
  FROM tastrade!Orders, tastrade!Order_Line_Items ;
  WHERE Orders.order_id = Order_line_items.order_id GROUP BY 1

****
=DBSetProp( 'SALES SUMMARY', 'View', 'UpdateType', 1 )
=DBSetProp( 'SALES SUMMARY', 'View', 'WhereType', 3 )
=DBSetProp( 'SALES SUMMARY', 'View', 'FetchMemo', .T. )
=DBSetProp( 'SALES SUMMARY', 'View', 'SendUpdates', .F. )
=DBSetProp( 'SALES SUMMARY', 'View', 'UseMemoSize', 255 )
=DBSetProp( 'SALES SUMMARY', 'View', 'FetchSize', 100 )
=DBSetProp( 'SALES SUMMARY', 'View', 'MaxRecords', -1 )
=DBSetProp( 'SALES SUMMARY', 'View', 'Tables', 'rectclass' )

*! Field Level Properties for SALES SUMMARY
* Props for the SALES SUMMARY.exp_1 field.
=DBSetProp( 'SALES SUMMARY.exp_1', 'Field', 'KeyField', .F. )
=DBSetProp( 'SALES SUMMARY.exp_1', 'Field', 'Updatable', .F. )
=DBSetProp( 'SALES SUMMARY.exp_1', 'Field', 'UpdateName', 'exp_1' )

* Props for the SALES SUMMARY.sum_unit_price field.
```

Continued on next page

```
=DBSetProp( 'SALES SUMMARY.sum_unit_price', 'Field', 'KeyField', .F. )
=DBSetProp( 'SALES SUMMARY.sum_unit_price', 'Field', 'Updatable', .F. )
=DBSetProp( 'SALES SUMMARY.sum_unit_price', 'Field', 'UpdateName', ;
   'sum_unit_price' )
```

This code defines relationships between tables using Alter Table statements.

```
*************** Begin Relations Setup **************
ALTER TABLE 'ORDER_LINE_ITEMS' ADD FOREIGN KEY TAG PRODUCT_ID ;
   REFERENCES PRODUCTS TAG PRODUCT_ID
ALTER TABLE 'EMPLOYEE' ADD FOREIGN KEY TAG GROUP_ID ;
   REFERENCES USER_LEVEL TAG GROUP_ID
ALTER TABLE 'ORDERS' ADD FOREIGN KEY TAG CUSTOMER_I ;
   REFERENCES CUSTOMER TAG CUSTOMER_I
```

Here, referential integrity rules are handled by opening the database as a table and using Replace to update the RIINFO field for each relationship record.

```
***** Referential Integrity Setup *****
CLOSE DATABASE
USE 'TASTRADE.DBC'
LOCATE FOR ObjectType = 'Relation' AND 'product_id'$Property AND
   'products'$Property AND 'product_id'$Property
IF FOUND()
   REPLACE RiInfo WITH 'CRR   '
ELSE
  ? "Could not set RI Information."
ENDIF
LOCATE FOR ObjectType = 'Relation' AND 'group_id'$Property AND
   'user_level'$Property AND 'group_id'$Property
IF FOUND()
   REPLACE RiInfo WITH 'CRR   '
ELSE
  ? "Could not set RI Information."
ENDIF
USE
```

13 Generated RI Code

The following code was generated by the RI Builder for the database described in the "Time to Play!" example at the end of Section 6. Comments have been added to help explain it, because it's quite dense and totally undocumented. Note that the code you see on screen may differ somewhat from the listing here, depending on any changes Microsoft makes to the RI Builder. However, the general concepts will be the same.

The following lines are put at the start and end of the inserted code block so the RI Builder can identify which code needs to be replaced when you regenerate the RI code.

```
**__RI_HEADER!@ Do NOT REMOVE or MODIFY this line!!!! @!__RI_HEADER**
**__RI_FOOTER!@ Do NOT REMOVE or MODIFY this line!!!! @!__RI_FOOTER**
```

Several routines appear at the start of the generated code. However, you'll look at those routines later because they are generic supporting routines called by the database-specific trigger routines. Here's the routine the RI Builder generated as the delete trigger for CLIENTS to cascade deleting a client record to the PROJECTS table:

```
PROCEDURE __RI_DELETE_clients
LOCAL llRetVal
llRetVal = .t.

* If we're in the first trigger routine (_TRIGGERLEVEL is a system memory variable
* containing the current trigger procedure nesting level), let's do some setup: start
```

Continued on next page

```
* a transaction, initialize some memory variables, set DELETED and EXACT the way we
* need 'em, and enable error trapping.

IF _triggerlevel=1
   BEGIN TRANSACTION
   PRIVATE pcRIcursors,pcRIwkareas,pcRIolderror,pnerror,;
   pcOldDele,pcOldExact,pcOldTalk
   pcOldTalk=SET("TALK")
   SET TALK OFF
   pcOldDele=SET("DELETED")
   pcOldExact=SET("EXACT")
   SET DELETED ON
   SET EXACT OFF
   pcRIcursors=""
   pcRIwkareas=""
   pcRIolderror=ON("error")
   pnerror=0
   ON ERROR pnerror=rierror(ERROR(),message(),message(1),program())
   IF TYPE('gaErrors(1)')<>"U"
      release gaErrors
   ENDIF
   PUBLIC gaErrors(1,12)
ENDIF first trigger

* Initialize some more memory variables.

PRIVATE pcParentDBF,pnParentRec,pcChildDBF,pnChildRec,pcParentID,pcChildID
PRIVATE pcParentExpr,pcChildExpr
STORE "" TO pcParentDBF,pcChildDBF,pcParentID,pcChildID,pcParentExpr,pcChildExpr
STORE 0 TO pnParentRec,pnChildRec
LOCAL lcParentID && parent's value to be sought in child
LOCAL lcChildWkArea && child work area handle returned by riopen
LOCAL lcParentWkArea
LOCAL llDelHeaderarea
lcStartArea=select()
llRetVal=.t.
lcParentWkArea=select()
SELECT (lcParentWkArea)
pcParentDBF=dbf()
pnParentRec=recno()
STORE CLIENT_NUM TO lcParentID,pcParentID
pcParentExpr="CLIENT_NUM"

* Open another copy of PROJECTS and set its order to the tag used by the relationship
* with CLIENTS. If we couldn't open the table, call RIEND to clean things up if we're
* the highest level trigger and return .F. so the trigger fails.

lcChildWkArea=riopen("projects","client_num")
IF lcChildWkArea<=0
   IF _triggerlevel=1
      DO riend WITH .F.
   ENDIF at the end of the highest trigger level
   RETURN .F.
ENDIF not able to open the child work area
```

Continued on next page

Continued from previous page

```
* Select the PROJECTS table, find the first matching record for the CLIENT we want to
* delete, and as long as we have matching records, call RIDELETE() to do the dirty
* work of cascading the delete.

pcChildDBF=dbf(lcChildWkArea)
SELECT (lcChildWkArea)
SEEK lcParentID
SCAN WHILE CLIENT_NUM=lcParentID AND llRetVal
   pnChildRec=recno()
   pcChildID=CLIENT_NUM
   pcChildExpr="CLIENT_NUM"
   llRetVal=ridelete()
ENDSCAN get all of the projects records

* Cleanup before returning: close the copy of PROJECTS we opened and call RIEND to
* finish things up like ending the transaction, resetting things we changed (such as
* DELETED and EXACT), etc.

=rireuse("projects",lcChildWkArea)
IF NOT llRetVal
   IF _triggerlevel=1
      DO riend WITH llRetVal
   ENDIF at the end of the highest trigger level
   SELECT (lcStartArea)
   RETURN llRetVal
ENDIF
IF _triggerlevel=1
   do riend with llRetVal
ENDIF at the end of the highest trigger level
SELECT (lcStartArea)
RETURN llRetVal
```

Here is the delete trigger for MANAGERS to restrict the deletion of any projects for the manager:

```
PROCEDURE __RI_DELETE_managers
LOCAL llRetVal
llRetVal = .t.

* If we're in the first trigger routine (_TRIGGERLEVEL is a system memory variable
* containing the current trigger procedure nesting level), let's do some setup: start
* a transaction, initialize some memory variables, set DELETED and EXACT the way we
* need 'em, and enable error trapping.

IF _triggerlevel=1
   BEGIN TRANSACTION
   PRIVATE pcRIcursors,pcRIwkareas,pcRIolderror,pnerror,;
   pcOldDele,pcOldExact,pcOldTalk
   pcOldTalk=SET("TALK")
   SET TALK OFF
   pcOldDele=SET("DELETED")
   pcOldExact=SET("EXACT")
   SET DELETED ON
```

Continued on next page

```
    SET EXACT OFF
    pcRIcursors=""
    pcRIwkareas=""
    pcRIolderror=ON("error")
    pnerror=0
    ON ERROR pnerror=rierror(ERROR(),message(),message(1),program())
    IF TYPE('gaErrors(1)')<>"U"
       release gaErrors
    ENDIF
    PUBLIC gaErrors(1,12)
ENDIF first trigger

* Initialize some more memory variables.

PRIVATE pcParentDBF,pnParentRec,pcChildDBF,pnChildRec,pcParentID,pcChildID
PRIVATE pcParentExpr,pcChildExpr
STORE "" TO pcParentDBF,pcChildDBF,pcParentID,pcChildID,pcParentExpr,pcChildExpr
STORE 0 TO pnParentRec,pnChildRec
LOCAL lcParentID && parent's value to be sought in child
LOCAL lcChildWkArea && child work area handle returned by riopen
LOCAL lcParentWkArea
LOCAL llDelHeaderarea
lcStartArea=select()
llRetVal=.t.
lcParentWkArea=select()
SELECT (lcParentWkArea)
pcParentDBF=dbf()
pnParentRec=recno()
STORE EMP_NUM TO lcParentID,pcParentID
pcParentExpr="EMP_NUM"

* Open another copy of PROJECTS and set its order to the tag used by the relationship
* with MANAGERS. If we couldn't open the table, call RIEND to clean things up if
* we're the highest level trigger and return .F. so the trigger fails.

lcChildWkArea=riopen("projects","emp_num")
IF lcChildWkArea<=0
   IF _triggerlevel=1
      DO riend WITH .F.
   ENDIF at the end of the highest trigger level
   RETURN .F.
ENDIF not able to open the child work area
pcChildDBF=dbf(lcChildWkArea)

* See if we can find any PROJECTS records that match the MANAGER we want to delete. If
* so, set llRetVal to .F. and give an error message.

llRetVal=!SEEK(lcParentID,lcChildWkArea)
SELECT (lcChildWkArea)
pnChildRec=recno()
pcChildID=EMP_NUM
pcChildExpr="EMP_NUM"
IF !llRetVal
   DO rierror with -1,"Delete restrict rule violated.","",""
ENDIF
```

Continued on next page

Continued from previous page

```
* Cleanup before returning: close the copy of PROJECTS we opened and call RIEND to
* finish things up like ending the transaction, resetting things we changed (such as
* DELETED and EXACT), etc.

=rireuse("projects",lcChildWkArea)
IF NOT llRetVal
   IF _triggerlevel=1
      DO riend WITH llRetVal
   ENDIF at the end of the highest trigger level
   SELECT (lcStartArea)
   RETURN llRetVal
ENDIF
IF _triggerlevel=1
   do riend with llRetVal
ENDIF at the end of the highest trigger level
SELECT (lcStartArea)
RETURN llRetVal
```

This section won't bother looking at the update trigger for CLIENTS (__ri_update_clients) because it's almost identical to the update trigger for MANAGERS. The MANAGERS update trigger cascades a primary key change to PROJECTS.

```
procedure __RI_UPDATE_managers
LOCAL llRetVal
llRetVal = .t.

* If we're in the first trigger routine (_TRIGGERLEVEL is a system memory variable
* containing the current trigger procedure nesting level), let's do some setup: start
* a transaction, initialize some memory variables, set DELETED and EXACT the way we
* need 'em, and enable error trapping.

IF _triggerlevel=1
   BEGIN TRANSACTION
   PRIVATE pcRIcursors,pcRIwkareas,pcRIolderror,pnerror,;
   pcOldDele,pcOldExact,pcOldTalk
   pcOldTalk=SET("TALK")
   SET TALK OFF
   pcOldDele=SET("DELETED")
   pcOldExact=SET("EXACT")
   SET DELETED ON
   SET EXACT OFF
   pcRIcursors=""
   pcRIwkareas=""
   pcRIolderror=ON("error")
   pnerror=0
   ON ERROR pnerror=rierror(ERROR(),message(),message(1),program())
   IF TYPE('gaErrors(1)')<>"U"
      release gaErrors
   ENDIF
   PUBLIC gaErrors(1,12)
ENDIF first trigger
```

Continued on next page

```
* Initialize some more memory variables.

PRIVATE pcParentDBF,pnParentRec,pcChildDBF,pnChildRec,pcParentID,pcChildID
PRIVATE pcParentExpr,pcChildExpr
STORE "" TO pcParentDBF,pcChildDBF,pcParentID,pcChildID,pcParentExpr,pcChildExpr
STORE 0 TO pnParentRec,pnChildRec
LOCAL lcParentID && parent's value to be sought in child
LOCAL lcOldParentID && previous parent id value
LOCAL lcChildWkArea && child work area handle returned by riopen
LOCAL lcChildID && child's value to be sought in parent
LOCAL lcOldChildID && old child id value
LOCAL lcParentWkArea && parentwork area handle returned by riopen
LOCAL lcStartArea
lcStartArea=select()
llRetVal=.t.
lcParentWkArea=select()
SELECT (lcParentWkArea)
pcParentDBF=dbf()
pnParentRec=recno()
lcOldParentID=OLDVAL("EMP_NUM")
pcParentID=lcOldParentID
pcParentExpr="EMP_NUM"
lcParentID=EMP_NUM

* If the primary key field for MANAGERS was changed, we'll have to cascade that change
* to PROJECTS. Start by opening another copy of PROJECTS and setting its order to the
* tag used by the relationship with MANAGERS. If we couldn't open the table, call
* RIEND to clean things up if we're the highest level trigger and return .F. so the
* trigger fails.

IF lcParentID<>lcOldParentID
   lcChildWkArea=riopen("projects")
   IF lcChildWkArea<=0
      IF _triggerlevel=1
         DO riend WITH .F.
      ENDIF at the end of the highest trigger level
      SELECT (lcStartArea)
      RETURN .F.
   ENDIF not able to open the child work area

* Select the PROJECTS table, find the first matching record for the MANAGER we want to
* update, and as long as we have matching records, call RIUPDATE() to do the dirty
* work of cascading the update.

   pcChildDBF=dbf(lcChildWkArea)
   SELECT (lcChildWkArea)
   SCAN FOR EMP_NUM=lcOldParentID
      pnChildRec=recno()
      pcChildID=EMP_NUM
      pcChildExpr="EMP_NUM"
      llRetVal=riupdate("EMP_NUM",lcParentID)
   ENDSCAN get all of the projects records

* Cleanup before returning: close the copy of PROJECTS we opened and call RIEND to
```

Continued on next page

Continued from previous page

```
* finish things up like ending the transaction, resetting things we changed (such as
* DELETED and EXACT), etc.

   =rireuse("projects",lcChildWkArea)
   IF NOT llRetVal
      IF _triggerlevel=1
         DO riend WITH llRetVal
      ENDIF at the end of the highest trigger level
      SELECT (lcStartArea)
      RETURN llRetVal
   ENDIF
ENDIF this parent id changed
IF _triggerlevel=1
   do riend with llRetVal
ENDIF at the end of the highest trigger level
SELECT (lcStartArea)
RETURN llRetVal
```

The following generic routines appear at the beginning of the generated code. These routines are called from various places in the trigger routines:

```
procedure RIDELETE

* This routine deletes a child record. If we can't lock the record, return .F.

local llRetVal
llRetVal=.t.
   IF (UPPER(SYS(2011))="RECORD LOCKED" and !deleted()) OR !RLOCK()
      llRetVal=.F.
   ELSE
```

```
* If the record hasn't already been deleted, delete it. This will cause the delete
* trigger for the child table to fire if there is one, causing a nesting of the
* trigger routines (_TRIGGERLEVEL is incremented). We don't see any of that here -- I
* just thought you might like to know! Unlock the record using the new RECORD argument
* for UNLOCK (which prevents unlocking other records that may have been locked by
* other routines) and return .T. if everything went OK.

      IF !deleted()
         DELETE
         UNLOCK RECORD (RECNO())
         llRetVal=pnerror=0
      ENDIF not already deleted
   ENDIF
return llRetVal
```

```
procedure RIUPDATE

* This routine changes the foreign key field in a child record to the specified new
* value. If we can't lock the record, return .F.

parameters tcFieldName,tcNewValue
local llRetVal
```

Continued on next page

```
llRetVal=.t.
   IF UPPER(SYS(2011))="RECORD LOCKED" OR !RLOCK()
      llRetVal=.F.
   ELSE
```

```
* If the field hasn't already been updated, replace it with the new value. This will
* cause the update trigger for the child table to fire if there is one -- see the
* comments for RIDELETE() for further information. Unlock the record and return .T. if
* everything went OK.
```

```
      IF EVAL(tcFieldName)<>tcNewValue
         REPLACE (tcFieldName) WITH tcNewValue
         UNLOCK RECORD (RECNO())
         llRetVal=pnerror=0
      ENDIF not already deleted
   ENDIF
return llRetVal
```

```
procedure rierror
```

```
* The error trapping routine. All it does is display a message (or it would if the
* MESSAGEBOX() code wasn't commented out) and return the error number, which causes
* V_ERROR to be set to that number since the ON ERROR statement is V_ERROR =
* RIERROR( ...
```

```
parameters tnErrNo,tcMessage,tcCode,tcProgram
local lnErrorRows,lnXX
lnErrorRows=alen(gaErrors,1)
if type('gaErrors[lnErrorRows,1]')<>"L"
   dimension gaErrors[lnErrorRows+1,alen(gaErrors,2)]
   lnErrorRows=lnErrorRows+1
endif
gaErrors[lnErrorRows,1]=tnErrNo
gaErrors[lnErrorRows,2]=tcMessage
gaErrors[lnErrorRows,3]=tcCode
gaErrors[lnErrorRows,4]=""
lnXX=1
do while !empty(program(lnXX))
   gaErrors[lnErrorRows,4]=gaErrors[lnErrorRows,4]+","+;
   program(lnXX)
   lnXX=lnXX+1
enddo
gaErrors[lnErrorRows,5]=pcParentDBF
gaErrors[lnErrorRows,6]=pnParentRec
gaErrors[lnErrorRows,7]=pcParentID
gaErrors[lnErrorRows,8]=pcParentExpr
gaErrors[lnErrorRows,9]=pcChildDBF
gaErrors[lnErrorRows,10]=pnChildRec
gaErrors[lnErrorRows,11]=pcChildID
gaErrors[lnErrorRows,12]=pcChildExpr
*=messagebox(str(tnErrNo)+" "+tcMessage+chr(13)+tcCode+chr(13)+tcProgram)
return tnErrNo
```

```
PROCEDURE riopen
```

Continued on next page

Continued from previous page

```
* Open another copy of a child table, set the order to the specified order, and update
* the V_RICURSORS string, which contains a list of the tables we opened and whether
* they're currently involved in a trigger or not. Here's an example of what
* V_RICURSORS might contain: PROJECTS*    1CLIENTS?    2. This indicates PROJECTS was
* opened in workarea 1 and isn't currently involved in a trigger (the *), and CLIENTS
* was opened in workarea 2 and is involved in a trigger (the ?). The reason for
* keeping a list of tables we opened is so we can reuse one we opened that isn't
* currently involved in a trigger (those that have ? in V_RICURSORS).

PARAMETERS tcTable,tcOrder
local lcCurWkArea,lcNewWkArea,lnInUseSpot
lnInUseSpot=atc(tcTable+"*",pcRIcursors)
IF lnInUseSpot=0
   lcCurWkArea=select()
   SELECT 0
   lcNewWkArea=select()
   IF NOT EMPTY(tcOrder)
     USE (tcTable) AGAIN ORDER (tcOrder) ;
       ALIAS ("__ri"+LTRIM(STR(SELECT()))) share
   ELSE
     USE (tcTable) AGAIN ALIAS ("__ri"+LTRIM(STR(SELECT()))) share
   ENDIF
   if pnerror=0
     pcRIcursors=pcRIcursors+upper(tcTable)+"?"+STR(SELECT(),5)
   else
     lcNewWkArea=0
   endif something bad happened while attempting to open the file
ELSE
   lcNewWkArea=val(substr(pcRIcursors,lnInUseSpot+len(tcTable)+1,5))
   pcRIcursors = strtran(pcRIcursors,upper(tcTable)+"*"+str(lcNewWkArea,5),;
     upper(tcTable)+"?"+str(lcNewWkArea,5))
   IF NOT EMPTY(tcOrder)
     SET ORDER TO (tcOrder) IN (lcNewWkArea)
   ENDIF sent an order
   if pnerror<>0
     lcNewWkArea=0
   endif something bad happened while setting order
ENDIF
RETURN (lcNewWkArea)


PROCEDURE riend

* A common cleanup routine: commit the transaction if everything worked and roll it
* back if it didn't. Reset the error handler, DELETED, and EXACT to their former
* settings and close every additional copy of a table we opened.

PARAMETERS tlSuccess
local lnXX,lnSpot,lcWorkArea
IF tlSuccess
   END TRANSACTION
ELSE
```

Continued on next page

```
   SET DELETED OFF
   ROLLBACK
   SET DELETED ON
ENDIF
IF EMPTY(pcRIolderror)
   ON ERROR
ELSE
   ON ERROR &pcRIolderror.
ENDIF
FOR lnXX=1 TO occurs("*",pcRIcursors)
   lnSpot=atc("*",pcRIcursors,lnXX)+1
   USE IN (VAL(substr(pcRIcursors,lnSpot,5)))
ENDFOR
IF pcOldDele="OFF"
   SET DELETED OFF
ENDIF
IF pcOldExact="ON"
   SET EXACT ON
ENDIF
IF pcOldTalk="ON"
   SET TALK ON
ENDIF
RETURN .T.


PROCEDURE rireuse

* Flag a table we opened as no longer being involved in a trigger (change the ? to a
* *), but leave it open in case another trigger in the nesting can use it.

PARAMETERS tcTableName,tcWkArea
pcRIcursors = strtran(pcRIcursors,upper(tcTableName)+"?"+str(tcWkArea,5),;
   upper(tcTableName)+"*"+str(tcWkArea,5))
RETURN .t.
```

Developing Client/Server Applications with Visual FoxPro and SQL Server

Robert Green

Introduction

When I first set out to write this report, I wanted it to be the definitive word on client/server applications. Shortly into the process, my editor Whil Hentzen and I decided the report would be more useful if it were aimed at Microsoft SQL Server novices. That means you won't find a lot of really advanced SQL Server information in this report.

This report is aimed at intermediate-level to advanced-level Microsoft Visual FoxPro developers who will be creating client/server applications, or who just want to know how to build them. It assumes you are familiar with SQL Server or another SQL-based DBMS (database management system).

If you are already a SQL Server expert, you may find that you know a lot of this material. However, you should be able to pick up some SQL Server tips in addition to learning a lot of Visual FoxPro techniques. Admittedly, this report is not the final word on client/server development. There are issues and more advanced techniques I would have liked to explore, but those will be left to future articles.

The report is designed to do several things to get you started building client/server applications with Visual FoxPro. It reviews techniques for connecting to servers, retrieving data, making changes to data then saving it back on the server, and constructing Visual FoxPro applications that use remote data.

It is also designed to provide an introduction to SQL Server for those who are only somewhat familiar with it. Of course, it's no substitute for a good SQL Server course or manual, but after reading this report you will no longer be a SQL Server neophyte. Even if you are not using SQL Server, you will still learn a lot of techniques to use on the front end, regardless of which back end you use.

This report also assumes that you know how to build a Visual FoxPro application. Of course, the way you build a FoxPro application has changed somewhat from the days of Microsoft FoxPro 2.x. Visual FoxPro's features are enhanced. To learn more about these changes, you can look at the sample code that ships with the product and the sample application for this report included on the accompanying disc. The basics of creating an application are still the same, but many of the techniques have changed.

Section 1 covers why you need client/server applications and discusses the additional components required for them. It also addresses several questions including why you should use SQL Server, what SQL Server features you should take advantage of, how Visual FoxPro talks to SQL Server, and the role Open Database Connectivity (ODBC) plays.

Sections 2 and 3 discuss how Visual FoxPro interacts with SQL Server. They address how data is accessed from the server, how Visual FoxPro retrieves and updates data, and the differences between using a remote view and SQL Pass-Through to talk to SQL Server.

Section 4 covers how a client/server application is structured. Visual FoxPro and SQL Server are very powerful database management systems, so this part features discussions on leveraging the strengths of each to create the most powerful client/server application. It also contains information about where data is stored, and where data validation and querying occur.

Section 5 covers the Upsizing Wizard and how to move Visual FoxPro data into SQL Server. Visual FoxPro makes it very easy to prototype a client/server application using local data, and then to deploy it using remote data. The Upsizing Wizard makes it simple to move that prototype (or at least its data) to SQL Server.

Section 6 covers the report's sample application. Here you will explore the actual code used in the sample client/server application. You'll also find explanations of how a user logs on to SQL Server, locates records, edits data, saves data, and runs reports. Finally, you'll find out how to structure an application so you can prototype it in Visual FoxPro and deploy it in SQL Server.

Components of a Client/Server Application

In this section you will see what makes up a client/server application. You already know about the front end, Visual FoxPro. Here you will learn about the back end, SQL Server. What are the features of SQL Server? What do you gain by combining it with Visual FoxPro? What is Open Database Connectivity (ODBC) and what role does it play? The information in this section is at an advanced introductory level. For additional information you can consult the SQL Server manuals.

Benefits of Client/Server Applications

In a traditional database application the data sits on the file server. The workstations send requests to the file server, which retrieves files or pieces of files and sends them to the workstation for processing. The file server does not know how to work with the data. Indeed, it may not know that the file requested is data. It does know that workstation X has asked for file Y. You can think of the file server as a clerk in a library. It goes into the "stacks," gets the "books" you asked for, hands them to you, and then looks for the next request to be filled.

Because the file server is the central point in the network, it is typically a more powerful machine than the workstations. It has a lot of memory; large, fast hard disks; and possibly some fault-tolerance features. Still, when it comes time to assist in the retrieval and processing of data, the file server says, "Here's the data you asked for. Enjoy!"

In a client/server architecture the data resides on a different kind of server—a data server. It is a DBMS (database management system) capable of querying and modifying data. In a client/server application the front end sends a request for data in the form of a SQL Select statement. That request goes to the back end, which then runs the Select statement. The rows of data returned by the Select are sent to the workstation. If the workstation modifies any of the rows, it can send a SQL Update statement to the server, which then changes the data.

Compare the two architectures. In the file server scenario, the workstation sends a request for a file to the file server. The file server sends the file to the workstation, which has to find the actual rows requested. If a modification is made, the file has to be sent back to the server. This process involves a lot of network traffic and workstation processing.

In the client/server example, the workstation sends a message to the data server. The data server processes the request, and only the results are sent to the workstation. If a modification is made, the workstation sends another message to the data server, which processes the request. This scenario involves a small amount of network traffic and significantly less workstation processing.

Some people with fast workstations that have plenty of memory might not mind processing large amounts of data on their workstations. Even though the price of computers continues to drop and the power of computers continues to rise, it is still true that the fastest machines are at the top end. Two years ago very few companies were buying 486/66s with a lot of memory. A basic workstation might have been a 486sx with 4 MB or 8 MB of RAM. While they may have been high powered when they were purchased, they certainly are not high powered today. If you are building a mission-critical application that will support 100 users, the chances are slim that they are all using Pentiums with 32 MB of RAM. In a client/server architecture you need only one very high-powered machine. The workstations can be less capable because they don't need to do the heavy data processing. If your workstations are high powered you can split the work between the front ends and back ends to gain significant performance improvements. This will be explored in more detail in the section "Designing a Client/Server Application."

You might think that the benefit of less network traffic will be outweighed by the fact that the data server has to do all of the work. This will occur only if the data server isn't up to the task. At a minimum your data server should be a Pentium PC with 32 MB of RAM, but the more memory and the more processors the better. If you have a multiprocessor Pentium or MIPS machine with 128 MB of RAM running SQL Server for Microsoft Windows NT, you would be hard pressed to tax it to the point where client/server applications were actually slower.

You might wonder why you need client/server applications when Visual FoxPro's Rushmore is so fast. This is a good point. Everyone knows that FoxPro is impossibly fast and Visual FoxPro is faster, even on a network or with very large tables. So what would it gain you if you moved an application from Visual FoxPro to SQL Server?

Querying

Querying might not be any faster. While SQL Server has an excellent query engine, Visual FoxPro's is at least as good. Suppose that your application involves downloading 100 MB of mainframe data in a batch on Sunday night, then letting 20 (or even 50) users query the data for the week. The users want to run existing queries as well as creating their own. They want to run reports and graph data, and want the ability to export to Microsoft Excel and Microsoft Word. Except for a few small corrections, they will not be changing the data. In this case it is unlikely that performance would be improved by moving this application to SQL Server.

Data Entry and Online Transaction Processing

Suppose, however, that you are writing an order-entry application. The company has tens of thousands of customers and hundreds of thousands of orders representing gigabytes of data. There are 50 order entry clerks need to add and retrieve orders for customers who call in. Response time is very important. The clerks work with one order at a time, a tiny fraction of the total. This application is an excellent candidate for a client/server environment. A very powerful data server can handle the simultaneous requests for data. Network traffic would not be a problem because small amounts of information are passed back and forth. The workstations would be processing only a small number of records at any time. Visual FoxPro would not fare as well in this type of situation. The number of users and size of the data would lead to lesser performance than in a client/server environment.

Table and Database Size

Tables in Visual FoxPro can contain up to 2 GB of data. If you are working with more data than that you will need to break your data up into multiple tables. SQL Server databases can be up to 8 TB in size.

Security

Visual FoxPro databases are not secure. The file format is well known and there is nothing to stop users from buying a copy of Visual FoxPro or from using ODBC to read the data. SQL Server data, on the other hand, is totally secure because the user needs a valid login ID and password to connect to the server. In addition, each user needs specific rights to view and modify data in a database. This will be explored in more detail later in the section "Security and Permissions."

Recoverability

Visual FoxPro databases are not immune to corruption. If the network was to crash, the data would be at risk. There is no way to guarantee data could be recovered after an interruption. However, SQL Server data is fully recoverable. All data modifications are recorded in a transaction log. When SQL Server is started it automatically makes sure that the data and the transaction log are in sync. This will be explored in more detail later in the section "Automatic Recovery."

Other Features

There are other reasons to move to a client/server architecture. SQL Server has online backup, which means that data can be backed up while it is being used. SQL Server has a more complete SQL implementation than Visual FoxPro and offers support for outer joins; correlated subqueries; correlated inserts, updates, and deletes; as well as fuller wildcard support. Finally, SQL Server is fully integrated with Microsoft Windows NT.

Overview of SQL Server Features

This discussion reviews the main features of SQL Server. In cases where the features are only in SQL Server 6 this will be noted. Some of the features are also found in Visual FoxPro. Other features are not in Visual FoxPro but may be in other SQL databases.

SQL Server Capabilities

SQL Server is a high-performance, multiuser relational DBMS. It is designed to support high-volume transaction processing such as online order entry. It is also well suited for decision support applications involving data querying. SQL Server can support up to 2 GB of memory, up to 8 TB of data storage per database, and up to 32,767 user connections.

Data Types, Defaults, and Rules

A DBMS must ensure data integrity. Ideally, this is done in the data dictionary so that integrity is automatically enforced when data is entered or modified. At the simplest level, SQL Server uses data types, defaults, and rules to enforce data integrity. Visual FoxPro also includes these features.

Data Types

SQL Server data types are used to enforce data integrity by restricting the type of data that can be placed in a column. Table 1-1 shows the SQL Server data types and the comparable Visual FoxPro data types.

SQL Server Data Type	Description	Range of Values	Visual FoxPro Data Type
char(n)	fixed length alphanumeric	up to 255 characters	character
varchar(n)	variable length alphanumeric	up to 255 characters	n/a
text	variable length alphanumeric	up to 2,147,483,647 characters	memo
int	integer	-2,147,483,648 to 2,147,483,647	integer
smallint	integer	-32,768 to 32,767	n/a
tinyint	integer	0 to 255	n/a
float	floating point number	1.7 E-308 to 1.7 E+308	numeric, float, or double
real	floating point number	3.4 E-38 to 3.4 E+38	n/a
numeric	exact numeric data type, precision increases with size of field (SQL Server 6 only)	-10 E38 to 10 E38 - 1	n/a
decimal	exact numeric data type, precision increases with size of field (SQL Server 6 only)	-10 E38 to 10 E38 - 1	n/a
money	monetary values	-922,337,203,685,477.5808 to 922,337,203,685,477.5807	currency

Continued on next page

Table 1-1.

SQL Server and Visual FoxPro data types

Continued from previous page

SQL Server Data Type	Description	Range of Values	Visual FoxPro Data Type
smallmoney	monetary values	-214,748.3648 to 214,748.3647	n/a
datetime	dates and time of day with accuracy of millisecond	1/1/1753 to 12/31/9999	datetime
smalldatetime	dates and time of day with accuracy of minutes	1/1/1900 to 6/6/2079	n/a
binary(n)	fixed length binary data	up to 255 bytes	n/a
varbinary(n)	variable length binary data	up to 255 bytes	n/a
image	variable length binary data	up to 2,147,483,647 bytes	general
bit	either 0 or 1	either 0 or 1	logical
timestamp	automatically updated each time a row is modified	any varbinary(8) data	n/a

In addition to system-supplied data types, you can create user-defined data types. A user-defined data type is always based on a system data type. For instance, you may want all of your ID fields to be six characters wide. To do this, you would have to remember every time you create a table that the ID field should be six characters wide. However, by using a user-defined data type six characters wide to create tables, you could ensure consistency across all of your tables.

The following code is used in SQL Server to create a user-defined data type. This new data type is then used in two newly created tables.

```
exec sp_addtype udtID 'char(6)'

Create Table employee
   (employee_id udtID,
   first_name varchar(30),
   last_name varchar(30),
   extension char(5),
   salary money
   language char(6) )

Create Table contact
   (contact_id udtID,
   company_id udtID,
   first_name varchar(30),
   last_name varchar(30),
   city varchar(30),
   region char(6),
   phone char(12) )
```

Defaults

If the user does not supply a value for new records, defaults cause SQL Server to automatically insert specified values in columns. A default can be an expression and can be bound to a specific column or to a user-defined data type. Suppose that most of your contacts are with Microsoft. You could create a default to name Microsoft as the default company for any new contact. The following code first creates this default and then binds it to the company_id column in the contact table.

```
Create Default dftMicrosoft As 'MSFT'
Exec sp_bindefault dftMicrosoft, 'contact.company_id'
```

Rules

Rules allow you to require that a value in a column is valid. They can also require that the value fall within a certain range, match a specific pattern, or match an entry in a list. A rule can be bound to a column in a table or to a user-defined data type. The following code creates a rule that says salary must be between $20,000 and $87 million and then binds the rule to the salary column in the employee table.

```
Create Rule rulSalary As @salary Between $20000 and $87000000
Exec sp_bindrule rulSalary, 'employee.salary'
```

The @ denotes a variable name so @salary is a variable just as lySalary would be a variable in Visual FoxPro. @salary is also a parameter. When the rule is bound to a column, the value in that column is passed to the rule and winds up in the @salary variable.

The following code creates a rule that forces all IDs to be two letters followed by four digits. This rule is then bound to the user-defined data type udtID.

```
Create Rule rulID As @id Like "[A-Z][A-Z][0-9][0-9][0-9][0-9]"
Exec sp_bindrule rulID, 'udtID'
```

The next code listing creates a rule that allows the language field to be only FoxPro or Lesser. This rule is then bound to the language column in the employee table.

```
Create Rule rulLanguage As @language = 'FoxPro' Or @language =
    'Lesser'
Exec sp_bindrule rulLanguage, 'employee.language'
```

Constraints

SQL Server 6 supports constraints. Constraints are defined at the table level, whereas rules and defaults are separate objects bound to columns or user-defined data types. Constraints can be used in the same manner as defaults and rules. They can also be used to enforce referential integrity and the uniqueness of rows in a table. The following code shows how to create a default constraint and a rule constraint.

```
Alter Table authors
Add Default 'unknown' For phone

Alter Table authors
Add Constraint ck_zip Check (zip Like '[0-9][0-9][0-9][0-9][0-9]')
```

Indexes

SQL Server uses indexes for the same reasons Visual FoxPro does. Indexes can be used to speed data retrieval, sort data, and enforce uniqueness of records. A SQL Server table can have up to 250 indexes, one of which can be a clustered index. With a clustered index SQL Server will physically sort the table so that the data is in the index order. Clustered indexes are best used when you need to retrieve ranges of data, for instance, all contacts with the last name Chang. A unique index can be used to enforce the uniqueness of rows. It is equivalent to the Visual FoxPro candidate index. You would typically create a unique index on the table's primary key.

The following code creates indexes for the contact table. It creates a clustered index on region, a unique index on contact_id (the primary key) and an index on last_name.

```
Create Clustered Index clContactRegion On contact (region)
Create Unique Index pkContact On contact (contact_id)
Create Index idxLastName On contact (last_name)
```

Views

A view is a Select statement that is used as an alternate way of looking at data, and can be used to simplify a user's access to data. For instance, a user may need to perform a three table join to get to all necessary data. This makes access to the data more difficult. You can create a view that will do the join behind the scenes, allowing the user to issue a simpler Select statement that references only the view. In addition, you can issue an Insert, Update, or Delete statement against a view.

The following code creates a view based on a Select statement to retrieve total orders by company. A Select is issued on the view to allow a user to see dairy product orders shipped to London. This view is much easier to use than the Select statement that comprises it.

```
Create view vwOrdersByCategory
As
Select city = orders.ship_to_city,
        category = category.category_name,
        product = products.product_name,
        total = Sum(order_line_items.quantity *
                    order_line_items.unit_price)
From orders, order_line_items, products, category
Where orders.order_id = order_line_items.order_id
   And order_line_items.product_id = products.product_id
   And products.category_id = category.category_id
Group By orders.ship_to_city, category.category_name,
        products.product_name

Select * From vwOrdersByCategory
Where category = 'Dairy Products'
   And city = 'London'
```

A view can also be used as a security measure. For instance, the employee table created earlier in this section has a salary field. You may not want all users to have access to that field so you can create a view that does not include the salary field. The Select for that view includes all of the fields in the employee table except the salary. You can then give some users rights to access the view but deny them the rights to access the employee table. In other words, they can issue a Select statement with the view but they cannot issue the Select statement from the table. This prevents them from seeing the salary field. The following code creates such a view.

```
Create View vwEmployee
As
Select employee_id, first_name, last_name, language
From employee
```

If a user issues a Select statement from this view, all of the employee fields except salary will be available.

> ### Tip!
> If the user inserts a row into the view the salary field will be empty. If the salary field is defined as Not Null in the table then the Insert will fail. You must provide a default for salary for an Insert into the view to succeed.

Views in Visual FoxPro are similar to SQL Server views. In both products a view is merely a Select statement that returns a result set. Visual FoxPro takes the concept further by storing the result set in an updatable cursor. Section 2, "Accessing Remote Data Using Views," covers remote views in great detail.

Programming Language

Transact-SQL, the programming language in SQL Server, is used to control the flow of program execution. Table 1-2 lists the Transact-SQL keywords in SQL Server.

Table 1-2.

Transact-SQL commands

Transact-SQL Keyword	Description
If ...Else	equivalent to FoxPro's If ... Endif
Begin ... End	used to have more than one statement execute as a group
While	equivalent to FoxPro's Do While
Break	equivalent to FoxPro's Exit
Continue	equivalent to FoxPro's Enddo
Goto	used to move program execution to a particular line of code
Return	equivalent to FoxPro's Return
Waitfor	used to pause execution until an event occurs
Declare	used to initialize variables
Print	used to print a message
Raiserror	used to create an error number
/* */	used to indicate comments

Stored Procedures

A stored procedure is a precompiled set of SQL statements. This can include Select, Insert, Update, or Delete statements, or any combination of these statements. For example, when you issue a SQL statement SQL Server has to parse the statement, validate the names of tables and columns, check to see if you have permission to view each of the tables, determine the optimal way of accessing the data (which index to use, and so forth), and finally compile the statement. If you create a stored procedure that runs this SQL statement, the parsing and validating occur when the stored procedure is created. The optimizing and compiling occur the first time the stored procedure is run.

As a result, the first time you run the stored procedure SQL Server has to locate the procedure, check permissions, substitute parameters (if necessary), then optimize and compile the SQL statement. The stored procedure is then stored in memory. The second time the stored procedure is run SQL Server retrieves it from the cache, then checks permissions and substitutes parameters.

> ### *Tip!*
> Stored procedures execute more quickly than ad-hoc SQL statements. If you create a stored procedure to insert rows into a table and run it once, the performance gain is minimal. However, if you create a stored procedure to insert rows and then use it 1000 times, the performance gain will be significant.

Previously, you created a view to retrieve total orders by city, category, and product. The following code creates a stored procedure to run this Select statement. The stored procedure is then run.

```
Create Procedure pOrdersByCityCatProd
As
Select city = orders.ship_to_city,
       category = category.category_name,
       product = products.product_name,
       total = Sum(order_line_items.quantity *
                   order_line_items.unit_price)
From orders, order_line_items, products, category
Where orders.order_id = order_line_items.order_id
   And order_line_items.product_id = products.product_id
   And products.category_id = category.category_id
Group By orders.ship_to_city, category.category_name,
       products.product_name

Exec pOrdersByCityCatProd
```

Stored procedures can receive arguments. The following code creates a stored procedure to return total orders by city and product for a particular category.

```
Create Procedure pOrdersByCityProd_OneCat
@acategory varchar(15)
As
Select orders.ship_to_city,
       category.category_name,
       products.product_name,
       total = Sum(order_line_items.quantity *
                   order_line_items.unit_price)
From orders, order_line_items, products, category
Where orders.order_id = order_line_items.order_id
   And order_line_items.product_id = products.product_id
   And products.category_id = category.category_id
   And category.category_name Like @acategory
```

Continued on next page

Continued from previous page

```
Group by orders.ship_to_city, products.product_name

Exec pOrdersByCityProd_OneCat 'Dairy Products'
```

Triggers

A trigger is a special type of stored procedure. Triggers are automatically executed when a data modification occurs. Each table can have three triggers: an insert trigger, an update trigger, and a delete trigger. These can be used to enforce referential integrity. An insert trigger can be used to prevent the insertion of a child record if the parent doesn't exist. It can also be used to add records to another table. For instance, it can be used to add a record to a follow-up table when a new customer is added. An update trigger can prevent changes to the primary key or it can cascade an update so that all child records have their primary keys changed. A delete trigger can prevent deletion of parent records with children. It can also be used to cascade a delete so that all child records are also deleted.

Triggers are also used to enforce business rules. A delete trigger can be used to prevent the deletion of companies with orders. An insert trigger can be used to prevent new orders from being placed for companies with outstanding balances.

Note that triggers are reactive. A data modification occurs, then the trigger is fired. If the trigger rejects a modification, that modification has to be reversed using a Rollback Transaction statement.

The following code creates a trigger that prevents an order from being placed for a non-existent customer.

```
Create Trigger trOrdersInsert
On orders
For Insert
As
If (Select Count(*)
    From inserted
    Where customer_id Not In (Select customer_id From
      customer) ) > 0
Begin
  Rollback Transaction
  Raiserror 90001 "This customer doesn't exist. You can't add
    this order."
End
```

The *inserted* table contains a copy of the order record that was just inserted. It is available only inside the code of a trigger. The table's purpose is to allow you to reference any records that were just added. In the trigger example just presented, you want to see if the customer_id for the record in the inserted table is also in the customer table. If it isn't, the customer_id is invalid. The Select statement in the trigger counts the number of records in the *inserted* table that are not also in the customers table. If this count is more than zero, the customer_id for the new order record is not valid. The Insert is reversed by the Rollback Transaction command. An error number and error message are then returned.

The next piece of code creates an Update trigger preventing the price of any product from being raised by more than 10 percent.

```
Create Trigger trProductsUpdate
On products
For Update
As
If (Select (inserted.unit_price - deleted.unit_price) /
            inserted.unit_price From inserted, deleted) > .10
Begin
  Rollback Transaction
  Raiserror 90002 'Prices can not be raised by more than 10
    percent.'
End
```

The *deleted* table contains a copy of deleted records. Like the *inserted* table, it is available only in trigger code. Each time an Update is issued, records appear in both the *deleted* and *inserted* tables because an Update is really the deletion of the old record followed by the insertion of the new record. Therefore, *inserted* contains the new data and *deleted* contains the original data. In the code just presented, the Select in the trigger calculates the percentage difference between the new price and the old price. If it is higher than 10 percent, the transaction (the Update) is rolled back and an error is returned.

Tip!
The *inserted* and *deleted* tables are available only in trigger code. The *inserted* table is created in Insert triggers and in Update triggers. The *deleted* table is created in Delete triggers and in Update triggers.

The following code creates an Update trigger preventing the primary key of the customer table from changing.

```
Create Trigger trCustomerUpdate
On customer
For Update
As
If Update (customer_id)
Begin
   Rollback Transaction
   Raiserror 90003 "You can't change the customer_id."
End
```

The Update() function in SQL Server will return true if a field has been changed in an Update statement.

Like SQL Server, Visual FoxPro also supports triggers. Each table can have an Insert, an Update, and a Delete trigger. The trigger code is, of course, Visual FoxPro code.

Declarative Referential Integrity

SQL Server 6 supports declarative referential integrity. In SQL Server 4.2 you have to write triggers to enforce referential integrity. Declarative referential integrity is enforced by the database engine and eliminates the need to write these types of triggers by hand. The following code defines a relationship between a publishers parent table and a titles child table.

```
Alter Table titles
Add Constraint fk_pub_id Foreign Key (pub_id) References
   publishers(pub_id)
```

Transaction Processing

A transaction is a unit of work consisting of one or more SQL statements that must work unanimously—either all should work or none should work. A classic example is transferring $50,000 from a savings account to a checking account. This is a two-step process. Step one is an Update statement that reduces the balance in savings by $50,000. Step two is an Update that increases the balance in checking by $50,000. If the first Update worked but not the second, the customer would be unhappy. If the second Update worked but not the first, the bank would be quite upset. Both Updates should work or neither should work.

An individual Insert, Update, or Delete is automatically a transaction. The Begin Transaction command can be used to start a user-defined transaction. Commit Transaction is used to signal that the transaction succeeded, while Rollback Transaction is used to restore the data to the state it was in before the transaction started.

The following code issues the two Updates but puts them in a transaction.

```
Begin Transaction
   Update savings Set balance = balance - 50000
   If @@Error <> 0
   Begin
      Rollback Transaction
      Return
   End
   Update checking Set balance = balance + 50000
   If @@Error <> 0
   Begin
      Rollback Transaction
      Return
   End
Commit Transaction
```

However, suppose that your bank has a rule that says you must keep at least $50 in your savings account. The next sample of code is an Update trigger for the savings table to enforce this rule.

```
Create Trigger trSavingsUpdate
On savings
For Update
As
If (Select balance From savings) < 50
Begin
   Rollback Transaction
   Raiserror 90004 'You must have $50 in your savings account.'
End
```

When the first of these two code samples is run, the first Update will work and the balance in savings will be reduced by $50,000. This fires the trigger to check the balance. If the balance is less than $50, the Rollback Transaction is issued. This causes the first Update to be reversed, putting the $50,000 back in savings. SQL Server then exits the transaction without running the second Update because the value of @@Error is a SQL Server global variable that indicates whether or not the last SQL statement executed successfully.

In SQL Server, transactions can be nested up to five levels. The data modifications will not be final until the last Commit Transaction command occurs.

Visual FoxPro also supports transaction processing with the use of the Begin Transaction, End Transaction, and Rollback commands. Transactions can be nested up to five levels in Visual FoxPro.

Automatic Recovery

Automatic recovery protects databases against system failures, operating system crashes, power outages, and other hazards. Automatic recovery occurs any time SQL Server is started; its key is SQL Server's transaction log. Whenever a data modification is made, SQL Server records the old and new data in the log in cache memory. The changes are then written to the database, which is also in cache memory. When a transaction is committed, the transaction log is written to the physical disk. At periodic intervals called checkpoints the database and the log are also written to the physical disk. If a system crash occurs, SQL Server will make sure that committed transactions are reflected in the database while uncommitted transactions are not.

The example of transferring money from savings to checking accounts can be used to demonstrate how automatic recovery works. Look at three scenarios.

Scenario 1: The system crashes before anything is written to the disk.
In Scenario 1 you have sent the Begin Transaction command to SQL Server where it is written to the transaction log in cache memory. Then the first Update is sent. It's written to the transaction log and the database in cache memory. Then the system crashes.

When SQL Server is restarted there is nothing you can do. Nothing has been written to the disk because a checkpoint has not yet occurred and the transaction was not complete. Because the changes were written only in cache, there is no record on the physical disk that this transaction was ever started. It is unrecoverable.

Scenario 2: SQL Server rolls back an uncommitted transaction.
In Scenario 2 you have sent the Begin Transaction to SQL Server where it is written to the transaction log in cache memory. The first Update is then sent. It is written to the transaction log and the database in cache memory. A checkpoint occurs and both the log and the database are written to the disk. Then the system crashes.

When SQL Server is restarted it looks in the transaction log and sees that a transaction was started but never finished. It then looks in the database and sees that the savings balance was reduced. This uncommitted transaction will be automatically rolled back. The savings balance will be restored and the database will be returned to its state before the transaction was started.

Scenario 3: SQL Server rolls forward a committed transaction.
In Scenario 3 you have sent the Begin Transaction to SQL Server
where it is written to the transaction log in cache memory. The first
Update is then sent. It is written to the transaction log and the
database in cache memory. The second Update is then sent. This is
written to the transaction log and the database in cache memory.
The Commit Transaction command is then sent, which causes the
log to be written to the disk. Then the system crashes.

When SQL Server is restarted it looks in the transaction log and
sees that a transaction was started and committed. It then looks in
the database and sees that this transaction is not reflected in the
database. The system crashed before a checkpoint occurred. This
committed transaction will be automatically rolled forward. The
savings account balance will be reduced and the checking account
balance will be increased. These changes will be written to the
database on the disk.

As you can see, if SQL Server crashes, you will lose only the
current transaction. As a result, keeping your transactions short
reduces the risk of losing data. This is why a transaction is not only
a unit of work, it is also a unit of recovery.

Visual FoxPro does not have recoverability, nor does it have a
built-in transaction log to record changes to the data. If the system
crashes there is no record of anything that has occurred since the
last backup. You could, of course, write a transaction log in a Visual
FoxPro application but it would be a drag on performance. Anytime
you made a change to data you would have to wait for the change
to be written to both the log and the database. Recovery would
also be a very time-consuming process because you would have to
recover every data modification since the last backup. SQL Server
needs only to recover transactions that are either incomplete or not
in the database.

Dynamic Backup

Backing up a database protects against media failure. SQL Server
allows you to back up an entire database as well as back up its
transaction log incrementally. In a typical backup scenario, you
might back up the entire database twice a week and back up the
transaction log twice a day. When the transaction log is backed
up, committed transactions are removed from it. Therefore, each
transaction log backup is an incremental backup. If a hard disk
goes down, you can first restore the most recent database backup.
Then you can restore from each of the incremental transaction
log backups.

> *Tip!*
>
> SQL Server backup is dynamic because databases can be backed up while they are in use. This means that you do not have to kick the users out of the system to back up a database. However this backup will take longer and the users will also experience a slowdown in performance.

SQL Server has the ability to back up a transaction log even if the database cannot be accessed. To do this, the log must be on a different hard disk. In such cases, you can lose the database but still be able to back up the transaction log. The only data lost will be the uncommitted transactions each user is working on.

Visual FoxPro has no built-in backup capabilities. Databases and tables can be backed up as part of the regular network backup. If a database or table is lost, everything after the last backup is gone.

Security and Permissions

To access SQL Server you need a login ID and password. When you connect to the server you have to log in. Successfully logging in, however, does not automatically allow you to use any databases. To access a database you have to be set up as a user of that database or the database needs to be set up with a guest user account. Within a database, users are given permission to use database objects. By default, a new user in a database has no right to use any database object. All rights must be explicitly assigned.

A user might have rights to Select from a table but not to use Insert, Update, or Delete statements. By the same token, a user might not have Select rights on a table but could have Execute rights on a stored procedure that runs a Select statement on that table, or the user may have Select rights on a View that includes some information from a table but not have Select rights on the table itself.

Visual FoxPro does not have built-in database-level security. You can, of course, build security into an application, but there is nothing to stop someone from using another copy of Visual FoxPro to read and change data. Also, someone could use Microsoft Access or Microsoft Visual Basic together with the Visual FoxPro ODBC driver to get at the data. As a result, Visual FoxPro data is not secure whereas SQL Server data is.

Integration with Windows NT

As the name makes clear, Microsoft SQL Server for Windows NT is a Windows NT application. It therefore takes advantage of Windows NT's robust features.

Windows NT Architecture

Windows NT is scaleable. It can be run on single-processor or multi-processor 486, Pentium, MIPS, or Alpha machines. Windows NT is a multithreaded operating system. To understand this you need to know a little terminology. In Windows NT a *process* is created when a program runs. A process can be an application, such as Word or SQL Server, or it can be an Windows NT service, such as Windows NT's event log. It can also be a subsystem, such as the print spooler. A *thread* is an object within a process that executes program instructions. Windows NT is multithreaded because a particular program can have multiple threads, which allows more than one instruction to be carried out at a time.

In a typical multiprocessor database, each process is bound to a specific CPU. This prohibits load balancing. One processor may be overburdened while another is sitting unused. In SQL Server for Windows NT, all processes are spread over all processors. Windows NT will dynamically allocate processes to CPUs for better performance.

Integration with Windows NT Utilities

SQL Server is an application but it is also an Windows NT *service*. A service in Windows NT is a process that performs a specific system function. Some other Windows NT services include the Event Log, the Net Logon, the Server, and the Workstation. One benefit to having SQL Server be an Windows NT service is that services can be set up through the Control Panel to automatically start when Windows NT starts. This allows you to have SQL Server automatically start when the machine is turned on.

Another benefit of SQL Server as an Windows NT service is that it can be monitored. The Windows NT Event Viewer logs messages for the Windows NT system, for security, and for applications. Because it is a service, SQL Server is an application. Therefore if problems occur (for instance if SQL Server cannot be started) the information is available in the Windows NT Event Viewer.

SQL Server performance can be monitored in the Windows NT Performance Monitor. You can monitor counters such as Cache Hit Ratio, Network Reads and Writes per Second, User Connections, and a host of others. The Performance Monitor allows you to view this data graphically in real time. You can create reports that can be printed and you can create a log file that can be exported to a spreadsheet or database. You can also create alerts, which will be triggered when a counter reaches a certain value. For instance, you can have an alert that fires when a database's transaction log is more than 70 percent full.

Integrated Security

Users of a network must log on to the network. By the same measure, if they then want to use SQL Server they have to log on to SQL Server. You can set up SQL Server so that it uses integrated security, allowing users to automatically use SQL Server once they log on to the network. However, you still decide what rights they have in SQL Server. Integrated security simply means that they do not have to log on twice.

Network and Connection Issues

This discussion will provide a quick overview of some of the plumbing issues involved in talking to SQL Server from a client workstation. Windows NT comes complete with network support for Netware, Banyan, Apple Talk, DEC Pathworks, Unix-based networks, LAN Manager, Microsoft Windows for Workgroups, Microsoft Windows 95, and Windows NT. Therefore, you can have a database server running SQL Server for Windows NT and be able to access it from workstations regardless of the network you are running.

SQL Server uses network libraries, which are Dynamic Link Library (DLL) files, to communicate with workstations across the network. Both the client and the server must have network libraries installed. The client libraries send requests to the server and receive data and messages from the server. The server library listens for these requests. As long as the client and the server are speaking the same language they can communicate. Technically, this means running the same network transport protocol. For instance, if the workstation is part of a Netware network running IPX/SPX, SQL Server has to have an IPX/SPX network library loaded.

Windows NT can have multiple protocol libraries loaded at one time. Therefore, SQL Server can talk to workstations running different protocols. Windows NT (and therefore SQL Server) is multilingual.

The server-side network libraries are installed automatically when you install SQL Server. You can add additional libraries at any time. When you install ODBC or an ODBC-enabled application, the appropriate client-side library for the protocol running on the client will be installed. If you change the protocol on the workstation (IPX/SPX to TCP/IP for instance), you would need to install additional network libraries to talk to SQL Server. You will also need to modify your ODBC settings to use the new library.

Open Database Connectivity (ODBC)

ODBC is the glue that holds a client/server application together. It is the communication mechanism between a client front end and a server back end. The client sends requests for data retrieval, data modifications, administrative functions, and so forth. The server hears these requests and acts on them, sending results (if appropriate) and messages or errors indicating success or failure. The client must then receive these result sets and messages or errors to act accordingly.

All SQL databases have a native language. In the case of SQL Server, this is called DB-Library. DB-Library is an API (application programming interface). It is implemented as a DLL and consists of a number of C routines for communicating with SQL Server. There are routines for establishing a connection to the server, sending SQL statements to the server, checking for error messages, receiving result sets from the server, disconnecting from the server, and so on.

It is not difficult for a good programmer to use DB-Library to write a SQL Server application. However, there are problems with that approach.

- Each DB-Library function deals with a piece of a puzzle. Each function call handles a specific task. There are often many tasks involved in what on the surface appears to be one task. For instance, there is more than one function call involved with connecting to the server or with retrieving a result set.

- Your application will work only with SQL Server. If you want to adjust your application to use Oracle, for instance, a huge rewrite would be involved. Different SQL databases have different capabilities. Your application would have to account for those differences. As an example, the function calls to talk to each server will differ. Also, the SQL syntax of each server will be different.

ODBC was invented to supply a single API that would allow multiple front ends to access data from multiple back ends. ODBC is middleware. It takes requests from front ends, translates them into a language the back end can understand, and passes them to the back end. It then repeats the process to send results and messages from the back end to the front end.

ODBC Architecture

There are four components to the ODBC architecture. These are shown in Figure 1-1.

The *application* uses ODBC to send SQL statements to a back end and receive results. The application is responsible for

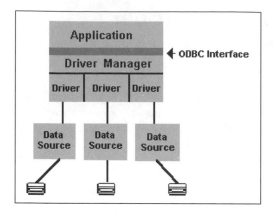

Figure 1-1.

The ODBC architecture

connecting to the data source; processing SQL statements; retrieving result sets, errors, and messages; ending transactions by either a commit or a rollback; and terminating the connection.

An application becomes ODBC-enabled by using the ODBC API, which consists of the ODBC function calls necessary to communicate with back ends. Available functions can connect to a data source, obtain information about a driver or data source, prepare and submit SQL statements, retrieve result sets and information about result sets, retrieve information about a data source's system tables, terminate SQL statements, and terminate connections.

You can use the ODBC API yourself to write applications. The ODBC Software Developer Kit (SDK) provides all of the functions and documentation for using them. This is a popular technique for writing Visual Basic client/server applications. You can also rely on the developers of your favorite database or spreadsheet to use the ODBC API to support accessing external data. As you probably know, Visual FoxPro is ODBC enabled.

The *driver manager* provides access to ODBC drivers. It loads the required driver and passes ODBC function calls from the application to the driver. It performs error checking and can log function calls in a trace file for debugging. There are two versions of the driver manager—a 16-bit version (the file ODBC.DLL) and a 32-bit version (ODBC32.DLL). The driver manager file is in your Microsoft Windows System directory. The driver manager is written by Microsoft but can be used by any application. It is automatically installed when the application is installed.

The *driver* processes ODBC function calls sent by the application. It then establishes a connection to the data source, translates SQL statements so the data source can understand them, submits or executes the SQL statements, and returns result sets, errors, and messages to the application.

Each back end that supports ODBC will have a driver. For SQL Server this is either the SQLSRVR.DLL (16-bit) or SQLSRV32.DLL (32-bit) file, which can also be found in the Windows System directory. The data source does not have to be a SQL database. There are ODBC drivers for numerous programs including FoxPro, Microsoft Access, Excel, Btrieve, dBASE, and Paradox. Each of these drivers is a DLL. While Microsoft supplies some drivers, it is mostly up to the database vendor or third parties such as Intersolv (formerly known as Q+E) to provide drivers.

There are two types of drivers—single tier and multiple tier. Single-tier drivers retrieve data from non-SQL data sources, such as Access, FoxPro, Excel, and Btrieve. They process ODBC function calls and are responsible for executing the SQL statement. For example, to process a Select statement the driver must first read the file containing the data, regardless of whether it is a DBF file (dBase or FoxPro), an MDB file (Access), or an XLS file (Excel). The driver will then extract the requested data and return it in a result set. In this case, the driver acts as the database engine.

Multiple-tier drivers retrieve data from SQL data sources such as SQL Server, Oracle, and DB2. The drivers process ODBC calls but do not execute SQL statements. The SQL statements are translated into the native syntax of the data source, then passed to the data source for execution. The driver retrieves the result set, errors, and messages. A two-tier driver talks directly to the back-end server. A three-tier driver uses a gateway to talk to the server. (You would use a three-tier driver if you wanted to talk to an AS/400 or an IBM 3090 mainframe.)

The *data source* is the back end containing the data. If the data source is a SQL database, it processes SQL statements passed to it from the driver; returns result sets, errors, and messages to the driver; and performs the usual DBMS functions such as logging. If the data source is not a SQL database, it allows the driver to retrieve data. The list of available data sources is stored in the ODBC.INI file under Microsoft Windows and in the registry under Windows NT and Windows 95.

How the Components Interact

It is important to understand that the application talks to the driver manager, never directly to the driver or to the data source. An application is ODBC enabled if it can talk to the driver manager. In turn, the driver manager does not talk to the data source. It talks only to drivers and applications. This process is necessary to achieve interoperability, allowing a single application to talk to many back ends.

ODBC is based on the SQL language. The ODBC version of SQL naturally includes Select, Insert, Update, and Delete statements, but it does not include any of the extensions to the SQL language found in specific SQL databases. The application does not need to know the data source's language. It talks to the driver manager using ODBC's SQL.

The driver manager does not need to speak the data source's language either but it does need to be able to work with the driver. The driver manager passes the ODBC SQL that came from the application to the driver. The driver then talks to the data source. The driver is the only piece of the chain that must speak the specific language of the data source. It must be able to translate SQL statements sent by the application into this language. For instance, the SQL Server driver uses DB-Library to talk to SQL Server while the Oracle driver uses Oracle Call Interface to talk to Oracle.

Remember that the data source does not have to use SQL. In fact, there is no requirement that the data source be a database at all. All that is necessary is that the driver be able to translate the SQL statements that come from the application into whatever language the data source understands, retrieve the data itself if the data source is not a SQL database, and package result sets to look as if they were returned by a SQL statement.

This allows you to have a single application talk to multiple back ends. You simply need to specify the data source. If you have an ODBC driver for the desired back end, you can access its data. The application sends a SQL statement and gets back data in the expected format.

Adding a SQL Server Data Source

Before you can access SQL Server data, or any ODBC data, you must add one data source for each type of data you want to access. This information is stored in the ODBC.INI file under Windows or in the registry under Windows NT or Windows 95. It is used by the driver manager to load the appropriate driver when an ODBC function call is received from the application. You add data sources so that the driver manager knows which drivers are available and what files they are.

To add a data source, double-click the ODBC icon in the Control Panel. This is shown in Figure 1-2.

Figure 1-2.

**The ODBC icon in
the Control Panel**

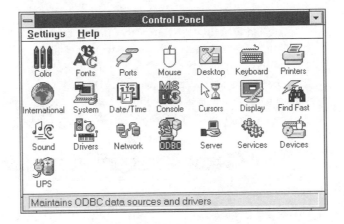

This brings forward the Data Sources dialog box shown in Figure 1-3, which contains a list of already installed ODBC drivers.

Figure 1-3.

**The ODBC Data
Sources dialog box**

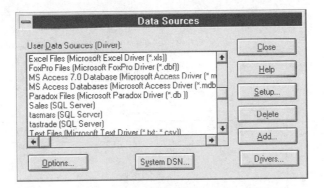

You can add a new driver by selecting Add. The Add Data Source dialog box will then supply a list of installed ODBC drivers. Select the driver you want to use and click OK. You will then see a setup dialog box for the chosen driver. The dialog box for a SQL Server driver is shown in Figure 1-4. After supplying the required information click the OK button to add this data source. When you return to the Data Sources dialog box you will see the new data source. If you want to modify an existing data source, select it and click the Setup button. You can use the Delete button to remove an existing data source.

Data Source Name and Description

The Data Source Name is the name by which you will refer to this data source. When you want to establish a connection to a data source you need to supply the Data Source Name, a user ID, and a password. The Description can be any text you want. For instance, you might have a data source named "Sales" with the description "Sales database on SQL Server Windows NT."

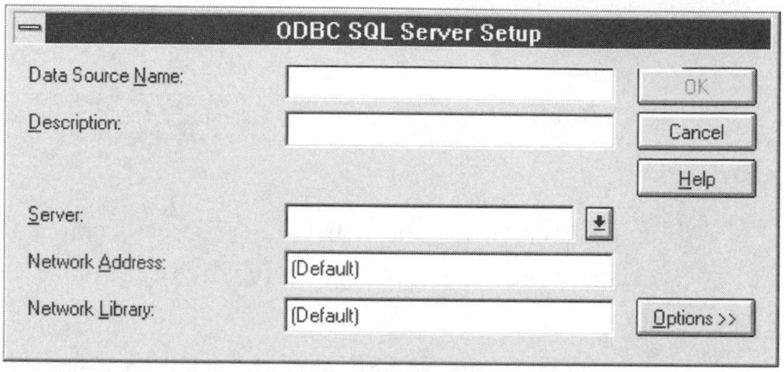

Figure 1-4.

The ODBC SQL Server Setup dialog box

Server

The Server is the name of the back-end database you want to connect to. Table 1-3 shows server names for various networks if the data source is SQL Server.

Table 1-3.

Network transport protocols and server names

Network/Transport Protocol	Server Name
Windows NT, Windows 95, Windows for Workgroups, LAN Manager, DEC Pathworks	The network name of the computer on which SQL Server is running.
Novell Netware	The name that SQL Server registers with the Netware Bindery. For SQL Server for Windows NT, this name is configured by SQL Server Setup.
Banyan Vines	The PC-based service name SQL Server registers with StreetTalk when it starts.
TCP/IP	If Sockets is running, enter an alias. If named pipes are running, enter the network name of the computer on which SQL Server is running.

If your workstation is running Windows NT you can install a copy of SQL Server locally and use that as your data source. In that case enter "(local)" as the Server name.

Network Address

The Network Address specifies the location of the data source on the network. You can usually leave this set to "(Default)." Table 1-4 shows network addresses for various networks.

Table 1-4.

Network transport protocols and network addresses

Network/Transport Protocol	Network Address
Windows NT, Windows 95, Windows for Workgroups, LAN Manager, DEC Pathworks	Enter "(Default)" to use the default named pipe (*<server>*\pipe\sql\query). To use another named pipe enter its name in the format *<server>*\pipe*<pipe name>*.
Novell Netware	The default network address is associated with a name stored in the Netware Bindery. To use that name enter "(Default)." To use another name enter that name.
Banyan Vines	The default network address is associated with a name stored in the Street Talk Directory service. To use that name enter "(Default)." To use another name enter that name.
TCP/IP	Enter an address of the Form IP-address, socket-address.

Network Library

The Network Library is the name of the network library that the data source uses to communicate with the network software. You can usually leave this set to "(Default)." Table 1-5 shows network libraries for various networks.

Table 1-5.

Network transport protocols and network libraries

Network/Transport Protocol	Network Library
Windows NT, Windows 95, Windows for Workgroups, LAN Manager, DEC Pathworks	Use the named pipes network library DBNMP3.DLL (16-bit) or DBNMPTW.DLL (32-bit). These ship with SQL Server and with FoxPro, Access, and Visual Basic, among other programs.
Novell Netware	Use the Novell IPX/SPX network library DBMSSPX3.DLL (16-bit) or DBMSSPXN.DLL (32-bit). These ship with SQL Server.
Banyan Vines	Use the Banyan Vines network library DBMSVIN3.DLL (16-bit) or DBMSVINN.DLL (32-bit). These ship with SQL Server.
TCP/IP	Use the Sockets network library DBMSSOC3.DLL (16-bit) or DBMSSOCN.DLL (32-bit). These ship with SQL Server.

Click the Options button on the ODBC SQL Server Setup dialog box to configure additional options for this data source. These options are shown in Figure 1-5.

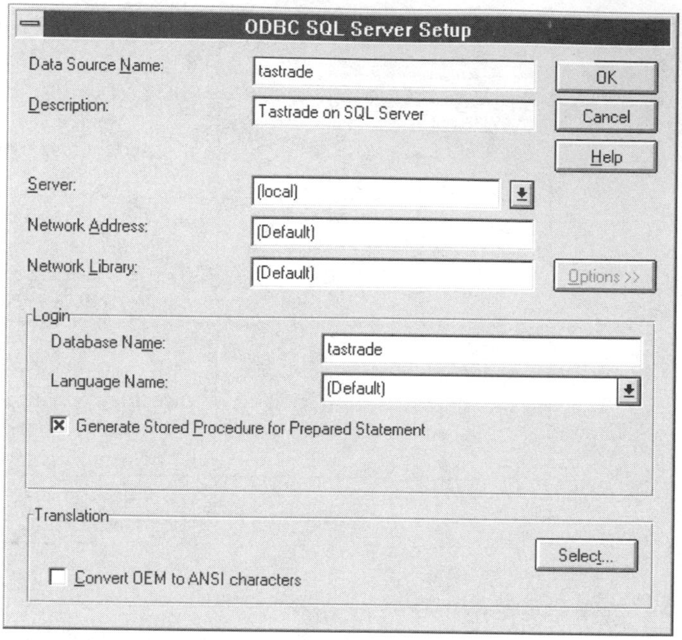

Figure 1-5.

The ODBC SQL Server Setup dialog box with options

Database Name
Setting a database name allows you to specify which database will be in use once the user logs in to this data source. If no database name is supplied, the user's default database will be in use. The default database is typically specified when the user's login ID is added to the server.

Language Name
The language name allows you to specify which language to use when sending SQL statements to SQL Server. SQL Server is installed with support for these languages and a default is specified at install time. To use the default language, leave this choice set to "(Default)."

Generating Stored Procedures for Prepared Statements
ODBC provides two ways for a SQL statement to be submitted to a data source for processing—direct execution and prepared execution. Direct execution is preferred for a statement that will be executed once. Prepared execution is beneficial if a statement will be executed

more than once. After receiving the SQL statement the data source compiles the statement and produces an action plan for execution. This plan is then used whenever the data source receives that SQL statement. If the Convert Stored Procedure for Prepared Statements CheckBox is checked, then stored procedures will be created on the data source for all prepared statements.

Be aware that preparing a statement requires a particular ODBC function call. This has to occur explicitly in the application. An ad-hoc SQL query will never be a prepared SQL statement.

Fast Connect Option

When an application connects to a data source it uses ODBC functions to query the system catalog of the data source. If the Fast Connect Option CheckBox is checked then these queries will not be run upon connecting. This reduces the amount of time required to connect, improving performance for applications that connect and disconnect repeatedly.

Translation

An application and a data source can store data in different formats. For instance, they might use different character sets or the data source may store data in a compressed or encrypted format. The driver can use a translation DLL to translate data that passes between the driver and the data source or to encrypt and decrypt or compress and decompress data.

The most common form of translation is a code page translation. To select a translator click the Select button. To select a code page translator, select MS Code Page Translator from the list of installed translators.

Converting OEM to ANSI Characters

If SQL Server and the workstation are using the same nonANSI character set, check the Convert OEM to ANSI Characters CheckBox. If they are using different character sets you must use a translator.

16-bit Versus 32-bit ODBC Drivers

ODBC drivers come in 16-bit and 32-bit flavors. 16-bit drivers are used in 16-bit environments such as Microsoft Windows 3.1 and Windows for Workgroups. 32-bit drivers are used in 32-bit environments such as Windows NT and Windows 95. Visual FoxPro is a 32-bit application that can run in either the 16-bit or 32-bit flavor of Windows.

You can use 16-bit ODBC drivers with Visual FoxPro in Windows 3.1 or Windows for Workgroups. Visual FoxPro uses the Win32s operating system extension to run in 32-bit mode. In this environment Visual FoxPro calls the 32-bit thunking version of the driver manager, which then uses a thunking DLL to call the appropriate 16-bit driver. A thunk occurs when a 16-bit function call is translated into a 32-bit function call and vice versa.

You can use 32-bit ODBC drivers with Visual FoxPro in Windows NT or Windows 95. Visual FoxPro calls the 32-bit driver manager which calls 32-bit drivers.

Suppose that you have Visual FoxPro running in Windows for Workgroups and you upgrade to Windows NT or Windows 95. You must then install the 32-bit version of ODBC, including the drivers. If you do not, your 32-bit applications will attempt to use the 32-bit thunking driver manager instead of the 32-bit driver manager. This will not work well and will lead to errors.

If you have both Windows for Workgroups and Windows NT on your computer and you dual boot, you must install ODBC under both operating systems. If you do not, your applications will attempt to use the wrong ODBC components. This will again lead to errors.

Where ODBC Information Is Stored

ODBC information is stored in several places. The bulk of the information on data sources is stored in the ODBC.INI file if you are running Windows and in the registry if you are running Windows NT or Windows 95.

The following code shows some lines from an ODBC.INI file for a Windows NT workstation. This represents a 32-bit application (Visual FoxPro) using 32-bit ODBC drivers and running in a 32-bit environment, Windows for Workgroups.

```
[ODBC 32 bit Data Sources]
Tastrade=SQL Server 2.0 (32 bit)
MS Access Databases=Microsoft Access Driver (*.mdb) (32 bit)
FoxPro Files=Microsoft FoxPro Driver (*.dbf) (32 bit)
dBase Files=Microsoft dBase Driver (*.dbf) (32 bit)

[Tastrade]
Driver32=C:\WINDOWS\System32\SQLSRV32.DLL
Driver=C:\WINDOWS\SYSTEM\SQLSRVR.DLL
Description=Tastrade on MARS
Server=MARS
FastConnectOption=No
UseProcForPrepare=Yes
Database=tastrade
OEMTOANSI=No
LastUser=RGreen
Language=
```

The next code sample shows a section of the WIN.INI file.

```
[SQLSERVER]
DSQUERY=DBNMP3
AutoAnsiToOem=off
```

Suppose you want to connect to the *Tastrade* data source, which represents the Tastrade database on the SQL Server called MARS. The driver manager looks in the ODBC.INI file for the Tastrade section. It looks for the Driver or Driver32 entry to find the 16-bit or 32-bit driver's DLL file. The driver manager then loads the driver. The driver looks in ODBC.INI for the Server entry and sees that the server is called MARS. It then looks in the WIN.INI for a SQLServer section. It finds the DSQUERY entry to find the network library to use to connect to the server, in this case DBNMP3.DLL.

Figure 1-6 displays a piece of a Windows 95 registry showing the Tastrade data source that uses the 32-bit SQL Server driver. Notice that the driver and server information are in there, just as in the ODBC.INI file. Windows 95 (and Windows NT) still look in the WIN.INI for the SQLServer section to find the network library.

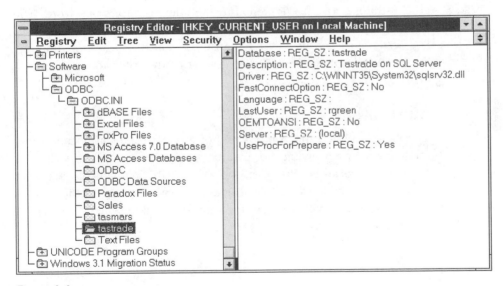

Figure 1-6.

The ODBC section of the Windows NT registry

> **Tip!**
> Note that Windows 95 and Windows NT still use WIN.INI files. Not everything is in the registry.

Preparing SQL Server for ODBC

When an application wants to query the data source's system catalog, it uses ODBC catalog functions. The data source has to be able to respond to these or the function calls will generate an error. SQL Server 4.2 is not installed with the system procedures necessary to respond to ODBC catalog functions. To install these you must run the INSTCAT.SQL script file. This file is installed with SQL Server and can be found in the SQL\INSTALL directory on the SQL Server machine.

SQL Server 6 has the catalog system procedures installed automatically. You do not need to install them.

The easiest way to install the required catalog stored procedures is to use the ISQL utility that ships with SQL Server. ISQL stands for *interactive SQL*. ISQL is a command prompt utility. There is also a graphical version called ISQL/W. To install the catalog stored procedures run the following code. This takes about 15 minutes.

```
isql -S<servername> -Usa -P<password> -i<path>instcat.sql
```

In this code, the "S" refers to the name of the SQL Server, and the "U" refers to a user ID. It is best to log in as the system administrator (sa). The "P" refers to the administrator's password. The "i" allows you to identify a script file to run. Script files consist of SQL statements and usually have an extension of SQL. After running the INSTCAT.SQL file SQL Server is now ready to be accessed via ODBC.

Summary

You have explored the components of a client/server application in this section by reviewing the features of SQL Server and how they compare to Visual FoxPro. You looked at ODBC, which plays a critical role in connecting Visual FoxPro to SQL Server. In the next two sections you will see how to connect and access SQL Server data from Visual FoxPro.

2 Accessing Remote Data Using Views

In this section you will make a connection from Visual FoxPro to SQL Server in order to access data. In a client/server application, most (if not all) of the data sits on the server. The server's main role is to receive requests from the clients for data. The client may want to ask questions of the data, such as "What were the total sales, by state, for the Eastern region of the United States in 1995?" Questions like this will be asked in the form of a Select statement.

There are two ways to access server back-end data in Visual FoxPro—remote views and SQL Pass Through. In this section you will explore remote views. In the next section you will use SQL Pass-Through.

A Visual FoxPro view is nothing more than a SQL Select statement that is stored in a database. You run a view in Visual FoxPro by issuing the Use command, just as you would with a table. When you invoke the Use command with a view, Visual FoxPro issues the Select statement that defines the view. The data is returned into a Cursor. This Cursor can be read/write in Visual FoxPro and changes made to the data can be sent to the back-end data. Remember that when you issued a Select statement in FoxPro 2.x, the results were returned to a read-only Cursor.

Visual FoxPro has two types of views, local and remote. Local views can use native Visual FoxPro tables as well as other local and remote views. A remote view uses ODBC to access non-native data. You can create both types of views with the View Designer.

In a client/server application, a user may want to add, edit, or delete rows of data. The client will typically request one or more rows from the server via a Select statement. After the client receives the data, it is then modified locally. The client then sends Insert, Update, or Delete statements back to the server, where the data is "officially" changed. As you will see, if you are using remote views to work with server data, Visual FoxPro will hide much of this activity in the background.

Using Remote Views

In SQL terms, a view is a Select statement that acts as a filter. Because huge amounts of data may reside on the server, you'll want to retrieve only the records that are needed at any particular time.

There are two important steps in creating remote views in Visual FoxPro. First you must create a connection for Visual FoxPro to use to talk to SQL Server. Then you must create the view and decide what parameters it will take. A parameter allows you to substitute different values into the Select statement. This is how you limit the amount of data that will be returned.

You can begin by creating a test project to store the database, connection, and views created in this section. Call the project "sqltest". In addition, create a database called "sqltest". You can leave it empty for now, as you will be using Tastrade data (the sample data customers and orders application that ships with Visual FoxPro) on SQL Server. This data needs to be moved to SQL Server. You can see how to do this in Section 5.

Creating Connections

Connections in Visual FoxPro use ODBC to enable a conversation between Visual FoxPro and a back-end database. You cannot create a remote view without a connection. When the conversation is established, Visual FoxPro will request data and send data back. In turn, SQL Server will receive requests for data and send data.

> ### Tip!
> Because you are using ODBC, the connection will work the same way regardless of the database used on the back end. If you have an ODBC driver, you can access the data supported by that driver. It doesn't matter if the back end is SQL Server, Oracle, DB2, Interbase, or FoxPro.

There are two ways to create connections, visually and programmatically. To visually create a connection, you will use the Connection Designer dialog box. This is shown in Figure 2-1.

Figure 2-1.

The Connection Designer

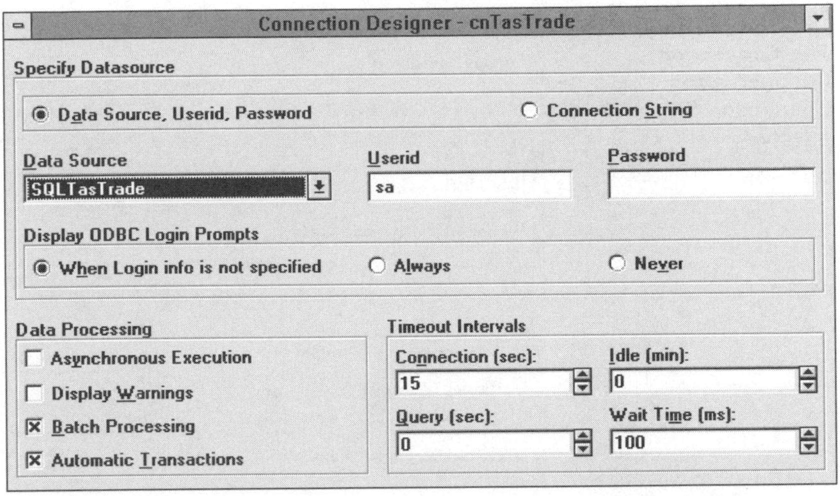

To invoke the Connection Designer you can type the following in the Command window:

```
Open Database sqltest
Create Connection cnTastrade
```

You must have a database open when you create a connection so that the connection will belong to the database. If you do not specify a name in the Create Connection command, you will be prompted for a name when you save the connection.

You can also create a connection from the Project Manager. Make sure the sqltest project is open. In the Data tab you will see the sqltest database. A database contains five different types of objects—tables, local views, remote views, connections, and stored procedures. Highlight the word Connections and click the New button to bring up the Connection Designer.

The Connection Designer allows you to base a connection on a preexisting ODBC Data Source Name (DSN) or on a connection string. If you select the Data Source, Userid, Password OptionButton, the Connection Designer will have a drop-down Data Source list and two TextBoxes, one for user ID and one for password. This is shown in Figure 2-1. If you select the Connection String OptionButton the Connection Designer will have one TextBox where you can enter the connection string. This is shown in Figure 2-2.

Figure 2-2.

The Connection Designer with Connection String selected

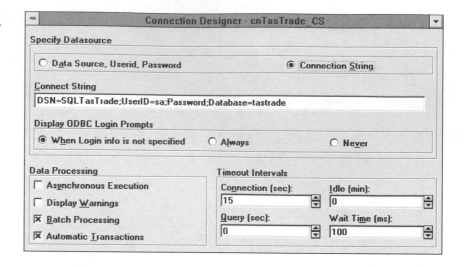

If your connection is based on an existing DSN simply select that from the drop-down list. You will see the same data sources you saw in the ODBC Data Sources dialog box. If you add new data sources they will appear in the drop-down list. Then you can supply a user ID and password. If you leave the password empty and the user ID has a password, the user will be prompted for a password at runtime.

If your connection is based on a connection string, you will need to supply four pieces of information: the Data Source Name, the user ID, the password, and the name of the back-end database you will be connecting to. For the report's sample application, the connection string would be as follows:

```
DSN=tastrade;UID=rgreen;PWD=bert;DATABASE=tastrade
```

Notice that no quotation marks are used here and that the arguments are separated by a semicolon.

Tip!
You can use the connection string to specify a different database than the default database defined in the ODBC data source.

> ### *Tip!*
> The meaning of the database name varies according to the program
> you are working with. For instance, if you are connecting to SQL
> Server or Oracle you will supply the name of the database that
> contains the data you want. With Visual FoxPro or Access, the
> database would be the name of the DBC or MDB file where the data
> resides, plus the fully qualified path. For FoxPro 2.x data, the
> database is actually the directory where the DBF files are stored.

To programmatically create a connection, you would use the
Create Connection command. Again, you can use either a DSN or
a connection string. You can use either of the two following
commands to create the connection for your application:

```
Create Connection cnTastrade DataSource 'tastrade' Userid 'rgreen' ;
                    Password 'bert'
```

or

```
Create Connection cnTastrade ;
   ConnString
   'DSN=tastrade;UID-rgreen;PWD=bert;DATABASE-tastrade'
```

This information is all you need to create a connection. Once
the connection is saved you can see it in the Project Manager. Figure
2-3 shows the new connection cnTastrade. This connection can be
used to access server data from Visual FoxPro. There are, however,
additional options that can be set for a connection either at the time
the connection is created or later using the DBSetProp() function.
This will be explored later in the section with the ShareConnection
CheckBox.

Figure 2-3.

*The cnTastrade
connection in the
Project Manager*

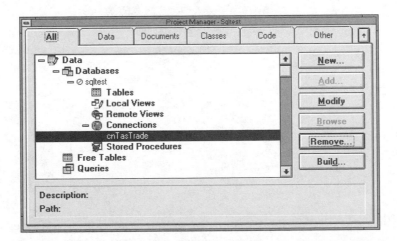

Figure 2-4.

**The New Remote
View dialog box**

Creating a View Visually

Views can be created visually or programmatically. To visually create
a remote view, have the Data tab active in the Project Manager.
Select Remote Views and click the New button. In the New Remote
View dialog box shown in Figure 2-4, choose whether you want to
create this view using a View Wizard or by hand.

> **Tip!**
> You might not be prompted to use a Wizard if you turned off the
> Prompt for Wizards CheckBox under the Projects tab of the Options
> dialog box.

Click New View to create the view by hand. Because this is a
remote view you need to supply connection information. In the Select
Connection or Datasource dialog box you will identify a connection

Figure 2-5.

**The Select
Connection or
Datasource dialog
box with list of
connections in this
database**

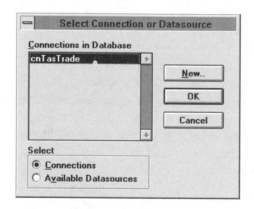

or ODBC data source to
use with this view. When
the dialog box appears it
will contain a list of
connections in this
database as shown in
Figure 2-5. To use an
existing connection, select
that connection and click
OK. Clicking the New
button will bring you into
the Connection Designer,
where you can create a
new connection. Select the
Available Datasources
OptionButton to choose
from a list of available
ODBC data sources. This
is shown in Figure 2-6.

Figure 2-6.

**The Select
Connection or
Datasource dialog
box with list of
available data
sources**

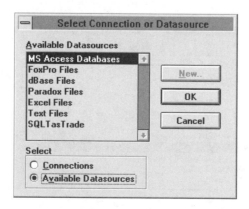

When you create a
new local or remote view,
Visual FoxPro will ask you
for a table to use in the
view. When local views
are created, these tables
are native Visual FoxPro

tables in the current database, tables in another database, free tables,
local views, or even other remote views. When remote views are

created, you are going to access tables that reside on the back-end server. Remote views always utilize an ODBC driver and never access other Visual FoxPro views. When you create a connection you either specify an ODBC data source or a connection string. Either way you can specify the database on the server to use. Visual FoxPro will connect to that database and retrieve a list of tables. These tables are displayed in the Open dialog box, which is shown in Figure 2-7. After a table is selected, Visual FoxPro will retrieve a list of columns for that table in addition to other information.

Figure 2-7.

The Open dialog box

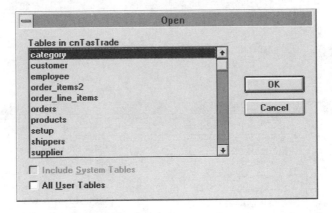

It's assumed that you have created views before and can step quickly through the basics. Doug Hennig's report *The Visual FoxPro Data Dictionary* contains a more in-depth treatment of creating views.

To create a view using the orders table in the Tastrade database on SQL Server you will use the cnTastrade connection. Select the orders table in the Open dialog box and click OK. The view will contain all fields in the table, so either double-click the asterisk in the field list or go to the Fields tab and click the Add All button.

In the Order By tab you can specify one or more fields to order the results of the Select statement. If you do not set an order, the default is that the rows are returned in the order they appear in the data.

Tip!

SQL Server supports clustered indexes. When you create a clustered index the data is physically sorted in the index order. If you then used a Select statement to choose rows from the table and you did not use an Order By clause, the data would be returned in the order determined by the clustered index.

The Update Criteria tab allows you to set update options for the view. When Visual FoxPro retrieves information on the table in the view, it checks to see if a primary key has been defined. In order for the view to be updatable, you must have a primary key defined in the view. In Figure 2-8 you can see that once you selected the orders table, Visual FoxPro was able to figure out that the order_id was the key field because it was defined as the primary key in the SQL Server table.

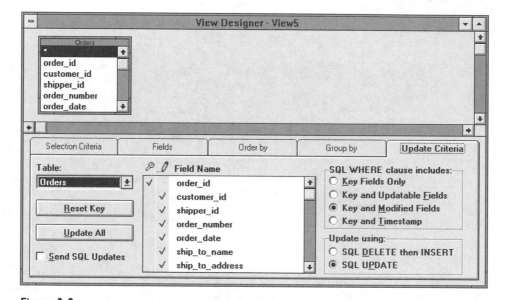

Figure 2-8.

The Update Criteria tab with order_id identified as the primary key

If no primary key is identified and you want to be able to update fields in the view, you must select one or more fields to be the primary key. If you click in the key column (the one with a key), a button will appear next to the selected field. Click this button to make that field the primary key. Select additional fields if the primary key is made up of more than one field.

If you have selected a primary key you can then mark fields as updatable. If you click the updatable column (the one with the pencil), a button will appear next to the selected field. Click this button to make that field updatable. You can make all fields updatable by clicking the Update All button.

> ### Tip!
> Clicking the Update All button will not mark the primary key as updatable. If you choose you can have the primary key updatable, although this is typically not a good idea. Having an updatable primary key opens a Pandora's box of issues including cascading updates, what it means to be a primary key, and a whole host of other issues that would fill up a good-sized book.

You must also check the Send SQL Updates CheckBox to enable updating in the view. When you create a new view, the Send SQL Updates CheckBox is not checked. If you set the primary key and mark fields for updating but do not check this box, any changes you make to the data contained in the view will not be sent to the back-end server.

> ### Tip!
> By default, a view's Cursor is read-only. To make it read and write you must identify the primary key, mark fields as being updatable, and check the Send SQL Updates CheckBox.

Creating a View Programmatically

The Create SQL View command is used to create a view programmatically. To specify that you are creating a remote view use the Remote keyword. You then need to supply a connection and the Select statement for the view. The connection can be a saved connection or an ODBC data source. For example, the following code shows a command that will create the vOrders2 view.

```
Create SQL View vOrders2 Remote ;
    Connection cnTastrade ;
    As Select * From orders
```

Notice that there are no quotation marks around the connection name and no quotation marks around the Select statement. If there is a database open and current, the view will be saved in that database. If there is no database open, you can create and use the view but you cannot save it.

The following code shows a more involved view that includes information from three tables.

```
Create SQL View vOrders3 Remote ;
  Connection cnTastrade ;
  As Select orders.order_id, customer.company_name, ;
      shippers.company_name, orders.ship_to_name, ;
      orders.ship_to_address, orders.ship_to_city, ;
      orders.ship_to_region, orders.ship_to_postal_code, ;
      orders.order_date, orders.ship_to_country, ;
      orders.deliver_by ;
    From orders, customer, shippers ;
    Where customer.customer_id = orders.customer_id ;
      And orders.shipper_id = shippers.shipper_id ;
    Order By customer.company_name, orders.order_id
```

Using Views

The view itself is merely a definition and is nothing more than a saved Select statement. To see the data, you have to run the view. In Visual FoxPro you can treat a view just like you treat a table. For instance, the following command runs the vOrders Select statement:

```
Use vOrders
```

Keep in mind that in this particular view there is no Where clause to limit the amount of data returned by the Select statement. All rows in the table will be sent to Visual FoxPro. This is acceptable when you're using this sample data, but you wouldn't want to do this with a production table of 85 million rows!

Because the view is treated like a table, you can use the Browse, Skip, Replace, Report, and Select commands with it. For instance, the next code sample will return all rows from the vOrders view that have London as the ship_to_city. Don't forget to have the view's database open at the time. If you don't, Visual FoxPro will think that vOrders is a table and it won't be able to find it.

```
Select * From vOrders ;
  Where ship_to_city = 'London'
```

There are actually two Select statements here because the view itself is a Select statement. Visual FoxPro will run the Select that comprises the view's definition and bring down all of the rows in the orders table. Then it will run the Select in the previous code from that result set. It is important to understand that Visual FoxPro does not flatten this into one Select with a Where clause and send that to the server. If you want only the London rows to be retrieved from the server, the Where clause would need to be part of the view's definition.

Parameterized Views

The Where clause of a Select statement limits the number of rows returned. Only those rows that match the Where clause criteria will be in the result set when the view is run. You can easily create a Where clause for a view. The following code creates two views, one that returns only orders that were shipped to London and one that returns only orders that were shipped to Chicago.

```
Create SQL View vLondonOrders Remote ;
   Connection cnTastrade ;
   As Select * From orders
     Where ship_to_city = 'London'

Create SQL View vChicagoOrders Remote ;
   Connection cnTastrade ;
   As Select * From orders
     Where ship_to_city = 'Chicago'
```

If you wanted to see orders shipped to Cairo, you could create another view with a different Where clause. Of course, if you created a new view each time you wanted to see the data from a different city, you would soon have more views than you could manage.

The solution is to create a parameterized view. This allows you to fill out the Where clause at runtime. You can create a parameterized view by using the ? symbol and a variable in the view's Where clause. Visually you can do this from the Selection Criteria tab. Create a view called vOrders_OneCity that shows orders for any given city. The view will be based on the orders table. In the Selection Criteria tab, choose orders.ship_to_city from the field name list, choose Like from the Criteria list, and then type ?pcCity in the Example TextBox. This is shown in Figure 2-9.

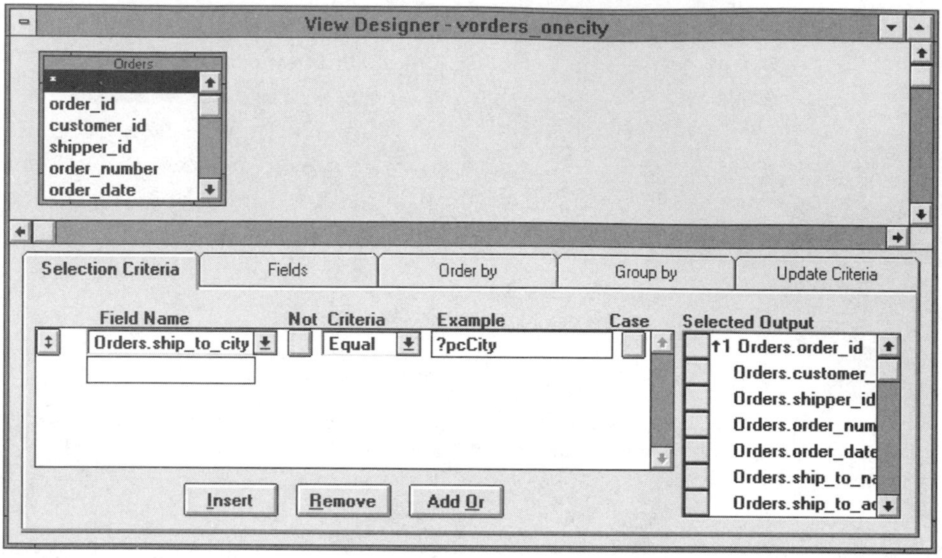

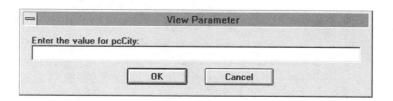

Figure 2-9.

A parameterized view in the Selection Criteria tab

When you use the view, Visual FoxPro checks to see if the variable pcCity exists. If it does, the variable's value is substituted into the Where clause. If it does not, you will be prompted to supply the value. This dialog box is shown in Figure 2-10.

Figure 2-10.

The View Parameter dialog box

The next code sample shows how to create this view programmatically. The parameter is then given a value and the view is run.

```
Create SQL View vOrders_OneCity Remote ;
   Connection cnTastrade ;
   As Select * From orders ;
      Where orders.ship_to_city = ?pcCity

pcCity = 'London'
Use vOrders_OneCity
Browse
```

Only the orders sent to London are brought back to Visual FoxPro and appear in the Browse.

You can use a parameterized view to return one row at a time. This is how you will build the sample application. The view vOrder takes an order ID as the parameter and then retrieves the single row that has an order ID equal to the parameter's value. This view is shown in the following code. Remember to make the view updatable by identifying the primary key, marking fields as updatable, and checking the Send SQL Updates CheckBox in the Update Criteria tab in the View Designer.

```
Create SQL View vOrder Remote ;
   Connection cnTastrade ;
   As Select * From orders ;
      Where orders.order_id = ?pcOrderid
```

Later you will base a Form on this view. To navigate from order to order the user will enter the order ID and then have the view refreshed.

A view can contain as many parameters as you wish. The next code sample shows a view that allows the user to see all orders in a particular city for a particular month and year.

```
Create SQL View vOrders_OneCityMonth Remote ;
   Connection cnTastrade ;
   As Select orders.order_id, orders.order_date, ;
      orders.deliver_by, ;
      customer.company_name, orders.ship_to_name, ;
      orders.ship_to_address, orders.ship_to_city, ;
      orders.ship_to_region, orders.ship_to_postal_code, ;
      orders.ship_to_country ;
      From orders, customer ;
      Where orders.customer_id = customer.customer_id ;
         And orders.ship_to_city = ?pcCity ;
         And DatePart(month, order_date) = ?pnMonth ;
         And DatePart(year, order_date) = ?pnYear
```

Tip!

Originally, this view was created with the Visual FoxPro Month() and Year() functions. However, when it was run it returned an error from SQL Server because Month() and Year() are not SQL Server functions. As a result, the SQL Server DatePart() function was used instead.

When the vOrders_OneCityMonth view is run, Visual FoxPro asks for the three parameters one at a time, then sends the Select to the server. Remember that if the variables pcCity, pnMonth, and pnYear exist and have values, Visual FoxPro does not need to ask the user for their values.

What happens if one of the parameters has the wrong data type? To test this, run the query and enter a value of 3 for the city and "London" for the month. Figure 2-11 shows the error message you will receive. Entering a value of 3 for the city is not a problem because city is a character field and accepts both letters and numbers. However, the DatePart function returns an integer while you entered letters. SQL Server will attempt to convert the letters to an integer. It will fail and respond with an error message.

Figure 2-11.

An implicit conversion from Varchar to Int error message

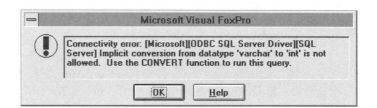

By default, there is no restriction on the value you store to a view's parameters. However, you can explicitly declare parameter types in the view's definition. The code to create a different view, vProducts_OverPrice, is shown.

```
Create SQL View vProducts_OverPrice Remote ;
   Connection cnTastrade ;
   As Select * ;
      From products ;
      Where products.unit_price >= ?pyPrice
```

In the SQL Server products table, unit_price is a money field, therefore you want the user to enter a currency value for pyPrice. To declare the parameter currency, select Query/View Parameters from the View Designer's menu. The View Parameters dialog box is shown in Figure 2-12. Enter pyPrice in the Name column and select Currency from the Type column. Now when you run the view you will be asked to enter a currency value. This is shown in Figure 2-13. If you enter a currency amount, then only products that cost more than that amount will be returned from the server.

Figure 2-12.

The View Parameters dialog box

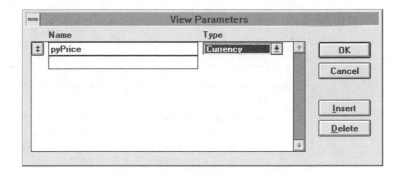

Figure 2-13.

The View Parameter dialog box

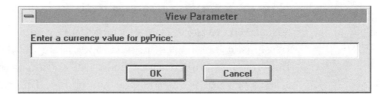

> **Tip!**
> Be aware that you could get unexpected results if you enter a noncurrency value. For instance if you enter "high" as the parameter value, Visual FoxPro will convert that to a currency. However, the currency value of "high" is 0. As a result all products with a price greater than 0 (presumably all of them) will be returned. To avoid this problem in an application, you could let the user enter the price by using a spinner control in a dialog window.

Using Wildcards in Parameter Views

You can use wildcards in parameters when you are looking for more than one record in a result set. The following code creates a view that lists customer information. The parameter allows the user to retrieve all customers whose company names match the parameter value.

```
Create SLQ View vCustomers_ByName Remote ;
  Connection cnTastrade ;
  As Select * ;
    From customer ;
    Where company_name Like ?pcCompName
```

Suppose you wanted all companies whose names begin with a C. For the parameter value you would enter "C%." The % in SQL Server acts like the * in Visual FoxPro. SQL Server returns all companies with names beginning with a C. Or, you might want all companies whose names begin with either an A, a B, or a C. To accomplish this, you could enter "[A-C]%" as the parameter.

> *Tip!*
>
> You must use the % not the * with remote data. If you entered "C*" as the parameter the view would not return rows.

> *Tip!*
>
> Notice that you used Like instead of Equal in the Where clause. This is because you must use Like with wildcards. If you used Equal and entered "C%" as the parameter, SQL Server would return all companies whose name was literally C%.

Row and Table Buffering with Views

Visual FoxPro adds row and table buffering and optimistic and pessimistic locking to the developer's bag of tricks. When data is buffered it is copied to a Cursor. All editing then occurs in the Cursor. To see if anyone else has changed the data in the meantime, you can compare the data in the buffer to the data on disk. Buffering takes the place of the Scatter and Gather developers typically have used in FoxPro 2.x multiuser applications. Each machine will have its own buffer, and you cannot compare one machine's buffer to another machine's buffer. You will typically use row buffering when editing a single record such as an invoice. You can use table buffering when editing more than one record at a time as with the invoice's detail records.

Visual FoxPro also supports optimistic and pessimistic locking. With optimistic locking, a record is locked when the user tries to save changes to that record. The record is unlocked after the changes are saved. With pessimistic locking, the record is locked once editing begins and remains locked until any changes are saved.

Buffering and locking are used together. You can buffer at the row or table level and you can lock optimistically or pessimistically. You cannot buffer without choosing a locking scheme, and you cannot choose a locking scheme if you are not buffering. Table 2-1 shows the possible buffering and locking combinations.

Table 2-1.

Buffering/locking combinations

Buffering/Locking	Description	Setting of Cursor's Buffering Property
No buffering	This is the default.	1
Pessimistic row buffering	The record is locked when editing begins. The lock is released when the pointer moves or TableUpdate() is issued.	2
Optimistic row buffering	The record is locked, changes are saved (if possible), and the record is unlocked when the pointer is moved or TableUpdate() is issued.	3
Pessimistic table buffering	Each record is locked when editing (of that record) begins. Locks are released when TableUpdate() is issued.	4
Optimistic table buffering	Records are locked when TableUpdate() is issued.	5

Visual FoxPro includes several functions designed to make multiuser programming much easier and more robust. Table 2-2 lists these functions.

Table 2-2.

Buffering functions

Function	Description
CurVal()	Returns a field value directly from disk or from a remote source.
OldVal()	Returns the original field value for a field that has been modified but not updated.
TableUpdate()	Commits changes made to a buffered row or a buffered table or Cursor.
TableRevert()	Discards changes made to a buffered row or a buffered table or Cursor and restores the OldVal() data for remote Cursors and the current disk values for local tables and Cursors.
GetFldState()	Returns a numeric value indicating if a field in a table or Cursor has been edited or appended, or if the deleted status of the current record has been changed.
GetNextModified()	Returns the record number for the next modified record in a buffered Cursor.
CursorSetProp()	Specifies property settings for a Visual FoxPro table or a Cursor.

Continued on next page

Continued from previous page

Function	Description
CursorGetProp()	Returns the current property settings for a Visual FoxPro table or a Cursor.
AError()	Creates a memory variable array containing information about the most recent Visual FoxPro, OLE, or ODBC error.

For native tables and local views, Visual FoxPro supports both row and table buffering and both optimistic and pessimistic locking. For remote views, Visual FoxPro supports both row and table buffering but only optimistic locking.

The easiest way to see how these features work is to use them from the Command window. To simulate a multiuser environment run two copies of Visual FoxPro. If you have 16 to 20 MB of memory or more, this works really well in Windows NT or Windows 95. It may not work so well in Windows if you don't have much memory. Of course, you can also try this on a real network.

To make things clear, change the name of each Visual FoxPro session. In the first session, type the following:

```
_Screen.Caption = 'Visual FoxPro 1'
```

In the second session type the following:

```
_Screen.Caption = 'Visual FoxPro 2'
```

Now you can clearly tell which session you are in.
Enter the following commands in both sessions:

```
Open Database tastrade
Set Multilocks On
```

Note that Multilocks must be set on if you use buffering (for any buffering setting other than 1).

Optimistic Row Buffering
In both sessions enter the following commands:

```
pcCity = 'London'
Use VOrders_OneCity
? CursorSetProp('Buffering', 3) && optimistic row buffering
```

The CursorSetProp() function allows you to set the properties for a table or Cursor. However, most of the properties you can set with CursorSetProp() apply only to Cursors. In fact, the only property you can set for a table is the buffering mode. Table 2-1 listed the five possible buffering modes and their values. In the code just presented, the Buffering property was set to 3, which indicates that optimistic row buffering is set. This allows two or more users to change the same record simultaneously.

You can test optimistic row buffering by having the address change in both sessions. The value of ship_to_address is currently "Fauntleroy Circus."

In Session 1 change the value of ship_to_address with the following code:

```
Replace ship_to_address With 'Picadilly Circus'
```

Now check for the value of ship_to_address in Session 2. It is still "Fauntleroy Circus." The change made in Session 1 was made only in that session's buffer. Return to Session 1 and skip to the next record. This moves the record pointer, which then causes Visual FoxPro to send the changed data in the buffer to SQL Server, physically updating the record.

Now return to Session 2 and check for the value of the address. It is still "Fauntleroy Circus." You are reading the value from the Session 2 buffer, which was copied before the change was made in Session 1. If this were a native Visual FoxPro table you could see the new data by moving off the record and then moving back, which recopies the data into the buffer. You could also see the new data by locking the record, which forces Visual FoxPro to recopy the data into the buffer. With remote data you need to issue either Refresh(), which refreshes the records in the view's result set, or Requery(), which produces a new result set. This is shown in the following code:

```
? ship_to_address      'Fauntleroy Circus'
? Refresh()            .T.  && refreshes the current record
? ship_to_address      'Picadilly Circus'
```

Requery() will reissue the view's Select statement and therefore bring all of the rows in the view back down to Visual FoxPro. Refresh() can be used to update one or more rows. The first two arguments of the Refresh() function specify the number of records to refresh and a record offset. The offset is the number of rows from the current row to begin refreshing. For instance, Refresh() and Refresh(0) will refresh only the data in the current row. If the current row is record 5, Refresh(10, 5) will refresh the data in rows 10 through 19.

Now look at what happens if two users change the address at the same time. Return to the first record in both sessions. In Session 1 change the address with the following code:

```
Replace ship_to_address With 'Buckingham Palace'
```

Then change the address in Session 2 with this code:

```
Replace ship_to_address With '10 Downing Street'
```

Now skip to the next record in Session 1. This sends the change to SQL Server. You can tell this is occurring because there should be a noticeable pause while the Update is sent to the server and Visual FoxPro waits for notification of success or failure.

One way to cause Visual FoxPro to update a record is to move the record pointer. The other way is to use the TableUpdate() function. TableUpdate() will return true if the changes are written to disk and false if they are not. This does not move the record pointer. The next code sample changes the address again and then saves the change using TableUpdate().

```
Go Top
Replace ship_to_address With 'Leicester Square'
? TableUpdate()
```

Here the TableUpdate() function returns true. These changes are sent to SQL Server and saved.

Now skip to the next record in Session 2. You will receive the update conflict error message shown in Figure 2-14.

Figure 2-14.

An update conflict error message

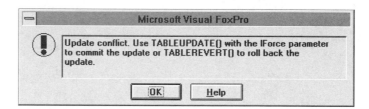

The message appears because Visual FoxPro automatically detects that a change has been made to the underlying data. Because there has been an update conflict, the data is not saved and you will receive the error message.

You can trap for this error. The function AError() creates an array containing information about the most recent error. The array contains six columns. Depending on the type of error, not all of these columns will be used. If a Visual FoxPro error occurs, the first column will contain the error number while the second will contain the error message. The remaining columns will be null. The following code shows how the resulting error can be trapped using AError().

```
lnError = AError(laError)
? lnError        returns 1
? laError[1]     returns 1585
? laError[2]     returns 'Update conflict. Use TABLEUPDATE() with
                 the lForce parameter to the update
                 or TABLEREVERT() to roll back the update.'
```

In Session 2, type the following:

```
? TableUpdate()
```

This code comes back false because the underlying data has changed.

You can find out what field changed by using the GetFldState() function, which returns a numeric value indicating whether you have changed a field. Type the following command:

```
? GetFldState('ship_to_address')
```

This function returns a value of 2, indicating that this field has changed. You can loop through each field, checking the value of GetFldState(). You can also issue the following:

```
? GetFldState(-1)
```

This returns a character value consisting of a string of numbers. In this example, the GetFldState() function returns the following:

```
1111111211111111
```

The first character refers to the deletion status of the record. GetFldState() will contain a value of 1 in the first character of the string if the record has not been deleted, a value of 2 if the record has been deleted, a value of 3 if the record has been appended, and a value of 4 if the record was appended and then deleted.

Each of the rest of the characters refers to a field in the table or view. GetFldState() will return a value of 1 if the field has not been edited, a value of 2 if the field has been changed, a value of 3 if the record is an appended record and the field has not been edited, and a value of 4 if the record is an appended record and the field has been changed.

In this example, the 2 in the eighth spot indicates that the seventh field has changed.

Now that you know what field or fields changed, you can use the CurVal() and OldVal() functions to get the current and original values of that field. If CurVal() and OldVal() are different, then someone else changed the data in that field.

```
* this reads out of the buffer
? ship_to_address                      '10 Downing Street'
* CurVal() returns the data on the server
? CurVal('ship_to_address')            'Picadilly Circus'
* OldVal() returns the original data before editing
? OldVal('ship_to_address')            'Picadilly Circus'
```

Notice that both CurVal() and OldVal() returned "Picadilly Circus." Why did the TableUpdate() fail if CurVal() and OldVal() are the same? If this were native Visual FoxPro data, CurVal() would return "Buckingham Palace." When used with local data, CurVal() reads the current data from the disk. When used with remote data, CurVal() returns the old data. CurVal() is automatically updated for local views and Visual FoxPro tables, but not for remote views. For remote views, you must issue either a ReQuery() or a Refresh() function before issuing the CurVal().

```
* this reads out of the buffer
? ship_to_address                      '10 Downing Street'
* this is the old data on the server
? CurVal('ship_to_address')            'Picadilly Circus'
* this refreshes the current row
? Refresh()                            returns 1
* this is the current data on the server
? CurVal('ship_to_address')            'Buckingham Palace'
* this is the original data
? OldVal('ship_to_address')            'Picadilly Circus'
```

Use the TableRevert() function to discard the changes that have been made. This restores the current disk values for local tables and Cursors. For remote Cursors it restores the OldVal() values.

```
? TableRevert()                        returns 1
? ship_to_address                      'Buckingham Palace'
? CurVal('ship_to_address')            'Buckingham Palace'
? OldVal('ship_to_address')            'Buckingham Palace'
```

You can force Visual FoxPro to overwrite the changed data by using the TableUpdate() function as follows:

```
? TableUpdate(.T., .T.)
```

The first .T. tells Visual FoxPro to update all buffered rows. This is redundant with row buffering. The second .T. tells Visual FoxPro to overwrite the data on the disk, despite the fact that it was changed by someone else.

Optimistic Table Buffering

Table buffering is useful in situations where child records are edited. More than one record can be buffered and edited at a time, and rows can be updated or reverted either one at a time or all at once. With optimistic table buffering, each of the records can be edited by more than one user at a time. To test table buffering you can use the vOrderItems_OneOrder view, which contains order detail records. This view is created as shown.

```
Create SQL View vOrderItems_OneOrder Remote ;
  Connection cnTastrade ;
  As Select *;
    From Order_line_items;
    Where Order_line_items.order_id = ?pcOrder
```

Now set the parameter and use this view in both of the sessions you created earlier. Remember to set MultiLocks on if you haven't already done so.

```
pcOrderID = ' 10001'
Use vrOrderItems_OneOrder
? CursorSetProp('Buffering', 5)
```

Setting the Buffering option to a value of 5 turns optimistic table buffering on. Each session will have three rows in the Cursor created by the view. In Session 1 enter the following commands:

```
Replace quantity With 51
Skip
Replace quantity With 56
```

In Session 2 enter the following commands:

```
Replace quantity With 31
Skip
Replace quantity With 36
```

Because table buffering is being used, moving the record pointer will not save the changes. Changes are saved only with the TableUpdate() function. Type the following in Session 1:

```
? TableUpdate(.T.)
```

This will return true. The .T. argument tells Visual FoxPro to update all rows in the table. If this argument is omitted, only the current row will be updated and the changes to the other row will not be sent to SQL Server.

In Session 2 the TableUpdate() will return false. With row buffering you know which record caused the conflict because you are working with only one record at a time. With table buffering any number of the records could have changed.

You can find the record that was modified by using the GetNextModified() function. Enter the following in Session 2 to find the first record modified:

```
lnModRec = GetNextModified(0)
```

This tells Visual FoxPro to start at the top of the view's Cursor and return the record number of the next modified record. In this example lnModRec would be equal to 1. You can then go to that record and compare OldVal() to CurVal() to see which field or fields caused the conflict. Remember to Refresh() or Requery() first to ensure that you have the most current data from SQL Server. You can also use GetFldState() to see if the value was also changed by the current user.

Next, type the following.

```
lnModRec = GetNextModified(lnModRec)
```

This will find the next modified record. In this example, lnModRec would now equal 2. When GetNextModified() returns 0, there are no more modified records. This allows you to loop through the table and identify all records that may have caused the conflict.

One important thing to keep in mind is that conflicts are based on individual records. If Session 1 changed the quantity in record 2 and Session 2 changed the quantity in record 3 then TableUpdate(.T.) would return true in both sessions. This is not considered a conflict because the two users did not change the same records.

Use the TableRevert() function to discard all of Session 2's changes. This can be done by typing the following in Session 2:

```
? TableRevert(.T.)
```

This will return 2, indicating that the changes in two rows were discarded. The .T. argument tells Visual FoxPro to discard changes to all rows in the table. If this is omitted, only the current row's changes will be discarded.

To force Session 1's changes to be overwritten, use TableUpdate() and supply .T. as the second argument. In Session 2 you would type the following to force the saving of changes to all rows:

```
? TableUpdate(.T., .T.)
```

The next code forces only the current row to save changes.

```
? TableUpdate(.F., .T.)
```

Pessimistic Row and Table Buffering

Pessimistic row and table buffering are not supported with remote views. This is because most SQL back ends do not pessimistically lock records. If a record is locked pessimistically it is locked as soon as the user begins editing and it is not unlocked until the user saves the changes to that record. SQL Server does not allow this type of locking. To change a record, you issue an Update statement. SQL Server locks the page of data the record is on for the length of time it takes to make the change, then it unlocks the data page. This is optimistic locking. You cannot pessimistically lock a record or a table in a Visual FoxPro remote view.

Setting View Properties

View properties determine how views behave. For instance, by setting a property you can control the number of records that will be brought down at a time when running a Select statement. By setting a different property you can control when to retrieve memo fields from the back end. In this discussion you will look at the various properties of views and explore how changing the values of these properties can affect the way views behave.

View properties can be set visually or programmatically. Setting a property visually is done through the View Designer's Update Criteria tab and the Advanced Options dialog box. Most of a view's properties can be set visually, both at the time a view is created and later after the view exists. Changing a property visually is a permanent change whereas changing a property programmatically can be either a permanent or temporary change.

The DBSetProp() function is used to set properties for databases and their objects. Database objects include connections, views, tables, and fields. The function takes four arguments: the name of the database object whose property you are changing, the type of object you are changing (database, connection, view, table, or field), the property you are changing, and the new value for the property. DBSetProp() is used to make permanent changes to database objects. The new setting is stored in the database and will be in effect the next time the object is used.

The DBGetProp() function is used to determine properties for database objects. You supply three arguments to the DBGetProp()

function: the name of the database object, the type of object, and the property whose value you want to know.

Update Criteria Tab

You saw earlier that the Update Criteria tab in the View Designer, shown again in Figure 2-15, is where you identify the primary key and updatable fields for a view. It is also where you can set view properties that determine how updates are handled.

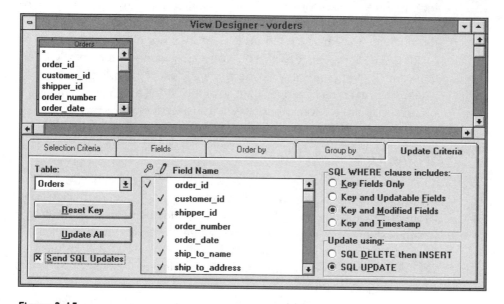

Figure 2-15.

The Update Criteria tab

SendUpdates Property

The SendUpdates property determines whether or not changes made in a view are sent back to the back-end server. If they are, a SQL Update will be sent from Visual FoxPro to the server. If this property is set to false, the view will be read-only. Check the Send SQL Updates CheckBox in the Update Criteria tab to make a view updatable.

The following code makes the vOrder view read-only, then sets it back to read and write.

```
= DBSetProp('vOrder', 'View', 'SendUpdate', .F.)
= DBSetProp('vOrder', 'View', 'SendUpdate', .T.)
```

WhereType Property

The WhereType property allows you to fine-tune the Update and to determine when an Update will fail. There are four choices for the WhereType property: Key Fields Only, Key and Updatable Fields,

Key and Modified Fields, and Key and Timestamp. Use the SQL Where Clause Includes OptionGroup to set this property visually.

Key Fields Only

If you select Key Fields Only, the Update will fail if any field involved in the primary key has been changed by another user. It's important for an Update to fail if the primary key is changed while a user is editing a record. How does the back end know where to put the user's changes? For instance, suppose the user changes the ship_to_name for a particular order. The Update statement sent to the server may look like the this:

```
Update orders
   Set ship_to_name = "B's Beverages Too"
   Where order_id = '      1'
```

This will fail if the order ID has been changed. There will be no records that match the Where clause and therefore no records to update. This setting is the bare minimum to allow Updates to occur.

Tip!

Notice that the only field being updated is the field that changed. In traditional FoxPro applications, developers have to use code to prevent unintentional overwriting of fields. For instance, if User 1 changes the ship_to_name immediately after User 2 changes the order_date you don't want User 1 to overwrite the order_date and set it back. In a remote view this is not an issue because the Update sent to SQL Server contains only the fields that actually changed. This also minimizes the amount of time the Update requires on the server.

If Key Fields Only is selected, there is no automatic change detection involved with saving the user's changes. Visual FoxPro would have no way of knowing if someone else changed data at the same time that you changed it.

You can test this by changing a row on SQL Server and then changing the same row in Visual FoxPro. From the Project Manager select the vOrder view and click the Browse button. In the parameter dialog box type, "   1" (with five spaces before the 1) to bring down that order.

You can use the ISQL/W facility that ships with the product to change the data on SQL Server. ISQL/W is the Windows version of the Interactive SQL command prompt utility. ISQL/W allows you to log on to the server and execute SQL statements. ISQL/W is automatically installed on the Windows NT server machine when SQL Server is installed. It can be installed on a client machine from the Windows 3.1 Utilities disks that ship with the product.

When you start ISQL/W you will be asked to connect to SQL Server. You identify the server itself and then supply a login ID and password. This is shown in Figure 2-16.

Figure 2-16.

The ISQL/W Connect dialog box

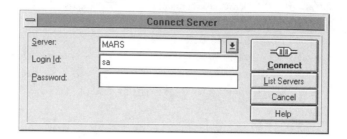

Once in ISQL/W you can type and execute SQL statements. For instance, Figure 2-17 shows the SQL statement to make the Tastrade database current and then run a Select statement. After clicking the Execute button, or pressing Ctrl-E, the query will be run and the results will be shown in the bottom half of the window.

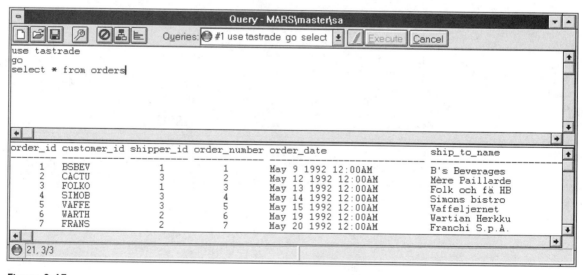

Figure 2-17.

The ISQL/W window

You now have a user in Visual FoxPro working with order information and a user working with the same data using a different front end. From ISQL/W, execute the following Update statement:

```
Update orders
   Set ship_to_name = "Bs Beverages Too"
   Where order_id = '     1'
```

In the ISQL/W results window you will see the following message:

```
(1 row(s) affected)
```

Now return to Visual FoxPro and, in the Browse window, change the ship_to_name for the order record to B's Beverages II. Move off the row. There will be no error message. Return to ISQL/W and execute the following Select statement:

```
Select * From orders Where order_id = '    1'
```

You can see that the ship_to_name was changed on the server to B's Beverages II. Visual FoxPro didn't warn you that it had been changed by a different user. There is no buffering so there is no change detection. When you move off the record, Visual FoxPro sends an Update statement to SQL Server. SQL Server doesn't care that data is being overwritten. Both users have the right to update data and SQL Server simply processes the Updates in the order it receives them.

The following code sets the WhereType property to Key Fields Only for the vOrder view.

```
= DBSetProp('vOrder', 'View', 'WhereType', 1)
```

Key and Updatable Fields

The other three choices for the WhereType property all detect changes. If Key and Updatable Fields is selected, the Update will fail if any field involved in the primary key has been changed by another user or if any of the updatable fields have been changed. For instance, suppose the user is editing an order_line_items record. The user changes the quantity. The Update statement sent to the server could look like this:

```
Update order_line_items
   Set quantity = 25
   Where order_id = '    1'
      And product_id = '    10'
      And unit_price = $31
      And quantity = 5
```

As you can see, this Update will fail if any field in this row has been changed on the server by another user.

To test this, use the vOrderItems_OneOrder remote view you created earlier. This is based on the order_line_items table in the Tastrade database. In the Update Criteria tab, you can see that order_id and product_id are the primary key and that unit_price and quantity are updatable. The Send SQL Updates CheckBox and the Key and Updatable Fields OptionButton should be selected. When you are back in the Project Manager, highlight the view and click the Browse button.

In ISQL/W execute the following Update statement:

```
Update order_line_items
   Set quantity = 20
   Where order_id = '      1'
      And product_id = '     10'
```

Now return to Visual FoxPro and change the quantity for the second record to 25. Move off the row and you will receive the following error message:

```
Update conflict. Use TABLEUPDATE() with the lForce parameter to
   commit the update or TABLEREVERT() to roll back the update.
```

When you moved off the record, Visual FoxPro sent the Update statement you just issued in ISQL/W. The order_id, product_id, and unit_price were the same but because the quantity changed, no record in the table matched the Where clause. As a result, the Update failed. Visual FoxPro detected this and reported the conflict.

In the error dialog box click the Revert button. Or, from the Command window, type the following.

```
=TableRevert()
```

This will return the quantity to its previous value of 5 and allow you to move to a different record.

The following code sets the WhereType property to Key and Updatable Fields for the vOrder view.

```
= DBSetProp('vOrder', 'View', 'WhereType', 2)
```

Key and Modified Fields

If Key and Modified Fields is selected, the Update will fail if the primary key or any of the modified fields has been changed by another user. Again, suppose the user changes the quantity for an order_line_items record. The Update statement sent to the server could look like this:

```
Update order_line_items
   Set quantity = 27
   Where order_id = '      1'
      And product_id = '     10'
      And quantity = 5
```

Notice that the unit_price is not in the Update statement because the user didn't change it. This Update will fail only if the primary key has been changed and the server can't find the old record, or if someone else changed the quantity at the same time the user was changing it. If the unit_price were changed while the user was changing the quantity there would be no conflict generated.

The following code sets the WhereType property to Key and Modified Fields for the vOrders view.

```
= DBSetProp('vOrder', 'View', 'WhereType', 3)
```

Key and Timestamp

If Key and Timestamp is selected, the Update will fail if the primary key or the table's timestamp has been changed by another user. A timestamp column is automatically updated each time a row in the table is updated or inserted. Again, suppose the user changes the quantity for an order_line_items record. The Update statement sent to the server could look like this:

```
Update order_line_items
   Set quantity = 27
   Where order_id = '      1'
      And timestamp = '0x0000000100004fa5'
```

If the row has been changed by another user, the timestamp will be different and the Update will fail, thereby notifying Visual FoxPro that a conflict has occurred.

Tip!
The Key and Timestamp option will be disabled if the table the view is based on does not have a timestamp column.

The following code sets the WhereType property to Key and Timestamp for the vOrder view:

```
= DBSetProp('vOrder', 'View', 'WhereType', 4)
```

UpdateType Property

The last option on the View Designer's Update Criteria tab is Update Using, which is used to set the view's UpdateType property. You can choose between two settings—SQL Delete then Insert and SQL Update. These options specify how you want the back-end server to perform a SQL Update. You can ask the server to delete the old record and insert the new record, or you can ask the server to update the existing record.

The default behavior for most SQL databases is to delete then insert when performing an update. SQL Server stores data on 2 K pages. If there are variable-length fields in a row, the length of each row can vary. Therefore, the number of rows that will fit on a page depends on the width of the rows. There would be a performance penalty if SQL Server had to check to see if the width of the updated row were less than, the same as, or larger than the width of the original row. If it were less than or the same, the updated row could go on the same page. If it were larger, SQL Server would either have to put the row on the last page or split the page the row was on. There is an added performance penalty to page splitting.

To enhance data modification performance, SQL Server deletes the old row and inserts the new row. If there is no clustered index on the table, the "updated" row goes on the last page. If there is a clustered index, the data is physically sorted by the order of the index. In that case, the "updated" row has to go in its proper place. If the modified row is larger than before, the page may need to be split.

If certain conditions are met, SQL Server for Windows NT will allow an Update in Place. The table must not contain an update trigger; variable length columns must not change in width; the changed columns cannot appear in the table's clustered index; the update must affect only one row; and the amount of data changed cannot exceed half the row size. If all of these conditions are met, SQL Server will replace the row rather than deleting it and reinserting it.

In reality, the setting of the UpdateType property in Visual FoxPro may not matter. The back end will decide how it wants to update rows.

The following code sets the UpdateType property to SQL Delete then Insert for the vOrder view. It then sets it back to SQL Update.

```
= DBSetProp('vOrder', 'View', 'UpdateType', 1)
= DBSetProp('vOrder', 'View', 'UpdateType', 2)
```

Advanced Options Dialog Box

The Advanced Options dialog box, shown in Figure 2-18, allows you to set properties that mainly determine how Visual FoxPro retrieves data from a back-end server.

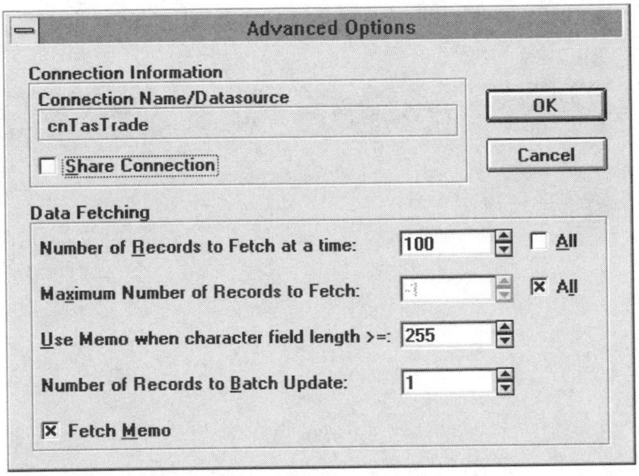

Figure 2-18.

*The Advanced
Options dialog box*

ShareConnection Property

This is the same as using the Share keyword in the Create SQL
View command. To make a connection shared, check the Share
Connection CheckBox. The following code makes the connection
shared for the vOrder view:

```
= DBSetProp('vOrder', 'View', 'ShareConnection', .T.)
```

Sharing a connection allows you to better manage user
connections on the server. In SQL Server, user connections are
preconfigured. The system administrator decides how much memory
to set aside for user connections. Each connection takes 18 K of
memory to be preconfigured and then about another 20 K of
memory when it is used. If you set SQL Server up to support 100
users, you would need 4 MB of RAM just for the connections.

Every time a view is used Visual FoxPro connects to the server
by default. To see this, you can look at the Sys Options/Active
Resources window in the SQL Administrator tool that ships with
SQL Server. This window shows the results of running the built-in
sp_who system procedure, and shows who is connected to the
server. Figure 2-19 shows the window before any views are used.

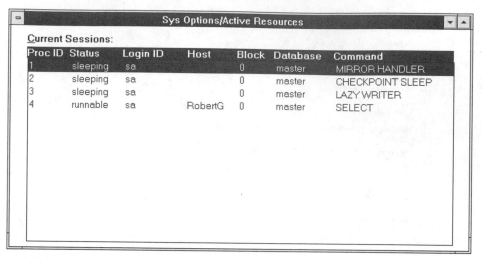

Figure 2-19.

The Sys Options/
Active Resources
window with no views
open

Now use the vOrder view. Figure 2-20 shows the window as it now stands. Notice that machine RobertG has two connections.

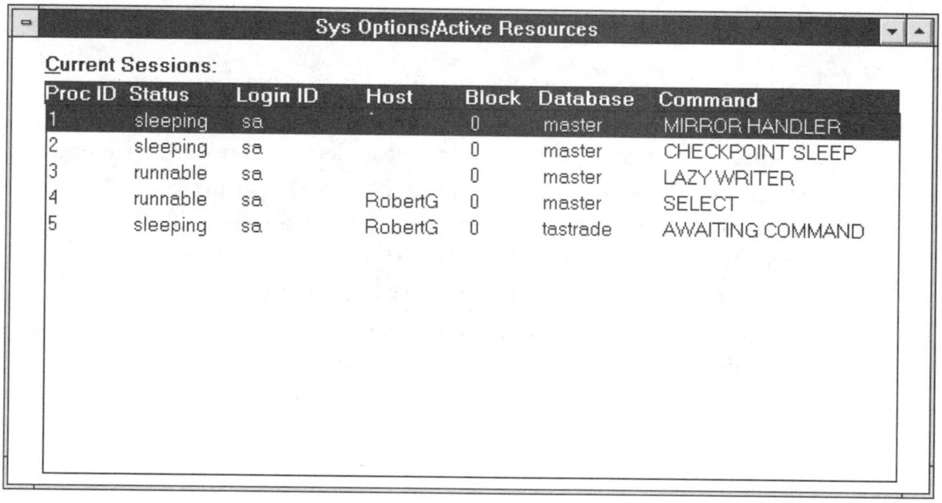

Figure 2-20.

The Sys Options/
Active Resources
window with one
view open

Now use the vOrders_OneCity view. Figure 2-21 shows the window as it now stands. Notice that machine RobertG has three connections.

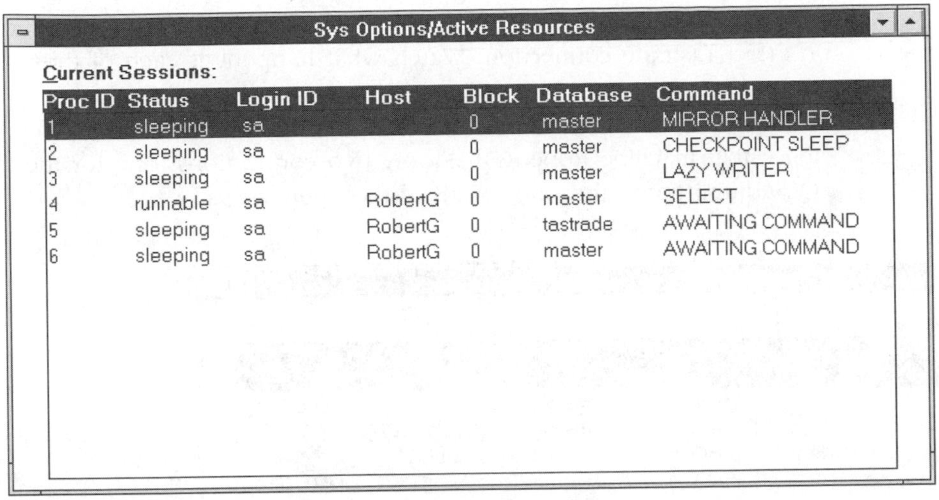

Sys Options/Active Resources

Current Sessions:

Proc ID	Status	Login ID	Host	Block	Database	Command
1	sleeping	sa		0	master	MIRROR HANDLER
2	sleeping	sa		0	master	CHECKPOINT SLEEP
3	sleeping	sa		0	master	LAZY WRITER
4	runnable	sa	RobertG	0	master	SELECT
5	sleeping	sa	RobertG	0	tastrade	AWAITING COMMAND
6	sleeping	sa	RobertG	0	master	AWAITING COMMAND

Figure 2-21.

The Sys Options/
Active Resources
window with two
views open

Now use the vCustomers_ByName view. Figure 2-22 shows the window as it now stands. Notice that machine RobertG has four connections.

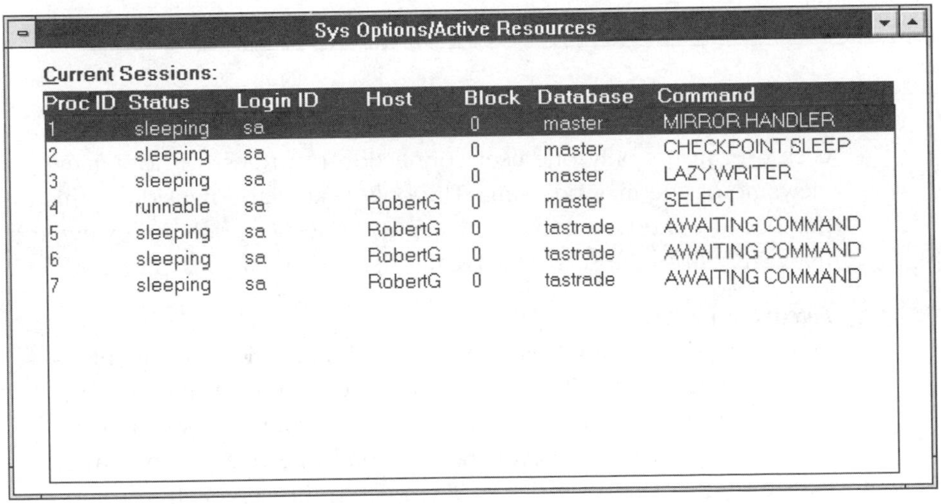

Sys Options/Active Resources

Current Sessions:

Proc ID	Status	Login ID	Host	Block	Database	Command
1	sleeping	sa		0	master	MIRROR HANDLER
2	sleeping	sa		0	master	CHECKPOINT SLEEP
3	sleeping	sa		0	master	LAZY WRITER
4	runnable	sa	RobertG	0	master	SELECT
5	sleeping	sa	RobertG	0	tastrade	AWAITING COMMAND
6	sleeping	sa	RobertG	0	tastrade	AWAITING COMMAND
7	sleeping	sa	RobertG	0	tastrade	AWAITING COMMAND

Figure 2-22.

The Sys Options/
Active Resources
window with three
views open

You can see that each view requires a connection to the server. If each user had three views open and SQL Server was configured to 20 user connections (the default for SQL Server 6), only six users could retrieve SQL Server data at a time.

To deal with this limitation, you can either reduce the number of connections used by each user or increase the number of preconfigured connections on SQL Server. The former takes good connection management, the latter takes memory. Each view is based on the cnTastrade connection. Watch what happens if each of the views shares the connection. Figure 2-23 shows the Sys Options/Active Resources window as it stands when all three views are open. Notice that machine RobertG has only two connections, one for the SQL Administrator and one for all of the open views.

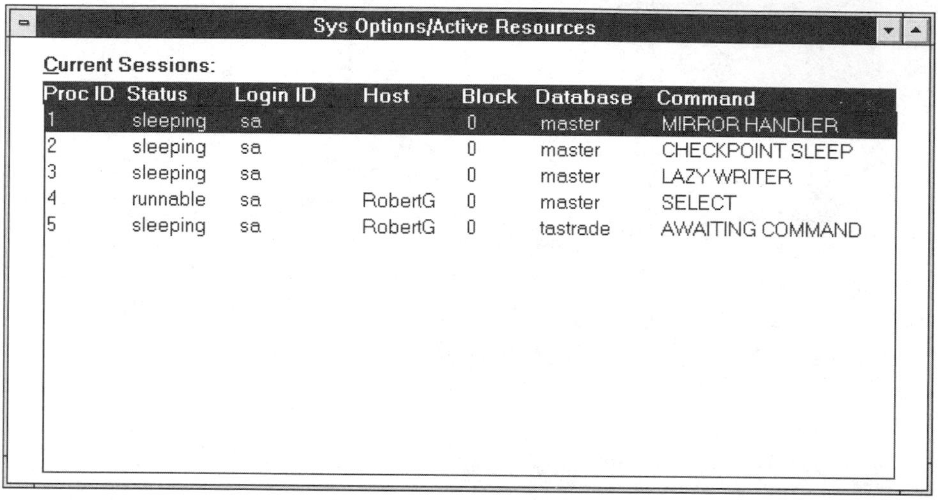

| Sys Options/Active Resources | | | | | | |

Current Sessions:

Proc ID	Status	Login ID	Host	Block	Database	Command
1	sleeping	sa		0	master	MIRROR HANDLER
2	sleeping	sa		0	master	CHECKPOINT SLEEP
3	sleeping	sa		0	master	LAZY WRITER
4	runnable	sa	RobertG	0	master	SELECT
5	sleeping	sa	RobertG	0	tastrade	AWAITING COMMAND

Figure 2-23.

*The Sys Options/
Active Resources
window with three
views open*

Because each view shares the same connection to SQL Server, each user needs only one user connection regardless of how many views he or she may be using. The only potential downside to this is that because the views share the same connection, only one view at a time can talk to the server. Typically this shouldn't be a problem.

FetchSize Property

When you Use a view, Visual FoxPro sends a Select statement to the back-end server. The server in turn sends the results of the Select to Visual FoxPro. You should design your views to return small amounts of data. If you need to edit one record, you should have only that one record sent down from the server. If you are viewing the detail rows for one order, you should have only those records sent from the server. This minimizes network traffic as well as the time Visual FoxPro takes to receive and prepare data.

However, there may be times when you need or want to work with large data sets. For instance, you might need to manually review last month's 8,000 order records to look for a mistake. In that case, your view will return a large data set in spite of the fact that it is parameterized.

Visual FoxPro uses progressive fetching when receiving rows from a server. Without progressive fetching you would have to wait until all of the rows had been retrieved before you could start working with or looking at the data. For a result set of 20 rows this is not a problem. If your result set is 8,000 rows, you could spend a significant amount of time staring at the screen wondering how long it's going to take before you see the data. With progressive fetching, Visual FoxPro retrieves the data in batches and allows you to work with the already retrieved data while it continues to fetch more rows in the background.

To see this, run the view vOrders, which retrieves all rows on the orders table. Highlight the view in the Project Manager and click the Browse button. There will be a pause while the Select is sent to the server and rows begin to be returned. When the Browse appears you can see in the status bar that there are 100 rows. The status bar text will read "Record: 1/100." Shortly thereafter, this display will change to "1/200," and then "1/300," and so on until it reads "1/1072." Visual FoxPro fetches data from the server 100 rows at a time.

The Browse will appear as soon as the first 100 rows have been fetched. The user can then scroll through the Browse and work with those 100 records. When the next 100 records are fetched they will be added to the Browse. The principle behind this is that the user probably wants to see the first records first and the last records last.

If you want to see the last records you have to wait for them to arrive. You can speed this process slightly by issuing the Go Bottom command. This will force Visual FoxPro to suspend progressive fetching and retrieve all of the rest of the rows at once.

To have Visual FoxPro fetch more or fewer rows at a time, change the Number of Records to Fetch at a Time in the Advanced Options dialog box. This will change the amount of time you must sit before being allowed to see the data. To disable progressive fetching, check the All CheckBox.

The following code changes the number of rows that will be fetched to 200 for the vOrders view. It then disables progressive fetching by setting the FetchSize property to -1.

```
= DBSetProp('vOrders', 'View', 'FetchSize', 200)
= DBSetProp('vOrders', 'View', 'FetchSize', -1)
```

The value of this property cannot be greater than the value of the MaxRecords property.

UseMemoSize Property

If a Select statement returns long character fields, Visual FoxPro can put them into memo fields. The UseMemoSize property determines how many characters wide a field can be before it is placed into a memo field. The default value for this property is 255. Therefore, if a character column of data is less than 255 wide it will be a character field in the Visual FoxPro result set Cursor. If it exceeds this length it will be a memo field.

To change this property in the Advanced Options dialog box, enter a number in the Use Memo when Character Field Length >= spinner.

The following code sets the maximum character field width to 150 for the vOrders_OneCity view.

```
= DBSetProp('vOrders_OneCity', 'View', 'UseMemoSize', 150)
```

This property can have a value from 1 to 255.

FetchMemo Property

In Visual FoxPro the only limit to the size of a memo field is disk space. In SQL Server a text column can hold up to 2 GB of data. Suppose that you have a view that includes a column of text data. When this view is run, the text data will be stored in a Visual FoxPro memo field. Similarly, long character fields (as defined by the UseMemoSize property) are stored in memo fields. The Fetch Memo on Demand property allows you to decide if text data is sent to Visual FoxPro for every row returned when a view is run.

If this property is set to true, which is the default, then the memo field data is retrieved only if the user asks for it. The user can ask by double-clicking the column in a Browse window or by displaying the contents of the memo field. If you have a Form that displays the memo field in an edit region, then the memo field for each record would be retrieved only when that record was displayed.

To turn this option off and have all memo field data retrieved at the time the view is run, uncheck the Fetch Memo on Demand CheckBox in the Advanced Options dialog box.

The following code sets the FetchMemo property to .T. for the vOrders_OneCity view.

```
= DBSetProp('vOrders_OneCity', 'View', 'FetchMemo', .T.)
```

MaxRecords Property

System administrators always worry about the dreaded run-away query. This occurs when a user issues a Select statement, the server begins processing, then, eight hours later, the server is still processing and has sent 28 million rows to the user's workstation. This all happens because the user forgot to put a Where clause on the Select statement. The MaxRecords property allows you to limit the number of records that Visual FoxPro will retrieve. The default is -1, or all.

Tip!

Regardless of the setting of MaxRecords, SQL Server will generate the complete result set for a Select statement. Visual FoxPro will fetch only the number of rows specified by MaxRecords. The rest of the rows will not be brought down to Visual FoxPro.

To change the property, uncheck the All CheckBox next to the Maximum Number of Records to Fetch spinner in the Advanced Options dialog box and enter the maximum number of records you want fetched.

The following code sets the maximum number of rows to fetch to 1,000 for the vOrders view.

```
= DBSetProp('vOrders', 'View', 'MaxRecords', 1000)
```

BatchUpdateCount Property

You have seen that changes made to the data in an updatable view are sent back to the server. Visual FoxPro will construct a SQL Update statement to send changes back. Each row changed generates an Update statement and, by default, each of the Updates is sent to the server by itself. There is overhead involved in sending a statement to the back end. Visual FoxPro must connect to the server and send messages (the Update statements), the messages must travel over the network, and the server must receive the messages. You can reduce this overhead by increasing the value of the BatchUpdateCount property of the view.

By default, the BatchUpdateCount is set to 1, which means each Update will be sent to the server by itself. Increasing the BatchUpdateCount to 5, for instance, would cause Visual FoxPro to send up to five Updates together as a single batch. This would reduce the overhead involved. However, the server still Updates the rows one at a time.

> ### Tip!
> If you make changes only to single records, changing this property will have no effect. However, suppose you are table buffering and you change 15 records. If BatchUpdateCount were set to a value of 5 then Visual FoxPro would send three batches of Updates (five per batch) to the server rather than 15 batches (one Update per batch).

To change this property, enter a number in the Number of Records to Batch Update spinner in the Advanced Options dialog box. The following code sets this property programmatically.

```
= DBSetProp('vOrderItems_OneOrder', 'BatchUpdate', 5)
```

Permanently and Temporarily Changing View Properties

The CursorSetProp() function is used to set properties for a Visual FoxPro table or Cursor. The function accepts three arguments: the table name (or Cursor name, alias, or work area), the property you are changing, and the new value for the property. The table or Cursor must be in use at the time you use CursorSetProp(). As a result, any changes made with this function are temporary.

The CursorGetProp() function is used to determine properties for a Visual FoxPro table or Cursor. The function takes two arguments: the table name (or Cursor name, alias, or work area) and the property whose value you want to know.

Most of the view properties discussed in this section can be set using either DBSetProp() or CursorSetProp(). When a property is changed using DBSetProp(), it is changed in the database. The property is actually changed in the view's definition and therefore becomes the default setting for that property the next time the view is used. When a property is changed using CursorSetProp(), it is changed only in the view's Cursor so the property is changed only for the current use of the Cursor. The next time the view is run, the property will revert to its default value.

Similarly, DBGetProp() will read the value of a property from the view's definition in the database, while CursorGetProp() will read the setting of that property for the Cursor currently in use.

You can see this in the following example code. The code first looks in the database and sees that in the definition of the vOrder view, the FetchMemo property is set to true. The view is then used and the value of the FetchMemo property is checked in the view's Cursor. It is true because that is the default for the view. The code then changes the FetchMemo property in the Cursor to false. In the view's definition, of course, it is still true. Because the property has changed in the view's Cursor, it will stay that way until it is either set back or the Cursor is closed. The code then closes the view and reopens it. You can see that the FetchMemo property is back to true, which is the default.

```
* What is FetchMemo in the view's definition?
?DBGetProp('vOrder', 'View', 'FetchMemo')          && returns .T.

Use vorder
* What is FetchMemo in the view's cursor?
?CursorGetProp('FetchMemo', 'vOrder')              && returns .T.
* Change FetchMemo in the view's cursor
?CursorSetProp('FetchMemo', .F., 'vOrder')         && returns .T.
* What is FetchMemo in the view's definition?
?DBGetProp('vOrder', 'View', 'FetchMemo')          && returns .T.
* What is FetchMemo in the view's cursor?
?CursorGetProp('FetchMemo', 'vOrder')              && returns .F.

Use
Use vorder
* What is FetchMemo in the view's cursor?
?CursorGetProp('FetchMemo', 'vOrder')              && returns .T.
```

Read-Only View Properties

The view properties in this discussion are all read-only. With the exception of the view's SQL and Comment properties, they can only be viewed programmatically.

SQL Property
The SQL property of a view is the Select statement that defines the view. This property is set visually by using the View Designer to construct the Select statement that defines the view.

The following code returns "Select * From orders."

```
? DBGetProp('vOrders_OneCity', 'View', 'SQL')
```

Comment Property
The Comment property contains the text of the comment associated with the view. This property can be set by selecting Query/ Comments from the menu when in the View Designer.

The following code returns "This view returns all orders for a particular city."

```
? DBGetProp('vOrders_OneCity', 'View','Comment')
```

Database Property
The Database property returns the name of the database a Visual FoxPro table or Cursor belongs to. If the Cursor is the result of

running a view, this function returns the name of the database that contains the view.

The following code returns "tastrade."

```
? CursorGetProp('Database', 'vOrders_OneCity')
```

SourceType Property

The SourceType property identifies whether a view is local or remote.

The following code returns a value of 2, telling you that the view is a remote view.

```
? DBGetProp('vOrders_OneCity', 'View','SourceType')
```

ConnectionHandle Property

A view's connection establishes the communication path between Visual FoxPro and ODBC, which then communicates with the back-end server. Each communication path is represented by a handle, which is merely a number. If you want to use a particular connection or change the properties of a connection, you need to know the connection handle. The ConnectionHandle property returns the handle used by a view's connection.

The following code might return a value of 1.

```
? CursorGetProp('ConnectionHandle', 'vOrders_OneCity')
```

ConnectName Property

The ConnectName property returns the name of the database connection used when a view is executed.

The following code returns "cnTastrade."

```
? CursorGetProp('ConnectName', 'vOrders_OneCity')
```

Setting Connection Properties

Connection properties determine how connections behave. For instance, the user ID and password used to log on to a back-end server are properties of a connection. In this discussion, you will look at the various properties of connections and how changing the values of these properties can affect the way connections behave.

Connection properties can be set visually or programmatically. The Connection Designer is used to set properties visually. Changing a property visually involves a permanent change whereas changing a property programmatically can be either a permanent or temporary change.

There are two functions that can be used to set properties for connections—DBSetProp() and SQLSetProp(). There are two corresponding functions that can be used to determine properties for connections—DBGetProp() and SQLGetProp(). You saw the DBSetProp() and DBGetProp() functions earlier in the section. They are used to change the default properties of a database object. The changes made with DBGetProp() are stored in the database.

The SQLSetProp() function is used to set properties for an active connection. Connections are identified by a connection handle. The function takes three arguments: the connection handle, the property you are changing, and the new value for the property. The connection must be in use at the time you use SQLSetProp(). Therefore, any changes made with this function are not permanent.

The SQLGetProp() function is used to determine properties for database objects. The function takes two arguments: the connection handle and the property whose value you want to know.

Connection Designer

In the beginning of this section you used the Connection Designer to create a connection that was then used in several views. The next part of the section reviews the connection properties that can be set both in the Connection Designer and programmatically.

DataSource Property

The DataSource property contains the name of the ODBC data source used in a connection. Remember that if the DataSource, Userid, Password OptionButton is checked, you can select an existing ODBC data source from the Data source list in the Connection Designer.

The following code first determines the connection handle used when the vOrder view is executed. SQLGetProp() is then used to find out the name of the view's data source. This code returns "Tastrade."

```
lnHandle = CursorGetProp('ConnectionHandle', 'vOrder')
? SQLGetProp(lnHandle, 'DataSource')
```

UserID Property

The UserID property contains the user ID stored in a view's connection. When the view is executed this ID will be sent to the server in an attempt to log in. If the DataSource, Userid, Password OptionButton is checked, you can type in the UserID in the Connection Designer. The following code changes the user login ID which will be sent to the server when any view using the cnTastrade connection is executed.

```
? SQLSetProp('cnTastrade', 'UserID', 'CChaney')
```

Password Property

The Password property contains the user password stored in a view's connection. When the view is executed, this password will be sent to the server in an attempt to log in. If the password is not valid for the user logging in, the connection will fail and the view cannot be executed. If the DataSource, Userid, Password OptionButton is checked, you can type in the password in the Connection Designer. The following code changes the password, which will be sent to the server when any view using the cnTastrade connection is executed.

```
? SQLSetProp('cnTastrade', 'Password', 'Formula1Fan')
```

This does not change the user's password on the back-end server. It merely changes the password that will be sent with the user ID in the attempt to log in to the server.

ConnectString Property

The ConnectString property contains the connection string belonging to a saved connection. The connection string contains the data source name, user ID, password, and database. If the Connection String OptionButton is checked, you can type in the connection string in the Connection Designer. The following code changes the connection string that will be used to connect to the server when any view using the cnTastrade connection is executed.

```
? SQLSetProp('cnTastrade' 'ConnectString', ;
       'DSN=MARS;UID=RGreen;PWD=Formula1Fan;DATABASE=tastrade')
```

DispLogin

In the Connection Designer there are three choices for Display ODBC Login Prompts. The default is When Login Info Is Not Specified. If this is selected, an ODBC Login dialog box will appear if either the user ID or the password is left out of the connection definition. This dialog box is shown in Figure 2-24. If Always is selected, the ODBC Login dialog box will always appear, even if the user ID and password are specified in the connection definition. This would allow you to have a default user ID and password while allowing the user to log in as a different person when accessing server data. If Never is selected, the ODBC Login dialog box will never appear, even if the user ID and/or password are not specified in the connection definition. In this case, an error will occur if the information is not supplied.

Figure 2-24.

The ODBC Login dialog box

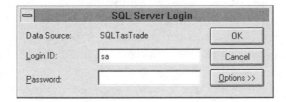

To set the Display ODBC Login Prompts property to When Login Info Is Not Specified, use the following command:

```
= DBSetProp('cnTastrade', 'Connection', 'DispLogin', 1)
```

To set the Display ODBC Login Prompts property to Always, use the following command:

```
= DBSetProp('cnTastrade', 'Connection', 'DispLogin', 2)
```

To set the Display ODBC Login Prompts property to Never, use the following command:

```
= DBSetProp('cnTastrade', 'Connection', 'DispLogin', 3)
```

Asynchronous Execution

Asynchronous execution determines whether Visual FoxPro has to wait for the back end to finish processing before it can continue. With synchronous execution, Visual FoxPro cannot continue with another task until it is done receiving data from the server. With asynchronous execution, control is returned to Visual FoxPro at intervals. This would allow you to send a long Select statement to the server and then periodically ask the user if he or she wants to continue processing. The default setting for this property is false, which means Visual FoxPro uses synchronous processing. However, the property is automatically set to true for all remote views. This allows progressive fetching to occur.

To change a connection's default to asynchronous execution, check the Asynchronous Execution CheckBox in the Data Processing section of the Connection Designer. The following code turns on asynchronous execution for any SQL statement using the cnTastrade connection.

```
? DBSetProp('cnTastrade', 'Connection', 'Asynchronous', .T.)
```

DispWarnings

Errors can occur when Visual FoxPro sends a SQL statement via ODBC. An error could be due to a faulty connection or a rejection of the data by the server. Most errors can be trapped. Trappable errors have an error number and message that can be determined via the AError()function. You can also use the older Error() and Message() functions. However, some errors are not trappable. The DispWarnings property determines whether nontrappable warnings are displayed. The errors would be displayed in a message box. The default setting for this property is true.

To enable nontrappable warnings to be displayed, check the Display Warnings CheckBox in the Data Processing section of the Connection Designer. The following code causes nontrappable warnings to not be displayed for the cnTastrade connection.

```
? DBSetProp('cnTastrade', 'Connection', 'DispWarnings', .F.)
```

BatchMode Property

The BatchMode property determines if multiple result sets are fetched all at once or in pieces (in batches). In other words, if you send three Select statements to SQL Server will Visual FoxPro receive them all at once or separately? The default for this property is .T., which means that Visual FoxPro fetches all of the result set rows for a query as a batch. If this setting is set to .F., Visual FoxPro fetches each result set one at a time. Because a view is based on a single Select statement, this property does not apply to views. It will be covered in more detail in Section 3 when SQL Pass-Through is discussed.

Transactions Property

Visual FoxPro supports transaction processing for remote data. The Transactions property allows you to determine whether a connection manages transactions automatically or manually. The default is for transactions to be managed automatically. Each Update, Insert, and Delete statement is treated as a single transaction. When you are working with a view you cannot create your own transaction, so this property is not applicable to views. It will be covered in more detail in Section 3.

ConnectTimeout Property

The ConnectTimeout property specifies in seconds the amount of time that Visual FoxPro will wait before timing out a connection. A connection timeout generates an error. The default value for this property is 0, which means that Visual FoxPro will never time-out a connection. If the connection is broken in the middle of a SQL statement, Visual FoxPro will not return an error and will wait indefinitely for results which will never arrive. This property can have values ranging from 0 to 600 seconds.

To visually change the timeout, set a value using the Connection spinner in the Timeout Intervals section of the Connection Designer. The following code sets the connection timeout for the cnTastrade connection to 30 seconds.

```
? DBSetProp('cnTastrade', 'Connection', 'ConnectTimeout', 30)
```

IdleTimeout Property

The IdleTimeout property controls how many seconds of idle time can pass before a connection is dropped. The default value is 0, which means Visual FoxPro will not drop a connection, regardless of how long it has been idle. Because connections take up memory and resources, this property can be used to drop an idle connection if it is not being used. Visual FoxPro will automatically reestablish the connection when it is needed. To change the idle timeout, set a value using the Idle spinner in the Timeout Intervals section of the Connection Designer. The following code causes the cnTastrade connection to be dropped any time it sits idle for five minutes.

```
? DBSetProp('cnTastrade', 'Connection', 'IdleTimeOut', 300)
```

QueryTimeout Property

The QueryTimeout property controls how many seconds of idle time can pass before a query is canceled. The default value is 0, which means Visual FoxPro will not cancel a query, regardless of how long it has been idle. The query timeout does not refer to the length of time it takes for Visual FoxPro to fetch all of the rows returned by the query. If fetching is occurring, no timeout will occur. A timeout can occur only if Visual FoxPro is waiting for results from the server. This could occur if the server requires a large amount of time to send the results. It could also occur if the server has stopped sending results. To change the query timeout, set a value using the Query spinner in the Timeout Intervals section of the Connection Designer. The following code causes any query using the cnTastrade connection to be canceled if one minute passes with no results sent from the server.

```
? DBSetProp('cnTastrade', 'Connection', 'QueryTimeOut', 60)
```

WaitTime Property

The WaitTime property controls how many milliseconds will pass before Visual FoxPro checks to see if a SQL statement has finished executing. The default value is 100, which means Visual FoxPro will check every 100 milliseconds. When using a view there may be no reason to change this property. In the next section you will use asynchronous processing with SQL Pass-Through and this property will more likely have some use. To change the wait time, set a value using the Wait Time spinner in the Timeout Intervals section of the Connection Designer. The following code causes Visual FoxPro to check every 200 milliseconds to see if any SQL statement using the cnTastrade connection has finished executing.

```
? DBSetProp('cnTastrade', 'Connection', 'WaitTime', 200)
```

Other Connection Properties

There are two connection properties that can be accessed only through code.

ConnectName Property

The ConnectName property returns the name of the connection used when a view is executed. This property is read-only. The following code first determines the connection handle used when the vOrder view is executed. SQLGetProp() is then used to find out the name of the view's connection. This code returns "cnTastrade."

```
lnHandle = CursorGetProp('ConnectionHandle', 'vOrder')
? SQLGetProp(lnHandle, 'ConnectName')
```

Comment Property

The Comment property contains a comment describing a connection. The following code changes the comment stored with the cnTastrade connection.

```
? DBSetProp('cnTastrade', 'Connection', 'Comment', ;
            'This connection is used by all of the views.')
```

Summary

In this section you saw how to access SQL Server data using remote views. Remote views are based on a Select statement and return data into a Cursor, which can be made updatable by setting a few key properties. Any data modifications made will automatically be sent back to SQL Server. For this reason, remote views will be ideal for the basic data entry in an application. All of the data entry forms in the sample application are based on remote parameterized views. In the next section you will see how to access SQL Server data programmatically using the SQL Pass-Through functions.

3 | Using SQL Pass-Through

In Section 2 you saw how to connect to back-end server data using remote views. A view is nothing more than a SQL Select statement. When the view is executed, Visual FoxPro sends the Select to the server and fetches the results. These results are placed in a Visual FoxPro Cursor. This Cursor will be read and write if you have defined a primary key, marked fields as updatable, and set the SendUpdates property to true for the view.

Another way to access back-end data is by using Visual FoxPro's SQL Pass-Through functions. These functions are used to connect to a back-end server and to send SQL statements directly to the server. These SQL statements can be Selects, Updates, Inserts, or Deletes. They can also be commands to run stored procedures or to take administrative actions such as backing up a database or adding users.

SQL Pass-Through Functions

Table 3-1 lists the 12 Visual FoxPro SQL Pass-Through functions.

Table 3-1.

SQL Pass-Through functions

Function	Description
Connection Management	
SQLConnect()	Connects to a back-end server using an ODBC data source, user ID, and password.
SQLStringConnect()	Connects to a back-end server using an ODBC connection string.

Continued on next page

Continued from previous page

Function	Description
SQLDisconnect()	Disconnects from a back-end server.
SQL Statement Execution	
SQLExec()	Sends a SQL statement to a back-end server for execution.
SQLCancel()	Cancels an executing SQL statement.
SQLMoreResults()	Fetches another result set from an executing query.
SQLCommit()	Sends a commit transaction request to a back-end server.
SQLRollback()	Sends a rollback transaction request to a back-end server.
Data Source Information	
SQLTables()	Returns a list of tables residing in a database on a back-end server.
SQLColumns()	Returns a list of columns in a table residing in a database on a back-end server.
Miscellaneous	
SQLGetProp()	Determines the value of a property of an active or saved connection or an active remote view.
SQLSetProp()	Sets the value of a property of an active or saved connection or an active remote view.

In this section you will see how to use these SQL Pass-Through functions to access remote data. You will also explore when to use SQL Pass-Through and when to use remote views.

Connecting to SQL Server

The SQLConnect() and SQLStringConnect() functions are used to establish a connection between Visual FoxPro and an ODBC data source.

SQLConnect() Function

The following code shows the syntax for SQLConnect().

```
Syntax:
SQLConnect([lcDataSource, lcUserID, lcPassword | lcConnection])
```

```
Arguments:
lcDataSource        An existing ODBC data source
lcUserID            The logon ID or name used to connect to the
                    back-end server
lcPassword          The password for the logon ID or name
lcConnection        A saved Visual FoxPro connection
```

```
Returns:
Numeric
```

To connect to a back-end server, you must supply the name of an ODBC data source, a user ID, and a password. If you do not supply any of these pieces of information up front, you will be prompted for them. For instance, the following code uses SQLConnect() but leaves all of the connection information empty.

```
? SQLConnect()
```

After issuing this command you will see the Select Connection or Datasource dialog box. This is shown in Figure 3-1. This dialog box is used to prompt the user for a data source or connection and has OptionButtons for Connections and Available Datasources.

Figure 3-1.

The Select Connection or Datasource dialog box with connections

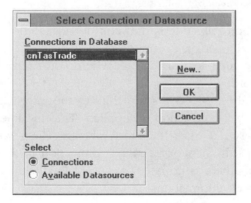

If there is currently a database open and that database has connections saved in it, this dialog box will have the Connections OptionButton selected and will display a list of saved connections in the database. You can use one of the saved connections or you can create a new connection by clicking the New CommandButton. This will bring forward the Connection Designer.

If you select the Available Datasources OptionButton, the dialog box will list all available ODBC data sources. This is shown in Figure 3-2. Note that the New button is now disabled as you cannot create new ODBC data sources from this dialog box.

Figure 3-2.

The Select Connection or Datasource dialog box with data sources

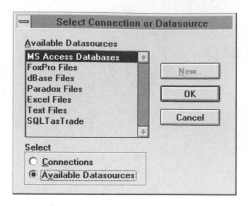

If no database is currently open you must use a data source to establish a connection. The Select Connection or Datasource dialog box will appear with the Connections OptionButton disabled.

If you use a saved connection with a user ID and password specified, you will not be prompted for any other information. If you use an ODBC data source or if that information is not saved in the connection, you will see the SQL Server Login dialog box. Enter the login ID and password to connect to the back-end server.

In the following code, more information is supplied to the SQLConnect() function. Specifically, a data source is specified, although no user ID or password is supplied.

```
? SQLConnect("tastrade")
```

When this code is run, you do not need to be prompted for a connection or data source. The first dialog box you will see is the SQL Server Login dialog box where you can enter the user ID and password.

In the next code sample, all of the information needed to establish a connection is supplied. The first line of code supplies a data source, user ID, and password. The second line of code supplies the name of a saved connection in the database. In cases like this there is no need for Visual FoxPro to prompt the user for additional information.

```
? SQLConnect("tastrade", "rgreen", "vfpgenius")
? SQLConnect("cnTastrade")
```

If the cnTastrade connection does not have the user ID and/or password specified, you will be prompted for the missing information.

If the connection to the back end was established, SQLConnect() will return a positive non-zero number. This number is a connection handle and represents a shorthand way of referring to the connection. All communication to the back end requires this handle. As a result, the handle should be stored to a memory variable, as shown in the following code. Typically, the first connection has a handle of 1, the second has a handle of 2, and so on. However, this is not guaranteed.

```
gnHandle = SQLConnect("cnTastrade"')
lcMessage = IIf(gnHandle < 0, "Connection didn't work.", ;
            "Welcome to SQL Server!")
= MessageBox(lcMessage)
```

If the connection cannot be established, SQLConnect() will return a negative number. If the saved connection or the data source specified does not exist, a -1 will be returned. If the connection or the data source is valid but the connection cannot be established for some other reason, a -2 will be returned. This could occur because of an invalid user ID or password. Perhaps the back-end server is not running or there are network problems.

You can trap for this error using AError() or Error() and Message(). For instance, the following code attempts to connect using a data source that does not exist. The error is then displayed, as is shown in Figure 3-3.

```
gnHandle = SQLConnect("myserver", "rgreen", "vfpgenius")
If gnHandle < 0
   lnError = AError(laError)
   = MessageBox(laError[2])
Endif
```

Figure 3-3.

The Data Source Name Not Found error message

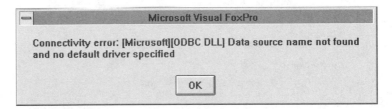

SQLStringConnect() Function

The SQLStringConnect() function can also be used to establish a connection to a back-end server. The following code sample shows the syntax for SQLStringConnect().

```
Syntax:
SQLStringConnect(lcConnectString)

Arguments:
lcConnectString            An ODBC connection string

Returns:
Numeric
```

The next code shows the use of this function to connect to SQL Server. As you can see, an ODBC connection string has the information you would expect—a data source name, user ID, password, and database.

```
? SQLStringConnect("DSN=tastrade;UID=rgreen;PWD=vfp genius;" + ;
                   "DATABASE=tastrade")
```

As is the case with SQLConnect(), if you do not supply all of the necessary pieces of the connection string, you will be prompted for the missing information. SQLStringConnect() returns a positive non-zero number if the connection is successful and a negative number if it is not.

Disconnecting from SQL Server

Before you see how to send SQL statements to the server and work with the results, you should learn how to disconnect from the server. Connections established with SQLConnect() or SQLStringConnect() are fairly resource intensive. If you make connections and leave them around, you could be using up valuable Windows resources. This is especially problematic if you are not using Windows NT or Windows 95, both of which have much larger resource pools.

The SQLDisconnect() function is used to break an existing connection. The following code shows the syntax for SQLDisconnect().

```
Syntax:
SQLDisconnect(lnConnectionHandle)

Arguments:
lnConnectionHandle      The handle number for an existing
                        connection

Returns:
Numeric
```

SQLDisconnect() returns a value of 1 if the connection was successfully terminated, a value of -1 if the termination failed due to a connection-level error, and a value of -2 if the termination failed because of an environment-level error. You can trap for the error, but there probably isn't much you can do about it. You can also assume that the connection is broken anyway, although the resources Visual FoxPro was using for it may not have been released. The next code sample shows code to connect to a server and then disconnect.

```
gnHandle = SQLConnect("cnTastrade")
If gnHandle > 0
  = MessageBox("Hello and goodbye from SQL Server")
  = SQLDisconnect(gnHandle)
Endif
```

> ### Tip!
>
> You should make gnHandle a public variable in your applications because you need to know the value of gnHandle to disconnect. For example, suppose you are connected to SQL Server and your application has an error. You receive the standard Visual FoxPro error message and use the Cancel command. You are then in the Command Window and you realize that you are still connected to SQL Server. In order to disconnect you need to know the value of gnHandle. However, unless gnHandle is public, the variable will be gone and the connection will remain.

The following sample code shows DISCONN.PRG, the program that will close existing connections. The program assumes the first connection is number 1. It keeps closing connections until it receives an error, presumably an invalid connection number. This program is not guaranteed to close all connections, but it should work most of the time.

DISCONN.PRG

```
lnHandle = 1
lnError = 0
On Error Do connerr
Do While .T.
  = SQLDisconnect(lnHandle)
  If lnError <> 0
    Exit
  Else
    lnHandle = lnHandle + 1
  Endif
Enddo

Procedure connerr
  lnError = Error()
EndProc
```

Executing SQL Statements

Once you have a connection to the back-end server established, you can send SQL statements to the server. These are "passed through" by Visual FoxPro without any front-end processing. The server takes the SQL statement, executes it, then sends the results to Visual FoxPro. It will also send errors and messages back if necessary. The following code shows the syntax for SQLExec().

```
Syntax:
SQLExec(lnConnectionHandle, lcSQL, [lcCursor])

Arguments:
lnConnectionHandle    The handle number for an existing
                      connection
lcSQL                 The SQL statement being sent to the
                      server
lcCursor              The name of a Visual FoxPro cursor to
                      store the results of a query

Returns:
Numeric
```

The SQL statement sent to the server can be any number of things: a simple Select statement, a complex Select statement, an Update or Insert statement, a command to run a stored procedure, or a command to perform an administrative function. If the server can understand and act on the statement, it will be run. If the server cannot run the statement, an error will be returned.

If the SQL statement is successfully executed, SQLExec() returns the number of result sets returned to Visual FoxPro. For instance, a single Select statement will return one result set consisting of all of the rows returned by the Select statement. If the SQL statement does not run, SQLExec() will return a negative number. If the error is at the connection level, SQLExec() will return -1. A connection level problem can be as simple as an improperly specified SQL statement or an attempt to Update a table to which you don't have rights. If the error is at the environment level, SQLExec() returns -2. An environment-level error could be a problem communicating across the network.

Select Statements

If the SQL statement returns results, they will be stored in a Visual FoxPro Cursor. When a Cursor name is not specified, Visual FoxPro will use a Cursor called *sqlresult*. Be aware that if a Cursor with that name is already in use it will be overwritten with the new results. The following code sends a Select to the server to bring down all orders shipped to London.

```
lnSuccess = SQLExec(gnHandle, "Select * From orders ;
                Where ship_to_city = 'London'")
```

When this code is run, the Select statement is sent to the server. If it works, lnSuccess will be equal to 1 and the London orders will be in a Cursor called sqlresult.

The next code sends the same Select statement but puts the results in a Cursor called c_London.

```
lnSuccess = SQLExec(gnHandle, "Select * From orders ;
                Where ship_to_city = 'London'", "c_London")
```

The following code sample sends two Select statements to the server. Because no Cursor name is specified, the results from the first Select will be in the Cursor sqlresult, and the results from the second Select will be in the Cursor sqlresult1.

```
lcSQL = "Select * From Where ship_to_city = 'London' ; " + ;
        "Select * From Where ship_to_city = 'Paris'"
lnSuccess = SQLExec(gnHandle, lcSQL)
```

Notice that the variable lcSQL contains two Select statements separated by a semicolon. Do not confuse this semicolon with the semicolon used as the Visual FoxPro line continuation character. When these Selects are sent to the server two result sets will be returned, each winding up in a different Cursor. In this case, lnSuccess will be equal to 2, the number of result sets that came back.

Tip!

The Cursor that contains the result set is read-only by default, although you will see later in the discussion "Updating Result Sets" that it can be made read and write.

In Section 2 you created parameterized views. By setting the value of a variable you could change the data a view returned. You can do the same with Select statements sent to the server with SQL Pass-Through. The following code shows the use of a parameter in a Select statement.

```
pcCity = "London"
lcSQL = "Select * From orders Where ship_to_city = ?pcCity"
lnSuccess = SQLExec(gnHandle, lcSQL, "c_orders_one_city")
```

Data Modification Statements

SQLExec() can be used to send Insert, Update, and Delete statements to modify data on the server. The next code sample sends an Update that will change the shipping name for all orders for the Seven Seas Imports company.

```
lcSQL = "Update orders Set ship_to_name = 'Six Seas Imports' " + ;
        "Where ship_to_name = 'Seven Seas Imports'"
lnSuccess = SQLExec(gnHandle, lcSQL)
```

If lnSuccess returns a negative number, the Update failed. This could be because of an error in the Update statement, insufficient update rights, or problems with the connection, among other reasons. If lnSuccess is equal to 1, the Update did not fail.

Be aware that if you look only at lnSuccess you can't say for sure that any data was changed. If 27 rows had a ship_to_name of "Seven Seas Imports," they would all be changed and SQLExec() would return a value of 1. If no rows had a ship_to_name of "Seven Seas Imports," there would be no rows to update. However, the Update still worked in the sense that SQL Server changed every row that met the condition in the Where clause. The fact that there might not be any rows to change does not mean the Update didn't work.

You can use the built-in SQL Server global variable @@Rowcount to see how many rows were updated. @@Rowcount returns the number of rows affected by the most recent SQL statement. The following code sends an Update to the server and then reports how many rows were affected.

```
lcSQL = "Update orders Set ship_to_name = 'Six Seas Imports' " + ;
        "Where ship_to_name = 'Seven Seas Imports'"
lnSuccess = SQLExec(gnHandle, lcSQL)
lnSuccess = SQLExec(gnHandle, "Select @@Rowcount", "c_numrows")
= MessageBox(Ltrim(Str(c_numrows.exp)) + " rows were updated.")
```

You can use @@Rowcount to see the number of rows affected after issuing any Select, Update, Insert, or Delete statement.

Stored Procedures

An excellent use of the SQL Pass-Through functions is running stored procedures. Stored procedures are precompiled SQL statements. There are two primary benefits to using stored procedures. The first is that they execute more quickly than ad-hoc SQL statements because they are precompiled and already optimized. The second benefit is that they can be used as a security measure. You can give a user the right to run a stored procedure, but not the right to query the underlying table or tables. That way the user can execute only the exact SQL statements he or she is given permission to run. The next code sample shows the SQL Server code to create a stored procedure. This stored procedure runs a Select statement to determine sales by year.

```
Create Procedure orders_by_year
As
Select Datepart(year, order_date), Sum(quantity*Unit_price)
From orders, order_line_items
Where orders.order_id = order_line_items.order_id
Group By Datepart(year, order_date)
```

The following Visual FoxPro code sends a request to SQL Server to run the stored procedure. The results will be stored in the Cursor c_order_by_year. This is shown in Figure 3-4.

```
lnSuccess = SQLExec(gnHandle, "Exec orders_by_year", "c_order_by_year")
If lnSuccess = 1
   Browse
Endif
```

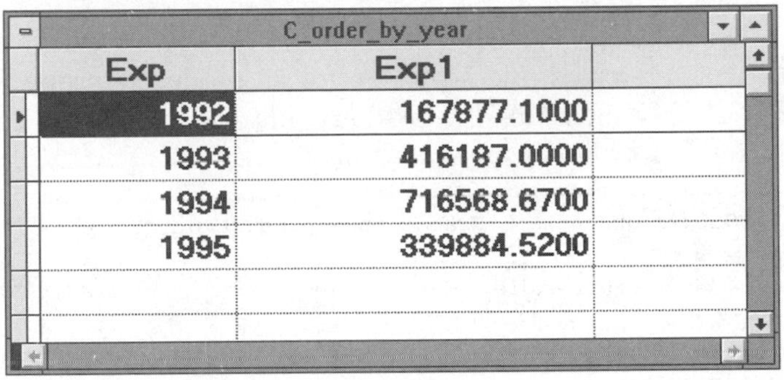

Exp	Exp1
1992	167877.1000
1993	416187.0000
1994	716568.6700
1995	339884.5200

Figure 3-4.

The c_order_by_year Cursor's browse

Stored procedures can take arguments. The next code sample creates a stored procedure that returns the total orders for one year.

```
Create Procedure orders_for_1_year
@ayear int
As
Select Datepart(year, order_date), Sum(quantity*Unit_price)
From orders, order_line_items
Where orders.order_id = order_line_items.order_id
   And Datepart(year, order_date) = @ayear
Group By Datepart(year, order_date)
```

The following code causes this stored procedure to be run for the specified year.

```
lnSuccess = SQLExec(gnHandle, "Exec orders_for_1_year 1993", ;
                     "c_orders1993")
If lnSuccess = 1
   Browse
Endif
```

Stored procedures are not limited to Select statements. A stored procedure can also be any combination of SQL statements. The following sample code creates a stored procedure that raises or lowers product prices for any products that cost less than a specified amount. The stored procedure takes two parameters, the percentage increase or decrease in price, and the price below which product prices will be changed.

```
Create Procedure change_product_prices
@apercent real
@apriceabove money
As
Update products
Set unit_price = unit_price * (1 + (@apercent/100))
Where unit_price <= @priceabove
```

The next code sample runs the previous stored procedure and raises prices by 50% for all products costing $25 or less. The code then uses the @@Rowcount variable to see how many product prices were changed.

```
lnSuccess = SQLExec(gnHandle, "Exec change_product_prices 50, 25")
If lnSuccess = 1
   lnSuccess = SQLExec(gnHandle, "Select @@Rowcount", "c_results")
   If lnSuccess = 1
      = MessageBox(LTrim(Str(c_results.exp)) + " prices were changed.")
      Use In c_results
   Else
   Endif
Else
Endif
```

Displaying Result Sets

The results of a Select statement sent to the server will be stored in a Visual FoxPro Cursor. You can programmatically access the data because it is in a Cursor and presumably you know what information is in each row and column. You can also display the information to the user.

The simplest way to see the data is to Browse it. The next code listing executes a Select statement to return all orders shipped to London. The data is stored in a Cursor called sqlresult. The Cursor is browsed and then closed.

```
lnSuccess = SQLExec(gnHandle, "Select * From orders ;
                     Where ship_to_city = 'London'")
Browse
Use In sqlresult
```

You can also create a Form to view the data. The Form
SPTORDER.SCX shown in Figure 3-5 displays orders information. The
data is retrieved by a Select statement and is stored in a Cursor. The
Form's TextBoxes each point to a field in the Cursor.

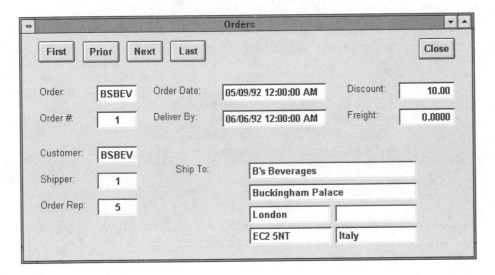

Figure 3-5.

**SPTORDER.SCX's
Orders Form**

The Select statement is run from the Form's Load event. This is
shown in the following code.

```
lnSuccess = SQLExec(gnHandle, "Select * From orders ;
                    Where ship_to_city = 'London'", ;
                    "c_LondonOrders")
```

The ControlSource property of each TextBox is set to the
appropriate field in the Cursor. For example, the ControlSource
property for the order_id TextBox is c_LondonOrders.order_id. You
can see this in Figure 3-6.

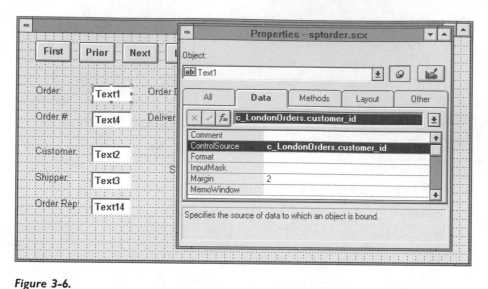

Figure 3-6.

**The TextBox
properties sheet**

The user can scroll back and forth among the records in the Cursor by using the record navigation CommandButtons. The Form's Unload event closes the Cursor. This is shown in the following code:

```
Use In c_LondonOrders
```

If you wanted the results of a sales-by-customer query to be printed in a report, you could do so with the next code listing. First a Select statement is run to retrieve sales by customer and then a report is run based on the resulting Cursor. The report is shown in Figure 3-7.

```
Wait Window "Retreiving results..." NoWait
lcSQL = "Select customer.company_name, Count(orders.order_id), " + ;
     "Sum(order_line_items.unit_price * ;
         order_line_items.quantity) " + ;
     "From customer, orders, order_line_items " + ;
     "Where customer.customer_id = orders.customer_id " + ;
     "  And orders.order_id = order_line_items.order_id " + ;
     "Group By customer.customer_id " + ;
     "Order By 3 Desc"
lnSuccess = SQLExec(gnHandle, lcSQL, "c_ordersbycomp")
Wait Window "Printing results..." NoWait
Report Form ordbycmp To Printer NoConsole

Use In c_ordersbycomp
```

Figure 3-7.

The Orders by Company report

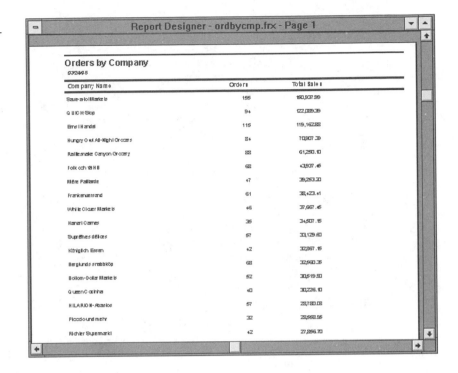

Finally, you might want to rely on some other software package to see the results. The next code sample uses OLE Automation to send the results of a sales-by-category query to Microsoft Excel. The data is stored in an Excel spreadsheet and is then graphed. The Excel spreadsheet is shown in Figure 3-8.

```
lcSQL = "Select category.category_name, " + ;
        "Sum(order_line_items.quantity * ;
            order_line_items.unit_price) " + ;
        "From products, order_Line_Items, orders, category " + ;
        "Where products.product_id = order_line_items.product_id " + ;
        "  And orders.order_id = order_line_items.order_id " + ;
        "  And category.category_id = products.category_id " + ;
        "Group By category.category_name"

Wait Window "Executing query..." NoWait
lnSuccess = SQLExec(gnHandle, lcSQL, "c_catsales")

If lnSuccess = 1
   *Report Form catsales Preview

   Wait Window "Starting Excel..." NoWait
   oXLSheet = CreateObject('Excel.Sheet')
   *oXLSheet.Application.Visible = .T.
   If Not Type('oXLSheet') = "O"
      = MessageBox("Problem starting Excel")
   Else
```

Continued on next page

Continued from previous page

```
      Wait Window "Moving query results to Excel..." NoWait
      oXLSheet.Cells(1, 1).Value = "Category"
      oXLSheet.Cells(1, 2).Value = "Sales"
      liCounter = 2
      Scan
         oXLSheet.Cells(liCounter, 1).Value = c_catsales.category_name
         oXLSheet.Cells(liCounter, 2).Value = c_catsales.exp
         liCounter = liCounter + 1
      EndScan

      Wait Window "Creating Excel chart..." NoWait
      oXLSheet.ChartObjects.Add(159, 25.5, 294, 168)
      oXLSheet.ChartObjects(1).Chart.ChartWizard(oXLSheetRange("A1:B9"), ;
         -4099, 4, 2, 1, 1, 2, "Total Sales by Category", "", "", "")
      oXLSheet.ChartObjects(1).Width = 450
      oXLSheet.ChartObjects(1).Height = 265.5
      oXLSheet.ChartObjects(1).Left = 114

      oXLSheet.SaveAs('c:\msoffice\excel\catsales.xls')
      Release oXLSheet
      Wait Window "Finished..." NoWait
   Endif

   Use In c_catsales
Endif
```

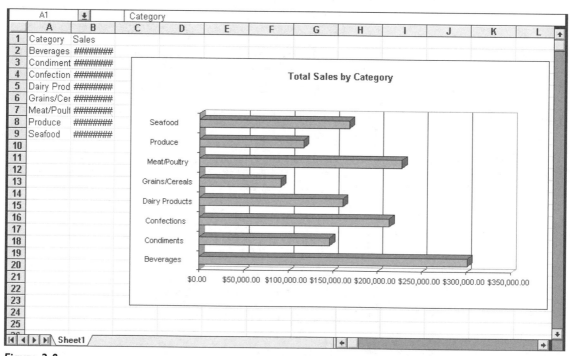

Figure 3-8.

An Excel spreadsheet and chart

Updating Result Sets

When you use SQL Pass-Through to send a Select statement to the server, the Cursor that stores the results is read-only. Actually, you can write to the Cursor but Visual FoxPro will not send your changes back to the server. By setting some important properties of the Cursor, you can turn it into a read-and-write Cursor. In Section 2 you looked at the properties of remote views and the Cursors they create. The Cursor created by SQL Pass-Through is the same type of Cursor with the same properties.

The following code sends a Select statement to the server and then tries to update a row in the resulting Cursor.

```
lnSuccess = SQLExec(gnHandle, "Select * From orders ;
                    Where ship_to_city = 'London'", ;
                    "c_LondonOrders")
Replace ship_to_name With "Devonshire"
```

The Replace seems to work. However, Visual FoxPro never actually updates the back end. If you ran the Select again, the changed row would once again have London as the ship_to_city.

In Section 2 you saw that views have many properties, one of which was the SendUpdates property. This property must be set to true for the view's Cursor to be updatable. Cursors also have properties. In fact, many of the properties of a view are actually properties of the Cursor created by the view. The five properties that must be set properly in order for a result set Cursor to be updatable are shown in Table 3-2.

Table 3-2.

Cursor properties that control updatability

Property	Description
SendUpdate	True if a SQL update query is sent to update remote tables. False otherwise.
Tables	A comma delimited list of the names of remote tables.
KeyFieldList	A comma delimited list of primary fields for the Cursor.
UpdateNameList	A comma delimited list of remote field names and the local field names assigned to the Cursor.
UpdatableFieldList	A comma delimited list of Cursor fields that can be updated.

The following code uses the CursorGetProp() function to determine the values of these five properties for the c_LondonOrders Cursor.

```
? CursorGetProp("SendUpdates", "c_LondonOrders")          && returns .F.
? CursorGetProp("Tables", "c_LondonOrders")               && returns blank
? CursorGetProp("KeyFieldList", "c_LondonOrders")         && returns blank
? CursorGetProp("UpdateNameList", "c_LondonOrders")       && returns blank
? CursorGetProp("UpdatableFieldList", "c_LondonOrders")   && returns blank
```

The most important property of these is SendUpdates. If this is false, updates will not be sent back to the server regardless of the settings of the other properties. However, setting SendUpdates to true is not enough to make the Cursor updatable. The other properties have to be set properly as well.

To make c_LondonOrders updatable, you first need to tell Visual FoxPro to send updates back to the server. You can do this as shown:

```
? CursorSetProp("SendUpdates", .T., "c_LondonOrders")
```

Then you need to tell Visual FoxPro that the remote table upon which this Cursor is based is the orders table. This can be done as follows:

```
? CursorSetProp("Tables", "orders", "c_LondonOrders")
```

Next, you need to identify the order_id field as the primary key as shown:

```
? CursorSetProp("KeyFieldList", "order_id", "c_LondonOrders")
```

Then you need to identify which fields in the Cursor can be changed. You can do so with this code:

```
? CursorSetProp("UpdatableFieldList", "ship_to_name, ship_to_address, ;
        ship_to_city", "c_LondonOrders")
```

Finally, you need to match the names of the updatable fields in the Cursor with the names of the fields on the server with the following syntax:

```
? CursorSetProp("UpdateNameList", "ship_to_name orders.ship_to_name, ;
        ship_to_address orders.ship_to_address, ;
        ship_to_city orders.ship_to_city , ;
        order_id orders.order_id", "c_LondonOrders")
```

All of these statements return true if the property is successfully changed.

Now you can update the record with the code shown.

```
Replace ship_to_city With "Devonshire"
```

An easy way to check that this worked is to close the Cursor and re-create it. As you will see, the change was sent back to the server.

Retrieving Information About Tables

The SQLTables() and SQLColumns() functions are used to retrieve information about tables in a database and about the columns in those tables. SQLTables() retrieves a list of all user tables, views, or system tables in a database. SQLColumns() retrieves a list of all columns in a particular table.

The following code shows the syntax for SQLTables().

```
Syntax:
SQLTables(lnConnectionHandle [, lcTableTypes] [, lcCursorName])

Arguments:
lnConnectionHandle        The handle number for an existing
                          connection
lcTableTypes              The type of table, can be 'TABLE',
                          'VIEW', 'SYSTEM TABLE'
lcCursorName              The name of a Visual FoxPro cursor
                          to store the results of the query

Returns:
Numeric
```

SQLTables() will return a value of 1 if the list was successfully retrieved, a value of -1 if a connection-level error occurs, and a value of -2 if an environment-level error occurs.

The SQLTables() function will return a list of user tables, views, or system tables, depending on the value of the lcTableTypes parameter. If you include two types of tables, the list will contain both of the table types. For instance, the first line of code in the following sample retrieves a list of user tables. The second line retrieves a list of user and system tables.

```
lnSuccess = SQLTables(gnHandle, "TABLE")
lnSuccess = SQLTables(gnHandle, "'TABLE', 'SYSTEM TABLE'")
```

Table 3-3 shows the structure of the Cursor created by the SQLTables() function.

Table 3-3.

The structure of Cursors created by SQLTables()

Column name	Description
Table_Qualifier	Table qualifier identifier
Table _Owner	Table owner identifier
Table _Name	The table name as it appears in the data dictionary
Table _Type	The table type as it appears in the data dictionary
Remarks	A description of the table

This code shows the syntax for SQLColumns():

```
Syntax:
SQLCOLUMNS(lnConnectionHandle, lcTableName [, FOXPRO | NATIVE] ;
          [, lcCursorName])

Arguments:
lnConnectionHandle      The handle number for an existing
                        connection
lcTableName             The name of the table whose columns
                        are retrieved
lcCursorName            The name of a Visual FoxPro cursor to
                        store the results of the query

Returns:
Numeric
```

SQLColumns() returns a value of 1 if the list was successfully retrieved, a value of -1 if a connection-level error occurs, and a value of -2 if an environment-level error occurs.

This function will return a list of the columns in a table as well as such information as the data type and width of the column. If you are using the function with native FoxPro data, specify it by passing "FOXPRO" to the function. If you are using the function with remote data, specify that by passing "NATIVE". The following code retrieves a list of columns for the products table in the SQL Server Tastrade database.

```
lnSuccess = SQLColumns(gnHandle, "products", "NATIVE")
```

Table 3-4 shows the structure of the Cursor created by the SQLColumns() function when it is used with remote data.

Table 3-4.

The structure of Cursors created by SQLColumns( )

Column name	Description
Table_qualifier	Table qualifier identifier
Table_owner	Table owner identifier
Table_name	Table identifier
Column_name	Column identifier
Data_type	Column data type
Type_name	Column data type name
Precision	Precision of the column
Length	Transfer size of the data
Scale	Scale of the column
Radix	Base for Numeric type
Nullable	Supports null values
Remarks	Description of the column

The Form DATASTRU.SCX is used to demonstrate the capabilities of these two functions. It is shown in Figure 3-9. A list box on the Form contains a list of user tables while a Grid on the Form contains column information for the selected table. As the user selects a different table, the Grid is updated with that table's column information.

Figure 3-9.

DATASTRU.SCX's Tastrade Data Structures Form

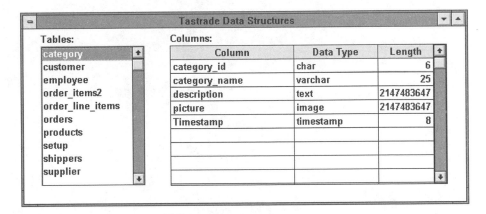

When the Form is first run, a connection is made to SQL Server and the SQLTables( ) function is used to retrieve a list of user tables. The results are stored in a Cursor. SQLColumns( ) is then used to retrieve column information for the first table in the list. This all occurs in the Load event of the Form, which is shown here:

```
Wait Window "Retrieving the list of tables..." NoWait

ThisForm.SQLHandle = SQLConnect("cnTastrade")

If ThisForm.SQLHandle < 0
  = MessageBox("Connect didn't work.")
  Return .F.
Endif

lnSuccess = SQLTables(ThisForm.SQLHandle, "table", "c_tables")
lnSuccess = SQLColumns(ThisForm.SQLHandle, c_tables.table_name, ;
                       "Native", "c_columns")
```

The RecordSource of the list box is the c_tables Cursor and the RecordSource of the Grid is the c_columns Cursor. The Grid has three columns, which contain the column_name field, the type_name field, and the precision field.

In the Init event of the Form, the first table in the list box is highlighted because that table's columns are in the Grid. In the InteractiveChange event of the list box, the SQLColumns() function is again used to retrieve the column information for the new selected table. This code is shown here:

```
Wait Window "Retrieving the table's column information..." NoWait

lnSuccess = SQLColumns(ThisForm.SQLHandle, ;
            ThisForm.lstTables.Value, "Native", "c_columns")

With ThisForm.grdColumns
  .DeleteMark = .F.
  .ReadOnly = .T.
  .RecordSource = "c_columns"
  .ScrollBars = 2
EndWith

With ThisForm.grdColumns.Column1
  .ControlSource = "c_columns.column_name"
  .Width = 171
EndWith

With ThisForm.grdColumns.Column1.Header1
  .Alignment = 2
  .Caption = "Column"
EndWith

With ThisForm.grdColumns.Column2
  .ControlSource = "c_columns.type_name"
  .Width = 117
EndWith

With ThisForm.grdColumns.Column2.Header1
  .Alignment = 2
  .Caption = "DataType"
EndWith
```

Continued on next page

```
With ThisForm.grdColumns.Column3
   .ControlSource = "c_columns.precision"
   .Width = 75
EndWith

With ThisForm.grdColumns.Column3.Header1
   .Alignment = 2
   .Caption = "Length"
EndWith

ThisForm.Refresh

Wait Clear
```

Tip!

When the RecordSource of the Grid changes, the Grid returns to its default behavior and shows every column in the Cursor. You need to reset all of the Grid's properties to see the three desired columns.

Synchronous and Asynchronous Processing

SQL Pass-Through functions all execute synchronously. This means that you have to wait until they are finished before you regain control of Visual FoxPro. This is fine most of the time. For instance, in the sample application there is a CommandButton on each Form that retrieves the total dollar amount of orders for the current record on the Form. Also, on each Form you can enter the ID of a record to which you want to go, and then you can click a CommandButton. The application sends a Select statement to the server to retrieve the information for the desired record.

In both of these cases the SQLExec() function is used to send a Select statement. The Select takes very little time to run so there is no problem making you wait for the results to come back.

There may be times, however, when you don't want to sit and wait for a SQL Pass-Through function to finish. You might want to use asynchronous mode to display a thermometer bar to monitor progress of a query. Perhaps you are retrieving a large number of rows and you want to work with the first group of rows while the rest are retrieved in the background. This is *progressive fetching*, which is automatic if you are using remote views. You might also want to have the ability to stop a query if it is taking too long or bringing back more rows than you wanted.

The Asynchronous property of a connection is used to enable asynchronous or synchronous processing. You can use DBSetProp() to change the default mode for a database connection, or use SQLSetProp() to change the mode for an active connection. The code shown here connects to SQL Server and then changes to asynchronous mode for that connection.

```
gnHandle = SQLConnect("cnTastrade")
lnSuccess = SQLSetProp(gnHandle, "Asynchronous", .T.)
```

The program ASYNCH.PRG is used to demonstrate using asynchronous mode to give the user the ability to cancel a query that is taking too long. This code is shown here:

ASYNCH.PRG

```
#Include misc\Foxpro.h
Wait Window "Connecting to SQL Server..." NoWait
gnHandle = SQLConnect("cnTastrade")
?SQLSetProp(gnHandle, "Asynchronous", .T.)

Wait Window "Executing SQL statement..." NoWait
lnExample = 3
Do Case
   Case lnExample = 1
      lcSQL = "Select DatePart(year, order_date), " + ;
              "DatePart(month, order_date), " + ;
              "Sum(unit_price*quantity) " + ;
              "From orders, order_line_items " + ;
              "Where orders.order_id = order_line_items.order_id " + ;
              "Group By DatePart(year, order_date), " + ;
              "DatePart(month, order_date)"
   Case lnExample = 2
      lcSQL = "Select customer.company_name, orders.order_id, " + ;
              "order_date, product_name, supplier.company_name " + ;
              "From orders, order_line_items, customer, " + ;
              "products, supplier " + ;
              "Where orders.order_id = order_line_items.order_id " + ;
              "And orders.customer_id = customer.customer_id " + ;
              "And order_line_items.product_id = products.product_id " + ;
              "And products.supplier_id = supplier.supplier_id "
   Case lnExample = 3
      lcSQL = "Select * From orders, order_line_items "
EndCase
lnStartTime = Seconds()
Do While .T.
   lnSuccess = SQLExec(gnHandle, lcSQL)
   If lnSuccess = 0 And Seconds() - lnStartTime > 10
      * The query is still running and at least 10 seconds have passed
      * since the query began or since the last time we checked.
      lnStartTime = Seconds()
If MessageBox("Still running. Do you want to continue?", ;
           MB_YESNO + MB_ICONQUESTION + MB_DEFBUTTON1) = IDNO
         If SQLCancel(gnHandle) = 1
           = MessageBox("SQL Statement cancelled.")
         Exit
      Else
```

Continued on next page

```
            = MessageBox("That's odd. The SQL Statement wouldn't cancel.")
         Endif
      Endif
   Else
      If lnSuccess < 0
         * There is an error.
         lnError = AError(laError)
         For i = 1 To ALen(laError,1)
            = MessageBox(laError(i, 2))
         Next i
         Exit
      Endif
      If lnSuccess > 0
         * The statement is finished executing.
         Exit
      Endif
   Endif
Enddo

= SQLDisconnect(gnHandle)
```

The SQLCancel() function is used to cancel the execution of the SQL statement. This function takes a connection handle as its only parameter. Whatever statement is executing on that handle will be canceled.

This program connects to the server and changes to asynchronous processing mode. A Select statement is then sent to the server. If the SQLExec() function returns a value of 0, the statement is still processing. The code then checks to see if 10 seconds have elapsed since the function began executing. If they have, the user is asked whether the SQLExec() should continue retrieving results. If they have not, the Select statement is canceled and the program is exited. The code always waits at least 10 seconds before asking the user whether or not to continue.

The program runs one of three Select statements, depending on the value of lnExample. The first Select returns 35 rows and takes well under 10 seconds to run, so the user is not prompted. The second Select returns 2820 rows. Depending on your hardware, this could take less than 10 seconds to run. If you change the code to wait only 5 seconds, the user should be prompted. The third Select is a Cartesian product. The orders and order_line_items tables are joined but there is no join condition. This Select would return 1078 times 2820 (or 3,039,960) rows. The user will be prompted repeatedly and, hopefully, will cancel the query before too long.

Batch Processing

The SQLExec() function can be used to send a single Select statement or multiple Select statments to the back end. If multiple Select statements are sent, they will be executed one at a time and so result sets will be returned to Visual FoxPro one at a time. By default, you will have to wait until all of the result sets are returned before control is returned to the application. The following code connects to SQL Server and sends two Select statements to be run. Notice the use of the semicolon to separate the two Select statements.

```
gnHandle = SQLConnect("cnTastrade")
lcSQL = "Select * From products ; Select * From supplier"
lnSuccess = SQLExec(gnHandle, lcSQL)
```

When you use the SQLExec() function you can either specify the name of the result set Cursor or you can let Visual FoxPro name it for you. If Visual FoxPro names it, the Cursor will be named sqlresult. If there is more than one result set, the first will be named sqlresult, the second sqlresult1, the third sqlresult2, and so forth.

Although you will sometimes want to wait for all of the result sets to be returned, there may be times when you want to execute code as each result set arrives. To do this, you must turn batch mode processing off. Batch mode is a property of a connection. By default, the BatchMode property of a connection is set to true, meaning that all result sets are retrieved in a batch and you have to wait for all of them to come back from the server.

The following code connects to SQL Server and then turns batch mode off for that connection.

```
gnHandle = SQLConnect("cnTastrade")
lnSuccess = SQLSetProp(gnHandle, "BatchMode", .F.)
```

The program BATCHON.PRG is used to demonstrate the ability to process result sets one at a time. This code is shown in the next code sample. The SQLMoreResults() function is used to see if more result sets are on their way. SQLMoreResults() returns a value of 1 if the next result set has been returned and a value of 2 if no more result sets are on their way. It returns a value of -1 or -2 if there is a connection-level error or environment-level error respectively.

BATCHON.PRG

```
Wait Window "Connecting to SQL Server..." NoWait
gnHandle = SQLConnect("cnTastrade")
?SQLSetProp(gnHandle, "BatchMode", .F.)

Wait Window "Executing SQL statement..." NoWait
lcSQL1 = "Select '1995', Sum(unit_price*quantity) " + ;
         "From orders, order_line_items " + ;
         "Where orders.order_id = order_line_items.order_id " + ;
         "And DatePart(year, order_date) = 1995"
lcSQL2 = "Select '1994', Sum(unit_price*quantity) " + ;
         "From orders, order_line_items " + ;
         "Where orders.order_id = order_line_items.order_id " + ;
         "And DatePart(year, order_date) = 1994"
lcSQL3 = "Select '1993', Sum(unit_price*quantity) " + ;
         "From orders, order_line_items " + ;
         "Where orders.order_id = order_line_items.order_id " + ;
         "And DatePart(year, order_date) = 1993"
lnSuccess = SQLExec(gnHandle, lcSQL1 + ";" + lcSQL2 + ";" + lcSQL3)
= MessageBox("Sales in " + exp + " were " + ;
             AllTrim(Transform(exp1, "$,$$$,$$$.99")))
Do While .T.
  lnMoreResults = SQLMoreResults(gnHandle)
  Do Case
    Case lnMoreResults = 1
      = MessageBox("Sales in " + exp + " were " + ;
                   AllTrim(Transform(exp1, "$,$$$,$$$.99")))
      Loop
    Case lnMoreResults = 2
      Exit
    Otherwise
      = MessageBox("Something happened.")
      = SQLCancel(gnHandle)
  EndCase

Enddo

= SQLDisconn(gnHandle)
```

This program connects to the server and turns batch mode processing off. Three Select statements are sent to the server via the SQLExec() function. Each Select returns the total sales for a particular year. When the SQLExec() is run, Visual FoxPro waits for the first result set. When it arrives, the program can run the next line of code to display the results of the first Select. Then, inside a Do loop, the SQLMoreResults() function is used to see when the next result set is returned. If it returns a value of 1, the next result set is available and the results are displayed. When it returns a value of 2, there are no more result sets, the Do loop is exited, and Visual FoxPro disconnects from the server.

Trapping for Errors

Visual FoxPro uses ODBC to send SQL statements to a back-end server. When the ODBC driver is finished processing a SQL statement, it returns a code to the application. The code indicates a few things: if the statement succeeded; if the statement succeeded and a message was generated; if the statement failed; if no data was found; if more information is needed from the application; or if the statement is still executing. In addition, if the driver was prevented from sending the statement to the data source, an error will be generated. Visual FoxPro automatically sends an ODBC error function to the driver manager to retrieve the information so it can be displayed to the user.

If the error originated in ODBC, indicating a programming error of some sort that prevented the SQL statement from reaching the server, the message will have the following form:

```
[vendor-identifier][ODBC-component-identifier]component-supplied
    text
```

An example is shown here:

```
[Microsoft][ODBC DLL]Function Sequence Error
```

If the error originated in the data source, the message will have the following form:

```
[vendor-identifier][ODBC-component-identifier][data-source
    identifier]data-source-supplied text
```

An example is shown here:

```
[Microsoft][ODBC SQL Server Driver][SQL Server]Invalid object name
    'ordres'
```

You can use AError() to trap for errors. AError() creates an array that stores error information. Each column in the array holds a different piece of information depending on where the error originated. Table 3-5 shows the information contained in the array if the error is a Visual FoxPro error.

Column	Contents
1	The error number
2	The error message
3	Either Null or Sys(2018)
4	Either Null or the work area where the error occurred
5	Either Null or the type of trigger that failed
6	Null
7	Null

The error number is stored in Column 1. This value is the same value you will get if you use the Error() function. Column 2 contains the error message, which is the same value you will get if you use the Message() function. Column 3 will usually be Null; however, some error messages need a parameter passed to them. A good example is an Alias Not Found error. Visual FoxPro will supply the error message with the name of the alias. This value will be stored in the third column, and is the same value as the value returned by the Sys(2018) function.

Column 4 will either be Null or it will contain the work area in which the error occurred. If this error was due to a trigger failing, Column 5 will contain a value of 1 if an insert trigger failed, a value of 2 if an update trigger failed, or a value of 3 if a delete trigger failed. If the error was not due to a failed trigger, Column 5 will be Null. Columns 6 and 7 are always Null if the error is a Visual FoxPro error.

The following code tries to select a work area that doesn't exist. The AError() function is used to populate an array with the error information. The contents of the error array are then displayed.

```
Select babaloo
? AError(laError)

LAERROR      Pub    A
   (   1,    1)    N  13              (          13.00000000)
   (   1,    2)    C  "Alias 'BABALOO' is not found."
   (   1,    3)    C  "BABALOO"
   (   1,    4)    C  .NULL.
   (   1,    5)    C  .NULL.
   (   1,    6)    C  .NULL.
   (   1,    7)    C  .NULL.
```

Table 3-6 shows the information contained in the array created by AError() if the error is an ODBC connectivity error (error number 1526).

Column	Contents
1	1526
2	The error message text
3	The ODBC error message text
4	The current ODBC SQL state
5	The error number from the ODBC data source
6	The ODBC connection handle
7	Null

The next code listing sends a Select statement to the server that references a table that does not exist. The AError() function is used to populate an array with the error information. The contents of the error array are then displayed.

```
lnSuccess = SQLExec(gnHandle, "Select * From prodcts")
lnError = AError(laError)

LAERROR      Pub    A
   (   1,   1)    N  1526          (      1526.00000000)
   (   1,   2)    C  "Connectivity error: [Microsoft][ODBC SQL
                                   Server Driver][SQL
Server] Invalid object
                                   name 'prodcts'."
   (   1,   3)    C  "[Microsoft][ODBC SQL Server Driver][SQL
                                   Server] Invalid object
name 'prodcts'."
   (   1,   4)    C  "S0002"
   (   1,   5)    N  208           (       208.00000000)
   (   1,   6)    N  1             (         1.00000000)
   (   1,   7)    C  .NULL.
```

Transaction Processing

A transaction is a unit of work. Everything in a transaction has to work successfully or none of it should work. For example, moving $5,000 from a savings account to a checking account involves two updates. First, the savings account has to be decreased by $5,000. Then the checking account has to be increased by $5,000. For obvious reasons, you either want both of these to occur or neither of these to occur. You would therefore make a transaction out of them. If something went wrong in between the updates, you would be returned to the point before any updates were made.

By default, every data modification statement in SQL Server is treated as a transaction. If you do a single delete or a single insert, that is considered a transaction. This is why you can issue a Rollback

Transaction in a SQL Server trigger. The trigger in the following code will reject any update to the product table that changes prices.

```
Create Trigger trProductsUpdate
On products
For Update
As
If Update (unit_price)
Begin
   Rollback Transaction
   Raiserror 99999 "You can't change product prices."
End
```

The Rollback Transaction in the trigger causes the Update that fired the trigger to be rolled back. The table is returned to the state it was in before the update occurred.

The SQL Server database used in the sample application has an orders table and an order_details table. Suppose you want to delete an order because it has been voided or is being archived. This will involve two deletes, one to delete the order and one to delete all of the detail records for the order. If you issue the first delete and then issue the second delete, you will have created two transactions, not one transaction with two deletes.

For this task you need to create a user-defined transaction. You don't want to delete the order but not the detail records, and vice versa. Visual FoxPro has a Begin Transaction command and an End Transaction command, but these work only with local data and cannot be used with remote data. However, you can use SQLSetProp() to set the Transaction property of a connection and start a transaction, then use either SQLCommit() to commit or SQLRollback() to roll back the transaction.

By default, the Transaction property of a connection is set to a value of 1, which denotes automatic transactions. This means every data modification statement is a transaction. To create your own transaction you need to set this property to a value of 2, which denotes manual transactions. This begins a transaction, and every data modification statement is added to the transaction until the transaction is ended with either a commit or a rollback.

Look at the following code to explore this further. It first checks to see if an order exists. Then it begins a transaction and deletes the order. The query is then run again to confirm that the order is gone, and then the transaction is rolled back and the query is run to prove that the order is not really gone.

```
? SQLSetProp(gnHandle, 'Transactions', 2)    && returns 1 for
                                                    success
? SQLExec(gnHandle, "Select Count(*) From orders " + ;
                "Where order_id = '    4'")
? sqlresult.exp   && returns 1 indicating the order is found

? SQLExec(gnHandle, "Delete orders Where order_id = '    4'")

? SQLExec(gnHandle, "Select Count(*) From orders " + ;
                "Where order_id = '    4'")
? sqlresult.exp   && returns 0 indicating the order is not found

? SQLRollback(gnHandle)

? SQLExec(gnHandle, "Select Count(*) From orders " + ;
                "Where order_id = '    4'")
? sqlresult.exp   && returns 1 indicating the order is found
```

The next code sample uses a transaction to delete both the order and the detail records. After each delete it checks to see if the delete worked. If anything went wrong the transaction will be rolled back. If everything appears to have worked the transaction will be commited.

```
? SQLSetProp(gnHandle, "Transactions", 2)    && returns 1 for
                                                    success
lnSuccess = SQLExec(gnHandle, "Delete orders Where order_id =
    '    4'")

If lnSuccess <> 1
  = SQLRollback(gnHandle)
  MessageBox("Something went wrong. The order was not deleted.")
  Return
Endif

lnSuccess = SQLExec(gnHandle, "Delete order_line_items " + ;
                                    "Where order_id =
    '    4'")

If lnSuccess <> 1
  = SQLRollback(gnHandle)
  MessageBox("Something went wrong. The order was not deleted.")
  Return
Endif

= SQLCommit()
= MessageBox("This order and all of its detail has been deleted.")
```

Controlling Connection and Cursor Behavior

In Section 2 you saw how to set properties of remote views. These properties can be changed in the view's definition with DBSetProp(), or for each use of the view with CursorSetProp(). In addition you saw how to set properties of a connection. These properties can be changed in the connection's definition with DBSetProp(), or for each use of the connection with SQLSetProp().

When you use SQL Pass-Through to access SQL Server data, you also use a connection. If you execute a Select statement, the results end up in a Cursor. You can change the properties of the Cursor using CursorSetProp() and you can change the properties of the connection using SQLSetProp().

This discussion covers some familiar material in a different context to give you a more complete understanding of the concepts. If some of the information in this part seems like it's being repeated from Section 2, that's a good sign. It means you understand that remote views and SQL Pass-Through are just two ways of executing SQL statements using the same connections and Cursors.

Connection Properties

Connections have default properties that can be viewed and changed in the Remote Data tab in the Options dialog box. This is shown in Figure 3-10. You can see that there are default properties for remote views and connections. When you create a connection using the Connection Designer, these will be the default properties. You can, of course, overwrite these properties for a particular database connection.

Figure 3-10.

The Remote Data tab in the Options dialog box

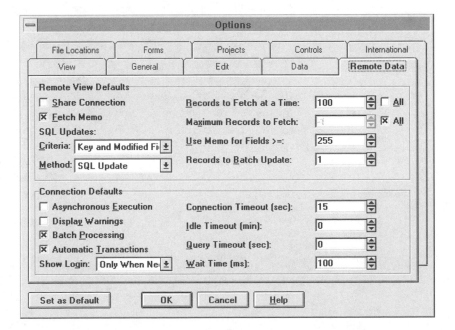

By specifying a connection handle of 0, you can set and change the connection default properties with the SQLSetProp() function. The following code uses SQLGetProp() to retrieve the default properties for connections.

```
? SQLGetProp(0, "ConnectTimeOut")      && returns 15
? SQLGetProp(0, "IdleTimeOut")         && returns 0
? SQLGetProp(0, "QueryTimeOut")        && returns 0
? SQLGetProp(0, "DispLogin")           && returns 1
? SQLGetProp(0, "DispWarnings")        && returns .F.
```

When you create a view or connect to the server, you can use a connection or an ODBC data source. If you use an ODBC data source, the connection will use the default connection properties. The next code sample connects to the server. It then uses SQLGetProp() to see the properties for the connection. They are the same as the defaults.

```
gnHandle = SQLConnect("tastrade", "rgreen", "bert")
? SQLGetProp(gnHandle, "ConnectTimeOut")    && returns 15
? SQLGetProp(gnHandle, "IdleTimeOut")       && returns 0
? SQLGetProp(gnHandle, "QueryTimeOut")      && returns 0
? SQLGetProp(gnHandle, "DispLogin")         && returns 1
? SQLGetProp(gnHandle, "DispWarnings")      && returns .F.
```

Now change some of the defaults. For instance, change the ConnectTimeOut to 30. This means that a connection time-out error will occur after 30 seconds (as opposed to never occurring if this property is set to 0). Also, change the DispLogin property. Currently the default is a value of 1, which means that the ODBC Login dialog box will be displayed only if the user leaves out the password, user ID, or data source. Change this property to a value of 2, which means the dialog box is always displayed, even if the user has filled in the expected information. The following code changes these default properties.

```
? SQLSetProp(0, "ConnectTimeOut", 30)    && returns 1, indicating success
? SQLSetProp(0, "DispLogin", 2)          && returns 1, indicating success
```

The next code sample connects to the server again. You can see in Figures 3-11 and 3-12 that even though you specified a data source you get the SQL Data Sources dialog box and then the SQL Server Login dialog box. The rest of the code in the sample shows that the new connection does have the new default properties.

```
gnHandle = SQLConnect("tastrade", "rgreen", "bert")
? SQLGetProp(gnHandle, "ConnectTimeOut")    && returns 30
? SQLGetProp(gnHandle, "IdleTimeOut")       && returns 0
? SQLGetProp(gnHandle, "QueryTimeOut")      && returns 0
? SQLGetProp(gnHandle, "DispLogin")         && returns 2
? SQLGetProp(gnHandle, "DispWarnings")      && returns .F.
```

Figure 3-11.

The SQL Data Sources dialog box

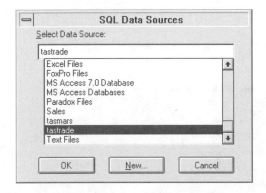

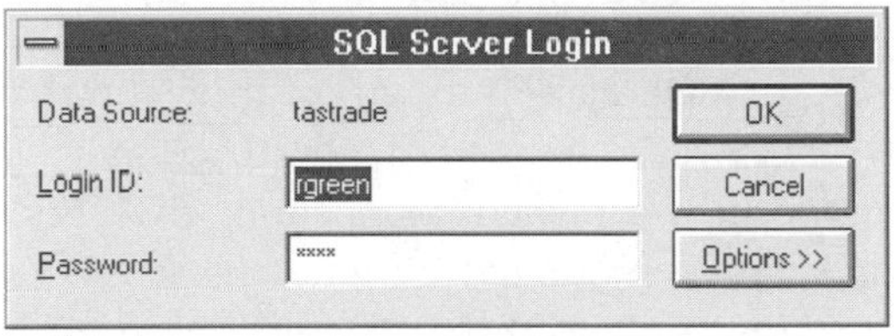

Figure 3-12.

The SQL Server Login dialog box

Now connect using a connection that is saved in the database. The following code connects using the cnTastrade connection and then looks at the connection's properties.

```
gnHandle = SQLConnect("cnTastrade")
? SQLGetProp(gnHandle, "ConnectTimeOut")    && returns 15
? SQLGetProp(gnHandle, "IdleTimeOut")       && returns 0
? SQLGetProp(gnHandle, "QueryTimeOut")      && returns 0
? SQLGetProp(gnHandle, "DispLogin")         && returns 1
? SQLGetProp(gnHandle, "DispWarnings")      && returns .F.
```

Notice that two of the properties, ConnectTimeOut and DispLogin, are different than the default connection properties you just set. If your connection is based on an ODBC data source, it will use the default connection properties. However, if you connect using a connection that is defined in the database, the properties come from the connection's definition. You can see in the Connection Designer shown in Figure 3-13 that the cnTastrade connection was created with a 15-second connection time out. Also, the login dialog box was set up to appear only if necessary information was missing.

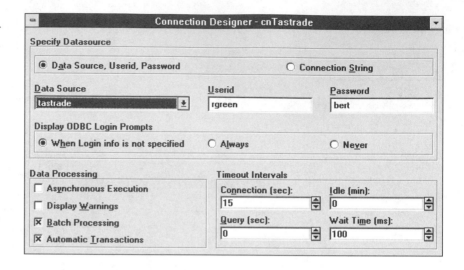

In the SQL Pass-Through examples in this section, you have used the SQLConnect() function to connect to a back-end server. You specified a named connection, cnTastrade, to use. The active connection, represented by gnHandle, uses the properties of the cnTastrade connection by default. These properties can be changed while the connection is in use. The following code establishes a connection and then uses SQLGetProp() to determine several properties of the active connection.

```
gnHandle = SQLConnect("cnTastrade")        && returns a connection handle
? SQLGetProp(gnHandle, "ConnectString")    && returns DSN=Tastrade;
                                           &&         UID=rgreen;
                                           &&         PWD=bert;
                                           &&         APP=Microsoft
                                           &&         Visual FoxPro;
                                           &&         WSID=ROBERTG;
                                           &&         DATABASE=tastrade
? SQLGetProp(gnHandle, "DataSource")       && returns Tastrade
? SQLGetProp(gnHandle, "UserId")           && returns rgreen
? SQLGetProp(gnHandle, "Password")         && returns bert
? SQLGetProp(gnHandle, "ConnectTimeout")   && returns 15
? SQLGetProp(gnHandle, "DispLogin")        && returns 1
? SQLGetProp(gnHandle, "DispWarnings")     && returns .F.
? SQLGetProp(gnHandle, "IdleTimeout")      && returns 0
? SQLGetProp(gnHandle, "QueryTimeout")     && returns 0
```

The values that are returned are the values set for the cnTastrade connection. Some of these properties, such as UserId, Password, and DataSource are read-only. These properties were used to make the connection and can't be changed in the middle while using that connection. Other properties can be changed. The next code sample changes some of the connection properties.

```
? SQLSetProp(gnHandle, "ConnectTimeout", 600)
? SQLSetProp(gnHandle, "DispWarnings", .T.)
? SQLSetProp(gnHandle, "IdleTimeout", 300)
? SQLSetProp(gnHandle, "QueryTimeout", 300)
```

Setting the ConnectTimeout property to 300 causes Visual FoxPro to wait 300 seconds, or 5 minutes, before generating a connection time-out error. Setting the DispWarnings property to .T. causes non-trappable warnings to be displayed. Setting the IdleTimeout property to 600 causes Visual FoxPro to wait 600 seconds, or 10 minutes, before deactivating the connection if it is not being used. Setting the QueryTimeout property to 300 causes Visual FoxPro to wait 300 seconds, or 5 minutes, before generating a general time-out error.

Cursor Properties

Just like connections, Cursors have default properties. By specifying a Cursor of 0 you can set and change the default Cursor properties with the CursorSetProp() function. The following code uses CursorGetProp() to retrieve the default properties for Cursors.

```
? CursorGetProp("BatchUpdateCount", 0)     && returns 1
? CursorGetProp("FetchMemo", 0)            && returns .T.
? CursorGetProp("FetchSize", 0)            && returns 100
? CursorGetProp("MaxRecords", 0)           && returns -1
? CursorGetProp("UpdateType", 0)           && returns 1
? CursorGetProp("UseMemoSize", 0)          && returns 255
? CursorGetProp("WhereType", 0)            && returns 3
```

If the Cursor comes from a view, the Cursor will use the properties set in the View Designer. If the Cursor comes from a SQL Pass-Through statement, it will use the default properties that you saw in the Remote Data tab in the Options dialog box. The next code sample connects to the server. You then use SQLGetProp() to see the properties for the connection. They are the same as the defaults.

```
lnSuccess = SQLExec(gnHandle, "Select * From orders Where " + ;
                    "ship_to_city = 'London'")

? CursorGetProp("BatchUpdateCount", "sqlresult")   && returns 1
? CursorGetProp("FetchMemo", "sqlresult")          && returns .T.
? CursorGetProp("FetchSize", "sqlresult")          && returns 100
? CursorGetProp("MaxRecords", "sqlresult")         && returns -1
? CursorGetProp("UpdateType", "sqlresult")         && returns 1
? CursorGetProp("UseMemoSize", "sqlresult")        && returns 255
? CursorGetProp("WhereType", "sqlresult")          && returns 3

Use
```

Now change some of the defaults. Change the FetchSize to 200. This means data will be brought into Visual FoxPro in chunks of 200 records instead of 100 records. Also change the UseMemoSize property. Currently the default is 255, which means that any character field over 255 in length will be stored in the Cursor in a memo field. You will change this property to 100. The following code changes these default properties.

```
? CursorSetProp("FetchSize", 200, 0)      && returns .T.
? CursorSetProp("UseMemoSize", 100, 0)    && returns .T.
```

The next code sample reruns the Select statement and re-creates the Cursor. You then use CursorGetProp() to show that the Cursor has the new default properties.

```
lnSuccess = SQLExec(gnHandle, "Select * From orders Where " + ;
                    "ship_to_city = 'London'")

? CursorGetProp("BatchUpdateCount", "sqlresult")   && returns 1
? CursorGetProp("FetchMemo", "sqlresult")          && returns .T.
? CursorGetProp("FetchSize", "sqlresult")          && returns 200
? CursorGetProp("MaxRecords", "sqlresult")         && returns -1
? CursorGetProp("UpdateType", "sqlresult")         && returns 1
? CursorGetProp("UseMemoSize", "sqlresult")        && returns 100
? CursorGetProp("WhereType", "sqlresult")          && returns 3

Use
```

Summary of View, Cursor, and Connection Properties

Table 3-7 lists view, Cursor, and connection properties; whether the property relates to views or connections; and which of the three functions can be used to set or read the property.

Table 3-7.

View, Cursor, and connection properties

Property	DBGetProp()	SQLGetProp()	CursorGetProp()
View Properties			
BatchUpdateCount	X		X
Buffering			X
Comment	X		
ConnectionHandle			X
ConnectName	X		X
Database			X
FetchMemo	X		X
FetchSize	X		X
KeyFieldList			X
MaxRecords	X		X
SendUpdates	X		X
ShareConnection	X		
SourceType	X		
SQL	X		X
Tables	X		X
UpdatableFieldList			X
UpdateNameList			X
UpdateType	X		X
UseMemoSize	X		X
WhereType	X		X
Field Properties			
KeyField	X		
Updatable	X		
UpdateName	X		
Connection Properties			
Asynchronous	X	X	
BatchMode	X	X	
Comment	X		
ConnectName		X	
ConnectString	X	X	
ConnectTimeout	X	X	
DataSource	X	X	
DispLogin	X	X	

Continued on next page

Continued from previous page

Property	DBGetProp()	SQLGetProp()	CursorGetProp()
DispWarnings	X	X	
IdleTimeout	X	X	
Password	X	X	
QueryTimeout	X	X	
Transactions	X	X	
UserID	X	X	
WaitTime	X	X	

Summary

In the last two sections you have seen how to access SQL Server from Visual FoxPro. You now know how to retrieve data from the server and view and edit it in Visual FoxPro. In the next section you will begin to design a client/server application.

4 | Designing a Client/Server Application

Before you start coding an application you need to design it. There are many steps involved with a proper design. You have to figure out the database structure and make several decisions: what tables will you need and how they are related? What Forms will you need and what can the user do on them? What reports will be needed and where will the data come from? Whether you are building a simple stand-alone application or a complex client/server application, you have to answer these questions before proceeding with coding.

When you are creating a client/server application you have additional issues, especially when the front end is an application as powerful as Visual FoxPro. In the early days of client/server development, the front end had no database capabilities of its own. It was a GUI design tool for creating the visual interface (the screens, menus, reports, and so forth). It had a scripting language that allowed you to move the cursor to a particular control, have a Form appear when the user clicked a CommandButton, and provide all of the other visual control you needed.

What the early front ends did not allow was the ability to split the data management work between the front end and the back end. The back end was the database, so all querying, data modification, data validation, and other tasks had to occur there.

Visual FoxPro is an excellent tool for designing GUI front ends. You could, if you wanted, use it to draw the forms and other visual elements of an application, relying totally on the back end for all data services. However, you can write a better client/server application if you take advantage of all of Visual FoxPro's capabilities.

In this section, you will not design the entire sample application. Instead, you will take the data as a given and use the Tastrade sample application that ships with Visual FoxPro. In the next section, you will upsize this data to SQL Server. In this section you will also design how to split the work between Visual FoxPro and SQL Server. Both have very powerful database engines and you want to leverage their respective strengths to come up with the best application.

Data Partitioning

Data can either be stored in SQL Server tables or Visual FoxPro tables. In a client/server application, data that changes frequently will typically be stored in SQL Server to take advantage of SQL Server's security and data integrity features. Static data should be stored in a way that strikes a balance between issues of performance and efficiency and issues of integrity, security, and ease of administration. The performance concerns involve network traffic as well as whether Visual FoxPro or SQL Server can perform an operation faster. The efficiency issue involves letting Visual FoxPro perform tasks to ease the processing burden on SQL Server. The integrity issue is concerned with maintaining data integrity, while the security issue involves keeping data secure. Finally, the administration issue involves minimizing the administrative burden of having things happen in both Visual FoxPro and SQL Server.

For example, suppose that an application requires a lookup table of zip codes. Instead of residing in SQL Server, this data can be stored in Visual FoxPro tables. This could improve application response time while reducing server traffic. Because the zip code table changes infrequently, there should be no adverse impact on application integrity and security if it is stored in a Visual FoxPro table.

Now suppose that an application contains a discount schedule table. The table is used when entering orders to determine the size of any discounts. Perhaps the discount schedule is updated on a weekly basis. Should this table be stored in SQL Server or in Visual FoxPro? Data entry speed may be improved if it is stored in Visual FoxPro. However, there is an administrative burden in having to update the Visual FoxPro table every week.

If storing static tables in Visual FoxPro gave no perceptible performance improvement, there would be little benefit to this splitting of data. Administration would be complicated by having the same data in two different places. However, if storing lookup tables locally reduced the time required to validate a zip code from two seconds to less than one second, it certainly might be worth trading off an increased administrative burden. The strength and power of the Visual FoxPro data engine gives the developer the flexibility of storing static tables in SQL Server or in Visual FoxPro.

However, if the data changes too often it might not be worth splitting, even if performance improves. Consider a table that contains daily interest rates. The administrative burden of having to update this table daily may offset any performance improvement.

Application Partitioning

There are many ways of setting up a client/server application. Consider several client/server application schemes. Scheme A involves one site with the data residing in Visual FoxPro. All data entry occurs in Visual FoxPro. The data is then exported to SQL Server in an overnight batch process. Querying is based either on the local Visual FoxPro data or on the remote SQL Server data.

Scheme B is a two-site version of Scheme A. It consists of a central office running SQL Server and field offices that enter data into Visual FoxPro during the day then upload it to the central office SQL Server at night. Querying at the field offices is based either on the local Visual FoxPro or on the remote SQL Server data.

Scheme C is a variation of Scheme B. It consists of a central office running SQL Server and field offices that enter data into Visual FoxPro during the day, then upload the data to a local SQL Server at night. The data is then exported from the local SQL Server to the central office SQL Server at night. Querying at the field offices is based either on local Visual FoxPro or on local or remote SQL Server data.

These three scenarios are not necessarily what people mean when they refer to a client/server application because the data is entered into Visual FoxPro and then exported to SQL Server. However, the client/server aspect is there because querying can be based on Visual FoxPro data or on SQL Server data.

In each of these three schemes data is exported to SQL Server in a batch process. This could be done with a series of Insert statements, although it would be more efficient to use the SQL Server Bulk Copy Program (BCP). To export data from Visual FoxPro to SQL Server, the data can be copied to text files and then imported into SQL Server. To export data from SQL Server to SQL Server, you can use the BCP or replication (if you are using SQL Server 6).

Another scenario, Scheme D, involves one site where the data resides on SQL Server. Data is entered into SQL Server through the

Visual FoxPro front end. Querying is based on the remote SQL Server data.

Scheme E is a two-site version of Scheme D. It consists of a central office running SQL Server and field offices that also run SQL Server with a Visual FoxPro front end. The field offices enter data into their local SQL Server throughout the day, then upload it to the central office SQL Server at night. Querying at the field offices is based either on local or remote SQL Server data.

Scheme D is the most common client/server implementation (especially for departmental applications), and represents the situation in the sample application in this report. Scheme E is a traditional distributed client/server implementation. In Scheme E, data is exported from the local SQL Server to the central office SQL Server. Again, this can be accomplished with the BCP or replication if SQL Server 6 is being used. Replication can be used to update one SQL Server with data from another. This could also be used in Schemes C and E. Replication can be scheduled to occur at set intervals, perhaps every two hours, or at a particular time, possibly each day at 9:00 P.M.

Data Validation

The Visual FoxPro language allows complex data validation to be coded into the front-end application. Does it make sense in a SQL Server application to have Visual FoxPro perform data validation? The following cases provide examples of what types of validation can best be performed in Visual FoxPro and which are best suited for SQL Server.

Case 1: Suppose one of the rules of the database is that zip codes must consist solely of numbers. In SQL Server this is a simple task. A rule that enforces numeric zip codes can be created, then bound to the zip code column in the appropriate tables. The following code creates such a rule and binds it to the postal_code column in the customer table:

```
Create Rule rulzipcode
As @zip Like "[0-9] [0-9] [0-9] [0-9] [0-9]"

sp_bindrule rulzipcode, "customer.postal_code"
```

If a record is inserted or updated and the zip code does not consist solely of numbers, SQL Server will reject the data because the zip code rule is violated. An error message would be returned to Visual FoxPro whether the user was in a view or the data was sent to SQL Server via the SQLExec() function.

In Visual FoxPro this is a also simple task. The zip code TextBox control on a Form can have its InputMask property set to "99999" to force the user to enter only numbers into the zip code field.

Even if there is a rule in the SQL Server table it makes sense to duplicate this on the Visual FoxPro Form. The effect of using an input mask in Visual FoxPro is immediate. Only numbers are accepted by the field. Relying on the SQL Server rule requires sending the entire record to the server and having it rejected for violating the rule. Visual FoxPro must then capture the error and inform the user why the data was rejected. By addressing validation up-front in the Visual FoxPro application, response time is improved and server traffic is reduced. The system also becomes easier to use.

Case 2: Suppose a system requires that data entry be validated against a zip code table. Once again the developer has a choice: the zip code table could be stored as a Visual FoxPro table on the network server or it could be stored on SQL Server. In either case, validation can be handled at the time of entry so that the user is informed immediately if there is an incorrect entry.

If the zip codes are stored in a Visual FoxPro table, the following code sample could be in the Valid event of the zip code TextBox.

```
Local lxRetVal, lcMessage
lxRetVal = .T.

Select city, state ;
From zipcodes ;
Where zip = ThisForm.txtZipCode.Value ;
Into Cursor c_zip

* Are the city or state on the form correct for this zip code?
If c_zip.city <> ThisForm.txtCity.Value ;
   Or c_zip.state <> ThisForm.txtState.Value
   lcMessage = "The zip code does not match the city and state."
   = MessageBox(lcMessage, MB_ICONEXCLAMATION)
   lxRetVal = 0
Else
   lxRetVal = .T.
Endif

* Close the cursor.
Use In c_zip
Return lxRetVal
```

If the zip codes are stored in a SQL Server table, the next code sample could be the code in the Valid event for the zip code control.

```
Local lxRetVal, lnResCode, lnError, lcMessage
lxRetVal = .T.

* Get city and state for this zip code from the
* zipcodes table.
lcSQL = "Select city, state From zipcodes " + ;
        "Where zip = '" + ThisForm.txtZipCode.Value + "'"

* Call the function SQLExec to send the SQL statement to the
* server.
lnResCode = SQLExec(gnHandle, lcSQL, "c_zip")

If lnResCode < 0
   lnError = AError(laError)
   = MessageBox(laError[2], MB_ICONINFORMATION)
   Return .F.
Endif

* Are the city or state on the form correct for this zip code?
If c_zip.city <> ThisForm.txtCity.Value ;
   Or c_zip.state <> ThisForm.txtState.Value
   lcMessage = "The zip code does not match the city and state."
   = MessageBox(lcMessage, MB_ICONEXCLAMATION)
   lxRetVal = 0
Else
   lxRetVal = .T.
Endif

* Close the cursor.
Use In c_zip
Return lxRetVal
```

These two versions of the zip code validation are very similar. The only difference is the source of the zip code data.

Storing lookup tables in Visual FoxPro tables may speed up application response time. With the proper indexes, Visual FoxPro may locate a record in less time than it takes SQL Server to perform the same process. In addition to the speed improvement, relying on Visual FoxPro for static lookups will reduce the processing burden on SQL Server, thereby improving overall application performance. Of course, performance considerations may in some cases be outweighed by integrity and security issues.

Case 3: Suppose there is a rule whereby the price of a product cannot be increased by more than $10. This kind of validation can be enforced in SQL Server by attaching a trigger to the products table. A trigger is a stored procedure that is automatically executed whenever changes are made to the data in a table. A table can have an insert trigger, an update trigger, and a delete trigger. The following code creates an update trigger that prevents the price of any product from being raised by more than $10:

```
Create Trigger update_price
On products
For Update
As
If (Select inserted.price - deleted.price
    From inserted, deleted
    Where inserted.title_id = deleted.title_id) > 10
Begin
  Rollback Transaction
  Raiserror 99999 "Can't raise the price of a product by more
    than $10."
End
```

The *deleted* table stores a copy of the original data for the product, while the *inserted* table stores a copy of the updated data for the product. When the user updates a product, SQL Server compares the before and after prices to see if the business rule has been violated. If so, the data will be rejected by SQL Server and an error message will be sent back to Visual FoxPro. As always, you can use AError() to determine the error message and then use MessageBox() to display it to the user. Notice the use of Raiserror to make the trigger return an error number. As long as the trigger returns an error number, Visual FoxPro will be informed that the trigger prevented the update.

This type of rule can also be programmed in Visual FoxPro. The code to compare the original price to the new price can be contained in the event code that saves the record and can be in the price control's Valid event. It can be a database stored procedure called from a validation rule. A benefit to using the Valid event is that the user is informed immediately if an invalid price is entered. If the SQL Server trigger is used, the user will not know that an invalid price was entered until the entire record is sent to the server and then rejected. The following Visual FoxPro code shows how to prevent a product's price from rising by more than $10. This code would be placed in the Valid event of the price field TextBox.

```
If price - OldVal("price") > 10
  = MessageBox("You can't raise the price of a product by " + ;
          "more than $10", MB_ICONEXCLAMATION)
  Return .F.
Endif
```

If the rule changes so that the price of a product may not be raised by more than 25 percent, the SQL Server trigger has to be updated. If the rule is also programmed into Visual FoxPro, then the Visual FoxPro code also has to be changed. This duplication of effort will often be unnecessary. The trigger will always reject invalid price increases, so there may be no need to duplicate the price checking in Visual FoxPro. If the validation code is in the Save button's Click event, the user is told after the Save button was clicked that the data was rejected. This is true regardless of how the validation is handled. However, if the ability to have data validation occur immediately is important, then duplicating the price rule in a Valid event may be a good plan.

Case 4: Suppose that there is a rule whereby new orders cannot be accepted if a customer has a balance of $10,000 more than 60 days overdue. This validation can be enforced in SQL Server by attaching a trigger to the appropriate table. If the user attempts to enter a new order, SQL Server checks the table that contains the receivables information to see if the order violates the rule. This type of rule can also be programmed in Visual FoxPro. When the user wants to save a new order record, Visual FoxPro can send a Select statement to SQL Server to return the customer's 60-day balance.

It rarely makes sense to maintain this type of rule in both places. Visual FoxPro cannot enforce the rule without querying the SQL Server tables, so there is no performance benefit to having Visual FoxPro perform the validation. Either way, the validation will occur as the record is being saved so it makes no difference to the user. Rather than maintain the rule in two locations, you should use only SQL Server.

Data and Referential Integrity

SQL Server supports referential integrity through the use of triggers tied to tables. A delete trigger can be written to delete all child records if the parent record is deleted. An insert trigger can be written to reject the insertion of a child record if the parent record doesn't exist. Once this type of trigger is in place, any changes to the data that violate integrity are rejected.

Tip!
SQL Server 6 supports declarative referential integrity. This removes the need to write triggers to enforce referential integrity.

The trigger in the following code prevents a product from being deleted if there are active order detail records for that product.

```
Create Trigger del_product
On products
For Delete
As
If (Select Count(*) From deleted, order_line_items
     Where order_line_items.product_id = deleted.product_id) > 0
Begin
   Rollback Transaction
   Raiserror 99999 "You can't delete a product with active orders."
End
```

When a Delete statement is sent to the server this trigger will be automatically executed. The *deleted* table stores a copy of the deleted product's record. The Select statement checks to see if there are any records in the order_line_items table for this product. If there are, then this product has active orders and the trigger rejects the deletion. The use of Raiserror ensures that SQL Server returns an error so that Visual FoxPro will know the Delete failed.

The trigger in the next code sample prevents orphan records by deleting information for an order from the orders table and from the order_line_items table (one row for each order).

```
Create Trigger del_order
On orders
For Delete
As
Delete order_line_items
From order_line_items, deleted
Where deleted.order_id = order_line_items.order_id
```

Visual FoxPro also supports referential integrity through triggers. These triggers will typically be stored procedures in the database. However, Visual FoxPro does not allow triggers on remote views. Relationships between SQL Server tables can only be enforced in Visual FoxPro through coding. Each of the previously mentioned triggers can be coded into a Visual FoxPro system. For instance, before sending the Insert statement to add a child record, Visual FoxPro can send a Select statement to retrieve the parent record. If the Select statement does not bring back any data, the parent record doesn't exist and the Insert statement would not be sent.

It would rarely make sense to enforce referential integrity in the front end rather than in the server. There is no guarantee that Visual FoxPro is the only front end used to access SQL Server. What happens if an Access application needs to use SQL Server data? If referential integrity is not maintained on SQL Server, it would have to be coded into the Access application. There's no point in writing this in every front end when you can write it once on the back end.

This type of protection needs to be at the server level so it is enforced regardless of how the data is accessed.

Enforcing referential integrity in both the front end and the back end simply makes you write a lot of code to do things that were going to happen anyway.

Data Security

Security can be built into a Visual FoxPro application. Upon entering the system, users can be presented with a sign-in screen that asks for a valid user ID and password. This can prevent unauthorized access to the system. Once inside the system, you can prevent users from performing specific actions by assigning them an access level and barring them from performing certain actions if they do not have the appropriate access level. This can also be accomplished by assigning users to a group and basing access to system features on the group level.

It's a straightforward task to deny access at the functional level, for instance preventing a user from accessing a screen or report. It is more difficult to deny access at the data level. Suppose that a user is not allowed to see a salary field. It's easy to set the field's Visible property to false on a screen. But what happens during the creation of ad-hoc reports and queries? How can the user be prevented from accessing the field? Ideally, security should occur at the data level, not at the process level. This is difficult to achieve in Visual FoxPro.

Visual FoxPro tables are not secure from prying eyes. The Visual FoxPro table format is well-known and therefore Visual FoxPro tables can be easily read by several other software packages. This could give someone the ability to bypass the system security and view the data directly using Access or Q+E. A way to reduce, but not eliminate, this problem is by encrypting the Visual FoxPro data. However, encryption imposes a performance penalty. It also makes it virtually impossible to give a user the ability to produce ad-hoc reports and queries. Unauthorized users can be denied rights to the network directory containing the data. However, this does not provide varying access to different files or to certain fields or records within a file.

Although there are a large number of applications that can access SQL Server data, SQL Server has very robust security built in. To connect to the server a user must supply a valid user ID and password. By default, a new user has no rights to view any data; all rights must be explicitly assigned. The system administrator can grant permissions to control access at the database, table, row, and column levels.

Security in SQL Server is at the data level. It is enforced by the data engine, not in code used to access the data. This centralization of security ensures that no matter how the SQL Server data is accessed the security scheme is in place. All front ends must respect the security that is set up in SQL Server.

Views

SQL Server views can be used to limit a user's access to certain rows or columns in tables. Views are SQL statements that act as filters. For instance, the customer table contains name and address information for each customer. In addition, there is information on the minimum order amount, maximum order amount, and discount for each customer. The following code could be used to create a view that excludes this additional information.

```
Create View vw_customer_name_address
As
Select customer_id, company_name, contact_name, contact_title,
       address, city, region, postal_code, country, phone, fax,
       sales_region
From customer
```

If a user is given access to the customer_name_address view and not to the customer table itself, that user will not be able to see the minimum order, maximum order, or discount fields. The user can enter new data and change existing data in the customer table as long as that data appears in the view.

Views can also be used to filter out rows. For instance, the next code sample creates a view that will exclude all customers who can't place orders for more than $1,000 and a view that will include only the rest of the customers.

```
Create View vw_small_customers
As
Select *
From customer
Where max_order_amt <= $1000

Create View vw_large_customers
As
Select *
From customer
Where max_order_amt > $1000
```

Suppose that you have two types of customers, large and small. Each type has different sets of reps entering orders. The reps who deal with small customers are not allowed to view large customer information, and the reps who deal with large customers are not allowed to view small customer information. You can accomplish this by giving small customer reps access to the vw_small_customer view while large customer reps have access to the vw_large_customer view.

Permissions

A rule of thumb in SQL Server is "You create it, you own it." The owner of a database is the person who created it. If the system administrator creates a database and its tables, by default the system administrator is the only one who can use the database. The fact that users can log in to SQL Server does not mean that they can use any particular database. If a user has explicitly been given access to the database (via the sp_adduser stored procedure) or if a "guest" user has been added to the database, that user can access the database. Only the system administrator or database owner can add someone to the list of users for a database.

Specific rights can be assigned or taken away by the system administrator or the database owner, and rights can be assigned to users or to groups. Each database has a Public group to which all users belong. In addition, each user can belong to one additional group in that database. A particular user could have Select rights on a table but not Insert, Update, or Delete rights.

When a user in the front-end application accesses some data, SQL Server can be queried to find out the permissions this user has regarding this data. If the user does not have Insert rights, the Add button on the Form can be disabled. You will see how to do this in Section 6, "Developing a Client/Server Application."

Stored Procedures

You saw that views can be used to limit the data a user can see. Giving the user permission to use the view but not the underlying table(s) is really the same as denying the user the right to see the data left out of the view. Another way to control what users can do is to use stored procedures. As an example, you might want certain users to be able to view customer name and address information, but not the other fields in the customer table. You could create a stored procedure that issues a Select statement, then give users permission to execute the stored procedure while withholding permission to Select from the table. The following code shows a stored procedure that retrieves company name and address information from the customer table.

```
Create Procedure customer_info
As
Select company_name, address, city, region,
       postal_code, country
From customer
```

If a user is allowed to use only the stored procedure, he or she is allowed to issue only the Select statement in the stored procedure. To be more flexible, you would probably create stored procedures that accept parameters. The next code sample creates stored procedures to retrieve the company name and address information for customers in one or more cities and in one or more countries. Each stored procedure is then executed to retrieve customers.

```
Create Procedure customer_info_city
@acity
As
Select company_name, address, city, region,
       postal_code, country
From customer
Where city Like @acity

Exec customer_info_city "London"
Exec customer_info_city "S%"

Create Procedure customer_info_country
@acountry
As
Select company_name, address, city, region,
       postal_code, country
From customer
Where country Like @acountry

Exec customer_info_country "Austria"
```

Stored procedures can also be used to control how data is modified. For instance, you might want to ensure that data is entered into tables in a particular manner, or you might wish to ensure that users enter all required information. Allowing users to insert only through a stored procedure and not directly into the underlying tables will ensure that Inserts occur as desired. For example, when an order is placed a row is added to the order_line_items table. The product also needs to have its units_in_stock figure adjusted.

The following code creates a stored procedure to ensure that the Insert statement in an order detail record is complete. A detail record is then added for order_id 1 and product_id 1. The stored procedure uses transaction processing to make sure that both actions are complete. If either the Insert or the Update fails, the whole transaction is rolled back.

```
Create Procedure insert_order_detail
@aorder_id char(6),
@aproduct_id char(6),
@aquantity float,
@aunit_price money
As
Begin Transaction
Insert Into order_line_items
   (order_id, product_id, quantity, unit_price)
   Values (@aorder_id, @aproduct_id, @aquantity, @aunit_price)
If @@Error <> 0
   Begin
      Raiserror 99999 "Something happened. The Insert was
         cancelled."
      Rollback Transaction
      Return
   End

Update products
Set units_in_stock = units_in_stock - @aquantity
Where product_id = @aproduct_id
If @@Error <> 0
   Begin
      Raiserror 99999 "Something happened. The Insert was
         cancelled."
      Rollback Transaction
      Return
   End
Commit Transaction

Exec insert_order_detail "     1", "     1", 10, $12.60
```

When this stored procedure is run, the order detail record is added and the product table is adjusted. Running this stored procedure guarantees that everything happens correctly.

> ***Tip!***
> Using stored procedures is an excellent way to reduce programming errors on the front end. If the front end inserts data through the stored procedure, there is much less of a chance of the insertion being coded incorrectly. You can write the stored procedure once on SQL Server and then use it repeatedly in front ends.

Using Remote Views or SQL Pass-Through

In Section 6, you will see how to combine remote views and SQL Pass-Through to build a client/server application. Remote views allow you to build an application that looks similar to the types of applications you have previously built in FoxPro. Remote views are easy to use and automatically handle sending data modifications back to SQL Server. For this reason, they give you less control over your application. SQL Pass-Through gives you total control because you can use the views and stored procedures discussed in this section to limit user access to data. However, SQL Pass-Through requires more work on your part. Rather than using TableUpdate( ) to send changes and receive conflict messages, you would have to send up Inserts, Updates, and Deletes using SQLExec( ), and then check the return value to see if the statement worked.

The sample application in this report uses remote views for data entry and SQL Pass-Through for read-only queries. This is the easiest way of writing a client/server application and because the purpose of this report is to get you started, this approach works best here. As you gain more experience with client/server applications you should explore the "harder" way of building client/server applications by relying more on SQL Pass-Through and less on remote views.

Querying

Visual FoxPro's support for the SQL Select statement and its data manipulation commands raise two questions: when should queries be conducted against data residing in SQL Server, and when can data be moved to Visual FoxPro so that queries are performed against Visual FoxPro tables? The issue is one of maximizing query processing performance.

Querying in SQL Server

Accessing data stored on the server will require sending a SQL statement to SQL Server. The results can be stored in Visual FoxPro Cursors and then used in whatever manner is necessary. You can use either a Visual FoxPro view or SQL Pass-Through to query back-end data. Either way, the result set is stored in a Visual FoxPro Cursor. As you saw in the previous sections, you can easily make each Cursor read and write by setting certain properties. If you want only to send a Select statement to the back end and view the results, you might want to use SQL Pass-Through instead of a view. Because views have automatic buffering and update capabilities, they also have more overhead. This means that a Select statement sent via SQL Pass-Through should have somewhat faster performance and require fewer resources than a Select statement sent via a view.

Suppose that you have a customer Form with a CommandButton on it to allow the user to see the total year-to-date orders placed for a customer. You could have a view that accepts a parameter and then runs a Select to sum orders for the customer whose ID is equal to the parameter. The resulting Cursor would have one row and one column. The total would be in that column. You could also use SQL Pass-Through to send the same Select statement. Again, the result goes in a Cursor with one row and one column. Either way you could then read the total out of the Cursor and display it to the user. The following code shows the Select statement for the view vCustomerOrderTotal. The Form ORDTOT1.SCX is used to demonstrate using this view to display the customer's total. The Form's Init event code and the CommandButton's Click event code are listed after that.

```
Select Sum(Order_line_items.unit_price*Order_line_items.quantity);
   From orders Orders, order_line_items Order_line_items;
   Where Orders.order_id = Order_line_items.order_id;
     And Orders.customer_id = ?pcCustID

* this code is in the form's Init event.
Use tastrsql!vCustomerOrderTotal NoData In 0

* This code is in the command button's Click event.
pcCustID = ThisForm.txtCust_ID.Value
= ReQuery("vCustomerOrderTotal")
= MessageBox("This customer has placed orders totaling " + ;
             AllTrim(Transform(vCustomerOrderTotal.exp, ;
                          "$,$$$,$$$.99")) + ".", ;
             MB_ICONINFORMATION)
```

The Form ORDTOT2.SCX is used to demonstrate using SQL Pass-Through to display the customer's total. The next code sample shows the Form's Init event code, the CommandButton's Click event code, and the Form's Destroy event code.

```
* this code is in the form's Init event.
ThisForm.handle = SQLConnect("cnTastrade")

* This code is in the command button's Click event.
lcSQL = "Select Sum(Order_line_items.unit_price * Order_line_items.quantity) " + ;
        "From orders, order_line_items " + ;
        "Where orders.order_id = order_line_items.order_id " + ;
        "And orders.customer_id = '" + ThisForm.txtCust_ID.Value + "'"

lnSuccess = SQLExec(ThisForm.handle, lcSQL, "totord")

= MessageBox("This customer has placed orders totalling " + ;
        AllTrim(Transform(totord.exp, "$,$$$,$$$.99")) + ".", ;
        MB_ICONINFORMATION)

* this code is in the form's Destroy event.
= SQLDisconn(ThisForm.handle)
```

The two Forms achieve the same result. Using SQL Pass-Through involves less overhead than using a view, although if the SQL Server tables are fairly small you probably won't notice much of a difference.

Pick Lists and Scrolling Through Records

In many applications, a user who wants to update records is first presented with a pick list of available records, for example, a pick list of companies. The pick list is typically in alphabetical order and includes some incremental search capabilities. In a client/server application this could be accomplished by first sending a Select statement to the back end that returns customer names and IDs. The results are stored in a Cursor that could then be the basis of a pick list. You could use a modal Form with a list box or a Grid that displays all of the customers. When the user selects a customer to edit, you could then send a Select to the server to bring down the one row for that customer. Or you could use a parameterized view.

Many applications allow users to scroll through the records. A typical Form will have First, Previous, Next, and Last buttons. When the user clicks the First button you could move to the first record in the Cursor, get the ID for that customer, and either requery the view with the new parameter or send a Select statement to get that customer. If the user clicks Next, you could use Skip in the Cursor and then get the information from the server for that customer.

There are some problems with this approach. If you had 5,000 customers, performance would probably be acceptable but there would be a noticeable pause while the initial Cursor was created. However, if you had a million customers or 25 million order records, you certainly wouldn't want to make the user wait the amount of time required to download all of that data to the workstation.

Another problem is that the Cursor is static. It reflects the customers or orders that existed at the time the view was requeried or the Select was sent to the server. As users scroll from record to record, they skip over new records because the records would not be reflected in the Cursor. If there is a Find button on the Form to bring up the pick list so the user can move to a new record without having to scroll one at a time, the pick list will be out of date. You could refresh it, but this would again subject the user to a long wait while the Cursor was re-created.

A different approach is needed. In a well-designed client/server application you will always have the minimum amount of data on the workstation. Ideally, you would have only the single customer or order record the user was working on. You would not want to maintain a static, out-of-date, large list whose sole purpose was navigation.

This begs the question of how navigation is handled. When you call the phone company to ask about your bill, you have to supply your phone number. You can be sure the operator doesn't do an incremental search on a huge pick list to get to your record. Using your unique identifier, the application goes directly to your record.

Now suppose that the phone company operator is done with you and is ready to deal with the next person. The odds are pretty slim that this person is the next (or previous, top, or last) record in the customer table. In that type of application the users would not even have a need for First, Previous, Next, and Last buttons. They would need a TextBox to enter a unique ID and a Locate button to go to that record.

They would also need limited search capabilities. Rather than supplying a list of every customer or order, you could allow a user to enter a search string, then bring down all records that match. If the user enters "Smi" you might bring down all customer records where the company name begins with "Smi." You could first check to see how many records matched the criteria. If there were too many, you could prompt the user for more letters to limit the result set. You could then display the matching records in a Grid or list box and let the user select the record to edit.

This solves the two problems. There is no large delay while huge numbers of records are brought down to the workstation, and there is no problem with out of date records because they are not maintained on the workstation.

The sample application for this report uses this approach. When users enter a Form, no data is displayed. If users know the ID of the record to edit, they can enter that and click the Locate button. If users don't know the ID, they can enter a search string and click the Locate button. A pick list of all matches will be presented and users can select the record to edit from that.

There may be applications where the user needs to scroll from record to record. A user might want to bring down a small number of records and work with all of them. For instance, in a contact management system the user may not know the exact name or ID of a contact. The user might want to enter a company code and bring down all of the contacts for that company, then scroll through them looking for the specific contact. In that case you could add navigation buttons to the Form.

Reports

In general, reports will be run using SQL Server data. You will use views or SQL Pass-Through to send Select statements that will be sent to the server. The results will be stored in Visual FoxPro Cursors. Reports will then be run against the Visual FoxPro data containing the results of the queries. Network traffic is kept to a minimum because only the results of the queries are sent back to Visual FoxPro from SQL Server.

There may be times when users want to share data. Suppose several users want SQL Server data to support a direct mail program. Each user can send a Select statement to SQL Server and then copy the results of the query to a Visual FoxPro table for storage. Because the data is in a table, it can be accessed by multiple users on the network. This table can then be used to print mailing labels, conduct mail merges, and perform other tasks.

Ad-hoc Reporting

A major strength of Microsoft Access is its ability to directly attach to SQL databases. This allows users to easily create ad-hoc queries and reports in Access that use SQL Server data. With Visual FoxPro remote views, you can create essentially the same environment. A user can use the Remote View Wizard to create new views that use SQL Server data. The user can also use the Report Wizard and base a report on an existing remote view. The user simply needs to know which connections or ODBC data sources to use.

You can include the ability to call wizards from the menu in your application. For the Query Wizard use Bar # _mwz_query, and for the Report Wizard use Bar # _mwz_reprt. Figure 4-1 shows the Wizards menu choices from a Quick Menu.

Figure 4-1.

The Quick Menu wizard choices

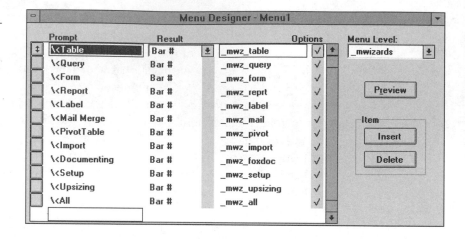

> **Tip!**
>
> Note that you cannot include the wizards if you are distributing your application. However, you should check into products such as Foxfire! and see if they allow you to specify remote views as well as tables. The file LICENSE.TXT in the Visual FoxPro root directory lists the files that cannot be included in distributed applications.

Querying in Visual FoxPro

It is possible to copy all the data from SQL Server tables to Visual FoxPro Cursors, copy those to tables, and then let the user query the tables from within Visual FoxPro. Security considerations aside, this makes sense from a performance standpoint whenever the amount of time saved by querying in Visual FoxPro is greater than the amount of time it takes to download the data to Visual FoxPro. All things being equal, Visual FoxPro's query speed can be faster than that of SQL Server. For instance, you could expect Visual FoxPro to retrieve data from a table with 100,000 records in only a few seconds. Of course, this depends on the complexity of the query and on network and workstation processing capabilities.

Suppose that it takes 20 minutes to download the SQL Server data to Visual FoxPro tables. If the user wants to know only the name of the customer with the most year-to-date orders, then there is little benefit in offloading the query. On the other hand, what if the user wants to spend all day querying the table? Perhaps a department head needs to do a financial analysis using the previous month's accounting data. The data can be offloaded to Visual FoxPro tables and the user can use the Query Designer to build queries that access this static data. The query results can be saved, sent through the Report Writer, and graphed. In this example, the user can create ad hoc queries within Visual FoxPro, thus freeing up SQL Server resources.

Of course, if a query needs to be run against changing data, then it is not feasible to download the data to Visual FoxPro for querying. The data could be obsolete before the downloading was finished. In addition, downloading the data might raise security concerns that could outweigh performance considerations. Queries that need to be run against changing data should occur in SQL Server.

Transaction Logging

In a mission-critical application, stability of the data is of paramount importance. Although Visual FoxPro tables are stable there is a risk of data loss. If the network crashes it is possible that the net result will be a corrupted table. It is possible to lose large amounts of data. Even if the table is backed up daily, a crash at 4:00 in the afternoon could result in the loss of the entire day's data. In many applications this would be unacceptable.

A transaction log keeps a record of all changes to the data as they occur. If a crash occurs, the data can be restored from the most recent backup tape. The contents of the log can then be used to restore the data to its state just before the crash. With an effective transaction log no data should be lost. The log itself can be backed up regularly and stored on a separate hard drive (or even a separate server) for extra security.

Although a transaction log can be built into a Visual FoxPro application, the impact on performance can be considerable. However, transaction logging is native to SQL Server. All Updates, Inserts, and Deletes are automatically recorded in the transaction log. This logging capability, combined with SQL Server's capability to perform online backups, provides a high level of assurance that data on the server can be completely recovered in the event of system failure.

> ### *Tip!*
> Note that the SQL Server transaction log is only for internal use. It can't be used to get a history of who made what changes when. If that capability is required it will have to be coded into the application.

Prototyping in Visual FoxPro

A major benefit to using remote views in a client/server application is the ability to prototype. One of the earliest steps in designing the application is to design the tables. You can build these in Visual

FoxPro and populate them with sample data. You can then construct a prototype of the application using local views. These local views will use local Visual FoxPro tables. The only difference between these views and the views in the final application is that they are local instead of remote. They can still be parameterized to return one row or a few rows at a time.

Visual FoxPro supports rules and triggers to enforce referential integrity and data validations. After the design phase you will know what rules and triggers you are going to need on the back end. You can write these into the Visual FoxPro database and therefore simulate the validations that will occur on the server. Be aware, of course, that you are writing these in Visual FoxPro code and will need to rewrite them in SQL Server code when the data is moved to the back end.

Once you have the tables and views you can build forms based on the views. These will be the same forms used in the finished application. Again, the only difference is that the data is local. You can build validations into the forms and trap for errors due to data violations that are enforced by the rules and triggers.

When it is time to convert your prototype to a client/server application, all you need to do is have Visual FoxPro use remote views instead of local views by changing the scope of the views. However, if you wanted to go back into prototyping mode you would have to change them back. A better idea would be to have two databases, each with the same set of views. The only difference between the two databases would be that one had local and the other had remote views. Then, if you want to prototype, you would open the local views database. If you wanted to use SQL Server data, you would open the remote views database. This allows you to quickly and simply change back and forth between local and remote data. You have one set of forms, and local or remote data will be used in those forms, depending on which database is open.

Another way to prototype is with remote views that use Microsoft Access data. You could create the tables with sample data in an Access database and use that for the prototype. Then you could set up relationships between tables in Microsoft Access and have Access enforce referential integrity. For instance, Access will prevent you from adding a child record with a nonexistent parent. You can take advantage of this data integrity in the Visual FoxPro front end. Access will behave the same way as SQL Server in that respect. This allows you to create the same environment that you will use in the production application.

This process has several benefits. First, it makes converting the prototype much easier. You have only to change the connection on the remote views from one that uses Access to one that uses SQL Server. You don't have to change the tables in the views or change the forms. Another benefit is that it allows you to use SQL Pass-Through in the prototype. In addition, you can build an ODBC/remote view-based prototype without needing SQL Server or Windows NT.

Tip!

If you don't have Microsoft Access you can use Visual FoxPro data. In other words, you would use ODBC to get to Visual FoxPro data from within Visual FoxPro. You can use triggers to enforce referential integrity and simulate the behavior of SQL Server.

Upsizing to SQL Server

The Upsizing Wizard is covered in detail in Section 5, "Moving Data into SQL Server." The wizard allows you to take a Visual FoxPro application and move it to SQL Server. The tables, indexes, defaults, rules, and triggers (including referential integrity triggers), will be moved to SQL Server. You can move the table structures but not the actual data if you prefer. The Upsizing Wizard can change your local views to remote views after upsizing the data.

Whether or not you automatically convert local views to remote views, the Upsizing Wizard is an excellent tool for moving local data to SQL Server. However, you need to understand how it works and how you will upsize the application before you start building your prototype.

Planning for Connections and Users

How many users will your application support? How many connections to SQL Server will there be? These are important questions because connections in SQL Server require memory and need to be allocated in advance. There is a configuration option in SQL Server for the number of user connections. The default is 10 (or 20 if you are using SQL Server 6), but you can set the number as high as 32,767. However, each connection requires about 40 KB of memory. Therefore, if you set this to 100 you need an additional 4 MB of memory on the server.

Each user who logs on to the server will use at least one connection. Each SQLConnect() requires a connection, and each remote view requires a connection, unless they are based on a shared connection. Suppose a user is running a Form that is based on three remote views, each of which uses the same shared connection. In addition, the Form uses SQL Pass-Through to derive some totals. This Form will therefore require two connections to SQL Server. If 25 users are simultaneously running this Form, 50 connections will be required.

This does not have to be a problem if you are aware of the resource requirements in advance. If your SQL Server machine has 16 MB of RAM and you have devoted only 4 of them to SQL Server, there is no way your application will be able to have 25 simultaneous users. You would want to add at least 8 more MB to the machine devoted to SQL Server, for a total of 12 MB. That way you could configure the 50 user connections and still have plenty of memory left over for SQL Server to cache data and perform other tasks.

Timetables, Conversions, and Implementation

Suppose your data is currently in a FoxPro 2.x application and you want to move it to SQL Server. Your first step, obviously, is to move the data into Visual FoxPro. This allows you to get experience converting your old applications to Visual FoxPro and prototyping the application. You can leave it in production in 2.x until it is moved to SQL Server, or you can move it to Visual FoxPro first and then move it to SQL Server.

Any scenario works, as long as the users can still use the system. However, you will need to decide how many steps you are going to take. You also need a timetable for each step. Will you convert the application to Visual FoxPro? How long will it take? Will that version go into production? If so, for how long? How long will it then take to convert from Visual FoxPro to SQL Server? When will that version go into production?

How much do you know about SQL Server? Are you going to be the system administrator? How long will it take you to come up to speed on SQL Server? Are you responsible for writing the SQL Server triggers and stored procedures? How long will it take you to learn enough Transact-SQL to write the code for the back-end part of the application? If it is not you, who will it be? You obviously need to work very closely with that person or team and the system administrator. Remember, you are writing one application. If the front end and the back end are developed and maintained in a vacuum, the project will not be very successful.

> **Tip!**
> It may sound basic, but keep in mind that the front-end team should know enough SQL Server to be helpful to the back-end team, and the back-end team should know enough Visual FoxPro to be helpful to the front-end team.

Summary

This section has served as an overview of design issues involved in building a client/server application. It has been an opportunity to think about where data is stored, where validations occur, and how to split up the work between the front end and the back end. In Section 6, "Developing a Client/Server Application," you will put this knowledge to use as you build a client/server application. In the next section you will use the Upsizing Wizard to move Visual FoxPro data to SQL Server.

5 | Moving Data into SQL Server

One of the least appreciated facts of application development is that the data has to get into the tables somehow. If the data doesn't exist, the users will have to enter it and there is not a lot left to talk about in this section. If the data already exists, it will have to be exported from its current home and imported into its new home. In this section you will see three ways to move data into SQL Server—by hand, with the Upsizing Wizard, or with the SQL Server Bulk Copy Program utility.

Moving Data by Hand

Suppose that you are upsizing an application from Visual FoxPro to SQL Server. The data currently exists in Visual FoxPro tables and you now want to move it to SQL Server. Suppose further that the database and all of the tables have been created in SQL Server. Now you want to transfer the data from Visual FoxPro to SQL Server.

A straightforward way to move the data is to do so manually. This can be accomplished with remote views. First, create a remote view for each empty SQL Server table. Include all of the fields in the table and be sure not to use a Where clause. That way all records will be included in the view. You must also remember to identify the primary key, make all fields updatable, and check the Send SQL Updates CheckBox. This will make the remote view updatable.

Now invoke the view with the Use command. Because the SQL Server table is empty, Visual FoxPro will create an empty Cursor.

The structure of the Cursor, of course, is the same as the structure of the SQL Server table. If the field names are the same in both tables, the transfer could be handled with a simple Append command. The following code shows how to move the shippers table from Visual FoxPro to SQL Server via the vShipperMove remote view.

```
Use vShipperMove
Append From shippers
```

If the fields in the Visual FoxPro table have different names than the fields in the SQL Server table, or if they are in a different order, you can't use a straightforward Append. However, you could use multiple Insert statements to move the data, looping through each record in the Visual FoxPro table and inserting it into the remote view. The next code sample shows how to move the shippers table if the fields names differ. Using Insert statements with the remote view causes Visual FoxPro to send an Insert to SQL Server with the same data. This code will copy the data from the Visual FoxPro shippers table to the SQL Server shippers table.

```
Use shippers
Scan
   Insert Into vShipperMove (shipper_id, company name) ;
      Values (shippers.ship_id, shippers.comp_name)
EndScan
```

Moving Data with the Upsizing Wizard

The code just presented will move your Visual FoxPro data up to SQL Server. You can then create the indexes for the tables and establish the defaults and referential integrity constraints. The technique requires that you create the database and the tables in SQL Server, then move the data in. There may be times when that is all you need. However, Visual FoxPro has a more robust tool to assist you in moving to the SQL Server world. The Upsizing Wizard allows you to move more than just the actual data.

Suppose you have created a prototype of your application in Visual FoxPro. You have data sitting in Visual FoxPro tables. You have defined persistent relations and referential integrity, and have written much of the application logic. You have a functioning prototype, and now you want to move that to SQL Server. The Upsizing Wizard will help you do this.

The Upsizing Wizard is an application consisting of a series of screens that ask questions about how you want to upsize a Visual FoxPro database. It consists of eight steps, some of which you may not see, depending on how you set up the upsizing process. These eight steps are explored in detail in the following parts.

Tip!

The Upsizing Wizard will only upsize data to Microsoft SQL Server, either version 4.2 or version 6. It will not upsize to any other DBMS.

Step 1—Local Database Selection

To use the Upsizing Wizard, select Tools/Wizards/Upsizing from the menu. Step 1, shown in Figure 5-1, asks which local (Visual FoxPro) database you want to upsize. All open databases will be shown in the list box. You can choose a database from there. The currently selected database will be displayed in the Database to Upsize TextBox. If no databases are open or if you want to choose a different database, click Open and choose the database you want to upsize.

Figure 5-1.

Upsizing Wizard Step 1—Local Database Selection

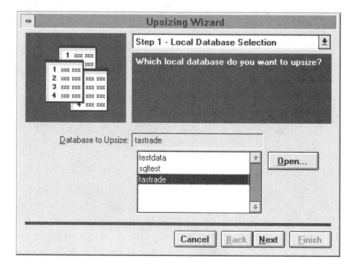

Step 2—Data Source Selection

Step 2, shown in Figure 5-2, asks how you want to connect to SQL Server. You can either use an ODBC data source or a connection stored in the database that will be upsized. If you select the ODBC Data Sources OptionButton you will see a list of all of your SQL Server ODBC data sources. If you select the Connections OptionButton you will see a list of all of the SQL Server connections stored in the selected database.

> ### Tip!
> Because the Upsizing Wizard only works with SQL Server, any ODBC data sources or connections that are not for SQL Server will not appear in the list box.

Figure 5-2.

Upsizing Wizard Step 2—Data Source Selection

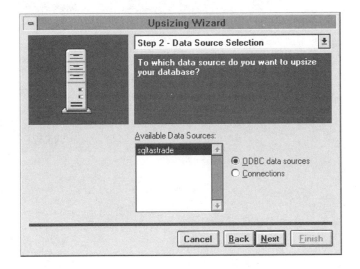

When you click the Next button, Visual FoxPro will attempt to connect to SQL Server using the data source or connection you specified. If you use an ODBC data source, you will see the SQL Server Login dialog box and you will be asked to supply a user ID and password. If you use a connection and the user ID and password are stored in the connection, you do not need to manually log in. If Visual FoxPro is unable to log you into SQL Server, you will get an error message. This could happen if your user ID or password is invalid or if SQL Server is not running.

Step 3—Target Database

After successfully logging in, the Upsizing Wizard will retrieve a list of all databases on SQL Server. Step 3, shown in Figure 5-3, asks which of these databases you want to upsize to. This database will then contain your tables, indexes, and data. You can choose an existing database from the drop-down list or, if you want to create a new database, choose New.

Figure 5-3.

*Upsizing Wizard
Step 3—Target
Database*

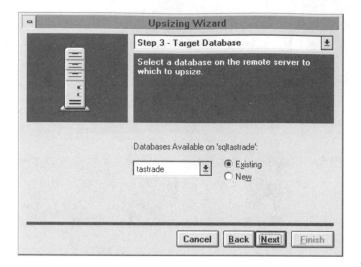

If you choose an existing database, you must have rights in that database. If you are not allowed to use a SQL Server database, you certainly won't be allowed to upsize to it. You need the rights to use the database as well as the rights to create tables and indexes and the rights to Insert into the tables.

If you choose to create a new database, you must have that right. By default, only the SQL Server system administrator can create databases. Although this right can be given to others, it usually isn't because creating a database requires allocating storage space.

> **Tip!**
> Be aware that SQL Server databases are fixed in size. If you try to upsize 50 MB of data into a 25 MB database the upsizing will fail halfway through. See the discussion "Estimating the Size of SQL Server Databases" later in the section to see how to estimate the amount of space required to store data.

Step 4—Database Device (SQL Server)

If you choose an existing database, you will be brought to Step 6. However, if you choose to create a new database you will be asked to supply the name of the new database. When you click the Next button you will then be brought to Step 4, shown in Figure 5-4. In this step you will identify the database device that will contain the new database. A database is stored on one or more devices in SQL Server. In Step 4 you choose a device for the new database.

Figure 5-4.

*Upsizing Wizard
Step 4—Database
Device (SQL Server)*

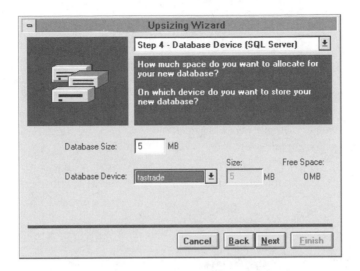

The Upsizing Wizard initially suggests that you use the default device. The default device can actually be more than one device, and is used only if you create a database and do not specify the name of a device to use or you explicitly specify the default device. Existing devices can be made default devices from within SQL Server.

Rather than use the default device, you can choose a specific existing device from the database device drop-down list. The size of each device and its free space are shown. The new database cannot be larger than the remaining space on the selected device.

> **Tip!**
> Keep in mind that you cannot specify more than one device when creating a database in the Upsizing Wizard. If you wanted the new database to span particular devices, you would have to create the database in SQL Server before you upsized. Then all you would need to do is choose to use the existing database.

If you have the proper rights, you can choose to create a new device by selecting Create New Device... from the device list. You will be prompted for the name of this device, then you will need to specify the size of the device. Finally, specify the size of the new database on this new device.

Be aware that only the system administrator has the right to create a device. This right cannot be assigned to any other user as creating a device actually creates a physical file. Only the system administrator can do this.

Step 5—Log Device (SQL Server)

When you have specified the name of the database to use or create, and the device it will reside on, click the Next button. This brings you to Step 5, shown in Figure 5-5. Here you are asked which device should hold the transaction log of the new database. You can choose the same device that holds the database, you can choose any of the other devices, or you can create a new device for the log. Unless the database is solely for testing purposes, its log should go on a separate device. There are two main reasons for this: reduced contention and the ability to back up the log separately.

Figure 5-5.

*Upsizing Wizard
Step 5—Log Device
(SQL Server)*

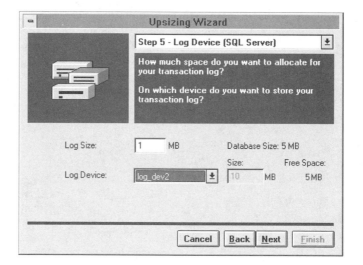

If the data tables, indexes, and log are all on the same device, they all use the hard disk the device is on. The transaction log is actually a system table called syslog, and all data modifications are written to the log. Therefore, every Insert, Update, or Delete statement is recorded in the log. More specifically, if you use Insert or Delete statements in one row, one row is added to the log table. If you use an Update statement on one row, two rows are added to the log—one for the deletion of the old row and one for the insertion of the new row. If a Delete statement deletes 50 rows, 50 rows are added to the log.

You can see that the most frequently used database table is the log table. Every data modification affects the log. Therefore, if it is placed on a separate device and this device is on a separate hard disk (ideally with its own controller), you can achieve a significant improvement in performance.

A backup of the database will back up all of the data tables and indexes. A very popular SQL Server backup scenario involves backing up the entire database once or twice a week and then cleaning out the transaction log, as it is not needed for recovery once the database has been backed up. The transaction log is then backed up once or twice daily. If the database crashes, the most recent database backup is restored, followed by each of the incremental transaction log backups.

Having the log on a separate device allows you to back up the log separately from the database. All committed transactions in the log will be backed up then deleted from the log. This allows you to perform incremental backups while keeping the size of the log down. If you put the transaction log on the same device as the database, you cannot back it up separately and therefore you cannot limit its size.

Tip!

The traditional SQL Server rule of thumb is that the size of the transaction log should be 10 to 20 percent of the size of the database. If you choose to locate the log on the same device as the database, you do not need to specify a size for the log.

Step 6—Tables to Upsize

After you have identified the SQL Server database you want to upsize to, and have identified the device it will use, you can click the Next button. You will then be brought to Step 6, shown in Figure 5-6. Here you are asked which Visual FoxPro tables you want to export to SQL Server. You can choose one, some, or all of them.

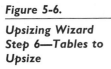

Figure 5-6.

Upsizing Wizard Step 6—Tables to Upsize

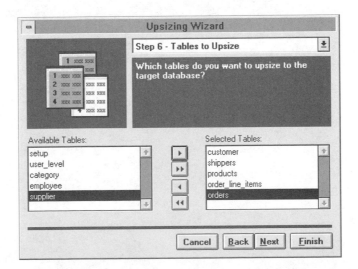

These tables are, of course, the ones in the Visual FoxPro database you are upsizing.

> ### Tip!
> Visual FoxPro will open the tables exclusively to upsize their data. If any of the tables are currently open, the Upsizing Wizard will close them and attempt to reopen them exclusively. If someone else is using them, an error will result.

Step 7—Field Data Types

After choosing the tables to upsize you are brought to Step 7, shown in Figure 5-7. Between Steps 6 and 7, Visual FoxPro analyzes the tables you want to upsize and maps Visual FoxPro data types to SQL Server data types for each table. Although SQL Server and Visual FoxPro do not have the same data types, they have many in common. For instance, both have character and datetime data types. However, Visual FoxPro has memo and general data types while SQL Server has text and image data types. Visual FoxPro has a currency data type while SQL Server has money and smallmoney data types. Table 5-1 shows Visual FoxPro data types and the SQL Server data types they will be mapped to by default.

Figure 5-7.

Upsizing Wizard Step 7—Field Data Types

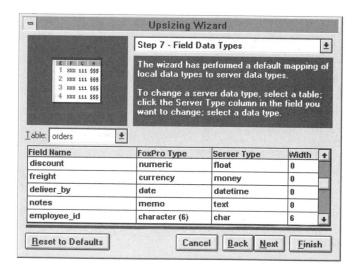

Table 5-1.

Default mapping of Visual FoxPro data types to SQL Server data types

Visual FoxPro Data type	SQL Server Data type
Character	char
Memo	text
Date	datetime
DateTime	datetime
Numeric	float
Double	float
Float	float
Integer	int
Currency	money
Logical	bit
General	image

In Step 7 you can change any of the data type mappings in any of the tables. For instance, in the Visual FoxPro customer table, the field company_name is a character field with a width of 40. By default this will be mapped to a fixed-width 40 wide character field in SQL Server. However, SQL Server supports variable-length character fields. You would probably want to change the company_name field to a varchar data type with a width of 40. To do this, select varchar from the Server Type drop-down list. This is shown in Figure 5-8.

Figure 5-8.

Changing SQL Server data types for upsized tables

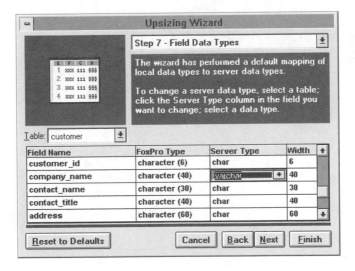

In the Visual FoxPro customer table, the combined width of the company_name, contact_name, contact_title, address, city, region, postal_code, and country fields is 225. Assume that, on average, half that space is needed to store that information. The rest of the space is empty because Visual FoxPro has fixed-width fields. Imagine that the customer table has 500,000 rows. Multiplying 500,000 by 112 bytes yields 54.7 MB. This is an estimate of the amount of disk space saved by using the varchar instead of char data type for those fields. This is an unscientific and inexact method, but it does suggest that changing the data type can potentially save large amounts of disk space.

Another example of a default data type you might want to change is a Visual FoxPro currency field that you know contains relatively small dollar amounts. By default, Visual FoxPro currency fields will be mapped to SQL Server money fields. The money data type in SQL Server holds values between -922,337,203,685,477.5808 and +922,337,203,685,477.5807 and requires 8 bytes of storage. However, the smallmoney data type holds values between -214,748.3648 and +214,748.3647 and requires only 4 bytes. There is no reason why the unit_price field in the products and order_line_items tables needs to be a money data type. Both of these can be smallmoney and store the same information. A salary or total sales field, on the other hand, may need to be created with the money data type.

The SQL Server datetime data type stores dates between January 1, 1753 and December 31, 9999 and is accurate to the millisecond. It requires 8 bytes of storage. The smalldatetime data type stores dates between January 1, 1900 and June 6, 2079 and is accurate to the second. It requires only 4 bytes of storage. The order_date and deliver_by fields in the orders table can be created using the smalldatetime data type instead of the datetime data type.

The Upsizing Wizard will map numeric fields to the SQL Server float data type. The float data type stores numbers between 2.23E - 308 and 1.79E 308 and requires 8 bytes of storage. Suppose that the discount field in the customer table is defined as numeric. When you upsize the data, this will be a float data type by default. However, the discount can only be between 0 and 100. The SQL Server tinyint data type stores numbers between 0 and 255 and requires only 1 byte of storage. The quantity field in the order_line_items table can use the smallint data type, which stores numbers between -32,768 and 32,767 and requires only 2 bytes of storage.

Tip!

Be sure that you give a lot of thought to each and every field in the tables you are upsizing. You can save significant amounts of disk space by using the smallest possible data type rather than the defaults.

Step 8—Upsizing Options

After adjusting the field data types, you are brought to Step 8, which is shown in Figure 5-9. Here you decide exactly what you want upsized and what changes you want to make to your local database.

Figure 5-9.

Upsizing Wizard Step 8—Upsizing Options

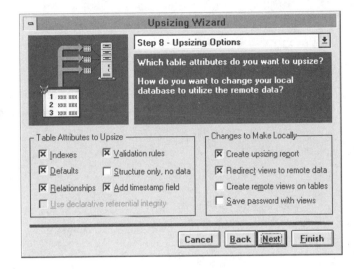

Table Attributes to Upsize

There are two sets of CheckBoxes in Step 8. The first set allows you to specify what parts of the table you want to upsize in addition to the data.

Indexes CheckBox

If you want the Visual FoxPro indexes to be upsized, check the Indexes CheckBox. Primary indexes will be upsized as SQL Server clustered unique indexes, while candidate indexes will be upsized as SQL Server unique indexes. Regular and unique indexes will be upsized as SQL Server nonclustered indexes. You can, of course, change these later by dropping any index and recreating it.

For instance, you would always want your primary key index to be unique. However, you do not always want it to be a clustered index. Remember that a clustered index physically sorts the data, therefore you can have only one clustered index per SQL Server table. If you are retrieving a single row from a table there is a trivial performance difference between using a clustered and a nonclustered index. However, if you are retrieving a range of data, a clustered index can dramatically outperform a nonclustered index. Because the primary key is unique, any query involving the primary key will bring back one row. If you also have queries that return ranges, placing the clustered index on the primary key is basically a waste of that index. You would be better off using it to improve the performance of the most important of your range queries.

As an example, suppose you have a parameterized remote view on the customer table that allows the user to retrieve all customers in a particular city. This will typically bring down more than one row. In addition, suppose you have a remote view that takes the customer ID as the parameter. This view returns one row at a time. Placing the clustered index on city rather than on customer_id will improve the performance of the first remote view significantly but won't noticeably affect the performance of the second remote view.

Defaults CheckBox

Defaults are used to insert a value into a field if the user doesn't supply a value. You can choose to have your Visual FoxPro defaults upsized to SQL Server defaults by checking the Defaults CheckBox. A default in Visual FoxPro can be a simple expression or built-in function. For instance, you could use USA as the default for a country field or Date() as the default for a date field. A default can also be a stored procedure.

If the default is an expression, there is a good chance that the Upsizing Wizard can translate it accurately into SQL Server's language. For instance, if your default is Date() it will become GetDate() in SQL Server. Table 5-2 shows the Visual FoxPro expressions that the Upsizing Wizard will convert to SQL Server expressions. If you use any of these Visual FoxPro expressions in a default, they will be successfully translated into a SQL Server expression.

Table 5-2.

Visual FoxPro expressions and their SQL Server equivalents

Visual FoxPro Expression	SQL Server Equivalent	Visual FoxPro Expression	SQL Server Equivalent
.T.	1	Day()	DatePart(dd, ...)
.F.	0	Dow()	DatePart(dw, ...)
#	<>	Dtoc()	Convert(varchar, ...)
.And.	And	Dtor()	Radians()
.Not.	Not	Dtot()	Convert(datetime, ...)
.Null.	Null	Hour()	DatePart(hh, ...)
.Or.	Or	Like()	PatIndex()
=<	<=	Log()	Log()
=>	>=	Minute()	DatePart(mi, ...)
Asc()	Ascii()	Month()	DatePart(mm, ...)

Continued on next page

Visual FoxPro Expression	SQL Server Equivalent	Visual FoxPro Expression	SQL Server Equivalent
At()	CharIndex()	Mton()	Convert(money, ...)
Cdow()	DateName(dw, ...)	Ntom()	Convert(float, ...)
Ceiling()	Ceiling()	Rtod()	Degrees()
Chr()	Char()	Str()	Str()
CMonth()	DateName(mm, ...)	Substr()	Substring()
Ctod()	Convert(datetime, ...)	Ttoc()	Convert(char, ...)
Ctot()	Convert(datetime, ...)	Ttod()	Convert(datetime, ...)
Date()	GetDate()	Year()	DatePart(yy, ...)
DateTime()	GetDate()		

If the Visual FoxPro expression you use for a default contains expressions that do not have a SQL Server equivalent, the Upsizing Wizard will not be able to create the default in SQL Server. The same thing will happen if you write Visual FoxPro code for your default. In the Visual FoxPro Tastrade database, some fields have a default of NewID(). This is a stored procedure in the database. When the Upsizing Wizard sees this it tries to find a SQL Server equivalent, but there is none. As a result the default will not upsize.

Tip!
Be careful not to use a Visual FoxPro procedure with the same name as a SQL Server function. For example, suppose you created a stored procedure called Degrees() and made it the default for a field in a Visual FoxPro table. When you upsized it, the default would be upsized but SQL Server would use its own built-in Degrees() function instead of the code stored in the Visual FoxPro database.

Relationships CheckBox

If you have persistent relationships defined in your Visual FoxPro database and you are enforcing referential integrity, you can upsize these by checking the Relationships CheckBox. Referential integrity is enforced in Visual FoxPro and in SQL Server 4.2 by the use of triggers. Referential integrity can be enforced in SQL Server 6 at the engine level. Although you do not need to write triggers, you can if you want support for cascading updates and deletes.

When you enforce referential integrity in Visual FoxPro, you decide whether to cascade updates and deletes or to restrict them. If you cascade updates, changing the primary key in the parent table will automatically change it in all child tables. If you cascade deletes, deleting a parent record will automatically delete all child records. If you restrict updates, you cannot change the primary key in the parent table. If you restrict deletes, you cannot delete a parent record if there are child records.

The Upsizing Wizard will create the necessary SQL Server triggers to enforce referential integrity based on how you enforce it in Visual FoxPro. For each parent table there will be an Update trigger to either prevent or cascade changes to the primary key. There will also be a Delete trigger to either prevent or cascade the deletion of a parent record if there are corresponding child records. For each child table there will be an Update trigger that prevents changes to the primary key. There will also be an Insert trigger that prevents the addition of child records without a corresponding parent.

A trigger is automatically run when a data modification is made. Suppose you change a record in a remote view and then move off the record. Visual FoxPro sends an Update statement to the back end. Suppose this causes a SQL Server Update trigger to run, and further suppose the Update trigger code needs to reject the Update. The trigger will contain a line of code to roll back the transaction. This causes the updated record to be restored to its original value. SQL Server lets Visual FoxPro know the Update failed by sending back an error number. This is accomplished with the SQL Server Raiserror statement.

The following code is an Upsizing Wizard-generated SQL Server Delete trigger that enforces referential integrity. The trigger does not allow more than one customer to be deleted at a time and it does not allow customers to be deleted if they have orders. If either of these cases occurs, the deletion is rolled back and an error is sent back to Visual FoxPro.

```
CREATE TRIGGER TrigD_customer ON customer FOR DELETE AS

DECLARE @status char(10)  /* USED BY VALIDATION STORED PROCEDURES */

/* PREVENT DELETEs AFFECTING MULTIPLE RECORDS */
IF @@ROWCOUNT>1
    BEGIN
        RAISERROR 44448 'DELETEs affecting multiple records in ''customer'' not
           allowed because of referential integrity constraints.'
        SELECT @status='Failed'
    END

/* PREVENT DELETES IF DEPENDENT RECORDS IN 'orders' */
IF (SELECT COUNT(*) FROM deleted, orders WHERE (deleted.customer_id =
  orders.customer_id)) > 0
    BEGIN
    RAISERROR 44445 'Cannot delete or change record.  Referential integrity rules
      would be violated because related records exist in table ''orders''.'
```

Continued on next page

```
    SELECT @status='Failed'
    END

/* ROLLBACK THE TRANSACTION IF ANYTHING FAILED */
IF @status='Failed'
ROLLBACK TRANSACTION
```

Table 5-3 shows the error numbers used by Upsizing Wizard when creating referential integrity triggers.

Table 5-3.

Referential integrity error numbers used in triggers

SQL Server Error Number	Caused by
4445	Rejected deletion
4446	Rejected update
4447	Rejected insert
4448	Update or Delete that affects more than one row

If you create persistent relationships in Visual FoxPro but do not enforce referential integrity, the Upsizing Wizard will not upsize your relationships. If you check the Relationships CheckBox you are actually asking the Upsizing Wizard to upsize your enforcement of referential integrity. If you are not enforcing referential integrity there is nothing for the Upsizing Wizard to do.

You must enforce referential integrity using the Visual FoxPro Referential Integrity Builder if you want the Upsizing Wizard to upsize your relationships. The Upsizing Wizard will upsize only triggers that start with ri_, in other words the triggers created by the Referential Integrity Builder. If you use your own triggers to enforce referential integrity, they will not be upsized.

Use Declarative Referential Integrity CheckBox

SQL Server 6 supports declarative referential integrity. This is accomplished by defining the primary key in the parent table and a foreign key in the child table, then relating the two tables. Once you have declared referential integrity you don't have to use triggers. The database engine enforces referential integrity automatically. The next code sample is SQL Server 6 code for creating a relationship between the customer and orders tables.

```
ALTER TABLE customer ADD CONSTRAINT pk_customer_id PRIMARY KEY (customer_id)

ALTER TABLE orders ADD CONSTRAINT fk_customer_id FOREIGN KEY
    (customer_id) REFERENCES customer (customer_id)
```

If you are upsizing to SQL Server 6, the Use Declarative Referential Integrity CheckBox will be enabled. Check it if you want your Visual FoxPro persistent relationships to use declarative referential integrity when they are upsized to SQL Server. Again, this will happen only if you are enforcing referential integrity in Visual FoxPro via the Referential Integrity Builder.

Validation Rules CheckBox

If you want to upsize your Visual FoxPro field and row level validation rules, check the Validation Rules CheckBox. Remember that SQL Server rules are not very robust and apply only to fields in a table. You can specify that a field satisfy an expression, for instance discount <= 100. You can specify that a field fall in a range, for instance Salary Between 25000 and 87000000. You can specify that a field be contained in a list, for instance Expertise In ("FoxPro", "SQL Server", "Access/Visual Basic", "Other"). Finally, you can specify that a field match a pattern, for instance Zip Like "[0-9][0-9][0-9][0-9][0-9]".

SQL Server rules cannot refer to other fields in the table, although check constraints can. However, neither can display custom error messages. For this reason, when you upsize Visual FoxPro rules, whether they are field or row level, they are converted to SQL Server stored procedures that are then called from Insert and Update triggers on the appropriate tables. If the trigger rejects the Insert or Update, it rolls back the transaction and uses Raiserror to send error number 44444 back to Visual FoxPro.

If your validation rule calls a Visual FoxPro stored procedure, the Upsizing Wizard will attempt to convert it to a built-in SQL Server function. For this reason, unless you are using very simple rules, your best bet would probably be to not upsize them. Instead you should rewrite them in SQL Server.

Structure Only, No Data CheckBox

If you only want to upsize database objects but not the actual data, check the Structure Only, No Data CheckBox. You might do this if you only wanted to test the upsizing and see what the Upsizing Wizard moves to SQL Server, or if you wanted only a small part of the data in SQL Server for testing purposes. You could upsize everything except the data, then add some test data afterwards.

You might do this if you prototyped the application in Visual FoxPro, but the data is actually coming from somewhere else (the mainframe or another DBMS). For example, suppose you are downsizing a mainframe application into Visual FoxPro with SQL Server as the back end. You could create the application in Visual

FoxPro with some test data and then upsize only the structures to SQL Server. The data could be moved from the mainframe after that.

Add Timestamp Field CheckBox

If you want timestamp fields added to your upsized tables, check the Add Timestamp Field CheckBox. A timestamp field contains a SQL Server-generated unique value that is automatically updated whenever any update occurs to each record in the table.

A major benefit to timestamps is that you can use them to see if a record has changed. Remember that the WhereType property of a view determines how Visual FoxPro checks to see if anyone else has changed a record while a user is working with it. If you choose Key and Updatable Fields or Key and Modified Fields, Visual FoxPro will check all fields that can be updated or were updated, respectively. This can be time consuming if the table has many fields. If you choose Key and Timestamp, Visual FoxPro will compare the timestamp when the row was retrieved to the current timestamp. If they differ, you know that someone else changed the record in the meantime.

This is particularly helpful if the data you want to compare is a text or image field. The time savings in checking only the timestamp can be substantial.

Tip!

The Upsizing Wizard will automatically add a timestamp to an upsized table if the table will use any of the following SQL Server data types: binary, varbinary, float, real, image, or text. This will happen even if you do not check the Add Timestamp Field CheckBox.

Changes to Make Locally

The second set of CheckBoxes in Step 8 allows you to determine what changes, if any, the Upsizing Wizard will make to the upsized Visual FoxPro database.

Create Upsizing Report CheckBox

If you check the Create Upsizing Report CheckBox, the Upsizing Wizard will create several upsizing reports. It will first create a subdirectory called upsize. It will then create a project called report. The Upsizing Wizard will create a database called upsize, which will contain tables named tables_uw, views_uw, fields_uw, indexes_uw, relationships_uw, and errors_uw. These tables supply the information for reports on upsized tables, views, fields, indexes, relationships, and referential integrity constraints, and for errors encountered during the upsizing process.

In addition to the tables that support the reports, the Upsizing Wizard will create two more tables. The table misc_uw contains information on which version of SQL Server you upsized to, what data source or connection was used, the name of the SQL Server database used and the Visual FoxPro database upsized, and other information specified in the various Upsizing Wizard steps.

The table sql_uw contains one row with one field. That field is a memo field containing the SQL Server commands used to create the upsized database structures. This code can be saved and run as a SQL Server script. This would allow you to upsize the structures again without having to run the Upsizing Wizard. It is also your documentation of what the Upsizing Wizard did.

Redirect Views to Remote Data CheckBox

As you prototype a client/server application in Visual FoxPro, you might use local views on local data. When this data is upsized, you can have your local views converted to remote views by checking the Redirect Views to Remote Data CheckBox. The local views are renamed by having "_local" added to the end of their names. Remote views with the same names as the original local views are then created. As you would expect, these remote views use the remote data.

Once the local views are converted to remote views, the application will use SQL Server data instead of Visual FoxPro data. However, if you still want to use Visual FoxPro data you will have to change all references to the views and use the _local versions. This makes it very difficult to switch back and forth between local and remote data. In the next section you will see an elegant technique for this switch.

Create Remote Views on Tables CheckBox

Check the Create Remote Views on Tables CheckBox if you want the Upsizing Wizard to create remote views for each of the tables you upsized. The remote views will have the same name as the tables. The Upsizing Wizard will rename the local Visual FoxPro tables by adding "_local" to the end of their names. If you have a Form in the application that was based on the Visual FoxPro table customers, it will now use the remote view customers, which means that it will now be based on the SQL Server table customers.

Bear in mind that these new remote views will not be parameterized views. They will be straight Select * statements with no Where clause. If you use the resulting views you will get all of the rows in the table sent from SQL Server. This does not make for an efficient client/server application. In Section 6 you will see how to base an application on parameterized views and retrieve one row at a time on Forms.

Tip!

You could use these remote views in an application if you were going to provide the users with ad-hoc querying and reporting capabilities. They could use the remote views in reports and queries in the same way they would use local tables. This is equivalent to Microsoft Access's ability to directly attach to SQL Server tables, which can then be used in Forms, reports, and queries.

Save Password With Views CheckBox

When you use a remote view you have to supply a user ID and password to log on to SQL Server. You can create a connection and store the login information in the connection. When you use a remote view based on that connection, Visual FoxPro will retrieve the login ID and password and use those. Only if this information is missing or proves to be incorrect will the user be prompted for login information. If the remote view uses an ODBC connection rather than a database connection, the user will be prompted for login information every time the view is used.

If you check the Save Password With Views CheckBox, your user ID and password will be stored in the Visual FoxPro database that contains the views. Therefore you won't have to supply the user ID and password when you use remote views in that database.

Step 9—Finish

The last Upsizing Wizard step is Step 9, which is shown in Figure 5-10. Now that you have selected all of your options you are actually ready to upsize. When Visual FoxPro upsizes the database it creates a script file that runs on SQL Server. This script file contains SQL Server commands to create the device and database (if necessary) and to create the tables, indexes, rules, defaults, and triggers that are being upsized. This script can be run in SQL Server at any time, even after you upsize. As previously mentioned, this script is stored in the sql_uw table.

In Step 9 you actually have three choices. Choose Upsize to have Visual FoxPro upsize the selected database but not save the SQL Server script. Choose Save Generated SQL to have Visual FoxPro create and save the SQL Server script but not upsize the database.

Choose Upsize and Save Generated SQL to have Visual FoxPro upsize the database and save the SQL Server script.

Figure 5-10.

Upsizing Wizard Step 9—upsizing options

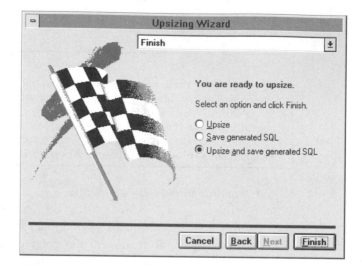

Upsizing Wizard Errors

Under what circumstances will the upsizing process fail or generate errors? There are three main sources of problems that can arise during an upsizing process: you can run out of room in the database, you can run out of room in the transaction log, or some of the data may not be upsized because of errors.

The Database Is Too Small

As part of the upsizing process you need to either specify an existing SQL Server database or create a new one. When a database is created you specify its size. This size is fixed unless you explicitly increase the database size with the Alter Database command. If you create a 25 MB database and you then try to upsize 30 MB of data, the upsizing process will fail after filling the database with the first 25 MB of data. You will need to increase the size of the database and either start the upsizing process over again or figure out which records did not make it and move those in separately.

The solution to this problem is to specify the correct size for the database. See the discussion "Estimating the Size of SQL Server Databases" later in the section to see how to estimate the amount of space required to store data.

The Transaction Log Fills Up

The Upsizing Wizard moves your data to SQL Server by using Insert statements. Each Insert statement adds a row to the transaction log. If you upsize 1 million rows from Visual FoxPro, there will be 1 million rows added to the log. When the database is created, you specify not only the size of the database but also the size of the log. If the log is on the same device as the database, it can use all of the free space in the database. If the log is on a separate device it can grow only as large as the space on that device allocated to it.

Suppose you create a 25 MB database with 20 MB for the data and 5 MB for the log. It is entirely possible that moving the 20 MB of data will require more than 5 MB of log space. However, you don't have it. Once the log fills up, the upsizing process will stop. No more Inserts can occur because they cannot be logged.

One solution to this would be to create a log large enough to record all of the required Inserts. The problem with this is that while the upsizing will work, once the data is in you now will probably have a log that is much too big for your application. You don't need a log that is as large as the data. The rule of thumb is that the log should be 10 percent to 20 percent the size of the database. This is too small to upsize a large amount of data, but is a good size once the data is in.

A better solution to this problem takes advantage of checkpoints. As discussed in Section 1, whenever a data modification is made, SQL Server records the old and new data in the log in cache memory. The changes are then written to the database, also in cache memory. When a transaction is committed, the transaction log is written to the physical disk. At checkpoints, the database and the log are written to the physical disk. If a system crash occurs, SQL Server will make sure that committed transactions are reflected in the database and that uncommitted transactions are not in the database. This is called automatic recovery.

Checkpoints occur periodically. By default, they occur often enough so that if the server crashes, it will take no more than five minutes per database to recover. If the Truncate Log On Checkpoint option is set to true in a database, the committed transactions in the log will be cleared out every time a checkpoint occurs. The Truncate Log On Checkpoint option is set using the sp_dboption system stored procedure.

To ensure that the upsizing process does not fill up the log, you can create the SQL Server database before you upsize. Then set the Truncate Log On Checkpoint option to true in that database. The log will be continuously emptied as the Upsizing Wizard inserts records.

It should never fill up. You can be doubly sure of this by using the sp_configure command in SQL Server to set the recovery interval to one minute. This will cause checkpoints to occur even more frequently, as SQL Server now expects to be able to recover each database in only one minute. The shorter the recovery interval, the more often the data has to be flushed to disk.

Tip!

You can leave the Truncate Log on Checkpoint option set to true during development. This allows you to test data modifications repeatedly without worrying about the log. However, make sure you set it to false when the system goes into production. Unless you have a reason to set it differently, you should also set the recovery interval back to five minutes.

Records Cannot Be Upsized Because of Errors

The Upsizing Wizard will create an export errors table for each upsized table. The name of the export errors table is "exporterrors_" followed by the table name. The records that were not able to be upsized will be copied into these tables. An error could occur if an inserted record violates a validation rule or is rejected by a trigger. For instance, if you have orphaned records in your Visual FoxPro tables, they will not make it up to SQL Server if you upsized your referential integrity constraints.

Moving Data with the Bulk Copy Program

A third way to move Visual FoxPro data to SQL Server is to use the SQL Server Bulk Copy Program. The BCP, as it is known, is a utility that ships with SQL Server. It is designed to import data into or to export data out of SQL Server. It can be used to move data from one SQL Server to another as well as to export SQL Server data into a text file or to import from a text file. The Bulk Copy Program is a command prompt utility. It is an executable file, BCP.EXE, installed on the SQL Server machine. It can also be installed on client machines.

You run the BCP by running the executable file and then specifying various parameters such as the table you are importing into or exporting out of, the name of the SQL Server, and your login ID and password. You can also add other parameters to fine tune the process. The following code shows the full syntax of the BCP utility.

```
bcp [[database_name.]owner.]table_name {in | out} datafile
[/m max number of errors] [/f format file] [/e error file]
[/F first row] [/L last row] [/b batch size]
[/n if native SQL Server format] [/c if character format]
[/E if identity values are imported]
[/t field terminator] [/r row terminator]
[/i input file] [/o output file]
/U login id [/P password] [/S server name]
[/v to report DB Library version] [/a network packet size]
```

To import using the BCP, the database and tables must already exist. You would therefore need to create them in SQL Server first. You could upsize the Visual FoxPro database, upsizing only the data structure, not the actual data. This will upsize the tables, indexes, and triggers. Make sure you have the Upsizing Wizard generate the SQL code.

To move Visual FoxPro data you would then copy that data to a text file and then use that to import the data into SQL Server tables. If there are no indexes, triggers, or constraints on the SQL Server tables, the BCP can insert data without recording that in the transaction log. This is the fastest way to move data into SQL Server using the BCP. If there are indexes, triggers, or constraints on the table, the Insert statements will be logged and the import will take longer.

You would therefore drop the indexes, triggers, and constraints before running the BCP. You also need to use the sp_dboption system procedure to set the Select Into/Bulk Copy option to true in the SQL Server database. If this option is set to true, and there are no indexes, triggers, or constraints on the table, BCP Inserts will not be recorded in the log. You would then use BCP to import the data into the SQL Server tables, and re-create the indexes, triggers, and constraints from the SQL code that the Upsizing Wizard generated. Finally, you would set the Select Into/Bulk Copy option back to false.

The next code sample shows how to use the BCP to import customer data. You need to run the BCP for each SQL Server table you are importing data into.

```
bcp tastrade..customer in customer.txt /m 50 /e custerr.txt /b 200
/c /t \t /r \n /Usa /P /SMars
```

The /m indicates that only 50 errors will be tolerated. If there are more errors the importing will stop. The /e directs errors to be written to the custerr.txt file while the /b directs SQL Server to import data in batches of 200. A batch is treated as a transaction, so if any batch fails, the whole batch will be rolled back. Also, if the maximum number of allowed errors is exceeded in a batch, the entire batch will be rolled back. The /c indicates that the data being imported is in character format, while the /t \t specifies that the fields are delimited with tabs. The /r \n specifies that rows terminate with a carriage return. The /U specifies the login ID, the /P the password, and the /S the SQL Server.

Tip!

The transaction log cannot be backed up if the Select Into/Bulkcopy option is set to true. So be sure to set it to false after importing all of the Visual FoxPro data.

Estimating the Size of SQL Server Databases

Before you upsize data from Visual FoxPro to SQL Server, you need to know how large to make the SQL Server database. You could add up the sizes of all of the Visual FoxPro tables, but SQL Server and Visual FoxPro store data in an entirely different manner. SQL Server stores data on pages that are 2k in length. It has variable length fields. In addition, rows cannot span pages. Visual FoxPro stores data in fixed-length rows made up of fixed-length fields. By understanding how SQL Server stores data you can fairly accurately estimate the size required for a database.

Calculating the Space Required for Tables

To calculate the size of a table you need to figure out how many 2 K pages will be required to store the data. To know the number of pages required to store a particular number of rows you need to know how many rows will fit on a page. As a result, the first step in calculating the space required for each table is to know how wide the data rows are.

To calculate the width of each row, add up the size of all of the fixed-width fields. Add to that each of the variable width fields. Use the average amount of data that will be stored in each field. Then add 4 bytes of overhead for the row and an additional 1 byte of data for each column that is variable length or allows nulls.

The following code shows the SQL Server code to create the customer table. Assume that each variable-length column will, on average, be half full. The width of each row in this table is 170, which is 10 (the two char fields) plus 8 (the two smallmoney fields) plus 1 (the tinyint field) plus 137 (sum the varchar fields and divide by two) plus 4 (standard overhead per row) plus 10 (1 byte overhead per variable-length field).

```
CREATE TABLE customer (customer_id char(6) NOT NULL,
     company_name varchar(40) NOT NULL,
     contact_name varchar(30) NOT NULL,
     contact_title varchar(40) NOT NULL,
     address varchar(60) NOT NULL,
     city varchar(15) NOT NULL,
     region varchar(15) NOT NULL,
     postal_code varchar(10) NOT NULL,
     country varchar(15) NOT NULL,
     phone varchar(24) NOT NULL,
     fax varchar(24) NOT NULL,
     max_order_amt smallmoney NOT NULL,
     min_order_amt smallmoney NOT NULL,
     discount tinyint NOT NULL,
     sales_region char(4) NOT NULL)
```

Of the 2 K pages where data is stored, 32 bytes of that amount is overhead, leaving 2016 bytes available to store data on a page. Divide that by the width of each row and you know how many rows will fit on each page for a table. For the customers table this is 28 (2016 divided by 170).

Divide the total number of rows in the table by the number of rows that fit on a page and you will know the number of pages required to store the data. Multiply by 2048 and that is the required number of bytes. If there are 10,000 customers, you will need 358 (10,000 divided by 28) pages. This requires 127,551 bytes.

Calculating the Space Required for Indexes

Indexes in SQL Server are also stored in 2 K pages. The leaf level of an index is where the data is sorted. The leaf level of a clustered index is the data itself, while the leaf level of a nonclustered index contains pointers to actual rows of data. On top of the leaf level there are several layers of nonleaf levels. The highest level in an index consists of one page of data. This is the root level of the index.

To calculate the size required by an index, you need to add up the number of pages in each level of the index. This is determined by the number of index entries that will fit on a page. This is 2016 divided by the index entry size. The index entry size is the width of the index key plus overhead. The overhead is 5 bytes for a clustered index nonleaf level page, 7 bytes for a nonclustered index leaf level page, and 11 bytes for a nonclustered index nonleaf level page.

As an example, consider an index on company_name. Company_name is varchar(40) in the customer table. Assuming that half of the column is full, each data page in the leaf level will store 74 index entries, or 2016 divided by (20 plus 7). There are 10,000 rows in the table, so 136 (10,000 divided by 74) pages are required in the leaf level of this nonclustered index.

The next level in the index is a nonleaf level. To determine the number of pages required, divide the number of leaf level pages by the number of index entries per page. This gives a value of 2, or 136 divided by 74. Finally, add one row for the root level and this index requires 139 2 K pages, or 284,672 bytes.

If you did these calculations for each of your tables and indexes, you would have a pretty good estimate of how large to make the database.

Tip!

For more information on how to estimate database size requirements see the SQL Server System Administrators Guide.

Summary

In this section you saw how to move data from Visual FoxPro into SQL Server. You can create a prototype of an application in Visual FoxPro using either sample data or even the real data. When you are ready to move the application up to SQL Server, you can use the Upsizing Wizard to fully automate the process or you can upsize only the data structures and move the data yourself. In the next section you will see techniques for building robust client/server applications.

6 | Developing a Client/Server Application

At this point, you can build a client/server application. You know how to create and use both local and remote views, and you also know how to make use of SQL Pass-Through. In this section you will build a client/server Tastrade application. You will design parameterized remote views to retrieve the data that can be viewed and edited, create the local data counterparts to these so you can prototype and develop using Visual FoxPro data, use SQL Pass-Through to retrieve read-only remote data, build queries and reports, and take advantage of SQL Server features such as security.

Before you begin, be aware that the files mentioned in this section are part of the source code disc and not the sample application. The data for the sample application is in the Tastrade database from the Visual FoxPro main sample application. It is found in the Vfp\Samples\Mainsamp\Data directory. Tastrade is an order entry system with customers placing orders. These orders have detail records that identify the products ordered and their cost. There is a products table with products that belong to categories and have suppliers. Orders are sent by shippers and are tied to sales reps. The sales reps are employees and belong to groups. Figure 6-1 shows the entity-relation diagram for this data.

To build the report's sample application you can take the Tastrade database as given. After all, Microsoft did such a nice job designing it and entering the data for you. The local Tastrade database has defaults, rules, triggers, stored procedures, and

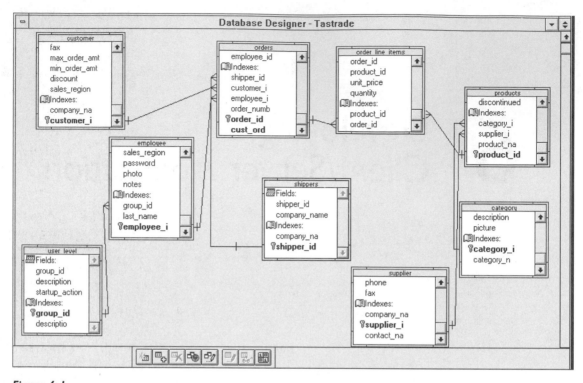

Figure 6-1.

The Tastrade entity relationship

persistent relationships already defined, as well as referential integrity triggers that were created using the Referential Integrity builder. In the previous section you saw how to upsize the Tastrade data to SQL Server.

The Application's Structure

A good application starts with a good class library. The application in this report starts with an application class library based on the one used in the Tastrade sample application. This is a very good example of how a Visual FoxPro application can be structured. It is not the purpose of this report to review the intricacies of this structure, but a few of the more important features can be covered.

Custom Application Classes

The highest level in the class hierarchy is the ccApplication class contained in the class library file TSGEN.VCX. This is a custom class and is designed to be a generic top level for any application you create. A major benefit to having an application class is that its properties and methods become application-wide. They are available throughout the application, can be used on any screen or in any code, and replace the global variables you have used in the past. The application class is responsible for things like environmental settings, setting the caption of the screen, opening the application's database, putting up the main menu, hiding Visual FoxPro's built-in toolbars when the application starts, bringing them back when the application is finished, and issuing the Read Events.

While the ccApplication class is application generic, the ccTastrade class is application specific. The ccTastrade class is a subclass of the ccApplication class, and is stored in the file MAIN.VCX. It inherits the properties and methods from the ccApplication class while adding its own properties and methods, which are specific to the report's sample application.

The properties and methods of the ccTastrade class are also application-wide. The ccTastrade class is instantiated in the main program of the application. This is shown in the following code. The object variable oApp refers to ccTastrade and is therefore the vehicle for running the methods and referring to or setting the properties of ccTastrade. It is made public so that it is always available. The Do method of ccTastrade is run to start the application.

```
Public oApp
oApp = CreateObject("ccTastrade")
If Type('oApp') = "O"
   oApp.Do
Endif
```

Form Template Classes

The Forms in the application share some common functions. The user needs to be able to identify a particular record to edit, and must be able to save, add, and delete records. The user is able to see related information in a Grid and can view the total dollar amount of orders for a record.

Some of the interface elements and coded routines on the Forms appear on every Form. Before the Forms are constructed, you should create classes and subclasses to handle these common elements. There are two Form templates used in the sample application—a generic Form template and an application-specific Form template. The generic Form template is vcFormTemplate in the file FORMS.VCX. This Form template is meant to be application generic because different code could be required for Save or Add buttons on any given Form in any given application. There is very little code in the vcFormTemplate class.

Each of the data entry forms in the sample application will be based on an application-specific Form template. In addition to all of the features of the generic Form template, this template will have features specific to this application. Therefore, vcFormTemplate will be subclassed to create vcAppForm, which is also stored in the file FORMS.VCX. The Form class vcAppForm is shown in Figure 6-2.

Figure 6-2.

The vcAppForm Form template

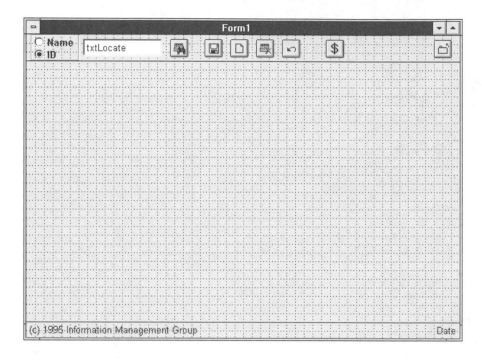

Each Form in the application will be based on vcAppForm, and every Form will use a PageFrame called pgfFormInfo. This provides consistency across all Forms and makes the coding in vcAppForm easier because the PageFrame on every data entry Form has the same name. The first page of the PageFrame contains the most common information for the entity being viewed or edited. For instance, the first page of the Customer Form will have the customer name and address. The first page of the Employee Form will have the employee's name and address.

Most of the Forms will give the user the ability to see related records in a Grid. For instance, on the orders Form the user will want to see all details for that order. On the shippers Form, the user can see all products for that shipper. The Grid will be on the last page in the PageFrame. The Forms will be set up so that the data in the Grid is not downloaded until it is needed. This means that the user must activate the page with the Grid to see it.

Forms will vary in page length depending on the amount of information. For instance, the orders Form has order information such as order date and amount on the first page, shipping information on the second page, and the detail records Grid on the third page. In the sample application no Form has more than three pages.

It is important to think about this up-front because most of the code for each Form will go in the vcAppForm template. There will be some Form-specific code in each Form, but most of what happens in a Form (retrieving a new record, adding a record, and checking for conflicts when saving a record) is the same from Form to Form. Specific code examples will be discussed later in the section.

Creating the Application's Views

What views are required to put together each of the forms in the application? Two types of views are needed in this sample application. The Customer Form will be used as the model to explain the purpose of each type of view. Both local and remote versions of the views will be created. This allows you to prototype and develop the application using Visual FoxPro data, then deploy it using SQL Server data.

The local views will be used in the version of the application that uses local data while remote views will be used in the version of the application that uses remote data. Because the remote data has the same structure as the local data, the remote views will have essentially the same Select statements and parameters as the local views. Both types of views bring back whatever records the user needs whenever they are needed. The remote views will have the same names as the local views. You will soon see why this is useful.

All remote views are based on the cnTastrade connection. To save resources, they all have the ShareConnection property set to true. Remember that to do this visually, you check the Share Connection CheckBox in the Advanced Options dialog box for each remote view. Sharing the connection allows each remote view to get its data from SQL Server without needing to establish a new user connection. This means that if a user has two remote views open, he or she will be connected to SQL Server once rather than twice. If there are 20 users simultaneously using the system, 20 connections to SQL Server will be required for views instead of 40. This saves a significant amount of SQL Server memory and resources.

Views for Viewing and Editing Form Information

The users want to be able to see and edit customer data, so you will need a view that returns the data in the customer table. Given that the users will be working with one customer at a time, you want a view that will return one record. The following code shows the SQL statement for the local version of the vCustomer view followed by the SQL statement for the remote version. These are parameterized views that will retrieve one customer record at a time when a customer's ID is stored to the pcViewParam variable.

```
* Local version
Select *;
   From tastrade!customer;
   Where Customer.customer_id Like ?pcViewParam

* Remote version
Select *;
   From dbo.customer Customer;
   Where Customer.customer_id Like ?pcViewParam
```

Because this customer data needs to be updatable on the Form, the view's Cursor should be read and write. This is accomplished in the Update Criteria tab by identifying the primary key, marking fields other than the primary key as updatable, and checking the Send SQL Updates CheckBox. This shown in Figure 6-3.

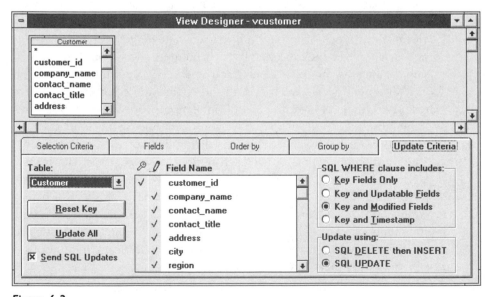

Figure 6-3.

The Update Criteria tab

Each table in the application has a corresponding Form that allows viewing and editing of the data in the table. The Customer Form is based on the customer table and uses the view vCustomer, the Orders Form is based on the orders table and uses the view vOrder, and so on for all of the data entry forms in the application. Table 6-1 lists each of the data entry forms in the application and the view that retrieves the main information displayed on the Form.

Table 6-1.

Data entry forms and their main views

Data Entry Form	Main View
Customer	vCustomer
Order	vOrder
Product	vProduct
Shipper	vShipper
Supplier	vSupplier
Category	vCategory
Group	vGroup

The order details table, order_line_items, does not have its own view because detail records are only viewed or edited in conjunction with an order. If you examine the SQL statements of the views you will notice that some of the views retrieve information from only one table while others retrieve information from more than one table.

Views to Display Related Information

The vCustomer view will take care of the main editing on the Customer Form. Suppose the user would also like to be able to see all of a customer's orders. There will be a Grid on the last page of the Customer Form that lists each of that customer's orders. As a result, you will need to create a parameterized view that retrieves all of the orders for one customer. The following code shows the SQL statement for the local version of the vOrdersOneCustomer view followed by the SQL statement for the remote version.

```
* Local version
Select Orders.order_id, Orders.order_date, Orders.deliver_by,;
    Sum(Order_line_items.unit_price*Order_line_items.quantity),;
    Sum(Order_line_items.quantity), Count(Order_line_items.product_id);
  From tastrade!customer, tastrade!orders, tastrade!order_line_items;
  Where Customer.customer_id = Orders.customer_id;
    And Orders.order_id = Order_line_items.order_id;
    And Customer.customer_id Like ?pcViewParam;
  Group By Orders.order_id;
  Order By Orders.order_date Desc
```

Continued on next page

Continued from previous page

```
* Remote version
Select Orders.order_id, Orders.order_date, Orders.deliver_by,;
     Sum(Order_line_items.unit_price*Order_line_items.quantity),;
     Sum(Order_line_items.quantity), Count(Order_line_items.product_id);
  From dbo.orders Orders, dbo.order_line_items Order_line_items,;
  dbo.customer Customer;
  Where Order_line_items.order_id = Orders.order_id;
     And Customer.customer_id = Orders.customer_id;
     And Orders.customer_id Like ?pcViewParam;
  Group By Orders.order_id, Orders.order_date, Orders.deliver_by;
  Order By Orders.order_date Desc
```

For each order, these return the order ID, the order date, the order's delivery date, the total amount of the order, the total quantity of items in the order, and the number of products involved in the order. When pcViewParam is set to the customer ID of the customer whose records are being looked at, the views can be requeried and the user can see that customer's orders.

On the Customer, Product, and Shipper Forms, the user will be able to see all orders for the customer, product, or shipper. On the Supplier and Category Forms, the user will be able to see all products for the supplier or category. On the Order Form, the user will be able to see all detail records for the order. On the Group Form, the user will be able to see all employees for the group.

Most of the Forms in the application allow viewing of related data in a Grid. Some of the Forms allow this data to be edited while others do not. Table 6-2 lists each of the data entry forms in the application and the view that retrieves the related information displayed on the Form.

Table 6-2.

***Data entry forms
and their related
information views***

Data Entry Form	Related Information View
Customer	vOrdersOneCustomer
Order	vDetailsOneOrder
Product	vOrdersOneProduct
Shipper	vOrdersOneShipper
Supplier	vProductsOneSupplier
Category	vProductsOneCategory
Group	vEmployeesOneGroup

Where Are the Views Stored?

All of the local views are stored in the Visual FoxPro database TASTRADE.DBC, which is part of the sample application. This database also contains the local Visual FoxPro version of the data (in other words, the original tables). This is the data that was upsized to SQL Server. All of the remote views are stored in the database TASTRSQL.DBC. This database contains no tables, only the remote views and the cnTastrade connection that is used by the remote views.

Why are two different databases being used? The remote views could be stored in the same database as the local views, but one of the goals of this application is that you should be able to switch back and forth between local and remote data easily. This makes it very easy to prototype the application using local data, then deploy it using remote data. It also makes it easy to switch back to local data for further modifications.

When remote and local views are in the same database they need to have different names. This makes it more difficult to switch between local and remote data. Also, when you distribute the application to someone using only SQL Server data, you distribute more views than are necessary.

If the remote and local views are stored in different databases and have the same names, you simply have to change the active database to switch between local and remote data. Consider the following code sample. The first time the vCustomer view is used, local data is retrieved. The second time the view is used, remote data is retrieved. That is because the vCustomer view in the Tastrade database is a local view and the vCustomer view in the tastrsql database is a remote view. Visual FoxPro will use the vCustomer view in whatever database is currently set. If you change that database, you change the view used. This makes it very easy to switch back and forth between local and remote data.

```
pcViewParam = "ALFKI"

Set Database To tastrade
Use vCustomer
Browse

Set Database To tastrsql
Use vCustomer
Browse
```

In the sample application, being able to switch back and forth between local and remote data is accomplished by changing the ccTastrade class's cDatabase property. This property stores the name of the database in use when the application is being run. If it is set to DATA\TASTRADE the data will be local. If it is set to DATA\TASTRSQL the data will be remote. This allows you to switch back and forth by changing only one property of the ccTastrade class.

Logging In To SQL Server

There are three things required for users to be able to use the sample application. First, they must be able to log in to SQL Server. This is taken care of in the Login Form, shown in Figure 6-4.

Figure 6-4.

The Login Form

Users enter their SQL Server login IDs and passwords. These are then sent to SQL Server using the SQLConnect() function. If the users can successfully log in, the connection handle is stored to the ccTastrade property nSQLHandle for use in all subsequent SQL Pass-Through functions. The code to log in is contained in the Click event of the Login Form's OK CommandButton.

```
oApp.nSQLHandle = SQLConnect("tastrade", ;
                            AllTrim(ThisForm.txtUserID.Value), ;
                            AllTrim(ThisForm.txtPassword.Value))
If oApp.nSQLHandle < 0
   lnError = AError(laError)
   = MessageBox(LTrim(Str(laError[1])))
   = MessageBox(laError[2])
   = MessageBox("Connect failed. Goodbye.", MB_ICONSTOP)
   oApp.lLoginSuccess = .F.
Else
   oApp.cUserID = AllTrim(ThisForm.txtUserID.Value)
   oApp.cPassword = AllTrim(ThisForm.txtPassword.Value)
   oApp.lLoginSuccess = .T.
Endif

ThisForm.Release
```

The second requirement for users to be able to use this application is that they must be allowed to use the SQL Server Tastrade database. To find out if they are allowed, the Do method of the ccTastrade class uses SQL Pass-Through to attempt to Use the Tastrade database. If it fails, the application will not run. This part of the ccTastrade Do method is shown here:

```
* Can this login id use the tastrade database?
lnSuccess = SQLExec(oApp.nSQLHandle, "Use tastrade")
If lnSuccess < 0
  = MessageBox("You're not allowed to use this data. Go away!", ;
          MB_ICONSTOP)
  This.Cleanup
  Return
Else
  = MessageBox("Welcome to Tastrade!", MB_ICONINFORMATION)
Endif
```

Finally, users must have explicit rights to use the database objects in the database, especially the tables. When users log into SQL Server they use their login IDs. However, when they use a database they use their database name. These may or may not be the same. All database object permissions are assigned based on a user's name in the database, not the login ID. Therefore the code must first determine the user's name. This part of the ccTastrade Do method is shown here:

```
* What is this user's name in the database?
lnSuccess = SQLExec(oApp.nSQLHandle, "Select user_name()")
oApp.cUserName = sqlresult.exp
```

The property oApp.cUserName will be used in each of the data entry forms to see if the user has the rights to edit, add, or delete records.

If the user owns the database the code does not need to check for permissions. The user name "dbo" denotes the owner of the database. In SQL Server, if you create something you own it, so the person who created the Tastrade database can do anything in it. There is no need to check for permissions.

In addition, users of the database can be aliased as the database owner. This is very useful if there is more than one person creating objects in a database. Life is a lot simpler if the dbo owns everything. If Gerhard creates (and therefore owns) half of the objects in the database and Pedro owns the other half, they will not be able to modify each other's objects. If Gerhard leaves the team, Pedro would not be able to work with Gerhard's objects. The solution is to alias all developers to the dbo and have the dbo own everything.

The Do method of ccTastrade checks to see if the user is the dbo or is aliased to the dbo. This part of the code is shown in the following code.

```
* Is this user the dbo?
lcSQL = "Select name From sysusers Where suid = " + ;
          AllTrim(Str(oApp.csUserID))
lnSuccess = SQLExec(oApp.nSQLHandle, lcSQL)
If sqlresult.name = "dbo"
  oApp.ldbo = .T.
Else
   * Is this user alisaed to the dbo?
   lcSQL = "Select * From sysalternates " + ;
           "Where altsuid In (Select suid From sysusers " + ;
           "Where name = 'dbo')"
   lnSuccess = SQLExec(oApp.nSQLHandle, lcSQL)
   If sqlresult.suid = oApp.csUserID
     * This user is the dbo.
     oApp.ldbo = .T.
   Else
     * What group is this user in?
     lnSuccess = SQLExec(oApp.nSQLHandle, "sp_helpuser " + ;
                         oApp.cUserName)
     oApp.cUserGroup = sqlresult.group_name
   Endif
Endif
Use In sqlresult
```

If the user is not the dbo and is not aliased to the dbo, the code then checks to see what group in the database the user belongs to. A group is a collection of users in a database. All users belong to the Public group. In addition, each user can belong to one additional group in each database. It is important to know what group the user belongs to because permissions can be granted to or revoked from a user or a group. In each Form, permissions are checked to see what the user is allowed to do on that Form. The code for that, which you will see later in the discussion titled "Checking Permissions," needs to check permissions for both the user and the groups the user belongs to.

The next part of the Do method is run if the application is using remote data. The code changes the user ID and password in the cnTastrade connection to the login ID and password entered by the user. The DBSetProp() function is used to change the Userid and Password properties of the cnTastrade connection. This code is shown here:

```
If oApp.cDatabase = "DATA\TASTRSQL"
   * Change the connection so that this user is the one that
   * logs in to SQL Server when the remote views are used.
   = DBSetProp('cntastrade', 'connection', 'userid', oApp.cUserID)
   = DBSetProp('cntastrade', 'connection', 'password', oApp.cPassword)
Endif
```

This step is necessary to support multiple users of the application. During development, somebody's user ID and password are put into the cnTastrade connection. However, during deployment you don't want every user logging in as this person. This would defeat the purpose of having various users. Therefore, each user will change these two connection properties to his or her own. Two thoughts might come to mind. First, how can this be done when the DBSetProp() function requires the database to be opened exclusively, and second, what if some other user is already using the cnTastrade connection?

Both of these issues are solved if each user has his or her own version of the tastrsql database. Each user will have the same remote views and, except for the user ID and password, the cnTastrade connections will all be the same. The tastrsql database contains only remote view definitions and a connection definition. You can therefore treat it just like an APP or EXE file, which is created once then given to each user to run locally.

Data Entry Forms

All of the data entry forms in the application are based on the vcAppForm class. There is quite a bit of code in the vcAppForm class. In fact, most of the code run from a data entry Form is stored in that class. This makes sense because the data entry forms basically do the same thing. The user selects a record and can view it, edit it, and delete it. The user can also add a new record and save changes, as well as view the total orders accounted for by the record. The procedures to do these things do not vary from Form to Form so the code should go in the Form class. The individual Forms will be created based on the Form class and will inherit the code from vcAppForm.

There turns out to be very little required to actually construct the data entry forms in this application. First, you need to make vcAppForm class the active Form template. This is accomplished in the Forms tab of the Options dialog box. That assures that each new Form will be based on vcAppForm and will inherit all of its visual elements, properties, methods, and event code.

There are typically two views needed for each Form. The first view contains the main record that the user is viewing or editing. The second view contains the detail information that will be displayed in the Grid on the last page of the Form. The class vcAppForm has two properties to store the name of each of these views. The property cMainView keeps the name of the view that will store the record currently being viewed and edited. The property cViewDetailGrid stores the name of the view that contains the detail records. These properties are created in vcAppForm and are set on each individual Form. Because each Form is based on vcAppForm, all Forms will inherit these properties.

The next step on each Form is to put a PageFrame with two or three pages on the Form. Most Forms have a Grid on the last page for viewing detail records. Several classes of PageFrames were created for this application because there are common PageFrames and Grids on Forms. These classes will be reviewed in more detail in the discussion "Displaying Related Information in a Grid." Once the appropriate PageFrame for a Form is selected and placed on that Form, the detail Grid needs to be tied to the appropriate data. The RecordSource property of the Grid is set to the appropriate detail records view and the ControlSource of each column is set to the appropriate field in the view.

Next, of course, the individual controls for viewing and editing the data have to be placed on the first (and if necessary the second and the third) page on the Form.

The final step is to set various properties of the Form. In particular, you need to identify the views that will be used in this Form, the Form used to display pick lists, and the main SQL Server table used by this Form. Figure 6-5 shows the Properties sheet for the Customer Form and the Form specific properties that are set for it.

In the Forms in this application, the views are not put into the DataEnvironment. This is because each Cursor in the DataEnvironment has a Database property. If you use the local version of vCustomer, for instance, the Database property will be set to DATA\TASTRADE.DBC. If you then set the current database to DATA\TASTRSQL.DBC and want to use the Form with remote data, you will receive an error because the view you are using is not from the same database as the view used to create the Form. You can get around this by changing this property at runtime, but the sample application avoids this issue by not including the views in the DataEnvironment.

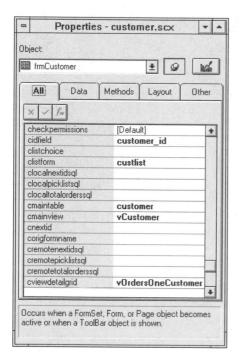

Figure 6-5.

The Customer Form's Properties sheet

Opening Data Entry Forms

The Load method of vcAppForm first runs the Load method of vcFormTemplate. It then sets the current database to whatever is in the cDatabase property of oApp. This property contains the name of the Visual FoxPro database containing either the local views and local data or the remote views. You could also explicitly identify the correct database by using Use (oApp.cDatabase)!vCustomer.

The Load code then opens the main view using the NoData clause. An empty Cursor will be created with the appropriate fields from the table or tables the view is based on. The Form opens with no data and the user will request a record to view and/or edit. The main view of the Form will use optimistic row buffering. Remember that remote views do not support pessimistic buffering. If the Form uses a detail records Grid, the cViewDetailGrid property will store the name of the view used to populate the Grid. If that property is not empty, the appropriate view is opened with no data and will use optimistic table buffering. The code for the Load method is shown here:

```
vcFormTemplate::Load

Set Database To (oApp.cDatabase)

Use (ThisForm.cMainView) In 0 NoData
=CursorSetProp("Buffering", DB_BUFOPTRECORD, ThisForm.cMainView)
If Not Empty(ThisForm.cViewDetailGrid)
   Use (ThisForm.cViewDetailGrid)In 0 NoData
   =CursorSetProp("Buffering", DB_BUFOPTTABLE, ThisForm.cViewDetailGrid)
Endif

Select (ThisForm.cMainView)
```

Checking Permissions

The CheckPermissions method of vcAppForm is run at the end of that class's Init method and is therefore run in the Init of each Form. CheckPermissions is used to see if the user has Update, Insert, and Delete rights on the SQL Server table used by the Form. If not, the appropriate CommandButtons should be disabled on the Form. The SQL Server system stored procedure sp_helprotect will return the rights granted or revoked for a particular database object. For instance, the following line of code will return permissions pertaining to the customer table.

```
sp_helprotect customer
```

A user can have permissions because they have been specifically granted to the user, because they have been granted to a group the user belongs to, or because the user is a guest user in the database and the guest user has been granted permissions. If the user is the dbo, he or she can do anything and there is no need to check permissions.

The CheckPermissions method first uses sp_helprotect to get a listing of permissions for the main table used by the Form. The results of this query are shown in Figure 6-6. The code then scans this result set to see if Update, Insert, and Delete rights have been granted to or revoked from the guest user, the Public group, any additional group the user belongs to, or the user.

> **Tip!**
> The order in which this code looks for permissions represents the SQL Server permissions hierarchy. Any permissions granted to or revoked from a user override any permissions granted to or revoked from a group that user belongs to.

Figure 6-6.

The browse results of sp_helprotect

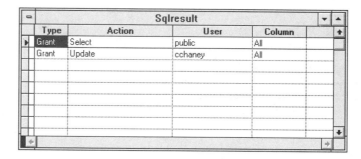

The Check Permissions method is shown here:

```
If oApp.ldbo
   * This user is dbo or aliased to dbo, so can do anything.
   ThisForm.lOKUpdate = .T.
   ThisForm.lOKInsert = .T.
   ThisForm.lOKDelete = .T.
   Return
Endif

ThisForm.lOKUpdate = .F.
ThisForm.lOKInsert = .F.
ThisForm.lOKDelete = .F.
* Get the protections for this form's main table.
lnSuccess = SQLExec(oApp.nSQLHandle, "sp_helprotect " + ;
            ThisForm.cMainTable, "c_protect")
Select c_protect
Scan
   * Can this user edit?
   If Type = "Grant" and Action = "Update" And user = "guest"
      ThisForm.lOKUpdate = .T.
```

Continued on next page

```
Endif
If Type = "Revoke" and Action = "Update" And user = "guest"
   ThisForm.lOKUpdate = .F.
Endif
If Type = "Grant" and Action = "Update" And user = "public"
   ThisForm.lOKUpdate = .T.
Endif
If Type = "Revoke" and Action = "Update" And user = "public"
   ThisForm.lOKUpdate = .F.
Endif
If Type = "Grant" and Action = "Update" And user = ;
      AllTrim(oApp.cUserGroup)
   ThisForm.lOKUpdate = .T.
Endif
If Type = "Revoke" and Action = "Update" And user = ;
      AllTrim(oApp.cUserGroup)
   ThisForm.lOKUpdate = .F.
Endif
If Type = "Grant" and Action = "Update" And user = ;
      AllTrim(oApp.cUserName)
   ThisForm.lOKUpdate = .T.
Endif
If Type = "Revoke" and Action = "Update" And user = ;
      AllTrim(oApp.cUserName)
   ThisForm.lOKUpdate = .F.
Endif

* Can this user insert?
If Type = "Grant" and Action = "Insert" And user = "guest"
   ThisForm.lOKInsert = .T.
Endif
If Type = "Revoke" and Action = "Insert" And user = "guest"
   ThisForm.lOKInsert = .F.
Endif
If Type = "Grant" and Action = "Insert" And user = "public"
   ThisForm.lOKInsert = .T.
Endif
If Type = "Revoke" and Action = "Insert" And user = "public"
   ThisForm.lOKInsert = .F.
Endif
If Type = "Grant" and Action = "Insert" And user = ;
      AllTrim(oApp.cUserGroup)
   ThisForm.lOKInsert = .T.
Endif
If Type = "Revoke" and Action = "Insert" And user = ;
      AllTrim(oApp.cUserGroup)
   ThisForm.lOKInsert = .F.
Endif
If Type = "Grant" and Action = "Insert" And user = ;
      AllTrim(oApp.cUserName)
   ThisForm.lOKInsert = .T.
Endif
```

Continued on next page

Continued from previous page

```
    If Type = "Revoke" and Action = "Insert" And user = ;
        AllTrim(oApp.cUserName)
      ThisForm.lOKInsert = .F.
    Endif

    * Can this user delete?
    If Type = "Grant" and Action = "Delete" And user = "guest"
      ThisForm.lOKDelete = .T.
    Endif
    If Type = "Revoke" and Action = "Delete" And user = "guest"
      ThisForm.lOKDelete = .F.
    Endif
    If Type = "Grant" and Action = "Delete" And user = "public"
      ThisForm.lOKDelete = .T.
    Endif
    If Type = "Revoke" and Action = "Delete" And user = "public"
      ThisForm.lOKDelete = .F.
    Endif
    If Type = "Grant" and Action = "Delete" And user = ;
        AllTrim(oApp.cUserGroup)
      ThisForm.lOKDelete = .T.
    Endif
    If Type = "Revoke" and Action = "Delete" And user = ;
        AllTrim(oApp.cUserGroup)
      ThisForm.lOKDelete = .F.
    Endif
    If Type = "Grant" and Action = "Delete" And user = ;
        AllTrim(oApp.cUserName)
      ThisForm.lOKDelete = .T.
    Endif
    If Type = "Revoke" and Action = "Delete" And user = ;
        AllTrim(oApp.cUserName)
      ThisForm.lOKDelete = .F.
    Endif
EndScan
Use In c_protect

If Not ThisForm.lOKUpdate
  ThisForm.cmdSave.Enabled = .F.
Endif
If Not ThisForm.lOKInsert
  ThisForm.cmdAdd.Enabled = .F.
Endif
If Not ThisForm.lOKDelete
  ThisForm.cmdDelete.Enabled = .F.
Endif

Select (ThisForm.cMainView)
```

Locating a Record

When a data entry Form is first opened, it will contain no data. This
is because there is no reason to assume that the user wants to look

at the first record in the table. The Form is brought up empty, then the user decides which record to retrieve. This avoids the overhead of actually bringing down data that is probably not the first record the user wants to see.

When users want to go to a particular record, they enter either an ID or some characters on which to base a pick list. Then they click the Locate button. The Click event code for the Locate button first checks to see if there is currently any data loaded in the Form. If there is, the code will check to see if the users made any changes. If they have, the users will be prompted to save the changes. If the users want to save the changes, the Save button's Click event code is run. If the users don't want to save the changes, the changes are discarded via the TableRevert() function. If the user had clicked the Add button but not entered any data, the appended record would be discarded from the buffer using TableRevert(). This part of the Locate button's Click event code is shown here:

```
If ThisForm.lDataLoaded And ;
    ("2" $ GetFldState(-1) Or "4" $ GetFldState(-1))
    * There is an edit pending.
    lnResponse = MessageBox("Changes have been made. " + ;
        "Do you want to save them?" , ;
        MB_YESNOCANCEL + MB_ICONEXCLAMATION + MB_DEFBUTTON3)
    Do Case
       Case lnResponse = IDYES
          ThisForm.cmdSave.Click
       Case lnResponse = IDNO
          * The connection is busy due to the pending edit.
          * The TableRevert ends the edit so we can requery.
          Select (ThisForm.cMainView)
          = TableRevert()
       Case lnResponse = IDCANCEL
          Return
    EndCase
Else
    If GetFldState(-1) = "3"
       * User pressed add before downloading any data.
       Select (ThisForm.cMainView)
       = TableRevert()
    Endif
Endif

If Not ThisForm.lOKToContinue
    = MessageBox("OKToContinue is False.")
    Return
Endif

Select (ThisForm.cMainView)
```

The grpLocate OptionGroup has one choice for ID and one for Name. You can see this OptionGroup in vcAppForm, shown in Figure 6-2. If ID is selected, the user can enter an ID in the txtLocate TextBox. This value is stored to pcViewParam and the LocateByID method is run. If Name is selected, the user can enter any number of characters in the TextBox. The SQL Server wildcard character % is added to what the user entered. This is then stored to pcViewParam. The GetPickList method of vcAppForm is run to retrieve the pick list records. This will be discussed in more detail shortly. The data is then displayed in a Grid in a pick list Form. The name of the Form to run is stored to the cListForm property. If the user selects a record and clicks OK, that record's ID is stored to pcViewParam and the LocateByID method is run to retrieve the record. This part of the Locate button's Click event code is shown here:

```
If ThisForm.grpLocate.Value = 2
  * Search by ID
  If Val(ThisForm.txtLocate.Value) > 0
     pcViewParam = PadL(AllTrim(ThisForm.txtLocate.Value), 6, " ")
  Else
     pcViewParam = AllTrim(Upper(ThisForm.txtLocate.Value))
  Endif
  ThisForm.LocateByID
  ThisForm.lDataLoaded = .T.
Else
  * Search by name
  pcViewParam = AllTrim(Upper(ThisForm.txtLocate.Value)) + "%"
  ThisForm.GetPickList
  ThisForm.cListChoice = "Cancel"
  Do Form (ThisForm.cListForm)
  If ThisForm.cListChoice = "OK"
     pcViewParam = Eval("c_PickList." + ThisForm.cIDField)
     ThisForm.LocateByID
     ThisForm.lDataLoaded = .T.
     ThisForm.txtLocate.Value = pcViewParam
     Use In c_picklist
  Else
     Use In c_picklist
     Return
  Endif
Endif
```

The LocateByID method is responsible for retrieving a single record to be displayed in the Form. It uses the Requery() function to requery the Form's main view with whatever ID has been stored to pcViewParam. The first page on the Form is made active and the Form is refreshed to show the new record. If no record is retrieved, the user is informed and can enter a different ID or create a new pick list. If a record is retrieved, it is displayed and the Cursor is placed in the first TextBox for editing. This is typically the TextBox that shows the name of whatever entity is on the Form. Following that, the caption of the first page is set to that name and the appropriate CommandButtons are enabled. The LocateByID method is shown here:

```
Local lcMessage, lnCount, i

If Empty(ThisForm.txtLocate.Value) And Not ThisForm.cListChoice = "OK"
   = MessageBox("Please supply an ID or name to search on.", ;
           MB_ICONEXCLAMATION)
   Return
Endif

= ReQuery(ThisForm.cMainView)
ThisForm.pgfFormInfo.ActivePage = 1
ThisForm.Refresh

If RecCount(ThisForm.cMainView) = 0
   ThisForm.pgfFormInfo.Page1.Caption = ThisForm.Caption
   lcMessage = "There is no " + Lower(ThisForm.Caption) + ;
              " with this id."
   = MessageBox(lcMessage , MB_ICONINFORMATION)
   ThisForm.cmdDelete.Enabled = .F.
   ThisForm.cmdSave.Enabled = .F.
   ThisForm.cmdUndo.Enabled = .F.
   ThisForm.cmdViewTotal.Enabled = .F.
   ThisForm.txtLocate.SetFocus
Else
   lnCount = ThisForm.pgfFormInfo.Page1.ControlCount
   For i = 1 To lnCount
     * This can be done by looking for the first control that begins with "txt".
     * It can be done by looking for "txtLocate".
     * It can be done by looking for TabStop = 1.
     If "txt" $ ThisForm.pgfFormInfo.Page1.Controls(i).Name
        Exit
     Endif
   Endfor
   ThisForm.pgfFormInfo.Page1.Controls(i).SetFocus
   ThisForm.SetPage1Caption
   ThisForm.EnableButtons
Endif
```

Pick Lists

Users want to be able to retrieve a customer record based either on the customer's ID or name. If the user knows and enters the ID, it will be stored to pcViewParam. The vCustomer view will then be requeried to get the data for that customer. However, sometimes users don't know customer IDs. They may not know how to spell the customer's complete name or may only know that the customer's name begins with "Micro" or "Info."

When this happens, you need to retrieve the records used in the pick list from the server. You could create and send a Select statement that returned customer ID and customer name for all customers sorted by name, but think about this for a second. Do you really want to bring all customers down from SQL Server? What if there are 250,000 of them? Although you could display all of them in a Grid it doesn't make sense to bring down this much data. The users probably don't really need or want to see all customers, only the customers they want to select from.

The most efficient way to do this is to give the user the ability to enter some characters, then show the user all customers whose name begins with those characters. So if the user enters M, the application will bring down all customers whose name begins with "M." If the user refines the search and enters "Micro," the application will bring down all customers whose name begins with Micro. That way it is up to the user to decide how many customers to view and how long it will take for them to be retrieved from the server.

The following code sample shows a Select statement that will create the customer pick list using local data.

```
Select Customer.customer_id, Customer.company_name, ;
        Customer.city, Customer.region ;
    From tastrade!customer ;
    Where Customer.company_name Like ?pcViewParam ;
    Order By Customer.company_name ;
Into Cursor c_picklist
```

The next code sample shows a Select statement that is sent to SQL Server using SQL Pass-Through to create the customer pick list.

```
lcSQL = "Select Customer.customer_id, Customer.company_name, " + ;
         "Customer.city, Customer.region " + ;
     "From customer " + ;
     "Where Customer.company_name Like '" + pcViewParam + "' " + ;
     "Order By Customer.company_name"
lnResult = SQLExec(oApp.nSQLHandle, lcSQL, "c_picklist")
```

The user will be shown the company name, city, and region in a Grid. When the user selects a customer, that customer's ID will then be stored in pcViewParam and the vCustomer view will be requeried to retrieve the information for the selected customer.

You need to be a bit clever about what is put into pcViewParam. Suppose the user enters "Micro." The Where clause would be as follows:

```
Where Customer.company_name Like "Micro"
```

Unless there is a customer literally named Micro, no records will be returned. You will need to supply a wildcard character to make this work as desired. pcViewParam should contain what the user entered plus a %, the SQL Server wildcard. It is equivalent to Visual FoxPro's *. The Where clause would then be as shown:

```
Where Customer.company_name Like "Micro%"
```

This will retrieve all customers whose names begin with Micro. If users really do want to see all of the customers, they can enter nothing. When the % is added to that, the Where clause would be as shown:

```
Where Customer.company_name Like "%"
```

This will return all customers. Of course, your code could prevent the user from doing this if you don't want unrestricted pick lists.

Figure 6-7 shows the customer pick list after the user entered "M."

Figure 6-7.

The customer pick list

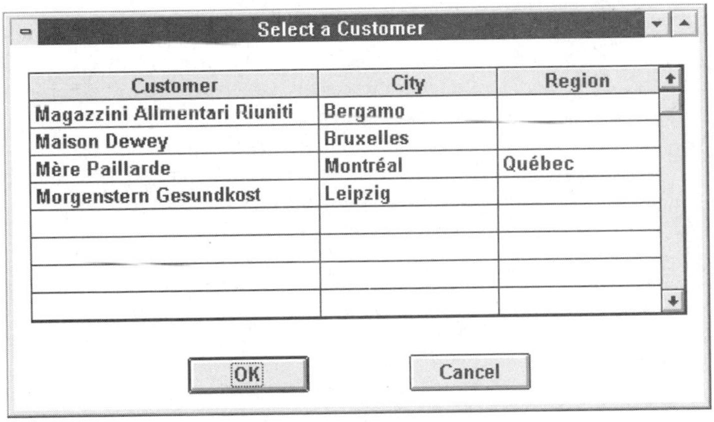

Customer	City	Region
Magazzini Allmentari Riuniti	Bergamo	
Maison Dewey	Bruxelles	
Mère Paillarde	Montréal	Québec
Morgenstern Gesundkost	Leipzig	

OK   Cancel

With the exception of the Order Form, all Forms allow the user to enter any number of characters and select from a pick list of all entities whose names begin with those characters. The Order Form does not allow this because orders are accessed by order number. It is expected that the user knows the number of an order.

The GetPickList method is used to retrieve the contents of the pick list. If the pick list comprises local data, a Visual FoxPro Select is used. If remote data is used, a Select is sent to SQL Server via the SQLExec() function. The GetPickList procedure is generic and is therefore a method of vcAppForm. The actual Select statements are Form specific and therefore stored in properties of vcAppForm. The cLocalPickListSQL property stores the local Select. The cRemotePickListSQL stores the remote Select. These properties are then set in the Init of each individual Form.

The GetPickList method is shown here:

```
If Upper(oApp.cDataSource) = "LOCAL"
   &ThisForm.cLocalPickListSQL
Else
   lnResult = SQLExec(oApp.nSQLHandle, ThisForm.cRemotePickListSQL, ;
                       "c_picklist")
   If lnResult < 0
      lnError = AError(laError)
      = MessageBox(LTrim(Str(laError[1])))
      = Messagebox(laError[2])
   Endif
Endif

Select (ThisForm.cMainView)
```

This code sample shows the part of the Init method of the Customer Form where the cLocalPickListSQL and cRemotePickListSQL properties are set.

```
ThisForm.cLocalPickListSQL = ;
   "Select Customer.customer_id, Customer.company_name, " + ;
   "Customer.city, Customer.region " + ;
   "From tastrade!customer " + ;
   "Where Customer.company_name Like ?pcViewParam " + ;
   "Order By Customer.company_name " + ;
   "Into Cursor c_picklist"

ThisForm.cRemotePickListSQL = ;
   "Select Customer.customer_id, Customer.company_name, " + ;
   "Customer.city, Customer.region " + ;
   "From customer " + ;
   "Where Customer.company_name Like '" + pcViewParam + "' " + ;
   "Order By Customer.company_name"
```

Table 6-3 shows each data entry Form, the Form used to display the pick list, and the information that is displayed to the user.

Table 6-3.

Data entry and pick list Forms

Data Entry Form	Pick List Form	Pick List Grid Columns	Column Captions
Category	catlist	2	Category, Description
Customer	custlist	3	Customer, City, Region
Employee	emplist	3	Last Name, First Name, Group
Group	grplist	1	Group
Product	prodlist	2	Product, English Name
Shipper	shiplist	1	Shipper
Supplier	supplist	3	Supplier, City, Region

Displaying Related Information in a Grid

Every Form will have a PageFrame on it. Most Forms will have a Grid with detail records on the last page. As a result, some of the Forms will have two pages while others will have enough information to require three pages. As you are constructing classes you should look for patterns and shared elements. The Product Form requires two pages and shows orders in the Grid on Page 2. The Shippers Form requires two pages and shows orders in the Grid on Page 2. The Category and Supplier Forms require two pages and both show products in the Grid. Classes should be made out of these shared elements.

This application uses a basic two-page page-frame class and a basic three-page page-frame class. These will not contain the actual Grids that appear on the last page. Rather, these classes will be subclassed and the subclasses will include the individual Grids. As always, the class contains the basic elements and the subclasses contain the exceptions.

The basic two-page page-frame class is called vcPageFrame_2Page and is stored in the file ELEMENTS.VCX. In the Activate event for the second page, the view that will be used to populate that page's Grid is requeried. The name of this view is stored in the Form property cViewDetailGrid. After the view is requeried, the page is refreshed. This code is shown here.

```
If Val(ThisForm.txtLocate.Value) > 0
   pcViewParam = PadL(AllTrim(ThisForm.txtLocate.Value), 6, " ")
Else
   pcViewParam = AllTrim(Upper(ThisForm.txtLocate.Value))
Endif

= ReQuery(ThisForm.cViewDetailGrid)

ThisForm.pgfFormInfo.Page2.Refresh
```

The basic three-page page-frame class is called vcPageFrame_3Page, and is stored in the file ELEMENTS.VCX. The Activate code for the second page refreshes that page. The code is shown in this code sample.

```
ThisForm.pgfFormInfo.Page2.Refresh
```

The Activate event code for the third page is basically the same as vcPageFrame_2Page's second page Activate code. This code is shown here:

```
If Val(ThisForm.txtLocate.Value) > 0
   pcViewParam = PadL(AllTrim(ThisForm.txtLocate.Value), 6, " ")
Else
   pcViewParam = AllTrim(Upper(ThisForm.txtLocate.Value))
Endif

= ReQuery(ThisForm.cViewDetailGrid)

ThisForm.pgfFormInfo.Page3.Refresh
```

The vcPageFrame_2Page and vcPageFrame_3Page classes have been subclassed to include the detail Grids on the last page. Each Grid is based on the built-in Visual FoxPro Grid. Table 6-4 shows each of these subclasses, the Forms that use the subclass, the detail that appears in the Grid, the number of Columns in the Grid, and the captions of the Columns.

PageFrame Subclass	Forms	Grid Detail	Grid Columns	Column Captions
vcpgfProductsGrid	category, supplier	products	4	ID, Product Name, English Name, Disc.
vcpgfOrdersGrid	customer, product, shipper	orders	6	Order, Order Date, Deliver By, Amount, Items, Quantity
vcpgfEmployeesGrid	group	employees	4	Last Name, First Name, Sales Region, Extension
vcpgfOrderDetailsGrid	order	order details	4	Product ID, Product, Price, Quantity

Table 6-4.

PageFrame subclasses

Saving Changes to the Data

As you learned how to access back-end data using remote views, you may have been struck by the similarities between using views (remote and local) and tables. Even though you are building a client/server application, in many ways it will look the same as an application that uses only Visual FoxPro data. This is particularly evident in the code used to manipulate records in a Form.

When the user clicks the Save button, the code in that button's Click event issues a TableUpdate(). Because the Cursor is from a remote view, Visual FoxPro sends an Update statement to SQL Server. The TableUpdate() will succeed if there are no conflicts. The setting of the remote view's WhereType property determines how Visual FoxPro checks for conflicts. Remember that the settings of this property can be one of the following: Key Fields Only, Key and Updatable Fields, Key and Modified Fields, and Key and Timestamp. The Update statement sent to SQL Server will succeed or fail based on the WhereType property of the view.

If the Update succeeds, the TableUpdate() will succeed. If the Update fails, the TableUpdate() will fail. In this regard, the only difference between using local data and remote data is where Visual FoxPro sends the Update. The TableUpdate() will succeed or fail regardless of where the data goes. Most of the Click event code for the cmdSave button on the Form template vcAppForm is shown in the following code. As you can see, much of this code is fairly generic Visual FoxPro Save button code.

```
If Not TableUpdate()
   lnError = AError(laError)

   * Did SQL Server reject the update?
   If laError[1] = 1526
     ThisForm.ParseSQLError(laError[3])
     Return
   Endif

   * Is this a new record?
   If Left(GetFldState(-1), 1) = "3"
       = MessageBox("Error " + AllTrim(Str(laError[1])) + ": " + ;
                 laError[2], MB_ICONINFORMATION)
     ThisForm.lOKToContinue = .F.
     Return
   Endif

   * Is there an update conflict?
   * Refresh the data so that CurVal is current
   =Refresh()
   lcChanged = ""
   For i = 1 To FCount()
     lcField = Field(i)
     If CurVal(lcField) <> OldVal(lcField)
        * The field has been changed by someone else.
        If GetFldState(lcField) = 1
          * You did not change it. Set your value to the
          * current value.
          Replace orders.&lcField With CurVal(lcField)
        Else
```

Continued on next page

Continued from previous page

```
                  * You also changed it.
                  Do Case
                    Case Type(lcField) = "C"
                      cString1 = AllTrim(OldVal(lcField))
                      cString2 = AllTrim(Eval(lcField))
                      cString3 = AllTrim(CurVal(lcField))
                    Case Type(lcField) = "N" Or Type(lcField) = "F" Or ;
                         Type(lcField) = "I" Or Type(lcField) = "B"
                      cString1 = LTrim(Str(OldVal(lcField), 20, 2))
                      cString2 = LTrim(Str(Eval(lcField), 20, 2))
                      cString3 = LTrim(Str(CurVal(lcField), 20, 2))
                    Case Type(lcField) = "Y"
                      cString1 = LTrim(Str(OldVal(lcField), 20, 4))
                      cString2 = LTrim(Str(Eval(lcField), 20, 4))
                      cString3 = LTrim(Str(CurVal(lcField), 20, 4))
                    Case Type(lcField) = "D"
                      cString1 = Dtoc(OldVal(lcField))
                      cString2 = Dtoc(Eval(lcField))
                      cString3 = Dtoc(CurVal(lcField))
                    Case Type(lcField) = "T"
                      cString1 = Ttoc(OldVal(lcField))
                      cString2 = Ttoc(Eval(lcField))
                      cString3 = Ttoc(CurVal(lcField))
                  EndCase
                  lcChanged = Proper(lcField) + " has been changed by "+ ;
                          "someone else. " + ;
                          Chr(10) + Chr(10) + ;
                          "It was " + cString1 + Chr(10) + ;
                          "You changed it to " + cString2 + Chr(10) + ;
                            "Someone else changed it to " + cString3
                  = MessageBox(lcChanged, MB_OK + MB_ICONINFORMATION)
               Endif
            Endif
     Next
     If Not Empty(lcChanged)
        * There is a conflict.
        If MessageBox("Do you want to save your changes and " + ;
                    "overwrite these?", ;
                       MB_YESNO + MB_ICONEXCLAMATION + ;
                          MB_DEFBUTTON2) = IDYES
           Select (ThisForm.cMainView)
           = TableUpdate(.T., .T.)
           = MessageBox("This record has been saved",
              MB_ICONINFORMATION)
           ThisForm.lDataLoaded = .F.
           ThisForm.EnableButtons
        Else
           Select (ThisForm.cMainView)
           = TableRevert()
           = MessageBox("This record has not been saved",
              MB_ICONINFORMATION)
```

Continued on next page

```
          ThisForm.Refresh
       Endif
    Else
       Select (ThisForm.cMainView)
       = TableUpdate(.T., .T.)
       = MessageBox("This record has been saved",
         MB_ICONINFORMATION)
       ThisForm.lDataLoaded = .F.
       ThisForm.EnableButtons
    Endif
 Else

 * There is code in here that you will see in the section on
 * adding a record.

    = MessageBox("This record has been saved", MB_ICONINFORMATION)
    ThisForm.lDataLoaded = .F.
    ThisForm.EnableButtons
 Endif
```

TableUpdate() is used to save the record. If it works, the user is informed. If it fails, the code needs to find out why. The code first checks to see if the Update failed because the record violated SQL Server data integrity. This will be explored in full detail shortly. If data integrity is not the problem, the code will then check to see if someone else made changes while this user was also editing the record. The CurVal() and OldVal() functions are used to compare the original and current values for each field. OldVal() returns the value of a field at the time it was copied to the buffer for editing. CurVal() returns the current value of a field. If they differ, then someone else changed the field.

When used with local data, CurVal() will read from the disk. When used with remote data, however, by default CurVal() will not read from the disk because the data is on the back-end server. Issuing the Refresh() function prior to using CurVal() will force Visual FoxPro to obtain the most current values from the server. This ensures that CurVal() uses the current data.

If a field was changed by someone else and the user didn't change it as well, the field in the user's buffer is set to the changed value. This way, the code can issue TableUpdate(.T., .T.) and force an override of the record. Because the field or fields changed by the other user are now changed in the current user's buffer, the override will leave the other user's changes alone while saving the current user's changes.

If both the current user and another user changed the same field(s), there would be a conflict. The original value, the current user's value, and the other user's value are displayed and the current user is asked whether the other user's changes should be overwritten. TableUpdate(.T., .T.) is used to force the current user's data to be saved.

Adding New Records

When the user clicks the Add button, an Append Blank is issued. Remember that the appended record is only in the view Cursor's buffer and has not been sent to SQL Server. If the user doesn't want to add the record, he or she can click the Undo button, which will issue a TableRevert() so that the new record is not written to the disk.

When the user saves the new record, a TableUpdate() is issued. This code is in the Click event of the vcAppForm Save button. However, this time Visual FoxPro sends an Insert statement instead of an Update to SQL Server. Before the Insert can be sent, there is a missing piece of information. Each record in each table has a unique ID. In most cases, this ID is a number. The ID of the added record should be one greater than the ID of the last record added.

The following code listing shows a piece of the Save button's Click event code. GetFldState() is used to determine if the user is currently adding a record. If so, the GetNextID method of vcAppForm is run to determine the ID of the new record. The code then has to update the value of the ID field with the next ID value before sending the Insert to SQL Server. TableUpdate() can then be issued to send the new record to SQL Server.

The ID field is the primary key. When the main view for this Form was created, the ID field was not marked as being updatable. It is always good practice to not let the users change the value of the primary key. Among other things, you don't have to worry about cascading the change to related tables. However, when adding a new record, the ID field must temporarily be made updatable. CursorSetProp() is used to accomplish this by adding the ID field to the updatable field list. This is shown in the second half of this code sample:

```
* If this is a new record, get the next id before saving.
If Left(GetFldState(-1), 1) = "3"
   llNewRec = .T.
   * There is an outstanding append blank.
   If Not "4" $ GetFldState(-1)
      * No data was entered in the new record.
      = MessageBox("There is nothing to save.", MB_ICONINFORMATION)
      Return
   Endif
   * Run the query to find out the last ID.
```

Continued on next page

```
    ThisForm.GetNextID
    * Put the new ID in the current record.
    Replace (ThisForm.cMainView + "." + ThisForm.cIDField) With ;
            ThisForm.cNextId
    * Make the primary key updatable.
    lcOrigFieldList = CursorGetProp("UpdatableFieldList", ;
                    ThisForm.cMainView)
    lcFieldList = ThisForm.cIDField + " " + lcOrigFieldList
    If Not CursorSetProp("UpdatableFieldList", lcFieldList, ;
                    ThisForm.cMainView)
       = MessageBox("Couldn't change updatable field list.")
       ThisForm.lOKToContinue = .F.
       Return
    Endif
Endif
```

After the new record has been sent to the server, the ID field
needs to be made read-only again. The code to accomplish this is
also in the Save button's Click event and is shown in the next code
sample. CursorSetProp() is used to set the UpdatableFieldList
property back to its original value.

```
If llNewRec
    * Make the primary key not updatable.
    If Not CursorSetProp("UpdatableFieldList", lcOrigFieldList, ;
                        ThisForm.cMainView)
       = MessageBox("Couldn't change back updatable field list.")
       ThisForm.lOKToContinue = .F.
       Return
    Endif
    * Display the new ID on the form.
    ThisForm.txtLocate.Value = ThisForm.cNextId
    lnCount = ThisForm.pgfFormInfo.Page1.ControlCount
    * Loop through each control on the form.
    For i = 1 To lnCount
       If "txt" $ ThisForm.pgfFormInfo.Page1.Controls(i).Name
          * This is the first text box control.
          Exit
       Endif
    Endfor
    ThisForm.pgfFormInfo.Page1.Controls(i).SetFocus
    * Display the name for this record in the tab for page 1.
    ThisForm.SetPage1Caption
Endif
```

The GetNextID method of vcAppForm is shown in the following
code sample. A Select statement is used to retrieve the next ID.
When the data is local the vcAppForm property cLocalNextIDSQL
stores the Select statement. When the data is remote the property
cRemoteNextIDSQL stores the Select statement. The ID retrieved by
the Select is changed by an increment of one and is stored in the

Form's cNextID property. This value is then put into the ID field in the Cursor's buffer and is sent to the server as part of the Insert when the TableUpdate() is issued.

```
If Upper(oApp.cDataSource) = "LOCAL"
  &ThisForm.cLocalNextIDSQL
Else
  lnResult = SQLExec(oApp.nSQLHandle, ThisForm.cRemoteNextIDSQL, ;
                     "c_lastid")
  If lnResult < 0
    lnError = AError(laError)
    = MessageBox(LTrim(Str(laError[1])))
    = Messagebox(laError[2])
  Endif
Endif

If Upper(oApp.cDataSource) = "LOCAL"
  ThisForm.cNextId = Padl(Int(Val(Eval("c_lastid.max_" + ;
                         ThisForm.cIDField))) + 1, 6, " ")
Else
  ThisForm.cNextId = Padl(Int(Val(Eval("c_lastid.exp"))) + 1, 6, " ")
Endif
Use In c_lastid

Select (ThisForm.cMainView)
```

The Cursor c_lastid has one field that contains the highest current ID. The field is called max_product_id if the data is local, and exp if the data is remote. To get the ID for the next added product, you simply need to add 1 to this number. Whether you add 1 in the Select statement or afterwards is a matter of preference.

The cLocalNextIDSQL and cRemoteNextIDSQL properties are set in the Init of each Form. The following code shows the part of the Init method of the Category Form where these two properties are set.

```
ThisForm.cLocalNextIDSQL = ;
  "Select Max(Category.category_id) " + ;
  "From tastrade!category " + ;
  "Into Cursor c_lastid"

ThisForm.cRemoteNextIDSQL = ;
  "Select Max(Category.category_id) " + ;
  "From category Holdlock"
```

The Select statement to get the last ID for the remote data uses the SQL Server Holdlock clause. Remember that data in SQL Server is stored on 2 K pages. As SQL Server reads each page, it locks it for the time it takes to read it. This lock is a *shared lock*, meaning others can read the page at the same time, but no one can write to the page. The lock is released when SQL Server is done with the page. If the Holdlock clause is used in a Select, SQL Server will not release the shared locks until it has read every page needed by the Select. While a user is reading the data to get the last ID, no one else can be adding a new record with the same ID.

This technique is not completely bulletproof. There is a gap between the time the Select finishes and the Insert is sent up and processed by SQL Server. If, in that time, someone else ran the Select they would get the same answer. As a result, it is possible that two users will send up a new record with the same ID. However, because each table has a unique index on the primary key, the second Insert will be rejected by SQL Server. All that is required is that the user rerun the Select to get a new ID, then resubmit the Insert.

In SQL Server 6, each table can have an identity column. SQL Server will autoincrement the value in the identity column each time a new row is inserted. If you made the ID field in each table the identity column, you would not need to determine the next ID number. You could let SQL Server determine it for you.

All of the Forms, except the Customer Form, run a Select to determine the last ID used when the user adds a record. In the Tastrade data, the customer IDs are not sequential numbers but are based on the customer's name. This is not a good idea because the customer ID is the primary key. However, the sample application takes the Tastrade data as a given. When the user adds a new customer he or she will have to supply the customer ID.

Deleting a Record

When the user wants to delete a record, the Visual FoxPro Delete command is used. Then a TableUpdate() is issued. Visual FoxPro sends a Delete statement to SQL Server to delete the current record. If the TableUpdate() fails, the user needs to be informed. The code first checks to see if SQL Server rejected the deletion, perhaps because of a referential integrity constraint. This is explored in full detail in the next part, "Checking for Rejected Updates, Inserts, and Deletes." The Delete button Click event code is shown here:

```
lcMessage = "Do you really want to delete this " + ;
           Lower(ThisForm.Caption) + "?"
If MessageBox(lcMessage, MB_YESNO + MB_ICONQUESTION + ;
           MB_DEFBUTTON2) = IDYES
  Delete

  If Not TableUpdate()
    lnError = AError(laError)

    If laError[1] = 1526
```

Continued on next page

Continued from previous page

```
      * SQL Server rejected the delete
      ThisForm.ParseSQLError(laError[3])
   Else
      = MessageBox(laError[3], MB_ICONINFORMATION)
   Endif
   Select (ThisForm.cMainView)
   = TableRevert()
Else
   lcMessage = "This " + Lower(ThisForm.Caption) + " has been
      deleted."
   = MessageBox(lcMessage, MB_ICONINFORMATION)
Endif
```

Checking for Rejected Updates, Inserts, and Deletes

When the user saves a record (new or old) or deletes a record, the TableUpdate() function is used to send the appropriate data modification statement to SQL Server. If SQL Server rejects the Update, Insert, or Delete, it will send an error message back to Visual FoxPro. This is why the TableUpdate() fails.

The AError() function can be used to determine if the TableUpdate() failed because SQL Server rejected the data modification. The first column of the array created by AError() will contain the error number. If SQL Server rejected the data, this column will contain 1526, the standard ODBC connectivity error number. The third column of the array contains the text of the error message from ODBC. This text string is passed to the ParseSQLError method of vcAppForm.

The ParseSQLError method is used to determine exactly what SQL Server error message was sent back to Visual FoxPro. It looks in the SQL Server error message for certain phrases to see what the cause of the data rejection was. The error message is parsed and reworded, then displayed to the user. The ParseSQLError method is shown here:

```
Parameter cSQLError

Local cMessage, cString, nPosition
cMessage = "The update was rejected because "

Do Case
   * Example: A column insert or update conflicts with a rule
   * imposed by a previous CREATE RULE command.
   * The conflict occurred in database 'tastrade', table
   * 'products', column 'unit_price'
   Case "CREATE RULE" $ cSQLError
      nPosition = At(", column", cSQLError)
```

Continued on next page

```
      cString = SubStr(cSQLError, nPosition + 10)
      cString - SubStr(cString, 1, Len(cString) - 1)
      cMessage = cMessage + "the data in " + cString + ;
                  " violates a database rule."

 * Example: UPDATE statement conflicted with COLUMN CHECK
 * constraint 'CK_unit_cost'.
 * The conflict occurred in database 'tastrade', table
 * 'products', column 'unit_cost'
 Case "COLUMN CHECK" $ cSQLError
      nPosition = At(", column", cSQLError)
      cString = SubStr(cSQLError, nPosition + 10)
      cString = SubStr(cString, 1, Len(cString) - 1)
      cMessage = cMessage + "the data in " + cString + ;
                  " violates a database constraint."

 * Example: DELETE statement conflicted with COLUMN REFERENCE
 * constraint. The conflict occurred in database 'tastrade',
 * table 'orders', column 'customer_id'
 Case "COLUMN REFERENCE" $ cSQLError
      nPosition = At("table '", cSQLError)
      cString = SubStr(cSQLError, nPosition + 7)
      nPosition = At("'", cString)
      cString = Left(cString, nPosition - 1)
      cMessage = cMessage + "there are related records in the " + ;
                  cString + "table."

* Other specific messages can be parsed in here.

  Otherwise
      nPosition = At("Server]", cSQLError)
      cMessage = cMessage + SubStr(cSQLError, nPosition + 8)
EndCase

= MessageBox(cMessage, MB_ICONINFORMATION)
```

The examples that follow look at various reasons why data modifications can be rejected. In each instance, the SQL Server error message that is returned is displayed. The ParseSQLError method takes these error messages and turns them into something more useful to the user.

Data Rejected Because a Rule Is Violated

Data rejection can occur because a rule has been violated. Rules are created on SQL Server with the Create Rule statement. The rules are then bound to a column in a table or to a user-defined data type. The following code shows a rule that keeps product prices less than or equal to $100.

```
Create Rule rul_product_price_change
As @price <= 100
```

If an Update is sent to SQL Server that changes a product's price to something more than $100, the Update will be rejected because of the rule. Figure 6-8 shows the error message sent back by the server.

Figure 6-8.

The SQL Server rule violation message

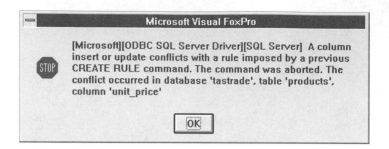

This is not the type of error message most users care to see. The ParseSQLError method will take this raw error message and turn it into something much more user friendly, as you can see in Figure 6-9.

Figure 6-9.

A user friendly rule violation message

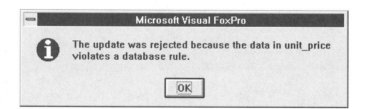

This error message does not say what rule has been violated. You could retrieve the rule definition with a Select and display that. You could also not use rules and just use triggers, as triggers allow you to return whatever error message you want.

Data Rejected Because a Constraint Is Violated

In SQL Server 6 you can define constraints. Constraints are similar to rules, but have a small amount of added functionality. The following code adds a constraint that prohibits the unit cost of any product from exceeding $100.

```
Alter Table products
Add Constraint ck_unit_cost
Check (unit_cost <= $100)
```

Figure 6-10 shows the error message returned by SQL Server when a constraint is violated.

Figure 6-10.

The constraint violation error message

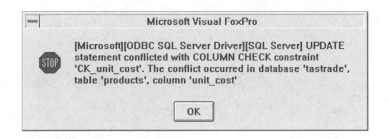

Figure 6-10.

The constraint violation error message

Data Rejected Because Declarative Referential Integrity Is Violated

SQL Server 6 supports declarative referential integrity. This allows you to have referential integrity enforced by the data engine rather than having to write triggers. The next code sample sets up a relationship between the customer and orders tables.

```
ALTER TABLE orders ADD CONSTRAINT fk_customer_id FOREIGN KEY
    (customer_id) REFERENCES customer (customer_id)
```

Figure 6-11 shows the error message returned by SQL Server when declarative referential integrity is violated.

Figure 6-11.

The declarative referential integrity violation message

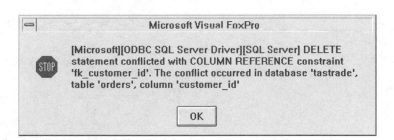

Data Rejected by a Primary Key Constraint

SQL Server 6 supports primary key constraints. This allows you to identify the primary key of a table in that table's definition. A unique index is created on the primary key to ensure that duplicates are not allowed in the table. The following code sets up a primary key constraint on the customer table.

```
ALTER TABLE customer ADD CONSTRAINT pk_customer_id PRIMARY KEY (customer_id)
```

Figure 6-12 shows the error message returned by SQL Server when a primary key constraint is violated.

Figure 6-12.

The primary key constraint violation message

Data Rejected by a Unique Index

In both SQL Server 4.2 and 6 the uniqueness of a table's primary key is physically enforced through the use of unique indexes. The following code creates a unique index for the customer table.

```
CREATE UNIQUE INDEX customer_id ON customer (customer_id)
```

Figure 6-13 shows the error message returned by SQL Server when a duplicate record is rejected by a unique index.

Figure 6-13.

The unique index violation message

Data Rejected by a Trigger

In SQL Server 4.2 and in SQL Server 6, you need to write triggers to enforce referential integrity. In addition, triggers are used to enforce data validation. The next code sample creates a trigger that prevents prices from being raised by more than 10 percent.

```
Create Trigger trProductsUpdate
On products
For Update
As
If (Select (inserted.unit_price - deleted.unit_price) /
            inserted.unit_price From inserted, deleted) > .10
Begin
  Rollback Transaction
  Raiserror 90002 'Prices can not be raised by more than 10
    percent.'
End
```

The Raiserror in the trigger causes SQL Server to let Visual FoxPro know that the data update failed. SQL Server will pass the trigger's error message to Visual FoxPro. Figure 6-14 shows this error message.

Figure 6-14.

The trigger error message

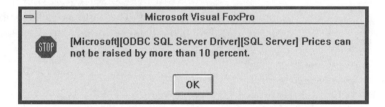

Retrieving the Total Dollar Amount of Orders

The cmdViewTotal CommandButton allows the user to see the total dollar amount of orders for the current record. The total is, of course, the sum of quantity multiplied by price for all order detail rows that belong to orders placed by that customer, product, shipper, and so forth. The Click event code for the View Totals button is shown here:

```
Local lcMessage, lnTotal
If Val(ThisForm.txtLocate.Value) > 0
  pcViewParam = PadL(AllTrim(ThisForm.txtLocate.Value), 6, " ")
Else
  pcViewParam = AllTrim(Upper(ThisForm.txtLocate.Value))
Endif

ThisForm.GetTotalOrders

If Upper(oApp.cDataSource) = "LOCAL"
  lnTotal = c_TotalOrders.sum_exp_1
Else
  lnTotal = c_TotalOrders.exp
Endif
If IsNull(lnTotal) Or lnTotal = 0
```

Continued on next page

Continued from previous page

```
       lcMessage = "No sales have been recorded for this " + ;
                    Lower(ThisForm.Caption) + "."
   Else
       lcMessage = "This " + Lower(ThisForm.Caption) + ;
                " has accounted for " + ;
                AllTrim(Transform(lnTotal, "$,$$$,$$$,$$$.99")) + ;
                " in sales."
   Endif
   = MessageBox(lcMessage, MB_ICONINFORMATION)

   Use In c_TotalOrders

   Select (ThisForm.cMainView)
```

The GetTotalOrders method of vcAppForm runs either a local or remote Select statement to figure out the total orders for the record. This figure is stored in the Cursor c_totalorders, which has one field containing the order total. The field is called sum_exp_1 if the data is local and exp if the data is remote. The code for the GetTotalOrders method is as follows:

```
If Upper(oApp.cDataSource) = "LOCAL"
   &ThisForm.cLocalTotalOrdersSQL
Else
   lnResult = SQLExec(oApp.nSQLHandle, ThisForm.cRemoteTotalOrdersSQL, ;
             "c_TotalOrders")
   If lnResult < 0
      lnError = AError(laError)
      = MessageBox(LTrim(Str(laError[1])))
      = Messagebox(laError[2])
   Endif
Endif

Select (ThisForm.cMainView)
```

Just like the Select statements to get the pick list records and to get the next ID, the Select statements to get the total orders are stored in properties of vcAppForm. These properties, cLocalTotalOrdersSQL and cRemoteTotalOrdersSQL, are set in the Init method of each Form. The following code shows the part of the Init method of the Category Form where these two properties are set.

```
ThisForm.cLocalTotalOrdersSQL = ;
   "Select Sum(Order_line_items.unit_price * " + ;
         "Order_line_items.quantity) " + ;
   "From tastrade!products, tastrade!order_line_items " + ;
   "Where Products.product_id = Order_line_items.product_id " + ;
   "And Products.category_id Like ?pcViewParam " + ;
   "Into Cursor c_TotalOrders"

ThisForm.cRemoteTotalOrdersSQL = ;
   "Select Sum(Order_line_items.unit_price * " + ;
         "Order_line_items.quantity) " + ;
   "From products, order_line_items " + ;
   "Where Products.product_id = Order_line_items.product_id " + ;
   "And Products.category_id Like ?pcViewParam"
```

Reports and Queries

The reports in this sample application are fairly simple. From the application's menu there are three report choices: total orders by customer, total orders by country, and total orders by employee. There is a PRG file to run each of these reports (ORDBYCUS.PRG, ORDBYCTY.PRG, and ORDBYEMP.PRG respectively).

To derive this information, Select statements are needed. What type of Selects should be used? For the local data, should views, queries, or the Select command be used? For the remote data, should views or SQL Pass-Through be used? The next code sample shows a statement that will create a remote view to see total orders by country.

```
Create SQL View vTotalOrdersByCountry ;
   Connection cnTastrade ;
   As Select Customer.country, Count(Orders.order_id) As ordcount, ;
      Sum(Order_line_items.unit_price * Order_line_items.quantity) ;
      As ordtotal ;
   From customer, orders, order_line_items ;
   Where Customer.customer_id = Orders.customer_id ;
      And Orders.order_id = Order_line_items.order_id ;
   Group By Customer.country ;
   Order By 3 Desc
```

This view shows each country, the number of orders placed in that country, and the total dollar amount of orders. The second and third fields have been renamed to allow control over the name. This data can also be retrieved by using SQL Pass-Through to send a Select statement. Either way, the data winds up in a Cursor.

Which method is better? There should be more overhead involved with a view that begins life as a read-and-write Cursor. In contrast, a SQL Pass-Through Cursor is read-only by default. Informal testing shows this to be true. The program PERFTST1.PRG provides a comparison of getting the total orders by employee information from SQL Pass-Through and getting it from a view. The SQL Pass-Through method is about 10 pecent to 15 percent faster when tested on a Pentium 75 with 24 MB of RAM and running Windows NT 3.51. The program PERFTST1.PRG is shown here:

PERFTST1.PRG

```
* In this program we test creating a total orders by employee report using a view vs
* using spt.

Set Database To tastrsql

* Create a view.
Create SQL View vTotalOrdersByCountry ;
   Connection cntastrade ;
   As Select Customer.country, Count(Orders.order_id) As ordcount, ;
      Sum(Order_line_items.unit_price * Order_line_items.quantity) ;
      As ordtotal ;
   From customer, orders, order_line_items ;
   Where Customer.customer_id = Orders.customer_id ;
      And Orders.order_id = Order_line_items.order_id ;
   Group By Customer.country ;
   Order By 3 Desc

time1 = Seconds()
* Use the view
Use vTotalOrdersByCountry
time2 = Seconds()

= MessageBox("The view took " + AllTrim(Str(time2 - time1, 7, 4)) + ;
             " seconds")

* Connect to SQL Server.
gnHandle = SQLConnect("cntastrade")

If gnhandle < 0
   = MessageBox("Could not connect")
   Return
Endif

lcSQL = "Select Customer.country, " + ;
        "Count(Orders.order_id) As ordcount, " + ;
        "Sum(Order_line_items.unit_price * " + ;
        "Order_line_items.quantity) " + ;
        "As ordtotal " + ;
        "From customer, orders, order_line_items " + ;
        "Where Customer.customer_id = Orders.customer_id " + ;
        "  And Orders.order_id = Order_line_items.order_id " + ;
        "Group By Customer.country " + ;
        "Order By 3 Desc"

time1 = Seconds()
```

Continued on next page

```
* Use SPT to send the Select
lnResult = SQLExec(gnHandle, lcSQL)
time2 = Seconds()

= MessageBox("SPT took " + AllTrim(Str(time2 - time1, 7, 4)) + ;
             " seconds")
```

The program ORDBYCUS.PRG is run when the user selects the Total Orders by Customer report from the menu. If the application is using remote data, SQL Pass-Through is used and the results are stored in a Cursor called c_results. If local data is used, a Visual FoxPro Select statement is used and the results are also stored in a Cursor called c_results. Either way, the column names are the same. This way, one report can be written and used regardless of the source of the data. The code for the program ORDBYCUS.PRG is shown here:

ORDBYCUS.PRG

```
Wait Window "Please wait while the report is prepared..." NoWait
If oApp.cDatabase = "DATA\TASTRSQL"
   lcSQL = "Select Customer.company_name, Count(Orders.order_id) " + ;
           "As ordcount, Sum(Order_line_items.unit_price * " + ;
           "Order_line_items.quantity) As ordtotal " + ;
           "From customer, orders, order_line_items " + ;
           "Where Customer.customer_id = Orders.customer_id " + ;
           " And Orders.order_id = Order_line_items.order_id " + ;
           "Group By Customer.company_name " + ;
           "Order By 3 Desc"

   lnResult = SQLExec(oApp.nSQLHandle, lcSQL, "c_results")

   If lnResult < 0
     lnError = AError(laError)
     = MessageBox(laError[3])
     Return
   Endif
Else
   Select Customer.company_name, Count(Orders.order_id) As ordcount, ;
          Sum(Order_line_items.unit_price*Order_line_items.quantity) ;
           As ordtotal ;
   From customer, orders, order_line_items ;
   Where Customer.customer_id = Orders.customer_id ;
      And Orders.order_id = Order_line_items.order_id ;
   Group By Customer.company_name;
   Order By 3 Desc ;
   Into Cursor c_results
Endif

Report Form ordbycus Preview

Use In c_results

Wait Clear
```

The other two report programs are structured the same. A single report handles both local and remote data because either way, the data is in the same Cursor.

Summary

In this section you have seen many techniques for building client/server applications using Visual FoxPro. As you look at the sample application you will notice how much of it is the same code you would use in a Visual FoxPro application that uses local data. This is the main benefit of using Visual FoxPro's remote views. Because they can be treated just like tables, they do not require dramatically different techniques for manipulating data. This application also makes good use of SQL Pass-Through to access read-only data.

Visual FoxPro Form Designer

Stephen Sawyer

Introduction

In developing a business application using any development product, the central pieces of the interface with the user are the *windows* or *boxes* on the computer monitor that present information to the user and accept input from the user. These things were called screens in releases of Microsoft FoxPro version 2 and later, and FoxPro provided a tool called the Screen Builder to create them visually.

Prior to FoxPro version 2, developers had two choices. They could laboriously code user interface screens line by line, or they could create or purchase some kind of screen painter to allow them to design their screens interactively and visually. The introduction of the Screen Builder and the ability to store all of a screen's design elements and program source code in a table during development were tremendous advancements in the art and practice of application development.

With the release of Microsoft Visual FoxPro 3, you are riding another wave of change. As with almost every other aspect of the product, Visual FoxPro's Form Designer bears only a passing resemblance to its predecessor, the Screen Builder.

This report will serve two needs. First, it will provide a more detailed examination of the Form Designer, Forms, and controls than is provided by the Visual FoxPro developer's guide. Second, it will provide a bridge between FoxPro 2.x screens and Screen Builder, and Visual FoxPro's Forms and Form Designer. I'll be discussing the similarities and differences, and explaining how things that you've done before (possibly with great difficulty) can be accomplished (hopefully with greater ease) using Visual FoxPro. Together with the other reports in this book, this report will provide you with a running start up the Visual FoxPro learning curve.

About This Report

My approach is hands on. There will be some example code on the source disc for this book, but most of the early "examples" will be created as you go. I recommend that you have your computer on and running Visual FoxPro once you reach Section 2. If I describe something that you're familiar with, skim the material. However, if it's something new to you, try it out! I've also included a few sidebars called "Let's Do It!" where I'll take you step by step through an example in a tutorial fashion. Beginning with Section 7, you will find that more sample forms are just explained. By that time you should be fairly comfortable with the techniques involved, so it won't be necessary for you to work through them step by step.

In researching this report I ran across some anomalous behavior in the released version of Visual FoxPro, as well as some problems that I hope to help you to avoid. You will find this information in the boxes labeled "Trap!"

All screen shots were done while running Visual FoxPro under Microsoft Windows 95, and with the screen resolution at 800 x 600 pixels.

Naming Conventions

Throughout this report I will be following the naming conventions that are found in the online help file under Contents...Technical Reference...Programming...Naming Conventions. If you are familiar with what is sometimes referrred to as "Hungarian notation," or the FoxPro naming conventions that have been popularized by Y. Alan Griver and Flash Creative Management, you will feel right at home with this scheme. If you're not familiar with this method, you should examine it in the FoxPro help file before proceeding.

I know that some developers really balk at the idea of adopting any kind of a standard. However, your development and code maintenance work will suffer if you don't maintain some kind of standard naming conventions in your development. I know my life has been made much easier by following a naming convention—I can tell at a glance the scope and data type of a variable, or the data type of a table field. Another advantage of adopting a commonly accepted naming convention is that when you read someone else's code, it looks like something you'd write, and you can grasp its intent and operation much more quickly.

In the case of objects, I feel that following naming conventions can be carried to an extreme. It makes little sense to rename a Label object to lblCustomer when it is never referenced in code. A similar situation exists when a particular object like a PageFrame or Grid is the only object of its type on the Form. In cases like this I am perfectly happy to allow Visual FoxPro to apply a default name to the object.

There are other habits that are becoming standard ways of communicating in code between developers that are also found in this report. First, methods, procedures, functions, and many Visual FoxPro keywords are all expressed in mixed case—ActiveForm instead of ACTIVEFORM, DockIt unstead of DOCKIT or dockit. This greatly enhances readability. Visual FoxPro commands and functions are expressed in uppercase—IF..ENDIF; ACTIVATE SCREEN; MODIFY COMMAND; UPPER().

Objects

Objects are an integral part of Visual FoxPro whether you get into object-oriented programming (OOP) and create your own objects, or stick with the objects that ship with the product. As a result, I will explain a great deal about objects and introduce a lot of object terminology. For instance, at runtime an object is *instantiated*, which is the OOP term for "created" or "run." Instantiated means to create an instance of an object from its definition, or *class*. Although you may not think of it in this way, when you design a Form in Visual FoxPro you are actually creating a design, a template, or, in object-oriented terms, a *class* for the Form. To familiarize you with this (and other) object-oriented terminology, I will use both the terms created and instantiated early in the report. However, by the end I'll use instantiated almost exclusively.

While I may try to avoid discussion of OOP in this report (leaving that topic to David Frankenbach's report in this book), do *not* infer from this that I believe that you can be a good developer without using Visual FoxPro's OOP extensions. You can develop some pretty good applications without creating any object classes or class libraries, but your efficiency in implementing an application is as much a part of your skill as a developer as your knowledge of application and database design. It is in this efficiency that OOP will have its greatest impact on your development skills. I encourage you to learn as much about OOP as you can and play with it a lot, as that is the only way you will learn how best to employ it in your development efforts.

Who Is This Report For?

This report concentrates on features that you are likely to encounter when you create *new* Visual FoxPro applications. For the most part, I have chosen not to dwell on features that are included for backward compatibility as these are of interest primarily for converting FoxPro 2.x applications to Visual FoxPro. While these features may be useful in certain circumstances, their functionality is usually better achieved through other methods specific to Visual FoxPro. They are fully documented in the Visual FoxPro language reference and in the Visual FoxPro online help.

This report assumes a familiarity with the Xbase language, but relevant Xbase extensions that are new to Visual FoxPro are discussed as opportunity permits. Some of the code examples will likely include FoxPro-specific Xbase language extensions, and numerous comparisons are made between Visual FoxPro and FoxPro versions 2.0 and later. This is for the benefit of those who can leverage knowledge of previous FoxPro versions in climbing the Visual FoxPro learning curve, and who may have to "unlearn" some of the concepts and techniques that have been replaced by more powerful capabilities in the new product.

Visual FoxPro is a complete rewrite of the FoxPro product, and while there is a great deal of backward compatibility built into it, anyone with some experience in an Xbase language should be able to gain a lot from this report. Familiarity with earlier FoxPro versions as well as Microsoft Visual Basic will also make it all a little easier.

Visual FoxPro Forms— An Overview

Contrasting Visual FoxPro Forms with FoxPro 2.x Screens

I'll begin by talking about some basic differences between Visual FoxPro and earlier versions of FoxPro.

Changed Terminology

The first change you'll notice about Visual FoxPro Forms is that they're not called "screens" anymore. This *does* take some getting used to, but it'll come a little more easily if you've been working with Visual Basic. Also, the objects that you placed on FoxPro 2.x screens and referred to as "fields" are now called "controls."

No Code Generation Step (No .SPR files)

A much more dramatic difference is that, unlike the FoxPro 2.x Screen Builder, the Visual FoxPro Form Designer does not generate any code. Visual FoxPro Forms are run directly from the .SCX table in which they are stored. The .SCX table now has an ObjCode field in which the compiled pseudocode is stored. This behavior is reminiscent of report Forms—there is no code-generation step when you use the Report Writer. The report is run directly from the .FRX table.

While you have the Form Designer open in Visual FoxPro, you can immediately run the Form by clicking the ! icon on the toolbar, or by selecting Form | Run from the menu. No code-generation step is necessary.

This means that, unlike .SPR code that is "run" (using DO <filename>.SPR) to display a FoxPro 2.x screen, a Visual FoxPro Form is not displayed by "running" any program code. The command Do Form <formname> displays a Form without executing a single line of code. To see what I'm talking about, create a FoxPro 2.x screen and generate the .SPR code from it. Make it a minimum screen—no fields, push buttons, or tables to open. Simply use the CREATE SCREEN TEST command and generate it. Open the trace window from the command window, DO TEST, and observe all of the lines of code as they are executed to save and change the environment settings, define the window, activate the window, and initiate the READ.

Now, do the same thing using Visual FoxPro. From the command window, use the CREATE SCREEN TEST command. While the Form Designer is displayed on the screen, open the trace window and run it by either selecting Form | Run from the system menu, or clicking the ! icon on the standard toolbar. (Remember, you don't have to do the generation step.) You'll see a line of code appear in the command window, (DO FORM C:\VFPSTUFF\TEST.SCX), but not a single line of code will appear in the trace window.

Forms as Objects

Another monumental change related to the fact that there is no generated code to run is that Forms are *objects,* hence the necessity of bringing a lot of object-speak into this report.

I'll talk more about what objects are and how they work in the discussion of object-based systems. At the moment you should realize something: all of the features that you put into the setup snippet of your screens (declaring variables that are used by the Form, opening tables, setting relations, and populating arrays) and all of the features that you put into the cleanup snippet of your screens (code for closing tables, and procedures and functions the Form needs) were placed there to resolve the variable scoping and calling-stack issues that you encountered in FoxPro 2.x screens. The issues still exist in Visual FoxPro, but you have different and better ways to deal with them.

No Read-Created "Wait State"

Assuming that you were suitably skeptical and tried the previous example, you have a simple Form to use for looking at another earth-shattering difference between FoxPro 2.x and Visual FoxPro.

When you ran the Visual FoxPro Form, you might have noticed that the command window was visible. In FoxPro 2.x the READ command activated the screen. The command inserted a wait state into the code that created the screen, allowing the user to interact with the screen while entering data, navigating a table, or performing some other task. The command window was closed during this Read-generated wait state, as it is while any program code is executing. Without the READ command, the screen code would continue to execute, the @...GET and @...SAY fields would never be activated, the window would flash momentarily on the monitor as it was activated, then the cleanup code would execute and dump you right back to the command window.

Remember that in Visual FoxPro the Form is an object. Once it's created, control is returned to the program that instantiated this object. In this case it was the command window.

While you have this Form on the Visual FoxPro Desktop, issue the DO FORM TEST command a few more times in the command window. Use your mouse to drag the four or five instances you created of this particular Form to different parts of the screen and amuse yourself for a few seconds by clicking back and forth between them.

Remember how hard this was to do in FoxPro 2.x?

Not only is the Form an object, but all of the controls you add to it—TextBoxes, EditBoxes, Spinners, and CommandButtons—are also objects. Most of the control objects are *visual objects* that can be seen on the Form at runtime. Some objects such as the Timer Control object may be visible at design time, but there is no visible representation of them on the Form when the Form is instantiated.

Old Functions, New Methods

Some features of Visual FoxPro Forms are very similar to those of FoxPro 2.x. For instance, the Read Show() function has been replaced by the form's Refresh() method, which performs a similar function. (A *method* is a fancy object-type name for a procedure or function.) The Activate() and Deactivate() functions are still there and are implemented as methods to perform a similar function.

"When" and "Valid" are still available for Visual FoxPro controls, and work the same way they did in FoxPro 2.x. They are used to do what they were designed for—validating a change to a field's value or preventing focus from moving to a particular field under certain conditions. More often, they were used to trap the event when the user moved the focus to or from a field. However, Visual FoxPro is a *real* Windows-based program, which means that it has an *event model* that allows you much finer control over your application's response to both user and system events. For instance, you now have a GotFocus event and a LostFocus event. You no longer have to use When and Valid to determine when the user moves from one control to another.

As Visual FoxPro Forms and the Form Designer are discussed in detail, you'll see that many features are familiar from your experience with FoxPro 2.x. However, there are also features that are totally new.

New Features in Visual FoxPro Forms
DataSessions

One of the thorniest problems in developing modeless event-driven applications in FoxPro 2.x was what is referred to as the *environment*. This means that certain features need to be set a specific way for a particular screen to work properly. These features include TALK, DELETED, NEAR, and EXACT, as well as the tables you're working with, their indexes, filters, and relations. Developers had to anticipate when users wanted to move the focus from one screen to another. They also had to be able to save and properly restore each screen's environment as users moved back and forth between them.

To make development of this type of application a hundred times easier, Visual FoxPro Forms have the option of creating a private *DataSession*. This makes it possible to allow the user to navigate from one Form to another (even to the command window) without having to do anything to save and restore each form's environment. Those tasks are all handled automatically.

Custom Controls

In FoxPro 2.x you had a finite set of fields available to you for designing your Forms. These fields included @...GET fields, CheckBoxes, push buttons, and edit fields, and encompassed the features that were deemed appropriate (and backwards compatible) with earlier versions of FoxPro. With Visual Basic, you have the option of purchasing (or, if you're a sharp C programmer, writing) custom-control libraries. This wasn't even an option with FoxPro 2.x.

All of that has changed in Visual FoxPro. With the new object-oriented extensions, it is now possible to customize the controls that you receive with Visual FoxPro, or to combine them to create your own controls. Creating completely original OLE controls will still be the province of the C-advantaged and suppliers of add-on libraries, but you have far more powerful tools in your hands than you did with earlier versions of FoxPro.

New and Enhanced Controls

For years, FoxPro developers have wished for the ability to place a Browse command into a screen. You still have Browse commands with Visual FoxPro, but the new Grid Control is all most of you have wished for and more.

ComboBoxes (long available to Visual Basic developers) make it into Visual FoxPro along with PageFrames (those neat little tabbed multi-page thingies), a Timer Control (a control that can execute code at particular times or intervals), and OLE Controls.

Visual FoxPro also provides improvements to old standards. This includes the ability to make multiple selections in list boxes, a change that will make your life a little easier and allow you to better meet your user's needs.

Data Buffering

Data buffering completely eliminates the old debate about using screens to edit data directly in the tables. You used to SCATTER to memvars, edit those memvars, and then GATHER them back. Now data buffering provides the buffering function that the memvars used to perform. You may never use SCATTER or GATHER again. This topic is covered in Doug Hennig's report in this book, *Visual FoxPro Data Dictionary.*

Runtime Adaptability

In FoxPro 2.x, changing the size, shape, color, or position of an object on one of your screens at runtime was not easy. It was possible, but it required some tricky programming. In Visual FoxPro, it isn't just possible, it's almost encouraged because most of the properties (another OOP word that will be discussed more) are exposed and available at runtime. If you haven't played with this on your own already, take the basic empty Form you created a few pages back and use the DO command from the command window.

You'll enter some commands in the command window to illustrate this capability, but first you need to learn to address the objects. The following names specify the custid field of the customer table and the name field of the vendor table:

```
customer.custid
vendor.name
```

Object syntax is similar to referencing fields in multiple tables. The object syntax is shown here:

<objectreference>.<property>

If you wanted to change one of your form's properties, you could do so using the following steps in the command window. Suppose you wanted to change a form's BackColor property to black. Create a new blank Form by entering CREATE FORM TEST into the command window. When you have the Form Designer open, immediately click the ! icon in the standard toolbar or select Form|Run from the system menu. Answer "Yes" when you are asked if you want to save the Form. Once the Form is running, give this a try:

```
Test.BackColor = RGB(0,0,0)
```

Voilà! The background of the Form is black. Now enter the following:

```
Test.AutoCenter = .T.
```

With this syntax, you're setting the AutoCenter property of the Form, causing the Form to center itself on the Visual FoxPro desktop. You can do this all day long—change label Captions, push button Captions, Form Captions, BackColors, ForeColors, Height, Width, position, Visible, and so forth. You can also use object syntax to query an object's properties. Again, enter the following code in the command window:

```
ACTIVATE SCREEN
? Test.Visible
```

This syntax will return .T.. This assumes that you haven't done anything to change the form's Visible property to .F.. We'll discuss the Visible property more fully in Section 3.

Object-Based Systems—An Overview

Even if you never intend to use Visual FoxPro's object-oriented language extensions, you must become conversant in some of the concepts of object-based systems to get up to speed with Visual FoxPro. As a result, the discussion will digress a bit here to cover some object talk that will relate to the remainder of this report.

Objects

Objects are "things"—Forms, TextBoxes (@...GET fields), ListBoxes, Labels (@...SAY fields), Spinners, or CommandButtons (push buttons).

In the context of the Visual FoxPro Form Designer, most of the objects you deal with are *visual* objects. A notable exception is the DataEnvironment object, an object that is part of every Form object. (As the author of this report, this is very convenient for me, as it's always easier to convey something that the reader can visualize). A software object is *the inseparable combination of data and the code to manipulate that data.* This is the central idea of object *encapsulation.* For objects, the data is stored as an object *property* and the code is stored in object *methods.* Objects can be *contained* within other objects (such as control objects in a Form). Objects can respond to *events* that trigger the code stored in some of their methods, and *messages* can be passed between objects. If you're confused, don't worry—the following discussions cover these ideas in greater detail.

Properties

You can visualize these Form objects, but what about data and code? Well, the *data* being referred to is one of two kinds—the memory variables you know and love, and properties that are an inseparable part of the object. Imagine your simple test Form from earlier in this section. What properties does it have? You know it has a property called BackColor because you changed it. It also has properties called Height, Width, Left, Top, WindowType, MinWidth, and Visible, among others.

Individual controls also have properties. For instance, a TextBox Control (what you used to call an @...GET field) has ForeColor, BackColor, Height, Width, FontSize, Name, and ReadOnly, among others.

Basically, a property is a memory variable that is attached to the object.

Can you add or remove the properties that Forms and Form controls possess? In the case of Forms, you can (at design time) add properties that you may need. In fact, if you think back to the discussion of the absence of setup code to establish memvars and arrays that need to be "scoped" to the Form, this is how it is done. If you need an array to populate a list box, you simply create an array as a property of the Form. Just like an instance when you declare an array in the setup code of a FoxPro 2.x screen, this variable or array is visible to any other control or method (code) in the Form. A property is just a variable. The difference is that the property is an inseparable part of the object (a Form in this case). You can change its value to .NULL., 0, or "", but as long as the object exists, its properties exist.

The objects that come "in the box" with Visual FoxPro are supplied as templates, definitions, or what OOP folks call *classes*. These definitions are contained in VFP.EXE, the FoxPro "engine," and are an inseparable part of Visual FoxPro. Because these classes are used by the OOP-enabled as foundations for their own classes, each of them is referred to as a *BaseClass*. You cannot remove any properties inherent in the Form (that is, part of the definition of the Form BaseClass), and you cannot add or remove properties of controls (such as the TextBox BaseClass or the CommandButton BaseClass) unless you create your own control classes by subclassing from the Visual FoxPro control BaseClasses. Doing this is beyond the scope of this report, so you are again referred to David Frankenbach's report on OOP in this book.

Unless otherwise specified, any discussion in this report of the properties of a Form object or a Control object will refer to the properties of the Visual FoxPro BaseClasses.

Events

Events are things that happen. They can be things that the user does, such as using the mouse to click a CommandButton or moving the focus from one Form to another, or they can be things under program control, such as the destruction of an object, the closing of a Form, or an error. Sometimes an event happens automatically as a result of another occurrence, such as a table that is opened automatically when a Form is run.

There are 41 events that can be trapped and acted upon in Visual FoxPro Forms or Form controls. However, not all objects can respond to all of these events. Also, the set of all events that occur and are detectable in Visual FoxPro is static—you cannot define general new events or new events for specific objects. In addition, because Labels cannot receive focus they cannot detect a GotFocus or LostFocus event. As a result, you cannot define such events for them, even if you create a user-defined class that is subclassed from the Label BaseClass. Further, you cannot trigger events except by specifically doing whatever it is that triggers that event. For example, you cannot trigger the Click event of a CommandButton except by moving the mouse pointer to the button and clicking it (or by moving the focus to the CommandButton and pressing Enter).

Methods

It was mentioned in the discussion of objects that they are inseparable combinations of data and code. Just as you have variables that are permanently linked to objects (these are called *properties*), you can also have procedures or functions linked to the object. These procedures or functions are called *methods*. For example, all Forms have a Release() method that releases the Form. To call an object's method, you use object syntax in a manner similar to the way you set or determined the value of an object's property. To release your "test" Form, first instantiate it by entering DO FORM TEST in the command window. Then enter the following code in the command window:

```
Test.Release()
```

In addition to releasing the Form, you could add to this method any code you wanted to execute. That way your code would execute whenever the method is called.

As is the case with properties, you can add user-defined methods to a Form, but you cannot remove any methods that are part of the definition of the Form BaseClass. Neither can you add or remove control methods without subclassing them. For example, you could add a method to a Form to determine whether any control values have changed and indicate that the user cannot close the Form without either saving or abandoning changes. You could call this method Changed(), and write code that would compare the values of all the controls to their original values, returning a .T. or .F. depending on whether any of the values were different. As you can see, the only difference between a method and a procedure or function is the way it is called. You can pass parameters to methods, return values from methods, and declare memory variables or arrays in methods. Methods are functions or procedures, but like properties they are an inseparable part of the object to which they belong. As long as the object exists, its methods will also exist.

As you explore the Form Designer, one potential source of confusion is that there are events and methods known by the same name. In fact, an object (whether it be a Form or a control) will have a method to correspond to every event that the object can detect. For instance, there are both Click events and Click() methods associated with many objects, including Forms, CommandButtons, CheckBoxes, and Labels. Keep in mind that the Click() method is triggered by the Click event. As with any other method, an object's Click() method can be called, executing the code it contains. As a result, if you *really* want that to happen, you don't have to trigger the Click event. Instead, you can simply cause the Click() method to execute as if the Click event had occurred.

Because there is a method for every event an object can detect, objects (including controls and Forms) can respond to these events and take appropriate actions. This report follows the habit of including a pair of parentheses [for example, Click() method or Changed() method] after a name when referring to a method. This makes it easier to see when you are referring to the event that triggers the method, or the method that is triggered by the event. The "()" is not necessary when calling a method unless you need to pass arguments to the method. As with function calls, these arguments are contained within the parentheses. However, you'll find that the habit of including the empty parentheses after methods is both a good practice and a good learning tool.

Encapsulation

The last OOP term to define is *encapsulation*. This simply means that an object wraps up the code (methods) and data (properties) into one neat package, and that it can hide or expose as much or as little of this to the outside world as is appropriate. In the case of the standard properties and methods available in Forms and Form controls, they are all *exposed*, or accessible, to external program code and objects. Note, however, that although these properties and methods are exposed, they are hidden from the rest of the system and cannot be changed, queried, or called without explicitly referencing the object of which they are members. (In the OOP world, a hidden property or method is truly hidden. It cannot be referenced from any code or object outside of the object of which it is a member.)

Containership

Methods, properties, and events are collectively referred to as *members*. An object can exist as a member of other objects, and some objects can have other objects as members. Objects capable of having other objects as members are referred to as *container objects*. A perfect example of this is the Form object, which can contain other control objects. The term *containership* is used in discussing the relationship between objects and their member objects.

When you design a Form, all of the controls you add are *contained by* the Form. The Form and its member objects have a parent-child relationship; if the Form is destroyed, then all of the objects it contains are also destroyed. Likewise, some objects are made up of other objects. For example, the Grid object is made up of other objects that include Columns and TextBoxes (for the cells of the Grid and which are contained by the Columns). This is important to understand in terms of an object's *reference* used to call its methods, and set or query its properties, and is inherent in the object syntax used to perform these functions.

For example, suppose you have a Form called MyForm. On that Form is a PageFrame Control called pgfSample that consists of 3 pages—pag1, pag2, and pag3. On page 3 of this PageFrame is a Grid Control named grd1 that has 3 Columns—grc1, grc2, and grc3. Each of these Columns has a corresponding Header named grh1, grh2, and grh3.

Now, suppose you need to refer to the Header on Column 3 of the Grid to change its caption property. If you're doing this from an object outside the Form, the reference of that object would be as follows:

MyForm.pgf1.pag3.grd1.grh3.Caption

Header grh3 is contained in grd1, which in turn is contained in pag3. This page is contained in pageframe pgf1, which is in turn contained in the Form MyForm.

Messages

Messaging is the process by which objects communicate. In strictly OOP terms, messages are calls to an object's methods (function calls). For example, if you wanted to send a message to a Form asking it to tell you whether it had changed (drawing from the previous hypothetical Changed() method example), you would call that form's Changed() method. The function call would return .T. if the Form had changed, and .F. if no changes had been made. If the Form were called MyForm, you would send the message with the following syntax:

llHasChanged = MyForm.Changed()

In some object-oriented programming languages, no properties are exposed. This means that you cannot directly determine the value of any property, nor can you change the value of any property. These properties are *protected*. Setting and getting the value of properties is accomplished only through methods. The exposed properties in Visual FoxPro provide you with flexibility. As a result, you can also talk about messaging in terms of setting properties or calling methods, but be aware that this may be frowned upon by folks who take their OOP straight.

Often an object on a Form will need to access its own properties, call its own methods, send a message to its Form, or send a message to another object in that Form. There are three keywords in Visual FoxPro that facilitate this kind of messaging.

- *This* refers to the current object. For example, if the line of code This.BackColor = RGB(0,0,0) were executed in one of an object's methods, that object's BackColor property would be set to black.

- *ThisForm* refers to the current Form, as in ThisForm.Move(0,0). If this line of code were executed either by one of a form's methods or in one of the methods of one of that form's controls, the Form would be moved to the upper left corner of the screen.

- *Parent* refers to the parent object of the current object. If the code This.Parent.BackColor=RGB(192,192,192) were to be executed by a CommandButton control's Click() method and the CommandButton were placed on a Form (rather than on a page of a PageFrame, for instance), it would cause the background color of the Form (the "parent object" of the CommandButton) to change to light gray. If the CommandButton were placed on a page in a PageFrame, the page's background color would change because the page is the parent object that contains the CommandButton.

If a "message" to change the forecolor property of a Grid Header on page 3 of a PageFrame was originating in the method of a CommandButton control on page 1 of the PageFrame, the message could be coded as follows to change the Header's text color to red:

    This.Parent.Parent.pag3.grd1.grh3.ForeColor = RGB(255,0,0)

In the line of code just presented, "This" represents the control sending the message (a CommandButton). The first occurrence of "Parent" represents the parent object of the CommandButton, which is pag1. The second occurrence of "Parent" stands for the parent of the CommandButton's parent object. In this case that is the PageFrame pgf1.

If you were to simply code pgf3.grh3.ForeColor = RGB(255,0,0), it would generate an error. This is because the CommandButton has no member object by that name, nor is there a memory variable in the CommandButton's method code that corresponds to that name.

An easier way of coding this message would be as follows:

    ThisForm.pgf1.pag3.Grid1.grh3.ForeColor=RGB(255,0,0)

This syntax avoids the potentially confusing "Parent.Parent" syntax.

If all of this seems a little unclear at the moment, keep in mind that you will be dealing with many of these issues in detail in future sections. These processes will eventually get to be a habit, but you might kick yourself more than once as you work to develop it. (I know *I* did!)

One other gotcha to be aware of is that Visual FoxPro uses the term "Parent" in two different contexts. As just described, "Parent Object" relates to the concept of containership. On the other hand, "Parent Class" relates to the concept of inheritance. Because this meaning is relevant to Visual FoxPro's object-oriented programming extensions, and the design of object classes, this report will not dwell on this usage of "parent." There is a ParentClass property for most Form-related objects. This is the only time that you will see the term "parent" used in this report in any context other than in that of containership.

2 | The Form Designer

By necessity, this report is more about the objects you create and how you make data entry and control Forms with the Form Designer than about the Form Designer tool itself. You would probably feel rather cheated if you looked at this report and found that it describes only how to use the Form Designer tool. However, the Form Designer is sufficiently different from FoxPro 2.x's Screen Builder that you really need to spend some time getting acquainted with it.

In describing the Form Designer interface, interface elements will be referred to by the Visual FoxPro term for that element. As a result, the item you used to refer to as a push button will now be called a CommandButton. This way you will become familiar with Visual FoxPro's new terminology and Form controls.

Starting the Form Designer

You can start the Form Designer in one of two ways:

1. Select File|New from the system menu. This brings forward a dialog box in which you can select one of several Visual FoxPro file types including "Form." Note that there are two large CommandButtons on the upper right of this dialog box. One is labeled New File and the other is labeled Wizard. While the real-world utility of FoxPro wizards has improved a great deal, in my opinion the Form Designer Wizard leaves much to be desired as a useful Form-creation tool, and is worth exploring only for

its educational value. This report therefore won't discuss any Visual FoxPro wizards. Select New File in the File | New dialog box to start the Form Designer.

2. Type MODIFY FORM, MODIFY SCREEN, or CREATE FORM in the command window. (Modify Screen is included to be backwards compatible for those of us who find it difficult to break old habits.) In the case of either of the MODIFY commands you will be prompted for a file name for either an existing or new Form file. (Note that Form files still carry the .SCX extension used in screen files in FoxPro 2.x.) In the case of CREATE FORM, you are immediately presented with a new Form in the Form Designer. If you provide a file name with MODIFY FORM or MODIFY SCREEN, you will load an existing Form file into the Form Designer, or you will be presented with a new Form that, if saved, will be assigned the name you specified. Using a file name with CREATE FORM will generate a message box, if an .SCX file with the name you've chosen already exists. A "<FileName> Already Exists. Overwrite it?" message box will appear. If you answer no, the specified file will be loaded instead of being overwritten with a new file.

Components of the Form Designer Interface

Once you have the Form Designer open, you should have at least three new objects on the screen in addition to the Visual FoxPro System Menu, the standard toolbar, and the command window. This is shown in Figure 2-1.

The new objects are:

- The Form Designer window in which you will be creating your Form. It is usually in the upper left of your screen.
- A property sheet to the right of the main Form Designer window.
- A Form Controls toolbar floating somewhere on top of everything else.

If the Form Controls toolbar doesn't appear, select View | Toolbars from the system menu, then check the box next to the Form Controls item in the list. While you're there, be sure that the Show Tooltips box at the bottom of the dialog box is checked. Alternatively, click the Form Controls Toolbar icon on the right side of the Form Designer toolbar if you have it displayed. (Use View | Toolbars to display the Form Designer toolbar and make sure ToolTips is turned on for this toolbar too.)

The toolbar can be dragged anywhere on the screen, and can be "docked" at the top, bottom, or either side of the screen. Also note

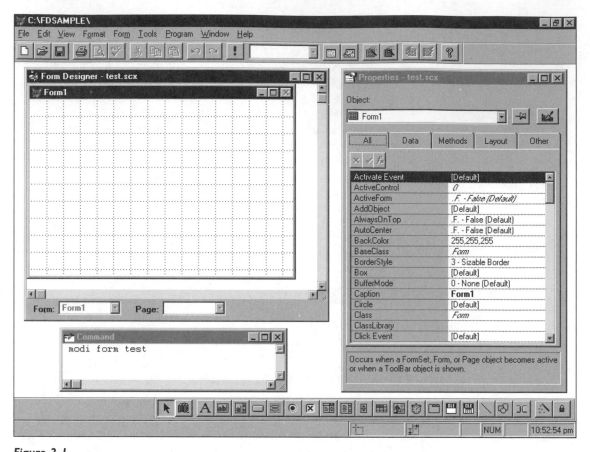

Figure 2-1.

The Form Designer Tool

that pausing with your mouse pointer on top of one of the buttons on the toolbar causes a yellow box to appear. This ToolTip box identifies the control that the button will invoke, a feature with which users of other Microsoft products are familiar.

The Property Sheet's Layout

If the property sheet didn't appear, use the right mouse button to click the blank Form to bring up a pop-up menu, then click the Properties option. In the Form Designer (as in most places within Visual FoxPro) using the right mouse button to click an object brings up a context menu. One of the options on this menu is to open the property sheet for that object. You can also open the properties sheet by clicking the Properties Window icon on the Form Designer toolbars.

The property sheet gives access to all members of the Form object, including any other control objects you may add to the Form. Some properties of Forms and Form Controls are not accessible at design time, or may be read-only properties. These properties are also listed in the property sheet, but are shown in italics to indicate that their values cannot be set from within the Form Designer.

At the top of the property sheet is an Object drop-down list box that shows all of the objects in the current Form except for the DataEnvironment object. To display the DataEnvironment object's property sheet, use the right mouse button to click the Form, then click the DataEnvironment menu option. The DataEnvironment design window will open, and the text in the property sheet's drop-down list box will change to DataEnvironment.

You can use the drop-down list box to select any of the objects on the Form, including the Form object itself. Also, notice that if you click any object on the Form, the object displayed in the drop-down list box on the property sheet changes to reflect the selected object.

To the right of the Object list box is what looks like a CommandButton. This is actually a *graphical CheckBox* (a CheckBox that looks like a CommandButton that "sticks in" and "pops up" when clicked) with a pushpin icon. Click this button a few times and notice that the appearance of the pushpin changes. When the pushpin is stuck in, it means that the property sheet is always on top. When the pushpin is unstuck, it means that other windows can overlap the property sheet.

The ComxmandButton next to the pushpin (the one with the bricks-and-trowel icon) is a Builder icon. Builders will be discussed in Section 11.

Below these three controls is a PageFrame control, which is a tabbed, multipage object. This is used to display all of the properties, events, and methods that are members of the object displayed in the drop-down list box object. Each page displays all of the properties, events, and methods in a Grid control (the new control that allows you to place a browse window onto a Form). The first page, named All, displays all object members. Each of the next four pages displays a subset (a filtered view) of the members listed on this page. The second page, Data, displays those properties that relate to the data which the control or Form displays or manipulates. The third page, Methods, displays all of the object's methods. The fourth page, Layout, displays properties that affect the object's physical appearance. The last page, called Other, is a catch-all for things that don't fall neatly into the other three subset pages.

> *Tip!*
> There's an oft-spoken piece of advice that should become apparent as you look at your computer's crowded screen. If you treat yourself to only one piece of hardware in the coming year, make sure it is a good 17" monitor and video card combination that can give you as many square pixels of sharp, clear screen real estate as you can manage! I find that when designing maximum 640 x 480 pixel forms, a screen resolution of 1024 x 768 allows the Form Designer, the property sheet, the command window, and all three Form Designer-related toolbars to coexist without anything overlapping. A 21" display at 1280 x 1024 would be absolute bliss, but unfortunately you have to eat and your kids have to wear shoes. Keep in mind that this is just for development—you can design for standard 14-inch or 15-inch 640 x 480 displays. Your users don't have to keep all those toolbars and property sheets on the screen!

The Property Sheet and Properties

Initially it's good to stick to the All page. This is because there are times when the page on which a property is displayed won't be immediately obvious. Everything can be found on the All page, and it's helpful to familiarize yourself with *all* of the many members of the objects with which you will be dealing. Here are some interesting facts to wow 'em with at your next cocktail party:

Number of Form and control members (Includes contained objects)	309
Maximum number of members for a single object (ComboBox):	119
Minimum number of members for a single object (relation):	13
Total number of different objects available in the Form Designer:	24
Total number of object/object-member pairs:	1,483

These numbers are presented to stress the importance of browsing the object members so that you know what's available. Also, any time you see an unfamiliar property (or an event or method in the property sheet), scroll to that item, or click it and press F1 to bring up the Help file entry for that property, event, or method. You can also find a brief description of the property, event, or method in the message box at the bottom of the property sheet.

To better illustrate the property sheet's capabilities, try the following experiment. If you haven't done so already, open a new, blank Form in the Form Designer. Be sure that you have the Form

Controls toolbar and the property sheet open. While you're at it, go to the View | Toolbars dialog box and open the Form Design toolbar and the Layout toolbar.

Find the TextBox icon on the Form Controls toolbar and click it. You'll notice that the mouse pointer changes to a small cross when you move it over the Form. Click somewhere on the upper left hand corner of your Form. This will change your mouse pointer back to an arrow, and drop a TextBox onto the Form. Now double-click the TextBox icon on the Form Controls toolbar. As you do so, notice that the Button Lock button at the end of the toolbar (it looks like a padlock) is automatically depressed. Click your Form twice more to place two more TextBoxes on it and then click the Button Lock icon on the toolbar to change the mouse pointer into an arrow again. As in FoxPro 2.x for Windows, clicking a control object allows you to place one of that type of object, while double-clicking (or clicking the Button Lock icon) allows you to place multiple objects of that type. If the properties sheet is in the way during this process, it can be minimized or closed. Alternatively you can click the pushpin button so that the Form Designer window can be on top.

Notice that each TextBox has some text in it—Text1, Text2, or Text3. Click the properties sheet, then click the arrow button on the right end of the Object drop-down list box at the top of the properties sheet. You should see the following list, shown in Figure 2-2.

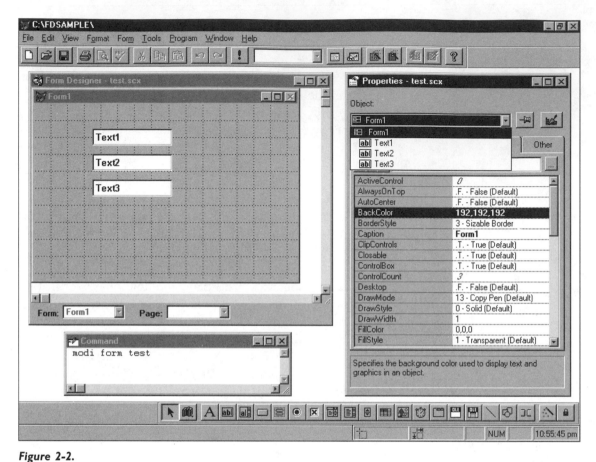

Figure 2-2.

**The Form Designer's
property sheet
showing the object
list**

Notice how the Form itself (*Form1*) and all of its member objects appear in the list. Select the Text3 item, then select the All page in the PageFrame below it. Scroll the list of TextBox object members until the Name property is visible. Notice that it says Text3. With the *Name property* highlighted, type "txtThird." Notice that you are typing into the TextBox that appears above the scrolling list of object members. When you are finished, press the Enter key, click another object member, or press an up or down arrow key. You'll notice that only at this point does the name property in the list change to reflect what you have typed. Pressing Esc cancels these changes.

You have just changed the Name property of the TextBox. This is not the same as the Caption property that some controls such as the Label or CommandButton have, but is the name by which the control is identified in the list of objects in the drop-down list box, and the name that you use to send messages to that object.

Now change a property of the Form itself. You could use the Object drop-down list box again, but this time, click the property sheet's pushpin to keep the sheet on top. Then reach over and click the Form (not one of the TextBoxes). Notice that the drop-down list box on the property sheet now shows Form1. Click one of the TextBoxes to select it, and note that the property sheet's drop-down list box shows the selected object. Click the Form again.

Click the property sheet, and scroll the list of properties until the BackColor property is visible. The property's value should be white (255,255,255). Type the value "192,192,192" in the data entry window and press Enter. You'll notice that the Form's background has changed to light gray.

Often a point-and-shoot dialog box is available to set a property. Notice that on the right side of the data entry TextBox there is a CommandButton with an ellipsis (...). Clicking this CommandButton brings up the Visual FoxPro color-picker dialog box. Click a color, then click OK, and you've changed the property again.

Scroll down to the next property (BaseClass). This item is in italics (*Form*) indicating that it isn't something you can set at design time. The data entry TextBox at the top of the page is also disabled. Scroll downward again to the Borderstyle property. This property is probably showing "3 - Sizeable Border." For this property, the data entry window has changed to a drop-down list box. You could type a 0, 1, 2 or 3, but how would you know that these were the only choices? How would you know what these choices meant? Click the down arrow on the right of the drop-down list box and then examine the available choices. Make a choice if you wish, and then continue to scroll through the list of members. You can watch how the data entry TextBox changes from a plain TextBox to a TextBox with a push button, then to a ComboBox, and finally to a drop-down list box.

Let's Do It!

If you're of the "old school" and prefer to work in code or from the command window rather than using visual tools, Visual FoxPro hasn't abandoned you. The following steps show how it is possible to modify properties and methods of Visual FoxPro Form controls from the command window.

Select one of the TextBoxes on your Form. Activate the command window, then type the following:

```
? ASELOBJ(aObject)
```

If you press Ctrl-Alt-Shift to make the screen visible, you'll see the number 1 on the screen. This means that you had one object selected. The number 1 means that a reference to that object has

Continued on next page

Continued from previous page

been stored in a one-element array called aObject. Now, type the following in the command window:

```
aObject[1].Name = "Hi_There"
```

See if you can set some other properties for this object, such as FontName, Width, Height, FontSize, and BorderWidth. Be sure you remember to use the proper object syntax: —<object>.<property>=<value>. Some examples of this syntax are shown:

```
aObject[1].FontName = "Terminal"
aObject[1].Width = 150
aObject[1].BorderStyle  = 0 (no border)
```

Be sure to check the Visual FoxPro documentation for ASELOBJ() when you have a chance!

To better understand what has just happened, think of it this way. In most cases Visual FoxPro creates a memory variable as a reference to an object. This happens whether the object is a Form, a Form Control, or some other type of object. You can determine or change an object's properties or can call its methods by using this variable reference. The Type() function returns an "N" for a variable that holds a numeric value, a "C" for a variable that holds a character value, and an "L" for a variable that holds a logical value. For a variable that holds an object reference, Type() returns a value of "O." The interesting thing is that when you have a variable x that holds a reference (in programming parlance, a *pointer*) to an object, assigning the value of x to y so that y = x, won't give you two objects. Instead you will have two *references* to the same object. You can set the object's BackColor property by using the following code:

```
x.BackColor = RGB(255,255,255)
```

or

```
y.BackColor = RGB(255,255,255)
```

Either command will set the object's background color to white. The ASELOBJ() function will create an array of references to all of the selected objects so that you can set their properties.

There is a quick way to navigate through the property sheet. Click the Form and open the property sheet. Select the All tab, and press Ctrl-Alt-R. You will move immediately to the first member that starts with an R. Pressing Ctrl-Alt-R again will advance you to the next member that begins with an R.

The Property Sheet and Methods

Now that you've looked at properties, you can turn to methods. Remember, methods are nothing more than functions, code that belongs to an object.

Select your Form either by clicking it, or by selecting it in the Object drop-down list box at the top of the property sheet. Then click the Methods tab of the PageFrame on the property sheet and examine all of the available methods. You'll notice that the methods that respond to an event are referred to as events (such as the Click event). Methods that do *not* automatically respond to some event are simply named.

Double-click the Click event. This opens the editing window shown in Figure 2-3, which allows you to type code that will execute when the Form is clicked. Notice that there is nothing in this method at the moment, which means that if you were to run this Form and click it, nothing would happen. The Click event would occur, of course, but because your Click() method doesn't contain any code, no action would be taken in response to the event. In the case of a CommandButton, something *would* happen in response to a click of the mouse despite the fact that you didn't have any code in the Click() method. The button would change its appearance to look as if it had been depressed. However, without any code in the Click() method, that's all it can do.

Figure 2-3.

The Form.Click( ) method editing window

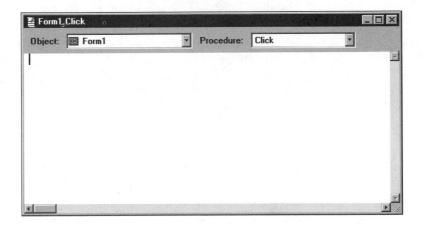

At the top of this editing window are two drop-down list boxes. One of these is labeled "Object" and shows "Form1." The second is labeled "Procedure," and shows "Click." You don't need to go back to the property sheet to look at another method. Click the Procedure drop-down list box and scroll down to the TextHeight method. You'll see some code already in the method:

```
LPARAMETERS cText
```

A method of a Form or control may require some parameters in order to perform default actions, and will have the LPARAMETERS line placed into the method by default. The presence of this line is required to avoid a No Parameter Statement Found error. (LPARAMETERS is a new Visual FoxPro keyword that allows parameters to be local variables. See the Visual FoxPro Help file under "Local" for more information.) This is very handy as a reminder that the default behavior of the method requires these parameters. Return to the property sheet for a moment, make sure that Form1.TextHeight is selected, and then press F1 to see what the default action is for the TextHeight() method.

It is possible to access the methods of an object without using the property sheet at all. To see this, close the property sheet. Select View | Code from the menu. (If "Code" does not appear in the drop-down View menu, click the Form Designer window first to make it active. The Visual FoxPro system menu will change drastically depending on which window is active. If you can't find a menu pad or an item on a drop-down menu, check to see which window is active.) After selecting View | Code, does the resulting window look familiar? It should—it's the same window you opened by double-clicking a method in the property sheet. The code-editing window can also be opened by double-clicking the Form or any object you've placed on the Form.

Click the Object drop-down list box and select the txtThird TextBox. Click the Procedure drop-down list box and scroll down to the DblClick() method. Type in some code. A simple comment like the one shown will do:

```
** This is a silly, do-nothing comment!
```

Then click the Procedure drop-down list box again. Scroll down to the GotFocus() method, and type in another comment. Scroll back to the first method in the list again, then scroll through the entire list of methods. As you do so, notice the appearance of DblClick() and GotFocus() in the list. These two events and methods always appear in the list, but because method code has been added, their appearance changes. They are now boldfaced, indicating that you've placed some code into them. Select the topmost method from the list, and press the PgUp and PgDn keys. Notice that as you page through, you go through only the populated methods. This makes it very easy to quickly focus on only the methods into which you have placed code.

Adding Properties or Methods to the Form

At this point you might wonder if you can add new properties or methods to objects. In the case of Forms, the answer is an unconditional yes. For other control objects, however, the answer is yes only if you create a new control object as a subclass of one of the Visual FoxPro BaseClass Controls. This process is covered in David Frankenbach's report on OOP in this book. Nevertheless, adding properties and methods to Forms does not require any object-oriented programming skills because the capability is built into the Form Designer.

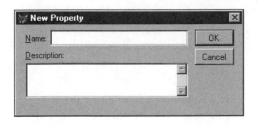

Figure 2-4.

New Property dialog box

With a Form open and the Form Designer window or property sheet active, select Form|New Property... from the system menu. Type "nMyProperty" into the Name TextBox on the New Property dialog box. This is shown in Figure 2-4. In the Description EditBox, type something like, "This is a demonstration of adding a property to a Form." Then click the *OK* button.

The Visual FoxPro help file doesn't contain a naming convention for object properties. Because properties are sometimes referred to as *instance variables* (variables that are scoped to the *instance* of an object), you will see properties with names like inMyProperty, where the "n" in the second character indicates a numeric data type. Some programmers use an "m" to denote an object member as in mnMyProperty. It's up to the individual developer. Some developers choose to have *no* character to indicate the scope of the variable for object properties, as in this example. Because this is the only case where they use no scoping initial character, they know by looking at the variable name that it is an object property, and they need to have an <objectname> in front of it! You should adopt whatever practice seems right to you and be consistent in its use.

Now that you've added a new property to the Form (presumably a property that will take a numeric value), click the property sheet, making sure that the Object drop-down list box shows Form1. Then click the All page tab, and scroll to the bottom of the Form object members list. Your new property should be at the bottom of the list. If you click it or scroll down to it with the down arrow key, you'll notice that the description you provided shows up in the message region at the bottom of the property sheet. User-added properties also appear on the "Other" page of the property sheet's PageFrame.

The initial value of any added property is .F. just as it is for any memory variable created with PUBLIC, PRIVATE, LOCAL, or DIMENSION. In the property sheet, you can change the value of nMyProperty to whatever initial value you want it to have. Note that even though the property is named to indicate a numeric value, it does not prevent you from leaving the value .F., or changing it to a character value, a date value, or even .NULL.. If you don't set an appropriate initial value for the property, you will need to do some type checking in your code before you use the property in any kind of operation. This helps you to avoid errors caused by an improper data type, so it's a good idea to initialize all property values.

The procedure for adding a new method to a Form is similar to the procedure for adding a property. Use Form | New Method... from the system menu. The new method will show up in the property sheet in the list on the All page, and again in the list on the Methods page.

You add code to user-added methods in the same way you add code to other methods already defined in the Form. You can double-click the method in the list on the property sheet, select View | Code from the system menu or double-click the Form. Then you can either use PgUp and PgDn to reach the desired method, or you can select the method from the Procedure drop-down list box at the top of the code editing window.

Selecting Form | Edit Property/Method brings up a dialog box that looks similar to the Add dialog box for properties and methods. However, instead of a TextBox for the property or method name, there is a drop-down list box that you can use to select a particular property or method to edit. In this case, editing doesn't amount to much—you can either change the description for that property or method, or remove the property or method from the Form. Remember that if you remove a property or method, all references to that property or method in your method code will also have to be removed or changed.

Search and Replace in the Visual FoxPro Editor

Now look at something on a related subject—the Visual FoxPro text editor. No applications developer ever includes every feature that all of their users want or expect. Visual FoxPro is no exception to this. For the most part, it has exceeded everyone's wildest expectations. Still, everyone has a couple of things on their wish list that didn't make it into the product. One of these items was an editor similar to the one included with Visual Basic. But alas, Visual FoxPro has basically the same clunky editor it's had since FoxPro 2 was released.

One nice feature that Microsoft *has* provided is the ability to do a search or a search-and-replace beyond the current method. The new feature can search all methods for the current object and all other objects in the Form. Open the code editing window, select Edit | Find from the system menu, and look at the Option Group at the bottom of the Find/Replace dialog box. There are three choices—Current Procedure, Current Object, and All Objects—which determine the scope of the search. This expanded feature is extremely useful. Imagine that you define a property as having numeric value (starting with an n). After you've referred to it in a couple dozen different methods, you discover that it contains character data. Some of the methods where you've used it are Form methods, and some are control methods. It's a simple matter to remove nMyProperty from the Form and add cMyProperty, but you'd *really* be cryin' the blues if you didn't have the ability to search for all occurrences of nMyProperty throughout all methods of the Form!

Form Designer Layout Tools

The last discussion of the Form Designer interface covers the layout tools available to the developer.

When you select Tools | Options... from the Visual FoxPro system menu, you are presented with a very complex, tabbed multipage dialog box that is used to set up the current Visual FoxPro session. You can also use it to make the settings the default for all future settings. For now, you'll focus on the items on the Form page, so select it by clicking the Form tab. (See Figure 2-5.)

Grid

In the upper left corner of the Form page are options for the Form Designer Grid. This is no different than that found in FoxPro for Windows 2.x. You can still use the arrow keys to nudge the position of objects, and use shifted arrow keys to nudge the size of objects one pixel at a time without regard to the Grid settings.

Show Position

At the upper right corner of this page is the Show Position CheckBox. Checking this activates two small windows on the right side of the Visual FoxPro status bar that show the position of the current object. FoxPro for Windows 2.x displayed this information as the top, bottom, left, and right coordinates of the object. Visual FoxPro displays this information as [left, top] positions in the first window, and [width, height] positions in the second. The small graphics to the left of the readings indicate which is [left, top] and which is [width, height], but it's sometimes difficult to remember which dimension is which within each window. It may help to remember the convention that you probably learned in high school or college geometry. If the horizontal axis is the x dimension, and the vertical axis is the y dimension, the object's position or dimensions are displayed in x,y order.

The Control object's position is displayed in reference to the Form with 0,0 as the Form's upper leftmost position. The units displayed are either pixels or foxels, depending on the Form's ScaleMode property. However, note that when the Form's ScaleMode is set to Foxels, the position readouts do not display fractional foxels. If you are new to development for the Windows platform, foxels are defined in the Visual FoxPro help file as being "equivalent to the average height and width of a character based on the current font of the Form in which an object is contained. Foxels are useful when developing cross-platform applications for character-based and graphical platforms." If you want more information on working with foxels, see "Foxels Demystified" by Randy Brown in the March 1993 issue of Pinnacle Publishing's *FoxTalk* newsletter.

ScaleMode

The next item on the Options dialog box sets your preference for the tab ordering method (which will be discussed in a moment), what default ScaleMode to use when creating a new Form, and the maximum design area.

Maximum Design Area

This last item is very important, especially as most of you are going to be developing applications using a much higher screen resolution than your clients and users. Setting the maximum design area ensures that your Forms will not be designed to be larger than the viewing area that your users have available.

Trap!

The Maximum Design Area feature is not a cure-all. For example, you will have a problem if you design a fixed-size Form for a 640 x 480 display that is designed to be exactly 640 x 480 pixels in size. In this case, not all of the Form will be visible. The Form's borders will extend slightly beyond each side of the screen, and the top of your Form will be positioned below the top of the screen to allow for the main Visual FoxPro window header, the system menu, and any toolbars that may be in use. As a result, the bottom of your Form will extend below the bottom edge of the screen. This means that the maximum design area is a theoretical maximum. It is meant strictly as a rough visual guide. Factors such as whether the system menu or status bar is on, whether there is a docked toolbar, or whether you're running under Windows 95 (which always maintains a visible taskbar at the bottom, top, or side of the screen), will all take something away from this maximum. At a resolution of 640 x 480, running under Windows 95 with no toolbars or status bar, the system menu "on," a sizeable or double-wide border on the Form, and the Windows 95 taskbar visible and docked at the bottom of the screen, the maximum size Form that can fit entirely within the remaining space on the screen is only 632 x 387 pixels! Note that this measurement does not include the left, right, and bottom borders and the title bar. Instead, it refers to the dimensions inside these boundaries.

Tab Ordering

The Tab Ordering drop-down list box gives two options—By List and Interactive. This determines which tool you should use for setting the order in which the Form controls receive focus. In FoxPro 2.x for MS-DOS, you are required to select the screen objects in the order that you want them to receive focus, and then use the Bring To Front choice on the Screen drop-down menu. FoxPro 2.x for Windows gave you a list which made it possible to determine the screen order by moving the various screen objects in the list. This is what you will have to work with if you select the By List option in the Tools|Options|Forms dialog box. The Interactive option is new, so you should explore it a bit.

Begin by creating a new Form in the Form Designer. Click the Button Lock icon on the Form Controls toolbar, then either click the TextBox icon, or double-click the TextBox icon and drop eight TextBoxes onto the Form in two columns. The names of these TextBoxes will be Text1 through Text8 (the default names assigned by Visual FoxPro). This numbering is handy for this exercise because it allows you to see the order in which the TextBoxes were created, and you can therefore see the current tab order. Next, scramble the TextBoxes by moving them so that they still appear in two columns but are no longer in their original order. If you have not set the tab order option to Interactive, open the Tools|Options dialog box, click the Forms tab, and set it, clicking the OK button so that any changes will take effect.

If you have the Form Design toolbar active, click the Set Tab Order icon. Otherwise, select View|Tab Order from the system menu. All of the controls will acquire a small white square with the control's current tab order number, and a small dialog box will appear on the Form Designer with the legend "Shift-Click To Select Tab Order," and two CommandButtons captioned "Reorder and Cancel." Move this dialog box out of the way and click the upper left TextBox. The Label on this TextBox will change to a value of 1, indicating that it will be the first control to receive focus. The remaining control Labels will become blank. Next, while holding down the Shift key, click the remaining controls in the order that you want them to receive focus. When you have them set, click the Reorder CommandButton on the Tab Order dialog box, and the tab orders will then be set.

Note that simply setting the Tab Ordering option to By List provides a much easier way to change the tab order of one or two items on a complex Form than having to click each object.

Template Forms

At the bottom of the Forms page of the Tools|Options dialog box are two TextBoxes in which you can specify a template for Forms and Form sets. You will see how to use these features in Section 4.

The last item on this page of the dialog box is Builder Lock. Leave this unchecked for now. It will be covered in the discussion of builders found in the upcoming "Potpourri" section.

Saving Option Settings

At the bottom of the Tools|Options dialog box is an OK CommandButton. When this is clicked, it sets all of the options you have chosen for the *current session only*. At the bottom left corner of the Tools|Options dialog box is a CommandButton with the caption "Set as Default." Clicking this CommandButton will save all of the settings as your default settings.

Trap!

Use caution when using the Set as Default CommandButton—it scts defaults for not only those items on the current active page of the PageFrame, but for all of the other pages including file locations. So, if your preferred default directory is C:\VFPSTUFF but you currently have it set to C:\VFPPJX, selecting Set as Default will change your default startup directory. Basically, Set as Default sets all of your current settings as defaults. If you want to change your default settings, it is a good practice to do so immediately upon restarting Visual FoxPro.

Formatting Tools

The last features in the Form Designer interface that will be explained are the new items available under the Format system menu pad. The Form Layout toolbar is a subset of these items, so these tools will be discussed from the menu options rather than the toolbar.

To demonstrate the Form layout options, go over the Form you've been working with (the one with the eight TextBoxes in two columns) and change the size and position of each TextBox. Change some by clicking them and dragging their control handles, and others by moving them with the arrow keys and sizing them while holding down the Shift key and using the arrow keys. (This allows them to be sized and positioned independent of the Grid.) As you work with the layout tools, you may occasionally have to go back and mess up your layout again.

Format | Align

Left Sides, Right Sides, Top Edges, and Bottom Edges
This is fairly self-explanatory. These options are enabled when you have either shift-clicked several controls, or "lassoed" several controls with the mouse by clicking and dragging a marquee that includes several controls. When aligning the left sides, the controls all line up with the leftmost control. Aligning the right sides lines up all controls with the rightmost control, while top edges aligns all with the highest-positioned control.

Align Vertical Centers and Align Horizontal Centers
This is enabled only when multiple controls are selected. If you're not careful, these options will make you frustrated enough to say bad words. What they mean is not "Align Vertical Centers," but "Align Horizontal Centers Vertically"; and not "Align Horizontal Centers," but "Align Vertical Centers Horizontally." If you find yourself confused by these terms, you'll come to love the Undo option on the Edit system menu.

Center Horizontally and Center Vertically
This is enabled only when at least one control is selected. This is also true of the entire alignment submenu. It centers controls in relation to the Form. If the Form is re-sized, the controls will have to be recentered.

Format | Size To Fit

The Visual FoxPro documentation says that this adjusts the control to fit the contents. This refers to the control's caption. As an example, add a Label to your Form. In the caption property in the property sheet, type "This is a Label with a loooong caption." Then observe that probably only the "This is" portion is visible in the Label. Select the Label, and select Format | Size | To Fit from the system menu. This works for any control such as CommandButtons, CheckBoxes, or Labels that have a caption property.

Format | Size To Grid

This snaps all of an object's control points to the nearest Grid point.

Format | Size To Tallest, To Shortest, To Widest, or To Narrowest

This is enabled only when multiple controls are selected. It's a good idea to re-size controls before any alignment operations.

Format | Horizontal Spacing and Format | Vertical Spacing

Make Equal, Decrease, Increase

If more than two controls are selected, the spacing between them is adjusted to that between the leftmost or topmost pair. You can use Increase and Decrease to make adjustments by spacing one pixel at a time.

Running Forms

So far, all you've done is play with design tools. At any time while developing a Form, you can run the Form to see if some piece of code is working right, or to see how the Form will look at runtime. As you'll remember from the introduction, there is no "generate" step in creating Forms. You can do so using any one of the three available methods. On the standard toolbar, click the ! icon, select Form | Run from the system menu, or use the right mouse button to click the Form to bring up the shortcut menu and select the Run option, and the Form will immediately execute.

3 | Common Members

There are 300 properties, events, and methods associated with Visual FoxPro Forms and Control objects. This section is a quick overview of some of the members that are common to many of these objects. Refer to the Visual FoxPro documentation for full details of these members, including parameters that methods receive in response to events, or that some methods require to perform their actions. Refer to Section 12 for a chart listing all object members and the Form-related objects in which they are found.

Common Properties

BackColor Property

This property represents the object's background color. For Forms and pages of PageFrames, this is the color of the background on which Control objects are placed.

For Labels, CheckBoxes (standard), OptionButtons, TextBoxes, EditBoxes, ComboBoxes, Grids, Grid Columns, Grid Headers, and spinners, the BackColor property is the background color on which the control's text appears. For graphical CheckBoxes (which appear as push buttons that remain depressed or pop back up when they are clicked with the mouse), the BackColor property has no effect because the background is not visible behind the graphical button.

For Option Groups and CommandGroups, the BackColor property is the color of the background frame on which the

CommandButtons or Option Buttons are placed. The property also sets the background color for individual OptionButtons.

For Shape Control objects, the BackColor property determines the color of the area inside the shape's boundary. The fill pattern is displayed against this background, which is visible unless the shape's FillStyle property is set to a value of 0 (Opaque).

Trap!

Depending on the characteristics of your (or your user's) display system, one object's BackColor may not match another object's BackColor, even when they are set to the same value. Some elements of the display have a broader palette of colors from which to choose. For instance, TextBoxes on some displays might be set to a light blue color with RGB(100,100,255). For a Form's BackColor, the same color setting might result in a "dithered" blue, which approximates the solid color displayed on the background of the TextBox but is very different in appearance.

BaseClass Property

All of the controls in this report will be based directly on the FoxPro BaseClass. As a result, the TextBox will have TextBox as its BaseClass, the Spinner will have Spinner as its BaseClass, and so forth.

BorderStyle Property

This property indicates the type of border around a visual object control. The online help or Visual FoxPro language reference provides details on the options available for a particular control. The BorderStyle property will also be discussed in the context of individual Form-related objects.

Caption Property

This property indicates the "text" on a CommandButton, Grid Header, Label, or OptionButton, or the tab on a page of a PageFrame. In the case of a Form, the caption is the text in the title bar.

Class Property

This property is the same as the BaseClass property for all Control objects that are not based on user-defined classes. This is true for virtually all of the Control objects discussed in this report. Again, this topic is the province of object-oriented programming, so further information is available in David Frankenbach's report in this book.

ClassLibrary Property

User-defined object classes can be stored in a class library. If the Control object or Form is based on a user-defined object class, this property shows where (in what class library) it is stored.

Comment Property

This property is similar to the comment snippet of FoxPro 2.x. It contains free-form descriptive text for whatever purpose you might have—to remind you of something that needs to be added or perhaps to document a control or Form.

Enabled Property

This property's setting indicates whether or not a control can receive focus. If it is set to 0 or .F., it prevents a control from receiving focus so that the control cannot be selected or changed. The control will then change its appearance to indicate that it is disabled. If the property is greater than 0 or is set to .T., the control can receive focus and can be selected or changed.

Font Properties

Font properties include the following:

- FontBold property
- FontItalic property
- FontName property
- FontSize property
- FontStrikethru property
- FontUnderline property

In the case of Forms, font properties set the font characteristics for anything output onto the Form. These are most commonly seen when the developer checks a value in the command window with "?" and forgets to use the ACTIVATE SCREEN command. For any other control that displays text, these properties set the appearance of that text.

ForeColor Property

This property determines the color of a control's or Form's text, and the color of graphic elements created on Forms using the Line(), Circle(), and Box() methods. However, it does not affect Shape or Line Control objects that have their own color properties. OptionGroups and CommandGroups that do not display text (the text is part of the individual OptionButtons and CommandButtons) do not have a ForeColor property.

Height Property

This property represents the height of a visible control in either pixels or foxels, depending on the ScaleMode property of the Form. Changing the ScaleMode of the Form from pixels to foxels or vice-versa does not change the size of the object, merely the units in which its size is expressed.

Help Contextid Property

This property provides a link into a Windows help file in order to provide context-sensitive help.

Left Property

Representing the leftmost position of a control, this property is expressed in relation to the Form on which it is placed. In the case of a Form object, it is expressed in relation to the Visual FoxPro Desktop. Units are expressed in pixels or foxels, depending on the Form or screen's current ScaleMode.

MousePointer Property

There are 13 different mouse pointer shapes available to the Visual FoxPro developer. As the mouse pointer moves over an object, you can use this property to change the pointer's shape to indicate what action the user can or cannot perform with the mouse. See the online help file for details.

Name Property

Each Control object on a Form or Form in a Form set can be referenced by its name property. However, a Form's Name property cannot be used to reference the Form, its methods, properties, or objects contained within the Form. In short, the Name property is important for Form Controls and other objects that are part of the Form, but is essentially useless for the Form itself. Don't be concerned though; there are simple methods for talking to a Form.

ParentClass Property

Objects are instantiated (created) from an object class. If an object is based on a user-defined class, the Class property indicates the name of the class. The ParentClass property is the next step up the class hierarchy from the class on which the object is derived. This is of interest only when using user-defined classes, and is explained more fully in David Frankenbach's report on OOP.

TabIndex Property

This property determines the tab order of Control objects on a Form. It's easier to use the tools the Form Designer provides to set tab order than it is to manually set this property. The use of these tools is explained in the section "The Form Designer."

TabStop Property

This property determines whether a control can receive focus when the user navigates around a Form with the Tab key.

Tag Property

This is an interesting property that can be used to hold any additional character information you would like to store. For instance, if you have a group of OptionButtons with numeric values (0 or 1), you can store the caption of the group's currently selected option to the group's Tag property.

Top Property

This property represents the topmost position of a control, and is expressed in relation to the Form on which it is placed. In the case of a Form object, it is expressed in relation to the Visual FoxPro desktop. Units are expressed in pixels or foxels, depending on the current ScaleMode of the Form or the screen.

Visible Property

This property determines the visibility of a Control object. It will be visible if this property is greater than 0 or is set to .T., or will be invisible if this property is 0 or .F..

Width Property

This property controls the width of a visible control. This will be measured in either pixels or foxels, depending on the ScaleMode property of the Form. Changing the ScaleMode of the property from pixels to foxels or vice-versa does not change the size of the object, merely the units in which its size is expressed.

Common Methods

AddObject( ) Method

This method is used to add an object to another object at runtime. It applies only to *container objects*, which are objects designed to hold other objects. Container objects are the Form object, CommandGroups (for adding additional CommandButtons), the DataEnvironment object, the Grid, Grid Columns (for adding controls like CheckBoxes or CommandButtons in place of TextBoxes), OptionGroups (for adding additional OptionButtons), PageFrame objects (for adding additional pages), or pages (for adding any kind of control object onto the page).

Move() Method

This method is used to change the position of a control object on a Form, or the position of a Form on the Visual FoxPro screen.

Refresh() Method

The Refresh() method causes the data being displayed in the object to be reread from its data source. The Refresh() method of container objects such as Forms, Grids, pages, and OptionGroups causes all member objects to be refreshed.

RemoveObject() Method

This method removes objects at runtime. See the preceding description of the AddObject() method for more information.

SaveAsClass() Method

This method is used for creating object classes. See David Frankenbach's report on OOP for more information.

ZOrder() Method

The ZOrder method changes the order of objects displayed on a Form in respect to the Z-axis. You can think of the Z-axis as an axis that is perpendicular to the screen. Passing an argument of 0 (<object>.ZOrder(0)) causes the object to move to the "front," putting it "on top" of any other objects that it may overlap. Passing an argument of 1 causes the object to move to the "back" of the Z-order, putting it "behind" any overlapping object.

It is important to note that while there is not a ZOrder Property, a Z-order attribute is inherent in an object's place within a container. This occurs when you place control objects within a Form. As explained in the discussion covering the sequencing of events, the contained objects are instantiated before the container object. Be aware that controls and other contained objects are instantiated in the Form Designer in the order that they are added at design time. Normally this is of little importance. However, if you have one control that has a property that makes reference to another control, you must ensure that the second control is instantiated before the first. Otherwise an error will result.

Common Events

Remember that for every event associated with an object, there is a method that can execute your code in response to that event. The following events include both events and the methods that respond to that event. Remember that when any of these methods are called, the code will execute as if the event had occurred *but the associated event will not occur.* For instance, calling an object's Destroy() method will not destroy or remove the object. It will only execute the code that would have executed if the object were destroyed.

Click Event

This event occurs when the mouse button is clicked while the mouse pointer is positioned over an object or Enter is pressed when the object has focus.

DblClick Event

This event occurs when the mouse button is double-clicked while the mouse pointer is positioned over an object.

Destroy Event

The Destroy event occurs when an object is destroyed.

Error Event

The Error event is triggered by an error that occurs within a control or Form object. If there is code in an object's Error() method, it will take precedence over any On Error command. If an error occurs in an object's Error() method, the error will then be trapped by the global ON ERROR. If an object has code in its Error() method and control is passed to another object that does *not* have code there, the handling of an error event in the second object is delegated to the Error() method in the first object.

GotFocus Event

This event occurs when a Control or Form object receives focus.

Init Event

The Init event occurs automatically during the process of a control or Form being instantiated.

KeyPress Event

This event occurs when a key is pressed.

LostFocus Event

The LostFocus event occurs when a Control or Form object loses focus.

MouseDown Event

This event occurs when a mouse button is depressed and held down. The associated method receives several arguments that indicate the mouse pointer's position, when mouse button is being depressed, and whether any "modifier" keys (Ctrl, Alt, Shift) were being pressed when the mouse button was depressed.

MouseMove Event

This event occurs when one or more mouse buttons are depressed and held down while the mouse is moved.

MouseUp Event

The MouseUp event occurs when a previously depressed mouse button is released.

RightClick Event

The RightClick event occurs when an object is clicked with the right mouse button.

4 | The Form Object

The Form is the first object that will be examined in detail. It is also the first object whose BaseClass definition includes another object.

The Form is a container object. Controls are added to and contained by the Form object. This is usually referred to as a parent-child object relationship. In FoxPro 2.x, you could define windows *in* another window so that the "child" window could not move outside of the "parent" window, and the child window would be closed, hidden, or removed from memory if the parent window was closed, hidden, or removed from memory.

Likewise, control objects such as TextBoxes and CommandButtons that are added to a Form at *design time* are created in the process of the instantiation of the Form. As children of the Form, they are destroyed when the Form is destroyed. Other objects that are added to a Form at *runtime* are also child objects. These objects are likewise destroyed with the Form.

As you'll remember, Forms are instantiated without the execution of any code. However, you needn't worry about how you'll open your tables or how you'll set up variables without setup code. These tasks have been provided for in Visual FoxPro.

First look at instantiation. All of the Visual FoxPro BaseClasses are defined in the Visual FoxPro code in Visual FoxPro.EXE. If you were to create your own user-defined object class, it would be stored in a class library, which is a table with a .VCX extension. Remember that each class (including Visual FoxPro BaseClasses) is simply a definition of the properties and methods for the object. If you were to look at the structure of the .SCX table in which your Form definition is stored, then you were to look at the structure of the .VCX tables in which user-defined object classes are stored, you'd see that the .SCX table is actually a superset of the .VCX table. Both tables store *definitions*. In object-oriented programming, this is called a *class*.

As a result, when you instantiate a Form, you create an object that uses the definition in the .SCX table as the template. The fact that this happens without the execution of a bunch of lines of code doesn't leave you on the sidelines. There is a whole series of events that occur in this process, and there is an opportunity to run some code for every event. This gives you an opportunity to do some of the housekeeping that you're accustomed to. The rest of this housekeeping can happen without your intervention.

The DataEnvironment Object

As part of the Form's BaseClass definition, the Form contains another object. This means that this object is present in any object based on the Form BaseClass, so you don't have to do anything to add this object to your Forms. The object is the DataEnvironment object. It opens tables and sets filters, indexes, and relations. In FoxPro 2.x, these tasks used to be done in a screen's setup code. Like all objects, the DataEnvironment object has members (a series of properties, events, methods, and objects) that are part of *its* definition.

Because some of the properties of the DataEnvironment interact with settings for the Form of which it is a part, the DataEnvironment object will be covered more closely in the next section.

Scoping Variables to the Form Object

Another thing that the setup code of your FoxPro 2.x screens used to deal with was setting up variables that needed to remain in existence and visible to all of the code in the screen's .SPR program. If the variable was initialized in the screen's Activate snippet, in a UDF in the screen's cleanup code, or in a Valid snippet for one of the fields, this variable would go out of scope and be removed from memory once that code module returned control to the calling program (in this case, the .SPR file). There were only two ways around this. One way was to declare the variable Public so it would remain in scope while the screen was active. However, you needed to remember to use the RELEASE command for the variable in the screen's cleanup code. Your other choice was to establish the variable in the setup code and let the variable naturally go out of scope when control returns to the calling program from the .SPR code.

Visual FoxPro does not have setup and cleanup snippets, so you must scope a variable to the Form differently. You do this by creating the variable by adding a new property to the Form. Just like any other variable, you can create an array, properties of any data type (numeric, character, logical, or date), or even another object. Any Form property is scoped to the Form, and therefore is accessible to the method code of any control object, the Form object, or any other object that is contained in the Form. It can also be assigned to a property of a control object. For instance, if you want to populate a list box using an array, you create an array property for the Form, and the list box can use this array as its list.

The Form Event Sequence

Because a sequence of events occurs when an object is instantiated, it is important to know what those events are and in what order they occur. Here is a rough outline of what happens when you instantiate a Form:

1. The Form loads.
2. All of the objects that the Form contains are created (instantiated).
3. The Form activates.
4. The When event of the first control object occurs.
5. The Form receives focus.
6. The first control object receives focus.

The *Init event* occurs for all objects as they are instantiated. Init is short for initialize. This causes some confusion because many people interpret this as the "initial" or "first" event and try to do all sorts of things to the Form, control objects, or data. Then they are surprised when there are problems. These problems occur because many events occur *before* the Init event.

To help you to conceptualize the sequence of events in the instantiation of a Form, it is best to think of the Init event as the "*Initialized*" event. To add to the confusion, the Init() method (which is triggered by the Init event) receives any parameter passed to the object when it is instantiated. This strengthens the impression that the Init() event is a Form's first event. It's not!

What follows is the sequence of events for running a Form, and then the sequence for closing it down again. Notations have been included to fit these events into the previous outline. To fully illustrate this sequence, the hypothetical Form being instantiated has a table specified in the DataEnvironment object, which creates an object identified as a Cursor in the DataEnvironment object. This way it is possible to illustrate the entire event sequence. For the same reason, the Form has two TextBox objects (Text1 and Text2) to allow you to see what events relate to the creation of control objects.

1. The Form loads
Form.DataEnvironment.BeforeOpenTables Event
Form.Load Event

2. All of the objects are instantiated
Form.DataEnvironment.Cursor.Init Event
Form.DataEnvironment.Init Event
Form.Text1.Init Event
Form.Text2.Init Event
Form.Init Event
(See the discussion that follows.)

3. The Form activates
Form.Activate Event

4. The When event of the first control object occurs
Form.Text1.When Event

5. The Form receives focus
Form.Gotfocus Event

6. The first control object receives focus
Form.Text1.Gotfocus Event

When the Form is closed, the next list of events occurs in the order shown (assuming that the Text2 TextBox has focus at the time the Form is closed):

Form.Text2.Valid Event
Form.Text2.Lostfocus Event
Form.Queryunload Event
Form.Destroy Event
Form.Text2.Destroy Event
Form.Text1.Destroy Event
Form.Unload Event
Form.Dataenvironment.Afterclosetables Event
Form.Dataenvironment.Destroy Event
Form.Dataenvironment.Cursor1.Destroy Event

Notice that the completion of objects' instances is done from the "inside out." The Init event for the DataEnvironment object occurs after the Init event of any Cursor objects it contains, and the Init event of the Form itself is the last to occur. This is because it is the "outermost" container object—all of the other objects that are contained in it must be instantiated before the Form can be initialized. If any object's Init() method returns a value of .F., the object will *not* be instantiated. If any of the objects contained by a Form fail in their instantiation, the Form's Init event will fail, and the Form itself will fail to instantiate. This is why the Init of the Form (or any container object) is the last Init to occur.

For quick reference, a table of the primary Form events sequence can be found in the Visual FoxPro online help file under Event Sequence.

Trap!

If you add objects to a container object at runtime using the AddObject() method and the instantiation of those objects fails, the Form will *not* automatically fail to instantiate! As the developer, you must take responsibility to ensure that these objects instantiate properly. Then, in the Init() method of your Form, you should use the Return .F. command if any of the instances fail.

If you try this, you may get an Object Is In Use error when you try to edit the Form. You could also get this error after an error occurs in a running Form. In these cases, issuing a CLEAR ALL command in the command window will remove the object references in memory, and allow the Form to be edited.

To illustrate why an awareness of this event sequence is important, suppose that you want to pass a parameter to a Form that affects which control objects are displayed. Just as in FoxPro 2.x, you can pass a parameter to a Form by issuing the following command:

```
DO FORM <formname> WITH <argument>
```

However, a parameter is received by the Form's Init() method (which is triggered by the Form's Init event). As you can see from the event sequence, it's a bit like closing the barn door after the horse has gotten out. It's much too late to affect the instantiation of the control objects. This is not to say that you can't modify (or add or even remove) objects as a result of a parameter passed to a Form. Just be aware that at the time the Init() method runs, all of the control objects are in place and have all of the properties that you set at design time.

It's always safest to examine and verify any assumptions you may make about any sequence of events. To assist in such an examination, the source disc for this book includes a Form called TestBed. You can use this Form for adding objects and examining event sequences and interactions between the Form and various control objects. (See Figure 4-1.)

Figure 4-1.

The TestBed Form

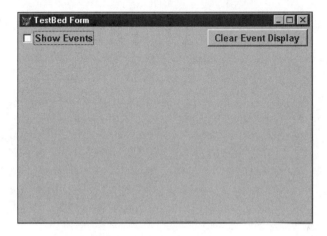

Let's Do It!

In this example you will change your default directory to the directory in which you installed the sample files. Begin by typing the following in the command window:

```
DO FORM testbed
```

Notice that the Form starts in the upper right corner of the screen. Clicking the Show Events CheckBox will cause selected events to "report" on the screen as they occur. You can practice this by clicking the Show Events CheckBox, then clicking the Form. Now resize the Form and drag it to a new position. Each event (in this case the Move event and the Resize event) is reported on the Visual FoxPro desktop. Clicking Clear Event Display clears the desktop.

Now suppose that you set a pseudo-system variable called _SHOWEVENTS to .T. before you started the TestBed Form. The Show Events CheckBox would be selected, and all events would be reported as the Form loaded and all of its objects were instantiated. Note that while the Form "exists" at the time that the DataEnvironment.BeforeOpenTables event occurs, the ShowEvent() method is not yet available so this event is not reported.

Now look at the TestBed Form by using the MODIFY FORM TESTBED command. Use the right mouse button to click the Form, and click Properties if the property sheet isn't already open. Select the Methods tab in the property sheet, then double-click the Click

Continued on next page

Continued from previous page

event to open the Click() method code in an editing window. Then add the following code in the editing window:

```
ThisForm.ShowEvent(PROGRAM())
```

When you add this code to the method code for any event of any object you place on this Form, the ShowEvent() method will "echo" the name of the event method to the Visual FoxPro desktop whenever the Show Events CheckBox is selected.

If you're interested, scroll to the bottom of the list of methods in the properties sheet containing the ShowEvent method. Double-click the method to see how ShowEvent does its thing.

Now that you see how you can trap and report these events, select the TextBox icon from the Form Controls toolbar, and drop a TextBox onto the Form. Next paste the following code into the Click() method, and the DblClick() method for the TextBox.

```
ThisForm.ShowEvent(PROGRAM())
```

You can run the Form by clicking the ! icon or selecting Form|Run from the system menu. Make sure that the Show Events CheckBox is checked, then double-click the mouse pointer in the TextBox.

Did you expect to see both the DblClick event *and* the Click event reported? If you included program code for both events expecting to trigger one method in response to a single click and the other in response to a double-click, you would get more than you bargained for!

There are a few other points to be made about the TestBed Form before you move on. (You'll be using the TestBed Form again in Section 5's "Let's Do It!" box.):

- If you create the variable _SHOWEVENTS and set it to .T. in the command window, you'll see all of the usual events fire as the Form loads and its objects are initialized. (The exception is the DataEnvironment BeforeOpenTables event.)

- You will also see one additional event—the Resize event. Because the Form can be resized, it is necessary to move the CommandButton around so that it remains visible. To position it properly when the Form activates, the Init() method calls the Resize() method. (Note that the Resize() method is being called even though the Resize event wasn't fired!) This is why the ShowEvent method of the Form reports methods and not events; there is no way of telling whether the method was triggered by the event with which it is associated, or whether it was simply called as a function.

- Because you probably haven't added any tables or view to the DataEnvironment object, you won't see any events associated with Cursor or Relation objects.

Continued on next page

> • The necessary code has not been placed in the events associated with the Show Events CheckBox and the Clear Event Display CommandButton, so events associated with these objects are not displayed. Feel free to change this if you wish.
>
>   If you want to explore events some more, take a look at CONTROLS.APP found in the \VFP\SAMPLES\CONTROLS directory that was created when you installed Visual FoxPro.

Now that you've examined some of the behind-the-scenes happenings, take a look at some of the Form's more tangible (visible) properties.

Primary Form Visual and Behavioral Properties

Begin by creating a new Form from the command window using whatever name you choose for your throw-away items (maybe something original like TEST). Then start setting some of the Form's properties to see their effects.

BackColor Property

One of the first things that you'll notice is that the Form in the Form Designer has a white background. If the properties sheet isn't visible, use the right mouse button to click the Form, then click Properties.... In the property sheet, select the Layout tab then select the BackColor property. You could type in a number to represent a color, or you can use an RGB() color triplet separated by commas (such as 192,192,192 for light gray). You can also click the CommandButton to the right of the property-value entry TextBox at the top of the properties list. This will bring forward the Visual FoxPro color-picker dialog box. Choose a color, then run the Form.

While the Form is running, note that all of the usual Windows operations are available. The window can be minimized, maximized, resized, moved, or closed via the control menu at the Form's upper left corner.

Close the Form, then reload it into the Form Designer by issuing MODI FORM <filename> in the command window.

Form State, Size, and Position Properties

- MinButton property
- MaxButton property
- WindowState property
- BorderStyle property
- AutoCenter property

In the property sheet, locate the entry for the MinButton property and the MaxButton property. Set them both to .F.. Note that the Minimize and Maximize buttons on the upper right of the Form no longer appear. Run the Form again. Now you can move, size, and close the Form, but the minimize and maximize options are no longer available and do not appear on the Form control menu. (The Form control menu is popped open by clicking the control-menu box at the Form's upper left corner.) Even though these options are not available to the user, the developer can maximize or minimize the Form under program control with the *WindowState property*. Setting the WindowState to 0 (normal), 1 (minimized), or 2 (maximized) will change the Form independent of the availability of the Minimize and Maximize buttons.

Close the Form and reload it into the Form Designer. Locate the BorderStyle property and look at the options available in the drop-down list box above the properties list. Alternatively, you could simply double-click the BorderStyle property and cycle through the available choices. These choices are shown here:

Setting	Effect
0	No border
1	Single line border
2	Double wide border
3	Sizeable border (default)

As you select an option other than "3 - Sizeable," you'll notice that the appearance of the Form in the Form Designer changes for each choice. You can also see that if you set the BorderStyle property to a static (nonsizeable) border, you can't change the Form size at design time. As a result, if you want something other than a sizeable border it's best to set this once the Form's layout is complete.

Another property that might be best to leave to the end of the design process is the *AutoCenter property*. As an experiment, change the AutoCenter property to .T. and observe how the Form is centered in the Form Designer window. Because the Form Designer window always shows the upper left corner of the "virtual screen," you will need to scroll the Form Designer window or move an AutoCentered Form for them to be visible.

An alternative to either of these options is to set these properties in the Init() method of the Form. You can first do this from the command window, then implement it in code.

Modifying Running Forms from the Command Window

- Deactivate event
- HalfHeight Caption property
- Caption property
- ControlBox property
- Release() method
- Closable property

Begin by restoring the Borderstyle to "3 - Sizeable," then setting AutoCenter to .F.. Open the Deactivate() method either by double-clicking the Deactivate event entry in the property sheet's All list, double-clicking Deactivate event in the property sheet's Methods list, or by first selecting View | Code and then selecting Deactivate from the drop-down list box on the upper right of the code editing window. Then add the following line of code to the method and run the Form:

```
ACTIVATE SCREEN
```

Placing this line of code in the Deactivate() method of your Form ensures that any output you generate by moving to the command window will go to the Visual FoxPro desktop, not onto your Form.

Move the Form over to the right side of the screen and size it so you can see the Visual FoxPro desktop. Enter the "Clear" and "Display Memory" commands in the command window. To interrupt the display, press Esc when you get the Press Any Key prompt. If your Form file is TEST.SCX, you will see in the memory display a line like this:

```
Test   Pub   O      Form
```

This line indicates that there is a public memory variable named Test. This variable is of type "O" (which stands for object), and this object is an instance of the class Form. This variable is an *object reference* and can be used to change the properties of the object to which it refers, or to call an object's methods. For this exercise, use the variable to call the object's methods.

Again, enter the following code in the command window. (This code assumes that your Form is named Test. Substitute the name of your Form if you've used something different.)

```
Test.BorderStyle = 1
Test.BorderStyle = 2
```

Once the code has been entered, the border of the Form will change first to a nonsizeable, single-line border with a pixel width of 1. Next the border will change to a double-width nonsizeable border, which has a width of 4 pixels. This width is the same as the sizeable border.

You should note two things about these borders. First, the Form width and height are the size of the Form *inside* the borders. Keep in mind that a single-line border adds two pixels to the over-all width of the Form, while the double-wide and sizeable borders each add eight pixels to the width of the Form. Also, note that BorderStyle = 0 and BorderStyle = 1 look the same. To see the Form without any border line requires that the Form's HalfHeightCaption Property be set to .T..

Now that you know how to do this, you can set some other properties. Begin with the following code:

```
Test.AutoCenter = .T.
```

You can still move the Form after setting AutoCenter = .T.. Resetting it again will re-center the Form.

Next, you can enter the following code to change the Form's Caption property:

```
Test.Caption = "My Visual FoxPro Form"
```

The next line of code sets the Form's ControlBox property. This causes the control-menu box and its associated menu to be removed from the Form.

```
Test.ControlBox = .F.
```

Looking back at what you've just done, you'll notice that you don't have controls on your Form such as OK or Cancel, a control-menu box you can double-click to close the Form, or a control menu to open and select Close.

Remember that once you know an object's reference, you can call methods of that object. It just happens that Forms have a handy method called Release() that closes Forms. From the command window, you can type the following code to send your Form to the bit-bucket:

```
TEST.RELEASE()
```

You can retain the control-menu box but prevent the user from either selecting Close on the control menu or closing the Form by double-clicking the control-menu box by setting the Form's *Closable Property* to .F..

Object (and Form) References

As long as you're this far, you can take a little side trip into object references. Begin by executing DISPLAY MEMORY in the command window. You'll notice that there is still a memory variable named Test. That variable is still public and still type O, but instead of being based on the Form class, it shows .NULL. This shows that you have destroyed the Form object, but not the variable that was used to refer to the object.

You might wonder if destroying the variable would mean destroying the object. In the case of a Form instantiated with Do Form <filename>, the answer is no. (This is not true for all objects. See David Frankenbach's report on OOP for more on object references.) However, it would make it difficult to refer to the Form. This will be covered further in the discussion of Form references.

Setting Form Properties at Runtime

- MinWidth property
- MinHeight property
- ScaleMode property

Earlier during the discussion of the AutoCenter property and the BorderStyle property, it was mentioned that you might want to leave AutoCenter set to .F. and BorderStyle set to 3 during design. There might be times when you really want a Form to have AutoCenter set to .T. and BorderStyle set to 2, but you don't want to have to remember to make these changes when you're ready to deliver your application.

To deal with this, open your Form in the Form Designer and set BorderStyle to 3 and set AutoCenter to .F.. Then close the Form Designer. Save your changes and reopen the Form, verifying that the Form is appearing in the upper left of the Form Designer window, and that the border is still sizeable. In the Form's Init() method, place the following lines of code:

```
ThisForm.AutoCenter = .T.
ThisForm.BorderStyle = 2
```

Now run the Form. You should have a centered Form with a double-width non-sizeable border.

Now try another exercise. Open the Form in the Form Designer and locate the *MinWidth* and the *MinHeight properties*. Set the

MinWidth property to 200, and the MinHeight to 150. This will prevent resizing the Form smaller than these dimensions. Set the Form's Caption property to "My VFP Form."

Next, suppose that you want to be able to dock the Form, reducing it to its minimum size (without actually minimizing it to an icon) and moving it to an out-of-the-way location on the screen.

To do this, you'll need to add a method to the Form. From the system menu, select Form | New Method.... In the dialog box that appears, enter the method name "DockIt," and click OK.

Next, go to the property sheet. Under the Methods tab, scroll to the bottom to find this new method. Double-click it, and enter the following code in your DockIt method:

```
ThisForm.Width = ThisForm.MinWidth
ThisForm.Height = ThisForm.MinHeight
ThisForm.Left = _SCREEN.Width - ThisForm.MinWidth - 8
ThisForm.Top = 0
```

This code sets the Form's Width property and Height property to their minimums. It then positions the left edge of the Form at a point that is equal to the screen's width less the Form's width plus eight pixels ($W_s - W_f + 8$ where W_s is screen width and W_f is Form width). Eight pixels were chosen because the properties that position the Form on the screen (Top and Left) refer to the *outside* measurements of the Form, while *height* and *width* refer to the Form's extent *inside* the borders. Since a sizeable border is four pixels wide, the eight pixels account for the left and right border widths.

Now you need some way of calling this method. You could call it from the command window with the following code:

```
Test.DockIt()
```

However, that's sort of dull. Instead, place the following in the DblClick() method for the Form:

```
ThisForm.DockIt()
```

As you run this Form, first verify that you can move it, resize it, and subject it to the minimum sizes specified. Then double-click the Form. The Form resizes to the minimum height and width, and should dock itself at the upper right corner of the screen.

Now look at another property of Forms, and see how you can break this little "docking" trick without changing a single line of code.

First be aware that the Visual FoxPro object _SCREEN that was referred to in the DockIt() method is indeed an object, and is based on the Form class. As a result, it shares many of the properties, events, and methods of Forms. One of these properties is the *ScaleMode property.*

That DockIt() code, which adjusted for an eight-pixel combined left and right border width, assumed that the ScaleMode property for the _SCREEN was "3 - Pixels." However, it *could* have been "0 - Foxels." In that case, the value of 8 in the code would have been interpreted very differently. Type the following in the command window:

```
_SCREEN.ScaleMode = 0
DO FORM test
```

Now, try to dock the Form by double-clicking it. It should end up hanging somewhere near or off the left side of the screen. The lesson here is that, any time you are positioning an object at design time or runtime that specifies a certain dimension in either pixels or foxels, you should take steps to make sure that the Form or screen is in the appropriate ScaleMode for the units you are using.

To see how this works, run the TestBed Form and double-click the Form background. You can observe that whatever value the _SCREEN's ScaleMode property is set to, the TestBed Form will move to the upper right of the screen when you double-click the Form's background. Check the code for the Park() method to see how this is implemented.

Lets's Do It!

Object References (Again)

Set the _SCREEN's ScaleMode back to "3 - Pixels," and instantiate your test Form from the command window with the following code:

```
DO FORM test
```

Now do this twice more.

```
DO FORM test
DO FORM test
```

Verify that you have three *instances* of your test Form available at the same time by moving them to different parts of the screen. To show that these Forms are independent, enter the following in the command window:

```
Test.BackColor = RGB(0,255,0)
```

Continued on next page

Continued from previous page

> This code makes the background of the first Form you instantiated turn green. Minimize all three Forms and use the Display Memo command. Note that you have one reference to a Form object, Test. You will remember there was some discussion about having a Form object with no variable reference. This is a naturally occurring example of that situation. You can reference only the second and third Forms you've instantiated with the _SCREEN's ActiveForm Property. Select one of the Forms that has not had its BackColor property changed and type the following in the command window:
>
> ```
> _SCREEN.ActiveForm.BackColor = RGB(255,0,0)
> ```
>
> Now select the remaining Form and type the following code in the command window:
>
> ```
> _SCREEN.ActiveForm.BackColor = RGB(0,0,255)
> ```

AlwaysOnTop Property

While you have three screens available from the Let's Do It box, take a look at how you can use the Always on Top feature that the Windows Help system offers. This is done by setting the Form's *AlwaysOnTop property*. Select one of the Forms and type the following in the command window:

```
_SCREEN.ActiveForm.AlwaysOnTop = .T.
```

Then select another Form and issue the same command.

You will be able to activate the third Form, but you will not be able to move it on top of the two Forms for which you have set the AlwaysOnTop property to .T.. However, either of the two windows with this property set can be placed in front of the other.

Icon Property

When a Form is minimized, by default it has a Fox-Head icon. If you want to specify a different icon for a specific Form, you can do so by indicating the .ICO file name in the Form's *Icon property*.

Additional Form Properties, Methods, and Events

KeyPress Event

- KeyPress() method
- KeyPreview property

A Form can trap a *KeyPress event* with code placed in the KeyPress method. However, under normal circumstances, the Form itself must have focus to trigger the KeyPress event. This is not normally the case because a control usually has focus. Setting the *KeyPreview property* of the Form to .T. allows any KeyPress event to be handled by the Form prior to being handled by the control.

To see when a KeyPress event occurs and in what order, open the TestBed example Form and place a TextBox on the Form. Place the reporting code [ThisForm.ShowEvent(PROGRAM())] into the KeyPress() method of the TextBox, and the KeyPress() method of the Form. Don't worry about the parameters at the moment.

Run the Form and check Show Events in the CheckBox. Then type a few characters into the TextBox. The ShowEvent() method should be reporting that the Testbed.Text1.KeyPress() method is executing for each keystroke. Now, from the command window, change the Form's KeyPreview property as follows:

```
TestBed.KeyPreview = .T.
```

Return to the TestBed Form and again type a few characters into the TextBox. You'll notice that the Text1.KeyPress() is still being executed, but now it is preceded by the TestBed.KeyPress() method. This ability is handy when you want to have a Form-level hotkey—it avoids having to write the code to handle the hotkey combination in every control object.

Hide( ) Method—Visible Property

Setting the *Visible property* of a Form to .F. does not destroy the Form or remove it from memory; it merely makes the Form invisible and inaccessible to the user. When the Form's Visible property is set to .F., it is still possible to access the Form's properties and methods as well as the properties and methods of its control objects from program code.

The *Hide() method* simply sets the Visible property to .F..

LockScreen Property—Refresh( ) Method

When the data being displayed by any control has changed (for instance, if the user has skipped to another table record), the control can be updated to reflect the change by calling the control object's *Refresh() method*. In calling the Form's Refresh() method, all of the control objects are refreshed and the Form is repainted.

While it is handy to simply refresh all of the control objects, it is much more efficient (when possible) to refresh only those objects that have changed.

In some cases, refreshing Form controls and changing numerous Form and Form-control properties can cause annoying visual effects as the various changed properties take effect on one property and one object after another. Setting the Form's *LockScreen property* to .T. prevents property changes from taking immediate effect, while setting LockScreen property to .F. causes all of the changes to take effect simultaneously and all of the controls to be refreshed. Note that setting LockScreen to .T. at design time is not usually a good idea because it will have to be reset to .F. before any controls or properties become visible. It is best to set LockScreen to .T. when updates are taking place, then change it back to .F. when the updates have finished.

QueryUnload Event—ReleaseType( ) Property

The *QueryUnload event* allows you to determine how a Form is being closed, and, if necessary, take actions based on this information. This is similar to (although not at all the same as) the Readkey( ) of FoxPro 2.x because it provides you with information about how the user is exiting a Form. The QueryUnload event is triggered any time the Form is released through the control menu (either by double-clicking the control-menu box or selecting Close from the control menu), if the Clear Windows or Clear All command is issued, or if Visual FoxPro is being exited using the Quit command. Closing the Form using the Form's Release( ) method does *not* trigger the QueryUnload event. The Visual FoxPro documentation states that the Release Windows command will also release the Form and trigger the QueryUnload. However this can be somewhat unreliable. Release Windows works as advertised in Windows 95 and Windows for Workgroups, but not under Windows NT Workstation. Carefully check the behavior of this command for the platform under which your application will run, or better yet, use a more reliable way of releasing a Form.

The QueryUnload event can be used to do things like save changes, prompt the user to save changes, or prevent closing of a Form in which the user has made changes to a table. It can also be used to prevent termination of a Visual FoxPro application until the user has closed all open Forms. When the QueryUnload is triggered, a property of the Form (the *ReleaseType property*) is automatically set and you can check the status of this property in your QueryUnload code. You can then take whatever action is necessary. Placing the following code in the QueryUnload method will prevent the user from exiting Visual FoxPro while the Form is active:

```
IF ThisForm.ReleaseType = 2
   NODEFAULT
ENDIF
```

The NODEFAULT Visual FoxPro keyword is used to prevent certain default behaviors from occurring. Consider the default behavior of a TextBox in response to the KeyPress event—the character that corresponds to the key being pressed is placed into the TextBox and the insertion point is moved one character to the right. The NODEFAULT keyword stops this default behavior of the TextBox BaseClass and prevents the typed characters from appearing in the TextBox, allowing you to insert characters of your choice.

The other methods of closing a Form listed previously will result in a ReleaseType of 1. As of this writing and contrary to the Visual FoxPro documentation, Release Windows has no effect on the Form. If you instantiate a Form with a linked reference variable, Release < reference name> will release the Form, but will not trigger the QueryUnload event. The code to instantiate the Form is shown here:

```
DO FORM <formfile> NAME <reference name> LINKED
```

Resize Event and Move Event

These two events allow you to take some programmatic action when a Form is resized or moved. You will probably use the Resize event more often.

If you haven't already thought of it, consider when you are likely to want your users to be able to resize a Form. Is there any advantage to allowing them to do so? Many Forms have a fixed number of objects placed upon them. Each object is painstakingly placed so as to be clear and uncluttered. Resizing a Form to a smaller size will obscure some of the controls, while resizing a Form to larger dimensions will create a lot of blank space below and to the right of your controls. As a result, you will probably want to select a non-sizeable BorderStyle property.

However, there are times when a resizeable border makes a lot of sense. This might be when a Form presents a list box that the user may want to be taller than you have specified in your design, or when a PageFrame contains pages of lists that could benefit from being sized as the user's needs change. For an example of such a Form, just look at the Form Designer's properties sheet.

The PageFrame, ComboBox, Drop-Down ListBox, and ListBox properties are not resized automatically. If you want to have a Form display this type of behavior, you will have to detect the Resize event and take appropriate action.

To see a simple example of this, run the TestBed sample Form. You'll note that as it is resized, the Clear Event Display CommandButton remains spaced three pixels from the right border of the Form no matter how the Form is sized. Here is the code that was placed in the Form's Resize() method:

```
LOCAL lnOldScaleMode
lnOldScaleMode = ThisForm.ScaleMode
ThisForm.ScaleMode = 3
ThisForm.Command1.Left = ;
   ThisForm.width - ;
   ThisForm.Command1.width - 3
IF ThisForm.ScaleMode # lnOldScaleMode
   ThisForm.ScaleMode = lnOldScaleMode
ENDIF
```

As in the Park() method with _SCREEN, care was taken in this method to ensure that the Form's scalemode was set to 3 (Pixels) before changing the Left property of the CommandButton. Note, too, that the TestBed Form's MinWidth property was established to take into account the space required for the Show Events CheckBox and the Clear Event Display CommandButton. You could just as easily change the dimension of control objects, the font size of the captions, or even the wording of the captions to accommodate a resized Form.

SetAll() Method

At times it might be convenient to set a property for multiple control objects to be the same value at the same time. The *SetAll() method* accomplishes this. To try it, place an additional CommandButton and CheckBox on to the TestBed Form. Change the BackStyle property of the CheckBox to 0 (transparent) and run the Form. Now issue several commands from the command window. The first command sets the text on all of the controls to red.

```
TestBed.SetAll("ForeColor",RGB(255,0,0))
```

The next command sets the text on all of the CommandButtons to black.

```
TestBed.SetAll("ForeColor",RGB(0,0,0),"CommandButton")
```

The third command sets the text on all of the CheckBoxes to green.

```
TestBed.SetAll("ForeColor",RGB(0,255,0),"CheckBox")
```

The fourth command sets the text of all of the controls back to black.

```
TestBed.SetAll("ForeColor",RGB(0,0,0))
```

This method is available for most of the container objects in Visual FoxPro including Forms, CommandGroups, OptionGroups, Grids, pages, and PageFrames.

WindowType Property—Show() Method

As in FoxPro 2.x, you have the option of creating a Form as a *modeless object* or as a *modal object.* In the case of a modeless Form, *WindowType property* is set to 0 and the execution of code that instantiates the Form object continues after the Form is displayed and activated. The user can either select another Form or make a selection from the system menu without closing the modeless Form. With a modal Form, the WindowType property is set to 1, causing code execution to stop or enter a wait state while the Form is active. The user is prevented from activating any other Form or initiating any other action through the system menu until a modal Form has been closed.

In all cases, calling a Form's *Show() method* causes its Visible property to be set to .T., making that Form the active Form. The Show() method can be used without arguments or with an argument of 1 or 2 to override the Form's WindowType setting. Show(1) causes the Form to be modal, Show(2) causes the Form to be modeless. Passing no argument defaults to the Form's WindowType property.

• *ShowTips Property*

An absolutely wonderful enhancement in Visual FoxPro is the ability to show ToolTips. If you've used other shrink-wrapped software products such as Microsoft Excel, Microsoft Word for Windows version 6, or even Visual FoxPro toolbars, you've seen these little black-on-yellow text flags that describe what the buttons on toolbars do. You simply have to pause with the mouse pointer over the toolbar button for the ToolTip to appear. This really helps the user figure out the "intuitive" icons they're faced with. Icons are great, but until you know that the little icon that looks kind of like a 3.5" diskette means "Save," you're really at a disadvantage compared with a nice clear textual description on a drop-down menu. Many Visual FoxPro control objects including TextBoxes, CheckBoxes, and

CommandButtons have a ToolTipText property that determines which ToolTip will be automatically displayed when the user pauses the mouse pointer over the control object.

However, remember that no matter how conscientious you are about placing ToolTipText into all of your control objects, it will all be for naught if you forget to set the Form's ShowTips property to .T..

In case you're wondering, the font, position, size, and color of the ToolTips is not under your control unless you create some kind of pop-up window of your own triggered by the MouseOver event.

- *DataSession Property*
- *BufferMode Property*

These two properties represent two of the greatest innovations in the creation of Visual FoxPro Forms.

The *DataSession property* takes two values; one is a default DataSession, and the second is a private DataSession. The default DataSession is the DataSession that you've been working in for many years. It includes the attendant concerns caused by multiple screens having multiple DataEnvironments that you would struggle mightily to protect from interacting with one another. Now it's simply a matter of giving Forms a private DataSession. All of the tables, relations, filters, views, and index orders are completely insulated from any other Form, report or action, even in the command window (at least without taking explicit steps to breach that insulation).

The *BufferMode property* allows you to determine whether the data that is displayed and edited in Form controls and Form code is buffered, and, if so, how it is buffered. For more information on the options available and their full implications, refer to Doug Hennig's report in this book on the Visual FoxPro Data Dictionary, and to the discussion of the BufferModeOverride property of the DataEnvironment object in the next section.

For now, it is enough to understand that turning data buffering on by setting the Form's BufferMode to 1 (the pessimistic setting that locks records when the data is read) or 2 (the optimistic setting that locks records only when data is written) completely eliminates the debate over direct edits of table data that used to keep developers amused for hours. With data buffering enabled, it is necessary to issue a TableUpdate( ) command to commit changes to the table. It is also possible to use TableRevert( ) to discard changes. It would be difficult to find a situation (other than in converting a legacy application or the quick-and-dirty examples included here) in which you would opt to turn data buffering off by leaving the Form's BufferMode property set to 0. This would force you to revert to tricks involving RLOCK(), SCATTER, and GATHER in order to protect data from unintentional changes.

Creating Form Templates

This topic is *really* the province of object-oriented programming, but it's so simple and useful that it'll be discussed here.

The discussion about the dialog box presented by selecting Tools|Options... from the system menu mentioned that we'd come back to discuss the Template Classes at the bottom of the Forms page. Well, here you go. Using the Options... Form, you can save yourself a lot of work by specifying a template to use when creating Forms.

As you've been working thus far, you may have found that you already have some preferences. Objects with 3-D effects often look best on a light gray background, so one of the most common preferences in a template is a BackColor of RGB(192,192,192). You might also want to include the ACTIVATE SCREEN line in the Deactivate() method. This allows the screen to become the output window whenever you move to the command window during development and testing.

If you have different types of Forms such as data entry Forms and dialog box Forms, you can create a template for each and give all of your dialog boxes a light yellow background.

To make a template, create a Form that has all of the features you want in your default Form, save it as a class in a class library, and specify that class as your template in the Options dialog box.

To try this yourself, begin by creating a new Form. Set the background to light gray. (Select the *BackColor property* in the property sheet, and click the "..." CommandButton to bring up the Visual FoxPro color-picker dialog box.) Next add ACTIVATE SCREEN to the Form's Deactivate() method. If you want to add items such as AutoCenter and DataSession to a template Form, go ahead and do so. You might also want to set WindowStyle to "1 - Modal" for a dialog box template. Note that because this Form will be saved as a class in a .VCX table instead of a Form in an .SCX table, you will not be able to save the DataEnvironment or any of its properties in a template.

Once you have all of the default property values established, save your Form as a template. Form templates are saved in a class library, so you have to create a class library in which to store this Form template. To do so, enter the following in the command window:

```
CREATE CLASSLIB \PTFFD\TEMPLATE
```

This will create an empty class library. Now, from the system menu, select File|Save As Class.... In the resulting dialog box, enter an appropriate name such as PTFFD_Template for the template and click the "..." CommandButton. Then find the TEMPLATE.VCX table you created from the command window, enter a description (if you wish), and press the OK button.

Close the Form Designer but do *not* save the Form. Select Tools|Options from the system menu, then select the Forms page in the Options dialog box. Under Template Classes, check the Form CheckBox. You will be presented with another dialog box showing a list of class libraries on the left. If necessary, navigate to the proper directory until you locate TEMPLATE.VCX. Click *once* on TEMPLATE.VCX, and you will see a list of the templates available in this class library in the window on the far right. At this point there should be only one, the PTFFD_Template you just created. Select this template, click the OK button, and again click the OK button in the Options dialog box.

Now when you use the Create Form Test command, the BackColor property and the code to ACTIVATE SCREEN when the Form is deactivated are already taken care of. This is starting to go beyond the scope of this report, but accept two cautions. If you make any changes to the class that you are using as a Form template, those changes will affect all the Forms that use that template. This is what is known as *inheritance* in the OOP world. Also, if you remove the template, you will not be able to access any of the Forms that were created using that template. You may be able to recover from such a situation, but it will probably require surgery on your .SCX table to do so.

5 | The Form's DataEnvironment Object

The DataEnvironment object handles all of the data tables that your Form needs to access. This section provides a listing of all of the properties, events, and methods that are members of the DataEnvironment object, its Cursor objects (one for each table or view in the DataEnvironment), and its Relation objects (one for each relation between tables in the DataEnvironment). Each name listed is accompanied by a brief description. After that, you will construct a DataEnvironment for a Form using the Form Designer's visual tools.

DataEnvironment Properties

First, look at DataEnvironment properties.

AutoCloseTables Property

The AutoCloseTables property determines whether tables opened by the DataEnvironment object will remain open after the object is destroyed. It defaults to .T.. Note that this property has no practical meaning if the Form is set up to have a private DataSession.

AutoOpenTables Property

This property determines whether tables specified in the DataEnvironment object are opened automatically. It defaults to .T.. If AutoOpenTables is set to .F., the tables can be opened by calling the DataEnvironment's OpenTables() method.

InitialSelectedAlias Property

This property is the alias of the Cursor (table or view) that is selected when the DataEnvironment is loaded.

DataEnvironment Events

AfterCloseTables Event

BeforeOpenTables Event

As you might guess, the BeforeOpenTables event is triggered just before tables and views are opened. The AfterCloseTables event is triggered just after tables are closed.

DataEnvironment Methods

There are two DataEnvironment methods to review.

CloseTables() Method

OpenTables() Method

These methods are used when AutoOpen and AutoCloseTables are set to .F..

Cursor Object Properties

Now look at several Cursor object properties.

Alias Property

This property represents the alias of the view or table.

BufferModeOverride Property

There are six different settings for buffering table data. They are either identified by the number set by the CursorSetProp() function, or they are returned by the CursorGetProp() function. These settings are as follows:

Setting	Effect
0	None
1	Use Form setting
2	Pessimistic row buffering (The record is locked when read.)
3	Optimistic row buffering (The record is locked only when written.)
4	Pessimistic table buffering (Multiple record locks are placed when read.)
5	Optimistic table buffering (Multiple record locks are placed when written.)

The Form has a BufferMode property that can be set to one of three values: 0 (No table buffering), 1 (Pessimistic buffering), or 2 (Optimistic buffering). These correspond to settings 0, 2, and 3 in the preceding list. The Cursor's BufferModeOverride property allows you to use table buffering. It also allows you to use different buffering modes on different tables or views. The settings for the BufferModeOverride property are as follows:

Setting	Effect
0	None
1	Use Form setting (default)
2-5	Same as the previous list for CursorSetProp()

For more information on data buffering, see Doug Hennig's report on the Visual FoxPro Data Dictionary in this book.

CursorSource Property

The CursorSource property contains the name of a view or the long name of a table in a database, or it contains the full path to a free table. (See Doug Hennig's report on the Visual FoxPro Data Dictionary in this book for more information.)

Database Property

If the entry in the CursorSource property is in a database container (a view or a table), this property will show the name of the database.

Exclusive Property

This property controls whether the table or tables that support a view are opened exclusively. Unless the Form's DataSession property is set to 2 (private DataSession), the Exclusive property will default to .T..

Filter Property

The Filter property is a logical expression that is used to filter the records in the table or view. It's the same as the expression used in the SET FILTER TO command.

NoDataOnLoad Property

This property is used when a view specified for the Cursor object results in a large number of records, or when it must access records from a back-end server. If it is set to .T., NoDataOnLoad allows the Form to load quickly without waiting for the data.

Order Property

The Order property is the controlling index tag for the Cursor; it is the same as the SET ORDER TO TAG command. This property is overridden when the ChildOrder property in the Relation Object is set.

ReadOnly Property

As you'd expect, a table or view is read-only when its ReadOnly property is set to .T..

Relation Object Properties

ChildAlias Property

The ChildAlias property specifies the alias of the table in the child position of a relationship.

ChildOrder Property

This property specifies the index order of the child table. It overrides the Order property of the Cursor object.

OneToMany Property

The OneToMany property has an effect identical to the SET SKIP TO <child table> command in FoxPro 2.x. An explicit SET SKIP TO command is necessary to gain this effect in a more complex relationships with more than two tables. This can be executed in the Form's Load() or Init() methods. The OneToMany property defaults to .F..

ParentAlias Property

This property specifies the alias name of the view or table in the parent position in the relationship.

RelationalExpr Property

When establishing a relationship between two tables in code, the following command is issued while the parent table is currently selected:

```
SET RELATION TO <cExpression> INTO <Alias>
```

The parent's alias is specified in the Relation Object's ParentAlias property. The alias of the child table is specified in the ChildAlias property. The index order of the child table is specified in the ChildOrder property. The only additional information needed to establish the relationship is the <cExpression> of the SET RELATION command shown. This expression is placed into the RelationalExpr property. It can be an individual field name or a more complex expression corresponding to the index expression of the child table.

Let's Do It!

Now that you've taken a look at all the individual pieces, you can put together a DataEnvironment for a Form.

For all of the examples in this report, you'll be using the database container (the .DBC table) and tables found in the \VFP\SAMPLES\DATA directory that was installed with Visual FoxPro. If you haven't already done so, create a DATA subdirectory in the \PTFFD directory (you should already have this). Then copy the contents of \VFP\SAMPLES\DATA to this directory.

Next, open the TestBed Form, use the right mouse button to click the Form, and select DataEnvironment from the resulting pop-up list. This opens the DataEnvironment window. Before proceeding further, take a look at the drop-down list box at the top of the properties sheet. At the moment, the only thing in the list is the DataEnvironment object. As you continue you'll be adding Cursor and Relation objects to that list.

Now use the right mouse button to click the DataEnvironment window. Then select Add... from the pop-up context menu. The resulting dialog box has a ComboBox at its top in which all open database containers are listed. No database containers are open now, but if any were a list of the tables in the current database container would be shown in the list box on the left. You could select the Other CommandButton and navigate to the Data subdirectory and select a table. Instead, you should select the Cancel CommandButton, go over to the command window, and type OPEN DATA TESTDATA. Then pop back over to the DataEnvironment window and bring up the Add... dialog box again. Then you'll see a listing of all the tables in the TestData database container.

Continued on next page

Continued from previous page

Select the Customer table in the Add... dialog box. A window representing the customer table will appear in the DataEnvironment window. This new window will have the heading "Customer," and will list all of the fields in the table. As you scroll the list of fields toward the bottom, you will see all four of the index tags for this table. Check the drop-down list box on the property sheet. It will now have two items, "DataEnvironment" and "Cursor1."

Use the right mouse button to select the Add... option again. This time, select the Orders table. A window representing this table showing all of its fields and index tags also appears in the DataEnvironment window. However something else will appear—a line between the Customer table and the Orders table. If you scroll down the Orders table a bit, you'll see that the line is connecting the cust_id field in the Customers table to the cust_id index in the Orders table.

This line represents the relationship between the two tables. While at first this might seem like magic, it is actually what is referred to as a *persistent relationship* established in the database. Don't be too concerned though; it is simply a default relationship at this point. You have complete freedom to set up any relationship you find suitable for your applications, so the persistent relationship established in the database (using the Database Designer) is not cast in stone.

If you had an appropriate field in the Customers table and a corresponding index in the Orders table, you could click the field in Customers and drag it to the index in Orders. This would establish a relation that was different than the default. In fact, you can try this now. Click the relation line (it will turn to a heavy line to indicate that it is selected) and press the Delete key. The line will disappear, indicating that you have broken the relation. Then click the Cust_id field in the Orders table and drag it to the cust_id index in the Customers table. You've just set up a relationship with the Orders table as the parent and the Customer table as the child.

Now put things back the way they were by repeating the process, deleting the relation, and dragging customers.cust_id to the cust_id index in Orders.

Check the drop-down list box on the DataEnvironment's property sheet. You will see four items—DataEnvironment, Cursor1, Cursor2, and Relation1. You can take a look at some of the properties that have been set in this process.

In the property sheet for the DataEnvironment object, the AutoOpenTables and AutoCloseTables are at their default values of .T., and the DataEnvironment's default name has been established. Note that the InitialSelectedAlias property is not set. You can set it as the Customer table either by typing in the name, or by clicking the ComboBox below the PageFrame tabs and selecting one of the aliases listed there.

Continued on next page

Figure 5-1.

The DataEnvironment Designer

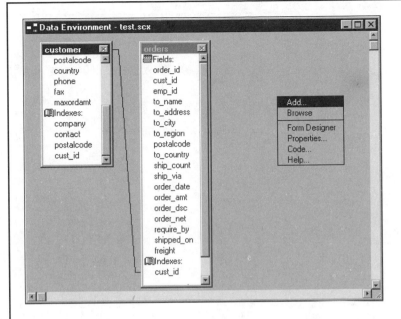

For Cursor objects, the alias, the CursorSource (a table in this case, but it could be a view), and the default name (Cursor1 or Cursor2) are specified. In addition, the database is filled in and the read-only property defaults to .F.. If you choose, you can change the name of the alias, however you must remember to go back and change the InitialSelectedAlias property in the DataEnvironment object. You can see that it's a little more convenient to set the aliases for the Cursors first, then select from the ComboBox available for the InitialSelectedAlias property. Because it is italicized, the NoDataOnLoad property shows that it is not available. If this Cursor represented a view (an updatable list of records created from a SQL query), this property would be enabled.

Continuing on to the Relation object, note that the ChildAlias, ParentAlias, ChildOrder, and RelationalExpr properties have been set by the visual placement of the tables into the DataEnvironment window. Instead of resetting the default relationship visually (deleting the existing relationship and then dragging from parent field to child index), you can change this relationship by selecting from the available fields in the parent table and the available index in the child table. However, if you are changing the parent-child relationship (as you did before, making Customer the child table to Orders), this must be done visually in the DataEnvironment. Notice that the ChildAlias and ParentAlias properties are disabled, and that the OneToMany property defaults to .F.. Leave it set this way.

By examining the DataEnvironment object and its child objects, you should be getting a feel for how objects work and how setting properties for objects affects the way that they behave. While

Continued on next page

Continued from previous page

you're examining the property sheets for the DataEnvironment and its child objects, try highlighting one of the properties, events, or methods in the list and pressing the F1 function key. This brings up the Visual FoxPro help file entry for that item. You should do this often, as it will further familiarize you with what properties are, what properties are available for different objects, which events different objects can respond to, and what methods are available for different objects.

6 | Basic Control Objects

In this section, you will begin to examine the following control objects available in Visual FoxPro and use them to assemble a working Form:

- Label Controls
- CommandButtons
- the CommandGroup
- TextBoxes
- EditBoxes
- Spinner Controls
- CheckBoxes
- the OptionGroup
- PageFrame Controls

Label Controls

Visual FoxPro Label Controls are used for the same purposes as the @...SAY fields you used in FoxPro 2.x. However, unlike the @...SAY fields, Label Control objects are much more flexible. At runtime you can change their color, font, size, and even the text that the label displays. This was not impossible with FoxPro 2.x, but it was very tedious. Furthermore, Label Control objects can respond to *events* such as clicks of the mouse button. FoxPro 2.x could not do that without resorting to very clever programming.

To practice using Label Controls, create a new Form, set the BackColor property to light gray, and select the Label Control from the Form Controls toolbar. Then, drop the Label somewhere on the Form.

- ***Name Property***
- ***Caption Property***

One of the first things that you will notice about the Label is that the *Name property* of the Label is "Label1." Visual FoxPro assigns a default name to every object you work with. If you were to add another Label, Visual FoxPro would name it "Label2." These are just convenient default names that you can change to something more meaningful. If you were to change the name of the first Label you placed on the Form, the next Label to be placed would be automatically titled Label1.

Now, place a second Label on the Form to illustrate a convenient feature of the property sheet. Select the Label1 object, open the property sheet (if necessary), and find the Name property of this object either on the All page or on the Other page. Change the Label's name to lblFirst. Don't forget to press Enter after typing in the new name. You'll notice that the appearance of the Label on the Form didn't change. That's because, in addition to a default name, Visual FoxPro also assigns a default *Caption property,* which determines the text that appears in the Label. The default value for this property is the same as the Label's name.

Now look at the drop-down list box at the top of the property sheet. You'll notice that the name of the current object appears now as "lblFirst." Click this drop-down list and select "Label2." You can see that the Name property is still highlighted in the list of properties below. You can also change objects while keeping the same property selected by clicking another object in the Form Designer. As long as the next object also has a property with the same name as the property that was selected for the previous object, this property will remain highlighted. This makes it very convenient to quickly change the same property on multiple objects. As you change the Name property for Label2 to lblSecond, note that lblSecond appears in the property sheet's drop-down list.

Change the Name property of the second Label to "Second Label" but don't press the Enter key yet. Note that the two push buttons to the far left are enabled when you are changing a property in the TextBox at the top of the properties and methods list in the properties sheet. One of these boxes has a check mark, while the other has an X icon. When you click the button with the check mark, you receive an "Expression Evaluated To An Illegal Value" dialog box. This is because object names cannot contain spaces. Click the OK CommandButton, reverting the Label's name to its previous value.

The function of the CommandButton with the X icon is illustrated with the following example. Suppose that it's about 1:00 A.M., and you're not paying close attention to what you're doing. You've selected Form1 in the drop-down list. You want to change the name of the Label to lblSecond and you start to type this into the TextBox. As you type, you realize that you're applying this name to the Form rather than the Label. Click the X icon, and the value will be restored to its previous value. You can then select the Label and continue with the operation.

Can you assign the same name to two Labels (or any two objects)? If you try to rename the second Label to lblFirst, you'll find that Visual FoxPro will not allow you to assign the same name to two objects. It will produce an error message and retain the second Label's old name.

Now you've changed the Name properties, but this property is completely separate from the Caption property that determines what a Label "says." Find the Caption property in the property sheet for the lblFirst object and type in "First Label." Do the same for the second Label and type in "Second Label."

- ***AutoSize Property***
- ***BackStyle Property***
- ***BorderStyle Property***

Continuing with the previous example, it's more than likely that not all of this text is visible in either Label. You could select the Label, grab the control points, and drag the border of the Label until all of the text is visible. Alternatively, you could select one or both Labels, then select Format | Size | To Fit from the system menu to resize the Labels to accommodate their captions. If you want to change the text of Labels at runtime, you can change the Label's *AutoSize property* to .T.. Find the AutoSize property for lblFirst, set it to .T., and run the Form.

Enter the following code from the command window:

```
Test.lblFirst.Caption = "This is a long caption"
```

Notice how the Label changed size to accommodate the new caption. As you enter the following code in the command window, you'll see that the Label (whose AutoSize property is set to .F.) did not resize.

```
Test.lblSecond.Caption = "Short"
```

If you followed the instructions to create a Form with a light gray background, the Labels might still look wrong to you because they have a white background. Close the Form, reload it into the Form Designer, and find the *BackStyle property* for one of the Labels.

In the drop-down list box at the top, you'll see that you have two choices, "0 - Transparent" and "1 - Opaque." Change the BackStyle property to "0 - Transparent" and see how it changes the appearance of the Label. You could also change the BackColor of the Label to that of the Form itself to achieve the same effect, but remember the cautions earlier about different color palettes being available to different objects depending upon the display system in use. It's always safest to make the BackStyle transparent so that it can blend in with the background.

If, on the other hand, you want to use a contrasting color behind your Labels, you can set the BackStyle property to "1 - Opaque" and set the BackColor to something bold like black. You can do this by selecting it from the color picker or by typing in "RGB(0,0,0)." You can change the ForeColor property to white by entering "RGB(255,255,255)." You can also select one of two *BorderStyle properties*—"0 - None" or "1 - Single." Single is used for a single-line black border.

- ## *Multiline Labels*
- ## *WordWrap Property*

Have you ever wanted to have a multiline @...SAY? You can by finding the AutoSize property for lblFirst and setting it to .F.. Then grasp one of the bottom handles on lblFirst with the mouse pointer and drag it downwards until the Label is about twice as high as it is wide.

Select the Caption property for lblFirst, and click the f_x icon that is immediately to the left of the TextBox where you can type the caption. This brings up the Visual FoxPro Expression Builder, something that should be familiar from FoxPro 2.x. Type the following code in the Expression Builder:

```
"The quick" + CHR(13) + "brown fox" + CHR(13) + "jumped " +
    CHR(13) + "over the" + CHR(13) + "lazy dog"
```

You'll notice that Visual FoxPro places an "=" in front of the resulting expression when the Expression Builder is closed. If you want to manually type in an expression without using the Expression Builder dialog box, remember that the = sign is necessary for Visual

FoxPro to interpret the expression as an expression instead of as a string literal. Run the Form, and see how all of the caption appears in the Label. (This will occur if you've dragged the Label to be large enough.)

There is an easier way to accomplish this. Close the Form and reload it into the Form Designer. Find the *WordWrap property* for lblFirst, and set it to .T.. Place something like "Hello" into the caption property and run the Form. Then type the following into the command window:

```
Test.lblFirst.Caption= "The quick brown fox jumped over the
   lazy dog"
```

The caption *automatically* wordwraps. However, you do have to ensure that the Label is sized vertically so that it can accommodate the caption.

Note that the AutoSize property is ignored if wordwrap is set to .T.. Also, you can use the first technique with the embedded carriage return characters (CHR(13)) in conjunction with AutoSize set to .T. to get a multiline Label that will automatically size itself both horizontally and vertically.

Alignment Property

You will usually want your Labels to be just large enough to display their captions. If you anticipate changing the caption at runtime, the AutoSize property is just the trick. However, you may want to use a Label as some kind of heading that should be aligned with some other object—a shape, a TextBox, or a Grid, for example. In that case you might want the Label text centered over the object. AutoSize = .T. allows the Label to resize, but the Label's Left and Top properties remain constant. As a result, the left side of the associated object will be under a shorter Label.

To deal with this, try the following exercise. Create a new Form and set the BackColor to light gray. From the Form Controls toolbar, select a shape object and place it on the Form, dragging and sizing it into a nice large rectangle. Be sure to leave some space above it on the Form. Next place a Label on the Form above the rectangle shape. Select both objects (either by lassoing them or by shift-clicking them individually), and select Format|Size|To Widest. Then choose Format|Align|Align Left Sides from the system menu. Select the Label1 object and set its BackStyle property to "0 - Transparent." Find the *Alignment property*, and change its value to "2 - Center."

Run the Form and notice that the Label's caption (Label1) is neatly centered above the rectangular shape object. To see this in

action and with the other Label alignment options, type the
following code into the command window:

```
Test.Label1.Caption="This is a long line of text"
Test.Label1.Alignment=0
Test.Label1.Alignment=1
Test.Label1.Alignment=2
```

Font Properties

In addition to being able to specify the caption text, alignment, and
color properties for the Label, you have full control over typeface
properties of the caption text. This includes the *FontBold, FontItalic,
FontName, FontSize, FontStrikeThru*, and *FontUnderline* properties.
Almost all of these properties default to .F. for Labels. The exception
is the FontBold property, which defaults to .T.. There are also
FontOutline and *FontShadow* properties that really won't be
applicable until Visual FoxPro is available for the Apple Macintosh.

Label Visibility and "Layering"

Label control objects have a *Visible property* that can be used to
make Labels visible or to make them disappear under program
control. Instead of simply disabling a Label (or any other control),
you can make it disappear so the user doesn't even know that the
control is available under other circumstances (or to other users).

   Before proceeding with the next exercise, place another Label
on the Form. Make sure that the three Labels are named lblFirst,
lblSecond, and lblThird. Change the caption on each to read First
Label, Second Label, and Third Label. Set the BackColor property
on each to a different light shade, and set the BackStyle property to
"1 - Opaque" so that the entire control is visible, and not just its
caption. Then select all three Labels and choose Format I Size I To Fit.

   Arrange the three TextBoxes so they are cascaded as shown in
Figure 6-1.

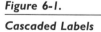

Figure 6-1.

Cascaded Labels

Make sure that "Third Label" is frontmost and overlaps "Second Label." First Label should be partially obscured by Second Label. Run the Form, then observe the effect of entering the following commands in the command window:

```
test.lblFirst.Zorder(0)
test.lblThird.Zorder(1)
```

You'll see that now First Label is frontmost and Third Label is in the back. If used with no argument or with an argument of 0, the Zorder() method will cause the object to move in front of any objects that overlap it. Calling an object's Zorder() method with an argument of 1 sends it to the *back* of the pile. Note that Zorder() is a runtime method of the Label Control (and most other visual Form objects), and does not affect the Z-order of the objects in your design.

The Label Object as a Control

Unlike FoxPro version 2.x, the Label object can detect and respond to certain events through code that the developer places in the associated method code. These events fall into two categories—user-generated events and non-user-generated (system) events. These are shown here.

User-Generated Events:

- Click
- DblClick
- RightClick
- Drag-and-Drop-related events
- MouseDown
- MouseMove
- MouseUp
- Move

Note that the Enabled property determines whether the Label can respond to user-generated events.

Non-User-Generated (System) Events:

- Init
- Destroy
- Error
- UIEnable

Note that the UIEnable event is applicable only when the Label is placed on a page of a PageFrame. This event is discussed fully in the section on advanced Control objects.

If you want to take advantage of a Label's ability to respond to an event, remember that the user will need some kind of visual cue that this is not a passive visual element, but an active control.

If you find the array of properties and methods that are associated with a control as simple as a Label somewhat daunting, realize that many of these options are common to other control objects. As a result, Name, Font, ForeColor, BackColor, Caption, Alignment, BackStyle, and BorderStyle properties will not be discussed again unless their behavior is significantly different than what has already been presented. Neither will the Zorder() method be discussed in the context of other controls. Refer to the chart in Section 12 for a cross-reference showing which properties, events, and methods are available for a particular control object.

CommandButton Control

Value Property

The CommandButton is the Visual FoxPro analog to the FoxPro 2.x push button @...GET field. In FoxPro 2.x, each control (or field) was represented by a variable, and a value was assigned to that memory variable. This would occur when a push button was selected, a CheckBox was checked, or a character value was typed into a textual @...GET field. In Visual FoxPro, control objects that have a value associated with them (like TextBoxes and CheckBoxes) do not have a conventional memory variable to store this value to. Rather, they have a *Value property* that holds this value.

While this explanation is getting a bit ahead of itself, you should be aware of a major difference in the way CommandButtons and FoxPro 2.x push buttons operate. With FoxPro 2.x push buttons, it was necessary to evaluate the value of the associated memory variable to determine what action to take. This was true even if you used single buttons rather than button groups. Also, the action was usually taken in the valid code snippet or in a UDF called by the valid code. Because Visual FoxPro CommandButtons do not have a value property, and because they can trap and give the developer an opportunity to write code to respond to events such as a mouse click or a key press, they can respond to these events directly in the events' associated method code.

For example, if you have an OK CommandButton whose action closes the Form it is on, simply place the following line of code in the CommandButton's Click() method:

```
ThisForm.Release()
```

With that code, the deed is done whenever the user clicks the mouse pointer on the CommandButton. Like Labels, CommandButtons have Height, Width, Left, Top, Caption, Font<attribute>, ForeColor, AutoSize, Enabled, and Visible properties.

• *Cancel Property*

• *Default Property*

With FoxPro 2.x push buttons, you had to make use of special characters in the prompts (\? and \!) to determine if the push button was a Default button or a Cancel button. A Default button is "pressed" if the user presses *Enter* in FoxPro for Windows (with KeyComp set to Windows) or Ctrl-Enter in FoxPro for MS-DOS. A Cancel button is "pressed" if the Esc key is pressed.

To this day, many programmers have difficulty remembering which of the two characters yields which result. For the typographically challenged, things are a little simpler in Visual FoxPro. CommandButtons have two properties, the *Cancel property* and the *Default property*.

To try these out, create a new Form and place a TextBox near the top center of the Form. Next, place three CommandButtons onto the Form in a row (from left to right) below the TextBox. Change the captions on Command1 to "\<Default," on Command2 to "\<Neither," and on Command3 to "\<Escape." Set the Default property for Command1 to .T. and the Cancel property for Command3 to .T.. Double-click Command1 (the caption should read "Default"), which will bring up the code editing window for the Click() method. Then add this line of code:

```
WAIT "Default" WINDOW
```

Select and copy the new line of code. Click the drop-down list at the top left of the window, select Command2, and paste the Wait...Window into this Click() method, changing the message to "Neither." Repeat the process for Command3, changing the message to "Escape." Use the Format|Align and Format|Size commands from the system menu to get everything looking nice. Now run the Form.

Because the controls were placed on the Form in your desired tab order, the TextBox should have focus. Notice that the leftmost CommandButton looks different, indicating that it's the Default button. Press the Enter key and verify that Command1 is actually designated as the Default button. Move the focus back to the TextBox using the Tab key, then press the Esc key and verify that Command3 is, indeed, designated as the Cancel button.

Move focus back to the TextBox once again with the Tab key. Notice that the \< character in front of the initial character of each caption property has resulted in an underline below the initial character of each CommandButton's visual caption. Press Alt-N and notice that the "Neither" button's Click() method has been triggered. While the focus is on the "Neither" button, press the Enter key. Notice that as long as a CommandButton has focus, the Default designation of another button is ignored.

When you are in design mode, setting any CommandButton's Default property to .T. changes the Default property of all other CommandButtons to .F.. It is possible to set the Cancel property of more than one CommandButton to .T., but the first button so designated in the tab order is the one whose Click() method will be triggered in response to the *Esc* key press. It is also possible to set a single CommandButton's Default *and* Cancel properties to .T..

- ***DisabledForeColor Property***
- ***Picture Property***
- ***DisabledPicture Property***
- ***DownPicture Property***
- ***StatusBarText Property***
- ***Enabled Property***

A CommandButton can be disabled by setting its *Enabled property* to .F.. When the button is disabled, the color of the caption defaults to a dark gray, but is under the developer's control through the *Disabled ForeColor property*.

It is also possible to have a picture in addition to, or instead of, a textual prompt on a CommandButton. To do this, you can specify a .BMP or .ICO file for the CommandButton's *Picture property*. If you want the picture to be different when the button is disabled (rather than simply "graying out"), you can use the *Disabled Picture property* to specify a different icon or bitmap file to be displayed when the control is disabled. While it is of most value with a graphical CheckBox, the CommandButton has a *DownPicture property*. This causes the image on the CommandButton to change when the button is depressed.

A Form (CMDGRAPH.SCX) is included on the source code disc that shows some of these features at work. It uses a combination of 16x15 pixel .BMP images (buttons #1 through #4), 32x32 pixel .BMP images (buttons #5 through #7), and a 32x32 pixel .ICO file (button #8). (See Figure 6-2.)

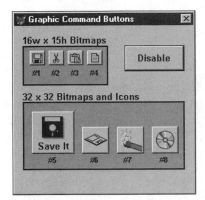

Figure 6-2.

CMDGRAPH.SCX at runtime

Each CommandButton has its ToolTipText property set to an appropriate description. If you pause the mouse pointer over any CommandButton, the small ToolTip window will appear. In the case of the small CommandButtons in the top row using 16x15 .BMP files for their pictures, the *StatusBarText property* is also set. You will see that a short description of the CommandButton's function appears in the status bar at the bottom of your screen either when the CommandButton receives focus from the Tab key on the keyboard, or when the mouse pointer is positioned over the CommandButton. Notice that the ToolTip text appears only in response to the mouse pointer, and does not appear when the user uses the Tab key to give a particular CommandButton focus.

CommandButton #5 illustrates that you can have both a picture and a caption on a single CommandButton.

It would be nice if a CommandButton could be set to a size that would neatly accommodate the picture when you used the Format | Size | To Fit command from the system menu, or when you set a CommandButton's AutoSize property to .T.. However, this does not appear to be the case. Using the AutoSize property or the formatting command on a CommandButton with a 32x32 .BMP or .ICO image yields a CommandButton of 61x54 pixels, a size much larger than necessary. Sizing picture-only CommandButtons to a size that exceeds the dimensions of the image by six pixels allows for a CommandButton of minimum size, but preserves the 3-D features of the button without cropping the image.

CommandButton #4 uses the DisabledPicture property. It changes its appearance from a lined document to a document with the "No" red-circle-and-diagonal-bar symbol superimposed when the CommandButton is disabled. By clicking the Disable CommandButton, all of the CommandButtons (except Disable) are disabled, and the caption of the Disable CommandButton changes to Enable. The code that performs this task is in the Click() method of the Disable CommandButton. It uses the Form's SetAll() method to set the Enabled property of all of the Form's CommandButtons to .F.. It then resets its own Enabled property back to .T.. The Click() method also uses the CommandButton's own Caption property to determine whether CommandButtons are enabled or disabled. That code is shown here:

```
DO CASE
   CASE This.Caption = "Disable"
      ThisForm.SetAll("Enabled",.F.,"CommandButton")
      This.Caption = "Enable"
   CASE This.Caption = "Enable"
      ThisForm.SetAll("Enabled",.T.,"CommandButton")
      This.Caption = "Disable"
ENDCASE
This.Enabled = .T.
```

- ### *MousePointer Property*

- ### *Style Property*

Two other properties that will be mentioned briefly are the *MousePointer property* and the *Style property*. The MousePointer property allows the developer to change the shape of the mouse pointer when it is over certain objects. There are 13 different choices. These include 0, which is the default value that allows the mouse pointer shape to be controlled by the object, and 12 others including various types of arrows, a "no drop" symbol, and so forth. Note that the MousePointer property for CommandButton #4 in the CMDGRAPH Form changes to an Icon shape.

The Style property has two values—"0 - Standard" and "1 - Invisible." It allows CommandButtons to have the same effect as FoxPro 2.x's "invisible" push button. With it, you can allow an area of your Form to respond to any event a CommandButton can detect.

- ### *SetFocus( ) Method*

The *SetFocus( ) method* is not unique to the CommandButtons. This method takes no arguments. It allows you to programmatically set focus to any control that has a SetFocus() method, whose Enabled and Visible properties are .T. , and whose When() method returns .T.. In FoxPro 2.x, it was necessary to set the value of _CUROBJ to the appropriate field number to perform this task.

It's a good idea for you to take a moment to look at this example Form. In particular, look at the tasks performed in the Init() method, the Destroy() method, and the cOldStatusBar property. If you want to jump ahead a bit, notice the properties specified for the two shape objects that are used to visually group the two rows of CommandButtons.

CommandGroup Control

- *BorderStyle Property*
- *SpecialEffect Property*
- *BorderColor Property*

Like a Form, the CommandGroup is a container object, but it contains only CommandButtons. In addition to all of the properties possessed by the individual CommandButtons that it may contain, the CommandGroup has a *BorderStyle property* that takes two values, "1 - Fixed Single" and "0 - None." The default is 1. The appearance of this border can be influenced by two other properties, the *SpecialEffect property*, which takes two values, "0 - 3D" and "1 - Plain," and the *BorderColor property*, which is ignored if SpecialEffect is set to "0 - 3D." The default for SpecialEffect property is 0.

- *ButtonCount Property*
- *Buttons Property*

When creating a CommandGroup on a Form, the CommandGroup's *ButtonCount property* determines the number of buttons in a group. Once you have set the number of buttons, you can use any of the formatting tools to change the size or alignment of the CommandButtons, or to size the group object that contains them.

When editing one of the CommandButtons within the CommandGroup, clicking the CommandButton with the mouse will *not* select that button. Instead, you can click the drop-down list box at the top of the properties sheet and scroll down until you can select the CommandButton that you want to edit. The desired CommandButton will then be selected. You can also use the right mouse button to click the CommandGroup, and select the Edit option from the pop-up menu. You will see a blue hashed border around the CommandGroup, which indicates that you now have mouse access to its contents. You will then be able to select any of the individual CommandButtons in the normal manner by clicking them with the mouse. This technique is applicable to all of the other container Control objects you will be dealing with—Grids, PageFrames, and OptionGroups.

As in the Form object, the CommandGroup object has a SetAll() method that can be used to set properties of all of the individual CommandButtons. However, there may be times when you want to set properties of only one or a few of the CommandButtons, or you might want to call the methods of one or more CommandButtons.

For this reason, the CommandGroup has a *Buttons property*, which is an array property whose elements hold a reference to each CommandButton in the group.

Data From CommandGroups

• *Value Property*
• *ControlSource Property*

Unlike the CommandButton object, the CommandGroup has a *Value property*. This property reflects the *index* or the *caption* of a CommandButton that has been activated. (The index of the CommandButton is its ordinal position within the CommandGroup.) Which data type the Value property contains is determined by the initial data type of the Value property. This data type can be established at design time and changed at runtime. If you assign a value of 0 to the Value property, it will then reflect the numerical index of the CommandButton last activated in the CommandGroup. If you assign a value of "" (an empty character string) to the CommandGroup's Value property, the Value property will reflect the *caption* of the last CommandButton activated.

These characteristics make it as easy to work with CommandGroups as it was to work with push buttons in FoxPro 2.x. A Do Case structure can be placed in the InteractiveChange method code of the CommandGroup, which can determine (from the CommandGroup's Value property) which button was activated. It can then perform an action based on this information.

If this "action" involves changing the value of a table field, another object's property, or a memory variable to correspond to the CommandGroup's Value property, there is an easier way to accomplish this than in the InteractiveChange() method code. The CommandGroup has a property that you will see in many other controls, the *ControlSource property*. This is the name of the memory variable, property, or field to which the value of this control is bound. Keep in mind, however, that this binding is a one-way proposition in the case of command-button groups. Changing the CommandGroup's value will automatically change the variable or field named in the ControlSource property, but changing the value of the variable or field will *not* change the Value property of the CommandGroup.

You can explore this by placing a CommandGroup onto the TestBed Form. This Form already has two properties to act as control sources in the absence of any open tables, nControlSource (for numeric values) and cControlSource (for character values). Change the CommandGroup's ButtonCount property to 3, then apply the Format | Size | To Fit command to the group from the system menu.

Set the CommandGroup's ControlSource property to:

```
ThisForm.nControlSource
```

Then run the Form. Next, click any of the CommandButtons in the CommandGroup, and type the following in the command window:

```
? Testbed.nControlSource
```

You will see that nControlSource reflects the index of the CommandButton most recently selected. Try this again, but first change the captions of the three CommandButtons to "First," "Second," and "Third." Also, change the control source to the Form's cControlSource property.

TextBox Control

The Visual FoxPro TextBox Control object is the direct analog to the FoxPro 2.x @...GET field. Some of the features of the TextBox will be discussed, then we can take a little break and start putting together everything that that has been covered up to this point. You will use this information to put together a working Form. Most of the propertics, events, and methods that apply to the TextBox Control also apply to the EditBox. The TEXTDEMO.SCX Form includes an EditBox so that you can compare the members of the two objects. (See Figure 6-3.)

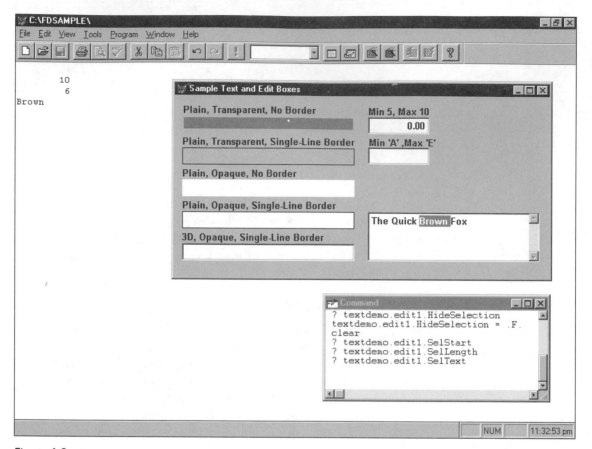

Figure 6-3.

**TEXTDEMO.SCX at
runtime**

TextBox Appearance

- *Margin Property*
- *SpecialEffect Property*
- *SelectedBackColor Property*
- *SelectedForeColor Property*

As in the case of the CommandGroup, the TextBox also has a
SpecialEffect property. The property affects the control's border and
can be set to 0 (3-D) or 1 (plain). A setting of 0 (3-D), which is the
default, causes the BorderColor property to be ignored. Likewise, a
BorderStyle of 0 (None) overrides a SpecialEffect setting of 0 (3-D).

The *Margin property* defaults to 2 and specifies, in pixels, the
margin between the text and both the top and left inside edges of
the TextBox.

The Form file TEXTDEMO.SCX, which is on the source code
disc, illustrates the various options for the appearance of a TextBox.
Of course, you have all the usual properties affecting font, color, and
so forth. Two additional color properties can be used to change the

color of selected text, the *SelectedBackColor property* and *SelectedForeColor property*.

Controlling TextBox Input

- *Format Property*
- *InputMask Property*
- *PasswordChar Property*
- *ReadOnly Property*

In FoxPro 2.x, you had a Picture clause that could be used to control what characters could be typed into an @...GET field. This clause could include a Format code to further control the text's appearance. These chores are now handled by the *Format property* and *InputMask property*, and use the same codes that were used in the Picture clause in FoxPro 2.x. However, it is unnecessary to embed the format code into the InputMask property with the "@" symbol; you simply assign the appropriate codes to the TextBox's Format property. Note in TEXTDEMO.SCX that the Format property for the Text1 object is set to "K." This selects the entire TextBox and makes the user aware of this otherwise invisible TextBox when it receives focus.

For some reason known only to the documentarians at Microsoft, not all of the Function and InputMask properties are documented under those entries. Instead, you must refer to the documentation for the @...GET TextBox. The following tables give the listing of all possible values for both properties from the online help:

Format Code	Purpose
A	Allows alphabetic characters only (no spaces of punctuation marks).
B	Left-justifies numeric data within the TextBox.
D	Uses the current Set Date format.
E	Edits date-type data as British date.
I	Centers text within the TextBox.
J	Right-justifies text within the TextBox.
K	Selects the entire TextBox when the cursor is moved to the TextBox.
L	Displays leading zeros (instead of spaces) in the TextBox. Use this with numeric data only.

Continued on next page

Continued from previous page

Format Code	Purpose
MList	Creates multiple preset choices. The list is a comma-delimited collection of items. Individual items within the list cannot contain embedded commas. If Object.Value does not contain one of the items in the list when it is instantiated, the first item in the list is displayed. To scroll through the list, press the space bar or type the first letter of an item. To choose one of the items and move to the next control, press Enter. Use this with character data only.
R	Displays a format mask in a TextBox. These mask characters are not stored to the ControlSource when you exit the TextBox. Use this with character or numeric data only.
Sn	Limits the TextBox to n characters. You can scroll within the region with the cursor control keys. Use this with character data only.
!	Converts alphabetic characters to uppercase. Use this with character data only.
^	Displays numeric data using scientific notation. Use this with numeric data only.
$	Displays currency symbol before numeric data. Use this with numeric data only.

InputMask Code	Purpose
A	Allows the entry of alphabetic characters only.
L	Allows the entry of logical data only.
N	Allows the entry of letters and digits only.
X	Allows the entry of any character.
Y	Allows you to enter Y, y, N, and n for the logical values true (.T.) and false (.F.), respectively.
9	Allows entry of only digits in character data; allows entry of digits and signs in numeric data.
#	Allows entry of digits, blanks, and signs.
!	Converts lowercase letters to uppercase letters.
$	Displays the current currency symbol specified by Set Currency. By default, the symbol is placed immediately before or after the numeric value. However, the currency symbol and its placement (Set Currency), the separator character (Set Separator), and the decimal character (Set Point) can all be changed.

Continued on next page

InputMask Code	Purpose
$$	Displays a floating currency symbol that is always adjacent to the digits in the spinner or TextBox.
*	Asterisks are displayed in front of a numeric value. Use with a dollar sign ($) for check protection.
.	A decimal point specifies the decimal point position.
,	A comma is used to separate digits to the left of the decimal point.

Another capability for TextBoxes that's new with Visual FoxPro is the *ReadOnly property.* In FoxPro 2.x, preventing changes to data required either having the field's WHEN snippet return .F. (this is still available in Visual FoxPro), or disabling the control. Although disabling the control is the most direct way of preventing user access to a field, the change in the control's appearance often made it difficult to read and required that you monkey with the disabled colors. The ReadOnly property provides yet another way to restrict user input. However, you should realize that setting a TextBox's ReadOnly property to .T. does not prevent the TextBox from receiving focus, and there is no visual cue to inform users that they cannot change the TextBox's contents. It's a good idea to make some visible change to such TextBoxes by changing the BackColor, BorderStyle, or SpecialEffect properties.

The *PasswordChar property* lets users hide their input from prying eyes by substituting whatever character is assigned to the TextBox's PasswordChar property for anything typed into the TextBox. Developers often use an asterisk (*), but it can be any valid character. This is only a *visual* alteration of the user's input—the Value property is set to what is actually typed, not what is being displayed.

Data From TextBoxes

- *Value Property*
- *ControlSource Property*
- *Refresh() Method*

Like the CommandGroup Control, the TextBox has a *Value property* that holds the contents of the TextBox instead of using a separate memory variable as in FoxPro 2.x. Also like the CommandGroup, it is possible to bind the TextBox's Value property to some other memory variable or table field by specifying this variable or field in the TextBox's *ControlSource property.*

Unlike the CommandGroup, the TextBox's ControlSource property establishes a two-way relationship between the variable or field specified in the ControlSource property and the TextBox's Value property. If the Value property of a TextBox changes, the variable or field specified by the TextBox's ControlSource property is also changed. However, if the variable or field's value changes, this is *also reflected in a change to the TextBox's Value property.* However, the TextBox's Value property is not immediately altered to reflect a change in the value of the variable or field specified in the TextBox's ControlSource property. This occurs only when the TextBox is *refreshed,* which occurs automatically when the TextBox receives focus. It can also be forced programmatically by calling the TextBox's *Refresh() method.*

All controls are refreshed by calling the Form's Refresh() method. However, if you have a very complex Form with a lot of controls, you can significantly improve the performance and responsiveness of a Form by refreshing controls selectively. This is accomplished with the individual controls' Refresh() methods, which are common to all visual data-bound controls. (See Section 12 for more information.)

Manipulating Text in Text Objects

- *SelStart Property*
- *SelLength Property*
- *SelText Property*
- *HideSelection Property*

TextBoxes, EditBoxes, and spinners have all four of these properties, while ComboBoxes have only the first three. These properties are probably most useful in the context of EditBoxes, but you should examine them here because they have the same effect in all of the controls.

If text is selected in a TextBox (or EditBox or ComboBox) the *SelStart property* indicates the position of the first character selected, the *SelLength property* indicates how many characters are selected, and the *SelText property* contains the actual text selected. If no text is selected, the SelStart property will indicate the insertion point, the SelLength property will be 0, and the SelText property will be the empty string.

These properties are unavailable at design time, and are read/write at runtime. This means that you can programmatically set the insertion point or select text in any of the three control objects that have these properties as members.

The fourth property is the *HideSelection property*. Normally when a control loses focus, the selected text no longer looks selected. If you want the selected text to retain its selected appearance after the control loses focus, changing the HideSelection property from .T. (the default) to .F. will accomplish this. Note that the ComboBox does not have a HideSelection property.

To try this, run the TEXTDEMO.SCX Form. In the second TextBox (Text2), type in "The Quick Brown Fox Jumped Over," then position the insertion point somewhere in the middle of the TextBox. In the command window, enter the following commands and observe the results:

```
? TextDemo.Text2.SelStart
* In my case this returned 9
? TextDemo.Text2.SelText
* an empty string - no text is selected
? TextDemo.Text2.SelLength
* 0 - again, no text is selected
TextDemo.Text2.SelStart = 4
TextDemo.Text2.SelLength = 5
* No visible change, but you can verify that the property
* has been changed - See following note
? TextDemo.Text2.SelText
* Returns "Quick"
TextDemo.Text2.HideSelection = .F.
* The selected text, the word "Quick" now appears selected
TextDemo.Text2.HideSelection = .T.
* The selected text, the word "Quick" no longer appears selected
```

TextBoxes and EditBoxes behave slightly differently when their HideSelection properties are set to .F.. In that situation, selected text will retain its selected appearance in both objects when focus is moved to another object on the Form. However, the TextBox's SelStart and SelLength properties will be reset to 0 if the focus returns to the TextBox. The EditBox, on the other hand, will retain its selected text when regaining focus. The insertion point will be at the end of the selected text, the exact position determined by the sum of the SelStart and SelLength properties. The SelStart, SelLength, and SelText properties are changed in an EditBox only when the insertion point is reset by clicking somewhere with the mouse or by navigating within the EditBox using the arrow keys.

If you want to try HideSelection with the EditBox object on the TEXTDEMO Form, be aware that HideSelection for TextDemo.Edit1 is set to .T. (the default).

Determining User Actions and Validation

- *InteractiveChange Event*
- *ProgrammaticChange Event*
- *Valid Event*
- *GotFocus Event*
- *RangeHigh Event*

- *KeyPress Event*
- *When Event*
- *LostFocus Event*
- *RangeLow Event*

In FoxPro 2.x, you could trap only two events. You could determine if the user was attempting to move the focus to a screen field (using the field's When clause), and, if they had made some change to the field variable, you could detect when the user moved the focus off of that field with the field's Valid clause.

In Visual FoxPro, however, you have a wealth of events that you can tie program code to. As with most objects that can accept user input rather than just responding to an action like the CommandButton, the TextBox has seven events for which you can place code in associated methods.

The *InteractiveChange event* is triggered whenever users actively change a control, for instance when they click a spinner, type a character into a text or EditBox, or select an item in a list box. By contrast, the *ProgrammaticChange event* is triggered when the value of a control is changed programmatically. Be cautious when writing code for objects such as TextBoxes and EditBoxes for the InteractiveChange event because the event will be triggered for *each keystroke*. If you have extensive code in this event's method, data entry will slow to a crawl.

The *KeyPress event* is triggered for each keystroke, but, unlike the InteractiveChange event, two parameters are automatically passed to the KeyPress event. This allows you to take action depending on which key (or key combination) was pressed. This is done with the following code:

```
LPARAMETERS nKeyCode, nShiftAltCtrl
```

The nKeyCode parameter indicates which key is pressed, and, in general, corresponds to the ASCII value of the key. The nShiftAltCtrl parameter indicates whether the Shift, Alt, or Ctrl key, or a combination of these keys is also being pressed according to the following scheme:

nShiftAltClr	Meaning
1	Shift
2	Ctrl
3	Shift+Ctrl
4	Alt
5	Shift+Alt
6	Ctrl+Alt
8	Shift+Ctrl+Alt

The *Valid event* and *When event* occur in the same manner as the code in which FoxPro 2.x When and Valid snippets would occur. If the When event code, which is triggered as the user tries to bring the focus to the control, returns a value of .F., the user is prevented from shifting focus to that control, and the *GotFocus event* does not occur. Likewise, if the user changes the value of the control and attempts to move the focus off of the control, the Valid event is triggered. The code in the associated Valid method is then executed. If this method code returns a value of .F., the user is prevented from moving off of the control and the *LostFocus event* can't occur. It may not be necessary to prevent access to the control or leaving the control, but you might want to take some action when the control either gains or loses focus. In such cases it is more appropriate to use the GotFocus and LostFocus events.

The last two events that will be discussed are not used by EditBoxes but are available in TextBoxes, ComboBoxes, list boxes, and spinners. These events behave differently in the context of ComboBoxes and list boxes, but this discussion is applicable to both TextBoxes and spinner objects.

You might think that Visual FoxPro would employ RangeHigh and RangeLow properties to replace the FoxPro 2.x RANGE clause. However, the development team at Microsoft has opted for a *RangeHigh event* and a *RangeLow event* instead. At its simplest, the code in the methods associated with RangeHigh and RangeLow is triggered as the user attempts to shift the focus off of the control. The value entered into the spinner or TextBox is compared to the value returned by the RangeHigh() and RangeLow() method code. If the first value is higher than the value returned from the RangeHigh() method or is lower than the value returned by the RangeLow() method, the user is prevented from leaving the control.

By performing this function in the context of an event and method rather than a property, it is easy to evaluate other values and to *calculate* the maximum and minimum values that a TextBox or spinner may take.

The RangeHigh and RangeLow can be used to limit a range of character or numeric data, as you can see by the two TextBoxes on the TEXTDEMO.SCX Form. One of these boxes is labeled "Min 5, Max 10," while the other is labeled "Min 'A', Max 'E'." If you look at the code for the RangeHigh and RangeLow events for these two TextBoxes, you'll see that they simply use the RETURN command to get the appropriate maximum or minimum value.

Now let me take this opportunity to pass along a bit of personal application design philosophy. In my applications I *seldom* (I want to say *never*, but it is such a big word) return an .F. value from a Valid method, or return a RangeHigh or RangeLow value.

To see why, run the TEXTDEMO Form, and tab to the TextBox labeled Min 5, Max 10. Type in a 0, then try to leave the field. Because the value entered is outside the range allowed, you cannot force the field to lose focus. When you try to close the Form, you'll see that you can't. At this point, you can't do anything other than be a good little user, do as you're told, and enter an allowed value in the TextBox. Only then are you allowed to do something else.

To my way of thinking, this is a distinctly user-hostile interface feature, and should be avoided. The principle of event-driven programming is to leave the user in control, and to minimize (or eliminate) messages that imply the user has done something wrong. I follow a policy of never doing field-level validation in forms. It is a simple task to evaluate the data entered into the various controls by the user, inform the user of any problem, and disable other controls (like a Save CommandButton) if the user has entered an inappropriate value. This leaves the user in control, and allows them at least to close a Form and go do something else until they have appropriate data to enter.

Let's Do It!

Now it's time to make a working Form.

Establishing a DataEnvironment

From the command window, select the *TESTDATA* database, which you should now have in a directory below the one you're using for the exercises in this report. Make sure that this DATA subdirectory is in your FoxPro path, and use the following code:

```
OPEN DATA testdata
```

This will make all of the tables in this database available to you.

Continued on next page

Next, create a new Form with the code shown.

```
CREATE FORM customer
```

Unless you're the bold type and have a Form template set up with a gray background, select the Layout tab on the properties sheet, double-click the BackColor property, and select the light gray color from the color-picker dialog box.

Open the Form's DataEnvironment object by using the right mouse button to click the Form, then select the DataEnvironment option. Use the right mouse button to click in the DataEnvironment workspace and select the Add... option. Select (double-click) the customer table in the list. Open the drop-down list box at the top of the property sheet and select Cursor1 from the list. Find the Order property under the All or Data tabs, then either double-click the Order property until Company appears or click the drop-down list box just above the properties list and select the Company option. This sets the index order for this table. Close the DataEnvironment workspace by double-clicking the control-menu box or selecting Close from the control menu.

Back in the Form, locate the Caption property under All or Layout and change it to Customers. Then locate the Name property under All or Other and change it to frmCustomerEdit. Find the DataSession property under the Form's All or Data tabs, double-click it, and change it to "2 - Private DataSession." Now take a look at what this last step will do for you.

Run the Form, and open the View window by selecting Window|View from the system menu. Note that the drop-down list box at the top of the View window labeled Current Session shows Default(1), and that no tables appear in the list box on the left side of the View window. Now move to the command window and enter the following code:

```
CLOSE DATABASE ALL
CLOSE TABLES ALL
```

This step would have caused havoc with a FoxPro 2.x screen. (That is, if you could have done it—remember, in FoxPro 2.x you wouldn't have access to the command window at this point.) This is because FoxPro 2.x had only one DataSession. As a result, the effect of the two commands would have been global and would have affected any running screens. Now return to the View window, click the drop-down list box, and select the entry there that reads frmCustomerEdit(2). You will see that the left-hand list box is populated with your customer table. (Notice, too, that the command SET DATASESSION TO 2 appeared in the command window. This will be covered in Section 10 under "Multiple Simultaneous Forms.") Click the Properties CommandButton and note that the Index Order in the resulting dialog box is just as you set it up; the company index tag is active. You can switch to the command window and use the BROWSE NORMAL command to

Continued on next page

Continued from previous page

look at the table. Had you done this prior to setting the DataSession the same as the Form's, you would have been prompted for a table to browse. Isn't that slick?

What you're seeing here is the barrier that a Form with a private DataSession has between itself and any other object that is not contained in the Form. You can do *anything* outside such Forms with respect to opening or closing tables, databases, setting filters, and changing index orders. Your actions will have *no effect* on the DataEnvironment of the Form.

Trap!

The documentation for the SET DATASESSION command mentions that it is intended for debugging purposes only (as you just did to verify that the DataEnvironment properties are as you intended them to be), and that SET DATASESSION TO should not be issued in code with an active Form. This caution is not just saying that you should be careful, know what you're doing, and take full responsibility for your actions. It seems that issuing SET DATASESSION TO in an application with an open Form introduces some instability into the system. You might completely crash your application and Visual FoxPro at some point down the road from the place at which you started playing with SET DATASESSION.

Adding TextBox Controls to the Form

Now you can start putting some controls onto the Form. First, close the Form and reopen it in the Form Designer. Click the TextBox icon on the Form Controls toolbar and drop a TextBox onto the Form. While this control is still selected, move to the properties sheet and locate the ControlSource property (look under the Data tab). Select CustID from the drop-down list above the property list. Note that all of the table's fields are listed in this drop-down list.

There is a way to do this in a single step. Open the DataEnvironment object, locate the Company field in the list of fields for the customer table, click it, and drag and drop the field onto the Form. Voila! You have a TextBox (Text2) placed on the Form. If you check the ControlSource property for this control, you'll see that it's already set to Customer.Company.

One disadvantage with this drag-and-drop technique is that the data type of the table field determines what control object is placed. This is usually OK, but if you want to place a date field that will be the control source for a ComboBox you'll get a TextBox by default instead. Also, if you are working with Form objects based on object classes that you have designed, there is at present no way to convince Visual FoxPro that you want to use *your* objects instead of Visual FoxPro's own BaseClass objects.

Continued on next page

Now continue using the drag-and-drop method. Place the following customer table fields onto the Form: address, city, region, postalcode, country, phone, and fax.

Next you should take care of the TextBox *names*—you'll have a heck of a time trying to do anything with them set to Text1, Text2, and so forth. Select the first (custid) TextBox and locate the Name property in the property sheet. (Look under the Other tab, or select the All tab and press Ctrl+Alt+N to move quickly to the Name property.) Change the name to *txtCustID*, then alternately click each of the TextBoxes and change its name to txtCompany, txtAddress, txtCity, txtRegion, txtPostalCode, txtCountry, txtPhone, and txtFax. As you do this, be sure that you're assigning the right name to the right TextBox. Scroll up to the ControlSource property if you need to check.

Now run the Form to see how it looks. Pretty ugly, isn't it? All of the TextBoxes have defaulted to the same length and are probably not arranged in a very attractive manner, so you should head back to the Form Designer.

Adjusting Control Fonts

You can deal with the fonts first. Select the txtCustId object, and change the FontName property to Courier New. Many developers prefer a monospaced font for data entry forms. This limits your choices to Terminal, Courier, and System. None of these are scaleable TrueType fonts, so your choice of point sizes is limited. Courier New is a fair compromise—it's a monospaced, scaleable TrueType font, but it isn't very attractive.

As you continue to change the typeface of all the other TextBoxes to Courier New, note that the FontBold property defaults to .T.. Leave it that way, and leave the FontSize at 10. Do you find this a bit tedious? Well, there was considerable complaint in the early stages of the Visual FoxPro beta testing about the lack of an easy way to set the properties of multiple objects simultaneously. The reasons behind the decision to use this method are a mystery, but it was amusing to see how these complaints quieted as folks discovered they could write their own tools to accomplish this task and perform jobs such as appropriately sizing the TextBoxes, setting input masks, and placing captions.

There are already public-domain tools like this available in the FoxPro forums on CompuServe. However, if you're interested in pursuing the development of your own tool along these lines, check the documentation on the ASELOBJ() function that was demonstrated in Section 2's "Let's Do It!" box. You might also want to look at John V. Petersen's article on ASELOBJ() and Builders in the June 1995 issue of the *FoxTalk* newsletter. Creating Builders is quite easy, and well worth the effort both in terms of enhancing your knowledge and experience and in providing a very handy tool for your own use.

Continued on next page

Continued from previous page

The next step is to appropriately resize the TextBoxes. Here is the structure of the fields you're dealing with at the moment:

```
1   CUST_ID       Character   6
2   COMPANY       Character   40
5   ADDRESS       Character   60
6   CITY          Character   15
7   REGION        Character   15
8   POSTALCODE    Character   10
9   COUNTRY       Character   15
10  PHONE         Character   24
11  FAX           Character   24
```

The Fontmetric() function will give you the maximum width of a character given a specific font name, point size, and style. That function is shown here:

```
FONTMETRIC(7,"Courier New",10,"N")
```

With the initial release of Visual FoxPro, Fontmetric() returns incorrect maximum width values for Courier New Bold and Courier New Normal. However, because the maximum width for a monspaced font is the same as the average width, you can use Fontmetric(6...) to determine the width of Courier New characters. Fontmetric() seems to be working properly with non-TrueType monospaced fonts such as Terminal and Courier. The correct character width for Courier New 10 point is eight pixels. Using this information, you can calculate the proper widths for each TextBox using the following formula:

$$(W_f \times W_c) + 2W_m + 2W_b$$

In this formula, W_f is the field-width in characters, W_c is the maximum character width for the current fontname, size, and style, W_m is the width of the TextBox's Margin property (which defaults to 2), and W_b is the TextBox's border width—two pixels for a 3-D border, one for a single-line border. Your field widths for this Form can be calculated as follows:

$$(W_f \times 8) + 8$$

You can get out your calculator and determine the appropriate widths for each TextBox, or you can simply enter =<fieldwidth>*8+8 into the width property for each TextBox, substituting the appropriate field width for each one (include the "=" but don't enter the quotation marks), or entering <fieldwidth>*8+8 into the Expression Builder.

If you make a habit of using a monospaced font for data entry, you may prefer to make your fields a little wider and change the previous formula to the following:

$$(W_f \times W_c) + 2W_m + \mathbf{3}W_b$$

Continued on next page

Now that you have all of your fields sized properly, you can lay them out in a pleasing manner. Use the Format|Align, Format|Horizontal Spacing, and Format|Vertical spacing tools to get everything to your liking. Be sure to leave sufficient space between the rows of TextBoxes for some labels. Remember that you'll need to adjust the size of the Form to accommodate the Address field.

Adding Labels to the Form

Place an appropriate Label above each TextBox, aligning it with the left edge of its associated TextBox, and making the BackStyle property transparent. You might find it easier to place the first Label on the Form, set its BackStyle, then copy and paste the other Labels. You can move each into position, then go back and change all of their Caption properties. You can also apply Format|Size|To Fit to all of the Labels at once.

As long as you're dealing with cosmetic issues, add the following to the Form's Init() method:

```
ThisForm.AutoCenter = .T.
ThisForm.BorderStyle = 2
```

Then add this code in the Deactivate() method:

```
ACTIVATE SCREEN
```

Now stop for a moment to get some instant gratification by running the Form and admiring your work.

Adding Navigation Methods (Code) to the Form

Now you can display and edit the information, but it'd be nice to look at more than just the first record. You could go to the command window, issue SET DATASESSION TO 2, then SEEK, LOCATE, SKIP, or GOTO TOP, and finally do a Customer.Refresh(), but it'd be tough to train your users to do that.

As a result, you'll need to add some navigation controls.

While developers may no longer argue about direct edits versus indirect edits of table data or about "de-snippetizing" their screens, folks will probably argue for some time about where to place navigation code. In this exercise, you are going to place some navigation CommandButtons on the Form, and you could very easily place the code to do the table navigation in the Click() method of the CommandButtons. However, some developers believe that the navigation code belongs with the Form. This is really an issue when you design reusable objects and when you provide the flexibility of using either toolbars or navigation buttons on your Forms. It's less of a concern when creating a one-of-a-kind Form as you are here. However, this discussion will step through the process of creating navigation methods as part of the Form object, as much as a way of illustrating the technique

Continued on next page

Continued from previous page

as anything else. You will probably come to your own conclusions as to what is the "right" thing to do in regard to this issue, and you are encouraged to do so. Placing your navigation code in the navigation CommandButtons isn't *wrong*, it's just a choice that you will eventually have to make. It's better to decide once and make exceptions rather than decide for every Form in every application that you develop.

You can start by opening the Form Designer and adding the following code to the Init() method of the Form. Because you have an active index for your customer table, it's highly unlikely that it will be in record order. As a result, you'll need to know when you are on the first and last record of the table so you can avoid an "End of File" error.

```
GOTO BOTTOM
ThisForm.nBottomRecord=RECNO()
GOTO TOP
ThisForm.nTopRecord = RECNO()
```

The nBottomRecord and nTopRecord properties for the Form object haven't been discussed because they don't exist at the moment. Select Form | New Property... from the system menu. Add the two properties, nBottomRecord and nTopRecord, then add a description if you wish. In the property sheet, scroll to the bottom of either the All page or the Other page for the frmCustomerEdit object, and you'll see the two properties you just added. Just to be anal retentive about it, set them both to 0. (They are numeric properties, after all.)

Next you'll need to add some methods. Go to the Form | New Method... option on the system menu and add four methods—GoToTop, GoToBottom, GoNext, and GoPrevious. Then add a description for each.

In the Form's property sheet, these new methods will appear first at the bottom of the list on the All page, then again at the bottom of the list on the Methods page.

Open the code-editing window either by double-clicking these methods in the property sheet, or by selecting View | Code from the system menu. If you select View | Code, you'll probably have to use the drop-down list box at the upper right of the code editing window to find the new methods.

Place the following code in the methods indicated:

```
* GoToTop
GOTO TOP

* GoToBottom
GOTO BOTTOM

* GoNext
SKIP
```

Continued on next page

```
* GoPrevious
SKIP -1
```

You could also have placed all of this into a single Go method with a character parameter of tcGoWhere, then used a DO CASE structure that would evaluate whether tcGoWhere was NEXT, PREVIOUS, or something else. After all, there's more than one way to skin a cat.

Calling Navigation Methods and Refreshing Controls
Now run your Form and play with it. From the command window, enter the following command:

```
customer.gonext()
```

Nothing happened to the Form. Remember that the table fields are the control source for the TextBoxes, and the TextBoxes now need to be refreshed. Also remember that if you encountered this situation in FoxPro 2.x, you would have had to issue a SHOW GETS command to refresh the fields. You must do the same here. Because it's likely that *all* of the fields have changed, it's appropriate to enter the following in the command window:

```
Customer.Refresh()
```

Now you can go back and add this line to all of your navigation methods. (This is another argument for placing all of this functionality into a single method!) Then place the following line as the last line in each of your navigation methods:

```
ThisForm.Refresh()
```

Now the following commands should yield the expected results:

```
Customer.GoNext()
Customer.GoPrevious()
Customer.GoToBottom()
Customer.GoToTop()
```

As you might expect, the following sequence of commands causes an error:

```
customer.gotobottom()
customer.gonext()
customer.gonext()
```

Adding Navigation Controls to the Form
You'll need to add something else to your method code, but first you can add the CommandButtons. Drop four CommandButtons onto the Form in a row at the bottom. Change their names to cmdTop, cmdPrevious, cmdNext, and cmdBottom. Then change their captions to the following:

"|<","<",">" and ">|"

Continued on next page

Continued from previous page

These CommandButtons look a little better with their FontSize set to 12. You can then use Format|Horizontal Spacing and Format|Align to get them all in a neat row, lasso all four of them, and position them at the bottom center of the Form.

In the Click() method of each CommandButton, place the appropriate line of code:

```
ThisForm.GoToTop()
ThisForm.GoToBottom()
ThisForm.GoNext()
ThisForm.GoPrevious()
```

Enabling and Disabling Navigation Controls

You still need to deal with that BOF() or EOF() condition, and you could add a check to the navigation code to enable and disable the CommandButtons. However, you need to set the status of the CommandButtons as soon as the Form starts. (The Form as designed is positioning the Form on the first record.) Instead, you'll add another method to the Form called SetButtons, placing the following code in it:

```
DO CASE
   CASE RECNO() = ThisForm.nTopRecord
      ThisForm.cmdTop.Enabled = .F.
      ThisForm.cmdPrevious.Enabled = .F.
      ThisForm.cmdNext.Enabled = .T.
      ThisForm.cmdBottom.Enabled = .T.
   CASE RECNO() = ThisForm.nBottomRecord
      ThisForm.cmdTop.Enabled = .T.
      ThisForm.cmdPrevious.Enabled = .T.
      ThisForm.cmdNext.Enabled = .F.
      ThisForm.cmdBottom.Enabled = .F.
   OTHERWISE
      ThisForm.cmdTop.Enabled = .T.
      ThisForm.cmdPrevious.Enabled = .T.
      ThisForm.cmdNext.Enabled = .T.
      ThisForm.cmdBottom.Enabled = .T.
ENDCASE
```

The last step is to call this method, both in the Form's Init() method and again in each of the navigation methods. This code is shown here:

```
ThisForm.SetButtons()
```

The finished Form should look something like the one shown in Figure 6-4.

Continued on next page

Figure 6-4.

The Customer Form

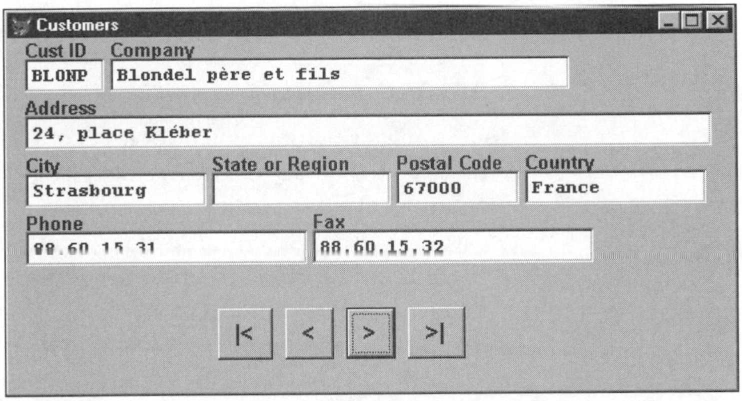

This Form isn't complete by any means. You have not enabled any table buffering, so if you make any changes to the value in the tables you're writing directly to the tables instead of to a data buffer. This doesn't give you any way of canceling those changes. In addition, there is no provision for adding a new record, and there are some assumptions in the code to enable and disable the CommandButtons (for example, what if you're adding the *first* record?). However, you should be getting a feel for how all this is fitting together. Save this Form because you'll be working with it again.

For the moment, run the Form and enjoy it.

EditBox Control

The EditBox Control shares most of the properties of the TextBox Control, but introduces three new ones. Normally, pressing the Tab key in a control (including an EditBox) causes the user to advance to the next control in the tab order. If you want the user to be able to place tab characters in an EditBox, set the *AllowTabs property* to .T.. Users can still advance to the next field, but they must use Ctrl+Tab to do so. It's a good idea to provide a Label that alerts them to this.

You can also limit the number of characters that can be entered into an EditBox by using the *MaxLength property*. Setting the MaxLength property to 0 removes any limits on the number of characters that can be entered.

When there is more data in the EditBox's Value property than can be displayed, setting the *ScrollBars property* to 2 (the default) automatically places vertical scrollbars to the right of the EditBox's window. If the ScrollBars property is set to 0, no scrollbars will appear. In that case, the only way of navigating in the EditBox is via the PgUp, PgDn, and arrow keys.

Spinner Control

The Spinner Control (which looks like a TextBox with a pair of vertically aligned arrows at the right edge) shares many of the properties, events, and methods that you've seen in the TextBox Control. However, there are some significant differences. First, the Value Property cannot accept a non-numeric value. Second, in addition to having the TextBox's RangeHigh and RangeLow methods, the spinner has a *KeyboardHighValue property* and a *KeyboardLowValue property.* As their names imply, these properties limit the range of values that can be typed into the Spinner object. They behave in exactly the same way as a value returned from a TextBox's RangeHigh and RangeLow methods. Typing a value into the spinner that exceeds these values prevents the user from doing anything further until they place an allowed value into the spinner.

A more user-friendly set of properties is the *SpinnerHighValue property* and the *SpinnerLowValue property,* which limit how high and how low the user can set the spinner object's value using the up and down arrow buttons on the right of the Spinner Control. Note that these values do not *override* the KeyboardHighValue and KeyboardLowValue. If the KeyboardHighValue is set to 10, and the SpinnerHighValue is set to 15, you can use the Spinner Controls to dial in a 15. However, the KeyboardHighValue will still trigger a user error message, and the user will be prevented from leaving the object until the value is adjusted.

The spinner's *Increment property* (default value 1) determines how the spinner's Value property is incremented (or decremented) with each click of the Spinner arrow buttons.

There are two events unique to the spinner, the *DownClick event* and the *UpClick event.* Triggered by clicking the up and down arrows on the spinner, these events allow you to write method code that is independent of changes to the spinner's value. Note that the InteractiveChange event occurs *before* the UpClick or DownClick events, and that if one of the spinner's control buttons is depressed and held down, the InteractiveChange event fires repeatedly. The DownClick or UpClick event does not fire at all until the mouse button is released. Also, the Click event will not be triggered at all unless the user uses the mouse to click in the text area of the Spinner Control.

While it may seem a limitation that spinner objects can take only numeric values, it's easy to use this value to increment or decrement the value of another control with a date type or character Value property.

CheckBox Control

A CheckBox Control's Value property can take a numeric, integer, or logical value. Its data type will reflect the data type of its ControlSource, or will retain whatever data type it was given at design time. If a CheckBox is checked, it will have a value of .T.. If its Value property is of type numeric or integer, it will have a value of 1. Setting the Value property of a CheckBox to any numeric value greater than or equal to 1 is interpreted as being checked.

The CheckBox can have two different appearances. The default appearance is a small square that can display a check mark with a caption to its right (specified by the CheckBox's Caption property). By changing the *Style Property* from "0 - Standard" to "1 - Graphical," the CheckBox changes to what appears to be a CommandButton. Its behavior is somewhat different because, when it is clicked with a mouse pointer, the depressed appearance persists until it is clicked again, visually indicating the CheckBox's current .T., .F., 0, or 1 value. The graphical CheckBox can be assigned a picture instead of (or in addition to) a textual caption. Like the CommandButton, the graphical CheckBox has a DownPicture property so that the image can change when the button is depressed (when the CheckBox's value is .T.). A perfect example of this behavior is in the graphical pushpin CheckBox on the property sheet that keeps the property sheet at the top of the stack when it is on.

OptionGroup Control

Like the Form and the CommandGroup, the OptionGroup is another container control. Unlike the CommandGroup whose members (the CommandButtons) can be used individually and apart from a CommandGroup, OptionButtons can only be contained in an OptionGroup. This is because the OptionGroup is the analog to FoxPro 2.x's radio buttons. Only one option in the group can be selected, and selection of one of the OptionButtons automatically removes the selection of all other options.

The number of buttons in the group is set by the *ButtonCount property*. To change the caption on individual OptionButtons in the group, you follow the same procedure described for the

CommandGroup. First use the right mouse button to click in the OptionGroup, then select the Edit option.

The OptionGroup's *SpecialEffect property* determines whether the border has a 3-D look, whereas the individual option's SpecialEffect property determines whether the push button has a 3-D look.

If the OptionGroup's Value property is set to a numeric value (the default) at design time, at runtime the Value property represents the ordinal position of the checked OptionButton. However, the Visual FoxPro documentation does not mention that if you set the Value property to a character-type value at design time, the Value property will reflect the caption of the selected OptionButton!

The individual OptionButtons also have a Value property, that can be assigned either a numeric value (the default) or a logical value at design time. A 0 or .F. indicates that the option is not selected, while a 1 or .T. indicates that the option is selected.

PageFrame Control

The PageFrame control is useful when you need to present more information than will normally fit onto a single Form. To deal with this in FoxPro 2.x, you either had to use multiple-screen sets or a third-party tool that would allow the emulation of tabbed pages. You've seen examples of PageFrames both in the Tools|Options... dialog box and in the property sheet. As an aid to seeing the features of the PageFrame Control in action, the PGFDEMO.SCX Form is included on the source code disc.

The PageFrame itself can be sized, and can be resized or moved at runtime. It can appear with tabs that can be used to select a page, or can be made to appear with no tabs. It can even be made effectively transparent so that users aren't even aware that they are viewing separate pages.

Each individual page has properties such as a Caption property that determine what text appears on that page's tab (if tabs are used) and what the background color will be. The individual pages can detect events such as Activate and Deactivate that allow the developer to take some action in response.

Many of the properties that are members of the PageFrame control and its pages are common to other objects and have already been discussed. (See Section 12 for a complete cross-reference of control object properties, events, and methods.)

PageFrame Appearance

* *Tabs Property*
* *PageCount Property*
* *TabStretch Property*

The most visible property of a PageFrame is its *Tabs property*. A page within a PageFrame that has visible tabs along the top (the Tabs property is set to .T.) can be activated by using the mouse pointer to click the appropriate tab. It can also be activated by executing the appropriate command in code. Without visible tabs along the top, the desired page can only be activated in code. This occurs when the Tabs property is set to .F..

When the PageFrame's Tabs property is set to .T., the PageFrame appears as rectangular region with a raised 3-D border effect. When the PageFrame's Tabs property is set to .F., however, the PageFrame's BorderWidth, BorderColor, and SpecialEffect properties all become enabled at design time. The SpecialEffect property can be set to a "0 - Raised," "1 - Sunken," or "2 - Flat" in appearance. The BorderColor property is ignored except when it is set to option "2 - Flat."

Tip!

The shape object that will be discussed in Section 9 cannot create a 3-D, raised, bevel-edged box. However, you can make an approximation by creating a PageFrame with Tabs property set to .F., PageCount property set to 1, SpecialEffect property of 0, and BorderWidth property set to a value that suits your preferences for the depth of the bevel effect. Unfortunately, the sunken effect isn't very effective.

The number of pages contained by a PageFrame is set by the *PageCount property*, which is available both at design time and runtime. The *PageHeight property* and *PageWidth property* are both read-only properties, and are useful for positioning objects within the PageFrame, particularly when the Form and PageFrame are resized. As with the Form's height and width, the PageHeight and PageWidth properties indicate the *inside dimensions* of the pages exclusive of any border that might exist for the PageFrame.

> **_Trap!_**
> While it may seem obvious, remember that if you reduce the PageCount property, anything on the removed page is lost forever! If you want to move objects from a page that you intend on moving to another page, you must select the objects then select Edit|Cut from the system menu. Then select another page, and choose Edit|Paste from the system menu. You can also use the Ctrl-X and Ctrl-V hotkeys. These options can move controls that you want to retain to a safe page before changing the PageCount property. Remember, you need to make any changes to control object references that might be made necessary by changing their location to another page.

The PageFrame's *TabStretch property*, which is available only when the Tabs property is set to .T., determines how the tabs are arranged if all of the tabs cannot be displayed without clipping their captions. A setting of 1 (the default) will clip the captions within the tabs and show as many of the characters as possible. A setting of 0 will stack the tabs into multiple rows as needed to allow the full captions to be displayed.

When the tabs are stacked, selecting one of the tabs that appears in the second (or higher) row will move all of the tabs in that row to the first (or bottom) row. This can be a bit confusing if the number of tabs in the second row is smaller than the number of tabs in the first row. To see this, run the sample Form PGFDEMO.SCX. Select the "8 Pages" option, click the graphical CheckBox labeled "Stack Pages," and leave the Tab Captions on "Standard." Pages one through five will appear in the lower row, and pages six, seven, and eight appear in the upper row. Clicking the tab for page six moves tabs six, seven, and eight into the lower row, but pages four and five remain in the lower row. (See Figure 6-5.) Compare this with the appearance when long captions are selected.

Figure 6-5.

PFGDEMO.SCX at runtime

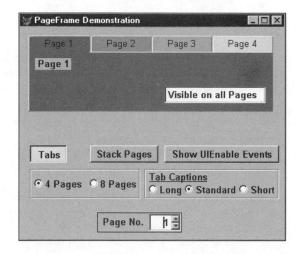

Using Program Code to Manipulate Pages

- *ActivePage Property*
- *Pages Property*
- *PageOrder Property*

You can change the active page on a PageFrame in code by setting the PageFrame's *ActivePage property* to the number of the page you want to activate. This is the only way that a page can be selected if you have a PageFrame with the Tabs property set to .F.. Run PGFDEMO.SCX, click the Tabs graphical CheckBox, and observe that any of the pages can be selected using the Spinner Control at the bottom of the Form.

The *Pages property* of the PageFrame object is identical in function to the Buttons property of the CommandGroup or OptionGroup—it is an array that contains a reference to each member object of the container. In this case, the Pages property is an array that contains a reference to each page in the PageFrame. The PGFDEMO.SCX Form uses this property to set the Caption property for all of the pages both in response to changing the length of the caption and to changing the number of pages from four to eight.

The preceding discussion related to the PageFrame object. However, the individual Page objects also have properties, events and methods, most of which have already been discussed. The behavior of the BackStyle property deserves some special mention. Its transparent setting causes the page to assume the same color as the Form (the PageFrame itself has no BackColor property), and the BackStyle property cannot be changed unless the Tabs property has been set to .F. for the PageFrame.

Another handy property of the Page object is the *PageOrder property*. You can change the order of the pages within the PageFrame by changing a page's PageOrder property to the ordinal position you want the page to acquire. Changing the property will automatically effect any necessary changes to the PageOrder property of other pages. Note that this does *not* change the name or the caption of any of the affected pages. Also, changing the PageOrder property does not change the index of the page in the Pages array property. However, it *does* change the page's designation when setting the PageFrame's ActivePage property.

For instance, suppose that you have a PageFrame with four pages named pagA through pagD, captions A through D, and PageOrder properties of 1 through 4. If you set the PageOrder property of pagC to 2, the pages will appear in the order A, C, B, D. Setting the PageFrame's ActivePage property to 2 will activate pagC, but accessing the second element of the PageFrame's Pages property (Pages[2]) will access pagB, even though that page's PageOrder property is now 3.

The UIEnable Event

The *UIEnable event* is not detectable by pages within a PageFrame, but it is a member of any object that can be placed *within* a page (including PageFrames). Each page has an Activate and Deactivate event for which you can write code to take necessary actions when these events occur. However, if you want to refresh only particular controls, you can place the code to do so in the UIEnable() method for those controls. The UIEnable event receives a logical argument from the page being activated or deactivated—a .T. if the page is being activated or an .F. if it is being deactivated.

The Labels on the first four pages of the PGFDEMO.SCX Form have code in their UIEnable() methods. If you click the Show UIEnable Events graphical CheckBox, this code will report each page activation and deactivation.

When dealing with PageFrames in the Form Designer, work with individual pages is accomplished in the same manner as individual CommandButtons in CommandGroups or OptionButtons in OptionGroups are accessed. You select the object in the drop-down list box at the top of the property sheet, or you can use the right mouse button to click the PageFrame to bring up the shortcut menu, then select the Edit option. You can then select one of the pages by using the mouse pointer to click it.

It is important to make sure that you do indeed have an individual page selected when you attempt to place a control object on it. Attempting to drop a TextBox onto a PageFrame rather than an individual page will actually place the TextBox on the Form in front of the PageFrame. Note that in the PGFDEMO.SCX sample Form that there is an "always visible" TextBox that was placed in just this way. This TextBox is different than the Labels that were placed on each individual page, which are visible only if the page that contains them is selected. It is *not* contained by the PageFrame of one of its Pages; it's contained by the Form itself and is positioned in front of the PageFrame.

7 The List Controls— ComboBox and ListBox Controls

A ComboBox is similar to what was called a pop-up in FoxPro 2.x. It looks like a TextBox with a small push-button control on the right end. When this push-button device is clicked, a list drops down and the user can make a selection from it. The ComboBox can behave in one of two different ways, depending on the setting of its *Style property*. Setting this property to 2 creates a drop-down list that allows the user a choice of items in a pre-defined list. Setting the Style property to 0 (the default) creates a drop-down ComboBox that allows the user to either make a selection from the list, or to type in the value they want to enter. There is a subtle difference in the appearance of these two objects. The drop-down ComboBox will have a small blank space between the TextBox and the "CommandButton" that drops the list down. In the case of the drop-down list box, the "CommandButton" butts up against the right edge of the TextBox.

Instead of dropping down the list of items, the ListBox Control presents the list in a scrollable window (if there are more items in the list than can be displayed), and the user can select one or more of the items presented.

Because much of the following discussion relates to all three controls, they will be referred to collectively as List Controls or List objects. When discussing a feature unique to one of the controls, the text will specify the control as the ListBox Control or the ComboBox Control (or more specifically, one of its two styles—the drop-down list or the drop-down combo).

Populating List Objects

- ***RowSourceType Property***
- ***RowSource Property***
- ***ListItem Property***
- ***ListItemID Property***
- ***List Property***
- ***ListIndex Property***
- ***ListCount Property***

The items displayed in lists are determined by the *RowSourceType property* and the *RowSource property*. The choices available for the RowSourceType property are as follows:

RowSourceType Setting	Description	RowSource
0	(Default) None. When this default value is used, fill the list at runtime using the AddItem( ) or AddListItem( ) method.	Blank
1	Value	A comma-defined list.
2	Alias. Use the ColumnCount property to select fields in the table.	A table (or view) alias.
3	SQL Statement.	A SELECT-SQL statement (use the Expression Builder).
4	Query (.QPR).	A file name with a .QPR extension.
5	Array.	The name of an array scoped to the Form. The name must include "ThisForm."
6	Fields.	A comma-defined list of fields. The fields may be prefaced by a period and the table alias.
7	Files.	A file skeleton or mask (such as *.DBF or *.TXT).
8	Structure. Fields from the table specified in RowSource.	Table name or alias.
9	Pop-up. This is included for backward compatibility.	

No matter how you populate your List Control, it maintains the data internally in an array-like property that can be referenced under two names, the *List property* and the *ListItem property*. Note that these properties were described as "array-like." They will be referred to as "arrays" (with the quotation marks) because while they have rows or rows and columns like an array, they cannot be handled strictly like an array. The features of these two properties differ from normal arrays in a few ways:

- The List property does not need to have DIMENSION used on it. It will accept a value assigned to it according to any specified row and column coordinates. Likewise, querying a List property value for row and column coordinates that don't exist does not cause a Subscript Out of Bounds error.
- The List property can contain only character data. If the ComboBox or list box is populated by an array, table, or query that contains numeric data, that data is converted to a character representation for display purposes. Any attempt to write anything other than character-type data to the List property will cause an error.
- The List property (and the ListItem property) cannot be manipulated using any of the array functions, such as ACOPY() or ADEL().

There is only one "array," but it can be referenced by two different property names, the *List property* and the *ListItem property*. When the user makes a selection from the list, three properties are set—the *ListIndex property*, the *ListItemID property*, and the *Value property*. The ListIndex property reflects the item's ordinal position in the list. If you change the position of an item in the list either by sorting, adding, or removing items from the list, the ListIndex property value associated with a particular item may change. The ListItemID property is a number that is unique to the item. An item's associated ListItemID will not change even if the order of the items in the list changes. The List property allows referencing of list items by the value of the ListIndex property. The ListItem property is actually the same "array," although it can be thought of as a copy of the List property "array." Its elements can be referenced using the ListItemID property.

Once a List object has been populated with list items, the number of items in the list can be determined by checking the *ListCount property*.

Because there are two "pointers" to the data in the List property (the ListIndex) and ListItem property (the ListItemID), the list controls provide methods to allow you to "translate" one reference to the other at any time by using the control object's *ItemIDToIndex() method* or the *IndexToItemID method*.

Populating a List Object Using "0 - None" as the RowSourceType

- *Sorted Property*
- *NewIndex Property*
- *NewItemID Property*
- *AddItem() Method*
- *AddListItem() Method*
- *RemoveItem() Method*
- *Clear() Method*

When specifying "0 - None" for the RowSourceType items in the List object, you can use the object's *AddItem() method* or *AddListItem() method* to populate the list. Both methods accept a character-type parameter with which you specify the character string to appear in the list. An optional second parameter accepts a numeric-type value that specifies either the index value (for the AddItem() method) or the ListItemID (for the AddListItem() method) of the added item.

If you use AddItem() and specify an index of an item already in the list, the item will be *inserted* into the list, and all items lower than the new item in the list will have their associated index values increased by one. If you use AddListItem() and specify an item ID that already exists, the new item *replaces* the existing item. With the foregoing caveat, you can specify any numeric value for the ListItemID when using the AddListItem() method. The same is not true of the AddItem() method. With it, you must either leave the nIndex argument blank, allowing AddItem() to place the new item into the next available position, specify an existing valid index value, or specify the next sequential index value available. If you have a list with 12 items, the following code will generate an error:

```
Form1.Combo1.AddItem("Last Item",15)
```

You can keep the list items sorted alphabetically by setting the List object's *Sorted property* to .T.. (This applies only if the RowSourceType is set to 0 or 1.) If the List object's Sorted property is set to .T., the AddItem() method (if used without the nIndex argument) and AddListItem() method will place the new item into the list in proper alphabetical order.

When using AddItem() and AddListItem() without the second (numeric) argument, both the associated ListIndex and ListItemID values will start at one. After that they will increment by one for each item added. You can determine the ListItemID and the ListIndex value associated with the last item added by the *NewItemID property* or the *NewIndex property*, respectively.

The AddItem() and AddListItem() methods also use a third argument, the column number of the added item. This is intended to enable the creation of a multicolumn list when the RowSourceType property is set to "0 - None." However, the behavior of AddItem() is not quite as simple as the Visual FoxPro documentation explains. Remember that AddItem() *always* inserts a value into the list. If no index value is provided, it will either insert a value at the end of the list or it will insert itself into the list at the point specified by a provided index value. Each time that AddItem() is called, *another item is added to the list*.

So while one might try to create a two-item, four-column list with the following code placed into the Init() method of a ListBox, you will not get what you expect:

```
This.AddItem["First",1,1]
This.AddItem["1",1,2]
This.AddItem["One",1,3]
This.AddItem["Numero Uno",1,4]
This.AddItem["Second",2,1]
This.AddItem["2",2,2]
This.AddItem["Two",2,3]
This.AddItem["Numero Dos",2,4]
```

Try creating a ListBox with the foregoing in the Init() method, set the ColumnCount property to 4 and run the Form. You will see the following in the ListBox:

```
Numero Uno
Numero Dos
Two|
2|
Second|
One|
1|
First|
```

To understand what's happening, adjust the ListBox's height and width properties to 250 pixels each. Then assign the value of "50,10,30,80" to the ColumnWidths property. You will see this:

```
                                        Numero Uno
                                        Numero Dos
                        Two |
                    2 |
          Second |
                        One |
                    1 |
          First |
```

As you can see, each time AddItem() was called, it inserted a new item, and inserted the desired text into the specified column.

To achieve a two-row, four-column List as intended, either of the following sections of code could be used in the ListBox's Init() method:

```
** Using AddItem(), NewItemID and AddListItem() **
This.AddItem["First"]
This.AddListItem["1",This.NewItemID,2]
This.AddListItem["One",This.NewItemID,3]
This.AddListItem["Numero Uno",This.NewItemID,4]

This.AddItem["Second"]
This.AddListItem["2",This.NewItemID,2]
This.AddListItem["Two",This.NewItemID,3]
This.AddListItem["Numero Dos",This.NewItemID,4]
```

or

```
** Using AddListItem() alone**
This.AddListItem["First",1,1]
This.AddListItem["1",1,2]
This.AddListItem["One",1,3]
This.AddListItem["Numero Uno",1,4]
This.AddListItem["Second",2,1]
This.AddListItem["2",2,2]
This.AddListItem["Two",2,3}
This.AddListItem["Numero Dos",2,4]
```

Another way to populate the List object with RowSourceType set to 0 is to directly write values to the List property. Placing the following code into the Init() method of a List object will create a three-row, two-column list:

```
This.List[1,1] = "First Item"
This.List[1,2] = "1"
This.List[2,1] = "Second Item"
This.List[2,2] = "2"
This.List[3,1] = "Third Item"
This.List[3,2] = "3"
```

Remember that the List property cannot accept any non-character (date, numeric, and so forth) values.

Because this option of populating a List object is intended to allow easy manipulation of the list data at runtime, the List objects also have a *RemoveItem() method* for removing list items by their associated ListIndex value. They also have a *RemoveListItem() method* for removing list items by their associated ListItemID value. All of the items can be removed from a List object by using the object's Clear() method. Note that this method is available only when the RowSourceType is set to "0 - None."

Populating a List Object Using "1 - Value" as the RowSourceType

While the AddItem() and AddListItem() methods are available when you select the "1 - Value" option for the RowSourceType property, this option is intended for short, static lists rather than lists that need to be created or modified at runtime. A comma-delimited list is assigned to the RowSource property, and this list is used to populate the List property "array." You can still create a multicolumn list using this RowSourceType property option by setting the List object's *ColumnCount property* to a value greater than 1. The ColumnCount property determines how many columns of a multicolumn list are displayed in the list. The ColumnCount property is discussed more fully in the upcoming discussion "Controlling the List's Appearance," but note that you can create a three-item, two-column list like the one in the previous example by specifying the RowSourceType property as "1 - Value," setting ColumnCount to 2, and placing the following character string into the RowSource property:

```
First Item,1,Second Item,2,Third Item,3
```

Populating a List Object Using "5 - Array" as the RowSourceType

• *Requery() Method*

The most important thing to remember when using an array to populate a List object is that the array needs to be *scoped to the Form*. This means that the array has to be created as an Array property of the Form. You can then populate or manipulate the array in any method of any object contained by the Form. To create an Array property, select Form|New Property... from the system menu while the Form Designer is open and selected. Specify the array name followed by brackets, as shown:

```
aListArray[1]
```

If you know at design time what the dimensions of the array property need to be, you can specify the dimensions in the property definition. Otherwise, you can use the DIMENSION command on the array at the time it's populated.

Once you have an array-type property for the Form, and specify "5 - Value" for the List object's RowSourceType, then you can indicate the name of the array to be used in the List object's RowSource property:

```
ThisForm.aListArray
```

Don't forget to include the scope of the array using ThisForm. There are two kinds of Visual FoxPro developers—those who have spent an hour trying to debug a List object in which they forgot to include ThisForm. in the RowSource property, and those who are going to spend that hour.

When you initially populate a Form array property for use in a List object, you need to be aware of the event sequence. If you first specify an array property as previously shown with a dimension of [1], then you write code in the Form's Init() method to DIMENSION this array to [10,3] and populate it, you may be puzzled that the List object shows only one item. Remember that all of a Form's controls are created *before* the Form's Init event. This means that the dimensions of the Form's array property have not yet been changed when the List object is instantiated. The List object thinks it's working with a one-element array.

There are a couple of ways to avoid this problem. The first is to make sure that the array is dimensioned and populated *before* the List object is instantiated. The Form's Load event is tailor-made to do this, so you could dimension and populate the array in the Load() method. However, there may be other circumstances when you want to manipulate an array that is specified as the RowSource for a List object. By necessity this could occur *after* the List object is instantiated, often while the Form is running and interacting with the user. In this circumstance, you might be tempted to use the Refresh() method on the List Object Control. The Refresh() will do what it's intended to do (refresh a control from the field or variable specified by its ControlSource property), but won't do what you need to accomplish.

The List objects all have a *Requery() method* that should be called any time you have either changed the RowSource property at runtime, or when you have changed the data in the source specified by the RowSource property. Remember that what is displayed by the List object is maintained in its internal List property. The only way to "refresh" this internal "array" is to do so using the Requery() method.

Populating a List Object Using Table Data for the RowSourceType

There are four RowSourceType options for populating a List object using table data—"2 - Alias," "3 - SQL Statement," "4 - Query," and "6 - Fields." These options populate the list object's List property directly from the table using the selected method. As an alternative to one of these methods, you *can* use table data to populate a list object by means of an array, using the steps outlined previously for setting the RowSourceType to "5 - Array." The array can be populated by issuing a SELECT - SQL statement INTO ARRAY <form array property>, or by using the COPY TO ARRAY command in method code.

The "Alias" option is the simplest approach, but it severely limits your ability to display table data. If the List object's ColumnCount property is set to 0 or 1, only the first field will appear in the list. If the ColumnCount property is set to a higher number, n, only the n leftmost fields will be displayed. This is fine if you want to display only the first n fields, but prevents you from displaying only the fourth and eighth fields.

The "Fields" option, on the other hand, allows complete control over which fields are used to populate the list by specifying the alias and field names in the RowSource property as a comma-delimited list. This code is shown:

```
customer.company,city
```

Notice that the alias is placed before only the *first* field in the list.

The SQL Statement and Query (.QPR) options provide even more control over the list items, including the ability to display data from more than one table. That cannot be accomplished using the "Fields" option. The "SQL Statement" and "Query (.QPR)" options are essentially identical. The only difference is that the SQL command resides either in the RowSource property itself or in an external .QPR file.

When you use "Fields," "SQL Statement," or "Query (.QPR)," be certain that you set the List object's ColumnCount property to the correct value to display the proper fields in the list.

Controlling the List's Appearance

In addition to all of the font properties, several other properties are critical in affecting the appearance of the list of items in a List object.

How Many Columns?

- *ColumnCount Property*
- *ColumnWidths Property*
- *ColumnLines Property*

If the RowSource of the List object creates a multicolumn list, the List object's *ColumnCount property* determines how many of those columns are displayed. In the case of the ComboBox Control, the contents of only the first column are displayed in the TextBox portion once a selection is made, but as many columns as you have specified in the ColumnCount property appear when the list is dropped down.

If you want to display only the first column for a ComboBox, set the ColumnCount property to 0. (Contrary to the Visual FoxPro documentation as of this writing, you cannot set the value of a List object's ColumnCount to -1, and setting it to 0 mimics FoxPro 2.x behavior.) Setting the ColumnCount property to 0 displays only the first column data in the List property. For a ComboBox Control, a ColumnCount of 0 will cause the dropped-down list to be as wide as the ComboBox Control on the Form, or as wide as necessary to accommodate the widest item in the list, whichever is greater.

When the ColumnCount property is set to a value greater than 0 and the List object's *ColumnWidths property* is left blank, each row in the List object will automatically allocate as much space as is needed for each column. You might want to choose this option when displaying information such as city and state names. In such cases, it is likely that the *ColumnLines property*, the property that places a vertical line between displayed columns, would be set to .F.. More common, however, is a desire to align the items in each column to the left, with the column lines forming a continuous vertical bar between each column.

The ColumnWidths property is a character string of comma-delimited numbers, each representing the width of a column expressed in the units specified by the Form's current ScaleMode property (foxels or pixels). An easy way to adjust these values is to create your Form with the List object, setting the ColumnCount property as appropriate. You can leave the ColumnWidths property blank, then run the Form.

Adjust the ColumnWidths property from the command window until you have the columns sized properly, then close the Form and paste the values that worked best into the property sheet.

Setting the ColumnCount to 1 for a ComboBox causes the drop-down list to make itself as wide as necessary to accommodate the longest entry in the visible list. As longer items appear when the list is scrolled, its width will change. This is strictly a cosmetic point, but you might find it visually unappealing and prefer to have the list sized consistently with the size of the unopened list control. Note that with the ListBox Control, the effect of setting the ColumnCount to either 0 or 1 has the same effect on the control's appearance. (See the upcoming discussion on the effect of ColumnCount > 0.)

Which Elements and Which Columns Are To Be Displayed?

• *NumberOfElements Property*
• *FirstElement Property*

If you have a ComboBox Control with a large number of items when you are using RowSourceType = 5 - (array), the list will normally drop down all the way to the bottom edge of the Form. You might want to limit the number of items that can be visible at any given time when the list is dropped down. This can be accomplished with the *NumberOfElements property*. The NumberOfElements property is also available to the list box when using an array as a RowSourceType. However, it usually makes more sense to leave NumberOfElements at its default value of 0, simply sizing the list as it is appropriate. The NumberOfElements property is ignored if the List object's ColumnCount property is set to a value greater than 0.

Another property applicable to List objects populated with an array is the *FirstElement property*. This property is used to determine which array element will appear first in the displayed list. The effect of setting the FirstElement property is not only to change the item displayed at the top of the list, but also to reduce the ListCount property—in other words, the effect of setting FirstElement the same as if the RowSource array was changed and the List object's Requery() method was called. For instance, if you have a 100-element array specified in the List object's RowSource and you set the FirstElement to 10, the ListCount property would reflect 90 items. Resetting the FirstElement property to 1 restores the ListCount property to 100, and the first array element again becomes the top item in the displayed list.

When you refer to an array "element," remember that you are not referring to the array element's row or row-and-column position, but to the element's ordinal position within the array. For example, suppose that the array used to populate a List object is a 100-row by 3-column array, the ColumnCount is set to 0, and the FirstElement property is set to 10. The value displayed at the top of the list will be the value in the array at row 4, column 1. If the FirstElement property is set to 12, the value displayed will be the value in the array at row 4, column 3.

Like the NumberOfElements property, the FirstElement property is ignored if the List object's ColumnCount is greater than 0, and can be used to display a column other than the array's first column. Again suppose that you have a 100-row, 3-column array as a List object's RowSource. The ColumnCount property is set to 0, and the FirstElement property is set to 3. The values in the array's third column will be displayed in the List object.

Trap!

Be aware of the execution order of method code and system events when you are populating arrays and List objects, and setting properties such as FirstElement and NumberOfElements. An error will occur if you set FirstElement or NumberOfElements to an array element that does not exist.

To avoid this, DIMENSION and populate the array in the Form's Load() method before the List object is instantiated, or set the List object's FirstElement and/or NumberOfElements properties in code after the array has been DIMENSIONed and populated.

Tip!

In addition to the FirstElement property (which can be used only when the List object's ColumnCount property is set to 0), it is also possible to control which columns are displayed in a List object by using the ColumnWidths property. Setting the width to 0 effectively hides the column from view.

Navigating in Lists

• *IncrementalSearch Property*

Another handy feature of Visual FoxPro List objects is the ability to enable incremental searching of the list items simply by setting the object's *IncrementalSearch property* to .T. (the default value). If the IncrementalSearch property is set to .F., each key press moves the selection to the next item in the list beginning with that letter. If incremental searching is enabled, typing a sequence of letters will position the selection to the first item that matches that letter pattern. The search is not case-sensitive.

You can either set or determine the item that is topmost in the current list display by using the *TopIndex property* or the *TopItemID property*. These properties reflect the ListIndex value or ItemID value associated with the item in the top of the list window. By setting either of these properties, the display can be made to scroll to a different portion of the list. Note that changing either property does not change the item selected, only the items displayed in the list.

Working with Data from List Objects

Which Column Is "Output"?

• *BoundColumn Property*
• *ColumnCount Property*

The List object's Value property reflects the item selected from the list. If you are working with a multicolumn list, specifying the column number in the control's *BoundColumn property* allows the Value property to assume the value of a column *other than the value in the first column*. The value of the BoundColumn property defaults to 1 and is, with one exception, completely independent of the List object's *ColumnCount property*. The ColumnCount property determines how many of the columns will be displayed in the list. This means that you can have a two-column List object in which only the first column is displayed in the list, while the second column actually controls the List object's Value property. Bring into play the List object's ControlSource property and you will be able to present the user with a natural-language list of options displayed in the first (and only visible) column. You will also be able to update a table field to the value in the second column, which can be a surrogate key.

There is one exception to the independent relationship between BoundColumn and ColumnCount. The BoundColumn is ignored if you are populating the List object from an array and you have the ColumnCount set to 0.

Which Item Is Selected?

• *ListIndex Property*
• *ListItemID Property*
• *DisplayValue Property*

It is possible to programmatically set the selection of any of the List objects by setting the ListIndex property or the ListItemID property to the value of the desired item. This is most commonly used to ensure that a drop-down List object displays the first list item. The drop-down list display is empty until the user drops the list down and makes a selection. You can set the ListIndex property of the List object to 1 if you want the first item in the list as the default choice.

This setting is also good if you want it to act as a cue that this is not a drop-down ComboBox, which users cannot use to type values into the display area. In the case of a List object with a RowSourceType of 0 (None) or 1 (Value), setting the Value property to the first (or any) item will insure that that item is the one initially displayed.

Another way to programmatically make a selection is to set the control's *DisplayValue property.* The DisplayValue property can assume a character-type value or a numeric value. Setting the DisplayValue property to a numeric value will select the item that corresponds to the specified ListIndex value. Once the DisplayValue property is set to a numeric value, it will change to reflect the ListIndex property. If the DisplayValue property is set to a character-type value that exists in the list of items in the first column of the List object, that item will be selected. Once the DisplayValue has been set to a character-type value, it will change to reflect the text in the selected item. Selecting an item programmatically by setting the DisplayValue to either a valid ListIndex value or a character value corresponding to an item in the list will also cause the List object's Value property to be updated.

User-Defined List Values (Drop-Down ComboBox)

Note that while the Value property can be set to a column other than column 1 by the BoundColumn property, a character-type DisplayValue always reflects the contents of the first column of the list. When you set the DisplayValue property to a nonexistent ListIndex (setting the DisplayValue to 10 for a five item list), none of the items will be selected and the List object's Value property will be set to the null string.

The default behavior is for the control's Value property to reflect the selected item in the list. However, in the case of the drop-down ComboBox, it is possible for the user to type something into the TextBox area of the control. This data is not reflected in the Value property, and therefore also does not affect any change in a field or variable specified in the ControlSource property.

There are several ways to deal with this, depending on whether you want to add the user's entry to the list of choices or whether the list should remain unchanged.

If you do not want to update the Value property to the text typed in by the user, you can check to see if this has already been updated by checking the value of ListIndex. A ListIndex value of 0 indicates that the user did not make a selection from the list so the DisplayValue can be used instead. If, however, you want the Value property to reflect the user's entry, and if you want to add the user's entry to the list of choices, refer to the following code. Placing this code in the LostFocus() method of the ComboBox will accomplish these tasks, as well as update the ComboBox's Value property and the ControlSource field or variable:

```
IF This.ListIndex = 0 AND ! EMPTY(This.DisplayValue)
   This.AddItem(This.DisplayValue)
   This.ListIndex = This.NewIndex
ENDIF
```

This bit of code uses the control's *NewIndex property*, which is the index of the last item added to the List property. It makes the new item the current selection and updates the Value and ControlSource properties.

You can use the following code if you don't want the item entered by the user to be added to the list but you need to update both the ComboBox's Value property and the target specified in the ControlSource property.

```
IF This.ListIndex = 0
   This.Value = This.DisplayValue
ENDIF
```

A problem with this approach is that the DisplayValue property is "blanked" as soon as its value is stored to the Value property. Changing the List object's Value property to a value that does not appear in the list will automatically change the List object's DisplayValue to the null string. This includes instances where you change the value of the field or memvar indicated by the List object's ControlSource property. After the Value property is updated with the DisplayValue property, the control is refreshed and the DisplayValue is reset to a null string. It's preferable to work with the DisplayValue property directly when necessary, or to add the DisplayValue property to the list as a new item.

Determining Numeric Values from List Objects

- *ListIndex Property*
- *ListItemID Property*
- *ItemData Property*
- *ItemIDData Property*

If the source for the data in the ComboBox or list box is a multicolumn source such as selected fields from a table, a two-dimensional array, or a multicolumn query, the numeric values that may be needed for calculations or other operations can be retrieved from the original data source. A numeric price in an array can be retrieved by using the List object's ListIndex as the array's row and using the appropriate column number for the column containing the price data. However, when using a List object that has a RowSourceType property of "0 - None" or "1 - Value," the Control's only possible value is stored in the object's List property. The property uses character data exclusively.

A numeric value is present in the form of the ListIndex or ListItemID properties, but these are somewhat limiting. The ListIndex values must be unique and sequential, and the ListItemID values must be unique.

To provide an opportunity to associate numeric values with list items in these situations, the List objects have two other "array-like" properties that can be referenced by two names in the same manner as List and ListItem properties. However, unlike the List and ListItem "array," these properties can contain only numeric data, are one-dimensional, and are not automatically populated along with the List and ListItem properties. *ItemData property* and *ItemIDData property* can be referenced by the item's ListIndex or ListItemID properties, respectively. Like the List and ListItem "array" properties, they are actually two different references to the same list. They must be manually populated with whatever numeric values are appropriate, but that can be easily accomplished by placing the code to populate either of the properties in the AddItem( ) or AddListItem( ) methods, and by making use of the NewIndex and NewItem properties.

The ListBox Control

In addition to all of the features just discussed, there are a few features that are unique to the ListBox Control.

- *MoverBars Property*
- *MultiSelect Property*
- *Selected Property*
- *SelectedID Property*

If you populate a list box while the RowSourceType property is set to "0 None" or "1 - Value," you have the option of setting the *MoverBars property* to .T.. This creates a rectangular button-like object to the left of each list item. A double-headed vertical arrow appears on the button corresponding to the item that is currently active. Clicking this button and dragging the item will allow the user to change the item's position within the list. This changes the item's visual order in the list as well as changing the item's associated ListIndex value.

Setting the list box's Sorted property to .T. will sort the items in the list, but their order can be changed using the mover bars. Setting the Sorted property to .T. will again re-sort the list alphabetically.

There will be times when you'll want the user to be able to select more than one item in a list box. Setting the list box's *MultiSelect property* makes this possible. Normally, clicking while the mouse pointer is on an item will de-select any other item. However, if the MultiSelect property is set to .T., users can hold down the Ctrl key and click multiple items. Alternatively, they can select an item, hold down the Shift key, and select another item as the last item. This selects both items and all of the items in between them.

Keep in mind that items being selected have no relation to the list box's Value property. The Value property simply represents the contents of the BoundColumn of the item currently active. Each list box can have only *one* value (regardless of the setting of the MultiSelect property).

To determine which of the items have been selected, the ListBox object also has a *Selected property* and a *SelectedID property*. The Selected and SelectedID properties are two ways to retrieve data from still another "array-like" feature of the list box. The Selected property will return .T. if it is passed the index of a selected item in the list, while the SelectedID property will return .T. if the ItemID of a selected item in the list is passed to it. This is accomplished from within a FOR...NEXT loop like the one shown:

```
FOR i = 1 TO This.ListCount
   IF This.Selected(i)
      * Take some action here like
      ThisForm.aSelectedArray[<next element number>] = ;
         This.List[i,]
   ENDIF
ENDFOR
```

Example List Form

Rather than walk through all of the steps to create a Form with some List objects, you will find a demonstration Form, LSTDEMO.SCX, on the source code disc. This discussion will examine some of the features of this Form, then it will cover how it was put together.

If you run LSTDEMO, you will see that it includes a PageFrame with four pages captioned Example 1 through Example 5. This section will examine each example individually after looking at the setup that was done to support all of the examples.

The first thing you'll notice is that there is a DataEnvironment established with a single table—the PRODUCTS.DBF table from the TESTDATA database.

For the Form, ShowTips is set .T., background color is set to cyan, and two properties have been added to the Form:

- aItems[1,0]. This is an array to use as a RowSource for the List objects in this Form.
- aSelected[1,0]. This is a target array for items selected in Example 4.

In addition, a new method called *GenParse()* has been added. This is a standard Xbase type of program that parses a string into an array.

```
LPARAMETERS tcParseString,tcSeparator,taArray
   lcParseString = ALLTRIM(tcParseString)
   DIMENSION taArray[OCCURS(tcSeparator,lcParseString)+1]
   STORE "" to taArray
   IF ! tcSeparator $ lcParseString
      taArray[1] = lcParseString
   ELSE
      lnOccurences = ALEN(taArray)
      FOR lni = lnOccurences to 1 STEP -1
         lnBeg = RAT(tcSeparator,lcParseString)
         lnEnd = LEN(lcParseString)
         taArray[lni] = SUBSTR(lcParseString,lnBeg+1)
         lcParseString = ;
            STUFF(lcParseString,lnBeg,lnEnd-lnBeg+1,"")
      ENDFOR
   ENDIF
   RETURN
```

In the Form's Deactivate() method, an ACTIVATE SCREEN command was placed so that you could easily check the value of any property from the command window.

In the Form's Init() method, AutoCenter is set to .T. and the BorderStyle is set to 2. Perhaps most importantly, the Form's aItems array property has been populated from three of the fields in PRODUCTS.DBF using a "SQL-SELECT statement."

```
ThisForm.AutoCenter = .T.
ThisForm.BorderStyle = 2
SELECT products.prod_name, ;
     products.product_id, ;
     products.eng_name ;
  FROM products ;
  ORDER BY prod_name ;
  INTO ARRAY ThisForm.aItems

ThisForm.PageFrame1.Page3.List1.Requery()
ThisForm.PageFrame1.Page2.Combo1.Requery()
ThisForm.PageFrame1.Page2.Combo1.ListIndex = 1
ThisForm.aSelected[1] = ""
```

Note that because all of the List objects on the Form are
instantiated at this point, it is necessary to call the Requery() method
of those objects populated by the aItems array property. Also, the
ListIndex property for the first item displayed has been set to 1
because the Page2.Combo1 object is a drop-down list. Finally,
because the second array property added to the Form (aSelected) is
not being populated, an empty character string was stored to its only
element to avoid having it appear with an .F. in the List object.

LSTDEMO.SCX Example 1

Figure 7-1.

LSTDEMO.SCX
Page I at runtime

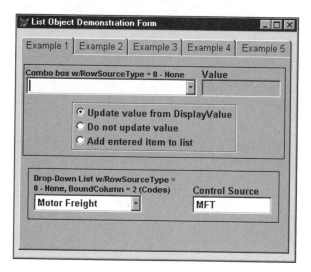

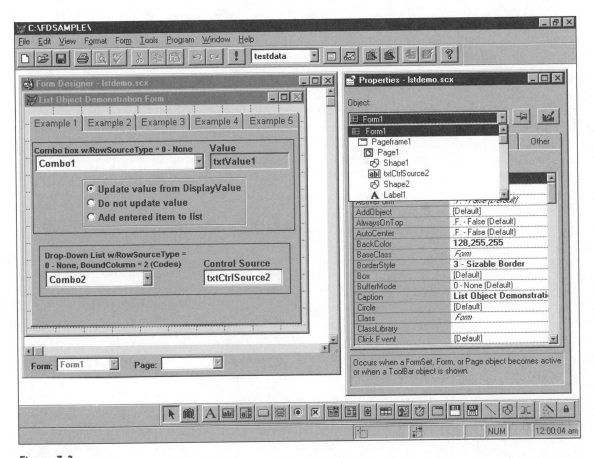

Figure 7-2.

LSTDEMO.SCX
Page I in the Form
Designer

If you haven't already done so, run LSTDEMO and look at the first page of the PageFrame for Example 1.

You will see two ComboBoxes on this page, Combo1 and Combo2. The first has its Style property set to 0, so it's a Drop-Down Combo Control. The TextBox to its right displays the Value property of this combo. Go down the list of items (First Item, Second Item, and so forth), and make a selection. You'll notice that the value of that item appears in the Value TextBox.

Below the Combo Control and its associated TextBox is an OptionGroup that determines how this Combo Control behaves when the user enters a value that is not in the control's list. If the Update Value From Display Value option is selected and the user types in an entry that is not in the ComboBox's list, the DisplayValue is transferred to the ComboBox's Value property. If Do Not Update Value is checked, the default behavior is observed—the DisplayValue shows what was typed while the Value property is blank. If Add Entered Item to List is selected, an entry made into the ComboBox that is not already in the list is added using the AddItem() method. Then the resulting item is selected so that both the DisplayValue and the Value correspond to the user's entry.

Programming Notes on Example 1

Combo1—ComboBox as Drop-Down Combo
The ComboBox is populated in its Init() method with the following code:

```
*** Combo1 Init() Method***
This.AddItem("First Item")
This.AddItem("Second Item")
This.AddItem("Third Item")
This.AddItem("Fourth Item")
This.AddItem("Fifth Item")
```

Here is the code for the InteractiveChange() method of this ComboBox:

```
***Combo1 InteractiveChange() Method***
This.Parent.txtValue1.Value = This.Value
```

Note how This and Parent are used to send a message to the TextBox displaying the value of the ComboBox.

```
***Combo1 LostFocus() Method***
DO CASE
CASE This.ListIndex = 0 AND ;
     This.Parent.OptionGroup1.Value = 1
   This.Value = This.DisplayValue
CASE This.ListIndex = 0 AND ;
     ! EMPTY(This.DisplayValue) AND ;
     This.Parent.OptionGroup1.Value = 3
   This.AddItem(This.DisplayValue)
   This.ListIndex = This.NewIndex
OTHERWISE
   * Do nothing
ENDCASE
This.InteractiveChange()
```

You'll notice that the LostFocus() method checks to see whether the ListIndex equals 0, whether the DisplayValue is empty or not (indicating that the user typed in a value that was not in the list), and what option was selected in the OptionGroup. Option 1 simply transfers the ComboBox's DisplayValue to its Value property. Option 3 causes the LostFocus() code to call the ComboBox's AddItem() method to add the contents of the DisplayValue property to the list, then it makes that item the current selection by setting the ComboBox's ListIndex property.

Combo2—ComboBox as Drop-Down List Box

The second ComboBox in Example 1 is configured as a drop-down list box, which means that the user is not allowed to type in a value that is not on the list. Once again, it is populated in its Init() method as a two-column list. The first column is a list of shipping methods, and the second is a list of associated 3-character codes for each method. Because the RowSourceType property is set to "0 - None" and you want a two-column list, you can use the AddListItem method to populate the list.

```
***Combo2 Init() method***
This.AddListItem("Motor Freight",1,1)
This.AddListItem("MFT",1,2)
This.AddListItem("United Parcel",2,1)
This.AddListItem("UPS",2,2)
This.AddListItem("Customer Pick-up",3,1)
This.AddListItem("CPU",3,2)
This.AddListItem("Customer Carrier",4,1)
This.AddListItem("YTK",4,2)
This.DisplayValue = This.List[1]
```

The last step in the object's Init() method sets the selected item to the first item in the list so that you can see right away that this is a drop-down list instead of a drop-down combo. That way, the box does not appear empty, which might imply that you can type an entry into it.

The ColumnCount for this ComboBox is set to 0, and the BoundColumn property is set to 2. This means that although only the first column is displayed, the ComboBox's Value property (and therefore the field or variable specified by the ControlSource property) reflects the contents of the second column in the list.

For the ComboBox in Combo1, the TextBox used to display the selected item (txtValue1) has been explicitly updated from the ComboBox's Value property in the ComboBox's InteractiveChange() method code. To display the selection in the second List object (Combo2), the ControlSource for this object is set to the Value property of the TextBox, txtCtrlSource2. This allows the TextBox to automatically be updated when a selection is made from the list box without the necessity of placing any method code into the InteractiveChange() method of Combo2. However, you can also type one of the three-character codes into the TextBox. Because this is specified as the ControlSource for the ComboBox, the selection of the ComboBox will change to the corresponding shipping method.

Z-Order and Interdependent Controls

In the second ComboBox of Example 1, you have a case of two controls that have some degree of interdependence and have a TextBox acting as the control source for a ComboBox. If you specify a ControlSource for an object that does not exist, any attempt to run that Form will fail. An error message will state that the control source was not found.

If the control source TextBox is added to the Form *after* the ComboBox, the TextBox has a Z-Order closer to the front and could have been placed in front of the ComboBox. This is a clue that you will experience an error because, as you'll remember, the control objects are instantiated in the order that they are added to the Form—in a "back-to-front" order. At the time that the ComboBox is instantiated, the TextBox does not yet exist. As a result, the error occurs.

Fortunately, you don't have to go around removing objects and adding them again to get them in the correct Z-Order. You can simply select the object, then select Send to Back or Bring to Front from the Format menu. Normally this is used to move one object behind another, but as you can see here, it can be useful in affecting the order in which objects are created.

If you're the adventurous type, open LSTDEMO in the Form Designer, select the txtCtrlSource2 TextBox, then select Format|Bring to Front from the system menu. This ensures that the TextBox will be instantiated *after* the ComboBox. Attempting to run the Form at this point will result in an error. Select the txtCtrlSource2 TextBox again, and select Format|Send to Back from the system menu. This forces the TextBox to be instantiated *before* the ComboBox, and the Form will run without an error.

LSTDEMO.SCX Example 2

On the second page of this Form, Example 2 presents a drop-down list populated by the aItems array that was created in the Init() method of the Form from the products table. Just below the drop-down list is a second drop-down list that controls which column is the BoundColumn, and therefore which column will update the TextBox at the bottom.

Drop the list down and scroll to one of the entries. For example, choose "Geitost." Change the BoundColumn to "2 - Product ID" and note that the text in the Control Source TextBox now shows "33." Change the BoundColumn to "3 - English Name," and you'll notice that the Control Source TextBox changes to show the English name of this product (stored in column three of the list), which is Goat Cheese.

Figure 7-3.

LSTDEMO.SCX
Page 2 at runtime

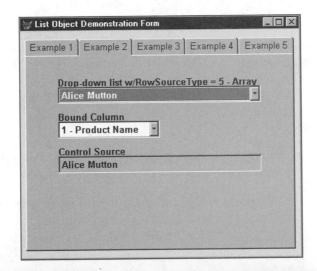

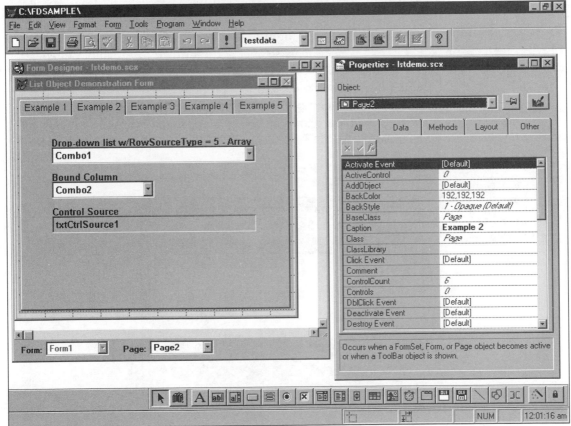

Figure 7-4.

LSTDEMO.SCX Page 2
in the Form Designer

Programming Notes on Example 2

Because it is populated from an array, the ComboBox Combo1 must have its ColumnCount property set to 1 (not 0 as was mentioned earlier) in order for the BoundColumn property to have any effect.

In order to *immediately* update the TextBox after changing the bound column using Combo2, the following code is placed in Combo2's InteractiveChange() method:

```
This.Parent.Combo1.BoundColumn = This.ListIndex
This.Parent.Combo1.ListIndex = This.Parent.Combo1.ListIndex
```

The second line of code has an effect similar to using a GOTO RECNO() method in a table: it "moves" the "record pointer" without actually moving it. This forces the TextBox that is acting as a control source to be updated with the data from the newly-specified column. This is the only way to accomplish this task. Refresh() has no effect.

The second ComboBox, Combo2, is used to select the BoundColumn of the drop-down list box. Its RowSourceType is set to "1 - Value." This setting is appropriate for a simple three-item list of this type. The three choices are entered as a comma-delimited string in the object's RowSource property.

Finally, instead of being made read-only, the TextBox has the When() method return .F.. In addition, the background is "grayed" to indicate that this is an output field instead of a data entry field.

LSTDEMO.SCX Example 3

Figure 7-5.

LSTDEMO.SCX
Page 3 at runtime

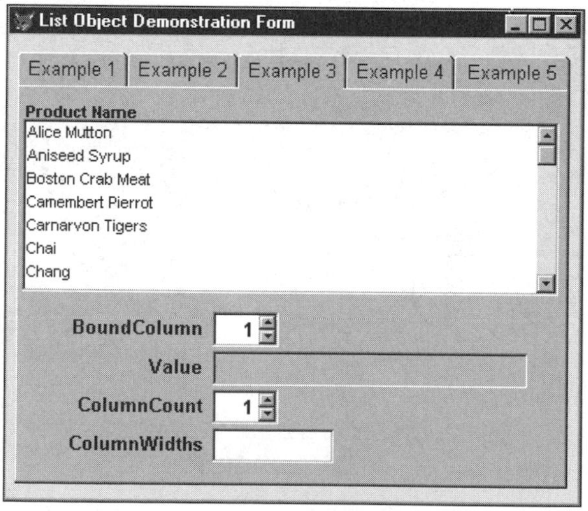

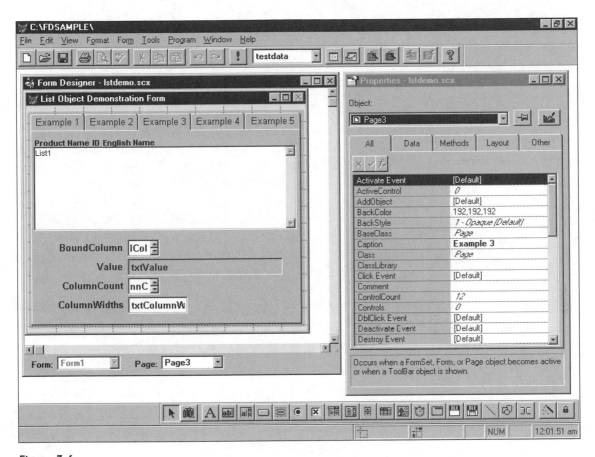

Figure 7-6.

LSTDEMO.SCX Page 3 in the Form Designer

Here is the first list box example. Again, it is populated from the altcms array that was created in the Form's Init() method. In this example, the user is able to determine the BoundColumn, the ColumnCount, and the ColumnWidths.

Before making any changes, note that when it is first started no items are selected, the Value property is empty, and the BoundColumn and ColumnCount are both set to 1.

Select an item (Chartreuse Verte, for example), change the BoundColumn spinner to 3, and observe that the value displayed in the Value TextBox is now the English name of the product. You can also see that the Value TextBox displays Green Chartreuse (Liqueur).

When you change the ColumnCount spinner to 2, you will observe that the second column of the list (the product_id values) is displayed with a vertical line separating each value in this column from the value in the first column. You will also observe that an ID label appears above the list, and that the alignment of the vertical lines between the columns is ragged.

Next, enter some values into the ColumnWidths TextBox. The proper way to enter the column widths is as a comma-delimited character string, so if you wanted to try column widths of 100 and 20 for columns 1 and 2 respectively, you would enter "100,20" into the ColumnWidths TextBox. Visual FoxPro apparently does the equivalent of applying the VAL() function to the values after parsing the string into its individual components. An alphabetical entry such as "100,hello" will be interpreted as a value of 0, and will cause the second column to have a column width of 0.

As you are determining the correct ColumnWidths entry to get the list displayed property, you will see that the ID label will line itself up with the left of the second column. You will also notice that you can enter *any* value for the second column; there is no maximum.

Now change the ColumnCount spinner to 3 and repeat the process. This time you will notice that an English Name label appears above the List object and positions itself to the left of its column. Changing the ColumCount spinner back to 2 will cause this label to disappear.

Programming Notes on Example 3

The TextBox "txtValue" is specified as the list box's ControlSource, so no special programming is needed for it to reflect the list box's current Value property.

Both Spinner Controls have a SpinnerHighValue property of 3 and a SpinnerLowValue property of 1. Notice that this is a user-friendly method that restricts keyboard input without resorting to use of the KeyboardHighValue or KeyboardLowValue properties, or without hard-coding a maximum and minimum value. The following code is from the spnrBoundColumn's IntractiveChange() method:

```
DO CASE
CASE This.Value > This.SpinnerHighValue
   This.Value = This.SpinnerHighValue
CASE This.Value < This.SpinnerLowValue
   This.Value = This.SpinnerLowValue
ENDCASE
This.Parent.List1.BoundColumn = This.Value
This.Parent.List1.listindex = This.Parent.List1.listindex
```

The last line is included to force the control source to "refresh" according to the newly specified BoundColumn property.

The code that creates the effect where column headings seem to magically appear and position themselves is very simple, and could have been placed in a Form method and called whenever the

ColumnCount or ColumnWidths properties were changed. However, since changes are often made to one page in a PageFrame that affect other pages, I chose to demonstrate how a control's UIEnable event can be used to "update" a page's display when that page is activated. The UIEnable event is triggered whenever the page that contains the control is activated. The following code is from the UIEnable() method of the lblEname object:

```
LOCAL ARRAY laPosition[1]
IF This.Parent.spnColumnCount.Value = 3
This.Visible = .T.
ThisForm.GenParse(This.Parent.List1.Columnwidths,",",;
  @laPosition)
IF ALEN(laPosition) .+ 2 AND VAL (laPosition[2]) > 0
  This.Left = MAX (101,VAL(laPosition[1]) + ;
    VAL(laPosition[2]) + ;
    This.Parent.List1.Left + 8)
  ENDIF
ELSE
  This.Visible = .F.
ENDIF
```

This code performs two operations. First, it makes the label that reads "English Name" visible only when the ColumnCount is set to 3. Second, it positions the label above the list column that contains the English name for the product, based on the column position specified in the ListBox's ColumnWidths property.

In the case of this example, the UIEnable() method is called whenever the value of the spnColumnCount control changes. (See the InteractiveChange() method of spnColumnCount.)

A new Form method could have been created to do the job for both the Product ID (lblID) and English Name (lblEname) labels. The code for each label could have been placed in its Click() method because the method isn't being used for anything else in this example. You also could have placed it in the Activate() method for Page 3 of the PageFrame, and coincidentally used the same code that would have been placed into a new Form method.

This looks like a good choice because it is possible that the ColumnCount of this control could be changed when this particular page is not active. When the page is activated, it then becomes necessary to either reveal and position these labels or to hide them.

More for the sake of illustration than anything else, the code was instead placed to reveal and position these two labels in each label's UIEnable() method. You'll remember that the UIEnable event occurs for each control whenever the page on which that control is placed is activated or deactivated, and an argument is passed to the

UIEnable() method to indicate whether the event is being triggered by the activation or deactivation of the page.

Here is the code that appears in the UIEnable() method of the lblID object:

```
***lblID.UIEnable()***
LPARAMETERS lEnable
   LOCAL ARRAY laPosition[1]
   IF This.Parent.spnColumnCount.Value >= 2
      This.Visible = .T.
      ThisForm.GenParse(;
         This.Parent.List1.Columnwidths,",",@laPosition)
      IF ALEN(laPosition) >= 1 AND ;
          VAL(laPosition[1]) > 0
        This.Left = MAX(86,VAL(laPosition[1]) + ;
           This.Parent.List1.Left + 6)
      ENDIF
   ELSE
      This.Visible = .F.
   ENDIF
```

This code checks the value of spnColumnCount and, if necessary, makes the label visible and parses the ColumnWidths property into a local array, laPosition. It then uses that array to calculate the position of the left edge of the label. A value of 86 is set as the minimum so that if a column is set to less than that value, the ID label will not print on top of the Product Name label.

The code in the InteractiveChange() method of the ColumnCount spinner ensures that the user does not type in a value outside the range allowed by the SpinnerHighValue and SpinnerLowValue properties. It then resets the ColumnCount of the list and calls the UIEnable() methods of the ID and English Name labels with the following code:

```
***spnColumnCount.InteractiveChange()***
DO CASE
CASE This.Value > This.SpinnerHighValue
   This.Value = This.SpinnerHighValue
CASE This.Value < This.SpinnerLowValue
   This.Value = This.SpinnerLowValue
ENDCASE
This.Parent.List1.ColumnCount = This.Value
This.Parent.lblID.UIEnable()
This.Parent.lblEname.UIEnable()
```

The LostFocus() method of the txtColumnWidths TextBox also sets the appropriate property of the list box and calls the UIEnable methods of the labels. This is more appropriate than placing the code in the InteractiveChange() method, as that would cause the code to be executed for every keystroke instead of waiting until the user has entered the entire ColumnWidths expression.

```
***txtColumnWidths.LostFocus()***
This.Parent.List1.ColumnWidths = This.Value
This.Parent.lblID.UIEnable()
This.Parent.lblEname.UIEnable()
```

LSTDEMO.SCX Example 4

Example 4 on page 4 of the PageFrame illustrates the MultiSelect and MoverBars properties. The list at the top of the page is populated manually using AddItem(), and its RowSourceType is "0 - None." The list presents a list of names, often referred to as "all the usual suspects". The CommandButtons just below it enable the user to clear the selected names or to sort the names alphabetically. There is also a label that displays the number of items selected.

Figure 7-7.

LSTDEMO.SCX
Page 4 at runtime

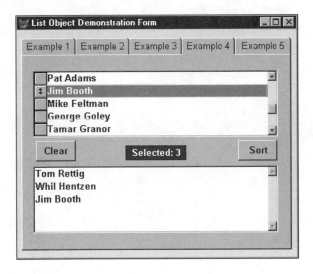

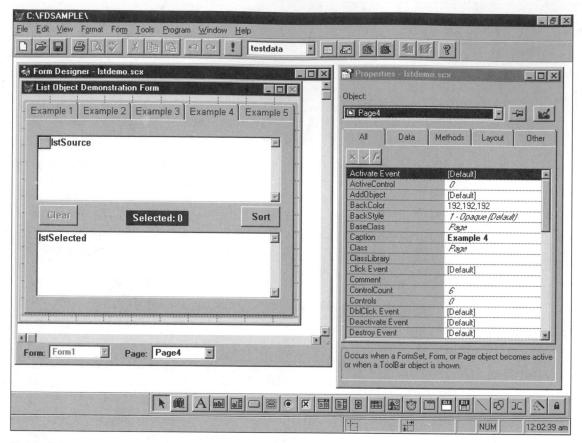

Figure 7-8.

LSTDEMO.SCX
Page 4 in the Form
Designer

The list box at the bottom of the page displays the selected items. If no items are selected, the Clear CommandButton is disabled. Any name can be moved to any position in the list by clicking and dragging the Mover icon to the left of that name. One item can be selected by clicking it, or, as is standard in Windows-based applications, multiple items can be selected by holding down the Ctrl key and clicking items. Alternatively, a block of items can be selected by holding down the Shift key and clicking the first and last items in the block.

The list of selected items at the bottom also reflects the action of selecting several items and changing their order either by using the mover bars or by sorting the list.

Programming Notes on Example 4

You might recall that there was an Array property created for this demonstration Form called aSelected, but that the array wasn't populated. This array is the RowSource for the bottom list box, lstSelected.

The meat of this example is in the Click() method of the top list box, lstSource. In turn, this populates the array that is specified as the RowSource for the lstSelected list box.

```
***lstSource.Click()***
LOCAL lnSelected
lnSelected = 0
* Loop through all the items in lstSource
FOR i = 1 to This.ListCount
    * If it's selected, increment the counter
    * (lnSelected), DIMENSION the array ThisForm.aSelected
    * (if necessary) then add the selected item to it
    IF This.Selected(i)
        lnSelected = lnSelected + 1
        IF ALEN(ThisForm.aSelected) < lnSelected
            DIMENSION ThisForm.aSelected[lnSelected]
        ENDIF
        ThisForm.aSelected[lnSelected] = This.List[i]
    ENDIF
ENDFOR &&* i = 1 to This.ListCount
* If no items are selected (the user cleared all selections)
* then re-dimension ThisForm.aSelected, and store an empty
* string to it for display purposes. If there are fewer
* items selected than there are elements in
* ThisForm.aSelected[], then re-dimension
* ThisForm.aSelected[] accordingly.
DO CASE
CASE lnSelected = 0
    DIMENSION ThisForm.aSelected[1]
    ThisForm.aSelected[1] = ""
CASE lnSelected < ALEN(ThisForm.aSelected)
    DIMENSION ThisForm.aSelected[lnSelected]
ENDCASE
* Enable/Disable the cmdClear Command Button
IF lnSelected = 0
    This.Parent.cmdClear.Enabled = .F.
ELSE
    This.Parent.cmdClear.Enabled = .T.
ENDIF
* Update the caption of the label reporting
* the number of items selected
This.Parent.lblSelected.Caption = "Selected: " + ;
    LTRIM(STR(lnSelected))
* Requery the lstSelected list (this is necessary as you've
* changed the RowSource array)
This.Parent.lstSelected.Requery()
```

The cmdSort CommandButton's Click() method simply sets the Sorted property of the lstSource list box to .T. and calls its Click()

method, which refreshes the lstSelected list box. That method is shown here:

```
This.Parent.lstSource.Sorted = .T.
This.Parent.lstSource.Click()
```

The cmdClear CommandButton's Click() method changes the lstSource list box's ListIndex to 0, then loops through all of the items and sets the list box's Selected property to .F. for each. It finishes by calling the lstSource list box's Click() method to refresh the lstSelected list box. The code for this method is shown here:

```
This.Parent.lstSource.ListIndex = 0
FOR i = 1 to This.Parent.lstSource.ListCount
   This.Parent.lstSource.Selected(i) = .F.
ENDFOR &&* i = 1 to This.Parent.lstSource.ListCount
This.Parent.lstSource.Click()
```

LSTDEMO.SCX Example 5

Example 5 is identical in function to Example 3, but it uses a table's fields (RowSourceType = "6 - Fields") instead of an array to populate the List object. The RowSource property is specified as follows:

```
Products.Prod_name,Product_ID,Eng_name
```

The only other difference between Example 5 and Example 3 is that Example 5 has an additional TextBox on the page that shows that the record pointer is being moved in the table as selections are made from the list. (The table record numbers do happen to correspond to the product_id value.)

Note that the list box is populated in record order. If you want the list to be sorted, you can set the appropriate index order in the Form's DataEnvironment.

8 | The Grid Control Object

For years FoxPro developers have been wishing for a Browse that could be placed in a screen. Finally, those wishes are fulfilled with Visual FoxPro.

The first thing you should know about the Grid Control object is that *it is not a Browse!* Approach this object as an entirely new species and you'll be much farther ahead.

Parts of a Grid—A Composite Object

Many of the Visual FoxPro BaseClass controls are templates for composite objects, objects that are not only able to contain other objects, but by default already do contain certain objects. The Form BaseClass automatically contains a DataEnvironment object, an OptionGroup automatically contains two or more OptionButton objects, and so forth. Similarly, a Grid object contains columns. Each of these columns contains a Header object and a default TextBox object. It is possible to replace the default TextBox object with one or more other controls if they are better suited to your purpose.

Initial Setup—Supplying the Grid with Data

- *RecordSource Property*
- *RecordSourceType Property*

Unlike the List object controls, the Grid can be only populated with table data. That data is not transferred into an internal representation like the List objects' List property, and therefore retains the original data's data type. RecordSourceType has only four settings. The "0 - Table" setting will automatically open a table specified in the Grid's RecordSource property, the "2 - Prompt" setting triggers a prompt dialog box that allows the user to specify which table to use, and the "3 - Query" setting runs the .QPR file specified in the RecordSource property. The most commonly used option for RecordSourceType is "1 - Alias," which happens to be the default value. This option populates the Grid with data from the table, Cursor, or view that has an alias specified in the RecordSource property. Note that with this option (unlike options 0, 2, and 3), the Grid relies on the fact that the specified table is already open. This implies that the Form on which it is placed has the necessary table as a Cursor member of its DataEnvironment, or that the necessary table, query-generated Cursor, or view is either opened or created in code prior to instantiating the Grid object.

Controls can be added to a Form by opening the DataEnvironment in the Form Designer and using drag and drop to move fields from one of the DataEnvironment's tables to the Form. Likewise, the easiest way of creating a Grid object and setting the RecordSource and RecordSourceType is to open the DataEnvironment in the Form Designer and drag and drop the entire table to the Form. The default object for an entire table is a Grid object.

Creating Grids

Now take a quick look at the Grid from the viewpoint of the Form Designer. Create a new test Form, add a table to the Form's DataEnvironment, then drag and drop this table from the DataEnvironment to the Form. Finally, size the Grid to fill most of the Form.

You'll notice that this isn't very interesting visually, as the Grid is represented by a blank square. If you drop down the object list while the Grid is selected, you will not see any headers, columns, TextBoxes, or any other objects that you were told are contained by the Grid. This is because the Grid's *ColumnCount property* is set to its default value of -1. With this setting, the ColumnCount property is adjusted at runtime to accommodate as many fields as exist in the specified RowSource, a header is automatically added to each column, and the control contained in each column is the default TextBox. When specifying a ColumnCount of -1, the properties of the individual columns, headers, and TextBoxes are not accessible at design time. However, when you change the ColumnCount property to 3, the columns, headers, and TextBoxes become accessible. Like other composite objects such as PageFrames and OptionGroups, clicking the Grid selects the entire Grid. Using the right mouse button to click the Grid and selecting Edit... from the shortcut menu makes it possible to gain access to the columns, headers, and contained controls. You can also select the contained controls from the drop-down list at the top of the property sheet.

Like all other Control objects, Grids, headers, columns, and contained controls all have a Name property. If the object is referenced in code, it may be convenient to name each object. Visual FoxPro assigns a default name to each so that your Grid now has three columns, each of which has a header named Header1, the default value of each header's caption property. You've seen this behavior before with Label objects. In fact, the Header object possesses a subset of the label's properties, events, and methods.

You can select individual columns or headers by selecting the Grid Control by clicking it with the mouse, then using the right mouse button to select Edit from the shortcut menu. Try this, then click various columns and headers. You'll notice a change in the object displayed in the property sheet. You will also see a tiny TextBox icon in each cell of the Grid. Selection of these or any objects contained in the column can only be made by selecting it in the property sheet's drop-down list.

Once a contained object such as the default TextBox is selected in the property sheet, moving the focus back to the Form Designer window will allow deletion of that object by pressing the *Delete* key. The object can then be replaced by clicking another object in the Form Controls toolbar, then dropping the new object into the cell previously occupied by the TextBox. When necessary, it is also possible to place more than one object in a Grid column using the same technique—select another control from the toolbar and drop it into the column in which you want the control used. Note that only one control will be visible in the Form Designer, which is also the case at runtime. Only one control at a time can be active in a given column. This can be changed at runtime using the DynamicCurrentControl property, which is discussed later under Column properties.

Give this a try, removing and adding control objects to the column until you are familiar with the technique.

Grid Properties
GRDDEMO1.SCX

The source code disc included with this book has four Forms that demonstrate Grids and their properties. GRDDEMO1.SCX demonstrates the most commonly used Grid and column properties. The RowSource for this Grid is the ORDERS table of the TESTDATA database. Before proceeding with this Form, you will need to modify the ORDERS table. Add the following captions to the fields indicated. If you already know how to do this, you can skip ahead. However, if this is unfamiliar to you, you can review the instructions in the box "Adding Field Captions to the Database."

Field	Caption
Order_ID	Order No.
Cust_ID	Customer No.
Emp_ID	Emp I.D.
Order_Date	Order Date
Order_Amt	Amount
Order_Dsc	Discount
Order_Net	Total
Shipped_On	Ship Date

Adding Field Captions to the Database

Make the directory in which you installed the sample files your current directory, and ensure that the DATA subdirectory is in your path. From the command window, enter the following commands:

```
OPEN DATABASE testdata
MODIFY DATABASE
```

Figure 8-1.

Changing a Field Caption in the Database Designer

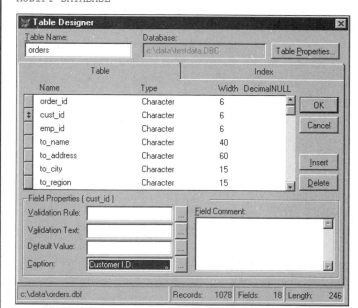

Continued on next page

This will open the Database Designer. Use the right mouse button to click the Orders table, then select Modify... from the shortcut menu to bring up the Table Designer dialog box shown in Figure 8-1. Select the fields specified in the table just presented, and type the indicated caption into the Caption TextBox at the lower left of the Table Designer dialog box. Once you have added the captions, click the OK CommandButton, and answer "Yes" in the Make Changes Permanent? dialog box.

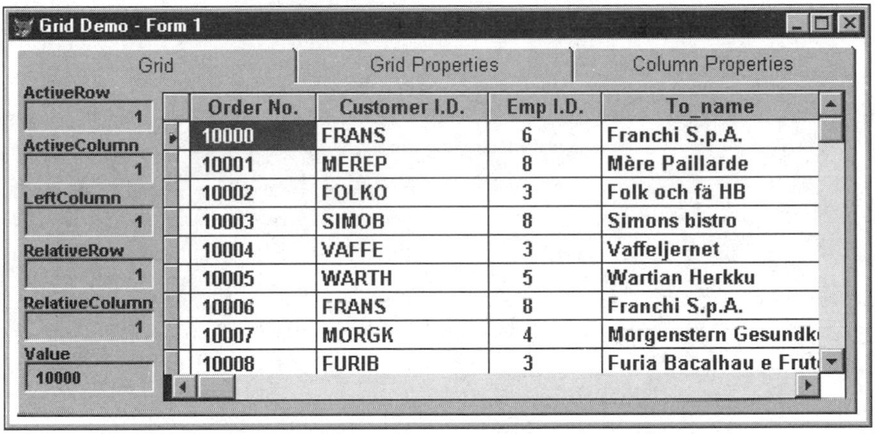

Figure 8-2.

GRDDEMO1.SCX
Page 1 at runtime

When GRDDEMO1.SCX is run, you will see a PageFrame with three pages captioned "Grid," "Grid Properties," and "Column Properties." The first Grid page also displays a group of Grid properties that are not available at design time and are read-only at runtime. These are the *ActiveRow, ActiveColumn, RelativeRow, RelativeColumn, LeftColumn*, and *Value properties*.

One of the first things you might notice is that the column headers display the field captions for those fields that have them. Otherwise, the field name is used as the default header caption.

Navigate around the Grid for a moment and observe the effect that this has on the displayed properties. Note that the Value property reflects the value of the current cell. The RelativeRow property and RelativeColumn property reflect the position of the active cell within the displayed rows and columns. This Form starts at its minimum size. If you size the Grid to its minimum dimensions and make active the cell at the lower right corner of the Grid (in the "Customer I.D." column), the RelativeRow and Relative Column TextBoxes will display the values of 9 and 2, respectively. Note that because the number of visible rows and columns can change if you resize the Form to be larger than its minimum size, the lower left cell's values in terms of the RelativeRow and RelativeColumn properties will therefore change. Making the top left cell active will change these two values to 1 and 1. It doesn't matter where you are in the table. Scroll the Grid all the way to the right so that the Freight column is visible. Then, scroll to the bottom of the table and make the top left cell active. RelativeRow and RelativeColumn will both continue to show 1. Making the bottom rightmost cell active will again cause 9 and 2 to be displayed.

By contrast, ActiveRow property and ActiveColumn property show the position of the active cell in relation to the table as a whole. Because there are 18 fields and 1078 records in this table, making the last row and last field active will cause ActiveRow to be 1078 and ActiveColumn to be 18. It is important to note that ActiveRow and ActiveColumn are completely independent of the order in which the rows and columns are displayed. In this example, if the active cell is in the rightmost column, ActiveColumn will be 18 even if it is the first field in the table. Likewise, if the active cell is in the 25th row of the table, ActiveRow will be 25 regardless of whether the table is in record order or if an active index or a filter is set.

You can verify this very easily. Scroll to the top of the table so that the first record is at the top of the Grid. Using the arrow keys, move down until the ActiveRow and RelativeRow both read 5. The Order No. should be 10004. Then type the following in the command window:

```
SET ORDER TO TAG cust_id
```

(Keep in mind that this Form does not employ a private data session to make this easy.) Reactivate the GRDDEMO1 Form by clicking its title bar. This will refresh the Grid and all other controls. Make sure that the active cell is still on the record for Order No. 10004, and note the ActiveRow property now reads 968.

As you navigate around the Grid using the scroll bars, you'll also notice that RelativeColumn will go negative as the active cell scrolls to the left of the Grid. However, RelativeRow will go to 0 when the active cell scrolls out of the Grid, and will remain at 0 until the active cell is scrolled back into the Grid.

The LeftColumn property displays the number of the leftmost column visible in the Grid. Like the ActiveRow and ActiveColumn properties, it is independent of the column actually being displayed. As with Browse windows, you can drag columns to different positions. Drag the Order No. column to the right by clicking its header until it is the third column. Make this column the leftmost visible column, then observe that the LeftColumn property displays 3 even though the Order_ID field is the first field in the table.

Absolute Referencing of Grid Columns

When you develop ways for your users to move the Grid Columns, you might want to have some way to reference a column without regard to its current position in the Grid. It is possible to reference the column by its Name property, and selecting names that adhere to the "Hungarian notation" used in this report makes this a bit easier (grcFreight, for example). However, the Grid has a *Columns property* that allows you to reference each object by a consistent numerical value. This is similar to properties for other composite objects such as the Pages property of a PageFrame, or the Buttons property of an Option or CommandButton Group. In this example Form, the ActiveColumn value will be 18 if the freight column has not been moved and becomes active. If the user drags this column to the first column position and makes it active, the ActiveColumn property will be 1. However, you can always reference the freight column as Columns(18) without regard to its position in the Grid.

You can try this yourself. With GRDDEMO1 running, drag the Freight column to some other position. Then enter the following in the command window:

```
grddemo1.pageframe1.page1.Grid1.columns(18).Backcolor =
   RGB(255,0,0)
```

> ### *Tip!*
> When manipulating many properties of an object such as the Grid in this example, you can save some typing by creating a reference to the object by assigning it to a memory variable:
>
> ```
> MyGrid = grdDemo1.PageFrame1.Page1.Grid1
> ```
>
> Thereafter, you can simply enter the code shown into the command window:
>
> ```
> MyGrid.Columns(18).BackColor = RGB(255,0,0)
> ```

The beginning of this discussion described all of the properties that are displayed on the first page of GRDDEMO1 as read-only at runtime. You should be aware that the Value property of a control object is normally read/write at runtime. The Visual FoxPro documentation does not state that it is read-only at runtime for Grids, however it has been my experience that setting the Grid's Value property will cause Visual FoxPro to crash under both

Windows 95 and Windows NT Workstation. These crashes occur both at runtime and at design time. While you may not experience the same problem, it might be safest to consider this a read-only property!

Setting Grid Properties

The second page of GRDDEMO1.SCX enables you to play with some of the properties of the Grid Control.

Figure 8-3.

GRDDEMO1.SCX at runtime

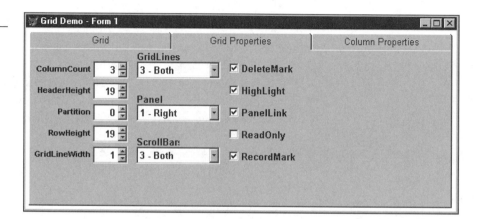

Numeric Valued Properties

First, try setting the Grid's ColumnCount property. You will probably notice that you can set the ColumnCount property to a value larger than 18. In such cases, the Grid is simply fleshed out with additional blank columns. Setting the ColumnCount property to something other than -1 will cause significant changes at design time, as you saw at the beginning of this section. Even at runtime, you'll see that the headers all default back to the "Header1" caption.

The Spinner Controls that set the *GridLineWidth property, HeaderHeight property,* and *RowHeight property* are all self-explanatory, and you can play with them to see their effects. The units for all of these are in pixels. For example, if the RowHeight property is set to 1 it will automatically size to fit the current FontSize for the Form.

To see how the *Partition property* works, return to the Grid page and click the black rectangle at the lower left of the Grid. Then drag it to the right, creating two panels for the Grid Control. Return to the Grid Properties page, and note the value shown in the Partition spinner. Change this value to some small value such as 5, and return to the Grid page to see the effect. The Partition property sets the location of the partition, in pixels, in relation to the left edge of the Grid. A value of 0 indicates that there is no partition.

The Grid also has a GridLineColor property that is not demonstrated here but can be modified from the command window easily by invoking the Visual FoxPro color picker dialog box with the following code:

```
grdDemo1.PageFrame1.Page1.Grid1.GridLineColor = GETCOLOR()
```

Properties with a List of Options

Two of the three drop-down lists on the Grid Properties page (for setting the *GridLines property* and the *ScrollBars property*) should be self-explanatory. Note that setting the ScrollBars property to "2 - Vertical" or "0 -None" also removes the rectangle used to drag the partition. However, it is still possible to set the Partition property in code, even if there is no horizontal scroll bar.

The third drop-down list for the *Panel Property* indicates whether the right or left panel is active when the Partition property is set to a value greater than 0.

Properties with On and Off Values

The CheckBoxes on the Grid properties page turn various features of the Grid Control on or off. The *DeleteMark property*, which defaults to .T., places a small rectangular column visible to the left of each record on the Grid's border. This column shows the DELETED() status of each record, and enables the deleting and recalling of records by clicking the DeleteMark column with the mouse.

The *HighLight property* either enables (.T.) or overrides (.F.) the Column object's SelectOnEntry property. The HighLight property defaults to .T., and therefore highlights the current cell when navigating with the arrow keys or the Tab key.

The *PanelLink property* determines whether the two panels that are created when you set the Partition property to a value greater than 0 are synchronized and scroll together. Note that in order to see the effect of setting this property to .F., you must scroll the current panel. Simply moving the record pointer will move the record pointer in *both* panels, creating the illusion that they are still synchronized. Once the record pointer is moved so that the current panel scrolls, you will see that the other panel does not and the two panels scroll independently.

When it is set to .T., the *RecordMark property* places a rectangular box with a 3-D look to the left of each record in the Grid. This indicates the current record with a small triangle.

The *ReadOnly property* determines whether the Grid can be used to edit table values, or if it is being used only for viewing the table. The Grid also has an Enabled property that prevents the Grid from receiving focus. You can also set the Enabled property for individual columns.

Principal Grid Events and Methods

While the Grid has a Click event, it is of extremely limited value. The only way the Click event can be triggered is by scrolling the Grid to its rightmost extreme to reveal the space beyond the last column. Then you must click that area. If you want to respond to the Click or DoubleClick event, you should do so in the object contained in the Grid's columns.

You can often achieve your intent by using the *MouseDown event* or *MouseUp event*. For an example of this, see the program notes for GRDDEMO1.SCX in this section.

The control object contained in the Grid column is the object used to populate the Grid cells. It retains all of its event-trapping capabilities, trapping events such as LostFocus, GotFocus, When, Valid, KeyPress, and Click. However, the Grid itself has two events, the *AfterRowColChange event* and the *BeforeRowColChange event*. These can be thought of as a cell-level GotFocus and LostFocus, respectively.

Trap!

The Visual FoxPro documentation states that an argument is automatically passed to the AfterRowColChange() method and the BeforeRowColChange() method, which is the column *index* of the active cell in which the event is triggered. The argument is referred to as nColIndex in the documentation, and is actually the value of the Grid's ActiveColumn property. This may simply be a case of a poor choice of words in the documentation, but describing this value as a column index implies that it can be used with the Grid's Column() property to determine which column the event has occurred in without regard to its position. As it stands, if the Column's Movable property is set to .T., the Column(nColIndex) in AfterRowColChange() or BeforeColChange() cannot be used to reliably return a reference to the current Column control object.

To see this behavior, place a Grid on a Form with the RecordSource set to the customer sample table. Set the ColumnCount to 5 and change the Header captions to "First" through "Fifth."

Continued on next page

> **In the AfterRowColChange() method, place the following code:**
>
> ```
> LPARAMETERS nColIndex
> WAIT CLEAR
> WAIT "AfterRowColChange - nColIndex: " + ;
>    LTRIM(STR(nColIndex)) + CHR(13) + ;
>    This.Columns(nColIndex) .Header1.Caption WINDOW NOWAIT
> ```
>
> **Run the Form and observe that the WAIT WINDOW accurately displays the column index and Header caption for the currently active column. Now drag one of the columns to a new position and note that moving the active cell to that column no longer accurately reports either value in the WAIT WINDOW.**

Which event you use in which situation depends on exactly when you want your method code to execute. The following list contains the event sequence for the Grid's AfterRowColChange and BeforeRowColChange, and a contained object's When, Valid, GotFocus, and LostFocus events. The list covers the sequence as the first cell of the Grid becomes active as the user tabs into the Grid, then moves to the next cell:

Order	Event
1	Contained object When event
2	Contained object GotFocus event
3	Grid AfterRowColChange event
4	Cell is active
5	Grid BeforeRowColChange event
6	Contained object Valid event
7	Contained Object LostFocus event

Notice that entering the Grid triggers the AfterRowColChange event, even though you may not think of the row or column as having been changed.

Other events that can be trapped and used to trigger the execution of code are the *Deleted event,* which occurs when a record is deleted, and the *Scrolled event,* which is triggered when the Grid display is scrolled up or down.

Navigating a Grid in Code

Two methods are available to allow you to perform navigation in a Grid. These methods are important because the RelativeRow, RelativeColumn, ActiveRow, and ActiveColumn properties are read-only.

The ActivateCell() method is useful for activating a specific cell that is visible in the Grid. This method accepts two arguments that correspond to the RelativeRow and RelativeColumn properties of the cell that you want to be active.

As with any table, Goto <Record No.>, Seek(), and Locate can be used to position the record pointer on a particular record. If any of these are used, it is necessary to call the Grid's Refresh() method so that the Grid changes to reflect the current record pointer. However, it is possible to use the Grid's DoScroll() method to scroll the Grid to the desired section of the table, then use the ActivateCell() method to make a particular cell active. DoScroll accepts a single argument that can be one of the eight different values shown in the following table.

Scroll command	Scroll action
0	Scroll up
1	Scroll down
2	Scroll page up
3	Scroll page down
4	Scroll left
5	Scroll right
6	Scroll page left
7	Scroll page right

Remember that these directions ("up" and "right") refer to the movement of the record pointer, or to shifts of the Grid's LeftColumn property.

Font Settings for the Grid

The Grid has the full complement of font settings, as does the column object. However, while the font properties of a contained object, a column object, and the Grid can all be set independently at design time, changing the Grid's font properties at runtime will override both the column and contained object's settings. Changing the column's font properties at runtime will override the contained object's settings.

Column Properties

You can manipulate some of the columns' properties on page 3 of GRDDEMO1.SCX, the Column Properties page.

Figure 8-4.

GRDDEMO1.SCX
Page 3 at runtime

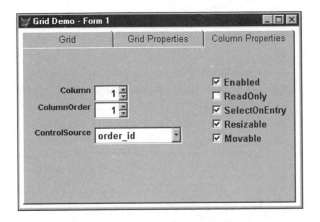

The Column spinner determines which column the other settings will affect. Note that as the column number is changed, the ControlSource property changes to show the specified column's ControlSource property. The ControlSource for a Grid column is the same in concept as the ControlSource for any other control, but in this case you must set the ControlSource to a field name.

Although it cannot be manipulated by this Form, each column also has a *Bound property.* The setting of this property determines if the ControlSource of the contained controls is set by specifying the ControlSource for the column, or if it is set by setting the property of the individual contained control. If the Bound property is set to .T., the ControlSource for the contained controls is the same as the one specified for the column. If the Bound property is set to .F., the ControlSource can be set for the individual controls.

When it is set to .T., the *Movable property* determines that the column can be dragged to a new position using the mouse. The *ColumnOrder property* changes the display order of a column and the value for Grid.ActiveColumn when that column is active. However, it does not change the column's position in the Columns property, nor does it change any of the column's heading properties. It is simply a way of programmatically achieving the same effect as dragging a column to a new position.

The *Resizeable property* determines whether the user can change the width of the column at runtime. The column has both an Enabled property and a ReadOnly property.

The Dynamic Column Properties

There are circumstances where it is convenient for certain properties to be evaluated automatically at runtime. The Grid column has a whole series of properties that are designed for just this purpose. All of these dynamic properties accept a character-type value. The character string stored to these properties is evaluated at runtime, and the result must be a data type appropriate to the property being dynamically set. To demonstrate some of these, you can enter some of the upcoming commands into the command window. You can get set up by running GRDDEMO1.SCX and making the following assignment:

```
oDemo = grdDemo1.PageFrame1.Page1.Grid1
```

Trap!

When you are making an assignment of a Form object to a memvar from the command window in this manner, you will not be able to release the Form by using the Close option from the control menu as you normally would. This is because there will still be an object reference to one of its objects. The Form will still appear to be active, and you will not be able to close it. When you're through with this exercise, issue a RELEASE oDemo in the command window *before* closing the Form. If you forget and try (unsuccessfully) to close the Form from the command menu, issuing the RELEASE oDemo command will allow the Form to close.

DynamicAlignment Property

```
oDemo.Columns(3).DynamicAlignment =
   "IIF(MOD(oDemo.ActiveRow,2)=0,0,1)"
```

You can use the Grd.MouseUp event to trigger the updating of the TextBoxes on the "Grid Properties" page that display the Partition, RelativeRow, and Relative Column properties in response to dragging the partition or columns to new positions.

DynamicBackColor Property

oDemo.Columns(2).DynamicBackcolor = ;
   "IIF(MOD(oDemo.ActiveRow,2)#0,RGB(0,255,0),RGB(255,255,255))"
oDemo.Columns(3).DynamicBackcolor = ;
   "IIF(MOD(oDemo.ActiveRow,2)=0,RGB(0,255,0),RGB(255,255,255))"
oDemo.Columns(1).DynamicBackcolor = ;
   "IIF(MOD(oDemo.ActiveRow,2)=0,RGB(0,255,0),RGB(255,255,255))"
oDemo.SetFocus()

These commands cause the odd-numbered cells in column 2 and the even-numbered rows in columns 1 and 3 to have a green BackColor. This creates a checkerboard effect.

While these examples use the ActiveRow property, any string expression that evaluates to an appropriate data type for the property being set can be used. The actual determination of the properties can be based on the value of a particular field, a public memvar, the record number, or the relationship between the values of two or more fields.

The full list of all the dynamic properties is as follows:

> DynamicBackColor
> DynamicForeColor
> DynamicAlignment
> DynamicCurrentControl
> DynamicFontBold
> DynamicFontItalic
> DynamicFontName
> DynamicFontUnderline
> DynamicFontStrikeThru
> DynamicFontSize
> DynamicForeColor
> DynamicFontOutline (FoxPro for the Macintosh only)
> DynamicFontShadow (FoxPro for the Macintosh only)

Programming Notes on GRDDEMO1.SCX

Much of what is used in this Form has been presented before in this report. You might want to review the code for the Form.Resize() method, which resizes the PageFrame, and the PageFrame1.Resize() method, which then resizes the Grid relative to the PageHeight and PageWidth properties.

New techniques presented with GRDDEM01.SCX include:

- The use of the Grid.MouseUp event to trigger the updating of the partition, RelativeRow display, and RelativeColumn displays in response to dragging the partition or columns to new positions.
- The use of the AfterRowColumnChange event to update all of the read-only properties that are displayed on the "Grid" page as the user navigates through the Grid. Of particular note is the use of the With...EndWith syntax for setting multiple properties or setting the properties of multiple objects contained within another object. The following code sets the Value property of six objects contained in the Grid's parent object. Notice that you only have to type "This.Parent" once!

```
WITH This.Parent
   .txtActiveRow.Value = This.ActiveRow
   .txtActiveColumn.Value = This.ActiveColumn
   .txtLeftColumn.Value = This.LeftColumn
   .txtRelativeRow.Value = This.RelativeRow
   .txtRelativeColumn.Value = This.RelativeColumn
   .txtValue.Value = This.Value
ENDWITH
```

- On "Page2," the Grid properties page of the PageFrame, the spnColumnCount.InteractiveChange() method code includes a line that sets the RecordSource for the Grid after the ColumnCount property has been changed. The Grid control does not have a Requery() method for the List objects, and calling the Grid's Refresh() method will not cause the Grid to reflect the change in the ColumnCount property. Whenever a change is made to the underlying table at runtime, you need to reset the Grid's RecordSource property. This includes changing the ColumnCount.

- The three drop-down list boxes are constructed in such a way that their ListIndex value can be used to set the appropriate Grid property.

- The spinners and ComboBox on Page3, the Column Properties page of the PageFrame, all use their UIEnable event to "self-refresh" when this page is activated. This is based on changes that may have occurred elsewhere in the PageFrame.

Using Grids to Display Data from Related Tables

GRDDEMO2.SCX and GRDDEMO3.SCX

The sample Forms GRDDEMO2.SCX and GRDDEMO3.SCX show how data from tables in a one-to-many parent and child relationship can be displayed using the Grid Control.

On both Forms, the Grid column widths and column orders are set at design time and are not meant to be changed at runtime. GRDDEMO2 is set up to allow navigation through the customer table using the navigation buttons at the bottom, and to display a list of each customer's orders in the Grid Control. The Grid Control in this Form is read-only.

GRDDEMO3 is a similar Form, but is set up so you can view individual orders. It shows each order's line items in the Grid Control. In this Form, the Grid allows table contents to be edited.

GRDDEMO3 can be launched from the command window in the way you have been doing throughout this report. It can also be launched from within GRDDEMO2 in two ways: by double-clicking a record in the Grid, or by clicking the Edit CommandButton at the lower right of the Form. Note that the Edit CommandButton shows which order it will display in GRDDEMO3 when it is launched. This way, the user knows what the Edit CommandButton will do even if the Grid does not have focus prior to selecting it.

The important feature in both Forms is that the relationship between the two tables is established in each Form's DataEnvironment. Once this is done, it is simply a matter of setting the parent table's fields as the ControlSource for the Form's TextBoxes and other non-Grid controls, and setting the child table as the RecordSource for the Grid.

Note that in the case of GRDDEMO2, the relationship is the default persistent relationship that can be seen in the Database Designer. The relationship is automatically established when the Customer and Orders tables are added to the DataEnvironment. However, in the case of GRDDEMO3, the relationship between Orders and Customers is established in the DataEnvironment, as you want the Orders table to be the master table in the relationship. Note that because the master table is specified as the InitialSelectedAlias property in the DataEnvironment, it is not necessary for the navigation code (the same code used in the customer editing example Form constructed at the end of the section on basic Control objects) to select a work area. This is because no change has been made to the work area anywhere else on the Form.

It is not necessary to establish the relationship in the DataEnvironment. There are three properties of the Grid Control object that can be used when the tables are not related in code or in the DataEnvironment. A Grid that will display the records of the child table can specify the appropriate index order for that table using the *ChildOrder property*, the alias of the parent table using its *LinkMaster property*, and the relationship with the parent table using the *RelationalExpression property*.

Programming Notes on GRDDEMO2.SCX

- A call to the Refresh() method of the cmdEdit button has been added to the SetButtons() method. The cmdEdit.Refresh() sets the caption of the cmdEdit button to "Edit" + orders.Order.ID. This is the same call that has been added to the Grid's AfterRowColChange() method.
- The Grid.Init() makes use of the SetAll() method to set the Movable and Resizeable properties of all of the Grid columns. That code is shown here:

```
This.SetAll("Resizeable",.F.,"Column")
This.SetAll("Movable",.F.,"Column")
```

- GRDDEMO3 is launched by the Click() method of the cmdEdit object:

```
DO FORM grddemo3 WITH orders.order_id
```

- As discussed previously, it is not practical to use the Grid's Click or DblClick events, so method code has been provided for the DblClick events of the five TextBox objects contained by the Grid's columns. Rather than write method code to perform the same task as the cmdEdit.Click() method, the TextBox's DblClick() method code simply uses the following syntax:

```
ThisForm.cmdEdit.Click()
```

GRDDEMO2.SCX makes use of another technique that bears some discussion.

As pointed out earlier in this section in the discussion about GRDDEMO1.SCX, setting the Grid's ColumnCount to -1 automatically creates as many columns as needed to display all fields of the table. This also has the added benefit of substituting the field names or the field captions (if any) for the default Header captions. This handy behavior is lost when the ColumnCount property is set to 1 or more.

It seems a shame to carefully establish a user-friendly caption for the table fields only to lose access to them in the Grid Control. However, don't worry. This capability hasn't been lost, it just isn't automatic.

To regain this behavior, you must retrieve the field captions from the database container or .DBC file where the information is stored. Visual FoxPro includes a DBGETPROP() function that can be used to return any database property stored in the .DBC. This includes field captions. Once you know how to use the function, it's simply a matter of placing the function with the proper arguments into the Caption property of your Headers using the Expression Builder.

If you look at the Caption property for any of the Headers in GRDDEMO2.SCX, and examine the line of code placed there in the Expression Builder, you will see the following:

```
DBGETPROP(This.Parent.ControlSource,"Field","Caption")
```

This command retrieves the field Caption property from the .DBC and uses it as the Header's caption. If there is no Caption property for a particular field, an empty string is returned.

Note that DBGETPROP() will trigger an error if there is no open database selected when it is called. Note that you must have the .DBC file open in order for the DBGETPROP() function to work. To accomplish this, the following code should appear in the BeforeOpenTables event method of the DataEnvironment object:

```
OPEN DATABASE testdata
```

The following code should appear in the AfterCloseTables event method of the DataEnvironment object:

```
SET DATABASE TO testdata
CLOSE DATABASES
```

Trap!

In the previous paragraphs, the term "should appear" was used, rather than "appears." This is because of a rather nasty bug that existed during the beta testing. Microsoft thought it was eradicated, but it appears to have survived in the initial release. This bug causes Visual FoxPro to swap the code in these two methods. Fortunately the methods aren't used too frequently, and there is an easy, albeit "kludgey," work-around. If you examine the BeforeOpenTables() and AfterCloseTables() methods of GRDDEMO2.SCX, you will see the following code in *both* methods:

```
DO CASE
CASE "AFTERCLOSETABLES" $ PROGRAM()
   SET DATABASE TO testdata
   CLOSE DATABASES
CASE "BEFOREOPENTABLES" $ PROGRAM()
   OPEN DATABASE testdata
ENDCASE
```

The advantage of using this technique is that if a field caption is changed at some future date, it will also change the Headers for columns bound to this field.

Finally, take a look at the InputMask and Format properties for Grid1.Column5.Text1, and the Sparse property for Grid1.Column5. The ControlSource for this column is Orders.Order_Net, which is a currency data-type field. The InputMask and Format properties allow the data to be displayed in the desired format. The importance of the Sparse property will be explained in the context of the next example, GRDDEMO4.SCX.

Programming Notes on GRDDEMO3.SCX

The Init() method code in both GRDDEMO2.SCX and GRDDEMO3.SCX should look familiar, as it's the same Init() code used in the Customer Editing Form constructed at the end of the section on basic control objects. This code sets the Form properties to keep track of the top and bottom record number so that the navigation buttons can be properly enabled or disabled. However, in GRDDEMO3.SCX it must be able to accept a parameter passed from GRDDEMO2.SCX that represents the order number, which should be initially displayed by GRDDEMO3.SCX. To do this, the code listed in boldface was added to the following code:

```
LPARAMETERS tcOrderNo
ThisForm.AutoCenter = .T.
ThisForm.BorderStyle = 2
GOTO BOTTOM
ThisForm.nBottomRecord=RECNO()
GOTO TOP
ThisForm.nTopRecord = RECNO()
IF TYPE("tcOrderNo") = "C"
   SEEK tcOrderNo
ENDIF
ThisForm.SetButtons()
```

This Form also has settings for Grid1.Column2.Text1.InputMask, Column2.Sparse, Column3.Text1.InputMask, Column3.Text1.Format, and Column3.Sparse.

Special Grid Features

GRDDEMO4.SCX

The next example Form demonstrates several additional features of the Grid Control, and displays data from the Products table. Run GRDDEMO4.SCX and observe the following:

- The font properties for the second (Description) column are set for a Times New Roman, 13-point, bold typeface.
- The "On Hand" column displays the table's numeric In_Stock field using a Spinner Control instead of a TextBox.
- The Grid's RowHeight property has been changed from the default value of 19 pixels to 25 pixels to accommodate the Spinner object.
- The Price column displays the table's currency-type Unit_Price field with only two of the four decimal places, and with the currency character displayed as specified by the current Set Currency setting.
- The Discontinued column displays the table's logical Discontinued field using a CheckBox.

The data displayed in a Grid cell whose column's *Sparse property* is set to .T. (the default) will display its data in an unformatted

TextBox until the cell becomes active. When the cell is active, the data is displayed using the contained control, and any formatting properties are applied. The Sparse property for the On Hand, Price, and Discontinued columns is set to .F.. As a result, all of the cells display each column's data using its contained control, and any InputMask and Format properties are also in effect for all cells.

While GRDDEMO4.SCX is running, make the cell at Row 1 and Column 1 active. Then change the Sparse property for Column 3 (the On Hand column) from .F. to .T. in the command window. Observe the effect:

```
GrdDemo4.Grid1.Columns(3).Sparse = .T.
```

You will see that all of the spinners in the third column will disappear, and each cell will instead display the In_Stock field's value in its native 12-digit, three-decimal, numeric format.

Now use the following code for the fourth (Price) column:

```
GrdDemo4.Grid1.Columns(4).Sparse = .T.
```

Because the contained control in Column 4 is a TextBox (the default control in the Grid column), this control doesn't change. However, note that the InputMask and Format properties are no longer applied, and the data from the Unit_Price field is again displayed in its native currency format.

Now that you have changed the Sparse property of these two columns, return focus to the Form and navigate to one of these columns with the mouse, the tab key, or the arrow keys. You will see that as each of these cells becomes active, the format of the data changes to reflect the contained object and its formatting.

Setting the Sparse property to .T., particularly for a Grid populated with many graphical controls, can improve the responsiveness and the speed of screen repaints.

Trap!

A problem can occur with CheckBoxes being used to display logical field data as in Column 5 of this example. If users use a mouse click to make a cell in Column 5 active, they will also be changing the value of whatever record they click.

Runtime Modification of the Grid

Close the GRDDEMO4.SCX Form. Then create a public variable from the command window with the following code:

```
_USERNAME = "GRUNT"
```

Rerun GRDDEMO4.SCX. The Form and Grid appear just as the did before.

Close the Form again, and, in the command window, change the value of _USERNAME as shown:

```
_USERNAME = "SUPERVISOR"
```

Now rerun the Form. You will see that a column displaying the table's Unit_Cost field has been added to the Grid. The *AddColumn()* *method* and *DeleteColumn() method* have been included in the Grid's Init() method for this purpose.

You can also add and remove controls from a column at runtime using the column's AddObject() and RemoveObject() methods. A column can actually contain more than one object. The total number of these is reflected in the column's ControlCount property. However, only one control can be active at any time. That control can be selected by the setting the CurrentControl property.

Programming Notes on GRDDEMO4.SCX

The Grid.Init() method code determines whether the additional sixth column (Unit Cost) should to be added, then it adds the column. Note the use of the With...EndWith syntax, and the adjustment of the second (Description) column's size.

```
IF TYPE("_USERNAME") = "C" AND ;
    UPPER(_USERNAME) = "SUPERVISOR"
  This.AddColumn(6)
  WITH This.Column6
    .ControlSource="Products.Unit_Cost"
    .BackColor = RGB(255,255,0)
    .Sparse = .F.
    .Width = 69
    .Movable = .F.
    .Resizeable = .F.
    .Header1.Caption = "Cost"
    .Header1.Alignment = 2
    .Text1.InputMask = "999.99"
    .Text1.Format = "$"
    .Text1.Alignment = 2
  ENDWITH
  This.Column2.Width = This.Column2.Width - 69
ENDIF
```

A Developer's Tool—NiceBrowser

This Form has been refined over several months and is a handy table inspection tool. It uses a Grid object in a Form to replace a program module that was used with FoxPro 2.x, and demonstrates several Visual FoxPro features that you might find useful in your production applications.

To use NICEBROW.SCX, you can open a table that you want to examine and then run NICEBROW.SCX. Alternatively, you can simply run NICEBROW.SCX from the command line and wait to be prompted for a table. Note that in Visual FoxPro, the USE ? command first prompts for a database container (.DBC file), and then it allows you to choose from one of the contained tables. If you want to select a free table, or to select a table without opening the database container first, select the Other CommandButton. To demonstrate this Form, open the Orders table that is part of the TESTDATA database.

Figure 8-5.

Browsing the Orders table with NICEBROW.SCX

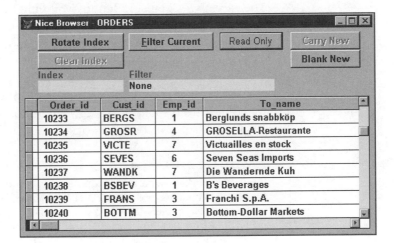

You are presented with a resizeable, centered Form with a Grid displaying the table contents. The Grid's ReadOnly property is set to .T., and all of the fields can be sized but not moved. If any index tags are in effect at startup, they will be cleared. The ColumnCount property is set to -1 so that all table fields are displayed.

At the top left is a graphical CheckBox with the caption "Rotate Index." Just below it is a disabled CommandButton with the caption "Clear Index."

The function of the "Rotate Index" CheckBox is to dynamically enable the automatic setting of the table's index order as the user moves from column to column. This works only for those index tags that have the same name as the current field. The "Clear Index" CommandButton, enabled when an index order is set, clears the current index. The Label just below these two controls shows the index tag currently in effect.

To the right of the "Rotate Index" CheckBox is a "Filter Current" CommandButton that filters the table according to the value of the currently active cell. When clicked, it sets the filter, refreshes the Grid, and changes its caption to "Clear Filter." Clicking it again clears the current filter. The Label just below this control shows the filter expression currently in effect. Note that a ToolTip for this control alerts the user to the availability of a hotkey (F12) to perform this function as well.

Next to the "Filter Current" CommandButton is a Read-Only CommandButton that toggles the ReadOnly property of the Grid. It also changes the BackColor property of the Grid to alert the user to the fact that they can modify the table.

The next two CommandButtons will either add a blank record or carry the contents of the current record to the new record. If the table being examined is part of a database and has a primary key, the Carry New CommandButton is disabled to avoid triggering the error that occurs if the uniqueness of a primary key is violated. More information on this and the other database container-related features of this Form can be found in Doug Hennig's report on the Visual FoxPro Data Dictionary in this book.

Trap!

If you are working with a table that is part of a database container (as are all the tables in the TESTDATA database), you could also trigger the "Uniqueness of <field name> Is Violated" error when using the Blank New CommandButton. If the table already has a record with a blank value in a primary key field, doing a second Append Blank will cause you to have two records with blank primary key field values. Then the error will occur.

Programming Notes on NICEBROW.SCX

In the Form.Load() method, the following code checks to see if a table is open. It then prompts the user for a table name. If the table is not free, the method ensures that the table's .DBC is opened so that the "Carry New" CommandButton can be disabled if necessary.

```
IF EMPTY(USED())
  USE ?
ENDIF
IF ! EMPTY(USED()) AND ! EMPTY(CURSORGETPROP("database"))
  OPEN DATA (CURSORGETPROP("database"))
ENDIF
```

To enable the F12 hotkey for setting a filter on the current Grid value, the following line is placed in the Form.Activate() method:

```
ON KEY LABEL F12 nicebrow.cmdFilter.click()
```

The following code is placed in the Form.Deactivate() method so that this hotkey is disabled when the Form loses focus. It also directs output to the Visual FoxPro _SCREEN instead of the Form:

```
ON KEY LABEL F12
ACTIVATE SCREEN
```

The Form.Init() method code disables the "Carry New" CommandButton when necessary. The DBGETPROP() function is used again, this time checking to see if the table has a primary key. Note that the "Carry New" button should also be disabled if the table has a candidate key (which also must be unique), but the DBGETPROP() function cannot return this information. However, the CANDIDATE() function could be used. The Init() method also checks to see if you still have not opened a table. If you haven't, it aborts the Form by returning a value of .F..

The Init() code finishes up by centering the Form and setting the Form's caption to the alias of the table. The Form's Resize() method is called to size the Grid within the Form. Also, any current filters or index tags are cleared.

```
IF EMPTY(USED())
  RETURN .F.
ELSE
  IF ! EMPTY(DBC()) AND ! ;
      EMPTY(DBGETPROP(ALIAS(),"Table","PrimaryKey"))
    ThisForm.cmdCarry.Enabled = .F.
  ENDIF
ENDIF
ThisForm.AutoCenter = .T.
thisform.caption = thisform.caption + " - " + ALIAS()
ThisForm.Resize()
SET FILTER TO
SET ORDER TO
```

Because the column properties cannot be set at design time when the ColumnCount property is set to -1, the following line in the Grid's Init() method sets all of the column's Movable property:

```
This.SetAll("Movable",.F.)
```

When you change the Grid's index order while the Grid has focus, the Grid attempts to retain the current record displayed in the Grid. Unfortunately, it does so by preserving the record displayed in the *first row* of the Grid, and allows the remainder of the displayed records to fall where they may. The net effect is that the record pointer is moved, which is not what you want. The following code, with comments, is placed in the Grid's AfterRowColumnChange() method to get the desired effect. That means that it retains the current record pointer as the user moves horizontally from one column to the next.

In a production application, this code might be better placed in the When() method of a contained control so that the ControlSource of the Control's column (the control's Parent object) can be determined. This makes it possible (if desired) to allow the user to change the position of the column and still be able to determine the likely name of the index tag associated with the current column.

This code keeps two pieces of information stored to two Form properties, cCurrField (the field name specified by the current column's ControlSource) and uCurrFldValue (the Grid's current Value property). This is done so that the information is preserved when the Grid loses focus.

```
PARAMETER pnColumn
* Store the current field and its value
thisform.cCurrField = this.columns(pnColumn).controlsource
thisform.uCurrFldValue = this.Value
* Check to see if you are "rotating" the index and
* if the current field name is also a valid index
* tag using the form's IsTag() method
IF ThisForm.chkRotate.Value AND ;
     ThisForm.IsTag(thisform.cCurrField)
  * Store the current record pointer
  lnRecNo = RECNO()
  * Store the current RelativeRow
  lnRelativeRow = This.RelativeRow
  * Change the index order
  SET ORDER TO TAG thisform.cCurrField
  * Lock the screen so the gyrations of the Grid
  * do not offend our aesthetic sensibilities
  ThisForm.LockScreen = .T.
  * Refresh the Grid
```

Continued on next page

```
this.refresh()
* At this point the record pointer has probably changed
* so you need to restore it
GOTO lnRecNo
* refresh the Grid again
this.refresh()
* In many cases the foregoing code has changed
* the RelativeRow, and you need to restore it to
* the value it had before you changed the table's
* index
DO WHILE This.RelativeRow < lnRelativeRow
   This.DoScroll(0) && Scroll up
ENDDO
DO WHILE This.RelativeRow > lnRelativeRow
   This.DoScroll(1) && Scroll down
ENDDO
* Now that you're through messing about with it,
* turn the screen back "on"
ThisForm.LockScreen = .F.
* Enable the cmdClearIDX CommandButton as
* you now have an index tag to clear
ThisForm.cmdCLearIDX.Enabled = .T.
* update the caption showing the current index order
ThisForm.lblIndex.caption=ORDER()
ENDIF
```

Here is the code in the Form's IsTag() method. It simply cycles through all of the table's index tags and determines if the current field matches with one of the tag names:

```
LPARAMETERS pcTag
LOCAL i, llRetVal
llRetVal = .F.
i=1
DO WHILE ! EMPTY(TAG(i))
 IF UPPER(pcTag) == TAG(i)
   llRetVal = .T.
   EXIT
 ENDIF
 i=i+1
ENDDO
RETURN llRetVal
```

The Click() method code of the "Filter Current" CommandButton performs a toggling operation on the Form property cFilteExp. cFilteExp is the value that would be returned by the Set("Filter") function on a filtered table. It then evaluates the data type and constructs an appropriate filter expression based on the name of the current field (Form.cCurrField) and the value of the currently active cell (Form.uCurrFldValue). Note that, if necessary, this code will have to be modified to accommodate the new Visual FoxPro data types such as Integer, Currency, and DateTime. As written here, it will filter only on character, logical, or numeric fields. This method code also changes the caption of the CommandButton to "Clear Filter" when a filter is applied to the table. In addition, it updates the label showing the filter expression and refreshes the Grid.

```
IF ! EMPTY(thisform.cFiltExp)
   thisform.cFiltExp = ""
ELSE
   DO CASE
   CASE TYPE("thisform.uCurrFldValue") = "C"
      thisform.cFiltExp= thisform.cCurrField + ;
         " = '" + thisform.uCurrFldValue + "'"
   CASE TYPE("thisform.uCurrFldValue") = "N"
      thisform.cFiltExp= thisform.cCurrField + ;
         " = " + LTRIM(STR(thisform.uCurrFldValue))
   CASE TYPE("thisform.uCurrFldValue") = "L"
      IF EVALUATE(thisform.uCurrFldValue) = .T.
         thisform.cFiltExp= thisform.cCurrField
      ELSE
         thisform.cFiltExp = "! " + thisform.cCurrField
      ENDIF
   OTHERWISE
      thisform.cFiltExp = ""
   ENDCASE
ENDIF
IF ! EMPTY(thisform.cFiltExp)
   lcFilt = thisform.cFiltExp
   SET FILTER TO &lcFilt
   thisform.lblFiltExp.Caption = thisform.cFiltExp
   thisform.cmdFilter.Caption = "Clear Filter"
ELSE
   SET FILTER TO
   thisform.lblFiltExp.Caption = "None"
   thisform.cmdFilter.Caption = "Filter Current"
ENDIF
thisform.Grid1.refresh()
```

The InteractiveChange() method of the Read-Only graphical CheckBox performs a series of property changes on both the Grid and itself, altering its Caption and ForeColor properties and changing the Grid's ReadOnly and BackColor properties.

```
IF this.Value = 1
    this.forecolor=RGB(255,0,0)
    this.caption="Read/Write"
    thisform.Grid1.backcolor=RGB(255,255,0)
    thisform.Grid1.ReadOnly=.F.
ELSE
    this.forecolor=RGB(0,0,0)
    this.caption="Read Only"
    thisform.Grid1.backcolor=RGB(255,255,255)
    thisform.Grid1.ReadOnly=.t.
ENDIF
```

Refreshing Grids When Changing Table Contents

One last point to make with regard to Grids is that the Refresh() method is not sufficient to update a Grid Control in some cases. Unlike the List objects, which have a convenient Requery() method that can be used to repopulate the list when a change is made to the underlying data source, you must employ a simple trick to accomplish the same task with a Grid.

This is often necessary when a Grid is populated by a query-generated or program-generated Cursor that may be rerun or rebuilt at some point. To demonstrate how the Grid is refreshed in this type of case, run NICEBROW.SCX again using the Orders table. Enter the following commands in the command window. (NICBROW.SCX does not employ a private DataSession, so you can manipulate the table from the command window.)

```
set fields to order_id, cust_id, emp_id
set fields on
nicebrow.Grid1.Refresh()
```

The last command will have no effect. As you will see when you reactivate the Form and navigate around the Grid, all of the fields are still visible. To get the Grid to refresh according to the field limitations you are trying to impose, issue the following command in the command window:

```
nicebrow.Grid1.RecordSource = "ORDERS"
```

This is somewhat akin to doing a Goto Recno() or doing a Combo1.ListIndex = Combo1.ListIndex. It makes no real change, but by setting the property Visual FoxPro is forced to update the control based on the "new" property setting.

9 | Special-Purpose Control Objects

Line Control

The Line Control appears at design time as a rectangular box, with the Line object appearing as a diagonal between two corners. Dragging the rectangular box into a single horizontal or vertical line creates a Line object that is horizontal or vertical. If you want a slanted Line object, you can determine the direction of the Line object's slant by using the *LineSlant property*. This can have one of two values, set by using either the backslash key (\) for lines sloping down and to the right, or the forward slash key (/) for lines sloping up and to the right.

The Line Control has a BorderStyle property that varies the line's appearance. The exception to this is a value of "0 - Transparent," which has an effect only when the object also has a BorderWidth property of 1. The settings are shown here:

Setting	Effect
0	Transparent
1	Solid (default)
2	Dash
3	Dot
4	Dash-Dot
5	Dash-Dot-Dot

The Line Control can respond to several events, including the DblClick, Click, RightClick, DragDrop, MouseUp, MouseDown, MouseMove, and UIEnable events.

The Line Control also possesses a somewhat arcane property, the *DrawMode property*. If you are an experienced Visual Basic programmer and have done a fair amount of work with graphic methods and animation, then the various DrawMode property values should be familiar to you. If not, however, you'll probably ignore this property until such a time when you really need to learn it.

Figure 9-1.

LINDEMO.SCX at runtime

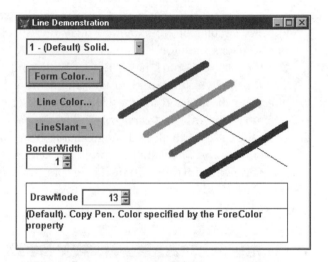

LINDEMO.SCX is a Form that demonstrates some of the properties of the Line Control. This includes the DrawMode property, which determines the interaction of the line and the object upon which it is drawn. In addition to using the LineSlant, ForeColor, BorderWidth, and BorderStyle properties, you should play around with the Form's BackColor property and the line's ForeColor property, observing the effect that the Line Object's DrawMode property has on the line's appearance.

The Shape Control

The Shape Control forms an object that can range from a rectangle to a circle or an ellipse. The outline of the shape is determined by the value of its *Curvature property*. This value can range from 0 (which causes the object to have right-angle corners), to 99 (which causes the object to have no straight sides and to appear as an ellipse or circle). It will appear as a circle only if the object's Height and Width properties are set to be *visually* equal. This is not the same as being set to the same pixel value! The aspect ratio of the pixels on a display are such that the width property of a perfect square or circle on the screen will be slightly larger than the value for the height property. The height-to-width ratio of 6 to 7 or .86 works fairly well. If you want a circular object 100 pixels high, it will need a horizontal dimension of about 116 pixels to appear circular. (Divide the height by .86 to derive the width, or multiply the width by .86 to derive the height).

If you do your development work at a screen resolution of 1280 x 1024 or higher, be aware that all lower screen resolutions have a slightly different aspect ratio to their pixels, so that what appears circular on your monitor may not appear perfectly circular on the user's monitor.

The Shape Control has a BorderWidth and BorderStyle property. The BorderStyle property can take the same values and has the same effects as those listed for the Line object. There is an undocumented seventh value of "6 - Inside solid" that appears in the property sheet, but it is virtually indistinguishable from the default setting of "1 - Solid." The SpecialEffects property, which allows either a flat or 3-D appearance for the border, is ignored unless the BorderStyle and the BorderWidth properties are set to 1, and the Curvature property is set to 0.

Figure 9-2.

SHPDEMO.SCX at runtime

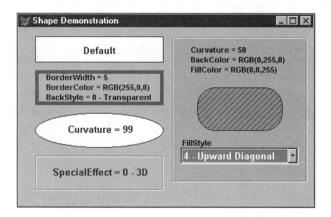

In addition to the border properties, a shape has a BackStyle property (opaque or transparent) and a BackColor property. The Shape object also has FillColor and FillStyle properties that determine the color or pattern that overlays the shape's background. The sample Form SHPDEMO.SCX illustrates the effect of these properties, and gives examples of shapes which use the properties that have been discussed.

Like the Line object, the Shape object can respond to events such as Click, DblClick, DragDrop, and UIEnable.

Image Control

The Image Control allows the placement of a bitmap image onto a Form. The name of the file containing the image to be displayed is placed in the Image Control's *Picture property*, and must be a .BMP file. The Image Control's *Stretch property* determines how the image is displayed, as shown in the following table:

Setting	Effect
0	Clip (default). The image is clipped to fit the control.
1	Isometric. The image resizes to fit the control while maintaining its original proportions.
2	Stretch. The image resizes to fit the control, but does not maintain its original proportions.

The default setting for the Stretch property, "0 - Clip," causes the control to automatically size itself to contain the image. Be sure that the Form design takes into account the size of the specified image.

The Isometric setting will resize the image to fit within the control while retaining the image's original aspect ratio. If the control's aspect ratio is different than that of the picture, the picture will size itself to be small enough to fit entirely within the control.

The Stretch setting allows the control's height and width settings to determine both the size and aspect ratio of the picture.

Figure 9-3.

IMGDEMO.SCX at runtime

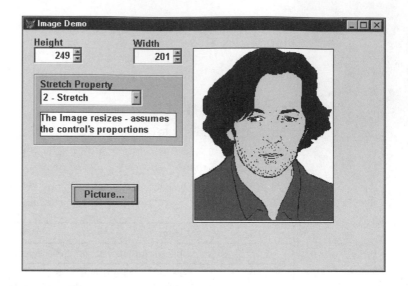

The included sample Form, IMGDEMO.SCX, allows you to see the effects of these three settings. The BorderStyle of the Image Control is set to "1 Fixed Single" so that you can see the relation of the Image Control's boundaries to the image which is placed in it.

If the Stretch property is set to clip the image, and the size of the image is changed using the height and width spinners, the significance of the term clip is evident. Note that setting the Stretch property to 1 or 2 and then resetting it back to 0 causes the Image Control to automatically resize itself, thereby displaying the entire image.

The picture used for this sample Form is TTSAMPLE.BMP, which is a portion of the SPLASH.BMP that ships with Visual FoxPro and is used in the Tastrade sample application. In addition to the bitmaps used for the CMDGRAPH demonstration Form (which you can select if you wish), two bitmaps that can be selected using the Picture... push button have also been included. You can display either CLAPTON.BMP or GATES.BMP, depending on your taste in heroes.

10 | Form Coordination and Interaction

While it is nice to have individual, independent Forms, the real world often dictates otherwise. For that reason, you need to understand how Forms can interact and communicate.

Multiple Simultaneous Forms

As demonstrated previously in Section 8, "The Grid Control Object," getting two or more Forms running simultaneously is child's play in Visual FoxPro. You have seen how you can launch one Form from within another while keeping the two Forms completely independent. This included keeping the Forms' DataEnvironments independent by setting each datasession property to "2 - Private."

While you will probably use Forms with private datasessions, there may also be times when you want to have the effect of two Forms that operate on the same DataEnvironment, or have two Forms that allow changes made in the first Form to affect the data displayed in the second.

Private datasessions are not barriers to achieving these effects.

Sharing a Private Datasession

If you instantiate a Form with a private datasession, and then instantiate a second Form that uses a public (default) datasession, you'll have two datasessions in use. However, if you launch a Form with a default datasession from within another Form that has a private datasession, the second Form will "share" the first Form's private datasession. If the second Form has a DataEnvironment that opens tables and sets relations, disaster may likely result when the second Form makes changes to the first Form's DataEnvironment.

If, on the other hand, the second Form has *no* tables or views open in its DataEnvironment, its controls can display and modify the tables that were opened by the first, or "launching" Form's DataEnvironment! This behavior is demonstrated in the two Forms MLTDEMO1.SCX and DISPLAY1.SCX.

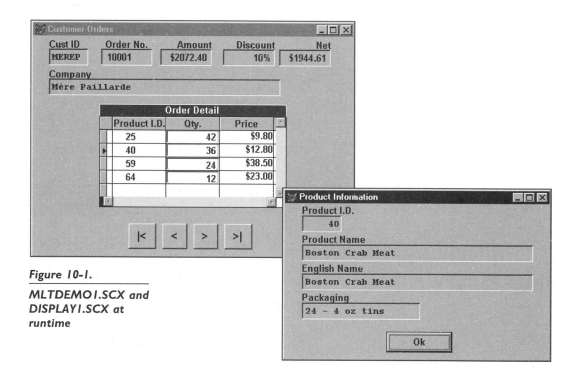

Figure 10-1.

MLTDEMO1.SCX and DISPLAY1.SCX at runtime

MLTDEMO1.SCX is a copy of the Form GRDDEMO3.SCX , which you saw in Section 8, "The Grid Control Object." GRDDEMO3.SCX displayed order information using a Grid to show the order details. It has been modified in two ways. First, another table (the Products table) has been added to the DataEnvironment. The relationship is established between the Product_ID of the OrdItems table and the ProductID of the Products table. Second, the DblClick() method for the TextBoxes contained within the Grid's columns have been given a single line of code:

```
DO FORM Display1
```

The Form DISPLAY1.SCX is about as minimalistic as you can get. It has four TextBoxes with their ControlSource properties set to the Products.Product_ID, Products.Prod_Name, Products.Eng_Name, and Products.No_In_Unit fields, and a single CommandButton that closes the Form. All of the fields have RETURN .F. in their WHEN() methods so that they cannot receive focus, and their BackColor properties are set to light gray as a visual cue that these are read-only fields. This Form also has its Datasession property set to "1 - Default" and its WindowType property set to "1 - Modal."

Running DISPLAY1.SCX from the command window will cause an Alias 'Products' Not Found error when it tries to instantiate the first TextBox. This should not be a surprise, as the Products table was not added to the DataEnvironment, nor was it opened in code in the Load() method or anywhere else.

However, if you run MLTDEMO1.SCX and double-click one of the rows of the Grid, DISPLAY1.SCX will be launched and will dutifully display the information for the product on the line of the Grid you clicked. Clicking the OK CommandButton will close the Form and allow you to return to the MLTDEMO1.SCX Form.

When using this technique, it's very important that the child Form is defined as *modal*. Otherwise, the user can close the parent Form, and take the child Form's DataEnvironment along with it!

These two example Forms illustrate another point that's important to the discussion of launching Forms from within Forms (either in this manner or as executed in Section 8, "The Grid Control Object"). In order to gain access to the command window while it's running, you can open DISPLAY1.SCX in the Form Designer and set its WindowType property to "0 - Modeless." Then close the Form Designer and save the Form. Run MLTDEMO1.SCX again. Launch DISPLAY1.SCX as you did before by double-clicking one of the items in the Grid Control.

If you've been checking and changing Form and Control properties from the command window as you've been reading this report, you might try to determine one of DISPLAY1's properties from the command window using this code:

```
? Display1.txtProductID.ControlSource
```

This will cause an "Alias DISPLAY Not Found" error, or, if you try to set one of the Form's properties, it will cause an "Object DISPLAY Is Not Found" error. This is because any reference variable for this Form is scoped to the method code in the TextBox's DblClick() method. Using the DO DISPLAY1 NAME frmDisplay syntax won't solve the problem either, because the variable frmDisplay will also be scoped to the DblClick() method.

Can you think of a way to solve this problem so that you can get a message to one of the DISPLAY1 Form's methods, or set one of its properties? If so, great! If not, never fear, you'll see how it's done in the next part.

Parent/Child Forms with Separate, Private Datasessions

The Forms MLTDEMO2 and DISPLAY2 are identical to the two Forms discussed in "Sharing A Private Datasession," but have been modified in several ways. They are both modeless Forms, and each has a private Datasession property. DISPLAY2 is launched from MLTDEMO2 just as it was in the previous example, displaying additional information about the products listed in the Grid Control.

In the case of these two Forms, reactivating MLTDEMO2 after launching DISPLAY2 and then navigating either from one record to another or from one cell to another in the Grid Control will refresh the display in DISPLAY2 to reflect the current product_ID. This product_ID is being displayed in the Grid's active row. The user can create only a single instance of DISPLAY2, and DISPLAY2 is automatically released when MLTDEMO2 is released.

For MLTDEMO2, the following changes were made:

- The Products table was removed from the DataEnvironment. DISPLAY2.SCX will have this table as part of its DataEnvironment.
- The property oChildForm was added, setting its value to an empty string. This property will serve as a reference to the child Form and enable MLTDEMO2 to determine if it has already launched the child Form. It will then enable the two to communicate.
- The code in MLTDEMO1's Grid.column.text1.DblClick() method was changed to the following:

```
IF TYPE("ThisForm.oChildForm") # "O"
   DO FORM DISPLAY2 WITH ThisForm, OrdItems.product_ID ;
      NAME ThisForm.oChildForm LINKED
ENDIF
```

This code first checks to see if the child Form is already running (oChildForm will have a type of "O" for "object" if it is). If the child Form has not been instantiated, the next line of code does so, using the NAME keyword so that it can be referenced by the parent Form's oChildForm property. The LINKED keyword will cause the child Form to be destroyed when the parent Form and its properties are destroycd.

- The following code was added to the Grid.AfterRowColChange() method:

```
IF TYPE("ThisForm.oChildForm") = "O"
   ThisForm.oChildForm.NewRecord(OrdItems.Product_ID)
ENDIF
```

This sends a message to the child Form, calling its NewRecord() method. This will move the record pointer in its DataEnvironment and refresh the controls.

The following changes were made to DISPLAY1.SCX for the DISPLAY2.SCX Form:

- The Datasession property was changed to "2 - Private."
- The WindowType was changed to "0 - Modeless."
- The Products table was added to the DataEnvironment with its order set to the Product_ID tag.
- The property oParentForm was added with its value set to an empty string.
- The following code was added to the Init() method:

```
LPARAMETERS toParentForm, tcProductID
ThisForm.oParentForm = toParentForm
SEEK tcProductID
```

This code stores a reference made to the parent Form to the oParentForm property of DISPLAY2. This enables DISPLAY2 to clear MLTDEMO2's oChildForm reference property when DISPLAY2 is closed.

- The following code was added to the Unload() method:

```
IF TYPE("ThisForm.oParentForm") = "O" AND !
ISNULL(ThisForm.oParentForm)
   ThisForm.oParentForm.oChildForm = ""
ENDIF
```

When an object is released, its reference variable remains, but with a .NULL. value. The preceding code checks to see if it is being unloaded as a result of the parent Form's destruction. If so, it doesn't need to do anything. If it is being closed and the parent Form is still instantiated, it needs to clear MLTDEMO2's oChildForm property so that MLTDEMO2 knows it can run DISPLAY2 if the user requests it.

- A new method was created. NewRecord() is shown here:

```
LPARAMETERS tcProductID
SEEK tcProductID
ThisForm.Refresh()
```

Form Sets

After reading the previous parts, you might wonder about screen sets.

Visual FoxPro does indeed have Form sets that conveniently allow multiple Forms to share a Datasession. However, it seems that their utility is greatly diminished given the greater flexibility outlined in the previous parts, the new private Datasession feature, and the new PageFrame Control.

As a result, the discussion of Form sets will not go into much depth, but will point out a few highlights.

A Form set is a composite object that is used to contain, or group, Form objects. It has its own DataEnvironment object, and can have a private Datasession. As with many other composite objects based on Visual FoxPro's BaseClasses, such as the PageFrame and the OptionGroup, the Form set has two properties that make referencing its Form members very easy: the *FormCount property* and the *Forms property*. The FormCount property indicates how many Forms are contained within a Form set, and the Forms property is an "array-like" property that holds a reference to each Form.

Forms can be added to and removed from Form sets at runtime using the AddObject() and RemoveObject() methods. Individual Forms can be made visible or hidden by using the Form's Show() and Hide() methods, and by using the Visible property.

Form sets are instantiated in the same way as a Form, by issuing the Do Form <formset> command.

Returning Values from Forms
RTNDEMO.SCX

If you are an experienced FoxPro developer, you have probably used a screen to return a value to a program. In FoxPro 2.x, it was simply a matter of placing a RETURN <expression> as the last line of the cleanup code.

Accomplishing this in Visual FoxPro is just as easy, but requires a slightly different approach.

A value is returned from a Form by placing the RETURN <expression> as the last line in the Form's Unload() method.

The expression that is returned cannot make reference to any control on the Form because all of the Form's objects have been destroyed by the time the Unload() method is triggered. This makes it necessary to store any value or values you expect to use in the Return expression in the Unload() method to a Form property.

Instead of calling the Form as a function as was done in FoxPro 2.x, a value can be returned from a Form in Visual FoxPro by using the following syntax:

```
DO FORM <form namd> TO <memvar>
```

When the Form is released, the value returned by the Unload() method is stored to the variable specified in the Do Form command.

Finally, the Form from which you are returning a value must be defined as a *modal* Form.

The sample Form RTNDEMO.SCX demonstrates this technique. To run it, execute the RTNDEMO.PRG program file, which will repeatedly call RTNDEMO to ask you a series of highly personal questions.

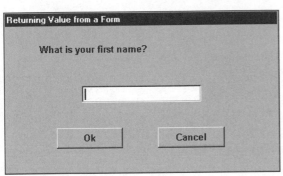

Figure 10-2.

RTNDEMO.SCX at runtime

There are several points about RTNDEMO.SCX that you should be aware of:

- Three arguments are passed—one to set the caption for the Form, one to set the caption for a message label, and one to set a string to be used as an InputMask for the TextBox. This parameter value not only formats the TextBox into which the user makes his entry, but is also used to size and center the field on the Form.

- If the Form does not receive three arguments from the calling program, it returns .F. from the Init() method so that the Form will not be instantiated.

- Even though the Form does not open any tables, the Datasession property has been set to "2 - Private." This enables you to use Set Confirm On and Set Bell Off in the Init() method, and not have to worry about saving or restoring these settings when the Form is released. Remember that these settings (among many others) are scoped to each datasession.

II Potpourri

This section will cover a bunch of miscellaneous Form and Form Designer features. While they are less central to the goal of bringing you up to speed with the Visual FoxPro Form Designer, these features are nonetheless important enough that you should become acquainted with them, even if it is for only a brief introduction.

Basic Drag and Drop

Drag and drop is one of Visual FoxPro's sexy new features. When it is carefully made part of the design, it brings a new level of intuitive user control to an application. Actual uses for drag and drop are almost literally limited only by your imagination.

DragMode Property

There are two ways to initiate a drag-and-drop action. The first and easiest way is to change an object's *DragMode property* from its default value of "0 - Manual" to "1 - Automatic." This automatically starts a drag operation when the user clicks an object. The user can then drag the object onto another object and release the mouse button, which triggers a *DragDrop event* (this will be explained shortly) for the object on which the dragged object is dropped. Then whatever code is contained in the DragDrop() method is executed.

The drawback of using this approach is that the Click event of the object is "intercepted" by the drag operation, and you cannot take any action exclusive of the initiation of the drag operation that you might want to be triggered by the Click event.

Drag() Method

The second way to initiate a drag-and-drop operation is to explicitly call an object's Drag() method. The Drag() method accepts the optional arguments shown in the following list:

Argument	Meaning
0	Cancel drag operation; restore original position of control.
1	Begin dragging the control (default).
2	End dragging; drop the control.

The Drag() method can be called at any time and from any method, but is usually called from the MouseDown() method code, or in some cases, in the MouseMove() method code.

DragDrop Event

The DragDrop event is triggered in the target object of a drag-and-drop operation. The DragDrop() method is automatically passed three arguments—a reference to the dropped object, and the x and y coordinates of the mouse pointer within the target object. The object reference of the dropped object is particularly useful as it gives the object for which the DragDrop event has been triggered access to all of the properties of the dropped object.

DragIcon Property

The default behavior of a dragged object is for it to appear as an outline of the object that can then be moved with the mouse pointer. The object itself does not move, only this outline representation. If you want to employ an icon in place of this outline, you can do so by specifying a Cursor (.CUR) file for the control object's DragIcon property.

Note that while the DragIcon property can be successfully changed at runtime, personal experience has shown that changing the property from a Cursor file to an empty character string (to restore the outline behavior) or vice-versa (to change the outline behavior to a the use of a special Cursor) does not work very well.

DragOver Event

The *DragOver event* is triggered in an object when another object is dragged over it. Its method is passed the same arguments that are contained in the DragDrop() method. However, the DragOver() method also has an nState parameter that determines whether the dragged object is entering the target object, leaving the target object, or is being moved within the target object. These arguments are shown here:

Argument	Meaning
0	Enter. The control is being dragged within the range of a target.
1	Leave. The control is being dragged out of the range of a target.
2	Over. The control has moved from one position in the target to another.

The DragOver event is particularly useful when you want to change a dragged object's DragIcon property to indicate to the user that the object can or cannot be dropped on a particular object.

It can also be used to change the appearance of the target object or other objects of the Form in response to the placement of an object being dragged.

Figure 11-1.

DNDDEMO.SCX at runtime

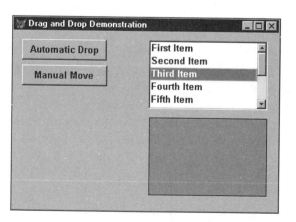

The sample file DNDDEMO.SCX demonstrates many of the drag-and-drop features. The Form consists of two CommandButtons captioned Automatic Drop and Manual Move; a list box with 10 items named First Item through Tenth Item; and a green Shape Control at the lower right.

The DNDDEMO.SCX Automatic Drop CommandButton

As you might suspect, the Automatic Drop CommandButton uses a DragMode setting of "1 - Automatic." Note that dragging and dropping the CommandButton to a different point on the Form, on the other CommandButton, or on the list box does not have any effect. This is because none of these objects have method code associated with their DragDrop events. However, the rectangular green Shape Control is a different story. You can see that dropping the Automatic Drop CommandButton onto this object does indeed evoke a response.

The DNDDEMO.SCX Manual Move CommandButton

The Manual Move CommandButton uses a setting of "0 - Manual" for its DragMode property. Its Drag() method is called by the MouseDown() method. The operation of this method code is simply to change the position of the control on the Form. Because the DragDrop() and MouseDown() methods are passed the coordinates of the mouse pointer and you want the control to assume the position of the outline, the MouseDown() method also uses the position of the mouse pointer to record the offset of the CommandButton's Top and Left properties. These values are stored to two Form properties, nXOffset and nYOffset. The MouseUp() method calls the Drag() method again, this time passing an argument of 2 to indicate that the object is being dropped.

The Form's DragDrop() method then verifies that it is indeed the Manual Move button that is being dropped. If it is, the method uses the mouse pointer's position and the Form's nXOffset and nYOffset properties to recalculate the Left and Top properties of the CommandButton.

Because you want to use the default outline appearance of this dragged object, you cannot (as already explained) assign it a DragIcon at runtime. However, you *can* change the appearance of a target object to indicate that the object cannot be dropped. Dragging the Manual Move CommandButton over the green Shape object causes the shape to change its color to red. Note that it is the mouse pointer, not the outlines of the object, that triggers this response.

The DNDDEMO.SCX ListBox Control

Unlike the Manual Move CommandButton whose Drag() method is called by the MouseDown() method, this technique won't have the desired effect for this control. You want to be able to select an item from the list, and in effect drag that one item. However, calling the

Drag() method from the MouseDown() method initiates the drag too soon because the item is not selected at that point. (Realize that even though it appears that only one item from the list is being dragged, the object being dragged is actually the entire list box.)

A new numeric property called nDragThreshold is established for the Form. Instead of calling the Drag() method from the MouseDown() method, it is called from the MouseMove() method as shown:

```
LPARAMETERS nButton, nShift, nXCoord, nYCoord
IF nButton = 1 && Left Mouse Button
   IF ABS(nXCoord - ThisForm.nMouseX) > ;
        ThisForm.nDragThreshold or ;
        ABS(nYcoord - ThisForm.nMouseY) > ;
        ThisForm.nDragThreshold
     This.Drag()
   ENDIF
ENDIF
```

The effect of all of this is that the user is able to select one of the items in the normal manner. However, if they keep the mouse button depressed and drag it more than the number of pixels specified in the Form's nDragThreshold property, the drag operation will be initiated.

When dragging begins, the mouse pointer changes to indicate this by using the DRAG1PG.CUR specified in the list box's DragIcon property. The list box's DragOver() event detects when the user drags the mouse pointer off of the list box because the nState parameter of the DragOver() event becomes 1. The list box's DragOver code then changes the list box's DragIcon to NODROP01.CUR, indicating that the user cannot drop the object on the Form.

Once the user drags the mouse pointer onto the green Shape object, the shape's DragOver event detects that the object being dragged can be dropped there. Once again it changes the list box's DragIcon to DROP1PG.CUR. Here is Shape1's DragOver() method code, which reacts to both the Manual Move CommandButton and the list box:

```
LPARAMETERS oSource, nXCoord, nYCoord, nState
DO CASE
CASE (nState = 0 OR nState = 2) AND ;
      UPPER(oSource.Name) = "CMDMANUALMOVE"
   This.BackColor = RGB(255,0,0)
CASE nState = 1 AND UPPER(oSource.Name) = "CMDMANUALMOVE"
   This.BackColor = RGB(0,255,0)
   ThisForm.lblDropped.ForeColor = RGB(255,0,0)
CASE nState = 0 AND UPPER(oSource.Name) = "LSTDROP"
   oSource.DragIcon = "DROP1PG.CUR"
CASE nState = 1 AND UPPER(oSource.Name) = "LSTDROP"
   oSource.DragIcon = "NODROP01.CUR"
ENDCASE
```

When the list box is dropped onto the shape, the shape's DragDrop() method executes the following code to determine which item on the list is selected. It then initiates the display that is seen when the drag-and-drop operation is completed:

```
CASE UPPER(oSource.Name) = "LSTDROP"
   FOR i = 1 to oSource.ListCount
      IF oSource.Selected(i)
         ThisForm.lblDropped.Caption = oSource.List(i,2)
         ThisForm.lblDropped.Visible = .T.
         This.Parent.Timer1.Interval = 200
      ENDIF
   ENDFOR
```

The call to the Timer object is discussed in this section *with the Timer Control.

Be aware that the wrong item will be dragged if the user clicks near the edge of an item in a list so that the Drag() method is not triggered until the pointer has actually moved to the adjacent item. You can minimize (but not prevent) "mis-selection" of items in a list like this by setting the nDragThreshold to a suitably small number (two pixels) as was done in this example. The downside is that this makes the control extremely sensitive to mouse movement. Users can find this annoying.

A better approach is to trigger the MessageBox() function in the target object's DragDrop() method. This confirms with the user which object is being dropped *before* the desired action is taken, and aborts the action if the user realizes that the wrong item from the list is being dragged.

The Timer Control

The DNDDEMO Form uses the Timer Control to achieve a nifty visual flashing effect. The Timer Control simply allows the execution of one of its methods at a regular interval.

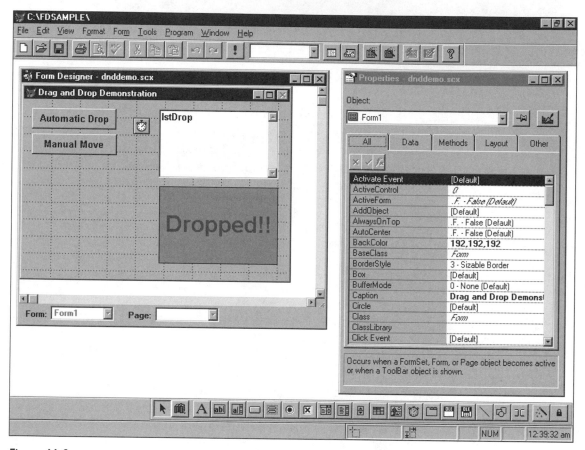

Figure 11-2.

DNDDEMO.SCX in the Form Designer

The interval is determined by the Timer's *Interval property*, which specifies how often the Timer Control's *Timer event* is triggered. The Interval property is expressed in milliseconds.

In this use of the Timer Control, the Interval property is set initially to 0. It is then reset to 200 in the DragDrop method, causing the Timer's Timer event to be triggered five times per second. Each time the Timer event is triggered, any program code in its Timer() method is executed. In this case, the Timer() method code stores a counter (as a character string) to the Timer's Tag property. If the Timer() method code determines that the VAL() of the string in the Tag property is 10 (the Timer has been running for two seconds), it resets the Timer object's Interval property to 0, effectively turning the Timer off.

Here is the Timer's Timer() method code in full:

```
IF VAL(This.Tag) > 10
   This.Tag = "0"
   This.Interval = 0
   WITH This.Parent.Shape1
      .BackColor = RGB(0,255,0)
      .FillStyle = 1
   ENDWITH
   ThisForm.lblDropped.Visible = .F.
   ThisForm.lblDropped.Caption = "Dropped!!"
ELSE
   This.Tag = LTRIM(STR(VAL(this.tag) + 1))
   IF MOD(VAL(This.Tag),2) = 0
      WITH This.Parent.Shape1
         .BackColor = RGB(0,255,0)
         .FillStyle = 1
      ENDWITH
   ELSE
      WITH This.Parent.Shape1
         .BackColor = 65535
         .FillStyle = 4
      ENDWITH
   ENDIF
ENDIF
```

It's important to be aware that the Timer does not mark actual time. If the Timer event initiates a process, for example a program that takes 10 seconds to execute, the Timer event will *not* occur during execution of that program. Certain user actions such as dropping down a menu pop-up or depressing and holding down a mouse button can also introduce a wait state that will interrupt the Timer. After dropping a control onto the shape in DNDDEMO.SCX, quickly click another control and hold down the mouse button. You will see that the flashing visual effect stops and does not resume until the mouse button is released.

OLE Controls

OLE Controls, which are introduced for the first time in Visual FoxPro, could be the subject of an entire book all by themselves. As a result, they'll be discussed only briefly. There are two different Visual FoxPro BaseClasses for OLE Control—the OLE Container Controls and OLE Bound Controls.

OLE Container Controls

An OLE Container Control is an installable control that is usually supplied by a third party. You can also write one yourself if you can program in C++ and have the professional edition of Visual FoxPro, which includes the Library Construction Kit. If you are familiar with Visual Basic, you are familiar with the custom controls that can be used on a Visual Basic Form. For versions of Visual Basic through version 3, these controls existed as separate files with a .VBX extension. For Visual FoxPro, OLE Controls are 32-bit objects, also contained in separate files, that have an .OCX extension. Four sample OLE Container Controls are shipped with Visual FoxPro. (This information came from the Visual FoxPro online help):

Type	File	Function
Communications	MSCOMM32.OCX	Provides serial communications for your application by allowing the transmission and reception of data through a serial port. (Installed only under Windows 95 and Windows NT)
Mail	MSMAPI32.OCX	Allows you to create a mail-enabled Visual FoxPro application.
Outline	MSOUTL32.OCX	Allows you to display items in a list hierarchically.
Picture Clipping	PICCLP32.OCX	Allows you to select an area of a source bitmap and then display the image of that area in a Form or picture box.

Each of these controls is documented in the Visual FoxPro manuals and online help.

Unlike Visual Basic VBX controls, OLE Container Controls can be subclassed and used in creating your own custom class library.

Microsoft intends to establish a standard to permit design of OLE objects that can be used in multiple development environments such as Microsoft Access, Microsoft Visual Basic 4, and Microsoft Visual FoxPro 3. In order to fully implement this standard, the OLE Container (the development environment) must provide an appropriate interface for the OLE Control. As with many fledgling standards, there are areas where the degree to which the standard is implemented or extended will affect the usability of the control.

With luck, this long-term strategy will lead to a wealth of third-party OLE Container Controls. In practice, the implementation of the OLE interface in Visual FoxPro and adherence to the OLE Control standard means that some OLE Controls that you develop yourself or from third parties may not work, or may not work properly in Visual FoxPro. However, it is reasonable to expect that you will see a refinement of Visual FoxPro's OLE interface and the OLE standard in future releases.

OLE Bound Controls

OLE Bound Controls enable developers to include OLE objects such as Microsoft Excel worksheets, Microsoft Word documents, Visio drawings, or Microsoft Paintbrush images into a Form. As you might expect with an OLE object, this enables the display and editing of the bound object from within Visual FoxPro.

If you've worked with Picture fields in FoxPro 2.x for Windows, you are familiar with the basic mechanics of an OLE Bound Control. The ControlSource for an OLE Bound Control is a general field in a table that either has the document embedded in it, or contains a link to the document located in a separate disk file.

Again, the use of OLE Bound Controls is fully documented in the Visual FoxPro manuals and online help.

Builders

Builders have been mentioned a couple of times in this report. Builders are development tools that automate the process of creating some part of an application. A large number of them are supplied with Visual FoxPro, and are contained in the Visual FoxPro application BUILDER.APP. Many (if not most) of these are tools to create Forms. If you check the value of the _BUILDER system memory variable from the command window, you will probably see something like this:

```
C:\VFP\BUILDER.APP
```

The value of this system memory variable also appears in the Tools|Options... dialog box, under the File Locations tab.

Builders are different than wizards because wizards are designed to create new entities: Forms, databases, and so forth. Builders, on the other hand, are often designed to be "re-entrant." That is, you can use a builder on an object that has already been created.

When you use the right mouse button to click a Form or a control in the Form Designer, a Builder item pops up in the shortcut menu. Selecting this option will invoke the builder for that object. You are then presented with one or more dialog boxes that allow you to set the properties for that object.

When you click the Builder Lock on the Form Controls toolbar (the icon that looks like a magic wand and stars—unfortunately, the same icon that is used elsewhere for wizards), the appropriate builder will automatically be invoked when you place a control on the Form. Some Form controls such as CommandButtons don't have builders, but many such as the CommandButton Group do.

While the builders that ship with Visual FoxPro are useful primarily as learning tools, the real power of builders lies in the opportunity for developers to use builders of their own design. A tutorial on this is unfortunately beyond the scope of this report. However, if you are interested in creating your own builders (and you should be), there is an excellent tutorial on this subject. The article "Use ASELOBJ() and Builders for Development" by John V. Peterson can be found in the June 1995 issue of the journal *FoxTalk* from Pinnacle Publishing.

You can also expect to see third party, freeware, shareware, and commercial builders become available. These should include builders that allow setting the properties of multiple screen objects, or automatically sizing screen objects to their bound data.

You can start getting an idea of how builders do their stuff by examining the Visual FoxPro function ASELOBJ() and the ReadExpression(), WriteExpression(), ReadMethod(), and WriteMethod() methods. These five functions and methods are available only at design time, and are designed exclusively for the purpose of writing builders. You can easily begin to explore the application of these language tools to a Form in the Form Designer from the command window.

NODEFAULT and the Scope Resolution Operator

The province of NODEFAULT and the Scope Resolution Operator are primarily in controlling method code execution in objects based on user-defined object classes subclassed from the Visual FoxPro BaseClasses. The only example of either in this report is to be found in the discussion of the QueryUnload event.

Still, it is important to know how they work so that when you find yourself in a situation where nothing else will do, you can reach into your toolbox and grab one of these babies.

Certain events cause specific default actions, even when you as the developer have not placed any code into the event's associated method. For instance, you do not need to specify that a KeyPress event in a TextBox causes the character associated with that key to be displayed in the TextBox. Likewise, you don't have to place code in the MouseDown() method of a list box to cause the item that the user just clicked to be selected. These actions occur by default.

If, on the other hand, you wanted to *prevent* the default behavior from occurring, you could place the NODEFAULT keyword into the method code. Then only the method code you placed in that method would execute. The default behavior of the control would be blocked. It doesn't matter *where* in the method the NODEFAULT keyword is placed, because the default behavior will occur *after* the execution of your method code. As a result, placing NODEFAULT anywhere in the method will stop the default behavior. Note, too, that once you have placed NODEFAULT in the method code, it is impossible to regain that default behavior. If you place NODEFAULT in the KeyPress() method of a TextBox, you must take steps to place a character into the TextBox's Value property.

Other times, you may not want to block a default behavior, but it may be convenient to get it to occur at a particular point in your method code instead of at the end. Doing this requires the use of the Scope Resolution Operator. It appears as a double colon (::).

For instance, if you wanted to force the selection of a list item before execution of your MouseDown() method code, you could place this code as the first line of the method:

```
ListBox::MouseDown()
```

This line of code says "Run the list box's default MouseDown code *NOW!*"

Much more information about the utility of the Scope Resolution Operator can be found in David Frankenbach's report on object-oriented programming in this book.

The Importance of Object-Oriented Programming

In preparing the examples for this report, the following code has been placed into the InteractiveChange() method of the spinner for every spinner that was placed on an example Form:

```
IF This.Value < This.SpinnerLowValue
   This.Value = This.SpinnerLowValue
ENDIF
IF This.Value > This.SpinnerHighValue
   This.Value = This.SpinnerHighValue
ENDIF
```

There were quite a few spinners in this report's examples! Every Form also has ThisForm.AutoCenter = .T. and ThisForm.BorderStyle

= 2 in its Init() method, and ACTIVATE SCREEN in the Deactivate() method. In addition, most of the examples have a BackColor property of light gray. All of the labels have had their BackStyles set to transparent. All of this resulted in a *ton* of redundant keystrokes.

At the very minimum, a set of simple modifications to the Visual FoxPro BaseClasses for Forms and controls can save you so much work over time that you really should at least stick a toe into the OOP waters. Keep in mind that these are reusable objects. Once you've decided what kind of behavior you want the controls to have, you can debug their methods and confidently drop them onto any Form without further thought.

Beyond these benefits, some much more complex reusable objects can be created. These include the following:

- Objects that save and restore environment information
- Objects that instantiate Forms and assist in coordination and communication between Forms, toolbars, menu selections, and so forth
- Objects that encapsulate a "mover" with two list boxes that use drag and drop to move items from one list to another
- Objects that encapsulate a series of navigation buttons and all of the methods necessary to navigate a Form object from record to record
- Objects that retrieve information from the .DBC and display it on a Form

This isn't just neat stuff—this is stuff that is going to make the difference between the productivity levels of you and your competitors, and can mean the difference between a bid of $20,000 and a bid of $30,000. This kind of power does not come without a price, however. It requires you to bring all of your experience to bear in creating a solid, robust set of reusable objects. The up-front effort is considerable, both in learning the methods of object-oriented programming and in designing (and discarding and redesigning) your class libraries (where your object definitions are stored). However, the effort will be well rewarded by tremendous productivity gains.

One last point about object-oriented programming. An application framework is going to assume much greater importance in Visual FoxPro development than it ever has with FoxPro 2.x and earlier versions. Successful developers will need to develop or adopt a robust, reusable set of objects in conjunction with standardized techniques for employing them in coordinating all of the elements of an application. A knowledge of OOP will be indispensable in using these frameworks, as object classes will play an important role in all of them. One such framework nearing completion now doesn't even use Forms (no .SCX files!), instead opting to store all Forms as object classes and instantiating them from their classes as needed at runtime.

To avoid learning about object-oriented programming in Visual FoxPro will be like avoiding use of the FoxPro 2.x Screen Builder—it can be done, but you're much more efficient and productive with it.

12 | Chart of Visual FoxPro Properties, Events, and Methods

Control Object

Member Name	Type	ComboBox	CheckBox	CommandButton	CommandGroup	Cursor	DataEnvironment	EditBox	Form	Column	Grid	Header	Image	Label	Line	ListBox	OptionGroup	OptionButton	Page	PageFrame	Relation	Shape	Spinner	Timer	TextBox
Activate	Event								●										●						
ActivateCell	Method										●														
ActiveColumn	Property										●														
ActiveControl	Property								●										●						
ActiveForm	Property								●																
ActivePage	Property																			●					
ActiveRow	Property										●														
AddColumn	Method										●														
AddItem	Method	●														●									
AddListItem	Method	●														●									
AddObject	Method				●		●		●	●	●						●		●	●					
AfterCloseTables	Event						●																		
AfterRowColChange	Event										●														
Alias	Property					●																			
Alignment	Property	●	●					●		●		●		●				●					●		●
AllowTabs	Property							●																	

Continued on next page

Control Object

Member Name	Type	ComboBox	CheckBox	CommandButton	CommandGroup	Cursor	DataEnvironment	EditBox	Form	Column	Grid	Header	Image	Label	Line	ListBox	OptionGroup	OptionButton	Page	PageFrame	Relation	Shape	Spinner	Timer	TextBox
AlwaysOnTop	Property								•																
AutoCenter	Property								•																
AutoCloseTables	Property						•																		
AutoOpenTables	Property						•																		
AutoSize	Property		•	•	•									•			•	•							
BackColor	Property	•	•		•			•	•	•	•	•		•		•	•	•				•	•		•
BackStyle	Property		•		•			•						•	•		•	•				•			•
BaseClass	Property	•	•	•	•	•	•	•	•	•	•	•	•	•	•	•	•	•	•	•	•	•	•	•	•
BeforeOpenTables	Event						•																		
BeforeRowColChange	Event										•														
BorderColor	Property	•			•									•	•	•			•			•			•
BorderStyle	Property				•			•	•						•	•						•			•
BorderWidth	Property														•				•			•			
Bound	Property									•															
BoundColumn	Property	•																							
Box	Method								•																
BufferMode	Property								•																
BufferModeOverride	Property					•																			
ButtonCount	Property				•												•								
Buttons	Property				•												•								
Cancel	Property			•																					
Caption	Property		•	•					•			•		•			•	•							
ChildAlias	Property																				•				
ChildOrder	Property																				•				
Circle	Method								•																
Class	Property	•	•	•	•	•	•	•	•	•	•	•	•	•	•	•	•	•	•	•	•	•	•	•	•
ClassLibrary	Property	•	•	•	•	•	•	•	•	•	•	•	•	•	•	•	•	•	•	•	•	•	•	•	•
Clear	Method	•														•									
Click	Event	•	•	•	•			•	•			•	•	•	•	•	•	•	•	•		•	•		•
ClipControls	Property								•																
Closable	Property								•																
CloseTables	Method						•																		

Continued on next page

Continued from previous page

Control Object

Member Name	Type	ComboBox	CheckBox	CommandButton	CommandGroup	Cursor	DataEnvironment	EditBox	Form	Column	Grid	Header	Image	Label	Line	ListBox	OptionGroup	OptionButton	Page	PageFrame	Relation	Shape	Spinner	Timer	TextBox
CLS	Method								●																
ColorScheme	Property	●	●	●				●						●		●			●			●	●		●
ColorSource	Property	●	●	●				●						●		●			●			●	●		●
ColumnCount	Property	●									●					●									
ColumnLines	Property	●														●									
ColumnOrder	Property									●															
Columns	Property										●														
ColumnWidths	Property	●														●									
Comment	Property	●	●	●	●			●	●		●	●	●	●	●	●	●	●	●	●	●	●	●	●	●
ControlBox	Property								●																
ControlCount	Property								●	●									●						
Controls	Property								●	●									●						
ControlSource	Property	●	●		●			●	●							●	●	●					●		●
CurrentControl	Property								●																
CurrentX	Property								●																
CurrentY	Property								●																
CursorSource	Property					●																			
Curvature	Property																					●			
Database	Property					●																			
DataSession	Property								●																
DataSessionID	Property								●																
DBLClick	Event	●	●		●			●	●		●	●	●	●	●	●	●	●	●	●		●	●		●
Deactivate	Event								●										●						
Default	Property			●																					
DeleteColumn	Method										●														
Deleted	Event										●														
DeleteMark	Property										●														
Desktop	Property								●																
Destroy	Event	●	●	●		●	●	●	●		●		●	●	●	●	●	●	●	●	●	●	●	●	●
DisabledBackColor	Property	●	●					●						●				●					●		●
DisabledForeColor	Property	●	●	●				●						●				●					●		●
DisabledItemBackColor	Property	●														●									

Continued on next page

Control Object

Member Name	Type	ComboBox	CheckBox	CommandButton	CommandGroup	Cursor	DataEnvironment	EditBox	Form	Column	Grid	Header	Image	Label	Line	ListBox	OptionGroup	OptionButton	Page	PageFrame	Relation	Shape	Spinner	Timer	TextBox
DisabledItemForeColor	Property	●														●									
DisabledPicture	Property		●	●														●							
DisplayValue	Property	●														●									
DoScroll	Method										●														
DownClick	Event	●														●							●		
DownPicture	Property		●	●														●							
Drag	Method	●	●	●	●			●			●		●	●	●	●	●	●	●			●	●		●
DragDrop	Event	●	●	●	●			●	●		●		●	●	●	●	●	●	●			●	●		●
DragIcon	Property	●	●	●	●			●			●		●	●	●	●	●	●				●	●		●
DragMode	Property	●	●	●	●			●			●		●	●	●	●	●	●	●			●	●		●
DragOver	Event	●	●	●	●			●	●	●	●		●	●	●	●	●	●	●			●	●		●
Draw	Method								●																
DrawMode	Property								●						●							●			
DrawStyle	Property								●																
DrawWidth	Property								●																
DropDown	Event	●																							
DynamicAlignment	Property									●															
DynamicBackColor	Property									●															
DynamicCurrentControl	Property									●															
DynamicFontBold	Property									●															
DynamicFontItalic	Property									●															
DynamicFontName	Property									●															
DynamicFontOutline	Property									●															
DynamicFontShadow	Property									●															
DynamicFontSize	Property									●															
DynamicFontStrikeThru	Property									●															
DynamicFontUnderline	Property									●															
DynamicForeColor	Property									●															
Enabled	Property	●	●	●	●			●	●	●	●		●	●	●	●	●	●	●	●		●	●	●	●
Error	Event	●	●	●	●	●	●	●	●		●		●	●	●	●	●	●	●	●	●	●	●	●	●
ErrorMessage	Event	●	●	●	●			●									●	●	●				●		●
Exclusive	Property					●																			

Continued on next page

Continued from previous page

Control Object

Member Name	Type	ComboBox	CheckBox	CommandButton	CommandGroup	Cursor	DataEnvironment	EditBox	Form	Column	Grid	Header	Image	Label	Line	ListBox	OptionGroup	OptionButton	Page	PageFrame	Relation	Shape	Spinner	Timer	TextBox
FillColor	Property								●													●			
FillStyle	Property								●													●			
Filter	Property					●																			
FirstElement	Property	●														●									
FontBold	Property	●	●	●				●	●	●	●	●		●		●							●		●
FontItalic	Property	●	●	●				●	●	●	●	●		●		●	●	●					●		●
FontName	Property	●	●	●				●	●	●	●	●		●		●	●	●					●		●
FontOutline	Property	●	●	●				●	●	●	●	●		●		●	●	●					●		●
FontShadow	Property	●	●	●				●	●	●	●	●		●		●	●	●					●		●
FontSize	Property	●	●	●				●	●	●	●	●		●		●	●	●					●		●
FontStrikeThru	Property	●	●	●				●	●	●	●	●		●		●	●	●					●		●
FontUnderline	Property	●	●	●				●	●	●	●	●		●		●	●	●					●		●
ForeColor	Property	●	●	●				●	●	●	●	●		●			●	●					●		●
Format	Property							●															●		●
GotFocus	Event	●	●	●				●	●							●		●					●		●
GridLineColor	Property										●														
GridLines	Property										●														
GridLineWidth	Property										●														
HalfHeightCaption	Property								●																
HeaderHeight	Property										●														
Height	Property	●	●	●	●			●	●		●		●	●	●	●	●	●	●	●		●	●	●	●
HelpContextID	Property	●	●	●	●			●	●		●		●	●	●	●	●	●	●	●		●	●		●
Hide	Method								●																
HideSelection	Property							●															●		●
Highlight	Property										●														
Icon	Property								●																
Increment	Property																						●		
IncrementalSearch	Property	●														●									
IndexToItemID	Method	●														●									
Init	Event	●	●	●	●	●	●	●	●		●		●	●	●	●	●	●	●	●	●	●	●	●	●
InitialSelectedAlias	Property						●																		
InputMask	Property																						●		●

Continued on next page

Control Object

Member Name	Type	ComboBox	CheckBox	CommandButton	CommandGroup	Cursor	DataEnvironment	EditBox	Form	Column	Grid	Header	Image	Label	Line	ListBox	OptionGroup	OptionButton	Page	PageFrame	Relation	Shape	Spinner	Timer	TextBox
InteractiveChange	Event	●	●		●			●								●	●						●		●
Interval	Property																							●	
ItemBackColor	Property	●														●									
ItemData	Property	●														●									
ItemForeColor	Property	●														●									
ItemIDData	Property	●														●									
ItemIDToIndex	Method	●														●									
KeyboardHighValue	Property																						●		
KeyboardLowValue	Property																						●		
Keypress	Event	●	●	●				●	●							●		●					●		●
KeyPreview	Property								●										●						
Left	Property	●	●	●	●			●	●		●		●	●	●	●	●	●		●		●	●	●	●
LeftColumn	Property										●														
Line	Method								●																
LineSlant	Property														●										
LinkMaster	Property										●														
List	Property	●														●									
ListCount	Property	●														●									
ListIndex	Property	●														●									
ListItem	Property	●														●									
ListItemID	Property	●														●									
Load	Event								●																
LockScreen	Property								●																
LostFocus	Event	●	●	●				●	●							●		●					●		●
Margin	Property	●						●															●		●
MaxButton	Property								●																
MaxHeight	Property								●																
MaxLeft	Property								●																
MaxLength	Property							●																	
MaxTop	Property								●																
MaxWidth	Property								●																
MDIForm	Property								●																

Continued on next page

Continued from previous page

Control Object

Member Name	Type	ComboBox	CheckBox	CommandButton	CommandGroup	Cursor	DataEnvironment	EditBox	Form	Column	Grid	Header	Image	Label	Line	ListBox	OptionGroup	OptionButton	Page	PageFrame	Relation	Shape	Spinner	Timer	TextBox
MemoWindow	Property																								●
Message	Event	●	●	●	●			●								●	●	●					●		●
MinButton	Property								●																
MinHeight	Property								●																
MinWidth	Property								●																
MouseDown	Event	●	●	●	●			●	●		●	●	●	●	●	●	●	●	●	●		●	●		●
MouseMove	Event	●	●	●	●			●	●	●	●	●	●	●	●	●	●	●	●	●		●	●		●
MousePointer	Property	●	●	●	●			●	●		●		●	●	●	●	●	●				●	●		●
MouseUp	Event	●	●	●	●			●	●		●	●	●	●	●	●	●	●	●	●		●	●		●
Movable	Property								●	●															
Move	Method	●	●	●	●			●	●		●		●	●	●	●	●	●		●		●	●		●
Moved	Event								●	●	●									●					
MoverBars	Property															●									
MultiSelect	Property															●									
Name	Property	●	●	●	●	●	●	●	●	●	●	●	●	●	●	●	●	●	●	●	●	●	●	●	●
NewIndex	Property	●														●									
NewItemID	Property	●														●									
NoDataOnload	Property					●																			
NumberOfElements	Property	●														●									
OneToMany	Property																				●				
OpenTables	Method						●																		
OpenWindow	Property																								●
Order	Property					●																			
PageCount	Property																			●					
PageHeight	Property																			●					
PageOrder	Property																		●						
Pages	Property																			●					
PageWidth	Property																			●					
Paint	Event								●																
Panel	Property										●														
PanelLink	Property										●														
ParentAlias	Property																				●				

Continued on next page

Control Object

Member Name	Type	ComboBox	CheckBox	CommandButton	CommandGroup	Cursor	DataEnvironment	EditBox	Form	Column	Grid	Header	Image	Label	Line	ListBox	OptionGroup	OptionButton	Page	PageFrame	Relation	Shape	Spinner	Timer	TextBox
ParentClass	Property	●	●	●	●	●	●	●	●	●	●	●	●	●	●	●	●	●	●	●	●	●	●	●	●
Partition	Property										●														
PasswordChar	Property																								●
Picture	Property	●	●	●					●				●			●		●	●						
Point	Method								●																
Print	Method								●																
ProgrammaticChange	Event	●	●		●			●								●	●						●		●
PSet	Method								●																
QueryUnload	Event								●																
RangeHigh	Event	●														●							●		●
RangeLow	Event	●														●							●		●
ReadOnly	Property					●		●		●	●												●		●
RecordMark	Property										●														
RecordSource	Property										●														
RecordSourceType	Property										●														
Refresh	Method	●	●	●	●			●	●	●	●	●				●	●	●	●	●			●		●
RelationalExpr	Property										●										●				
RelativeColumn	Property										●														
RelativeRow	Property										●														
Release	Method								●																
ReleaseType	Property								●																
RemoveItem	Method	●														●									
RemoveListItem	Method	●														●									
RemoveObject	Method				●		●		●	●	●						●		●	●					
Requery	Method	●														●									
Reset	Method																							●	
Resizable	Property									●															
Resize	Event								●	●	●									●					
RightClick	Event	●	●	●	●			●	●		●	●	●	●	●	●	●	●	●	●		●	●		●
RowHeight	Property										●														
RowSource	Property	●														●									
RowSourceType	Property	●														●									

Continued on next page

Continued from previous page

Control Object

Member Name	Type	ComboBox	CheckBox	CommandButton	CommandGroup	Cursor	DataEnvironment	EditBox	Form	Column	Grid	Header	Image	Label	Line	ListBox	OptionGroup	OptionButton	Page	PageFrame	Relation	Shape	Spinner	Timer	TextBox
SaveAs	Method								●																
SaveAsClass	Method	●	●	●	●			●	●		●		●	●	●	●	●	●		●		●	●	●	●
ScaleMode	Property								●																
Scrollbars	Property							●			●														
Scrolled	Event										●														
Selected	Property	●														●									
SelectedBackColor	Property	●						●															●		●
SelectedForeColor	Property	●						●															●		●
SelectedID	Property	●														●									
SelectedItemBackColor	Property	●														●									
SelectedForeColo	Property	●														●									
SelectOnEntry	Property									●															
SelLength	Property	●						●															●		●
SelStart	Property	●						●															●		●
SelText	Property	●						●															●		●
SetAll	Method				●				●	●	●						●		●	●					
SetFocus	Method	●	●	●				●			●					●		●					●		●
Show	Method								●																
ShowTips	Property								●																
Sorted	Property	●														●									
Sparse	Property									●															
SpecialEffect	Property	●	●		●			●								●	●	●		●		●	●		●
SpinnerHighValue	Property																						●		
SpinnerLowValue	Property																						●		
StatusBarText	Property	●	●	●				●			●					●		●					●		●
Stretch	Property												●												
Style	Property	●	●	●														●							●
TabIndex	Property	●	●	●	●			●	●		●			●		●	●	●		●			●		●
Tabs	Property																			●					
TabStop	Property	●	●	●				●	●		●					●		●		●			●		●
TabStretch	Property																			●					
Tag	Property	●	●	●	●			●	●		●		●	●	●	●						●	●	●	●

Continued on next page

Control Object

Member Name	Type	ComboBox	CheckBox	CommandButton	CommandGroup	Cursor	DataEnvironment	EditBox	Form	Column	Grid	Header	Image	Label	Line	ListBox	OptionGroup	OptionButton	Page	PageFrame	Relation	Shape	Spinner	Timer	TextBox
TerminateRead	Property	●	●	●	●			●								●	●	●					●		●
TextHeight	Method								●																
TextWidth	Method								●																
Timer	Event																							●	
ToolTipText	Property	●	●	●				●			●					●		●				●	●		●
Top	Property	●	●	●	●			●	●		●		●	●	●	●	●	●		●		●	●	●	●
TopIndex	Property	●														●									
TopItemID	Property	●														●									
UIEnable	Event	●	●	●	●			●			●		●	●	●	●	●	●		●		●	●		●
Unload	Event								●																
UpClick	Event	●														●							●		
Valid	Event	●	●	●	●			●			●					●	●	●					●		●
Value	Property	●	●		●			●			●					●	●	●					●		●
View	Property										●														
Visible	Property	●	●	●	●			●	●	●	●		●	●	●	●	●	●		●		●	●		●
When	Event	●	●	●	●			●			●					●	●	●					●		●
Width	Property	●	●	●	●			●	●	●	●		●	●	●	●	●	●		●		●	●	●	●
WindowState	Property								●																
WindowType	Property								●																
WordWrap	Property													●											
ZOrder	Method	●	●	●	●			●	●		●		●	●	●	●	●	●	●	●		●	●		●

Object-Oriented Programming with Visual FoxPro

David Frankenbach

Introduction

To start with the basics, this report is about objects. It will cover what they are, why you need them, how you create them, and how you use them.

On the other hand, this report is *not* a rehash of the Help file or printed documentation, nor is it about every property and method of every object. It's not meant to overlap with the other reports in this book—Steve Sawyer's *Visual FoxPro Form Designer,* Doug Hennig's *Visual FoxPro Data Dictionary,* or Robert Green's *Developing Client/Server Applications with Visual FoxPro and SQL Server.* The bottom line is that this report is not designed to show significant database access or to build the kinds of all-encompassing applications you'll eventually be developing. However, it will help equip you for these tasks.

Practical and Startup Uses of Object-Oriented Programming

This report is designed to cover the beginning through intermediate levels of object-oriented programming. That means that you should be familiar with FoxPro 2.x and have a good working knowledge of the FoxPro Power Tools (the Screen Builder, Report Writer, and so forth). In Microsoft Product Visual FoxPro, these tools have been renamed "designers." Here, you'll focus on the Class Designer, the Form Designer, and the Project Manager. As a result, if you are still hand coding @SAY and GETs, you need to break your old habits and learn to use the designers to improve your productivity. Most of the early examples will be .PRG-based, but that is only because you are probably most familiar with this format and it's easier to put into printed form. In all of my *real* work with Visual FoxPro, I use the designers everywhere that I can.

Microsoft has made a tremendous step forward by incorporating object-oriented programming into Visual FoxPro. Object-oriented programming offers many benefits, and while some of the new terminology may seem daunting at first, you'll probably find that you've already been using some object-oriented concepts in FoxPro 2.x.

Microsoft has also made Visual FoxPro a very "visual" tool. You'll spend a lot of time playing with it in hands-on sessions. I've tried to minimize the number of "forward references," places where a term is mentioned before it's been covered in detail. However, that's not always possible because many of the concepts are so intertwined. In those cases, I'll mention the term and say it will be covered more later. In light of this, it's a really good idea for you to read this report more than once. You'll cover a lot of ground in these pages, and some of the concepts are hard to grasp until you actually see them at work (which may happen in a later section of the report). Some of the concepts might not become clear until you've gotten significantly into your first or second object-oriented application. For me, object-oriented thinking has occurred in several "Aha!" points. I read several books and a lot of articles, but the concepts were just words until I'd really started to try to use object-oriented programming. But when I'd managed to successfully use one of the object-oriented concepts in a real program, the concept became wonderfully clear. I hope this report can lead you to those Aha! points a little more quickly than I came to them.

Benefits of Object-Oriented Programming

I'd like to use two Microsoft Windows application projects that I've worked on to illustrate the productivity gains that object-oriented programming offers. The first project used Microsoft C/C++ 7.0. We were on a tight schedule so we decided to stay away from learning C++ for the project, and we basically modified one of the SDK sample applications. The code had a minimum of Windows functionality and was 9800 lines long. A year later another application was added to the system, and we decided to try using the newly released Microsoft Visual C++ with the Microsoft Foundation Classes. This application had all of the features of a

Windows application, a toolbar, and a status bar. It had a Multiple Document Interface (MDI), contained a Dynamic Data Exchange (DDE) class that I designed, and took 6400 lines of code. About 1/2 of the code was automatically generated for us by Visual C++, so we had to write only 3200 of the lines of code! It took about the same amount of time to develop and learn the Microsoft Foundation Class application architecture and to get the DDE client to talk to an odd DDE server, but the Microsoft Foundation Class application has been much easier to maintain.

Will the Long Learning Curve Be Worth It?

Object-orientation has been around for quite a while, and its benefits are covered in great detail by authors far more accomplished than yours truly. Object-oriented programming is only one part of object-orientation. Object-oriented analysis and object-oriented design are more important. You can begin hacking out code, but if the object-oriented building blocks are poorly designed you will not realize the fundamental benefits of increased reuse and reduced or easier maintenance. You should also read other object-oriented books. Most of the concepts and issues are the same and apply equally whether the language is C++ or Visual FoxPro. The differences are simply a matter of language syntax differences in the program examples that are presented. A lot can be gained by pulling your head out of the Xbase sand every once in a while and seeing what's going on in the rest of the programming world. In fact, Visual FoxPro is a wonderful environment in which to learn object-oriented programming. Because objects can be created and manipulated in the command window, it becomes *very* easy to play with objects.

Reuse

Reuse is more than just having a procedure library of black box routines or cutting and pasting code or controls from one place to another. Objects are easier to reuse than straight library code because objects have a better defined interface and carry out better defined functions. Reuse is also easier because objects are used to build other objects. This makes the lower level objects much better tested and therefore much more reliable over time. You need to design the system with reuse in mind or reuse just won't happen. Reuse hinges on good and accessible documentation of the class libraries you develop.

Maintenance

Any significant project, one that will be used by more than one person or used more than once, needs to be maintained. Maintenance has two aspects—bug fixing and functional changes. For many projects, maintenance consumes more resources than the initial development. Object-oriented systems try to ease the burden of maintenance. Bug fixes can be reduced because the system is better designed at the start, and because you are building on other, more reliable objects. Functional changes tend to be easier because the functions are more localized to a set of objects that are easier to extend.

You Don't Have to Totally Object-Orient Yet

You don't *have* to totally embrace the object-oriented paradigm right from the start and you don't ever have to create your own class to build fully functional applications, but if you don't you won't gain the benefits of increased reuse and reduced maintenance. Visual FoxPro lets you mix object-oriented code in with your old procedural code. In some cases this might be your best solution. I think it is pretty safe to say that you won't be "porting" very much of your old code to Visual FoxPro. To gain all of the benefits of object-orientation you'll be more successful starting over from scratch.

The techniques you learned in structural programming are still very valuable. You're still programming, but object-oriented programming tends to deal with smaller code segments that range from one line to a couple of pages. However, the code still needs to be well structured.

I hope that by the end of this report you start to see some of the power that object-orientation brings to Visual FoxPro. After that, I'm sure that you'll want move to object-oriented development.

Object-Oriented Programming Concepts

This section will define object-oriented programming concepts and terminology as they relate to Visual FoxPro. It will use concrete examples rather than esoteric ones and will define the terms using the actual syntax of Visual FoxPro. It will also illustrate how some of these concepts relate and can be applied to make FoxPro 2.x object-like.

Pre-Object-Oriented Concepts

Abstraction

Abstraction is how humans take a complicated system and break it down into smaller, more easily understood components. These components are generally self-contained entities that hold information and know how to do things with that information. These components will interact with other components. You've used abstraction all of your life and you have used it in every program you've ever written. Most of the people reading this book are programmers, so take a look at programmers as an illustration of abstraction. A simple abstraction might look like the diagram in Figure 1-1.

In this diagram, the programmer has two inputs: a program specification and food. It also has one output: a working application. The particular way that program specifications and food are converted into working applications is abstracted into this thing called a programmer.

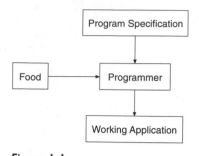

Figure 1-1.

Abstraction of a programmer

You also use abstraction while designing database applications when you abstract the data of the system into fields, combine the fields into tables, and add tables to a database. You use abstraction to simplify the functional details of a system until you get to something that can be expressed as a block of code. In procedural languages you abstract systems into processes and procedures. In object-oriented languages you abstract the system into objects.

Abstract Data Types (Data Structures at Last!)

Abstract data types allow you to create new data types that are composed of native data types (numeric, character, logical, and so forth). They also allow you to make your data model match the real world data. Many other programming languages have supported abstract data types for a long time. You could create a Person abstract data type by combining two character variables and a date variable: cFirstName, cLastName, and dBirth. Section 5 contains more detail on creating two abstract data types.

The "Big Three" Object-Oriented Concepts

For a language to be considered object oriented, it must support the concepts of *encapsulation, polymorphism*, and *inheritance*. Encapsulation is combining code and data into an object. Polymorphism is giving different objects similar internal structures. Inheritance is building new objects from other objects. Take a look at each concept in more detail.

Encapsulation

Encapsulation extends the abstract data type by adding code that manipulates the abstract data. Before you can go much further in your exploration of encapsulation, polymorphism, and inheritance, you need to become familiar with the "thing" that these concepts relate to—the Object.

Objects

You interact with real world objects every day. As an example, examine two common objects—a car and a personal computer. Both of these objects encapsulate many sub-objects and hide the infinite numbers of details that actually make them work. Take a look at two parallel examples:

- Your car is an object. When cars were first developed, it took an auto mechanic to keep such a complex machine operating properly. Car objects have evolved to the point that they can be used very easily and can reliably transport you from one place to another. Now you simply put your key into the ignition switch, turn it, and the engine begins to run. You don't need to think about the complex electrical, mechanical, and chemical processes occurring inside an internal combustion engine. All of these details are encapsulated for you by the car. You simply interact with the car object's standard interfaces such as the ignition key, the gas pedal, the brake pedal, and the steering wheel.

- Your personal computer is also an object. When personal computers were first developed, it took an electronic hobbyist to actually build the machine using a soldering iron, integrated circuit (IC) chips, and circuit boards. But even at the start, you could use standard IC objects; you didn't need to build the memory chips from the raw silicon dioxide. Personal computer objects have evolved to the point that you can simply turn one on and use it. You don't need to think about the complex physics involved in getting electrons to flow through semiconductor gates in the CPU or to fly from an emitter at the back of the monitor, strike the electron of a phosphor atom, and cause a photon to be released as the excited phosphor electron returns to its normal state. All of these details are encapsulated for you. You only have to perform easier tasks such as looking at words and pictures presented on the monitor, or manipulating buttons on the keyboard or mouse.

Computer and automobile manufacturers don't start from scratch every time they build a computer or car. They take reusable components off the shelf and put them together in a standard manner so they can produce more computers and cars in a shorter amount of time. This reuse component extends to the point that the same engine is used in many different kinds of cars and the same disk drive is used in many different kinds of computers.

Visual FoxPro objects are similar. You can build complex objects that hide the details of how the data gets from a table into an input field on a Form. In order to use the object, you don't have to fully understand everything that goes on inside it. You only need to know the object's proper interface. Once you "turn the object on," it handles the rest of the details of its existence. As you begin to build your own set of reuseable objects you can apply the same object to different programs. Right now you are an "object mechanic" with a lot of work to do to get your objects built and running reliably. It's time to get out your wrenches and oscilloscopes and begin building some objects.

Start with the fundamental aspects of objects. It's too soon to go into all of the details and ramifications of some aspects, so they'll be briefly presented here and will be discussed in more depth later. For the moment, take a look at an object. Its components will be explained step-by-step. Look at the object in Figure 1-2.

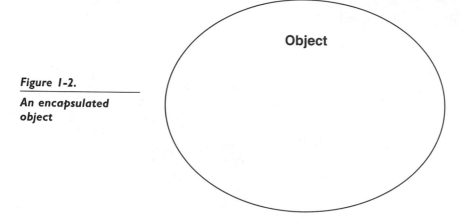

Figure 1-2.

An encapsulated object

Initially there doesn't seem to be much to the object shown. Object-oriented programming is going to be easier than you thought! The ellipse represents the encapsulation of the object. This encapsulation bounds everything an object is and does, and how it appears to the outside world.

The first components of an object to examine are its properties, which are represented in Figure 1-3.

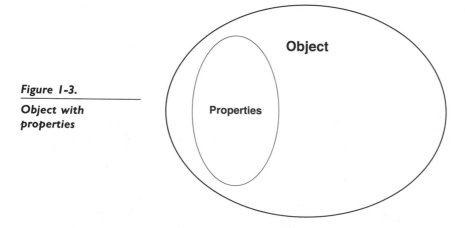

Figure 1-3.

Object with properties

A *property* is the information (data) that an object "knows." Properties include:

- nouns;
- attributes that describe an object;
- groups of memory variables of the same type; and
- numbers, character strings, logicals, or other objects.

Some example properties and sample values are shown:

- ForeColor   rgb(128, 128, 0)
- Height   47
- FontName   "Arial"
- Enabled   .T.

Properties contain the same kind of data you stored in memory variables in FoxPro 2.x, but in Visual FoxPro they are encapsulated within the object. This limits the access the outside world has to the property. Encapsulating the properties also prevents changes to other objects or programs that can unknowingly interfere with the object's properties. By encapsulating the object's properties, you protect them from interference that could occur when you make changes to other objects or programs. How many times has your FoxPro 2.x code failed because of memory variable scoping problems? Objects greatly reduce this kind of error.

A class is the blueprint used to build objects. This will be discussed in more depth shortly. Different objects created from the same class will typically have different values for some or all of the properties. For example, two different CommandButtons on a Form will have different Captions. One might be "OK" and the other "Cancel."

Although it's great that you can put all of these properties into an object, information without the ability to manipulate it is of limited use. As a result, the next object components to be discussed are methods. These are represented in Figure 1-4.

A *method* is a function that can be performed by an object. Methods include:

- verbs
- behaviors
- programs (code, functions, procedures, and subroutines)

They can manipulate the object's properties and are used to communicate with other objects.

Some example methods are:

- Click()
- Valid()
- Show()
- Move()
- InteractiveChange()

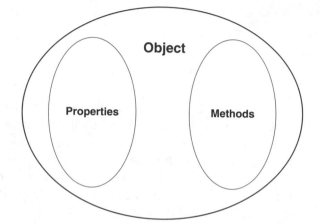

Figure 1-4.

Object with methods

Different objects created from the same class will all share the *exact same* methods.

A good way to conceptualize objects is to view them as living entities. In Peter Coad's *Object-Oriented Programming*, he proposes the following principle:

> *The "I'm alive!" principle*. Objects can be better understood by thinking about them as talking about them in the first person-"I know my own _____ and I can _____ myself.

The first blank represents the object's properties. The second blank represents the object's methods.

The next object components to look at are messages and events. These are represented in Figure 1-5.

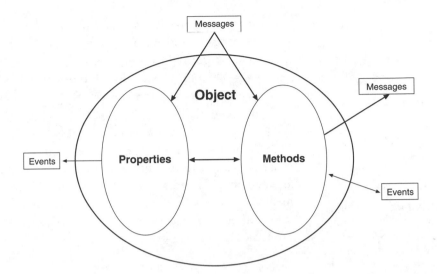

Figure 1-5.

Object messages and events

Messages are the only mechanisms used to communicate with objects. They are the only things that can cross the object's encapsulation boundary. Messages are used to change properties, return properties, and execute methods (subroutine calls).

Some sample messages are:

- cmdOk.Top = 0
- m.lnHeight = txtName.Height
- CustomerForm.Refresh()

Messages interact with an object's properties and methods. Messages look like structured data element references and use a '.' to separate the parts of the name. Messages can also look like function calls. (Note that you *cannot* use the Xbase DO command to execute DO CustomerForm.Refresh and similar methods.)

Some people restrict the use of the term message to calling an object's methods. This conflicts with the fact that property values can be manipulated from outside the object's encapsulation boundary. This report will define a message as any reference to an object's properties or methods.

An *event* is a user action or system event that causes a message to be sent to an object. Events are the primary driving force of a Visual FoxPro application. Events are interrupts and special case messages; they're handled by an object's method.

Some sample events include:

- pressing the left mouse button
- pressing and releasing the T key
- an input field losing focus
- a 500-millisecond timer interval that has elapsed
- the creation of an object

Objects can receive messages from other objects, from code in a .PRG, or even from the command window. These messages can change the value of a property, return the value of a property, or cause a method to execute. The object can also send messages to another object. Events primarily interact with methods. Events cause methods to execute, and, in some cases, code within a method can cause other events to occur. It is also possible that changes to properties can cause events to occur.

Example 1-1: Playing with the Basics
Now that you have the basic building blocks, take a few minutes to play with them. The following examples will focus on the basics: objects, properties, methods, events, and inter-object messages.

Before you start, be aware that receiving any of the following errors during this example probably means that you've made a typo:

- Unknown member ???.
- Object ??? is not found.
- Property ??? is not found.

The ??? represents the object, property, or method name that you've mistyped.

Begin by typing the following code in the command window:

```
do form sample
```

This will bring up the Form shown in Figure 1-6.

Disk Note: *The files to run the samples on pp 662-667 were inadvertently omitted from the CD for this book. You can obtain the files from Pinnacle Publishing's FTP site (ftp.pinpub.com, in directory ptvf_oop) or from Pinnacle's Compuserve section ("Go Pinnacle"). If you'd prefer to have the files mailed to you, call Pinnacle at 1-800-788-1900, 206-251-1900, or write to Pinnacle Publishing, Inc., PO Box 888, Kent, WA 98035-0888.*

Figure 1-6.

A simple Form object

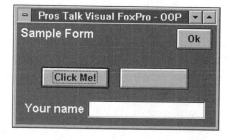

The command runs a Form named sample and creates a Form object named (surprisingly enough) Sample. You can use the following command to see what's in memory:

```
display memory like s*
```

This causes the following information to be displayed:

SAMPLE   Pub   O   Form

This information shows that Sample is a public object of type Form. You can begin by concentrating on this object's properties. First send the object (Form) some messages by typing in the following code:

```
sample.Top = 50
```

This sends a message to the Form telling it to change its Top property to 50. The Form will move down so that its topmost row of pixels is 50 pixels from the top of the main Visual FoxPro window. Now ask the Form to tell you something about itself by entering the following code:

```
nHeight = sample.Height
? m.nHeight
```

This will display the current Height of the Form. To change it, enter the following code:

```
sample.Height = 20
```

The Form then changes its Height to 20. You can restore the original height with the following code:

```
sample.Height = m.nHeight
```

Now enter the next code sample to change the Form's background color to red:

```
nColor = sample.BackColor
sample.BackColor = rgb( 255, 0, 0 )
```

Entering the next code sample will put your name up in lights:

```
sample.Caption = "<insert your name here>'s really cool Form!"
```

The following code minimizes the Form:

```
sample.WindowState = 1
```

To counteract the last code sample and restore the Form, enter the following:

```
sample.WindowState = 0
```

Now restore the Form's color with this code:

```
sample.BackColor = nColor
```

These examples should help you get the idea that you change an Object.Property by putting it on the left side of an = symbol. By doing so, you are sending the object a message to change the value of one of its properties. Putting the Object.Property on the right side of an = symbol asks for the current value of the property. Now you are sending the object a message requesting it to return the current value of one of its properties.

Now concentrate on some of the object's methods. To start, do something drastic. Terminate the Form with the following code:

```
sample.Release()
```

Now you can check the memory with the following command:

```
display memory like s*
```

This code elicits the following response:

SAMPLE   Pub   O   .NULL.

The sample memory variable is still in memory and is still a public object, but its value is now .NULL. instead of Form. It is no longer pointing to an object. Now get the Form back:

```
do form sample
```

Next, enter the following code:

```
sample.Move( 100, 10 )
```

Notice that the upper left corner of the Form has moved to 100, 10. Does this mean that the Move() method alters the object's Top and Left properties? You can verify that hypothesis with the following code:

```
? sample.Left
? sample.Top
```

You'll notice that they are now the values sent to the Move() method. Grab the Form's title bar and drag the Form to a new position on the screen. You can look at what this did to the Top and Left properties by entering these commands:

```
? sample.Left
? sample.Top
```

The properties reflect the location where you dropped the Form. Now try some of the new graphics methods. You can create a wide red line across the Form by using the following code.

```
sample.DrawWidth = 10
sample.ForeColor = rgb( 255, 0, 0 )
sample.Line( 0, 0, sample.Width / 2, sample.Height )
```

To create the line, the code needed to change two properties (DrawWidth and ForeColor), get the current value of two properties (Width and Height), and called one method (Line). Now try removing the OK button with the following code sample:

```
sample.RemoveObject( "cmdOk" )
```

This means that the button was really an object within another object, the Form. You've just seen an important concept: An object can contain other objects. This will be covered in more detail throughout the rest of the report.

Execute a method of one of the button objects by typing this in the command window:

```
sample.cmdLeftButton.Drag( 1 )
```

As you move the mouse, you will drag the form's button. Click anywhere and the button will return to the Form. However, the button won't have Drag and Drop functionality until more code is put into other methods of the button as well as the object onto which the button is being dropped.

Type your name into the input field, then enter the following code:

```
sample.txtName.ForeColor = rgb( 255, 0, 0 )
```

To see what's going on, read the last line of code backwards. The code sends a message to change the ForeColor property of an object named txtName, which is within another object named sample.

Now look at another line of code:

```
sample.txtName.BackColor = GetColor()
```

This syntax calls up the Visual FoxPro common dialog box to pick colors and puts the color you picked into the TextBox.

If you haven't already played with the two CommandButtons in the middle of the Form, here's your chance. If you click the one that has a Caption, a Click event will occur, causing the button to run the code in its Click() method. It will clear its own Caption, disable itself, tell the other button to display its Caption, and enable that button. When you click the other button, it follows the same process in reverse. It takes only four lines of code in the Click() method of each button to accomplish this task. The actual code for this will be covered in the "Special Object References" section. Remember that each of the buttons are themselves objects within the Form object. This is a good example of how objects talk to each other by sending messages.

If you haven't tried this yet, click the Label "Sample Form." Every time you click it, the case of its letters will change. This shows that the Label object can respond to events. Now click the Form somewhere where there is no control. The Form object can respond to events, and you can finally move the WAIT WINDOW around.

These simple examples should begin to show you some of the power that event-driven, object-oriented programming can provide.

Instance (Instantiate)

When you create an object in memory, that object is one instance of a class. The verb for this is "to instantiate," and the process is called instantiation. You can create more than one instance of a class in memory at a time. Each of these instances is separate and distinct from any other instances.

Now take a few minutes to play with this concept. This example will focus on multiple instances of a class and inter-object messages. Begin by creating two instances of the SAMPLE Form you used earlier. You can begin testing them by entering the following code:

```
do form sample name o1 linked
do form sample name o2 linked
display memory like o*
```

This code runs the Form twice, but names the Form objects o1 and o2 instead of creating a memory variable that is named sample like the one you saw earlier. You can now distinguish one Form object from the other. Both Forms are active, but the o2 Form is on top of o1. This is because they both instantiate from the same .SCX file so they both have the same values for Top and Left. You can move them apart with this command:

```
o1.Top = 50
o1.BackColor = rgb( 255, 0, 0 )
```

This code lowers the first Form on the screen and changes its color. You used the name o1 to manipulate the first object. Now use o2 to manipulate the second.

```
o2.Left = 0
```

This moves the second Form to the left side of the screen. As you click either Form's buttons, notice that they do not affect the buttons of the other Form. The same goes for the input field—each one is a distinct object in memory. Input some different text into each field, then enter the code shown:

```
clear
? o1.txtName.Value
? o2.txtName.Value
```

This code will display the current input you've typed in for each Form. You can even have the two Forms talk to each other as shown in the following code:

```
o1.txtName.Value = o2.txtName.Value
```

The textbox's value on the first Form changes to the current contents of the textbox on the second Form. This sends a message to retrieve the Value property of the txtName object within the object o2, then sends a message to change the Value property of the txtName object within the object o1. Because you used the LINKED clause in the DO FORM command, you can get rid of the Form objects by using the following code:

```
release o1, o2
```

The LINKED clause tells Visual FoxPro to tie the lifetime of the Form to the lifetime of the variable used by the NAME clause. Without the LINKED clause, the RELEASE command used with o1 and o2 would not have terminated the two Forms. However it would have removed the two memory variables o1 and o2, getting rid of names you used to reference the Form objects.

The ability to create multiple instances of Forms combined with the data buffering and private data sessions within Visual FoxPro eases the burden of giving your end users the ability to edit one record, open another Form to look at another record, and come right back to where they left their original edit. For more information on this, see Steve Sawyer's report on the Visual FoxPro Form Designer.

FoxPro 2.x Design Surface Objects

In FoxPro 2.x you've been using pseudo-objects within the design surfaces such as the Screen Builder and the Report Writer. These objects had properties like Font, Text Alignment, and Fill Color. Objects on a screen also had methods such as When(), Valid(), Message(), and Error(). In FoxPro 2.x, the properties and snippets were converted into clauses of various FoxPro 2.x commands by the GENSCRN program. Even though the FoxPro 2.x menu item was labeled Object they were not objects in an object-oriented sense. The distinction comes from the fact that you can't use these "objects" to derive new objects. This concept, called inheritance, will be covered later in this section.

Information Hiding

Another aspect of object-oriented programming is called *information hiding*. Information hiding is the ability to prevent outside forces access to parts of the object. This is strongly tied to encapsulation, and prevents the outside world from seeing all of the implementation details of a class. In Visual FoxPro, this is accomplished by using the PROTECTED keyword. If a property or method is declared protected, nothing any subclass does can expose it to the outside world.

Figure 1-7 represents how hiding affects our object drawing. Basically, it allows you to subset an object's properties.

Figure 1-7.

Object with public and protected properties

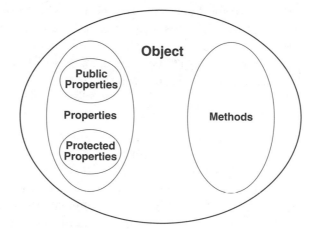

Properties are public by default, so you need to explicitly declare them protected. The entire "world" has read/write access to an object's public properties. However, protected properties are properties that have very limited outside access. Exactly who has access will be discussed more later. In general, you should leave a property public unless you have a real need to protect it. If your object's user has legitimate reasons to see the value of a protected property, you'll need to create a method that returns the current value. These methods will usually be named *Get*SomeProtectedProperty(). You can allow your object's user to change the value of a protected property only under circumstances that you control. Those methods are usually named *Set*SomeProtectedProperty().

Some people say you should protect everything and allow access only via Get() and Set() methods, however that can be too restrictive, create too much busy work (writing all those Get() and Set() methods), and can cause object bloat. It's simplest to protect properties only when the object will become invalid or incapable of performing properly if the user mucks with it. (For an illustration, see the Lock class in Section 3.)

As with properties, access to methods can be limited. This is shown in Figure 1-8.

Figure 1-8.

Object with public and protected methods

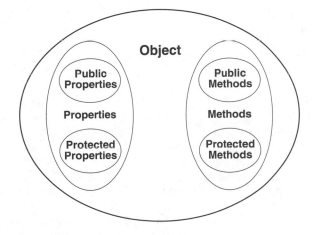

Like properties, methods are public by default, so you need to explicitly declare them protected. The entire world has access to an object's public methods. Protected methods are methods that your object will use internally.

As Figure 1-9 shows, designating a property or method public or protected doesn't really affect internal access to the object.

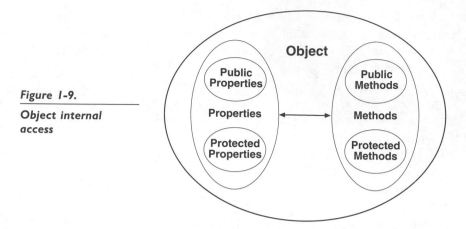

Figure 1-9.

Object internal access

All the methods in Figure 1-9 have full read/write access to all the properties. Inside the object the public and protected settings mean nothing. However the settings do have an impact on how the outside world sees the object. Figure 1-10 shows how messages and events deal with public and protected properties and methods.

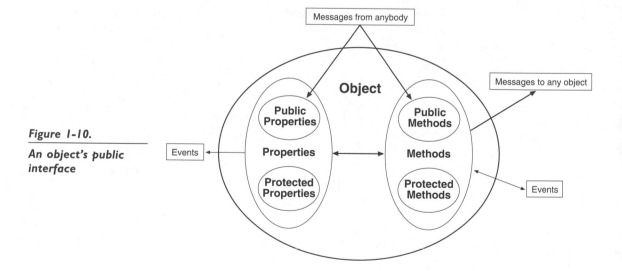

Figure 1-10.

An object's public interface

Starting at the top of the diagram, *Messages From Anybody* are those messages an object receives from another object, from code in a .PRG, or even from the command window. These messages can change the value of a public property, return the value of a public property, or cause a public method to execute. *Messages to any object* are those messages that methods send to another object. No outside entity has access to the protected properties or methods of the object.

Hiding allows the designer of a class to change the internal details of a class freely without worrying about breaking the applications that have used the class. For example, suppose that a class is going to store a series of names. You might begin to implement this design using an array. If the array (maName) was not hidden from outside view, some of the class's users might begin to write their code using direct access to the array rather than going through the normal public interface methods (GetName() and SetName()) that you set up. Now assume that several applications have been developed using this class. Most of the applications are well designed and use your GetName() method. A couple of applications were developed by a more cavalier programmer and they use the array maName directly. Later, to improve performance for long lists of names, you decide to change the implementation to use a SQL cursor instead of the array. You change the code in the GetName() and SetName() methods as needed to work with the cursor and you put the new version of the class into the company production class library. All of the applications that use the public interface methods still work properly, but the applications that relied on the maName array are now broken. If you had completely hidden the implementation details in the initial design, the array would have never been exposed and it never would have been "mis-used."

In summary, encapsulation is the object-oriented concept that lets you combine data and code together in a single unit. Encapsulation provides a boundary that controls how the outside world "sees" an object. The properties and methods that are not hidden constitute the public interface to the object. You need to treat the public interface as though it were cast in stone. Consider an automobile manufacturer that wanted to change some feature of the engine of one of its car models. However, in adding the new feature it needed to swap the positions of the gas and brake pedals. Imagine the problems caused by this little change to the auto's public interface!

Once you've established your public interface, it needs to be maintained. This means that you need to think about it very carefully at the beginning. Remember that good object-oriented programming requires a lot of work in the design stage of the project.

Polymorphism

Polymorphism comes from two Greek words: poly, which means many, and morphos, which means form. It means that a single token or name can have many different meanings based on the context in which the token is found. In Visual FoxPro this means that more than one class can have a property or method with the same name. For example, both Forms and CommandButtons have Caption properties. When a Form object gets a message to change its Caption, it changes the text that appears in the Form title bar. When a CommandButton gets a message to change its Caption, it changes the text that appears on the button. Similarly, both TextBoxes and Pages have Click() methods, but each does something different when it gets a Click message. This allows you to have fewer names to remember and improves your productivity.

Polymorphism is also useful when you want to "broadcast" a message to several kinds of objects. If they all share the same name for a property or method, this broadcast is achieved very easily. Suppose that one set of classes has a property named Enabled and another set of classes has a property named Disabled with a similar purpose but an opposite meaning. This situation would greatly complicate being able to enable or disable all controls on a Form.

FoxPro 2.x Using Runtime Type Information for Polymorphism

One method to achieve polymorphism in FoxPro 2.x was to use runtime evaluation of the type of argument sent to a routine to determine how to handle the data. Suppose that you wanted a routine that converted different input arguments into a character string but you didn't want to create individual routines for each data type (NumericToString and LogicalToString). Instead, you wanted one routine named ToString. This could be done with the following code:

```
* tostr.prg  25-Jan-95

* Convert the input argument to a string

function ToString
parameters puArg

private lcType, lcRetVal

lcType = type( "puArg" )

do case
  case ( m.lcType == 'C' )
    lcRetVal = m.puArg
```

Continued on next page

```
    case ( m.lcType == 'N' )
      lcRetVal = str( m.puArg )

    case ( m.lcType == 'L' )
      lcRetVal = iif( m.puArg, "True", "False" )
  endcase

  return ( m.lcRetVal )
```

If this routine ever changed, you would run the risk of introducing an error that could break any other code that uses this routine the next time the other code was recompiled. For all you know, the next compile could occur several months after your change when another programmer makes an enhancement in an unrelated area. That programmer would get the call from the irate user. You can imagine the problems if the error was caused by your change to the library routine. With object-oriented programming this kind of problem is reduced because you don't need to change library code. Instead you derive a new class and put any changes in the new class.

FoxPro 2.x Using the Call Stack for Polymorphism in FoxPro 2.x
In FoxPro 2.x you could also use a kind of polymorphism by using the call stack. For example, the function expression Validate() could be used as the valid clause on every @GET with a separate Validate routine handling all of the validations for each screen. This is an example of one screen's Validate routine.

```
function Validate
private lcVar, luReturnVal

lcVar = varread()            && get current read variable
luReturnVal = .t.            && default

do case
  case lcVar == "FIRSTNAME"
    luReturnVal = ! empty( m.FirstName )

  case lcVar == "SHOESIZE"
    luReturnVal = ( m.ShoeSize > 10 )
endcase

return (luReturnVal)
```

This Validate() function existed in a .PRG file that had the same filename as the .SPR. Without this function, a lot of development time is consumed by GENSCRN, and even changing a typo in a valid clause requires wading through endless modal dialog boxes in the Screen Builder. The Validate() routine can also be placed in the Cleanup snippet in of the FoxPro 2.x screens, but putting it there does not solve the screen generation delay problem.

You might wonder how FoxPro resolves the different Validate() routines for each screen at runtime, particularly if one screen calls another. Suppose that you have an application structured as shown:

> *Warning:* This is FoxPro for Windows code and should be run only under FPW2.X. It has not been converted to run properly under Visual FoxPro!

```
* CallStck.PRG  14-mar-95

* Program to Illustrate Calling Stack Polymorphism

do .\scr\Screen1.PRG
return
```

The screen driver program for Screen1 is shown here:

```
* Screen1.PRG  14-Mar-95

m.FirstName = "Wendy"
m.ShoeSize = 7.5

do .\scr\Screen1.SPR

return


function Validate
private lcVar, luRetVal

lcVar = varread()
luRetVal = .t.

do case
   case lcVar == "FIRSTNAME"
      luRetVal = ! empty( m.FirstName )

   case lcVar == "SHOESIZE"
      luRetVal = ( m.ShoeSize > 3.5 )

   case lcVar == "PBSCREEN1A"
      do .\scr\Screen1A.PRG
endcase

return (luRetVal)
```

A second screen can be added with this driver program:

```
* Screen1a.PRG  14-Mar-95

m.lbShoe = int( rand() * 4 ) + 1
m.lbMusic = int( rand() * 4 ) + 1

do .\scr\Screen1a.SPR

return


function Validate
private lcVar, luRetVal

lcVar = varread()
luRetVal = .t.

do case
  case lcVar == "LBSHOE"

  case lcVar == "LBMUSIC"
    do case
      case m.lbMusic = 1
        wait window "Rollover Beethoven!" nowait

      case m.lbMusic = 2
        wait window "Yee Haa!" nowait

      case m.lbMusic = 3
        wait window "I can hear the violins now." nowait

      case m.lbMusic = 4
        wait window "When did you lose your dog?" nowait
    endcase
endcase

return (luRetVal)
```

In the command window, you can execute a DO CALLSTCK command to cause the first screen to appear. Before you do anything on the screen, the call stack will look like this:

```
screen1.spr
screen1.prg
callstck.prg
```

When the push button Do Screen1A is pressed and released, the valid clause will execute. It calls the routine named Validate. However, there is no routine named Validate in SCREEN1.SPR, so FoxPro looks down the call stack to find it. It finds the routine in SCREEN1.PRG. The CASE statement then calls SCREEN1A.PRG. After the second screen appears, the call stack looks like this:

```
screen1a.spr
screen1a.prg
screen1.spr
screen1.prg
callstck.prg
```

If you make a change to the Music Preference radio button, its valid clause is executed and calls a routine named Validate. There is no routine named Validate in SCREEN1A.SPR, so once again FoxPro searches down the call stack to find it. It finds the routine in SCREEN1A.PRG. Notice that once the routine is found, FoxPro stops searching and you don't collide with the Validate routine in SCREEN1.PRG. Being able to use the same name for a similar function routine but having different routines execute is one kind of polymorphism.

In Visual FoxPro there is no need to desnippetize your Forms (screens) because there is no code generation phase. The Forms run directly from the compiled .SCX and .SCT files, and there are no more .SPR files. In addition, object-oriented principles require you to encapsulate this kind of code with the data.

For an example of these screens in Visual FoxPro, look at the VFPPOLYM project file included on the source code disk.

Inheritance

Hopefully you don't start every new project completely from scratch; instead you use your black-box library routines across multiple applications. You might have developed your own application framework or purchased a third-party framework that allows you to simply plug in application screens and reports. However it can be time-consuming to find existing code and figure out if it does what you need. It might seem simpler in the short run to rewrite the routine yourself than to decipher 100 lines of code that someone else wrote. This inhibits the ability to reuse your company's prior work effort, and today it is critical that we deliver more reliable systems much faster than you have in the past.

Class—The Object-Oriented Building Blocks

If you are coming from FoxPro 2.x, you are familiar with the DEFINE WINDOW command, which is used to define the attributes of the window. When DEFINE WINDOW is executed, it creates the window in memory but doesn't cause the window to be displayed. The window does not appear on the screen until you execute an ACTIVATE WINDOW command. The DEFINE MENU and DEFINE

POPUP commands are basically identical commands to define either a menu or a pop-up list.

In Visual FoxPro, the DEFINE CLASS command is used to define the attributes (properties and methods) of the class. Unlike the DEFINE WINDOW command, the DEFINE CLASS command does not instantiate an object of the class. Also, the flow of program execution does not flow through the DEFINE CLASS command.

Inheritance is the primary way that reuse is accomplished within an object-oriented programming language. Inheritance allows new classes to be built upon, or *derived* from, existing classes. The new classes are called subclasses. The subclass inherits all of the properties and methods of its ParentClass. The subclass can adapt and extend the existing classes to fit the needs of the new class. When you build new ones from other well tested classes, you also inherit the reliability of the other classes.

Some people compare object-oriented programming inheritance with biological inheritance. This analogy fails on a few major points.

1. I inherited the shape of my nose from my father, my fair skin color from my mother, and my red hair from my maternal grandmother. Biological inheritance causes me to get a random one-half of my father's DNA and a random one-half of my mother's DNA. Object-oriented inheritance, on the other hand, passes everything on to the new class. If biological inheritance passed everything on, I would have multiple noses—all of my mother's noses and all of my father's noses.

2. Biological inheritance also deals with the dominance of one gene over another. In my case, I wound up with two recessive-trait hair color genes that gave me my grandmother's red hair instead of my mother's brown hair or my father's black hair. There is no dominance in properties or methods; a new class gets all the properties and methods exactly as they are in its ParentClass.

3. Biological inheritance can't be completely overridden. Overridden means replaced, a concept that will be discussed in the next part. I can temporarily override my hair color by using dyes. I can override my inherited near-sightedness with glasses. In this case, though, I don't totally replace my eyes. I still use them but augment their behavior with glasses.

Ideally programming will get to a point where there is a class named MyMultipurposeFinishedApplication and all you'll have to do is point an instance of this class at a database to complete the whole application. Until then, you have a lot of work ahead of you.

Now that inheritance and derived classes have been defined, the diagram of the object can be finished. This is shown in Figure 1-11.

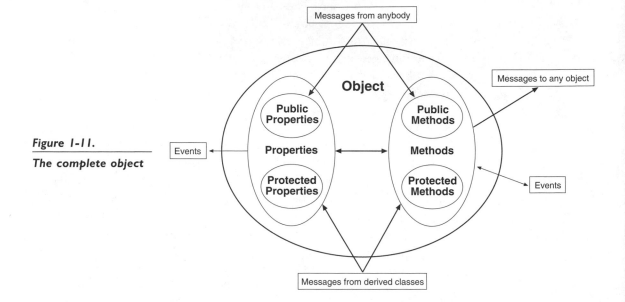

Figure 1-11.

The complete object

Messages From Derived Classes indicates that derived classes have access to all properties and methods, even the protected ones.

Override

The *override* feature allows subclasses to change the properties and methods that they inherit. Inheritance would not be useful without the ability to override, because otherwise you'd be stuck with only what the ParentClass gave the derived class. Overriding methods is what makes object-oriented programming more extensible than procedural programming. That extensibility also leads to better reuse. Unfortunately, the term "override" carries with it a negative connotation in the English language. In the object-oriented world, override is a good thing. It is what allows a subclass to do more than its ParentClass.

Overriding a property means that the derived class supplies a value for that property that has already been defined by one of its ParentClasses. Overriding a method means that the derived class puts code into a method that has already been defined by one of its ParentClasses.

The Visual FoxPro CommandButton class has a default FontName of Arial. By using an override, you can change the font of your

button to WingDings if you like. The CommandButton Click()
method does nothing. By using an override in the Click() method,
you can make the button do the work you need when it is clicked.

At times you might see people referring to an override as
"breaking inheritance." This is simply not true. When you derive a
subclass from a ParentClass, you always inherit everything from the
ParentClass. Inheritance is a general object-oriented concept that
gives the subclass access to everything that is in the ParentClass.
Inheritance is not the mechanism used to pass messages through the
class tree. When you override a method of a subclass, the message
is first received by the overridden method. Normally the overridden
method will also want to take advantage of the method it inherited,
so the message can be passed on to the ParentClass for additional
processing by using the scope resolution operator ::, which will be
discussed more later. If for some reason the overridden method does
not want the ParentClass behavior to occur, it does not have to pass
the message to the method it inherited. This gives you a tremendous
amount of flexibility in your class designs.

Class Tree (Is-A)

The inheritance of classes can be viewed in a hierarchy called a
class structure, which represents the *"Is-A"* relationships between
classes. This hierarchy is also called a *class tree*, and shows how the
classes are built. New classes (subclasses) are derived from other
classes, which become the ParentClass or superclass of the new
class. This is usually illustrated in a hierarchical drawing that shows
how each class is derived. Visual FoxPro implements the single
inheritance object model. This means that each class can be derived
from only one other class. Most class structures are set up as
generalization-specialization hierarchies, which
means that a general class is at the root of
the hierarchy and more specialized classes
are derived from the more general classes.
Specialization is accomplished by overriding
properties and methods, or by adding new
properties and methods that are not present
in the ParentClass.

Figure 1-12 illustrates that an OK button
is-a button, a Navigation Button is-a button,
the Top button is-a Navigation button, and
the Bottom button is-a Navigation button. The
most general class is the Button class. It has
properties such as size, color, and font. It has

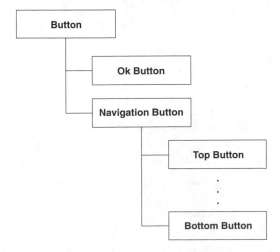

Figure 1-12.

A button class tree

methods that perform tasks such as changing a button's image when it's pushed. An OK button is a more specialized kind of button. It has all the properties a button has, but it could have a smaller size. It knows how to do everything a button does, but the OK button also knows how to close a Form when it is clicked.

The Navigation button knows about table navigation, and deals with things such as selecting the proper table and handling EOF() and BOF() conditions. The Top button is-a more specialized kind of Navigation button. The Top button inherits everything a Navigation button has, but additionally it knows how to make a table go to its beginning. Similarly, the Bottom button is-a Navigation button, but it knows how to make a table go to its bottom.

Figure 1-13 shows how you might design a person class. An Employee is-a Person, a Dependent is-a Person, and a Retired Employee is-an Employee. The most general class is the Person class. It would have the properties and methods that are common to every kind of person. Some of its properties might include First Name, Last Name, Date of Birth, and Sex. A Person might have methods such as Work, Play, Eat, and Sleep.

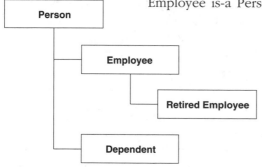

Figure 1-13.

A person class tree

If the Person class was used in a business application, you would need to make two more specialized versions of Person, Employee and Dependent. Remember that Employee and Dependent would inherit all of the properties and methods of the Person class. The Employee class would add properties such as Employee ID, Job Title, Salary, and Hire Date. The Employee class would also override the Work() method. The Dependent class would add properties such as Fulltime Student and Parent ID, as well as methods such as Study(). The Retired Employee class is a more specialized Employee class. It would add properties such as Retirement Date and Monthly Pension, and would override the Work() and Play() methods.

The farther to the right that you go in a class tree, the more specialized the class becomes. This is also known as the *depth* of the class tree. The guidelines for well designed class trees say the maximum tree depth should be 7±2. It begins to get unwieldy to find properties and methods during the design phase when the class tree gets too deep. The class tree for the Visual C++ MFC 2.1 goes to a maximum depth of eight levels, and the average depth is about four levels. However, everything is derived from a root class of CObject, so practically speaking the first level doesn't really count.

The classes supplied with Visual FoxPro are equivalent to classes at the fourth level in the MFC hierarchy.

At times you might see a class tree drawn like the one in Figure 1-14.

However, class trees drawn like the one in Figure 1-12 are easier because they don't get as wide as the style shown in Figure 1-14.

Now take a few minutes to play with the concepts just covered.

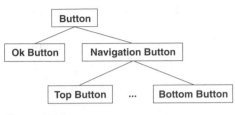

Figure 1-14.

An alternate class tree layout

Example 1-2: Inheritance, Overrides, Objects, and Classes
This example will focus on showing inheritance, overrides, and the difference between objects and classes. It will also provide your first peeks at the Class and Form Designers.

Begin by using the following command in the command window:

```
do form clastre1
```

This runs an example Form that looks like Figure 1-15.

Figure 1-15.

Sample Form to illustrate inheritance

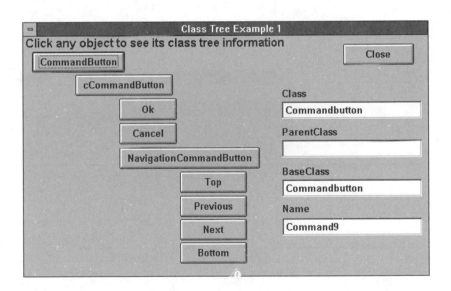

This Form has several CommandButtons on it arranged to display their class tree structure, some Labels, and TextBoxes. The button arrangement on the Form has *no* impact on the button inheritance. They were laid out like this for visual effect. The class tree is shown in *Figure 2-4*, which is a more formal extension of the class tree in Figure 1-12 that uses the Visual FoxPro BaseClass CommandButton.

If you click any of the objects (remember that the Form itself, the TextBoxes, and the Labels are all objects), the TextBoxes update to show relevant information about the clicked object. The mechanics of this Form will be discussed later.

Take a couple of minutes to click around the Form, then enter the following code in the command window:

```
clastre1.cmdOk.ForeColor = rgb(255,0,0)
```

The code changes the color of the Caption on the OK button. However nothing is derived from cmdOk, so try changing one of the buttons from which something is derived:

```
clastre1.cCommandButton.ForeColor = rgb(255,255,0)
```

Notice that only one button changed. The others did not because you changed only the property of an object, you didn't change the class definition, which is what affects inheritance. Now try making a change to the cCommandButton class, which will override one of the properties. You can do so by entering this command:

```
modify class cCommandButton of clastre1
```

This should bring up the error dialog box shown in Figure 1-16.

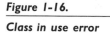

Figure 1-16.

Class in use error

Click OK to dismiss the dialog box. This box appears because the class definition is being used by an existing object, and that object must be released before you can edit the class.

Now clear the class from the memory cache with the following command:

```
clear all
```

Try changing the cCommandButton class by modifying class cCommandButton of clastrel.

If it's not already open, open the property sheet and go to the ForeColor row. Then enter 255, 0, 0. You should now see the button turn red in the Class Designer window. Finally, close the Class

Designer Window. Congratulations! You've just modified your first class. Now let's see if it worked by using this code:

```
do form clastre1
```

Now all of the buttons derived from cCommandButton have inherited the change you made to the class. But why didn't the CommandButton or the Previous buttons change? Click the CommandButton and look at its class information. It didn't change because it's an instance of one of the Visual FoxPro BaseClass controls. You can tell this because it does not have a ParentClass. Now click the Previous button. Its ParentClass is NavigationCommandButton. That button inherited the change, so why didn't the Previous button? To find that answer, you need to look at the Previous button in the Form Designer. You can do this by entering the following code:

```
modify form clastre1
```

Then click the Previous button to select it. As you look at the ForeColor Line in the property sheet, you'll notice that it has a value of 0,0,0 and uses a bold font. The bold font is an indication that the value is overridden. Next, use the right mouse button to click the ForeColor row in the property sheet. Then choose the Reset To Default item. You'll notice that the value changes to 255,0,0 but it's displayed in a normal font. This indicates it is no longer overridden; it is the normal value as defined by the ParentClass. Finally, close the Form Designer and save the changes.

```
do form clastre1
```

If everything went as planned, only the CommandButton will be black. To make that button red, you'd have to override its ForeColor property on the clastre1 Form. You might be asking "Why can't I just modify the class definition of the CommandButton class?" That has a two-fold answer. First, Microsoft didn't give you the source code to the BaseClass objects. Second, it's not the object-oriented way to solve the problem. The object-oriented way is to subclass the class you need to modify, then make the changes to your subclass. This fundamental object-oriented concept will be discussed in depth later.

Additional Object-Oriented Concepts
Containership (Has-A)

An object-oriented system can also be viewed using another hierarchy that is called an *object structure*. It represents the "Has-A" relationships between objects, which are also called *aggregation* or *containership*. This hierarchy looks at how the parts, or objects, are combined in the system.

Figure 1-17 illustrates that an application is composed of four parts: a Database, Forms, Reports, and Menus. Each of these parts is further decomposed into smaller and smaller parts until you get to an element small enough to be programmed.

Figure 1-17.

An application container

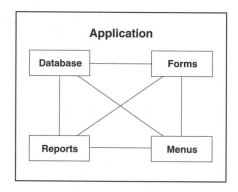

Figure 1-18 illustrates that a Form "Has" a name field, an address field, a birthdate field, an Ok Button, and a Cancel button.

Figure 1-18.

A Form container

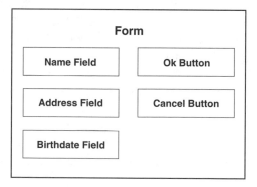

Class Library

The term class library has two meanings. The first is that it's what you call your whole collection of reusable classes. The second (and the definition that will be used most often) applies to the way that Visual FoxPro stores classes. Visual FoxPro provides two formats for storing class libraries: .VCXs and .PRGs. Most of Visual FoxPro is geared towards using class libraries stored in the .VCX format rather than classes in .PRGs. Just as FoxPro 2.x stores screens, reports, and menus in tables, the .VCX is a FoxPro table. Each class is stored as a record in the table. The Columns in the .VCX are identical to the Columns in the Visual FoxPro .SCX file, which has changed significantly from the FoxPro 2.x structure. Some documentation is available in the \VFP\FILESPEC\30SCX.DBF file supplied with Visual FoxPro. Forms are just special case classes that have additional records in the table to store information about the DataEnvironment and its Cursors and Relations. Here's a warning about USEing the .VCX and mucking around with it by hand: do this only on a backup copy. If you incorrectly change the contents of some of the fields, Visual FoxPro may not be able to load the classlib. In some cases this can crash your system all the way back to MS-DOS. Don't be too afraid to poke around in there, all of the listings of the methods and properties that appear in the reportare the output of a program that was written to read the .VCX or .SCX to make it easier to get the running code into this report.

This report has used separate class libraries for each of the examples. In some cases this has resulted in classes being duplicated in one or more class libraries. This was done so there wouldn't be any dependencies between the examples where code for one example would possibly break another example. You should *not* follow this example when developing your class libraries.

While you are learning object-oriented programming, you are probably going to make some mistakes in the way you develop your class libraries. It is not uncommon to have to throw-away your first couple of attempts at a class library. Don't feel that your work was not worth the effort. This experience will make your successive generations of classes better structured and much more reusable.

2 | Techniques and Details

Naming Conventions

Before you start creating names for your class properties and methods, you should study the property and method names used by Visual FoxPro. Whether you like them or not, they are the convention. If your class is going to have a property that contains foreground color, you should use the standard name ForeColor instead of your own name like ForegrndColor. The same rule applies for methods. If one of your class methods is used to display an object to the user, name the method Show() instead of Display(). Following this rule will reduce the amount of time you spend looking through class library documentation for property and method names. Using the same name for properties and methods is also consistent with the polymorphic nature of object-oriented programming languages. In addition, it will aid other programmers in using your class libraries.

I generally follow the naming conventions described in the Naming Conventions part of the Visual FoxPro Help file under the Technical Reference and Programming subheads. My conventions have been slightly modified based on my preferences and programming habits developed over the last 20 years. This naming convention is based on Hungarian notation in honor of the legendary Microsoft programmer Charles Simonyi. Fundamentally it prefixes "data type" information to a name. Hungarian notation is designed to reduce errors that occur when you pass invalid data types to functions or when you perform operations with incompatible data types (for example, adding a string to a number). Because Xbase is a weakly typed language, the severity of this problem depends on your viewpoint. In C/C++, it is usually a terminal mistake to pass the wrong type of argument to a Windows API routine, but C/C++ is also capable of insuring data type correctness at compile time. In Xbase you must wait for these failures to occur at runtime. Using a naming convention helps avoid the problem. Initially I disliked the thought of using the prefixed names primarily because of the large FORTRAN and pre-Windows C projects I'd worked on. A variable cross-reference listing was really needed in those environments, and in Xbase I thought it would be pretty useless to have all of the variables sorted by type rather than by name. In the five years that I've been working with Xbase, I've encountered only one or two instances where a variable cross-reference listing was of any use at all. As a result, the prefix naming convention is not nearly the problem I thought it would be.

My naming convention is just that—it's *my* naming convention. It's influenced by the fact that I also program in other languages and I like to provide as many similarities as possible in my work. This makes it easier to switch back and forth between languages. You may like it or hate it. Whether you use, change, or ignore my system, I strongly urge you to follow some sort of convention. That being said, take a look at some specific details.

An identifier name is composed of three parts: <scope prefix><type prefix><Identifier>.

Scopes:
The meanings of scope prefixes are listed in Table 2-1.

Scope Prefix	Meaning
g	global (PUBLIC)
l	LOCAL (and PRIVATE for compatibility with my FoxPro 2.x code)
m	member
p	parameter
r	reference parameter

Table 2-1.

Scope prefixes

I use an "m" as an object scope identifier. This is done to be consistent with Visual C++ and MFC, which I also use. It makes all of my names more consistent, and it helps to remind me that there needs to be an object reference in front of any "m" names. I use "p" instead of "t" for parameters from my pre-FoxPro Xbase habits. I added "r" to help note where a parameter was passed by reference instead of by value.

Types:
The meanings of type prefixes are listed in Table 2-2.

Table 2-2.

Type prefixes

Type Prefix	Meaning
a	array
b	double
c	character
d	date
f	float
i	integer
l	logical
n	numeric
o	object
t	datetime
u	unknown
y	currency

Identifiers:
An identifier is the name you give to a variable. I use internal capitalization to separate the "words" within the identifier. With FoxPro 2.x, you needed to be very creative with variable and routine names to work within the limit of 10 significant characters. I've always used names longer than 10 characters in Xbase, and I'm grateful the Visual FoxPro has increased the number of significant characters in names. I'd have been happy with 32, but the new limit of 254 should keep even the most verbose programmer happy. The only people that'll have problems are those who used names longer than 10 characters but weren't always consistent beyond the tenth character. In Visual FoxPro each name is now unique, which will cause the code with those inconsistencies to fail.

Here are some examples of variable names:

- laFiles   local array of files
- mcLastName   member character that holds a LastName
- pnItemId   parameter numeric ItemId
- glIdiotUser   global logical indicating the user is an idiot
- i   I refuse to give 'significant' names to simple loop counters

Objects:

For objects within containers, the <scope prefix> is dropped: <object prefix><Identifier>. The meanings of object prefixes are shown in Table 2-3.

Table 2-3.

Object prefixes

Object Prefix	Meaning/BaseClass
chk	CheckBox
cbo	ComboBox
cmd	CommandButton
cmg	CommandGroup
cnt	Container
ctl	Control
edt	EditBox
frm	Form
frs	FormSet
grd	Grid
grc	Column
grh	Header
img	Image
lbl	Label
lin	Line
lst	ListBox
olb	OLEBoundControl
ole	OLE
opt	OptionButton
opg	OptionGroup
pag	Page
pgf	PageFrame
sep	Separator
shp	Shape
spn	Spinner
txt	TextBox
tmr	Timer
tbr	toolbar

I don't have an object prefix for Custom because I haven't needed one yet, because the object usually winds up being named something like moContextMenu or loFont. For my subclasses of the

Visual FoxPro BaseClasses, I don't create a special object prefix. I use the same prefix as the BaseClass.

Here are some sample object names:

- txtLastName   TextBox for LastName
- opgReportDestination   OptionGroup that selects the report destination
- cmdHelp   CommandButton that launches Help

For Class names I use a similar method of prefixing. I prefix the "specialization" to the "general" class name it is derived from:

EditBox	The Visual FoxPro BaseClass
cEditBox	My custom EditBox
ContextMenuEditBox	An EditBox that has ContextMenu capabilities
TextBox	The Visual FoxPro BaseClass
cTextBox	My custom TextBox
ReadOnlyTextBox	A read-only TextBox

This prefixing follows the class naming conventions used by Visual C++ and MFC. For any class derived from cEditBox, I drop the "c" as redundant because I always derive other classes from my custom class rather than from the Visual FoxPro BaseClass. Each of the classes in the last example would use "edt" or "txt" as their object prefixes when they were put onto a Form.

Some authors add the specialization of the class as a suffix instead of a prefix. I present this to make you aware that there are always alternate ways of doing things. As a result, the class names would look like:

EditBox	The Visual FoxPro BaseClass
EditBoxRalph	An EditBox that Ralph likes
EditBoxRalphBlue	An EditBox that Ralph likes that is Blue

This report will follow the prefix convention because that's the one I like the best.

If the class is a single-purpose object that can be used directly on a Form, I go ahead and name it accordingly by using the object prefix at the beginning of the name:

CommandButton	The Visual FoxPro BaseClass
cCommandButton	My custom CommandButton
cmdOk	A functional Ok button

A cmdOk object can be dropped onto a Form and be fully functional as is. The cmdOk class has a Click() method that contains the code necessary to release the Form it is on. A cCommandButton that's dropped on a Form would need code attached to its Click() method before it would do any specific work when it was clicked. I also rename the button on the Form to fit the three-letter prefix Form, changing it from cCommandButton1 to cmdWhateverFunctionThisButtonPerforms.

All of my "c" classes are stored in the CCONTROL.VCX class library. That way I only have to go to one place to maintain my custom base classes. This also provides a single point, maintaining a consistent look and behavior.

I also use the diagram conventions in Figure 2-1 to draw class trees:

Figure 2-1.

Class diagram conventions

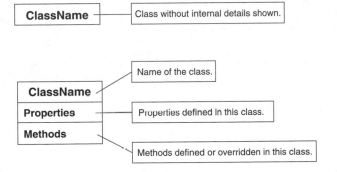

I use the undivided box when the overall class structure is more important than the internal details of each class. I'll use the divided box when you need to see what is inside each class.

Visual FoxPro Classes

The Base Classes

Visual FoxPro provides a set of fully functional classes that it calls the base classes. If you are a C++ programmer, this term conflicts with the C++ definition of base class. The C++ base class is called the ParentClass in Visual FoxPro. What Visual FoxPro calls a base class is simply a C++ class that is not derived from any other class. This report will use the term BaseClass when talking about these built-in classes. Visual FoxPro requires that any class you create must be derived from another class. This differs from C++ where classes do not have to be derived from a class.

Table 2-4 maps the Visual FoxPro BaseClasses to their FoxPro 2.x equivalents:

Table 2-4.

*Visual FoxPro and
FoxPro 2.x equivalents*

BaseClass Name	Closest FoxPro 2.x Equivalent	Description
CheckBox	@GET - Check Box	A yes/no control.
Column	BROWSE FIELD	A Column Container within a Grid.
ComboBox	@GET - Popup	A drop-down list control.
CommandButton	@GET - Push Buttons	A push button control.
CommandGroup	@GET - Push Buttons	A container for multiple CommandButtons.
Container		A class that contains other classes.
Control		A class that contains other classes but restricts access to the contained classes.
Cursor		A class representing one of the tables used by the DataEnvironment.
Custom		A user-defined container class.
DataEnvironment		A class that represents the data used by a Form.
EditBox	@EDIT	An input control for a multiple line edit region (memo field).
Form	A Screen	A container class for most of the other objects in this table.
FormSet	A Screen Set	A container of Forms.
Grid	BROWSE	An object that can display rows and Columns of data. A container for Column controls and Header controls.
Header	BROWSE :H=	The heading of a Grid Column control.
Image	@SAY - Bitmap	A picture display control.
Label	@SAY	A text display control.
Line	@ ... BOX	A line control. This is no longer restricted to being vertical or horizontal.
ListBox	@GET - List	A control with a list of items. It can have multiple Columns.
OLEControl		A control for OLE objects not bound to a General field.
OLEBoundControl	@SAY OLE Object	A control used to display the contents of an OLE object (such as from Microsoft Word and Microsoft Excel) from a General field of a table.
OptionButton		A control within an OptionGroup control.
OptionGroup	@GET - Radio Buttons	A "choose one" control. This is a container of OptionButton controls.

Continued on next page

BaseClass Name	Closest FoxPro 2.x Equivalent	Description
Page		A page within a PageFrame.
PageFrame		A tabbed display control. A container for Page controls.
Relation		A class representing the relation between two Cursors in the DataEnvironment.
Separator		A control that separates controls in a toolbar.
Shape	@ ... TO	A control for boxes, ellipses, and circles.
Spinner	@GET - Spinner	A numeric spinner control.
TextBox	@GET or @SAY	A text input control.
Timer		A control that can execute code at programmable timed intervals.
Toolbar		A container for creating free-floating and dockable Forms.

Container and Control Classes

Classes within Visual FoxPro are divided into two types: containers and controls. Container classes can contain other objects, support the ADD OBJECT command, and have AddObject( ) methods. A Form is a container class because it can contain control and container objects, and a PageFrame is a container class that can contain Page classes. The Control BaseClass is a special kind of container that prevents all external access to its contained objects. Most control classes create objects the user will interact with. These include TextBoxes (similar to @GETs) and CommandButtons (@GET - Pushbutton). The Timer control does not support any type of user interaction.

Visual Classes and Non-Visual Classes

Classes within Visual FoxPro are also divided into two other types: visual and non-visual. Objects created from visual classes can be seen (for example, the CommandButton). Objects created from non-visual classes cannot be seen (for example, a Timer). Non-visual classes (except FormSet) do not have a Refresh( ) method or a Visible property. The FormSet class does not have any visual presentation of itself; only the Forms it contains can be seen. The FormSet.Refresh( ) method and Visible property are items that allow you access to all the contained Forms.

In keeping with the fine Xbase tradition that brought you such memorable commands as WAIT WINDOW NOWAIT and EDIT ... NOEDIT, you can design non-visual classes using the visual class

Table 2-5.

Class groupings

designer. Table 2-5 lists the Visual FoxPro base classes. It shows whether they are controls or containers and whether they are visual or non-visual:

BaseClass Name	Control	Container	Visual	Non-Visual	Notes
CheckBox	✓		✓		
Column		✓	✓		1,3
ComboBox	✓		✓		
CommandButton	✓		✓		4
CommandGroup		✓	✓		4
Container		✓	✓		
Control		✓	✓		
Cursor	✓			✓	1
Custom		✓		✓	
DataEnvironment		✓		✓	1
EditBox	✓		✓		
Form		✓	✓		
FormSet		✓		✓	
Grid		✓	✓		3
Header	✓		✓		1,5
Image	✓		✓		
Label	✓		✓		
Line	✓		✓		
ListBox	✓		✓		
OLEControl	✓		✓		
OLEBoundControl	✓		✓		
OptionButton	✓		✓		1,7
OptionGroup		✓	✓		7
Page		✓	✓		1,2
PageFrame		✓	✓		2
Relation	✓			✓	1
Separator	✓		✓		
Shape	✓		✓		
Spinner	✓		✓		
TextBox	✓		✓		
Timer	✓			✓	
Toolbar		✓	✓		6

Here are a few notes on Table 2-5.

1. Subclasses of these classes cannot be created in the Class Designer. Subclasses of them can be created within .PRG files. For example, you cannot create a class cPage of ccontrol as a Page. If you try to do so, you will get the dialog box in Figure 2-2.

Figure 2-2.

The Class Designer cannot handle some classes.

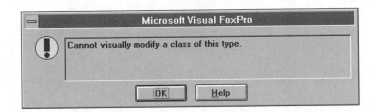

However, you can define a class cPage inside a .PRG:

```
define class cPage as Page
enddefine
```

2. PageFrames can contain only Pages, and Pages can be added only to PageFrames. For example, you cannot:

```
define class cPageFrame as PageFrame
  add object cmd OK as Command Button
enddefine
```

Trying to do so will get you the dialog box shown in Figure 2-3.

Figure 2-3.

Some containers restrict the type of contained objects.

3. Columns can be put into Grid container classes only. Columns can contain Headers and any other objects except Forms, FormSets, Columns, and Toolbars.

4. CommandGroups can contain only CommandButton classes.

5. Headers can be contained only in Column classes.

6. Toolbars can contain any Control class, PageFrame class, or container class.

7. OptionGroups can contain only OptionButtons.

Class Relationships

Given the part of a class tree shown in Figure 2-4, you can examine the relationships between each class.

Figure 2-4.

A button class tree

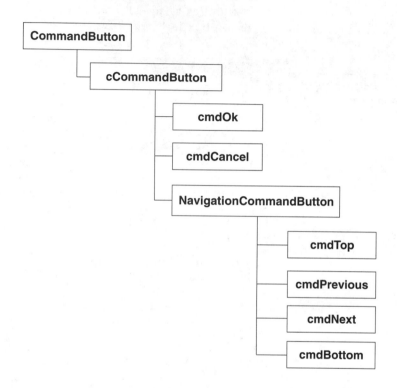

This is the code that creates the class tree:

```
* CLASTRE1.PRG   16-may-95

define class cCommandButton as CommandButton
enddefine

define class cmdOk as cCommandButton
Caption = "Ok"
enddefine

define class cmdCancel as cCommandButton
Caption = "Cancel"
enddefine

define class NavigationCommandButton as cCommandButton
enddefine

define class cmdTop as NavigationCommandButton
Caption = "Top"
enddefine
```

Continued on next page

```
define class cmdPrevious as NavigationCommandButton
Caption = "Previous"
enddefine

define class cmdNext as NavigationCommandButton
Caption = "Next"
enddefine

define class cmdBottom as NavigationCommandButton
Caption = "Bottom"
enddefine
```

Table 2-6 shows you the class and its ParentClass, any subclasses that are derived from it, and its BaseClass.

Class	ParentClass	Subclass	BaseClass
CommandButton	A Visual FoxPro BaseClass does *not* have a ParentClass	cCommandButton	CommandButton
cCommandButton	CommandButton	cmdOk cmdCancel NavigationCommandButton	CommandButton
cmdOk	cCommandButton		CommandButton
cmdCancel	cCommandButton		CommandButton
NavigationCommandButton	cCommandButton	cmdTop cmdPrevious cmdNext cmdBottom	CommandButton
cmdTop	NavigationCommandButton		CommandButton
cmdPrevious	NavigationCommandButton		CommandButton
cmdNext	NavigationCommandButton		CommandButton
cmdBottom	NavigationCommandButton		CommandButton

Table 2-6.

Class Relationships

The ParentClass is the class from which the class is derived. The subclass Column indicates any subclasses that a class may have. A class has *no* information about the subclasses derived from it; the subclasses are listed here only to familiarize you with the terminology. Notice that each one of these classes has CommandButton as its BaseClass. It doesn't matter how many levels down a class tree any given class is located; its BaseClass will always be the built-in Visual FoxPro BaseClass that is at the root of the class tree.

Object References

Object references are memory variables or object properties that contain a *pointer*, or reference, to an object. As you will see in the next two example sessions, you must know the object's .Name to create these references.

Special Object References

While you are creating a class and putting code into a method, you don't have any idea what the .Name of the object will be. Because of this, Visual FoxPro has a special set of "keywords" that serve as object references. *These are valid only while a class method is executing.*

this

While you are inside an object's methods, you refer to the object itself by the object reference keyword *this*. The keyword represents the name of the object, which is unknown until runtime.

thisform

Objects that are contained within a Form object can use the object reference keyword *thisform* to reference the properties and methods of the Form object. Again, this is because the class developer will not know the name of the Form object. Note that while you are in a Form method, *this* is equivalent to *thisform*.

thisformset

Objects that are contained within a FormSet object can use the object reference keyword *thisformset* to reference the properties and methods of the FormSet object. Again, this is because the class developer will not know the name of the FormSet object at design time. Note that while you are in a FormSet method, *this* is equivalent to *thisformset*.

parent

Any object contained in a container object can use the keyword *parent* to reference the properties and methods of that container object. The documentation lists parent as a property, but it doesn't appear as a property in the output of the AMEMBERS() function.

The this, thisform, and thisformset object references are available only while a method of an object is executing, so you can't use them in normal UDFs. They can also be passed as arguments to a UDF. However they can be used in the command window or debug window if you've suspended execution while you are in a method.

_screen.ActiveForm

In the command window or from within other code, you can reference the Form that has focus by using the ActiveForm object reference contained in the _screen object.

_screen.ActiveForm.ActiveControl
In the command window or from within other code, you can
reference the control that has focus on the Form that has focus by
using the ActiveControl object reference contained in the ActiveForm
object of _screen.

Now go back to the SAMPLE Form discussed earlier in which
two buttons were sending messages to each other. Here's the
cmdLeftButton.Click() method:

```
thisform.cmdRightButton.Caption = "Now Click Me!"
thisform.cmdRightButton.Enabled = .t.
this.Caption = ""
this.Enabled = .f.
```

The button uses the thisform reference to address the
cmdRightButton and alter its Caption and Enabled status. It then
uses "this" to change its own properties. The cmdRightButton has
a similar Click() method.

Example 2-1: Classes and Inheritance
Now take a few minutes to play with these concepts. Begin
this example by entering the following command in the command
window:

```
do form clastre1
```

This brings up a Form that shows objects from the CLASTRE1.VCX
visual class library. The buttons are arranged on the Form to illustrate
the structure of the class tree. While this Form is running, you can
click each item, including the TextBoxes and Labels, and that item's
Class, ParentClass, BaseClass, and Name will be displayed.

Now look at how easy it was to get each object to display the
information about itself. Begin by opening the CLASTRE1 project.
Expand the Class Library Item, then expand CLASTRE1 class library.
Next, highlight the CCOMANDBUTTON class and click the Modify
button. Now open the code window and select the GotFocus()
method. You'll see the following code:

```
thisform.DisplayObjectInfo( this )
```

This code passes a reference to the button (this) to the Form
method DisplayObjectInfo(). The DisplayObjectInfo() method places
the values of the button's properties into the appropriate property
of the Form. Normally a Generic class wouldn't have such intimate
knowledge about the Form, but this is a special case class for this

illustration. As this class is now coded, it can be used only on a Form that has a DisplayObjectInfo() method.

Now that a cCommandButton "knows" how to display its information, cmdOk will also automatically know how to display its information. When you open the GotFocus() method of the cmdOk class, you will find that it's empty. This is a benefit of inheritance. Because cmdOk is subclassed from cCommandButton, it automatically inherits the behavior of its ParentClass. Every subclass derived from cCommandButton will inherit the new GotFocus() method.

However the TextBoxes and Labels do not inherit the GotFocus() method of cCommandButton. You will have to duplicate that code in cTextBox and cLabel. Because a Label cannot get focus, the code is put into its Click() method.

This class tree in Figure 2-4 also illustrates the use of NavigationCommandButton as an *abstract class*. An abstract class is a class that will not have instances; it is used only to derive other classes (cmdTop, cmdNext, and so forth) that will be instantiated within an application. The NavigationCommandButton class would have basic table navigation functions such as checking for BOF() and EOF() that each button would use. In this case, rather than having each navigation button do its own checking and having the same (or very similar) code appear in each of the four buttons, you promote the common code up the tree to a higher class. Combining and moving the code to another class will simplify the code's debug and maintenance process. When the code is changed in the NavigationCommandButton, it's automatically inherited by the subclasses.

Example 2-2: Object References
Now try something else. You can begin a second example by entering this code:

```
do form objref
```

This brings up the Form shown in Figure 2-5. As you click the buttons, they update their own Captions and send messages to the adjoining TextBox, which updates its Value. Discussion of the contained objects and the control object will be postponed until later.

Figure 2-5.

OBJREF sample Form

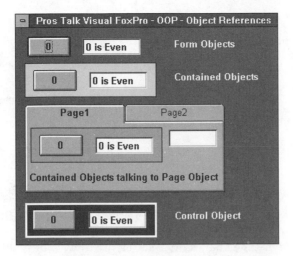

The Form's Init() method shows two equivalences:

```
* frmObjectReference.Init
* since you are in a Form method THIS == THISFORM

   this.AutoCenter = .t.
thisform.AutoCenter = .t.

   this.BorderStyle = 1
thisform.BorderStyle = 1
```

Inside Form methods, I normally use the this object reference instead of thisform. The two are equivalent in a Form method. Normally the thisform object reference is only used in methods of objects contained within the Form when they need to reference a Form property, method, or another Form object.

This example also illustrates two useful design time shortcuts. First, set the AutoCenter property when the Form initializes rather than setting it to .T. at design time. This is done because setting it to .T. at design time causes the Form to appear in the center of the Form Designer instead of the upper left corner, where it is easier to work with. Second, if the BorderStyle is set to 1 at design time, you can no longer use the mouse to drag it to the size and shape you want. As a result, you can leave it set to the default value during design and change it when the Form initializes.

The Click() method of the upper left CommandButton is shown here:

```
* cmdFormCount.Click

cmdCount::Click()

* These are all equivalent ways to send the current value of
* the button count to the txtFormEvenOdd object.

thisform.txtFormEvenOdd.mnNumber = this.mnCount

this.parent.txtFormEvenOdd.mnNumber = this.mnCount

_screen.ActiveForm.txtFormEvenOdd.mnNumber = this.mnCount

thisform.Refresh()
```

This code used the thisform object, but this.parent is more useful when you're talking about additional layers of object containers such as Pages of PageFrames and Grids. Using _screen.ActiveForm is sometimes necessary, but it's not always desirable because the Form in which this object is located might not be the active Form when this method is called. For example, you could start another Form and make it active. However, if you typed objref.cmdFormCount.Click() in the command window, the _screen.ActiveForm line would fail because the objref screen is not the currently active Form.

Object Reference Counter

Objects have an internal reference counter that keeps track of how many references there are to the object. Normally an object will have only one reference, but it is possible to have more than one. When an object has multiple references to it, it cannot be released from memory until all of the references are removed.

Example 2-3: The Object Reference Counter
Now take a few minutes to play with this information. Begin the example by entering the following code:

```
do objref
```

The code for this program is shown:

```
set safety off

o1 = createobject( "ObjectRef" )      && create an object
o2 = o1
   && create two references
o3 = o1

display memory like o* to file objref.1 noconsole
modify file objref.1 nowait

display objects like o* to file objref.2 noconsole
modify file objref.2 nowait
```

Continued on next page

```
? o1.mcValue, o2.mcValue, o3.mcValue

o3.mcValue = "Changed"

? o1.mcValue, o2.mcValue, o3.mcValue

release o1

? type( "o1.mcValue" )

? o2.mcValue, o3.mcValue

o2 = .null.

? o3.mcValue

release o3

define class ObjectRef as custom
   mcValue = "Test"

procedure Destroy()
? "I'm outta here!"
endproc

enddefine
```

The screen output will look like this:

```
Test Test Test
Changed      Changed      Changed
U
Changed      Changed
Changed
I'm outta here!
```

Only one object was created in memory, but three memory variables reference the object. This illustrates that when o3.mcValue is set to "Changed," all of the references are pointing to the same object whose value is altered. When all three references are released, the object is really destroyed. Notice that you can remove a reference by changing the value of the referencing memory variable to o2 = .null. (o2 = .f. would also work).

Now enter the following command:

```
do catch22
```

This next program creates an object that has a reference to itself as one of its properties. This will prevent the object from being released when you expect.

```
clear
o1 = createobject( "Catch22", "o1" )
? "Now you see it:"
display memory like o*

release o1
? "Now you don't:"
display memory like o*

? "Notice the Destroy() event did NOT occur."
? "But our only way to reference the object has been wiped out!"

o2 = createobject( "Catch22", "o2" )
? "Now you see it:"
display memory like o*

o2.moSelf = .null.                && remove internal object ref

release o2
? "Now you don't, because it has been destroyed:"
display memory like o*

? "This will finally destroy o1:"
clear all
return

define class Catch22 as custom
   mcName = ""
   moSelf = .null.

procedure Init( pcName )
this.moSelf = this               && create a reference to myself
this.mcName = pcName
?
? "Creating a Catch22 object named:", this.mcName
endproc

procedure Destroy()
? "Object named:", this.mcName, " being destroyed"
endproc

enddefine
```

This code can also cause problems if you are setting a Form property to one of the contained objects of the Form. In this case, the Form will not release until you reset the property to a non-object reference value. For example, if you want to be able to move the cursor to the first control on a Form, you don't want to hard code the object name because the first control might change as the Form is being designed. You could create a Form property named moFirstControl and assign it a reference to the object with .TabIndex = 1 during the Form Init() method. This code is shown:

```
* cForm.Init

cForm::Init()

local i
for i = 1 to this.ControlCount
   if ( this.Controls[i].TabIndex = 1 )
      this.moFirstControl = this.Controls[i]
      exit
   endif
endfor
```

However, when you issue a thisform.Release(), the Form will stay on the screen. Now try entering the following code:

```
do form catch22
```

This brings up the Form in Figure 2-6.

Figure 2-6.

Form with internal self references

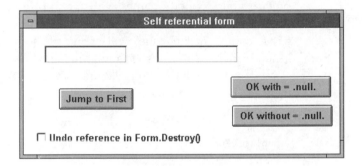

The cursor will return to the first TextBox control whenever you click the Jump To First button. However, if you click the Ok Without = .null. button or double-click the control menu, the Form Destroy() method will run but the Form will not close. If you click the control menu, you'll notice that it no longer has a Close option. The Form is now stuck! If you click the Ok With = .null. button, the Form will close because the reference has been removed in the Click() method. However, if you use the control menu to close the Form, it won't close because the Ok button Click() method does not occur. The only practical place to remove the reference is in the Form Destroy() method:

```
* cForm.Destroy

wait window "Form.Destroy" nowait

if ( this.chkUndo.Value  )
   this.moFirstControl = .null.
endif

cForm::Destroy()
```

The CheckBox controls whether or not the Destroy() method removes the reference. If the checkbox is checked, any way that the user has to close the Form it will successfully close.

Properties Versus Memvars

As you begin working with classes, you will probably to tear some of your hair out over the issue of using properties or memvars. While you are inside your method code, you *must* remember to preface your property names with the appropriate object reference (this, thisform, and so forth). If you don't, Visual FoxPro (being an Xbase-compliant language) will create memory variables whenever it needs them. This is especially confusing when you are creating classes in .PRG files, setting default values, and perhaps changing them in the Init() method as shown:

```
* nothis.prg  13-Aug-95

public oForm
oForm = createobject( "MyForm" )
oForm.Show()

define class MyForm as Form
Caption = "My Form"
BackColor = rgb( 255, 0, 255 )

procedure Init
Caption = "Hi There"
BackColor = rgb( 0, 255, 0 )
endproc

enddefine
```

When you run the code, the Form will still be purple and have the Caption My Form. You can open the Trace window and step through each line of code. Then watch Caption and BackColor in the debug window. When the Init() method runs, you will see Caption change to "Hi There" and BackColor change to 65280 (rgb(0,255,0)), but the Form will not change. In this case, Xbase is at fault, not object-oriented programming. When the Init() method runs and Visual FoxPro sees the line Caption = "Hi There", it sees that you want to create a new private memory variable named Caption and assign it a value. It doesn't see that you want to set the Caption property of the current object. If that is what you wanted, you'd have put a *this*. in front of it.

The proper Init() method should be as shown:

```
procedure Init()
this.Caption = "Hi There"
this.BackColor = rgb( 0, 255, 0 )
endproc
```

The ways to avoid this memory variable vs. property problem are to:

- Always remember to use *this*.
- Try to avoid setting initial values in both the default values and the Init() method.
- Avoid cutting or pasting code from the default values to the Init() method.
- Use a visual class library. You never directly work with the default values code because it comes from the property sheet, but this problem can still occur within any method code in which you forget the object reference.

Constructor and Destructor Methods

When an object is being created in memory, it is being instantiated. In most object-oriented languages, object instantiation is handled by the "constructor," which builds the object in memory. In C++, this is the constructor method; in Visual FoxPro, this method is named Init(). Likewise, when an object is being removed from memory, a method is used to "destruct" the object. In C++, this is the destructor method; in Visual FoxPro, this method is named Destroy(). Generally these methods let the object initialize its properties and clean up after itself.

Details of Object Instantiation

The next example will focus on object construction, default property values, and object memory use. If you compare the C++ constructor with the Visual FoxPro Init() method, there are a few differences. The C++ constructor allocates memory, initializes values, and can execute any other code placed in the method. The Visual FoxPro constructor has many internal steps which handle all of the low-level details for you. The memory allocation is out of your control and happens before the Init() method runs. The property default values are set, then the Init() method is called. If the Init() method returns .F., the object does not instantiate and the memory is released. The

Destroy() method does not run if the object does not instantiate.

Now examine these processes in closer detail to see exactly what happens when an object is instantiated. Use the following class as an illustration:

```
* hal9000.prg  07-Jul-95

* Sample class to illustrate memory use and default vs. Init()
* values
define class HAL9000 as custom
   mcText   = "I was defined in Lynchburg, Virginia"
   mtAware  = {7/7/95 19:57}
   mtDefault = datetime()
   Name     = "HAL9000"

procedure Init
   this.Show( .t. )
   this.mcText         = "I became a sentient, instantiated
   object"
   this.mtAware        = datetime()
   this.Show( .f. )
endproc

procedure Destroy
   ? "Stop, Dave. "
   this.Age()
   this.mcText         = "My existence ended"
   this.mtAware        = datetime()
   this.Show( .f. )
endproc

procedure Show( plDefault )
   ? " I am a", this.Name, padr( this.mcText, 40 ), this.mtAware
   if ( m.plDefault )
      ?? " mtDefault =", this.mtDefault
   endif
endproc

procedure Age
   ?? "I have existed", alltrim( str( datetime() -
      this.mtAware ) ), "seconds."
endproc

enddefine


define class SAL9000 as HAL9000
   mtDefault = datetime()
   Name = "SAL9000"
enddefine
```

This code defines two classes that assign default values to the properties, set some of the properties in Init(), set some of the properties in Destroy(), and prints information about the object to the screen.

The following test driver instantiates two objects of each class with a three-second delay between objects.

```
* haltest.prg 07-Jul-95

? datetime()
set procedure to hal9000
? datetime()

= inkey( 3 )
x1 = createobject( "hal9000" )

= inkey( 3 )
y1 = createobject( "sal9000" )

= inkey( 3 )
x2 = createobject( "hal9000" )

= inkey( 3 )
y2 = createobject( "sal9000" )

release y2
release x2
release y1
release x1

clear class sal9000
clear class hal9000
set procedure to
```

Now look step by step at what happens in memory:

Code	What happens	What is in memory
set procedure to hal9000	hal9000.fxp is loaded into memory.	
x1 = createobject("hal9000")	The HAL9000 default values are calculated. Memory is allocated to hold x1. The default values are assigned to x1.	HAL9000 default values and methods x1. mcText = "I was defined in Lynchburg, Virginia" x1.mtAware = {7/7/95 19:57} x1.mtDefault = datetime() x1.Name = "HAL9000"
	The HAL9000 Init() method executes.	x1.mcText = "I became a sentient, instantiated object" x1.mtAware = datetime()

Continued on next page

Continued from previous page

Code	What happens	What is in memory
y1 = createobject("sal9000")	The SAL9000 default values are calculated.	SAL9000 default values and methods
	Memory is allocated to hold y1.	

	The default values are assigned to y1.	`y1. mcText   = "I was defined in Lynchburg, Virginia"`
		`y1.mtAware   = {7/7/95 19:57}`
		`y1.mtDefault = datetime()`
		`y1.Name      = "HAL9000"`

	The SAL9000 Init() method executes.	`y1.mcText  = "I became a sentient, instantiated object"` `y1.mtAware = datetime()`
x2 = createobject("hal9000")	Memory is allocated to hold x2.	

	The default values are assigned to x2.	`x2. mcText   = "I was defined in Lynchburg, Virginia"`
		`x2.mtAware   = {7/7/95 19:57}`
		`x2.mtDefault = datetime()`
		`x2.Name      = "HAL9000"`

	The HAL9000 Init() method executes.	`x2.mcText  = "I became a sentient, instantiated object"` `x2.mtAware = datetime()`
y2 = createobject("sal9000")	Memory is allocated to hold y2.	

	The default values are assigned to y2.	`y2. mcText   = "I was defined in Lynchburg, Virginia"`
		`y2.mtAware   = {7/7/95 19:57}`
		`y2.mtDefault = datetime()`
		`y2.Name      = "HAL9000"`

	The SAL9000 Init() method executes.	`y2.mcText  = "I became a sentient, instantiated object"` `y2.mtAware = datetime()`
release y2	The SAL9000 Destroy() method executes.	`y2 = .null.`
release x2	The HAL9000 Destroy() method executes.	`x2 = .null.`
release y1	The SAL9000 Destroy() method executes.	`y1 = .null.`
release x1	The HAL9000 Destroy() method executes.	`x1 = .null.`
clear class sal9000	The class SAL9000 is released from memory.	

Continued on next page

Code	What happens	What is in memory
clear class hal9000	The class HAL9000 is released from memory.	
set procedure to	hal9000.fxp is released from memory.	

There is only one copy of the default values and methods for each class in memory. The objects of a given class do not get their own copies of the methods, instead they all share the one copy that was loaded when the first object of the class was instantiated. This works just like a UDF. There is only one copy of a UDF in memory even though there may be many references to it by many other procedures. However, each object does have its own set of properties in memory.

This also points out a misconception that occurs when cookie cutters or blueprints are used as examples to illustrate a class. When you stamp out a cookie, you create a whole stand-alone cookie. Individual cookies are not dependent upon a set of cookie methods such as GetStale() or EmitSmell() that exist out in the kitchen somewhere. When you build a house from a blueprint, you have a whole stand-alone house. Each house is not dependent on a global Bathroom() method located somewhere in the neighborhood. In a class, each object is dependent on a set of object methods located somewhere else in memory. This doesn't affect object encapsulation in any way, it is just a practical matter of minimizing the amount of memory that objects consume.

The following output is the result of running the HALTEST2 program two times in a row with a few seconds of delay between the runs. This is a second test driver that does not clear the class from memory at the end.

```
08/08/95 01:40:08 AM
08/08/95 01:40:08 AM
   I am a HAL9000 I was defined in Lynchburg, Virginia      07/07/95 07:57:00
PM mtDefault = 08/08/95 01:40:11 AM
   I am a HAL9000 I became a sentient, instantiated object  08/08/95 01:40:11 AM
   I am a SAL9000 I was defined in Lynchburg, Virginia      07/07/95 07:57:00
PM mtDefault = 08/08/95 01:40:15 AM
   I am a SAL9000 I became a sentient, instantiated object  08/08/95 01:40:15 AM
   I am a HAL9000 I was defined in Lynchburg, Virginia      07/07/95 07:57:00
PM mtDefault = 08/08/95 01:40:11 AM
   I am a HAL9000 I became a sentient, instantiated object  08/08/95 01:40:19 AM
   I am a SAL9000 I was defined in Lynchburg, Virginia      07/07/95 07:57:00
PM mtDefault = 08/08/95 01:40:15 AM
```

Continued on next page

Continued from previous page

```
   I am a SAL9000 I became a sentient, instantiated object  08/08/95 01:40:23 AM
Stop, Dave. I have existed 0 seconds.
   I am a SAL9000 My existence ended                        08/08/95 01:40:23 AM
Stop, Dave. I have existed 4 seconds.
   I am a HAL9000 My existence ended                        08/08/95 01:40:23 AM
Stop, Dave. I have existed 9 seconds.
   I am a SAL9000 My existence ended                        08/08/95 01:40:24 AM
Stop, Dave. I have existed 13 seconds.
   I am a HAL9000 My existence ended                        08/08/95 01:40:24 AM
08/08/95 01:40:41 AM
08/08/95 01:40:42 AM
   I am a HAL9000 I was defined in Lynchburg, Virginia      07/07/95 07:57:00
PM mtDefault = 08/08/95 01:40:11 AM
   I am a HAL9000 I became a sentient, instantiated object  08/08/95 01:40:45 AM
   I am a SAL9000 I was defined in Lynchburg, Virginia      07/07/95 07:57:00
PM mtDefault = 08/08/95 01:40:15 AM
   I am a SAL9000 I became a sentient, instantiated object  08/08/95 01:40:49 AM
   I am a HAL9000 I was defined in Lynchburg, Virginia      07/07/95 07:57:00
PM mtDefault = 08/08/95 01:40:11 AM
   I am a HAL9000 I became a sentient, instantiated object  08/08/95 01:40:53 AM
   I am a SAL9000 I was defined in Lynchburg, Virginia      07/07/95 07:57:00
PM mtDefault = 08/08/95 01:40:15 AM
   I am a SAL9000 I became a sentient, instantiated object  08/08/95 01:40:57 AM
Stop, Dave. I have existed 0 seconds.
   I am a SAL9000 My existence ended                        08/08/95 01:40:57 AM
Stop, Dave. I have existed 4 seconds.
   I am a HAL9000 My existence ended                        08/08/95 01:40:57 AM
Stop, Dave. I have existed 9 seconds.
   I am a SAL9000 My existence ended                        08/08/95 01:40:58 AM
Stop, Dave. I have existed 13 seconds.
   I am a HAL9000 My existence ended                        08/08/95 01:40:58 AM
```

It's important to note that while every HAL9000 object has the same mtDefault value and every SAL9000 object has the same mtDefault value, HAL9000 and SAL9000 objects have different mtDefault values. This shows that the default values assigned within the DEFINE CLASS command (or on the Property sheet in the Class Designer) mtDefault = DATETIME() are evaluated only when the *first* object of a class is instantiated. All subsequent objects get the same value as the first object. The class definition is cached in memory for performance reasons. The caching even survives the SET PROCEDURE command of the second run. However, when the expression mtAware = DATETIME() is used within the Init() method, the expression is evaluated when each object is instantiated. Note the mtDefault value is not evaluated when the class definition is loaded into memory with the SET PROCEDURE or SET CLASSLIB commands.

Gotcha!

Don't use instantiation-time-dependent expressions on the property sheet.
Where does this class-definition-caching behavior cause problems? Suppose that you created a class SetDeleted that was responsible for saving and restoring the current SET DELETED state. It would probably work the first time you used it because the = SET("DELETED") would get the current value. However, the next time you instantiated one of the objects it would not get the current value; it would have the value in effect when the first object was instantiated. The bottom line is that you should avoid putting dynamic expressions on the property sheet. Put code in the Init() method instead.

Gotcha!

Be careful when you use the property sheet Expression Builder.
This is another (somewhat) related issue I ran into while putting the BinaryTree class (covered in Section 5) into a class library. If you use the Expression Builder to create the default values for properties, it puts an = in front of the expression. For example, if you are assigning a default value of .NULL. to the moLeftChild and moRightChild properties in the BinaryTree, the Expression Builder will put =.NULL. into the field. However, when you try to use the class you will be able to create the first and second nodes but you will not be able to add a child node to the second node. It turns out that this problem occurs only when the =.NULL. value is replaced by an object reference. It took quite a few messages on the beta forum to finally isolate the cause of the problem, but now it works if the property value is set as .NULL. without the = that the Expression Builder was adding.

Scoping Issues and Object Lifetime

This next example will focus on the constructor Init() method and the destructor Destroy() method. It will also cover object lifetime and scope, object references, and object names.

Objects have a finite lifetime that is controlled by the location where an object is created. This lifetime is essentially the same as the lifetime of other memory variables. When an object is created in a procedure, the object ceases to exist when the procedure returns. Here's a class in a .PRG that simply prints to the screen when objects are being created and destroyed:

```
* lifetime.prg  12-Jun-95

* This class illustrates object scope and lifetime
define class Lifetime as custom
x1 = time()
x2 = ""
  procedure Init
    this.x2 = time()
        ? "A Lifetime object:" + this.Name + " is being created!"
  endproc

  procedure Destroy
        ? "A Lifetime object:" + this.Name + " is being destroyed!"
  endproc
enddefine
```

First, play with this class from the command window. Enter the following code:

```
set procedure to lifetime
o1 = createobject( "Lifetime" )
```

You will see this appear on the screen:

A Lifetime object:Lifetime1 is being created!

Using the Display Memory command will confirm the existence of o1 as a Lifetime object. To destroy the object, enter the following code:

```
release o1
```

Afterwards you will see this on the screen:

A Lifetime object:Lifetime1 is being destroyed!

Using the Display Memory command will confirm that object o1 is gone. Whenever an object is created, its Init() method is executed. Whenever an object is released, its Destroy() method is executed. Now take a look at the object lifetime in a program:

```
* life1.prg  12-Jun-95

* This program creates an object that goes out of scope
* automatically when this program returns

release all
clear all
clear

set procedure to lifetime.prg additive

o1 = createobject( "Lifetime" )
return
```

If you use do Life1 in the command window, you'll see the created message immediately followed by the destroyed message. The CreateObject() call will create a Lifetime object and the Init() method will be called. Then the "created" message will appear and the return value of createobject() will be assigned to a private memory variable o1. The variable is private by default because it isn't declared local or public. When the RETURN statement is executed, the private variable o1 goes out of scope and is automatically released. When the object is released, its Destroy() method is called and the "destroyed" message appears.

Because object references are memory variables, you can declare them PUBLIC to give them a scope outside the currently executing program:

```
* life2.prg  12-Jun-95

* This program creates a public object that won't go out of
* scope when this program ends

release all
clear all
clear

set procedure to lifetime.prg additive

public o1
o1 = createobject( "Lifetime" )
return
```

This creates o1 again and you see the "created" message. However, the RETURN command does not cause the object to go out of scope so you don't get the automatic "destroyed" message. You can use the following command to get rid of the object as you did before:

```
release o1
```

After that, the "destroyed" message will appear. Now look at how this scope issue applies to subroutines:

```
* life3.prg  12-Jun-95

* This program creates several objects within subroutines to
* show object scope

release all
clear all
clear

set procedure to lifetime.prg additive
```

Continued on next page

Continued from previous page

```
o1 = createobject( "Lifetime" )
do Sub1

? "leave main"
return

procedure Sub1
? "In Sub1"
local o1
o1 = createobject( "Lifetime" )

do Sub2

? "leave Sub1"
return

procedure Sub2
? "In Sub2"
local o1
o1 = createobject( "Lifetime" )
o2 = createobject( "Lifetime" )

do Sub3

? "leave Sub2"
return

procedure Sub3
? "In Sub3"
? "I can see o2! Its name is:", o2.Name
? "leave Sub3"
return
```

If you use do Life3 in the command window, you'll get the following output:

```
A Lifetime object:Lifetime1 is being created!
In Sub1
A Lifetime object:Lifetime2 is being created!
In Sub2
A Lifetime object:Lifetime3 is being created!
A Lifetime object:Lifetime4 is being created!
In Sub3
I can see o2! Its name is: Lifetime4
leave Sub3
leave Sub2
A Lifetime object:Lifetime4 is being destroyed!
A Lifetime object:Lifetime3 is being destroyed!
leave Sub1
A Lifetime object:Lifetime2 is being destroyed!
leave main
A Lifetime object:Lifetime1 is being destroyed!
```

In all cases, the objects created within a subroutine go out of scope when that subroutine ends. They are then destroyed. Sub1 and

Sub2 use the LOCAL command to create their own objects named
o1. When Sub2 ends, the objects are destroyed in the reverse order
of their creation. Inside Sub3, the o2 object is visible like any other
private memory variable.

Now go back to the first case to discuss object references versus
object names. Enter this code in the command window:

```
set procedure to lifetime
o1 = createobject( "Lifetime" )
? o1.Name
```

Because you didn't give your class an explicit value for its Name
property, Visual FoxPro obliged and created one automatically. To
do so, Visual FoxPro took the ClassName of the object and added a
serialized instance number to it to create the name. In this case it
comes up with Lifetime1 as a name. The thing called o1 isn't the
name of the object, it's a memory variable that references an object.
You can't use the object name for anything right now, but you'll see
where the object name is used later.

Gotcha!

Be aware of the object destruction order.

There's a significant difference between the way that objects
automatically go out of scope and the way that the RELEASE ALL
command works. When objects go out of scope, they are destroyed
in last-in-first-out (LIFO) order. The last object created is the first
object destroyed. However, RELEASE ALL destroys objects in one of
two orders: in first-in-first-out (FIFO) order or in alphabetical order
by object reference name. Examine the following program:

```
* life4.prg  12-Jun-95

* This program illustrates the difference between RELEASE ALL
* and an object going out of scope.

release all
clear all
clear

set procedure to lifetime.prg

? "create some objects"
z1 = createobject( "Lifetime" )
o1 = createobject( "Lifetime" )
o2 = createobject( "Lifetime" )
a1 = createobject( "Lifetime" )

? "release all"
? "These objects are released in FIFO order"
```

Continued on next page

Continued from previous page

```
release all

?
? "create them again"
z1 = createobject( "Lifetime" )
o1 = createobject( "Lifetime" )
o2 = createobject( "Lifetime" )
a1 = createobject( "Lifetime" )

? "out of scope release"
? "These objects are released in LIFO order"

return
```

For example, using do Life4 in the command window will yield this output:

```
create some objects
A Lifetime object:Lifetime1 is being created!
A Lifetime object:Lifetime2 is being created!
A Lifetime object:Lifetime3 is being created!
A Lifetime object:Lifetime4 is being created!
release all
These objects are released in FIFO order
A Lifetime object:Lifetime1 is being destroyed!
A Lifetime object:Lifetime2 is being destroyed!
A Lifetime object:Lifetime3 is being destroyed!
A Lifetime object:Lifetime4 is being destroyed!

create them again
A Lifetime object:Lifetime1 is being created!
A Lifetime object:Lifetime2 is being created!
A Lifetime object:Lifetime3 is being created!
A Lifetime object:Lifetime4 is being created!
out of scope release
These objects are released in LIFO order
A Lifetime object:Lifetime4 is being destroyed!
A Lifetime object:Lifetime3 is being destroyed!
A Lifetime object:Lifetime2 is being destroyed!
A Lifetime object:Lifetime1 is being destroyed!
```

That example shows RELEASE ALL using FIFO destruction, but the destruction will sometimes occur in alphabetical order by the object reference memory variable names. There is nothing you can do to control this order of automatic destruction. There is also no guarantee that the next version of Visual FoxPro will work this way. As a result, if you create classes that depend on one another and there is an order dependency in their construction and destruction, you need to explicitly control the destruction order with your own RELEASE commands.

Getting Useful Work Done Automatically

This next example will focus on environment save and restore, the constructor Init() method, the destructor Destroy() method, and object lifetime and scope. Think for a moment about how the automatic call of the Init() and Destroy() methods can be put to good use. To see how, step back and look at a FoxPro 2.x code fragment you are probably familiar with:

```
* set.prg  12-Jun-94

private lcDeleted

lcDeleted = set( "deleted" )
set deleted off

* do some processing

if ( lcDeleted == "ON" )
   set deleted on
endif
```

This code saves the current value of DELETED, sets it to OFF, and sets it back to ON if necessary. There are several variations to this code. Some people use & macro expansions while others use a logical memory variable to hold the original state, but all of these methods are structured the same way: save, change, do some work, and restore. They also all have a serious flaw: they require you to *remember* the restore step. If the processing code is a page or longer, it's easy to forget. This problem becomes even more severe when one method of the class does the SET and another method is responsible for the restore step. The first two are easy to remember because your code won't work without them. Failing to execute the restore step doesn't break your code so it doesn't show up in your testing, but it will break your caller's code!

CSet Class
Objects can come to the rescue and solve the restore step problem quite nicely. You can put the save and change steps into the Init() method, then put the restore step in the Destroy() method. That way the restore will *never* be forgotten because it will happen automatically. Another benefit is that this code fragment goes from seven lines of code to the three shown:

```
local loDeletedSave

loDeletedSave = createobject( "CSet", "deleted", "off" )

* do some processing
```

Now look at the CSet class:

```
* 12-Dec-94  cset.prg

* This class provides SET environment save/set/restore capabilities

* When the class is instantiated, the current SET environment is saved and set to the
* desired value. When the instantiated object goes out of scope the environment is
* restored.

* Usage:
*
* CreateObject( "CSet", cSet, cNewValue | nNewValue [, cSecondaryValue] )
*
*   cSet                = One of the SET commands
*   cNewValue           = Appropriate character value for the SET command
*   nNewValue           = Appropriate numeric value for the SET command
*   cSecondaryValue  = Optional character value for SET commands that
*                         are both ON | OFF and have another value like
*                         ALTERNATE
*
* Examples:
*
* loDeletedSave    = createobject( "CSet", "deleted", "on" )
* loDecimalsSave   = createobject( "CSet", "decimals", 5 )
* loAlternateSave  = createobject( "CSet", "alternate", "on", "a.txt" )

define class CSet as custom

* Protected Data Members ==============================================
protected mcSet                          && SET command
protected muOrgValue                     && Original value of the SET
protected muOrgValue1                    && Original secondary value of the SET
protected mlNoTO                         && no TO keyword

* Public Data Members ================================================
* NONE

* Protected Function Members ==========================================

* Constructor Method -------------------------------------------------

protected function Init( pcSet, puNewValue, pcSecondaryValue )

local  nParmCount                        && number of parameters sent to init
local  cSetCommand                       && constructed SET command

lnParmCount = parameters()

* Default the data members
this.mcSet = ""
this.muOrgValue = ""
this.muOrgValue1 = ""

* save current environment

this.mcSet           = lower( pcSet )
this.mlNoTo = inlist( this.mcSet, "compatible", "talk" )
```

Continued on next page

```
this.muOrgValue       = set( pcSet )
this.muOrgValue1      = set( pcSet, 1 )
if ( this.muOrgValue == this.muOrgValue1 )
   * throw this away because you don't need it
   this.muOrgValue1 = ""
endif

if ( lnParmCount = 3 )
   * optional argument handling
   if ( empty( this.muOrgValue1 ) )
      * you need to save this blank value state for restoring later
      this.muOrgValue1 = " "
   endif
   lcSetCommand = pcSet + " to " + pcSecondaryValue
   set &lcSetCommand
endif

if ( type( "this.muOrgValue" ) == 'C' )
   * character type of SET
   lcSetCommand = puNewValue
   if ( ! inlist( this.muOrgValue, "ON", "OFF" ) )
      * not a simple ON|OFF so add a TO keyword
      lcSetCommand = "to " + puNewValue
   endif
else
   * numeric type of SET
   lcSetCommand = "to " + str( puNewValue )
endif

lcSetCommand = pcSet + " " + lcSetCommand
set &lcSetCommand                                  && change the SET

endfunc


* Destructor Method -------------------------------------------------

protected function Destroy

if ( empty( this.mcSet ) )
   return
endif

local lcSetCommand                                 && constructed SET command

if ( type( "this.muOrgValue" ) == 'C' )
   * character type of SET
   lcSetCommand = this.muOrgValue
   if ( ! inlist( this.muOrgValue, "ON", "OFF" ) )
      * not a simple ON|OFF so add a TO keyword
      lcSetCommand = "to " + this.muOrgValue
   endif
else
   * numeric type of SET
   lcSetCommand = "to " + str( this.muOrgValue )
endif
```

Continued on next page

Continued from previous page

```
  lcSetCommand = this.mcSet + " " + lcSetCommand
  set &lcSetCommand                               && restore the SET

  if ( len( this.muOrgValue1 ) > 0 )
     * restore secondary SET information
     lcSetCommand = this.mcSet + iif( this.mlNoTo, " ", " to " ) + ;
                 this.muOrgValue1
     set &lcSetCommand
  endif

endfunc


* Public Function Members ===========================================

* Value Method --------------------------------------------------

* Return the current values of the protected data members in a comma delimited string.

function Value
local lcReturnValue

if ( type( "this.muOrgValue" ) == 'C' )
   lcReturnValue = this.mcSet + "," + this.muOrgValue
else
   lcReturnValue = this.mcSet + "," + alltrim( str( this.muOrgValue ) )
endif

if ( ! empty( this.muOrgValue1 ) )
   lcReturnValue = lcReturnValue + "," + this.muOrgValue1
endif

return lcReturnValue
endfunc

enddefine
```

The CSet class is derived from the Custom BaseClass. The Custom class is the simplest class from which you can derive your own subclasses. The CSet class has three protected properties—mcSet, muOrgValue, and muOrgValue1. These properties are used to save the original values so they can be restored when the object is released. They are protected because you don't want anybody to alter the values and thus prevent the object from properly restoring the environment when the object is released. Notice that the Init() method is also protected to prevent the object from later harm. In the Init() method, these properties are given default values. Then the current value of the set command is saved in them.

The class then checks to see if the optional third argument was passed to handle setting multiple values such as ALTERNATE. This gives you the ability to remove another two lines of "old-method" code. Look at the following samples:

```
set alternate to "somefile.txt"
set alternate on

* output to the file

set alternate off
set alternate to
```

With CSet, this code becomes:

```
loAlternateSave = createobject( "CSet", "alternate", "on",
  "somefile.txt" )

* output to the file
```

In this case, & macros are used to build and execute the SET statement. You don't do state changing inside a program loop because of the negative performance impact, so the macro expansion time should be acceptable in most cases. The rest of the code constructs the appropriate SET commands and executes them.

The Destroy() method basically uses the values saved in the object properties to restore the environment. Because the properties are protected, it was useful to add a Value() method to return the state saved by the CSet object. Here's the test driver for the cSet class:

```
* 25-Jun-95  cset3.prg

* Driver program to test CSet class

set procedure to CSet additive

_tabs = "5, 10, 65"
#define TAB chr(9)
clear
_screen.FontUnderline = .t.
? "Where", TAB, TAB, 'set( "deleted" )'
_screen.FontUnderline = .f.

set deleted on                        && start it out on for testing

? "Main", TAB, TAB, set( "deleted" )
do SomethingThatWantsDeletedOFF
? "After SomethingThatWantsDeletedOFF", TAB, set( "deleted" )
do Somemore
return

procedure SomethingThatWantsDeletedOFF
local loDeletedSave

? TAB, "Initial value in SomethingThatWantsDeletedOFF", TAB, set("deleted")

loDeletedSave = createObject( "CSet", "deleted", "off" )
? TAB, "Saved Value:", loDeletedSave.Value()

? TAB, "After object created", TAB, set("deleted")
```

Continued on next page

Continued from previous page

```
do SomethingElseThatWantsDeletedON
? TAB, "After SomethingElseThatWantsDeletedON", TAB, set("deleted")

* loDeletedSave now goes out of scope so the destructor gets called
return

procedure SomethingElseThatWantsDeletedON
local loDeletedSave

? TAB, TAB, "Initial value in SomethingElseThatWantsDeletedON", TAB, set( "deleted" )

loDeletedSave = createobject( "CSet", "deleted", "on" )

? TAB, TAB, "Saved Value:", loDeletedSave.Value()

? TAB, TAB, "After object created", TAB, set( "deleted" )

* loDeletedSave now goes out of scope
return

procedure SomeMore
local loDecimalSave
local loAlternateSave
local loSafetySave

loDecimalsSave = createObject( "CSet", "decimals", 4 )

loSafetySave = createobject( "CSet", "safety", "off" )
loAlternateSave = createObject( "CSet", "alternate", "on", "alter.txt" )

release loAlternateSave          && manually release these just for the fun of it
release loSafetySave

* loDecimalSave now goes out of scope
return
```

If you use do cSet3, you'll see the screen update with the DELETED status as the subroutines change it. It would be a good exercise for you to put Set("deleted") in the Debug window and use the Trace window to go through this program and watch as the steps happen.

The output should look like this:

```
Where                                               set( "deleted" )
Main                                                       ON
   Initial value in SomethingThatWantsDeletedOFF           ON
   Saved Value:  deleted,ON
   After object created                                    OFF
      Initial value in SomethingElseThatWantsDeletedON  OFF
      Saved Value:  deleted,OFF
      After object created                                 ON
   After SomethingElseThatWantsDeletedON                   OFF
After SomethingThatWantsDeletedOFF                         ON
```

There is no foolproof way of mimicking this class in FoxPro 2.x. The Init() and Destroy() methods could be put into a UDF() (user defined function), but there's no way to get the restore part to be automatically called. You still have to rely on your memory to call that code.

Even if you don't start to use object-oriented programming across your entire application, you can start using this class today. The code is in the CSET.PRG file as well as in the Visual Class Library CSET.VCX.

What Happens if Init( ) Fails?

This next example will focus on conditional object instantiation. There might be times when you only want an object to instantiate if it can successfully allocate some system resource that may or may not be available. Alternatively, you might not want to instantiate an object unless valid parameters were passed to the Init() method. You can return .F. from the Init() method to indicate there was a problem instantiating the object. To try this out, begin by using this line of code:

```
do form InitFail
```

As you click the buttons on InitFail, the Forms in Figure 2-7 through Figure 2-10 will attempt to run. In each case they will have an object that returns .F. from its Init() method.

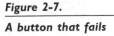

Figure 2-7.

A button that fails

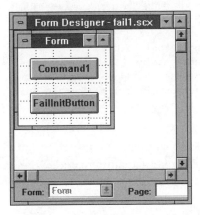

The Form in Figure 2-7 never displays because when the FailInitButton doesn't instantiate, the Form Init() fails. That sequence of events is as follows:

```
Form Load()
Form.Ccommandbutton1 Init()
Form.Failinitbutton2 Failing Init()
Form.Ccommandbutton1 Destroy()
Form Unload()
```

Note that the Form.Destroy() method does not execute because the Init() failed.

Figure 2-8.

A container that fails

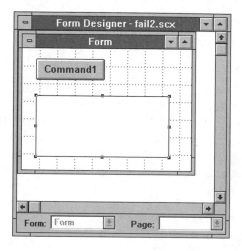

The Form in Figure 2-8 fails because the container attempts to use AddObject() to add two buttons. One of the two will have its Init() method fail. That sequence of events is shown:

```
Form Load()
Form.Ccommandbutton1 Init()
Form.AddObjectContainer Init()
Using AddObject() to add objects
Form.AddObjectContainer.mogoodbutton Init()
Form.AddObjectContainer.mobadbutton Failing Init()
Form Init()
```

The Form appears because the code failed to verify that the dynamic objects were actually created. When you close the Form, the rest of the sequence of events is as follows:

```
Form Destroy()
Form.AddObjectContainer Destroy()
Form.AddObjectContainer.mogoodbutton Destroy()
Form.Ccommandbutton1 Destroy()
Form Unload()
```

If you are creating objects that could have their Init() methods fail, you are responsible for testing to be sure that they really did instantiate. The code from the FailAddObject.Init() method looks like this:

```
set classlib to failinit additive

activate screen
? FullName( this ) + " Init()"
? "Using AddObject() to add objects"

this.AddObject( "moGoodButton", "cCommandButton" )
this.moGoodButton.Visible = .t.

this.AddObject( "moBadButton", "FailInitButton" )

if ( m.glVerify )
   return ( ( type( "this.moBadButton" ) == 'O' ) and
   ( ! isnull( this.moBadButton ) ) )
endif
```

Note that the AddObject() method does not return the value from the Init() method of the object it is creating. If it did, it would be easier to detect the failed Init(). Instead you have to test the type of the object reference and verify that it isn't null.

If the Verify CheckBox is checked, the following sequence will be displayed:

```
Form Load()
Form.Ccommandbutton1 Init()
Form.AddObjectContainer Init()
Using AddObject() to add objects
Form.AddObjectContainer.mogoodbutton Init()
Form.AddObjectContainer.mobadbutton Failing Init()
Form.AddObjectContainer.mogoodbutton Destroy()
Form.Ccommandbutton1 Destroy()
Form Unload()
```

The Form does not appear on the screen. Notice that the Form Init() and Destroy() messages do not appear because these events do not occur.

Figure 2-9.

A custom class that fails

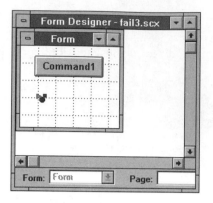

The Form in Figure 2-9 fails because the custom object attempts to use CreateObject() to add two buttons. One of the two buttons will have its Init() method fail. With the Verify CheckBox unchecked, the sequence of events is as follows:

```
Form Load()
Form.Ccommandbutton1 Init()
Form.CreateObjectCustom Init()
Using CreateObject() to add objects
ccommandbutton Init()
failinitbutton Failing Init()
Form Init()
```

At this point, the Form appears. When it is closed, the following sequence of events occurs:

```
Form Destroy()
Form.CreateObjectCustom Destroy()
ccommandbutton Destroy()
Form.Ccommandbutton1 Destroy()
Form Unload()
```

If you turn on the verification, the Form will not appear because of the failed Init().

```
Form Load()
Form.Ccommandbutton1 Init()
Form.CreateObjectCustom Init()
Using CreateObject() to add objects
ccommandbutton Init()
failinitbutton Failing Init()
ccommandbutton Destroy()
Form.Ccommandbutton1 Destroy()
Form Unload()
```

Figure 2-10.

A contained object that fails

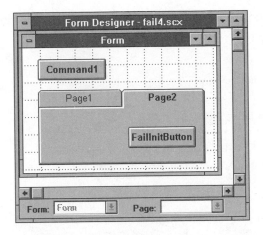

The Form in Figure 2-10 illustrates a problem with failing objects within containers such as a Page. This Form will not fully create, but it also doesn't fully release until you use CLEAR ALL The sequence of events is as follows:

```
Form Load()
Form.Ccommandbutton1 Init()
Form.Pageframe1.Page2.Failinitbutton1 Failing Init()
```

After you dismiss the MessageBox and enter CLEAR ALL in the command window, the rest of the sequence occurs:

```
Form.Ccommandbutton1 Destroy()
Form Unload()
```

There is no way to effectively trap this failure because the contained objects Init() before their container(). In this case, the container Init() doesn't even execute. You need to be very careful if you are going to use conditionally instantiated objects.

Parent Versus ParentClass

As confusing as it sounds, both Parent and ParentClass are parents. Visual FoxPro chose to give these two rather dissimilar things very similar names. You'll be using both intensely, so you'll need to understand the distinctions. The ParentClass is the class from which another class is derived. It's in the Is-A hierarchy of a class, and is directly involved in the inheritance of properties and methods. On the other hand, the Parent is a container object that holds other objects. It's in the Has-A hierarchy of objects, and is not involved in inheritance although contained objects can use its properties and methods. A simple example is in the P_V_PC.PJX project files. Take a look at the class tree in Figure 2-11.

Figure 2-11.

Is-A class tree

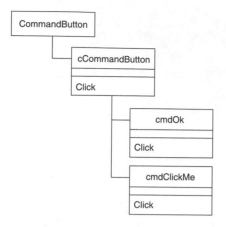

Now look at the containership hierarchy in Figure 2-12.

Figure 2-12.

Has-A containership

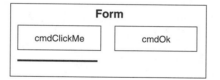

If you DO FORM P_V_PC and click the left button, the Line will change length. The Ok button will close the Form. Both of these buttons are derived from cCommandButton, which has an overridden Click() method that beeps when the button is clicked. Both of the buttons show interaction with both their ParentClass and Parent.

```
* cmdok.Click

cCommandButton::Click()

thisform.release()
```

The Ok button first sends the message to its ParentClass so that the button will beep. Then it sends a message to its Parent. In a method of an object contained by a Form, thisform is equivalent to this.parent.

```
*  cmdClickMe.Click

cCommandButton::Click()

if ( this.parent.linHowBig.Width = this.Width )
   this.parent.linHowBig.Width = this.parent.Width
   this.parent.linHowBig.Left = 0
else
   this.parent.linHowBig.Width = this.Width
   this.parent.linHowBig.Left = this.Left
endif
```

The Click Me button first sends a message on to its ParentClass so the button will beep. It then tests the Width of linHowBig, which is another of its parent's contained objects. Finally it sends the Line object two messages that control the object's size and position. As you can see, the cmdClickMe button can use some of its parent's properties (this.parent.width).

Event Versus Event Method

As you already know, an event is something that happens as a result of a user action such as a keypress or a system event such as a timer expiring. In addition to sending a message to an object, these events trigger various behaviors of the BaseClass. The message that is sent to the object causes the appropriate event method to execute. The name of the method is the same as the name of the event, but on the property sheet these methods have "event" at the end of their names. The only thing that distinguishes these methods is that they are called by messages outside of the code that you've written. These methods are provided so that you can hook into the event to provide special or additional handling. It is also possible for you to send a message to these methods the same way that you send a message to any other method. When the event method gets the message, it executes its code regardless of whether your code or the system sent the message. However, when you send the message you are not causing the event itself to occur. This is a critical distinction—by sending a message yourself you really aren't causing everything that would occur if the real event had occurred.

For example, suppose that you have a TextBox named txtFirstName. Somewhere in code (for example, in the Click() method of a CommandButton) is the command TXTFIRSTNAME.KEYPRESS(65). You are not triggering the event of the A key being pressed, but the TextBox doesn't know or care if the key was pushed by the user. It only sees an A coming and does whatever the KeyPress() method is programmed to do.

However, this does not include the function of adding A to the txtFirstName.Value property or of updating the display. This part of the KeyPress event handling happens outside of the code you put into an overridden KeyPress() method.

You can cause events to occur programmatically by using the KEYBOARD, MOUSE, and ERROR commands. In the previous example, if the code were KEYBOARD 'A' it would have caused the actual event to occur, which would in turn add the A to the .Value and send the message to the KeyPress() method.

The project EVENT.PJX has an illustration of this on the EVENT Form shown in Figure 2-13.

Figure 2-13.

Event handling

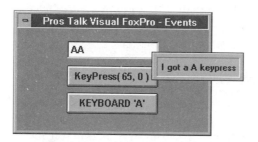

This screen shot reflects the state that exists after the KEYBOARD 'A' button has been clicked twice. The KeyPress button sends a KeyPress(65, 0) message to the TextBox above it. The TextBox responds with the WAIT WINDOW, but A does not show up in the TextBox. The KEYBOARD button actually causes a KeyPress event by putting an A into the keyboard buffer. The TextBox then displays the WAIT WINDOW and the A shows up in the TextBox.

:: Scope Resolution Operator

As was discussed in the previous section on override, overriding a method affects the way that method messages flow through a class tree. When an object receives a message, it is handled by the first method from the object class up to the BaseClass that has code in it. That method receives the message. If there is no overridden method for the message, it is handled by the BaseClass. The overridden method that gets the message must make sure that the rest of the class tree sees the message. If it doesn't, the inherited behavior in the rest of the class tree will not be executed. The behavior is restored by using the :: scope resolution operator to pass the message up to the classes' ParentClass. The **::** operator is a bit like DO X IN Y because it points to a class higher up the inheritance tree.

For example, examine the class tree in Figure 2-14.

Figure 2-14.

Class tree for ::
demonstration

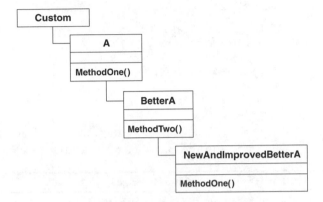

The following code will create the class tree of Figure 2-14, instantiate one object of each class, and send messages to each of the methods:

```
* override.prg  08-Sep-95

* Illustrate method overrides and ::

? "oA1"
oA1 = createobject( "A" )
oA1.MethodOne()
*oA1.MethodTwo()       && Error A does not have MethodTwo()

?
? "oA2"
oA2 = createobject( "BetterA" )
oA2.MethodOne()
oA2.MethodTwo()

?
? "oA3"
oA3 = createobject( "NewAndImprovedBetterA" )
oA3.MethodOne()
oA3.MethodTwo()
return

define class A as Custom
procedure MethodOne()
? "A::MethodOne()"
endproc
enddefine
```

Continued on next page

Continued from previous page

```
define class BetterA as A
procedure MethodTwo
? "BetterA::MethodTwo()"
endproc
enddefine

define class NewAndImprovedBetterA as BetterA
procedure MethodOne()
? "NewAndImprovedBetterA::MethodOne()"
BetterA::MethodOne()
endproc
enddefine
```

Table 2-7 explains how the messages flow through the class tree when you run the program with do override.

Code	What Happens To The Message
oA1.MethodOne()	The message goes directly to A::MethodOne().
oA1.MethodTwo()	Error! Class A has no MethodTwo defined.
oA2.MethodOne()	The message goes to BetterA::MethodOne. It is not overridden so it is automatically passed on to A::MethodOne().
oA2.MethodTwo()	The message goes to BetterA::MethodTwo().
oA3.MethodOne()	The message goes to NewAndImprovedBetterA::MethodOne(). It is then explicitly passed on to BetterA::MethodOne(). This has no overridden MethodOne(), so the message is passed on to A::MethodOne() automatically.
oA3.MethodTwo()	The message goes to NewAndImprovedBetterA::MethodTwo(). It is not overridden so it is automatically passed on to BetterA::MethodTwo().

Table 2-7.

Message flow through a class tree

In the last code sample you saw that the overridden methods follow a rule and only use the **::** operator to pass messages up to the ParentClass. These messages are not passed any higher. If the ParentClass does not override the method, the message is automatically passed on to the ParentClass's ParentClass. For example, NewAndImprovedBetterA's MethodOne() passes a message to BetterA::MethodOne, not to A::MethodOne(). Remember that even though BetterA does not override the MethodOne() method now, it might at some time in the future. As a result, if you did not send the message from NewAndImprovedBetterA to BetterA, you would not be able to use the new functionality of the BetterA class.

In human terms this means that you should not talk to your grandparentclass; you should talk only to your parentclass and let it talk to its parentclass. While you are designing your classes you need to understand what each level of inheritance is giving your class. However, when you are coding your methods you need to interface only with the ParentClass, knowing that it will interface to its ParentClass.

You cannot use the **::** operator to call a method of another class tree. For example, a class derived from the TextBox class cannot call a method from a class derived from the CommandButton class. This would be multiple inheritance which Visual FoxPro does not support. As another example, the following code will cause a runtime error:

```
define class txtOne as TextBox
   procedure Init()
      CommandButton::Init()
   endproc
enddefine
```

Realize that the code just presented is not the same as:

```
define class txtTwo as TextBox
   procedure Init()
      this.parent.cmdTwo.Init()
   endproc
enddefine
```

The second code sample would be properly sending a message to another instantiated object.

NODEFAULT

All of the Visual FoxPro BaseClasses have built-in default behavior attached to their methods. These default behaviors handle the mundane user-interface details. For example, if a MouseDown event occurs on a CommandButton, the image of the button changes to the DownPicture image. If a KeyPress event occurs in a TextBox, the character that represents the key that was pressed is added to the end of the Value property and the character is echoed to the screen. At times, the default behavior of the BaseClasses is to do nothing. For example, the default behavior of the Click() method of a CommandButton doesn't do anything.

In Visual FoxPro, the BaseClass method code is automatically called when a message is received. This occurs even if a subclass has an overridden method for the message. The default behavior happens after your overridden method code executes. This works differently than C++. In C++, all messages have to be explicitly sent from an overridden method to the superclass.

The NODEFAULT command prevents default behavior when you don't want the default behavior of the BaseClass methods to execute.

This would this be useful if you had a memo field that you wanted to be read-only. You could set its ReadOnly property to .T. to prevent the field from being edited, but if the user browsed through the field and happened to press a key, the computer would beep at them. You could just set the Enable property to .F. and the DisabledForeColor to RGB(0,0,0) so the field doesn't look disabled. That would prevent the beeps, but it would also prevent the user from scrolling the EditBox. Another solution would be to just throw the keystroke away using the NODEFAULT command in the KeyPress() method.

The next example focuses on NODEFAULT, BaseClass::Method() calls, and ParentClass::Method() calls. Begin by entering the command:

```
do form nodef1
```

Figure 2-15 shows the Form after clicking the NODEFAULT checkbox.

Figure 2-15.

Using NODEFAULT

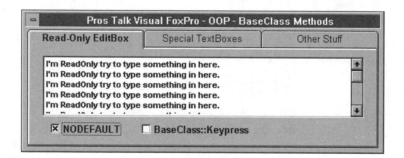

The EditBox at the top of this Form has its ReadOnly property set to .T.. The NODEFAULT and BaseClass::KeyPress CheckBoxes control whether or not the NODEFAULT command and an explicit call to the BaseClass method will execute.

The edtReadOnly.KeyPress() method code is shown here:

```
* edtReadOnly.KeyPress

LPARAMETERS nKeyCode, nShiftAltCtrl
if ( thisform.pgfMain.pagReadOnly.chkNoDefault.Value = 1 )
   nodefault
endif

if ( thisform.pgfMain.pagReadOnly.chkBaseClass.Value = 1 )
   EditBox::KeyPress( nKeyCode, nShiftAltCtrl )
endif
```

Now try playing with the CheckBoxes and pressing a key while the EditBox has focus. You will notice that the number of beeps varies depending on the combination of the two CheckBox values.

NODEFAULT	BaseClass::KeyPress	Number of Beeps	What Causes the Beeps?
☒	☐	0	NODEFAULT prevents the automatic call.
☐	☐	1	The automatic call causes it.
☒	☒	1	NODEFAULT prevents the automatic call, explicit call causes it.
☐	☒	2	Both the automatic and explicit calls yield a beep.

Table 2-8.

Effects of NODEFAULT and BaseClass::Method()

On the second page of the PageFrame you'll see some special TextBoxes. These are shown in Figure 2-16.

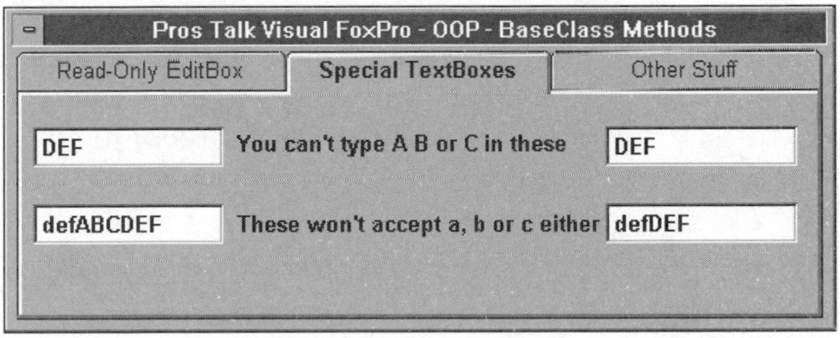

Figure 2-16.

Trying to inherit NODEFAULT

The two TextBoxes are more examples of using NODEFAULT to selectively eliminate some keystrokes from the inputting process. The top NoABCTextBox and GoodNoABCTextBox classes remove the input characters A, B, and C. The bottom two classes are derived classes that attempt to also eliminate the a, b, and c characters. However, as you can see from the screen shot in Figure 2-16, it was not very effective at removing the uppercase characters from the lower left TextBox. It appears that the NODEFAULT can be issued only by the first overridden method that gets the message. If NODEFAULT is issued in a ParentClass method when the derived class also overrides the method, NODEFAULT is ignored. If you need multiple levels of NODEFAULT action, you'll have to do something like returning .F. and testing for it in the derived classes. This is how the TextBox classes on the right side of the Form in Figure 2-16 handle the problem. Visual FoxPro 3.06 also fixes this problem.

The third page of the PageFrame shows another example, which is displayed in Figure 2-17.

Figure 2-17.

Click( ) versus MouseUp( )

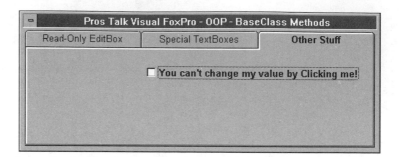

The CheckBox uses NODEFAULT to prevent it from being changed by a mouse click. However, you don't put NODEFAULT in the Click() method as you'd first think. Instead, you need to put the NODEFAULT in the MouseUp() method.

You can also use the NODEFAULT command to change the order of the default behavior's execution. There might be times when you want the default behavior to occur before your overridden method code. In such cases you would structure your code as shown:

```
BaseClass::Method()      && explicitly call default behavior
your code goes here
NODEFAULT                && prevent BaseClass::Method() from
                            running a second time
```

Finding Out About the Object

Visual FoxPro has added one command and two functions that are used to get information about objects. These are the DISPLAY OBJECTS command, the AMEMBERS() function, and the ACLASS() function. This discussion will look at these new commands and functions.

Using DISPLAY OBJECTS

You can begin by using the CLASTRE1 Form as an object to view.

```
do form clastre1
display objects like clastre1 to file dispobj.txt noconsole
modify file dispobj.txt
```

To view the output file properly use the Format menu, Font... submenu and select a fixed space font like Courier New or Fixedsys.

After the code is entered, you'll see the object's class tree, its properties with values, its member objects, and its methods and events.

```
Object: CLASTRE1                    Pub       O    FORM

Class Tree:
        FORM

Properties:
      ACTIVECONTROL                 (None)
      ACTIVEFORM                    (None)
      ALWAYSONTOP                   L     .F.
      FORECOLOR                     N     0         (0.00000000)
      ...
      HALFHE...APTION               L     .F.
      HEIGHT                        N     330       (330.00000000)
      ...
      WINDOWSTATE                   N     0         (0.00000000)
      WINDOWTYPE                    N     0         (0.00000000)

Member Objects:
      CCOMMANDBUTTON                CCOMMANDBUTTON
      CLABEL1                       CLABEL
      ...
      TXTMCNAME                     CTEXTBOX
      TXTMCP...TCLASS               CTEXTBOX

Methods and Events:
      ACTIVATE       ADDOBJECT      BOX            CIRCLE
      CLICK          CLASS          DBLCLICK       DEACTIVATE
      DESTROY        DISPLA...CTINFO DRAGDROP      DRAGOVER
      ...
      SAVEAS         SAVEASCLASS    SETALL         SHOW
      TEXTHEIGHT     TEXTWIDTH      UNLOAD         ZORDER
```

As you look at this output, notice that any name longer than 15 characters shows only the first six characters, "...", then the last six characters. This is done to save display space, but it forces you to know what the ellipses are replacing. This means that you've got to have the class definition handy, which can be quite inconvenient. It's also annoying if your names aren't necessarily unique in the first six and last six positions. For example, a TextBox has properties of SELECTEDFORECOLOR and SELECTEDBACKCOLOR that are displayed as SELECT...ECOLOR and SELECT...KCOLOR respectively. The DISPLAY OBJECTS command also has a lot of excess white space between its columns. To see the entire output of the command, you must have a wide window. The size also makes it hard to see which value goes to which property.

Using AMEMBERS()

AMEMBERS() gives you the names of an object's properties and methods. Its code is shown here:

```
? amembers( laMembers, clastre1 )
display memo like laMembers
```

When the code is executed, the following display is shown:

```
73
LAMEMBERS               Pub          A
                ( 1)                 C     "ACTIVECONTROL"
                ( 2)                 C     "ACTIVEFORM"
                ( 3)                 C     "ALWAYSONTOP"
                ...
                ( 72)                C     "WINDOWSTATE"
                ( 73)                C     "WINDOWTYPE"
```

This is a simple alphabetical list of the Properties of the clastre1 object. Now modify the first AMEMBERS() code and enter the following:

```
? amembers( laMembers1, clastre1, 1 )
display memo like laMembers1
```

This code brings up this display:

```
137
LAMEMBERS1              Pub          A
            ( 1,    1)               C     "ACTIVATE"
            ( 1,    2)               C     "Event"
            ( 2,    1)               C     "ACTIVECONTROL"
            ( 2,    2)               C     "Property"
            ( 3,    1)               C     "ACTIVEFORM"
            ( 3,    2)               C     "Property"
            ( 4,    1)               C     "ADDOBJECT"
            ( 4,    2)               C     "Method"
            ( 5,    1)               C     "ALWAYSONTOP"
            ( 5,    2)               C     "Property"
                ...
            ( 128,  1)               C     "TXTMCBASECLASS"
            ( 128,  2)               C     "Object"
            ( 129,  1)               C     "TXTMCCLASS"
            ( 129,  2)               C     "Object"
                ...
            ( 135,  1)               C     "WINDOWSTATE"
            ( 135,  2)               C     "Property"
            ( 136,  1)               C     "WINDOWTYPE"
            ( 136,  2)               C     "Property"
            ( 137,  1)               C     "ZORDER"
            ( 137,  2)               C     "Method"
```

In addition to the information in the first display, this display includes the names of the objects, methods, and events. The second column of the array tells if the name is an Event, Method, Object, or Property. If you are interested only in the objects contained within an object, you send two as the optional third argument:

```
? amembers( laMembers2, clastre1, 2 )
display memo like laMembers2
```

This code brings up the following display:

```
20
LAMEMBERS2              Pub         A
                ( 1)                C    "CCOMMANDBUTTON"
                ( 2)                C    "CLABEL1"
                ( 3)                C    "CLABEL2"
                ( 4)                C    "CLABEL3"
                ...
                ( 14)               C    "COMMAND9"
                ( 15)               C    "DATAENVIRONMENT"
                ( 16)               C    "NAVIGATIONCOMMANDBUTTON"
                ( 17)               C    "TXTMCBASECLASS"
                ( 18)               C    "TXTMCCLASS"
                ( 19)               C    "TXTMCNAME"
                ( 20)               C    "TXTMCPARENTCLASS"
```

This output simply shows the names of the member objects contained within object.

Using ACLASS()

ACLASS() is used to get the class tree of an object.

```
? aclass( laClass, clastre1)
display memo like laClass
```

This code brings up an uninteresting display:

```
1
LACLASS                 Pub         A
                ( 1)                C    "FORM"
```

This tells you that clastre1 is derived from the Form class. The next code sample triggers a more interesting display:

```
? aclass( laClass, clastre1.cmdBottom )
display memo like laClass
```

```
4
LACLASS                  Pub          A
                ( 1)                  C     "CMDBOTTOM"
                ( 2)                  C     "NAVIGATIONCOMMANDBUTTON"
                ( 3)                  C     "CCOMMANDBUTTON"
                ( 4)                  C     "COMMANDBUTTON"
```

This display provides the class tree from the Bottom button all the way to the BaseClass CommandButton.

Container Classes

Container classes are those classes that can contain other objects. In order to identify them, take a look at a simple example 3-D label. Some programmers used to use GENSCRNX and 3-D drivers to simplify the work associated with making FPW2.X screens pretty. Now GENSCRNX is no longer a useful tool because Visual FoxPro doesn't generate screen code. However, you can still create 3-D labels by dropping a Label object on the Form, copying it, and adjusting the position of the copy, but that's a lot of work. It's simpler to create a new Label3D class that will create the copy at runtime.

```
create class Label3D of 3d as cLabel from ccontrol
```

You can use the following code to make its Init() method:

```
thisform.AddObject( "Hilite", "label" )
with thisform.Hilite
    .Caption = this.Caption
    .Top = this.Top + 2
    .Left = this.Left + 2
    .Alignment  = this.Alignment
    .AutoSize   = this.AutoSize
    .BackStyle  = 0
    .FontBold   = this.FontBold
    .FontItalic = this.FontItalic
    .FontName   = this.FontName
    .FontSize   = this.FontSize
    .WordWrap   = this.WordWrap
    .Visible    = this.Visible
endwith

this.ZOrder( 0 )   && bring real label back on top of the shadow
```

This code creates a new Form object named Hilite, copies the Caption, offsets the shadow by two pixels, then copies the other relevant properties of the Label object. The ZOrder(0) call is necessary because otherwise the shadow would appear over the top of the label. It works well, but this class is limited because you can use only one of these Label3D objects on a Form. A second 3-D label would be unable to create the Form object Hilite because one already exists. You can remove this limitation in one of two ways. First, you could build a unique name using something like this.Name + sys(2015), but there would be no guarantee that the user didn't have an object named lblMyLabel_R2K0SERG0. You'd have to check just in case. A better solution is to use a container to hold the Label3D object and its shadow. These commands will get rid of the old version and create a new version.

```
remove class Label3D of 3d
create class Label3D of 3d as container
```

As long as you're going to this much work anyway, try making this class a little more functional by adding the following properties to the container:

```
mnTopOffset
mnLeftOffset
mnShadowColor
```

These allow the shadow offset distance, direction, and color to be specified when the Form is designed. Now set these properties for the container:

```
      Name: Label3D of 3d.vcx
ParentClass: Container
  BaseClass: Container

Custom Properties and Methods:

    Public     Property mnLeftOffset  Offset of shadow from the Left
    Public     Property mnShadowColor Color of shadow
    Public     Property mnTopOffset   Offset of shadow from the Top

Property Values:

    Width = 71
    Height = 19
    BackStyle = 0
    BorderWidth = 0
    mnTopOffset = 2
    mnLeftOffset = 2
    mnShadowColor = (rgb(0,0,0))
    Name = "label3d"
```

Now you can use the following code in the Container Init():

```
* Label3D.Init

this.Height = this.Label.Height + abs( this.mnTopOffset )
this.Width  = this.Label.Width  + abs( this.mnLeftOffset )

if ( this.mnTopOffset < 0 )
   this.Top = this.Top - this.mnTopOffset
endif

if ( this.mnLeftOffset < 0 )
   this.Left = this.Left - this.mnLeftOffset
endif
```

Next, drop a cLabel from ccontrol.vcx into the Label3D container. You can set the following properties for the label:

```
      Name: Label of 3d.vcx
ParentClass: cLabel of ccontrol.vcx
  BaseClass: Label
     Parent: Label3D

Property Values:

   Caption = "Label1"
   Name = "Label"
```

Put this code in the Label Init():

```
* Label.Init.

this.parent.AddObject( "Hilite", "label" )
with this.parent.hilite
   .Caption = this.Caption
   .Top = this.Top + this.parent.mnTopOffset
   .Left = this.Left + this.parent.mnLeftOffset
   .ForeColor  = this.parent.mnShadowColor

   .Alignment  = this.Alignment
   .AutoSize   = this.AutoSize
   .BackStyle  = 0
   .FontBold   = this.FontBold
   .FontItalic = this.FontItalic
   .FontName   = this.FontName
   .FontSize   = this.FontSize
   .WordWrap   = this.WordWrap
   .Visible    = this.Visible
endwith

this.ZOrder( 0 ) && bring real label back on top of the shadow
```

The only real difference between this class and your first attempt is that instead of using thisform you use this.parent. This is because the shadow is being added to the container, not to the Form. Now you can use as many 3-D Labels on a Form as you'd like. To use the Label3D class, you simply have to select the contained label and set properties such as Caption, FontSize, and ForeColor. If you want to be able to see the entire label, you need to drag the container to the right size. However the container adjusts its size to fit at runtime. This code also uses the WITH...ENDWITH command to set multiple properties of the shadow without using the full object reference on every line. Using WITH when you are setting more than a couple of parameters can improve performance.

Now go back to the Form that was presented in the object reference discussion to talk about the details of the containers on that Form. Enter these commands in the command window:

```
modify project objref
expand the Documents/Forms and Class Library sections of the
  project manager window
edit the objref form
```

You'll notice that the CommandButton/TextBox pairs above the PageFrame and on the pages are boxed. That's because they have been put into a container class. You can begin working with the yellow container. If you open the code window and select the cntFormGroup, neither it nor any of its contained objects have any method code. The code resides in the cntGroup class. Next, close the Form Designer.

```
edit the cntGroup class
```

If you open the code window, only the cmdCount.Click method will have any code. This is shown here:

```
* cmdCount.Click

cmdCount::Click()
this.parent.txtEvenOdd.mnNumber = this.mnCount
this.parent.Refresh()
```

Because you are overriding the Click() method, you need to have the button pass the message to its ParentClass. It then uses this.parent (the container) to send a message to the other object in the container (txtEvenOdd). Next it tells the container to Refresh(), which in turn distributes the Refresh() message to all of the contained objects. This causes the txtEvenOdd object to actually change the displayed value. You could have also sent the Refresh() message to the txtEvenOdd object directly with this.parent.txtEvenOdd.Refresh(). However, it would not be practical to use thisform in the container because that would require that you know the name of the container, in order to get to txtEvenOdd. Using thisform also presents a problem because this container might have been placed within several other containers on the Form (the containers on the pages for example). While you could go up the this.parent chain until you got to the top, there is really no need. This container is designed to be self-sufficient.

Close the Class Designer, then prepare to edit the Form. Select the cntPage2Group object. None of its methods are overridden so, like the container placed at the Form level, this container on a page within a PageFrame works all by itself.

Next, select the cntPage1Group object. This container has to do some additional work, it also talks to the txtPageCopy object. Open the cmdCount.Click() method and you will see the following code:

```
* cntPage1Group.cmdCount.Click

* use :: to call the container behavior

  cntGroup::cmdCount.Click()
* --------                  container class name (NOT object name)
*           --------        object name within the container class
*                   ------- method to run

* cntGroup.cmdCount::Click()  && equivalent to above


* now also do something here local (form specific) with the button click

* These are all equivalent ways to send the current value of the button count to the
* txtPageCopy object.

  this.parent.parent.txtPageCopy.Value = this.Caption
*      ------                           "up" to container
*             ------                    "up" to page
*                   ----------------    object.property within the page

  this.parent.parent.parent.pagOverrideContainer.txtPageCopy.Value = this.Caption
*      ------                                    "up" to container
*             ------                             "up" to page
*                   ------                       "up" to pageframe
*                         --------------------   "down" to page
*                                             ---------------- object.property

      within the page

thisform.pgfMain.pagOverrideContainer.txtPageCopy.Value = this.Caption
```

Because you still want the container to operate as before, you need to use the :: scope resolution operator to call the Click() method of the button within the container. After that, the code uses two object references to get the txtPageCopy object. The first object reference is the simplest—this.parent goes to the container, and the next parent goes to the page that is the parent of the container, then to the object within the page. The second, more convoluted object reference goes all the way up to the PageFrame, then back down to the page. (The page Name is hard coded in this example, which prevents this from being a reusable class.) Finally, it goes to the txtPageCopy object. The third example starts from the Form all the way down to the TextBox. Needless to say, the first reference is better and faster.

Control Classes

A control class (not to be confused with the controls classes like CommandButton and TextBox) is a specialized container class; it's a more encapsulated version. If you select the ctlGroup object on the OBJREF Form, you'll see that the contained objects of the control do not show up as they do for the container version. The control class prevents all outside access to the contained objects. Because there is no access to the button, it can't talk to any other Form objects. Any "conversations" would have to be done with a method of the control class that could be queried and would return the current value to the sender of the message. In general, a control class needs a very well defined and documented public interface to be used. To examine a control class, close the Form Designer, and open the class designer on the CtlGroup class.

You can see that the cmdCount has exactly the same code as the container version. However, by putting the CommandButton and the TextBox into a control class, you've provided a level of protection to the internals of the class. These internals are also unavailable to subclasses that are derived from a control class.

Class Browser

The Class Browser that ships with the Professional Edition of Visual FoxPro is a tool that lets you see your class libraries and Forms in their full class hierarchies. The Project Manager only allows you to see the classes by their alphabetical names without any indication of what each class is derived from. Classes can be dragged out of the Class Browser and dropped onto Forms in the same way they are dragged and dropped from the Project Manager.

The Class Browser also allows you to export your class or Form into a "readable" source code file. This file is not executable as a .PRG because of the way it outputs container objects such as PageFrames and Grids, but it is very useful for those people that miss seeing real code emitted by the FoxPro 2.x GENSCRN program.

One feature of the Class Browser is the Redefine command. This allows you to change the ParentClass of a class. When you Redefine a class, the new ParentClass needs to have the same BaseClass at its root. You can not, for example, change a class from CommandButton to CheckBox. The only other way to do this is to hand edit the .VCX. The Class Browser can also move classes from one class library to another.

Another of the Class Browser's functions is Clean Up Class Library, or pack. This is necessary because sometimes Visual FoxPro can't get exclusive use of the class library while the Class Designer is in use. This prevents the Class Designer removing the deleted records (earlier versions of an edited class). If you don't pack a class and then build an application, all of the deleted records in the .VCX will also be included, needlessly bloating the application. You can also pack the class libraries with the BUILDAPP program that wraps the BUILD command.

One little annoyance in the Class Browser is the amount of screen space consumed by "non-essential" information. After a discussion of property sheet enhancements in the VFOX forum on CompuServe, Steve Black, a FoxPro developer from Toronto, posted a routine that eliminates most of the wasted space. It was a pretty neat idea, so here is a modified version of the routine:

```
* browmod.prg  15-Sep-95

* This code modifies the class browser object
* It basically reduces it to the hierarchical outline

* Based on a CompuServe message posted by Steve Black
* CompuServe address 76200, 2110

IF (TYPE( "_oBrowser") <> "O")
     * browser not running so start it up
   do (_BROWSER)
ENDIF

with _oBrowser
   .Visible    = .f.
   .Height     = 330
   .Width      = 339
   .MinButton = .f.
   .MaxButton = .f.
   .BorderStyle = 2       && make non-resizeable to disable resize
                             calcs
                          && which hose the OLE scrollbar

   .SetAll( "Visible", .F., "Editbox")
   .SetAll( "Visible", .f., "TextBox" )
   .SetAll( "Visible", .F., "OptionGroup")
```

Continued on next page

```
      with .lblClassType
         .FontBold = .t.
         .Left = 50
      endwith

      with .cboClassType
         .Left = 85
         .FontBold = .t.
         .Width = 130
      endwith

      .chkEmpty.Visible = .f.
      .chkProtected.Visible = .f.

      .imgClassIcon.Top = .cboClassType.Top
      .cmdClassIcon.Top = .imgClassIcon.Top

      .pgfMembers.Visible = .f.

      with .OLEClassList
         .Left = 3
         .Top = 60
         .FontBold = .t.
         .Height = _oBrowser.Height - .Top - .Left
         .Width = _oBrowser.Width - 2 * .Left
      endwith

      .Visible = .t.
   endwith

RETURN .T.
```

To use the program you simply type do browmod. You may want to experiment a little with the values selected to make them more "comfortable" for your video system.

The Class Browser is also an open architecture tool, which makes it extensible. You can find the details in the Visual FoxPro Help file under the search topic "Browsing Classes."

3 | Applying Object-Oriented Programming

Lock Class

The next example will focus on several items: protected properties, protected methods, inheritance, generalization, specialization, overriding, and using the scope resolution operator.

To begin, look at why it's a good idea to protect properties and methods. This can be illustrated with a class of locks. You're familiar with locks, but how can they be abstracted? There are many kinds of locks—some have keys, some have combination dials, and others have timers that restrict the time of day the lock can be opened. Each lock is either locked or unlocked, and it must have some way to change from one state to the other.

You can turn this lock abstraction into a computer model by starting with the things that are common to all locks. The "state" of the lock can be represented by a logical variable (mlLocked = .T. if it is locked, mlLocked = .F. if it is unlocked). To make the lock "secure," you need to protect mlLocked. Otherwise anybody could unlock the lock by setting mlLocked to .F.. The lock will need a Lock() method to lock it and an Unlock() method to unlock it. Because the state of the lock is hidden in the protected mlLocked property, you'll also need two methods (IsLocked and IsOpen) to tell the outside world about the lock's state. These methods will become your generalized lock class.

The ability to encapsulate and hide the property mlLocked is what makes it possible to create a lock in Visual FoxPro. This example would be impossible to construct in FoxPro 2.x because of the visibility of memory variables.

You can specialize the general lock class to make it into a combination lock by adding a property that will hold the combination of the lock, and by having the Unlock() method check the trial combination before actually unlocking the lock. You can specialize a combination lock and make it a time lock by adding properties that denote when the lock can be opened, and by having the Unlock() method check the time before checking the trial combination.

Just for fun, a BrokenLock class is included to illustrates some class design problems. Functionally, a BrokenLock is modeled as a combination lock that's always unlocked. Figure 3-1 shows the class tree for the locks.

Figure 3-1.

Lock class tree

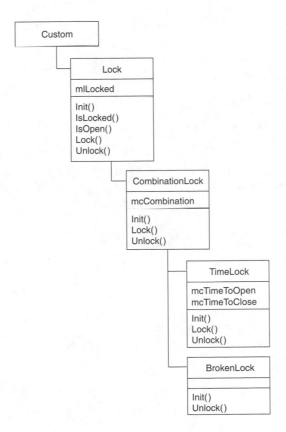

Drawing the class tree like this helps illustrate the generalization and specialization of the class hierarchy. Each class is drawn below the class it is derived from, its ParentClass. The farther to the right a class is, the more specialized it becomes.

Here's the code that creates the class tree in Figure 3-1.

```
* lock.prg 27-Feb-95

define class Lock as Custom
   protected mlLocked
   mlLocked = .null.

   protected procedure Init
      this.Lock()
   endproc

   procedure Lock
      this.mlLocked = .t.
   endproc

   procedure Unlock
      this.mlLocked = .f.
   endproc

   procedure IsLocked
      return( this.mlLocked )
   endproc

   procedure IsOpen
      return( ! this.IsLocked() )
   endproc
enddefine


define class CombinationLock as Lock
   protected mcCombination
   mcCombination = .null.

   protected procedure Init( pcCombination )
      Lock::Init()
      this.mcCombination = m.pcCombination
   endproc

   procedure Unlock( pcTestCombination )
      if ( type( "m.pcTestCombination" ) == type( "this.mcCombination" ) )
         if ( m.pcTestCombination == this.mcCombination )
            * combination is correct so send the message on up the class tree
            Lock::Unlock()
         endif
      endif
   endproc
enddefine


define class TimeLock as CombinationLock
   protected mcTimeToOpen
```

Continued on next page

```
    protected mcTimeToClose

    protected procedure Init( pcCombination, pcTimeToOpen, pcTimeToClose )
        CombinationLock::Init( m.pcCombination )
        this.mcTimeToOpen  = m.pcTimeToOpen
        this.mcTimeToClose = m.pcTimeToClose
    endproc

    procedure Unlock( pcTestCombination, pcTimeNow )
        if ( ( type( "m.pcTimeNow" ) == type( "this.mcTimeToOpen" ) ) and ;
             ( type( "m.pcTimeNow" ) == type( "this.mcTimeToClose" ) ) )
            if ( ( this.mcTimeToOpen <= m.pcTimeNow ) and ;
                 ( m.pcTimeNow <= this.mcTimeToClose ) )
                * time is correct send the combination on up the class tree
                CombinationLock::Unlock( m.pcTestCombination )
            endif
        endif
    endproc
enddefine


define class BrokenLock as CombinationLock
    protected procedure Init
        Lock::Init()
        this.mlLocked = .f.
    endproc

    procedure Unlock( cCombination )
        * no need to bother the sending the Unlock message on since this lock is
        * broken anyway.
    endproc
enddefine
```

Now take a moment to dissect the code. It starts by defining the generalized lock, which is derived from the BaseClass Custom. The lock state variable mlLockcd is declared protected and is given an initial value of .NULL.. Next comes the Init() method. Notice that Init() has also been protected; the reason for doing this will become clear when other locks are discussed. The Lock() and Unlock() methods simply put the appropriate value into the mlLocked property. The IsLocked() and IsOpen() methods provide public "read" access to the protected mlLocked property.

Example 3-1: The Lock Class
Now take a few minutes to play with this Lock class. Begin by running this program:

```
    do tlock
```

This test program simply creates one object of each kind of lock for you to experiment with in the command window. Begin by entering the following command:

```
display memory like o*
```

This will bring up the following display showing the four locks in memory.

```
OLOCK1   Pub   O              LOCK
OLOCK2   Pub   O              COMBINATIONLOCK
OLOCK3   Pub   O              TIMELOCK
OLOCK4   Pub   O              BROKENLOCK
```

Next, type in this command:

```
? oLock1.IsLocked()
```

This prints .T. because the lock you're working with is initially locked. You can unlock it with the code shown:

```
oLock1.Unlock()
? oLock1.IsLocked()
```

This prints .F. because you unlocked the lock. You can lock it again with this code:

```
oLock1.Lock()
? oLock1.IsLocked()
```

As you'd expect, this prints .T..

Now look back at the code for Figure 3-1's class tree, which was presented at the beginning of this chapter, and focus on the CombinationLock. It is derived from Lock which means that it will automatically inherit everything that is in the Lock class. CombinationLock begins as a functional lock, but without specialization it won't behave like a combination lock. To get that behavior, you need to add another protected property called mcCombination and modify (override) the Init() method and Unlock() method to handle the mcCombination property.

The Init() method receives the proper combination as an argument. You will override the Init() method by putting code into it. Overriding the method means that the default behavior provided by the Lock class is not automatically called. However, you're trying to *add* functionality to the Init() method, not to *replace* it. To regain the default behavior, you use the scope resolution operator :: to pass the message on to the Lock class. The Lock::Init() line does this, then the Init() method copies the combination argument to the property.

If the CombinationLock::Init() method was not protected, at anytime anyone could send an Init message to the lock object and supply a new combination for it. That is not very secure. By protecting the Init() method, you remove it from public view. You can set a lock's combination only when it is created.

Now take a look at the Unlock() method, starting with the innermost code. Again, you are overriding the method but you want the Lock class Unlock() method to run so you need to explicitly send the message Lock::Unlock(). The inner IF will unlock the lock only if the pcTestCombination is the correct combination for the lock. The outer IF is necessary because of the way that Visual FoxPro handles errors within methods. This issue will be covered later.

The mcCombination property doesn't have any effect on being able to lock the lock because you don't need to know the combination in order to lock a combination lock; you simply close the shackle and it will be locked. Likewise, you don't need the combination to see if the lock is locked or unlocked. This means that you don't have to do any coding for these methods in CombinationLock. The methods inherited from Lock will work just as you need them to.

Now try to unlock the CombinationLock without any combination:

```
oLock2.Unlock()
? oLock2.IsLocked()
```

This prints .T.. Next try using an invalid argument:

```
oLock2.Unlock( 4 )
? oLock2.IsLocked()
```

This also prints .T.. Finally, try using the correct combination:

```
oLock2.Unlock( "1R 32L 5R" )
? oLock2.IsLocked()
```

This prints .F., indicating that the lock is finally open. It can be locked again with this code:

```
oLock2.Lock()
? oLock2.IsLocked()
```

This prints .T.. Remember that because the CombinationLock class does not have an overridden Lock() method, the message is handled by the Lock() method within the Lock class. Now see what happens if you try to see what the combination of the lock is:

```
? oLock2.mcCombination
```

This results in the dialog window in Figure 3-2.

Figure 3-2.

*Trying to look at a
protected property*

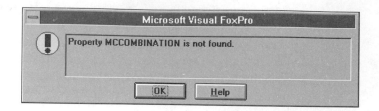

Because the property is protected, it is "hidden" from your view
and Visual FoxPro will tell you it doesn't know what mcCombination
is. Next try looking at the lock state:

```
? oLock2.mlLocked
Property MLLOCKED is not found
```

You find that you can't see it either! Now move to the TimeLock
class. TimeLock is derived from the CombinationLock class, which
means that it has all of the properties and behaviors of the
CombinationLock. You'll need to further specialize this to include the
time that the lock is allowed to open. You do this by adding two
protected properties to hold the mcTimeToOpen and mcTimeToClose
values. You also need to extend the functionality of the Init() and
Unlock() methods to handle the time values, but you can use the **::**
operator to pass the handling of the Combination to the
CombinationLock methods. Try entering this command:

```
? oLock3.IsOpen()
```

This prints .F.. Now try to open the lock early:

```
oLock3.Unlock( "2L 45R 77L 0R", "0859" )
? oLock3.IsOpen()
```

This prints .F., indicating that you can't open it early. Next,
attempt to open it within the allowed time:

```
oLock3.Unlock( "2L 45R 77L 0R", "0901" )
? oLock3.IsOpen()
```

This prints .T., indicating that the lock is open.

Now take a look at a bad class example. oLock4 is an instance
of a BrokenLock class. This class was created to show a few
problems. The code for the BrokenLock class is in the LOCK.PRG
program presented near the beginning of this chapter.

First, the Init() method of the BrokenLock class bypasses calling the ParentClass (CombinationLock::Init) and calls the Lock::Init() method directly. While this is legal from a Visual FoxPro sense, it's a really bad programming practice. If you find yourself wanting to call methods farther up the class tree than the ParentClass, you should closely examine the class tree because it's probably not designed correctly. If this kind of call is *really* necessary, it must be clearly documented. Another problem with calling back beyond the ParentClass is that when you do so, you cannot inherit any new functionality that might be added to the ParentClass's methods.

Second, the Unlock() method in the BrokenLock class is overridden with no executable code. This will cause the BrokenLock class to do nothing when it receives an Unlock() message. This is not bad in and of itself, but there will be times when you need to remove the functionality of the ParentClass. Once again, you need to closely examine why you are doing this and document it.

Third, the BrokenLock class shows an incomplete class derivation. Init() sets mlLocked to .F. and disables the Unlock() method, but what about the Lock() method? Think about this one for a minute.

```
? oLock4.IsLocked()
```

This code prints .F. because the BrokenLock class overrides the Init() method and explicitly unlocks the lock by setting mlLocked to .F.. Now try this line of code:

```
oLock4.Lock()
```

With that code, the BrokenLock class does not override the Lock() method. This means that the message goes all the way up the class tree until it gets to the Lock::Lock() method, which locks the lock. Now try this code:

```
? oLock4.IsLocked()
```

This prints .T. to show that the lock is locked. Now enter this:

```
oLock4.Unlock()
? oLock4.IsLocked()
```

Because you've disabled the Unlock method, you have no way of unlocking the lock once it's locked. This shows that the BrokenLock class was not properly designed. Now enter this command:

```
display objects like ol* to file olock.txt
modify file olock.txt
```

With this, you see all of the public properties and methods of the lock objects but you don't see any of the protected properties or methods. While this is what you are trying to achieve in this example, doing it this way makes it *very* hard to debug these classes. As a result, during development you may want to leave the properties and methods public until you are ready to release the class. Then you can switch them to protected. To clear the lock objects from memory, enter this in the command window:

```
release all
clear all
```

Now, because it will be important during development, take a few minutes to go back and cover the issue of errors within methods and Cancel in more detail.

Gotcha!

Watch out for errors within methods
If an error occurs within an object's method and you select Cancel from the Cancel/Suspend/Ignore dialog box, you are canceling only that method. That method will then stop running for the rest of the lifetime of the object.

Be aware that if a user attempts to unlock a combination lock and sends the wrong type of argument, the Unlock() method could stop functioning. As a result, the arguments are validated using the TYPE() function.

If a method is canceled, the "it stops working" behavior occurs at the object level, not the class level. If you have two objects of the same class and one errors with a subsequent Cancel, the other object will still work properly. To illustrate this, modify the CombinationLock::Unlock() method and comment out the IF (TYPE("M.PCTESTCOMBINATION") == TYPE("THIS.MCCOMBINATION")) and its ENDIF. Then do this code:

```
set classlib to lock
o1 = createobject( "CombinationLock", 123 )
o2 = createobject( "CombinationLock", "abc" )
o1.Unlock( "abc" )
```

When the Cancel/Suspend/Ignore dialog box appears, select Cancel.

```
?o1.IsLocked()
```

This prints .T. to show that it's still locked. Try to unlock it again with the correct combination:

```
o1.Unlock( 123 )
? o1.IsLocked()
```

Notice that the error dialog box does not appear this time. .T. is still printed because the Unlock() method for the o1 object has been disabled. However o2's Unlock() is still working:

```
o2.Unlock( "abc" )
? o2.IsLocked()
```

This prints .F., indicating that the failure in o1 has not affected the operation of the o2 object. This gives you another reason to provide an overridden Error() method in all of your custom baseclasses: to prevent the possibility of a user being able to cancel a method. While this method deactivation may seem odd at first, it actually can serve a purpose during development. If an error does occur, you can cancel so the error will not pop up again. Then you can continue testing other parts of the object.

One final note about protected members: Once a property or method has been declared PROTECTED, it cannot be made public by a subclass. For example:

```
define class X as Custom
   protected PropertyX        && protect this
   PropertyY = 1              && this is public
enddefine

define class X1 as X
   PropertyX = 1              && does NOT make PropertyX public
enddefine

define class X2 as X
   protected PropertyY        && does make PropertyY protected
enddefine
```

2-D Graphics Classes

This next example will focus on polymorphism, inheritance, override, and the scope resolution operator ::. A sample set of classes for dealing with 2-D graphics shapes are shown in Figure 3-3. You'll design an (x,y) point, circle, and rectangle classes. It starts with a simple XY point class.

Figure 3-3.

XY point class tree

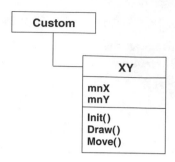

This class has two properties, mnX and mnY, to store the (x,y) coordinates of the point. These are set in the Init() method. The Draw() method uses the _screen.PSet() method to display the point on the screen. A Move() method changes the (x,y) coordinates by adding an ΔX and a ΔY.

The class is defined in the following code:

```
* xy.prg  18-Jul-95

define class XY as custom
   mnX = 0
   mnY = 0

procedure Init( pnX, pnY )
   this.mnX = m.pnX
   this.mnY = m.pnY
endproc

procedure Draw
   _screen.PSet( this.mnX, this.mnY )
endproc

procedure Move( pnDeltaX, pnDeltaY )
   this.mnX = this.mnX + m.pnDeltaX
   this.mnY = this.mnY + m.pnDeltaY
endproc
enddefine
```

As you can see in Figure 3-4, the Circle class is derived from the XY class.

Figure 3-4.

Circle class tree

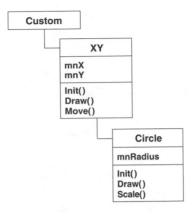

The Circle class inherits an (x,y) coordinate pair that will be used as the center of the circle. It adds a property mnRadius to store the circle radius. The Init() method first uses the scope resolution operator **::** to pass the center coordinates to the XY::Init() method, then it sets the object's radius. The Draw() method is overridden to use the _screen.Circle() method. The XY::Draw() method is not called because you don't want the center point drawn. The circle does not need its own Move() method because the XY:Move method does everything you need to move a circle. A Scale() method is created and is used to change the size of the circle by multiplying the radius by a scale factor; polymorphism allows you to use the same name for the Draw() and Scale() methods. Both XY and Circle objects can receive Draw() messages, but each one knows how to handle the details of drawing itself. You can contrast this polymorphism to the distinct names (like DrawXY and DrawCircle) these functions would need in FoxPro 2.x.

```
* circle.prg  18-Jul-95

define class Circle as XY
   mnRadius = 0

procedure Init( pnX, pnY, pnRadius )
   XY::Init( m.pnX, m.pnY )
   this.mnRadius = m.pnRadius
endproc

procedure Draw
   _screen.CurrentX = this.mnX
   _screen.CurrentY = this.mnY
   _screen.Circle( this.mnRadius )
endproc
```

Continued on next page

Continued from previous page

```
procedure Scale( pnScaleFactor )
   this.mnRadius = this.mnRadius * m.pnScaleFactor
endproc
enddefine
```

> ## Gotcha!
>
> ### There are class library class name restrictions for the Circle class.
>
> This class can be created only as a .PRG class. It cannot be stored as a .VCX class because the Class Designer will not accept Circle as a class name. In order to use the Class Designer, this class would need a different name like InfiniteSidedPolygon.

A rectangle whose sides are restricted to being parallel to the X-Y axis can be represented by using the two opposite corners. The Rectangle class presents a few implementation choices:

- **Implementation 1**. Derive the Rectangle class from XY and use height and width properties.
- **Implementation 2**. Derive the Rectangle class from the Custom class and use ADD OBJECT to add two XY objects.
- **Implementation 3**. Derive the Rectangle class from the XY class and use ADD OBJECT to add one XY object.

Figure 3-5.

Two possible rectangle abstractions

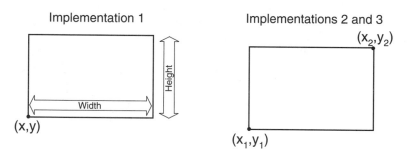

Figure 3-5 graphically illustrates the three possible implementations of the two abstractions.

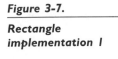

Figure 3-6.

Rectangle methods

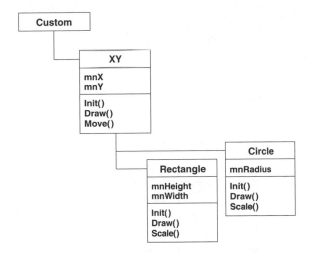

Move(100, -40)   Scale(2.0)

Figure 3-6 shows the behavior of the Move() and Scale() methods. Now take a look at the object details of each implementation:

IMPLEMENTATION 1. Here you derive the Rectangle class from the XY class and use height and width properties. This class hierarchy is shown in Figure 3-7.

Figure 3-7.

Rectangle implementation I

In this implementation, the Rectangle class inherits an (x,y) coordinate pair from the XY class that will be used to store one corner of the rectangle. By using the height and width to store the other corner, the XY::Move() method works well as it is. The Scale() method is easier here than it is in the other two implementations, but the Draw() method is slightly more complex.

> ### Gotcha!
>
> *Restrict your use of Custom class property names.*
> You can't reliably use the Top, Left, Height, and Width properties
> of the Custom base class. Visual FoxPro has a bug that sometimes
> changes these values behind the scenes in some sort of attempt to
> convert from pixels to foxels. As a result, it's best to simply avoid
> using them. In light of this "gotcha" these properties are named
> mnX, mnY, mnHeight, and mnWidth respectively, according to the
> naming standard.

The Init() method first passes the pnX and pnY coordinates
to the XY::Init() method, then it sets the object's height and width.
The Draw() method is overridden to use the _screen.Box() method.
The Rectangle class does not need its own Move() method because
the XY::Move() method does everything needed to move a rectangle.
A Scale() method is created and used to change the size of the
rectangle by multiplying the height and width by a scale factor.
The Rectangle class is defined in this code:

```
* rect.prg  18-Jul-95

define class RectangleHeightWidth as XY
   mnHeight = 0
   mnWidth = 0

procedure Init( pnX, pnY, pnWidth, pnHeight )
   XY::Init( m.pnX, m.pnY )
   this.mnHeight = m.pnHeight
   this.mnWidth  = m.pnWidth
endproc

procedure Draw
   XY::Draw()
   _screen.Box( this.mnX + this.mnWidth, this.mnY +
   this.mnHeight )
endproc

procedure Scale( pnScaleFactor )
   this.mnHeight = this.mnHeight * m.pnScaleFactor
   this.mnWidth  = this.mnWidth * m.pnScaleFactor
endproc
enddefine
```

IMPLEMENTATION 2. This option derives the Rectangle class
from the Custom class and uses ADD OBJECT to include two XY
objects. The class and container hierarchies are shown in Figure 3-8.

Figure 3-8.

Rectangle implementation 2

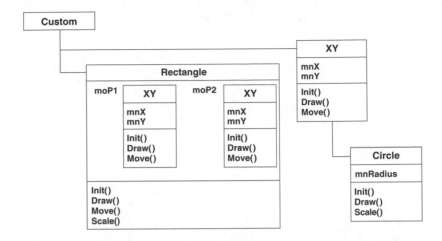

Gotcha!

The Custom class versus the Container class in the Class Designer.

This Rectangle class can be created only as a .PRG class and cannot be stored as a .VCX class. This is because the Class Designer will not allow you to visually add objects (moP1 and moP2) to a Custom class. To use the Class Designer, you need to derive Rectangle from the Container base class instead.

This Rectangle class uses ADD OBJECT to create the two XY objects so it can hold the (x,y) coordinates of two opposing corners of the rectangle. In the Init() method, the (x,y) coordinates are sent to their respective XY::Init() methods. The Draw() method calls the first corner's Draw() method. This moves the screen cursor to the first corner of the rectangle, then sends the second corner to the _screen.Box() method. Because you have the real (x,y) coordinates of the corner, you don't need to perform the addition necessary in the first Rectangle class. The Scale() method is much more complex. The Move() method is necessary because the Rectangle class isn't inheriting a Move() method from its ParentClass, Custom. Its contained XY objects have a Move() method, but you need to create a Move() method for the Rectangle class and pass the move message on to each of the contained XY objects. Here is the code for the second Rectangle class implementation:

```
* rect1.prg  18-Jul-95

define class RectangleAddObject as custom
   add object moP1 as XY
   add object moP2 as XY

procedure Init( pnX1, pnY1, pnX2, pnY2 )
   this.moP1.Init( m.pnX1, m.pnY1 )
   this.moP2.Init( m.pnX2, m.pnY2 )
endproc

procedure Draw
   this.moP1.Draw()
   _screen.Box( this.moP2.mnX, this.moP2.mnY )
endproc

procedure Scale( pnScaleFactor )
   this.moP2.mnX = this.moP1.mnX + ( this.moP2.mnX - this.moP1.mnX ) * m.pnScaleFactor
   this.moP2.mnY = this.moP1.mnY + ( this.moP2.mnY - this.moP1.mnY ) * m.pnScaleFactor
endproc

procedure Move( pnDeltaX, pnDeltaY )
   this.moP1.Move( m.pnDeltaX, m.pnDeltaY )
   this.moP2.Move( m.pnDeltaX, m.pnDeltaY )
endproc
enddefine
```

IMPLEMENTATION 3. This implementation derives the Rectangle class from the XY class and uses ADD OBJECT to include one XY object in the class tree. This hierarchy is shown in Figure 3-9.

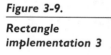

Figure 3-9.

Rectangle implementation 3

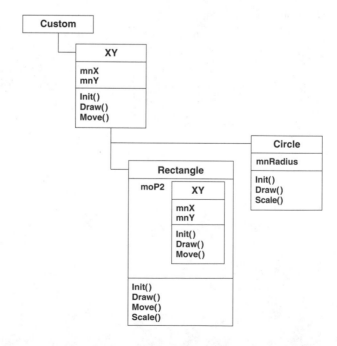

This implementation is being presented only because you *can* do it this way; however it's not recommended. It is basically the same as the second class in function, but each method has a class that is difficult to maintain and understand. Notice that each method uses the class's inherited method or property and the contained object's method or property. The code for this class implementation is shown:

```
* rect2.prg  18-Jul-95

define class RectangleMixed as XY
  add object moP2 as XY

procedure Init( pnX1, pnY1, pnX2, pnY2 )
  XY::Init( m.pnX1, m.pnY1 )
  this.moP2.Init( m.pnX2, m.pnY2 )
endproc

procedure Draw
  XY::Draw()
  _screen.Box( this.moP2.mnX, this.moP2.mnY )
endproc

procedure Scale( pnScaleFactor )
  this.moP2.mnX = this.mnX + ( this.moP2.mnX - this.mnX ) * m.pnScaleFactor
  this.moP2.mnY = this.mnY + ( this.moP2.mnY - this.mnY ) * m.pnScaleFactor
endproc

procedure Move( pnDeltaX, pnDeltaY )
  XY::Move( m.pnDeltaX, m.pnDeltaY )
  this.moP2.Move( m.pnDeltaX, m.pnDeltaY )
endproc
enddefine
```

Generally, the first implementation is the best. The second implementation is acceptable, but you should run away from any class structured like the third implementation.

Here's a little test program that tests each class:

```
* tgraph.prg  18-Jul-95

clear
set procedure to xy, circle, rect, rect1, rect2 additive

_screen.DrawWidth = 2

p1 = createobject( "XY", 80, 100 )
p1.Draw()
p1.Move( -15, -15 )
p1.Draw()

c1 = createobject( "Circle", 65, 45, 25 )
=Test( c1 )
```

Continued on next page

Continued from previous page

```
r1 = createobject( "RectangleHeightWidth", 10, 100, 30, 40 )
=Test( r1 )

r2 = createobject( "RectangleAddObject", 10, 200, 40, 240 )
=Test( r2 )

r3 = createobject( "RectangleMixed", 10, 300, 40, 340 )
=Test( r3 )
return

procedure Test( roGraph )
roGraph.Draw()
roGraph.Scale( 1.33 )
roGraph.Draw()
roGraph.Move( 50, 25 )
roGraph.Draw()
_screen.CurrentY = _screen.CurrentY - 16
_screen.Print( roGraph.Name )
endproc
```

This creates the image shown in Figure 3-10.

Figure 3-10.

Output of TGRAPH.PRG

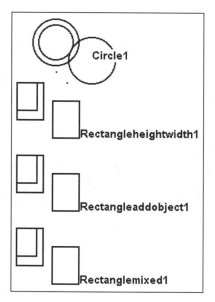

Preview—A Picture Viewer

This next example will focus on the Class Designer, the Form Designer, creating classes, using classes on Forms, and creating resizeable Forms and objects. This part covers how to use the Class Designer and the Form Designer. You'll also see that the Class Designer and Form Designer are the same tool for all practical purposes. You can tell which of them you are running by looking at the window titles and at whether the menu has a Class or Form item. It is also worth noting that the internal structure of the class library and Form tables are the same.

As you go through this example, you are going to make some intentional mistakes. These are to show you the error dialog boxes that Visual FoxPro produces, which aren't always as helpful as they could be. They will also show you some of the things that can go wrong, what the symptoms are, and how to correct these problems. These are the kind of things that you will probably run into. If you spot the errors before they are exposed, you have a good grasp of the issue, but you should go ahead and make the mistake anyway.

The report will now begin to concentrate on using the designers instead of typing code into a .PRG. The designers relieve you of some of the more mundane tasks such as typing the DEFINE CLASS...ENDDEFINE and PROCEDURE...ENDPROC. The designers also apply a little more structure to the class library. This structure allows the class library to be presented in a hierarchical display by the Class Browser. The hierarchy information can then be easily looked up in a couple of table fields instead of having to parse the source code to find it. The downside to using the designer is that the code can no longer be viewed or edited as a monolithic source code file. The Class Browser gives you the ability to generate a source code file that you can view. There are also third party products that should help the "editable" area.

This program will solve a problem that is in one of the Visual FoxPro dialog boxes. You will also build a couple of useful classes in the process. First, look at the problem with one of the new built-in functions GetPict(). In the command window, enter = `GetPict()`. This opens a dialog box that lets you pick either a .BMP or .ICO file. The dialog box has a preview area, but in order to see any particular image you need to pick the file, move to the Preview button box, and click it. If the image is not what you want, you have to keep going back and forth across the dialog box, picking files and clicking Preview until you find the image you want. This is especially annoying if you are working on a notebook with a TrackPoint type of pointing device. It would be better if the dialog box behaved like the dialog box in FoxPro 2.x in which, after a slight delay, the image would appear while you were scrolling through the file list. Another potential pet peeve deals with the fixed size dialog boxes that display selection lists. These dialog boxes are sized to fit the lowest common denominator, 640x480. Many programmers stopped using 640x480 about three years ago, and now run at either 1280x1024 or 1024x768.

Having all of that unused screen real estate is annoying, but you can fix that problem as well. Yes, user resizing of running Forms is possible in Visual FoxPro.

For brevity, the dialog box is simplified a little. You'll need to make the Form, then you can make it resizeable. The objects you'll need are listed in Table 3-1.

Object	Name	ParentClass	Description
Form	frmPreview	cForm	The Form
TextBox	txtFileSpec	cTextBox	Input field for the user-entered filespec
ListBox	lstFiles	cListBox	List of files meeting the filespec
CommandButton	cmdOk	cCommandButton	A button to end this Form
CommandButton	cmdDirectory	cCommandButton	A button to launch the built-in GetDir dialog box
Image	imgNormalSize	cImage	The image you want to see
Image	imgLargeSize	cImage	The image large enough to see
Label	lblFileSpec	cLabel	Text above txtFileSpec

Table 3-1.

Objects for the Preview Form

First you'll have to create "custom" base classes to avoid using the Visual FoxPro BaseClasses directly. This is done for two reasons: Visual FoxPro BaseClasses don't all work exactly the way you'd like them to, and inserting your own layer allows you to make system-wide changes easily.

The reason you'll want to create a custom Form base class is that a raw Form has one small problem that can be bothersome during development. To discover what it is, modify the Form Junk in the command window. Next, click the ! (run) button. Then click back to the command window and enter the following:

```
display memory
```

The output of the command appears in the Form window, but that's not where you normally want the output to appear. How do you fix this? Remember your new motto: if it doesn't work exactly the way you want, you can subclass it. Begin by entering this command in the command window:

```
create class cForm of cform.vcx as form
```

This will launch the Class Designer, allowing you to create a new class named cForm, store it in CFORM.VCX, and derive the class from the BaseClass Form. Then you'll do only one thing to your cForm class. Use the right mouse button to click the Form and select the Code... menu item. Then select the Deactivate() method and change it to:

```
* send output to the screen when this form is not active
activate screen
```

You can document this by adding a class description. From the menu, choose Class then Class Info.... You'll see the dialog box in Figure 3-11.

Figure 3-11.

The Class Info dialog box

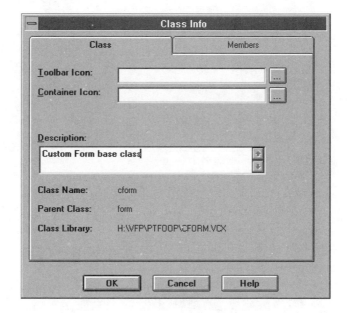

Then, enter this into the dialog box for the Description: Custom Form base class.

Close the Class Info dialog box and the Class Designer, saving all of the changes. Now you want to make cForm the default Form to use when creating new forms. Go to the Tools menu and select Options.... Then choose the Forms tab. You will see the dialog box in Figure 3-12.

Figure 3-12.

Form designer options

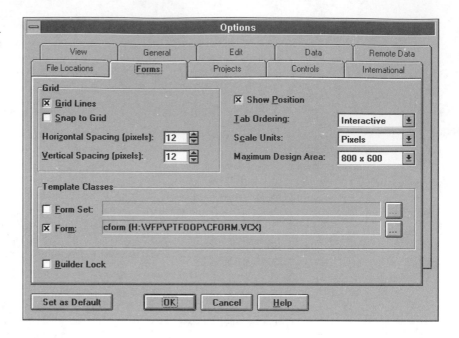

Under the Template classes, check the Form CheckBox and click the ... button. Then select cform.vcx as the class library and cForm as the class. When you select the class, you'll see that the description you entered earlier is below the Class Name ListBox. The dialog box should look something like the one shown in 3-13.

Figure 3-13.

Setting a template Form

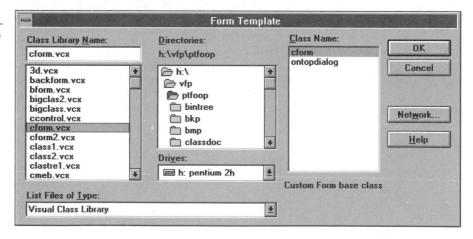

Then click OK. Any new Form you create will now be based on cForm instead of on the Form BaseClass. The template Form is only used by the Form Designer when a Form is first created. This means that you are free to change the Form template to a different class of Forms as you develop various application Forms. When the Form Designer opens an existing Form to edit that Form, ParentClass will not be changed even if a different template Form is currently set.

Now you can create the cCommandButton. Begin by entering this command:

```
create class
```

This opens the dialog box shown in Figure 3-14.

Figure 3-14.

New Class dialog box

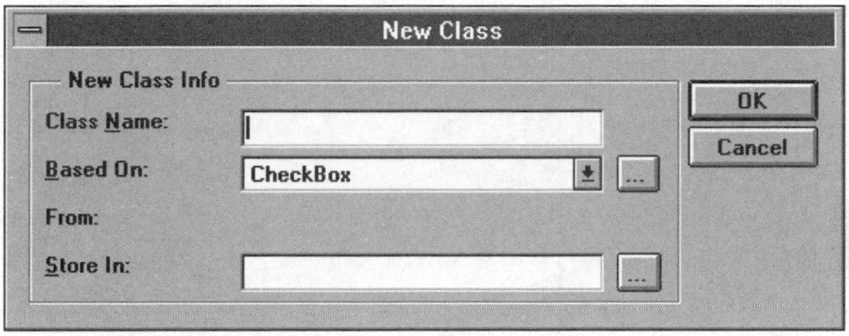

You can fill the dialog box with this:

```
Class Name=cCommandButton
Based on=CommandButton
Store in=ccontrol.vcx
```

That is equivalent to this command line:

```
create class cCommandButton of ccontrol as CommandButton
```

Make the class description: Custom CommandButton base class.

Now close the Class Designer. (You don't need to override any of the CommandButton properties or methods yet.) Next you can create the cLabel class using YAWTDSIVFP (Yet Another Way To Do Something In Visual FoxPro). Under the File menu, select New. Then choose Class and click the New button in the dialog box. This brings up the New Class dialog box. Enter the following information:

```
Class Name=cLabel
Based on=Label
Store in=ccontrol.vcx
```

This time you will override a property. Activate the property sheet and set the AutoSize property to .T..

You use this because you always want the label to be big enough for the Caption. Figure 3-15 shows the property sheet. This is followed by some explanations of what appears on it.

Figure 3-15.

The property sheet

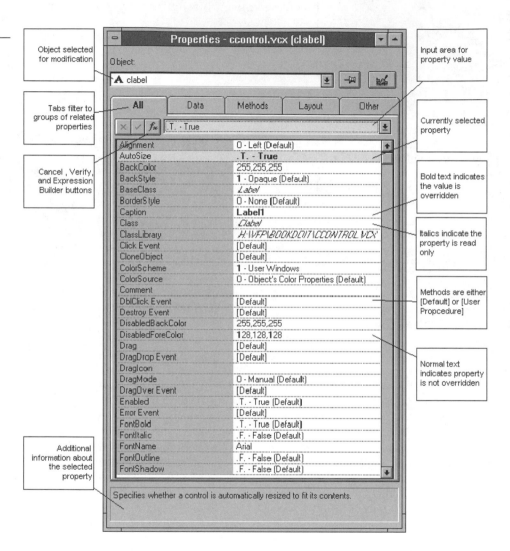

Class/Class Info.../Description=Custom Label base class

Close the class designer and save changes. Create the cTextBox next:

```
create class cTextBox of ccontrol as TextBox
Class/Class Info.../Description=Custom TextBox base class
```

Close the class designer and save changes. Create the cImage class next:

```
create class cImage as Image of ccontrol
Class/Class Info.../Description=Custom Image base class
```

Close the class designer and save changes. Create the cListBox class next:

```
create class cListBox as ListBox of ccontrol
```

Drag the listbox to a more useful size. Close the class designer and save changes.

Now that you're done creating your first class library, you can start to build the Form:

```
create form preview
```

Notice in the property sheet that this Form has a Class property and its value is "cForm." Now you can see if your cForm class really works. Click the ! button on the standard toolbar, then use the display memory from the command window. If the code worked the output will not show up in the Form. To close the Form, simply double-click its Control Menu. Use the following code to get the Form back into the Form Designer:

```
modify form preview
```

This Form will need a couple of custom properties and methods in order to work. These include a string for the filespec (mcFileSpec), a string for the directory (mcDirectory), and an array to hold the files to display in the ListBox (maFiles). You'll also create a method to set the array contents (UpdateFiles). To add these custom properties and methods, select New Property from the Form menu. This will bring up the dialog window shown in Figure 3-16.

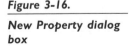

Figure 3-16.

New Property dialog box

New Property

Name: |

Description:

OK

Cancel

☐ Protected

Then enter the following data:

```
Name=mcFileSpec
Description=input filespec
```

Now repeat that process two more times.

```
Name=mcDirectory
Description=current directory, holds output of GetFiles()

Name=maFiles[1,2]
Description=Array of files, holds output of ADIR()
```

Entering the "[1,2]" is required to let Visual FoxPro know that the property is an array. Like any FoxPro array we can change its dimensions at runtime, so the [1,2] is merely a placeholder.

Now select New Method... from the Form menu. This brings up the window in Figure 3-17.

Figure 3-17.

New Method dialog box

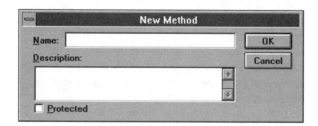

Notice that the New Property and New Method dialog boxes differ only by their titles.

Table 3-2.

Properties for the Form

```
Name=UpdateFiles
Description=This method updates the array and controls
```

Now change the Form properties as listed in Table 3-2.

Property	Value	How To/Notes
BackColor	192,192,192	You can either input the value or click the ... button to launch the color picker dialog, or use the Palette Toolbar to do this.
Caption	Image Preview	type it in
Name	frmPreview	type it in
ShowTips	.t.	
mcDirectory	" "	default to "current" directory
mcFileSpec	*.bmp	this will be default filespec

Notice that as you change these properties, the changes are immediately seen in the Form Designer window. Now you can start putting controls on the Form. If the Controls toolbar is not visible yet, turn it on with this code:

```
View/Form Controls Toolbar
```

However you *don't* want to use controls from this toolbar. These controls are the Visual FoxPro BaseClass controls, and you want to use your custom controls. Click the second button from the left on the toolbar (View Classes), chose Add..., and select the ccontrol.vcx. The toolbar will now redraw, and its new incarnation will contain your custom controls. Drop the controls on the Form and make it look like the one in Figure 3-18.

Figure 3-18.

The first attempt at the Preview Form

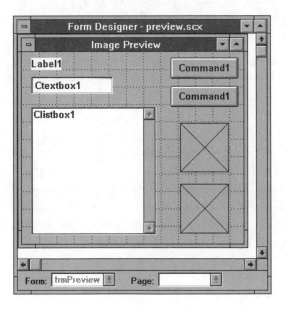

Now everything looks great except for Label1. Labels default to having an opaque background, which doesn't work for Forms with background colors. However, fixing this problem won't involve subclassing it a second time. It's better to have your base class cLabel default to Transparent. To do so, go to the command window and enter the following:

```
modify class cLabel of ccontrol
```

Visual FoxPro responds to this with an error dialog box that you might not expect. This is shown in Figure 3-19.

Figure 3-19.

Class in use error

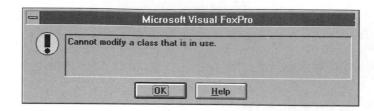

The dialog box is telling you that the cLabel class is being used by the Form Designer, so the Class Designer can't edit the class. This is because the Form Designer has actually instantiated each of the objects on the Form. To do this, it opened the classlib to create the objects. To get around this, you need to close the Form. Click OK and close the Form Designer.

```
modify class cLabel of ccontrol
change the property: BackStyle to 0 - Transparent
```

Then close the Class Designer and modify the Preview Form again.

The Form now shows the new transparent version of cLabel. When you dropped the objects onto the Form, Visual FoxPro generated a unique name for each object. It then takes those class names and appends serial numbers to them. This can be confusing for objects such as the button and the Form itself that have Captions. These names are adequate, but it's better to give each object a name that's a little more representative than cCommandButton2. You can change the name of each object to meet your naming conventions by selecting the cTextBox1 object. Then click the Other tab of the property sheet to filter out some of the chaff. Finally set the name property to txtFileSpec.

Now you can either click another object on the Form or select another object from the object drop-down list on the property sheet. You'll stay on the Name entry on the property sheet so the task will go pretty quickly. Select each control and name it according to Table 3-1. You don't need to bother with naming labels unless the label is going to respond to user actions. In this case you'll be using the label as a hotkey for the txtFileSpec, so you should change the name cLabel1 to lblFileSpec. Make the top button the cmdDirectory, and the top image imgNormalSize.

You might want to give the input control the same name as the property you are using as the data source, but you can't. If you try to name the txtFileSpec textbox mcFileSpec, you'll get the error dialog box shown in Figure 3-20.

Figure 3-20.

Dialog box from conflicting names

This dialog box might be a little misleading. It is actually complaining because a property (not an object) named mcFileSpec already exists.

Now you can make the cmdOk button functional. Begin by selecting it using the information in Table 3-3.

Property	Value	How To/Notes
AutoSize	.t.	When you press ".", the value will toggle between .F. and .T.. You can also double-click it to toggle it.
Caption	\<Ok	Type in the value. The \< makes the O the hot key just as it did in FoxPro 2.x
Click Event	thisform.Release()	Double-Click the Click event row and a code window will appear. You can also click the right mouse button on the Form and select Code..., or click the Code Window button on the standard toolbar. You'll notice that after the code is entered the property sheet displays [User Procedure] to indicate that it has been overridden.
Default	.t.	This makes cmdOK the default button when Enter is pressed.

Table 3-3.

cmdOk properties and method

Now test your Form to see if the cmdOk button works. Begin by clicking the ! button. The Form should go away when you click the OK button. Go back to editing the Form.

Finding the Files

Now enable the cmdDirectory button using the information in Table 3-4.

Property	Value	How to/Notes
Caption		Press the delete key to clear the Caption.

Click Event	`local lcDirectory`
	
	`m.lcDirectory = thisform.mcDirectory`
	`m.lcDirectory = getdir( m.lcDirectory, "Pick a directory" )`
	`if ( ! empty( m.lcDirectory ) )`
	   `thisform.mcDirectory = m.lcDirectory`
	   `thisform.UpdateFiles()`
	`endif`	

Picture	\ptfoop\bmp\open.bmp	This displays the open file folder picture.
ToolTipText	Choose directory	

Table 3-4.

cmdDirectory properties and methods

The local memory variable lcDirectory is used in case the user selects Cancel from the GetDir() dialog box. If a directory is selected, the Form property mcDirectory will be set and you can call the Form UpdateFiles() method. However, nothing will happen because you haven't put anything in the UpdateFiles() method.

Now make the two buttons of the same size. Open the Layout toolbar and click the cmdOk button. Then shift-click the cmdDirectory button so both the cmdOk and cmdDirectory buttons are selected. Finally click the Same Size button on the layout toolbox.

You test to see if the cmdDirectory button works by going to the Tools and Debug window and entering preview.mcDirectory. Then click the ! button. Finally, click the cmdDirectory button. After you select a directory you should see the value appear in the Debug window. Now close the Form.

You can get the UpdateFiles() method working by editing the Form again:

Then use the right mouse button to click the Form someplace where there is no control. Select Code..., then select the UpdateFiles() method. Finally, enter the following code:

```
* put the files matching the filespec into the array, update the listbox size

this.lstFiles.NumberOfElements = adir( this.maFiles, this.mcDirectory +
   alltrim( this.mcFileSpec ) )

if ( this.lstFiles.NumberOfElements > 0 )
   * at least one file matches
   this.lstFiles.ListIndex = 1        && point at the first
   this.lstFiles.Enabled = .t.        && enable the listbox
else
   * no files match
   this.lstFiles.ListIndex = 0        && so listbox doesn't have hilite bar

   * adjust listbox & array to indicate no files
   this.lstFiles.NumberOfElements = 1
   dimension this.maFiles[1,4]
   this.maFiles[1,1] = "No Matching Files"

   this.lstFiles.Enabled = .f.        && disable the listbox
endif

this.lstFiles.InteractiveChange()     && update images
this.lstFiles.SetFocus()              && move the cursor to the listbox
this.lstFiles.Refresh()               && redisplay it
```

Now you need to hook the lstFiles control to the maFiles array. Begin by selecting the lstFiles control using the information in Table 3-5.

Property	Value
ColumnCount	1
RowSource	maFiles
RowSourceType	5 - Array

When you try to run the Form you will get the dialog box shown in Figure 3-21.

Figure 3-21.

What do you mean it's not an array??

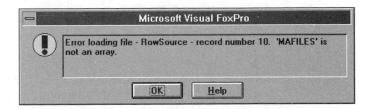

If you go back and check you'll find that you do indeed do have an array maFiles. Visual FoxPro is complaining because you didn't properly identify the array. The array is a property of the Form object, so you need to reference the Form using thisform. This is one of the reasons I use 'm' as an object scope. With it, I won't forget to put an object reference in front of the property. Change the RowSource property to thisform.maFiles and try running the Form again.

Hooking Up the Images

At this point you can finally get around to seeing some results from all of this effort. The next code sample will set the Picture property of the two image controls at the selected file in the ListBox. Select the lstFiles control and enter this code in its InteractiveChange() method:

```
local lcFile

if ( ( this.ListIndex > 0 ) and ( this.ListIndex <= alen( thisform.maFiles, 1 ) ) )
  m.lcFile = thisform.mcDirectory + thisform.maFiles[this.ListIndex,1]
else
  m.lcFile = ""
endif

thisform.imgNormalSize.Picture = m.lcFile
thisform.imgLargeSize.Picture = m.lcFile
```

Select the imgNormalSize control and change it using the information in Table 3-6.

Table 3-6.

imgNormalSize properties

Property	Value
Height	64
Width	64

Next, select the imgLargeSize control and change it using the information in Table 3-7.

Table 3-7.

imgLargeSize properties

Property	Value
Height	64
Stretch	1 - Isometric
Width	64

These images are 64x64 because most of the images viewed by this tool are 16x16. The imgLargeSize view will then be four times larger than normal. Now run the Form and select a directory with bitmaps or icons (\ptfoop\bmp or \vfp\samples\graphics\bmps\fox). As you move through the ListBox, each image will display in the two Image controls.

Now you only have to hook up the txtFileSpec control and you'll be done. Select the txtFileSpec and change it with the information in Table 3-8.

Table 3-8.

txtFileSpec properties and methods

Property	Value
DataSource	thisform.mcFileSpec
Valid	thisform.UpdateFiles()

Then select the lblFileSpec and change it with the information in Table 3-9.

Table 3-9.

lblFileSpec properties

Property	Value	How To/Notes
Caption	File \<Name	This will allow the label to act as the hotkey for the txtFileSpec control (provided it's next in the tab order)

Click the Set Tab Order button on the Form Designer toolbar and click each little box to set the tab order of the controls. You'll need to click the first object and then shift-click the other controls in the order you want. The tab order should be set as follows:

```
lblFilesSpec, txtFileSpec, lstFiles, cmdOk, cmdDirectory.
```

Now run your Form. It should look similar to the one in Figure 3-22.

Figure 3-22.

A working previewer

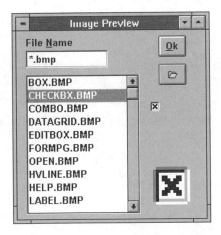

Making the Form Resizeable

Notice that although the Form window is resizeable, the objects don't yet know how to resize along with the Form. For this example, you'll resize only the ListBox so that it will get taller as the Form gets taller. You'll also set the Form so that it cannot be made any smaller than its "as designed" size; you don't want it to get any wider, narrower, or shorter than it already is. If the Form is made smaller, some of the controls will be clipped off. You can let the Form get as tall as the user's screen resolution will allow. There are four properties that control the Form resize limits—MaxHeight, MaxWidth, MinHeight, and MinWidth. If you look at them now in the property sheet you'll see that they have values of -1, which means that there are no limits on the Form's size. For this exercise you'll leave MaxHeight alone, because you don't want to limit the user's Form height selection.

You have two choices of how to change the other properties. You can set their values now, or you can set them at Form.Init() time. Both methods work, but the first method isn't very flexible and will cause you more work during the design process. For example, look at your Form's Height and Width properties. Take your current Height value and enter it in MinHeight. Then take your Width value and put it into MinWidth. Now run the Form and resize it. You'll be able to drag it taller and wider, but the Form cannot be made shorter or narrower than the size you just specified. Close the Form, and change the MaxWidth so that it also equals the Width. Run the Form again and you won't be able to resize the width at all. And to think that you got all of this functionality by filling in only three properties!

However, if you decide at design time to move elements around to make the Form a little narrower, you'll find that you can no longer drag the window to different sizes in the design window. You have to set then to -1, resize the Form, then reset them to the new Form size values. That seems like a lot of busy work. A better solution is to leave MaxWidth, MinHeight, and MinWidth set to the default during the design stage and have the Form set them whenever the Form object is initialized. You can do this by resetting the MaxWidth, MinHeight, and MinWidth properties to -1, then changing the frmPreview.Init() code to match the following:

```
this.mcDirectory = sys(5) + sys(2003)

* Limit the form size

this.MaxWidth  = this.Width
this.MinHeight = this.Height
this.MinWidth  = this.Width

this.UpdateFiles()
```

Now you have free reign to change the Form in any way you choose in the Form Designer. Whatever sizes you pick will be used to limit the Form at runtime. Now, to make the ListBox resize along with the Form, you will want to put some code into the ListBox

Resize() method. Begin by using the right mouse button to click the 1stFiles control. Then select Code... and open the Resize() method. There is no built-in Resize method for a ListBox, but object-oriented programming will come to the rescue! You can add your own Resize method.

With the lstFiles control still selected, go to the Form menu and select New Method....

```
Name = Resize
Description = Handle listbox resizing
```

After using this code, the dialog box in Figure 3-23 will appear.

Figure 3-23.

Method name conflict

This error message is telling you that the Form already has a Resize() method. This might seem unrelated to your adding a Resize() method to the selected ListBox, however you can't add properties and methods to objects on a Form. New Property and New Method are used to attach properties and methods to the Form, not to the objects contained in the Form. In order to get the Resize() method attached to a ListBox class, remember your motto and subclass the ListBox. Using the following instructions, you can make your own new kind of ListBox that "knows" how to resize itself.

Begin by creating a class. When that dialog box appears, fill in the class name as ResizeableListBox. Then click the ... button next to Based On and select the ccontrol classlib and clistbox class. Then, store this control in a different classlib called resize. When you're done, the dialog box should look like the one in Figure 3-24.

Figure 3-24.

Creating a Resizeable ListBox Class

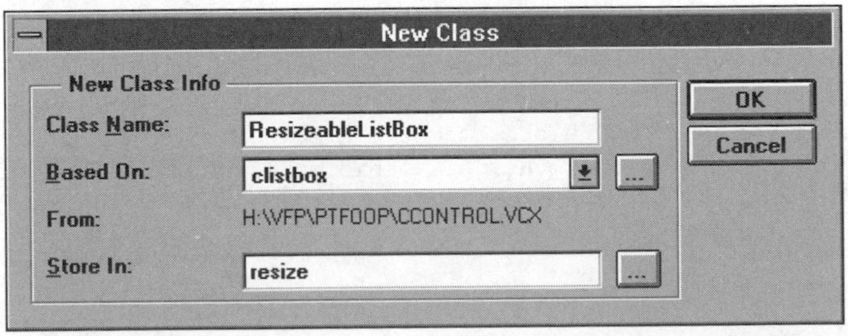

You've just created a new subclass of one of your own classes and stored it in a new classlib. The new class tree is shown in Figure 3-25.

Figure 3-25.

ResizeableListBox class tree

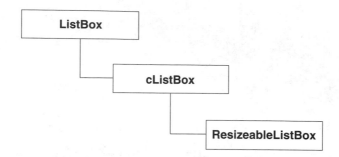

Notice that this class tree diagram does not represent the class library files used to store the classes. cListBox is stored in CCONTROL.VCX and ResizeableListBox is stored in RESIZE.VCX. This is important information, but it doesn't affect the class tree. You might want to put the classlib name in parentheses to show where the class is physically stored.

In order to make this ListBox smart enough to be resizeable, it will first have to have some way of knowing how big it is relative to the Form it's on when the Form is instantiated. Then it will have to adjust itself when the Form is resized.

To hold the size difference, give this ListBox a new property. Begin by selecting New Property... from the Class menu. Name the Property mnHeightDifference and put in this Description: Difference in height between the Form and this listbox on the property sheet give it an initial value of 0.

Put this code in the Init method:

```
cListBox::Init()
this.mnHeightDifference = thisform.Height - this.Height
```

Select New Method... from the Class menu. Name the method Resize, and put this in for the description: Handle the resize of the listbox.

Put this code in the Resize() method:

```
* calculate a new listbox height, limit minimum size
this.Height = max( ( thisform.Height - this.mnHeightDifference ), 50)
```

The benefit to doing the resize this way is that it gives you much more freedom at design time to move and change the size of the controls on the Form. You could determine at design time that frmPreview.Height - (lstFiles.Top + lstFiles.Height) was 10 pixels, then enter 10 as a value for mnHeightDifference and not calculate it inside the Init() method. This would work, but if you changed the size of the ListBox on the design surface, you'd have to remember to recalculate and change the mnHeightDifference property.

If you wanted to add a File Type drop-down list under the ListBox, you would make the Form taller and add a drop-down control. With a "hard-coded" 10 pixels on the property sheet, the ListBox would get too big and display over the top of the drop-down control the first time you resized the Form. By calculating the difference at runtime, the ResizeableListBox will always stay above the drop-down control.

Now close the Class Designer. You need to replace the cListBox on the Form with your new and improved ResizeableListBox. It's time to bring the Project Manager into the picture. Create a project, expand the Documents item by clicking its + button. Select Forms and click the Add button. Then select preview.scx. When you expand the Forms item, you'll see that preview has been added. At this point, you can let the Project Manager do some work for you. Click the Build button, then click OK. You'll notice that the Class Library item had a + button added to it. Click the + button to expand it (there isn't a keyboard shortcut).

After the build process finishes, you'll see that the cform and ccontrol class libraries have been added to the project. Because you haven't used a class from the resize class library, it didn't get added automatically.

Now make sure that you are on the Class Libraries row and click the Add button. Select resize.vcx and click the OK button. As you expand each library you'll see that all of the classes within the library are displayed in alphabetical order.

Next, double-click the preview Form to make it come up in the Form Designer. In the Project Manager, click the resizeablelistbox, then drag and drop it onto the Form.

Now you need to move the code stored in your existing lstFiles.InteractiveChange() method to the new ListBox. You can do this in a few steps. Open the code window and select the lstFiles object and go to its InteractiveChange() method. Then select all of the text and copy it to the clipboard. Select the resizeablelistbox1 object and go to its InteractiveChange() method. Then, paste the code in the method. On the property sheet select the resizeablelistbox1 object and hook it up like the original lstFiles. This is described in Table 3-10.

Table 3-10.

Properties for the new ListBox

Property	Value
ColumnCount	1
RowSource	thisform.maFiles
RowSourceType	5 - Array

Click the lstFiles control on the Form and press the *Delete* key. Change the name property of resizeablelistbox1 to lstFiles and move the new listbox to the correct position. Then drag the ListBox to the desired size. To see how all of this works, enter the following items in the debug window:

```
preview.lstFiles.mnHeightDifference
preview.lstFiles.Height
preview.Height
```

Now run the Form and resize it. There are good values displayed in the debug window. In spite of this, the Form resized but the ListBox didn't. This is because you never sent the ResizeableListBox a message to resize. The fact that ResizeableListBox has a Resize() method doesn't mean that it's automatically going to get messages. To fix this, change the frmPreview.Resize() method:

```
thisform.lstFiles.Resize()    && pass this message on to the
                                 listbox
```

Now when you run the Form, it will finally work just as it should. Or does it? It looks like it works, but you need to make a change to the cForm class to see the problem. In the Project Manager, double-click the cform class in the cform classlib to launch the Class Designer. Then put this code into the Init() method:

```
wait window "cForm.Init()"
```

Then put this code in the Activate() method:

```
wait window "cForm.Activate()"
```

Finally, put this code in the Resize() method:

```
wait window "cForm.Resize()"
```

Close the Class Designer and create a new Form named junk2, then run that Form. At this point you'll see the Init message and the

Activate message. When you resize the Form, you'll see the Resize message.

Now run the preview Form. Because frmPreview is derived from cForm, you should see the same messages appear. However, only the Activate message will appear. The reason for this lies in the fact that you overrode the Init() and Resize() methods in frmPreview. When you override a method, the code of the ParentClass is no longer automatically called. You must explicitly call it using the **::** scope resolution operator. To do this, double-click the Preview Form in the Project Manager.

Then change the Init() method:

```
cForm::Init()

this.mcDirectory = sys(5) + sys(2003)

* Limit the form size

this.MaxWidth  = this.Width
this.MinHeight = this.Height
this.MinWidth  = this.Width

this.UpdateFiles()
```

Next change the Resize() method to the following:

```
cform::Resize()            && call parentclass
thisform.lstFiles.Resize() && pass this message on to the
                              listbox
```

When you run the Form again, you will see the messages from the cForm class methods.

Generally you'll want to call the ParentClass() method before your code. There are cases where you'll want to call the ParentClass code after your code, but either way you'll need to know what the default code does in order to determine where the call should be placed. There are also cases where the ParentClass code needs to be skipped, but, as mentioned in the Lock example, these cases must be clearly documented.

Now close the Form. You'll need to remove the wait windows from the cForm class. You can easily do this by clicking the Methods tab in the property sheet and using the right mouse button to click the Activate(), Init(), and Resize() rows. Then choose Reset to Default. Don't reset the Deactivate() method. Remember that it contains the `activate screen` code.

Getting Information Back from Preview

Now you can give this Form the ability to return the picked filename back to you. To do this, use a .PRG to "wrap" the Form and to provide a place to hold the value. Right now it's kind of nice that the Preview dialog box is entirely modeless. You can start it, run other programs, and use the Form Designer on another Form, then you can pop right back into preview to look for an image. You could even start two instances of preview and use them to compare bitmaps from different directories. However as preview stands, if you find the image you want for a button on another Form you either have to retype the name or click the ... button to use the GetPict() dialog box. You might also want to use Preview as a modal dialog box asking your user for input. However while you are developing your program, you don't want to be forced into using preview modally. There are several ways give preview a multiple personality, one of which will be presented here. Create PREVIEW.PRG with a MODI COMM PREVIEW and enter this code in the edit window:

```
lparameter pnModal

if ( parameters() = 1 )
   local lcFileName
   do form preview with .t. to lcFileName
   return ( lcFileName )
else
   do form preview
endif
```

This code will look for the existence of a parameter. If one exists, then the Form will be run with a parameter and will use the TO clause. Using the TO clause requires that the Form is modal. If no parameter was passed, then the Form will be run (modelessly) as it has been so far.

Now add a Form property:

```
Name=mcReturnValue
Description=this will be used to hold the filename being
   returned to the calling program.
```

Then change the frmPreview.Init() as follows:

```
lparameter puReturnValue

if ( parameters() > 0 )
   * make this form modal
   this.WindowType = 1
endif

cForm::Init()          && call parentclass

this.mcDirectory = sys(5) + sys(2003)

* Limit the form size

this.MaxWidth  = this.Width
this.MinHeight = this.Height
this.MinWidth  = this.Width

this.UpdateFiles()
```

This code will check for the existence of a parameter sent to the Form. If one exists, the Form will be switched to modal. You then override the frmPreview.Unload() method with this code:

```
cForm::Unload()

if ( this.WindowType = 1 )
   return( thisform.mcReturnValue )
endif
```

The Unload() method is the last method to run in a Form. It returns the value to the calling program. Note that you cannot simply use the Value of a control in the Unload() method. By the time Unload() runs, the Form no longer contains any objects. The only "things" the Form has left are its properties. As a result, you need to copy the return value to a Form property while the Form is running so you have something to return.

Now change the lstFiles.InteractiveChange() method as follows:

```
local lcFile

if ( ( this.ListIndex > 0 ) and ( this.ListIndex <= alen( thisform.maFiles, 1 ) ) )
   m.lcFile = thisform.mcDirectory + thisform.maFiles[this.ListIndex,1]
else
   m.lcFile = ""
endif

thisform.imgNormalSize.Picture = m.lcFile
thisform.imgLargeSize.Picture = m.lcFile

if ( thisform.WindowType = 1 )
   * running modal so update the form return value
   thisform.mcReturnValue = m.lcFile
endif
```

This code will keep the return value up-to-date as the user selects each image. The code could have also been put in the lstFiles.Destroy() method. Now override the lstFiles.DblClick() method with this code:

```
ResizeableListBox::DblClick()
_cliptext = thisform.mcDirectory + thisform.lstFiles.DisplayValue
```

This code will put the file name into the clipboard when the ListBox is double-clicked. From here, you can paste it while you are designing other Forms. You could have put this code into the lstFiles.InteractiveChange() method, but the code has the potential to destroy important information that you've cut to the clipboard and haven't pasted yet. You will need to weigh whether the value of checking for clipboard contents and asking about overwriting them is worth the effort. This example has put the code into the DblClick method so that it will take a definite action before the clipboard contents are replaced. Now enter the following in the command window:

```
=preview()
```

Next, open the debug window and put _cliptext into it. If you double-click a .bmp in the listbox, you'll see _cliptext change. Then close the Form. Next you'll want to modify Form junk. Drop an Image control on the Form and select the property sheet. (The Picture property should already be selected.) Finally, press Ctrl-V. This procedure pastes the selected image filename into the image.Picture property. You've tested that preview will still run modeless, but what about modal? Enter the following in the command window:

```
? preview( 1 )
```

The Form is now running modal. You can't execute any commands in the command window, nor can you do anything else. When you select any .bmp and click OK the filename will display on the desktop. Now you have a modal dialog box that you can call from within another application.

There's one more thing to cover in this example. As you've put all of that work (one line of code) into that little cmdOk button, it would be nice if you had a way to reuse it on the next Form you design. You would reuse the button in FoxPro 2.x by opening two screens, copying the OK button to the clipboard, and pasting it into the buttonless screen. However, cutting and pasting is not real reuse. If the original button had an error in it, you would then have two

screens with the error and two screens to fix the error in. Visual
FoxPro provides a much better way to reuse the button.

In Visual FoxPro, you modify the Form preview and select the
cmdOk button. Then go to Save As Class in the File menu. This
results in the dialog box in Figure 3-26 after the necessary
information has already been filled in.

Figure 3-26.

***Saving an object as a
class***

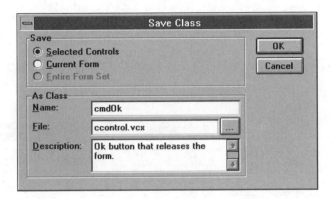

If you look back in the Project Manager window, you'll see the
cmdOk class in the CCONTROL class library. However the button
on your Form is still a cCommandButton. You didn't change it, you
simply saved a copy of it to a class library. Now you need to delete
the button from the Form and use the class you just created.

To do this, put the focus on the Form Designer window and
select the cmdOk button. Then press the Delete key. Finally, drag
and drop a cmdOk class from the Project Manager window back
onto the Form.

If you look in the property sheet, you'll notice that its
ParentClass is cmdOk instead of cCommandButton. While you're in
the property sheet, change its name from Cmdok1 to cmdOk. As you
open the code window for the button, you'll notice that the Click()
method is empty. That's because the thisform.Release() is now part
of the cmdOk class and your cmdOk button object inherits the
behavior. Now you can drop one of these cmdOk classes onto any
Form. If you happen to have made a mistake in the implementation
of the cmdOk class, you simply need to fix the class and every Form
that ever used the cmdOk class will also be fixed.

Have you noticed how nice it is not having to constantly build
projects or run GENSCRN on the screens? The fact that Forms and
classes run directly from their .SCX and .VCX files really makes the
prototype and test phases of designing much more rapid. The ease

and speed of switching from design mode to run mode makes incremental building and testing more practical. Most of the code you've written so far is in those nasty little snippets, but in Visual FoxPro they really aren't as limiting as they were in FoxPro 2.x. You might even learn to love them (or at least not hate them).

Fun with Forms!

This example will focus on Form classes. These Form classes are more for fun and because you *can* do them more than for any other reason. However, they show how to work with Form classes and could spark some novel Form ideas of your own. You can start by seeing what they look like in Figure 3-27 and Figure 3-28.

Figure 3-27.

A yellow legal pad Form

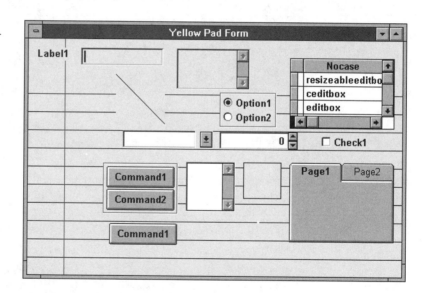

Figure 3-28.

A COBOL programmer's Form

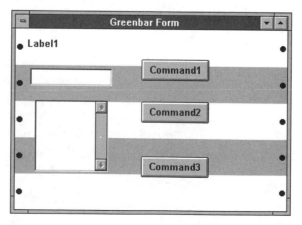

These Forms and class libraries are in the FUNFORMS.PJX project file. The class hierarchy for these Forms is shown in Figure 3-29.

Figure 3-29.

Forms class tree

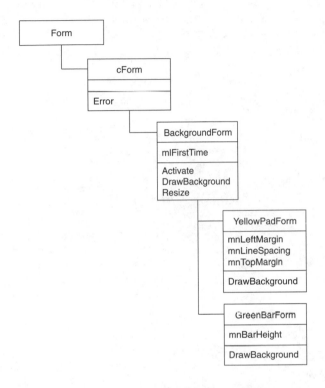

These Forms all use new graphic methods such as Line() and Circle() to draw the backgrounds. The drawing can't be done in the Load() or Init() methods because the Form doesn't visually exist yet, so the next logical place would be the Activate() method. However, you don't want the backgrounds to be drawn each time the Form becomes the active Form, so you can set up a property mlFirstTime that is initially set .T.. When the Activate() method runs, it tests mlFirstTime. It then calls the DrawBackground() method and resets the mlFirstTime flag.

When you read the help documentation for the graphics methods, it will lead you to believe that there are two graphics planes within the Form—one for the controls and one for the output of the graphic methods. The graphics plane is not behind the controls plane, so the output of the graphics methods draws over the top of the controls. When the YellowPad Form runs, this visual effect can be hidden by using the thisform.LockScreen property. The GreenBar Form can't use the LockScreen because it needs to use the Cls() method in order to remove the tractor feed holes. The YellowPadForm and GreenBarForm class's DrawBackground() methods are responsible for drawing their respective backgrounds. The BackgroundForm class's DrawBackground() method uses the Form's Controls[] array to bring the controls back to the top of the graphic method output. This method draws the lines across the Form:

```
* YellowPadForm.DrawBackground

local i, j, lnSaveForeColor, lnSaveDrawWidth, lnSaveDrawStyle

thisform.LockScreen = .t.

lnSaveForeColor = this.ForeColor
lnSaveDrawWidth = this.DrawWidth
lnSaveDrawStyle = this.DrawStyle

this.ForeColor = rgb( 0, 0, 255 )
this.DrawWidth = 1
this.DrawStyle = 0

for i = this.mnTopMargin to this.Height step this.mnLineSpacing
   this.Line( 0, i, this.Width, i )
endfor

this.ForeColor = rgb( 255, 0, 0 )
this.Line( this.mnLeftMargin, 0, this.mnLeftMargin, this.Height )

this.ForeColor = m.lnSaveForeColor
this.DrawWidth = m.lnSaveDrawWidth
this.DrawStyle = m.lnSaveDrawStyle

BackGroundForm::DrawBackground()

thisform.LockScreen = .f.
```

The following method brings the controls back above the lines:

```
* public method BackgroundForm.DrawBackground

* Handle object refresh

local i

* This will send the top control to the bottom of the array, so
* we only need to work on the top location for the number of
* controls.

for i = 1 to this.ControlCount
   this.Controls[1].ZOrder()
endfor
```

Notice that this routine iterates for the number of controls on the Form, but it always uses a value of 1 as the subscript into the Controls[] array. This is because the ZOrder() method changes the order of the objccts in the array and puts the object at the bottom of the array.

In order to use one of these Form classes for a Form you have to select Options... from the Tools menu. Select the Forms page and select the desired Form as the Form Template Class. Then choose the one you want to use.

4 | The Object Inspector

Visual FoxPro provides a good set of design tools for creating classes and forms, but the runtime tools (the debug window or ? in the command window) to examine them are pretty inadequate. In this section you'll build a better tool to work with objects at runtime. You can use Visual FoxPro's AMEMBERS() and ACLASS() functions to get information about the objects, but you can't easily manipulate the objects with them. To do that, you have to go to the command window and type the full object name, which can be ridiculously long if you have a Grid on a Page of a PageFrame. You can also use the following code to create intermediate object references to reduce some of the burden:

```
x = _screen.ActiveForm.pgfMain.Page1
x.FontName = "WingDings"
x.cmdOne.ForeColor = rgb(0,255,0)
```

Looking at the debug window's maximum of 32 items can get pretty old when most objects have more than 50 properties. Here you'll see how you can use the new internal functions to build an Object Inspector. Begin by running the Inspect tool:

```
do form clastre1
= inspect( clastre1 )
```

After that you'll see the Object Inspector shown in Figure 4-1.

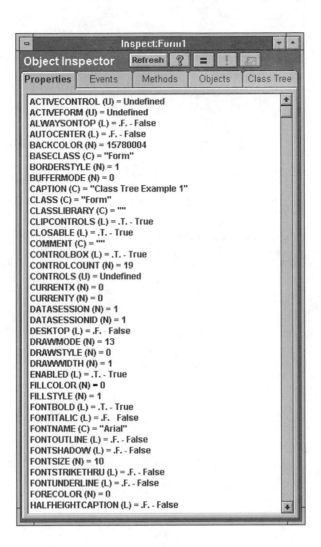

Inspect() has several key features, including:

- Runtime access to all of an object's properties, events, methods, and contained objects
- The ability to view all of the properties in the scrollable EditBox
- The ability to change the properties with a modeless dialog box launched from this window (= button)
- The ability to call the events and methods from another modeless dialog box (! button)
- The ability to inspect contained objects in another Inspect window (button)
- The ability to call up the Visual FoxPro help system to obtain detailed information on each entry (? button)

- The ability to resize the Form
- The ability to implement a right-click context menu to change font and colors and set Inspect options
- Persistence (it remembers its last size and position)
- The ability to see the effect of changes to objects at runtime with live data

This tool itself could justify the cost of this book!

Getting Started

You will not build this application step by step as you did with PREVIEW, but you will learn about the significant issues underlying the inner workings. The main Form that does all the work is wrapped by inspect.prg:

```
* inspect.prg   07-Feb-95

* Visual FoxPro Object Inspector

* Copyright 1995, DF Software Development, Inc.

* Usage: = inspect( SomeObject )

lparameter rObjectRef, roParent

if ( pcount() = 0 )
   * default this to a reasonable value
   if ( type( "_screen.activeform" ) != 'U' )
     rObjectRef = _screen.activeform
   endif
endif

do form inspect with rObjectRef, roParent
return
```

This takes an object reference as a parameter; the second parameter is used internally when additional child inspectors are launched. If no parameters are passed, it defaults to inspecting the current Form. The object is then passed on to the Form where the object is inspected. You might also want to set up an ON KEY LABEL x =inspect(_screen.ActiveForm.ActiveControl) to get right to the current control. The wrapper .PRG also serves a purpose because Forms cannot receive parameters when they are marked as the Main file in a project. This limit exists because of the way that Visual FoxPro creates an application when a Form is the main file. Behind the scenes, it creates a dummy program to launch the Form. This dummy program doesn't accept parameters.

Persistent Properties

When the Form initially loads, it takes care of some housekeeping
issues:

```
* frmInspect.Load

cForm::Load()

set talk off
set memowidth to 256

if ( ! file( "appset.dbf" ) )
   * table doesn't exist so create one
   create table appset;
     (;
     RecType C(1),;
     Id      C(64),;
     Value   C(254);
     )
   index on RecType               tag RecType
   index on upper( Id )           tag Id
endif

if ( ! used( "appset" ) )
   use appset in 0 shared
endif

* so persistent objects can be created in Init() of other objects

set classlib to persist.vcx additive
```

The table APPSET is used to store the persistence data. If the
table can't be found on the path, a new table is automatically
created. This also allows you to have multiple Inspect setups
because the first one that is found will be used. Persistent data refers
to storing the values of properties when an object is destroyed, then
restoring them when the object comes back into existence. This lets
Inspect remember where it was on the screen and how big it was
when you last used it.

This information could also be stored in an .INI file or in the
Microsoft Windows registry by using API calls. You might find that
using a table works well as a standard location to store application
configuration information, which is a little more secure inside a
table than an .INI file.

The code also adds the PERSIST class library to the environment
so the persistent objects can be added to the Form dynamically. You
need to open the APPSET table and set the classlib in the Form
Load() method rather than its Init() method because the EditBox
used to display the object information also has persistent font and
color properties. The EditBox Init() method executes before the

Form Init() method, which prevents contained objects from having access to things done by the container's Init() method. This is important enough to mention again:

Gotcha!

Contained objects are initialized before their container is initialized.
This might seem backwards at first, but it is quite workable. Typically contained objects don't need to talk to their container at Init() time, but they do have access to the container's default property values. From the container's point of view, having each contained object already initialized allows it to manipulate the contained objects during its initialization.

The issue of establishing the PERSIST class library is also important. There are several ways to accomplish the overall objective of objects that have persistent properties:

- **Implementation 1**: Use a Form-level persistent handler object that is put on the Form at design time.
- **Implementation 2**: Use dynamic persistent objects.
- **Implementation 3**: Wrap an object that wants to have persistence in a container with a persistent object.
- **Implementation 4**: Use a global persistent handler object.

Now take a moment to examine the advantages and disadvantages of each implementation. In the following diagrams, the persistent user object is an object that wants to use a persistent object to save and restore one of its properties. For example, the Inspect Form object wants to save and restore its Top, Left, Height, and Width properties.

IMPLEMENTATION 1: This Form-level persistent handler object is represented in Figure 4-2.

Figure 4-2.

Persistent implementation 1

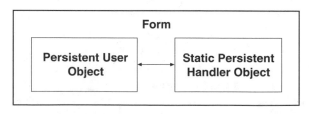

To simplify this explanation, the drawbacks and their explanations have been listed in columns:

Drawbacks	Reasoning
This implementation is Init()-order dependent.	The persistent object handler must be initialized before any object that wants to use it. This means that you must be cognizant of the design surface ZOrder of each object, and that's just too much work.
Objects that want to use it must know its Name.	This is what makes it hard for general class library classes to use the persistent object handler. If you have a PersistentEditBox class, you can hard code the handler's Name into the class, which means that you have to give the handler the same name on every Form. This is an inflexible design. Your other options are to search for the handler using AMEMBERS(), which takes too much CPU time, or to pass a reference to the handler in an overridden Init() method, which requires overriding every time you use a PersistentEditBox.
You must remember to put one of the objects on the Form.	Remember, you don't want to rely on your memory.
The handler is more complicated.	Because one handler object is going to be used for multiple persistent properties, it must keep up with each one in a dynamic array. Why should you make it that complicated?

IMPLEMENTATION 2: This dynamic persistent handler object is represented in Figure 4-3.

Figure 4-3.

Persistent implementation 2

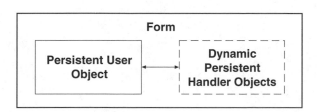

This is the technique that was used in this report.

Advantage	Reasoning
The user object knows the persistent object's Name.	The user object creates the persistent object via a thisform.AddObject() method call. When it does this, it names the object.
The user object is fully self-contained.	Because the user object creates the persistent object, it doesn't rely on any pre-existing outside objects and doesn't need to be hooked to outside objects. You can simply drop one of your user objects onto the Form and it will be ready to go.
The persistent object is less complicated.	It has to keep track of only one persistent property.
The persistence work is done automatically.	The Init() method can be used to read the saved value, and the Destroy() method writes the data. You don't need separate Read() and Write() methods.
You don't need a lot of custom objects laying around on the Form design surface.	If the object handles only one persistent property, then you'd need to put one object on the Form for each property you wanted to make persistent. Custom classes, which are shown in the Form Designer as , tend to clutter things up.

Drawback	Reasoning
You leave a SET CLASSLIB in the environment.	Because the persistent object is created at runtime, the class definition needs to be available. And, because multiple objects may need the classlib, you can't release it out from under the other objects, which may not be finished using the handler yet.

IMPLEMENTATION 3: This container and persistent object option is represented in Figure 4-4.

Figure 4-4.

Persistent implementation 3

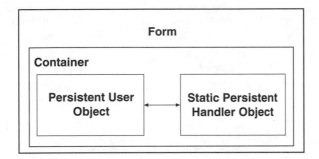

This technique is a good second choice.

Advantage	Reasoning
The user object knows the persistent object's Name.	Because the two objects are in the same container, the name will be known at design time.
The composite object is fully self-contained.	You can simply drop one of your user objects onto the Form and it will be ready to go.
The persistent object is less complicated.	The same simple persistent class created for Implementation 2 works in this implementation.
Doesn't need the SET CLASSLIB.	Because the object is defined in the Form at design time, the classlib is implicitly loaded for you.

Drawback	Reasoning
Many classes created resulting in some duplication.	You'd need to create one of these composite classes for each kind of user object and this can become unmanageable quickly.
The user object is more complicated.	You have to bundle the user object and the persistent object into a container object, which affects the design layout.
It adds another layer of containership.	This isn't a major issue, it just means more typing.

IMPLEMENTATION 4: This global persistent handler option is shown in Figure 4-5.

Figure 4-5.

Persistent implementation 4

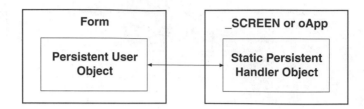

Drawback	Reasoning
The handler object has to exist.	This seems rather obvious, but it means that each object that wants to use it must check for its existence. If it doesn't exist, the user object needs to create it. Because you don't have multiple inheritance, you would have to call a common function to avoid having the verify or create code placed into each kind of persistent object you want to create.
Objects that want to use it must know its Name.	The reasoning is similar to the logic behind Implementation 1. However this also constrains the user object so that it is useable only inside a single framework designed to provide these support objects.
The handler is more complicated.	Because one handler object is going to be used for multiple persistent properties, it must keep up with each one in a dynamic array. Why should you make it that complicated?

You should realize that each of these four techniques works. The dynamic object and container versions are better choices because they make the object more self-contained, which in turn makes them easier to use.

Now look at the implementation details of the Persistent class. Just like the CSet class, it does all of its work in the Init() and Destroy() methods.

```
           Name: Persistent of persist.vcx
    ParentClass: cCustom of ccontrol.vcx
      BaseClass: Custom

Custom Properties and Methods:

    Public     Property mcId       Id to lookup in appset.dbf
    Public     Property mcItemName  Runtime resolvable name of
    the item that you want to be persistent

Property Values:

    mcItemName = .NULL.
    mcId = .NULL.
    Name = "persistent"
```

The object stores both an Id value used to register the persistent property in the APPSET table and the runtime name of object that can be used to read and write the property.

```
* Persistent.Init

lparameters pcProperty, pcControlName, pcObjectName

* a persistent object is being created

if ( ! empty( m.pcControlName ) )
   pcProperty = m.pcControlName + '.' + m.pcProperty
endif

local luVar
luVar = m.pcObjectName + '.' + m.pcProperty
this.mcItemName = m.luVar

this.mcId = upper( this.parent.name + '.' + this.parent.class + '.' + m.pcProperty )
select appset
locate for RecType = 'P' and Id = upper( this.mcId )

if ( found() )
   * this persistent property has been saved before so get the old value
   local lcType
   lcType = type( m.luVar )
   do case
     case m.lcType = 'C'
        store alltrim( appset.Value ) to &luVar
     case m.lcType = 'L'
        store ( alltrim( appset.Value ) == '1' ) to &luVar
     otherwise
        store val( alltrim( appset.Value ) ) to &luVar
   endcase
endif
```

When the object is created, it searches in the APPSET table for a previously stored value. If it finds one, the value is stored to the object property. If no value is found, the current property value will not be changed.

```
* Persistent.Destroy

* a persistent object is being destroyed so save it to appset
* table

if ( IsNull( this.mcId ) )
   * a null persistent object has nothing to save
   return
endif

select appset
locate for RecType = 'P' and Id = upper( this.mcId )
if ( ! found() )
   * this persistent property has never been saved before
   * so create a new entry in the appset table
   insert into appset values ( 'P', this.mcId, '' )
endif

local lcType, luVal
lcType = type( this.mcItemName )
luVal = evaluate( this.mcItemName )

do case
   case m.lcType = 'C'
      replace appset.Value with m.luVal
   case m.lcType = 'L'
      replace appset.Value with iif( m.luVal, '1', '0' )
   otherwise
      replace appset.Value with alltrim( padr( m.luVal, 20 ) )
endcase
```

When the persistent object is destroyed, it carries out the task of saving the state of the user object. This code checks to see if there's valid data to be stored. It then looks for the APPSET record. If the record is not found, then a new record is inserted into the table and the property value is finally stored to the table.

The first time you run Inspect it uses the default property values that are in the Form Designer. If you move or resize the Form and then close it, the values will be stored in the APPSET table for the next time Inspect is run.

Inspect Startup Code

Now look at the Form Init() method:

```
* frmInspect.Init

parameter pObjRef, poParent

* 25-Sep-95 added mlInspectLaunched
* 26-Sep-95 added mlAllObjects

cForm::Init()

if ( type( 'pObjRef' ) != 'O' )
   = MessageBox( "Sorry you didn't give me an object to inspect.", MB_ICONEXCLAMATION )
   thisform.cmdHelp.Click()
   return .f.
endif

this.mlInspectLaunched = ( ( type( 'poParent' ) == 'O' ) and ( ! IsNull( m.poParent ) ) )

if ( this.mlInspectLaunched )
   local loFont
   set classlib to font additive
   loFont = createobject( "font" )
   with poParent
      * this Inspect was launched from another instance so shift it down and left
      this.Top = .Top + sysmetric( 9 ) + sysmetric( 4 )
      this.Left = .Left + sysmetric( 5 ) + sysmetric( 3 )
      this.Height = .Height
      this.Width = .Width

      * copy menu selections

      this.mlAutoFontResize = .mlAutoFontResize
      this.mlInPlaceObject  = .mlInPlaceObject
      this.mlAllObjects     = .mlAllObjects

      * adjust edtmValue

      loFont.CopyFont( this.edtmValue,  .edtmValue )
      with .edtmValue
         this.edtmValue.ForeColor = .ForeColor
         this.edtmValue.BackColor = .BackColor
      endwith
   endwith
else
   * setup persistent properties for Form size/position

   this.AddObject( "moPersistTop",    "Persistent", "Top",    "", "thisform" )
   this.AddObject( "moPersistLeft",   "Persistent", "Left",   "", "thisform" )
   this.AddObject( "moPersistHeight", "Persistent", "Height", "", "thisform" )
   this.AddObject( "moPersistWidth",  "Persistent", "Width",  "", "thisform" )

   * setup persistent properties for Inspect options

   this.AddObject( "moPersistmlAutoFontResize", "Persistent", "mlAutoFontResize", "",
   "thisform" )
   this.AddObject( "moPersistmlInPlaceObject",  "Persistent", "mlInPlaceObject",  "",
   "thisform" )
   this.AddObject( "moPersistmlAllObjects",     "Persistent", "mlAllObjects",     "",
   "thisform" )
```

Continued on next page

Continued from previous page

```
  endif

* clip Inspect window to screen limits

local nLimit
nLimit = sysmetric( 22 ) - ( this.Top + this.Height )
if ( m.nLimit < 0 )
   if ( this.Height > abs( m.nLimit ) )
      this.Height = this.Height + m.nLimit
   endif
endif

nLimit = sysmetric( 21 ) - ( this.Left + this.Width )
if ( m.nLimit < 0 )
   if ( this.Width > abs( m.nLimit ) )
      this.Width = this.Width + m.nLimit
   endif
endif

* send the Form size through the rest of the objects

this.Resize()

* copy parameter to Form property

this.moObject = pObjRef

* create Cursor to hold object information, one record per type of information

this.mcCursorName = sys(2015)

set blocksize to 4
create cursor (this.mcCursorName) ;
   ( ;
   cType c(1), ;
   mValue m ;
   )

select (this.mcCursorName)
insert into (this.mcCursorName) ( cType, mValue ) values ( 'P', "" )
insert into (this.mcCursorName) ( cType, mValue ) values ( 'M', "" )
insert into (this.mcCursorName) ( cType, mValue ) values ( 'O', "" )
insert into (this.mcCursorName) ( cType, mValue ) values ( 'E', "" )
insert into (this.mcCursorName) ( cType, mValue ) values ( 'C', "" )

index on cType tag cType
set order to cType

this.GetObjectInfo()
```

The method starts out by making sure that the first parameter (pObjRef) is the object that has been sent for it to inspect. If it hasn't, an error message is displayed. Then the method "clicks" the form's cmdHelp button to display the internal text-based help file.

The second optional parameter (poParent) is checked to see if this inspector is being launched from another inspector. If it is, then this Form is moved down and to the left so it doesn't completely cover the existing Form. This inspector's properties are loaded from the Launching Inspector. The Form then uses the Resize() method to adjust the sizes of the Form objects based on the persistent Height and Width properties.

If the inspector was started from the command window, some Persistent objects are added to the Form to handle Form size and position memory. The objects are added to the Form object with the AddObject() method. The Form object moPersistTop is added to retrieve and store the thisform.Top property; the form's Left, Height, and Width properties use three other persistent objects. Three Form custom properties, mlAutoFontResize, mlInPlaceObject, and mlAllObjects are also made persistent.

The line "this.moObject = pObjRef" illustrates an important issue. You need to copy a parameter passed from a Form to a Form-level property. This is an issue involving asynchronous execution of methods. When the Init() method ends, the parameter no longer exists. If the parameter is needed by another method at a later time, the parameter is no longer available because the Init() method is no longer running. This is a sharp contrast to the way FoxPro 2.x screens could have memvars created at screen setup time and available to all snippets. This was possible because of the calling stack. In Visual FoxPro you need to create form-level custom properties instead. This is much better because they then become encapsulated by the Form object.

A temporary cursor is created to hold object information. One record's memo field is used for the properties, one for the methods, one for events, and so on. At the end of Init(), the GetObjectInfo() method is called to actually get all the information from the object. The code for GetObjectInfo() is shown:

```
* public method frmInspect.GetObjectInfo

* method to put the object information into the Cursor

* 23-Sep-95 additional handling on Controls[], Pages[], etc.
*           added PARENT to Objects page

* 26-Sep-95 added mlAllObjects, split Object code from here

if ( IsNull( this.moObject ) )
   * this object has been released out from under us
   = MessageBox( "Sorry, the object no longer exists!" + chr(13) + ;
                "Data NOT refreshed", MB_ICONEXCLAMATION )
   return
endif
```

Continued on next page

Continued from previous page

```
select (this.mcCursorName)
replace all mValue with ""

local lnMembers, laMembers[1], i, lcType, lcValue, CRLF, lcVar, ;
      lcBaseClass, llSeeObjects

CRLF = chr(13) + chr(10)

lnMembers = amembers( laMembers, this.moObject, 1 )
for i = 1 to lnMembers
   do case
      case ( laMembers[i,2] == "Property" )
         lcType = 'P'
         lcVar = "this.moObject." + laMembers[i,1]
         lcValueType = type( lcVar )
         lcValue =  laMembers[i,1] + " (" + lcValueType + ") = "
         do case
            case ( lcValueType == T_CHARACTER )
               lcValue = lcValue + '"' + evaluate( lcVar ) + '"'

            case ( lcValueType == T_NUMERIC ) or ;
                 ( lcValueType == T_DOUBLE ) or ;
                 ( lcValueType == T_CURRENCY )
               lcValue = lcValue + alltrim( str( evaluate( lcVar ) ) )

            case ( lcValueType == T_DATE )
               lcValue = lcValue + dtoc( evaluate( lcVar ) )

            case ( lcValueType == T_DATETIME )
               lcValue = lcValue + ttoc( evaluate( lcVar ) )

            case ( lcValueType == T_UNDEFINED )
               * 23-Sep-95 added additional handling of array properties
               llSeeObjects = .f.
               lcBaseClass = upper( this.moObject.BaseClass )
               do case
                  case ( m.lcBaseClass == "PAGEFRAME" )
                     llSeeObjects = ( laMembers[i,1] == "PAGES" )

                  case ( m.lcBaseClass == "FORM" )
                     llSeeObjects = ( laMembers[i,1] == "CONTROLS" )

                  case ( m.lcBaseClass == "FORMSET" )
                     llSeeObjects = ( laMembers[i,1] == "FORMS" )

                  case ( m.lcBaseClass == "OPTIONGROUP" )
                     llSeeObjects = ( laMembers[i,1] == "BUTTONS" )

                  case ( m.lcBaseClass == "COMMANDGROUP" )
                     llSeeObjects = ( laMembers[i,1] == "BUTTONS" )

                  case ( m.lcBaseClass == "GRID" )
                     llSeeObjects = ( laMembers[i,1] == "COLUMNS" )

               endcase

               if ( m.llSeeObjects )
```

Continued on next page

```
                  lcValue = lcValue + "See objects page"
              else
                 if ( type( lcvar + "[1]" ) != T_UNDEFINED )
                    lcValue = lcValue + "Array"
                 else
                    lcValue = lcValue + "Undefined"
                 endif
              endif

           case ( lcValueType == T_MEMO )
              lcValue = lcValue + "Memo"

           case ( lcValueType == T_GENERAL )
              lcValue = lcValue + "General"

           case ( lcValueType == T_LOGICAL )
              lcValue = lcValue + iif( evaluate( lcVar ), ".T. - True", ".F. - False" )

           case ( lcValueType == T_OBJECT )
              lcValue = lcValue + "Object"
        endcase

     case ( laMembers[i,2] == "Method" )
        lcType = 'M'
        lcValue = laMembers[i,1]

     case ( laMembers[i,2] == "Object" )
        * this function moved to GetAllObjects()
        loop

     case ( laMembers[i,2] == "Event" )
        lcType = 'E'
        lcValue = laMembers[i,1]
   endcase
   = seek( lcType )
   replace mValue with mValue + lcValue + CRLF
endfor

* build the class tree

lnParentClass = aclass( laParentClass, this.moObject )
lcValue = ""

local lcIndent

lcIndent = ""
for i = lnParentClass to 1 step -1
   lcValue = lcValue + lcIndent + laParentClass[i] + CRLF
   lcIndent = lcIndent + chr( 9 )
endfor
= seek( 'C' )
replace mValue with lcValue

this.GetAllObjects()

= seek( 'P' )  && start on the property page
this.pgfMain.ActivePage = 1
```

Continued on next page

Continued from previous page

```
if ( type( "this.moObject.Name" ) == 'C' )
   * object has a .Name so display it in the caption
   * 27-Sep-95 Limited caption Length because only 78 characters show up
   this.Caption = "Inspect:" + fullname( this.moObject )
   if ( len( this.Caption ) > 78 )
      i = at( '.', this.Caption )
      this.Caption = left( this.Caption, i ) + ".." + right( this.Caption, 76 - i )
   endif
endif
```

In this code, the Form property this.moObject is first checked to make sure that the object being inspected hasn't been released. The cursor memo fields are cleared because this method is also called to update the object properties, which can change over time. A call to AMEMBERS(,,1) is used to get the names of all the object's properties, events, methods, and contained objects. For the properties, EVALUATE() is used to get the value of each property. The values are then converted into character strings based on the property's type. Each line is then added to the appropriate memo field at the bottom of the loop. It became obvious during the development of another Visual FoxPro application that had a Grid on a PageFrame that the inspector needed to be able to automatically drill down through an object. Inspect can now optionally find all of the contained objects and display them in their containership hierarchy. This allows you to get directly to any contained object, saving you a few mouse clicks. Next, ACLASS() is used to get the object's class tree information. Note that the array laParentClass is processed backwards so the hierarchy display will appear the way you are used to seeing it. At the bottom, you see a test to check if the object has a Name property. If it does, then the form's Caption is altered to display the object's full containership name. Now take a look at FullName():

```
* fullname.prg  13-Jun-95

* Generate an object's full containership name

function FullName(  roObject )

if ( type( "roObject.Parent" ) == 'O' )
   return ( FullName( roObject.Parent ) + "." + roObject.Name )
else
   return roObject.Name
endif
```

The FullName() routine uses recursion to prepend the name of the Parent container to the object's Name property. Now look at the GetAllObjects() method:

```
* public method frmInspect.GetAllObjects

* Driver for recursive GetObjects

local lcValue

wait window "Getting Objects" nowait
lcValue = ""
lcValue = this.GetObjects( this.moObject, "" )

* 23-Sep-95 added to allow easier access back up to parent
if ( type( "this.moObject.parent" ) == 'O' )
   lcValue = "PARENT" + chr(13)+chr(10) + m.lcValue
endif

select (this.mcCursorName)
seek 'O'
replace mValue with m.lcValue

wait clear
```

The GetAllObjects() method is mostly a starting point for the recursive GetObjects() method. Next you can see how the GetObjects() method processes each level of container:

```
* public method frmInspect.GetObjects

* Get the contained objects

lparameter roObject, pcPrefix

local lnObjects, laObjects[1], i, CRLF, loObject, lcValue
CRLF = chr(13) + chr(10)

lnObjects = amembers( laObjects, m.roObject, 2 )
lcValue = ""
for i = 1 to m.lnObjects
   loObject = evaluate( "m.roObject." + laObjects[i] )
   lcValue = lcValue + m.pcPrefix + m.loObject.Name + m.CRLF
   if ( this.mlAllObjects )
      lcValue = lcValue + this.GetObjects( loObject, m.pcPrefix
   + chr(9) )
   endif
endfor

return m.lcValue
```

The GetObjects() method uses AMEMBERS(,,2) to find the contained objects of the current object, then it loops through them and adds their Name to the lcValue memory variable. If mlAllObjects is turned on, it then adds the result of recursing with contained object and another level of tab. For the OBJREF Form, it yields the following:

```
cmdFormCount
cntFormGroup
   CMDCOUNT
   txtEvenOdd
ctlGroup
DataEnvironment
Label1
Label2
Label3
pgfMain
   pagContainer
      cntPage2Group
         CMDCOUNT
         txtEvenOdd
      Label4
   pagOverrideContainer
      cntPage1Group
         CMDCOUNT
         txtEvenOdd
      Label4
      txtPageCopy
txtFormEvenOdd
```

Changing Property Values

Now take some time to play with Inspect. Begin by clicking the Properties page. This allows you to scroll through all of the Form's properties. Next, click the Events page. This allows you to see all of the Form events. When you click the Methods page, you will be able to see all of the form's methods. Clicking the Objects page lets you see all of the objects contained in the Form. Finally, clicking the Class Tree page enables you to see the form's class tree.

When you've finished experimenting with these options, enter the following in the command window:

```
clastre1.Caption = "OOP Rules!"
```

You'll see the caption change on the Form, but the Inspect properties page will not show the change. That's what the *Refresh* button is for. Click it and Inspect will make another call to its GetObjectInfo() method to requery the object's properties.

At this point you've been given only a paged view of the AMEMBERS and ACLASS functions. There's more. Double-click the BACKCOLOR listed on the Properties page. Then either press the = key, or click the right mouse button or click the = button. Either of these will bring up the dialog box in Figure 4-6.

Figure 4-6.

Property Change dialog box

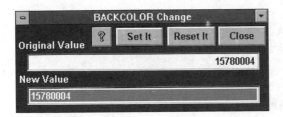

Now type 255 and either press Enter or click the Set It button. The form's BackColor property will change to the new value. If you click the Reset It button, the Original Value will be restored. Clicking the ♔ button will launch the Visual FoxPro help window, which enables you to find all of the details on the BackColor property while you are playing with it. The New Value field will also accept any expression that can be sent to EVALUATE(), so you could enter RGB(0,128,128) to get dark cyan. Alternatively, you can use the object reference THIS in the expression and it will be changed to a reference of the object being inspected by the cmdSetIt.Click() method code:

```
* cmdSetIt.Click

local lcVar

lcVar = "thisform.moObject." + thisform.mcProperty

if ( type( "thisform.muNewValue" ) == 'C' )
   thisform.muNewValue = alltrim( thisform.muNewValue )
endif

if ( type( "thisform.muCurrentValue" ) == T_NUMERIC )
   * eval() the input to allow things like rgb(0,0,0) or 5 + 2
   local lcExpr
   m.lcExpr = strtran( lower( thisform.muNewValue ), "this.", "thisform.moObject." )
   store evaluate( m.lcExpr ) to &lcVar
else
   store thisform.muNewValue to &lcVar
endif

thisform.txtNewValue.SetFocus()
```

Move the BACKCOLOR Change window out of the way and launch one on the CLOSABLE property and another on the CAPTION property. You can launch as many of these dialog boxes as your system resources will allow. When a logical property is inspected, the dialog box changes itself to look like the one in Figure 4-7.

Figure 4-7.

Logical Property Change dialog box

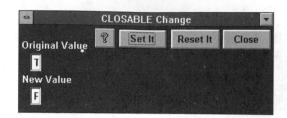

The New Value field automatically gets the inverse of the current value. If you click the Set It button and then click the form's Control Menu, you'll see that the Close item has been removed. If you click the Reset It button, the Close menu item will be restored. The code to control the input field is in the Form GETVALUE in the Init() method:

```
* frmGetValue.Init

lparameter poObject, pcProperty

if ( type( 'poObject' ) != 'O' )
   * didn't get an object
   return .f.
endif

this.moObject = poObject
this.mcProperty = alltrim( pcProperty )
if ( empty( this.mcProperty ) )
   * didn't get a property
   return .f.
endif

if ( type( "this.moObject." + this.mcProperty ) $ T_UNDEFINED + T_OBJECT )
   * can't modify array or object properties
   = MessageBox( "Can't alter this property", MB_OK + MB_ICONEXCLAMATION )
   return .f.
endif

this.muCurrentValue = evaluate( "this.moObject." + this.mcProperty )
this.muNewValue = this.muCurrentValue

do case
   case ( type( "this.muNewValue" ) == T_LOGICAL )
      * since this is a logical just set the new value to the opposite,
      * disable and resize the input field
      this.muNewValue = ! this.muNewValue
      this.txtNewValue.Enabled = .f.
      this.txtNewValue.Width = 18
```

Continued on next page

```
      this.txtCurrentValue.Width = this.txtNewValue.Width
   case ( type( "this.muNewValue" ) ) == T_NUMERIC )
     * convert to string so you can use expressions
      this.muNewValue = alltrim( str( this.muNewValue ) )
endcase

this.Caption = this.mcProperty + " Change"

this.AutoCenter = .t.    && 06/28/94 so you can design @0,0 but center it at runtime
```

Notice that these are all modeless windows. Even after you close the Inspect Form these Change dialog windows remain open so you can continue manipulating the inspected object.

If you happen to pick one of the properties that are read-only at runtime and click either the Set It or Reset It buttons, an error will be generated. The error occurs while a button method is in control so the button gets the error message. Because the buttons are derived from cCommandButton (which has an error handler), the Error() method of each button is overridden to reroute the error to the Form.

```
   * cmdSetIt.Error

   LPARAMETERS nError, cMethod, nLine

   * route the error to the Form error handler

   thisform.Error( nError, cMethod, nLine )
```

The Form Error() method then checks to see if it is the ReadOnly error. If it is, it displays an appropriate dialog window. Otherwise, it hands the error off to the OnTopDialog Error() handler, which ultimately sends it to the ObjError UDF.

```
* frmGetValue.Error

LPARAMETERS nError, cMethod, nLine

if ( nError = 1743 )
   = MessageBox( "Sorry this Property is Read-Only.", MB_OK + MB_ICONINFORMATION )
else
   OnTopDialog::Error( nError, cMethod, nLine )
endif
```

So now you can easily modify each of an object's properties. This can be a useful tool to see what effect various properties have on a Form with live data. For example, you could inspect the PREVIEW Form and play with changing the ListBox's ColumnCount, ColumnWidth, and Width properties to see if you'd like it to display the other columns that ADIR() returns.

Calling Methods

You can already manipulate object properties, so now you'll learn how easy it is to call method code and event code. Begin by clicking the Methods tab. Double-click the Line method, then either press the = key or click the right mouse button or click the **!** button. This brings up the modeless dialog box shown in Figure 4-8.

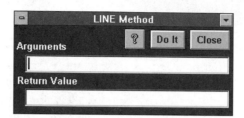

When this dialog window is started, the parameters are validated and the Form caption is altered so you know what method or event the dialog window is attached to:

```
* frmGetMethod.Init

lparameter poObject, pcMethod, pcWhich

OnTopDialog::Init()

if ( type( 'm.poObject' ) != 'O' )
   * didn't get an object argument
   return .f.
endif

this.moObject = m.poObject
this.mcMethod = alltrim( m.pcMethod )
if ( empty( this.mcMethod ) )
   * didn't get a method name
   return .f.
endif

this.mcWhich = m.pcWhich
this.Caption = this.mcMethod + " " + this.mcWhich
this.AutoCenter = .t.
```

To see how this works, enter "0, 0, 50, 50" (without the quotes) in the input field, then click the Do It button. After that, you'll get a line across the Form. The arguments you type are put inside parenthesis and concatenated to an expression that can be sent to the EVALUATE() method. The return value from the method or event code is stored to the muReturnValue property and displayed. All of this happens in the cmdDotIt.Click() method:

```
* cmdDoIt.Click

local lcVar

lcVar = "thisform.moObject." + thisform.mcMethod + "(" + thisform.mcArguments + ")"

thisform.muReturnValue = evaluate( lcVar )
thisform.Refresh()
```

The 🔮 button will send you to the help topic for the method or event so you can see what the valid arguments are. Like the property change dialog box, this dialog box can also be launched for multiple methods and events.

When using Inspect on an Event method, you need to realize that you are only causing the event handler (code within the overridden event method) to execute. You are *not* causing the event to occur.

Inspecting Contained Objects

Next, take a look at how to drill down and inspect a form's contained objects. There are two methods for doing this—the hard method and the easy method.

To use the hard method, click the Clastre1 Form to bring it into focus. Then press the Tab key until the cmdOk button has focus. Finally, enter the following in the command window:

```
= inspect( _screen.ActiveForm.ActiveControl )
```

To use the easy method, click the Objects page, then double-click the cmdOk line. Next, either press V, or click the right mouse button or click the 🔳 button. After this, another instance of the Inspect window will be open showing the cmdOk object. This inspector is independent of the first inspector and gives you full access to the button's properties, methods, and events.

The clastre1 Form isn't too complex, but using Inspect to drill down to contained objects will become very useful if you want to inspect a Form that has PageFrames and Grids.

You can also use Inspect on itself! This is a very useful process that's a bit like using C to write a C compiler. Close all of the other Forms and Inspect windows, then enter the following code:

```
= inspect( _screen )
= inspect( _screen.ActiveForm )
```

This gives you an inspector for the first inspector that's looking at the _screen object. Now click the Objects page then double-click the pgfMain row. Then click the right mouse button.

This gives you an inspector for the PageFrame of the inspector for the _screen object. Next, click the Objects page then double-click the pagProperty row. Click the right mouse button.

You now have an inspector for the Page of the PageFrame for the inspector of the _screen object. Finally, double-click the ForeColor property and click the right mouse button.

You now have a dialog window allowing you to modify the ForeColor property of the Properties Page of the inspector of the _screen object. Change the forecolor to some new value, then bring the _screen inspector on top of all the others to see the change you made to the color of the tab text. This makes Inspect a very powerful tool, and demonstrates the need for higher screen resolutions during development.

All of the code that launches the property and method dialog windows and inspects contained objects is in the KeyPress method of the EditBox:

```
* edtmValue.KeyPress

LPARAMETERS nKeyCode, nShiftAltCtrl

select (thisform.mcCursorName)

if ( ( ( nKeyCode = EQUALS_KEY ) and ( cType $ "PME" ) ) or ;
     ( inlist( nKeyCode, V_KEY, S_V_KEY ) and ( cType == 'O' ) ) )

  * = pressed on Properties/Methods/Events page
  * V or v pressed on Objects page

  local lcItem, i, j, k

  if ( cType != 'O' )

    * P/E/M Pages

    if ( ( empty( this.SelText ) ) or ( "=" $ this.SelText ) )

      * either nothing is selected or whole line selected

      if ( thisform.SelLength = 0 )
        * no text selected so select the first word on this line

        * look backwards for first non name character
        i = this.SelStart
        this.SelLength = 1
        do while ( this.SelStart > 0 ) and ( this.SelText > ' ' )
          this.SelStart = this.SelStart - 1
          this.SelLength = 1
        enddo
        k = 0
        if ( this.SelStart > 0 )
          k = this.SelStart + 1
        endif
```

Continued on next page

```
         * look forwards for next non name character
         j = len( this.Value )
         this.SelStart = i
         this.SelLength = 1
         do while ( this.SelStart <= j ) and ( this.SelText > ' ' )
            this.SelStart = this.SelStart + 1
            this.SelLength = 1
         enddo

         j = this.SelStart - k
         this.SelStart = k
         this.SelLength = j
      else
         * get selected text saved by Form to work around RightClick problem
         this.SelStart = thisform.SelStart
         this.SelLength = thisform.SelLength
      endif
   endif

   lcItem = chrtran( alltrim( this.SelText ), chr(13)+chr(10), "" )
else
   * Objects Page
   wait window "Finding object" nowait  && with lots of objects this takes a while

   * count how many lines down the SelStart Cursor is

   k = occurs( chr(13)+chr(10), left( this.Value, this.SelStart ) ) + 1

   * create array of every object up to this one

   local laObjects[k]
   for j = 1 to k
      laObjects[j] = mline( mValue, j )
   endfor

   lcItem = laObjects[k]

   i = occurs( chr(9), lcItem ) - 1
   if ( i > -1 )
      * this is a contained object, so work back up the array looking for its
      * parent objects, each parent will be the first one found at the next
      * lower indent level, till you get to the topmost parent
      j = k-1
      lcItem = chrtran( lcItem, chr(9), "" )
      do while ( i > -1 ) and ( j > 0 )
         if ( occurs( chr(9), laObjects[j] ) = i )
            lcItem = chrtran( laObjects[j], chr(9), "" ) + '.' + lcItem
            i = i - 1
         endif
         j = j - 1
      enddo
   endif
   wait clear
endif
```

Continued on next page

Continued from previous page

```
      do case
         case ( ( cType == 'P' ) and ( type( "thisform.moObject." + lcItem ) != 'O' ) )
            * this property is not an object
            do form GetValue with thisform.moObject, lcItem

         case ( ( cType == 'O' ) or ( type( "thisform.moObject." + lcItem ) == 'O' ) )
            * on Objects page or you have an object property
            if ( ! empty( lcItem ) )
               lcItem = "thisform.moObject." + lcItem
               if ( thisform.mlInPlaceObject )
                  * just change this inspector to look at a new object
                  thisform.moObject = &lcItem
                  thisform.GetObjectInfo()
                  this.Refresh()
               else
                  * launch another inspector
                  = inspect( &lcItem, thisform )
               endif
            else
               = MessageBox( "Sorry you didn't give me an object to inspect.",
                  MB_ICONEXCLAMATION )
            endif

         case ( cType == 'E' ) or ( cType == 'M' )
            if ( ! empty( lcItem ) )
               do form GetMeth with thisform.moObject, lcItem, iif( cType == 'E', "Event",
                  "Method" )
            else
               = MessageBox( "Sorry you didn't give me a method to run.",
                  MB_ICONEXCLAMATION )
            endif
      endcase

      nodefault              && prevent EditBox::KeyPress from firing
      return
   endif

if ( this.SelLength > 0 )
   local lcText
   lcText = alltrim( this.SelText )

   do case
      case cType == 'P'
         lcText = lcText + " Property"
      case cType == 'E'
         lcText = lcText + " Event"
      case cType == 'M'
         lcText = lcText + " Method"
      otherwise
         lcText = lcText + " Object"
   endcase

   help &lcText
   nodefault              && prevent EditBox::KeyPress from firing
endif
```

This is quite a mouthful of code, so chew it well before swallowing. You can begin with the bottom IF, which looks to see if any text is selected. If there is text selected (SelLength > 0), it builds an appropriate help topic and launches a help window. The code gets rid of the keypress with the NODEFAULT line, which tells Visual FoxPro *not* to call the BaseClass EditBox KeyPress() method, and return.

Now go back to the beginning of the code. The first big IF tests to see if the = key was pressed while focus was on the properties, events, or method pages, or if the v or V keys were pressed while focus was on the Objects page. If the correct key for the page is pressed, the code then looks to see if this.SelText is empty. If this.SelText is empty, a Form-level property SelLength is tested to see if it is 0. This is done to work around a problem with the RightClick() method, which will be discussed later. If no text is selected, the code uses SelStart to find the first word on the line. Notice that while the code manipulates SelStart, you need to reset SelLength to 1 each time because changing SclStart causes SelLength to be set to 0. Otherwise, if there is selected text in the Form properties, the EditBox selected text is set. lcItem is then created from the selected text and any carriage returns and line feeds are stripped off using CHRTRAN().

Next, the code goes into a CASE statement to determine what record you are looking at so you can decide what to do with the lcItem value. If the Properties page is selected, the inspected object (thisform.moObject) and the desired property name are sent to the GetValue Form. If the Object page is selected, lcItem is modified to prepend the proper object reference name. If the Form property mlInPlaceObject is set, then the inspected object is changed and the inspector is updated. Otherwise a new inspector will be started. If the Event or Method page is selected, then the inspected object and the desired method name are passed to the GetMeth Form.

If you select some text in an EditBox either by dragging the mouse across the text, double-clicking a word, or triple-clicking a line, clicking the right mouse button will deselect the selected text. This makes it difficult to implement a RightClick-based context-sensitive menu. To work around this, a Form-level set of properties (SelStart and SelLength) was added to track the same values from the EditBox. In the EditBox Click() method the Form values are reset as follows:

```
* edtmValue.Click

ContextMenuResizeableEditBox::Click()

* reset the Form level selected text properties

thisform.SelStart = 0
thisform.SelLength = 0
```

In the DblClick() method, the Form values are set as follows:

```
* edtmValue.DblClick

ContextMenuResizeableEditBox::DblClick()

* copy DblClick selected text properties to Form level properties

* you need to do this because a DblClick followed by a RightClick
* are seen as a TripleClick which selects the whole line

thisform.SelStart = this.SelStart
thisform.SelLength = this.SelLength
```

Context Menus

Now take a look at the context-sensitive menus in Inspect. With no text selected in the EditBox, use the right mouse button to click the EditBox.

Figure 4-9.

EditBox Context Menu

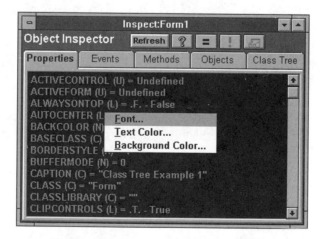

Figure 4-9 shows the pop-up menu from which you can change the font used as well as the foreground and background colors of the EditBox. If you select the Font... item, you'll be presented the built-in GetFont() dialog box. However, notice that the initial values displayed in the dialog box are the current font of the EditBox. If you select either of the color items, the built-in GetColor() dialog box will be called. It also initializes to the current color.

Two important questions that arise here: how do the dialog boxes get initialized, and how is the menu created in the first place?

The GetColor dialog box is easily initialized by sending it a parameter with the current color. The GetFont() dialog box is a little tougher. I built the Font class to aid in some of the translation issues between Visual FoxPro commands that use fonts and objects that have font properties. Take a look at the Font class and its SetFont() method:

```
* public method Font.SetFont

* Calls a dialog box to set an object to a new font

* SetFont Method  25-Mar-95

* DOC
*    Procedure: SetFont
*   Parameters: roObject - an object that will have its font changed
*       Return: .t. if the font was set
* Description: This routine calls the GetFont dialog box to change an object's
*              font.
*     Revision: 25-Mar-95 Initial Release
*              06-Jul-95 changed to work with release build of VFP

lparameters roObject

if ( type( "roObject.FontName" ) == 'U' )
   * didn't get a object with font properties
   return .f.
endif

* The common dialog box GetFont gets its initial values for the pick lists from the
* current window font, so you change the _screen to the font properties of the
* roObject.

local xFontSave

xFontSave = createobject( "CommandButton" )    && create an object with font properties

this.CopyFont( xFontSave, _screen )
this.CopyFont( _screen, roObject )
activate screen

local lcFont, llRetVal

lcFont = GetFont()
llRetVal = ! empty( lcFont )

this.CopyFont( _screen, xFontSave )

if ( llRetVal )
   * the user picked some font so parse the return value
```

Continued on next page

Continued from previous page

```
      local i
      i = at( ',', lcFont )
      roObject.FontName = left( lcFont, i - 1 )

      lcFont = substr( lcFont, i + 1 )
      roObject.FontSize = val( lcFont )

      * B Bold
      * C Condense (FoxPro for Macintosh only)
      * E Extend (FoxPro for Macintosh only)
      * I Italic
      * N Normal
      * O Outline
      * Q Opaque
      * S Shadow
      * - Strikeout (Visual FoxPro and FoxPro for Windows only)
      * T Transparent
      * U Underline

      roObject.FontBold      = ( "B" $ lcFont )
      roObject.FontItalic    = ( "I" $ lcFont )
      roObject.FontOutline   = ( "O" $ lcFont )
      roObject.FontShadow    = ( "S" $ lcFont )
      roObject.FontStrikethru = ( "-" $ lcFont )
      roObject.FontUnderline = ( "U" $ lcFont )
      roObject.Refresh()
   endif

   return llRetVal
```

To use this method, instantiate a Font object and call that Font object's SetFont() method with an object that wants its font changed. The method first checks to see if an object with font properties has been sent to the method. It does this by checking TYPE("roObject.FontName"). Next, it uses the fact that the GetFont() dialog box is initialized from the current window's font properties, so it temporarily changes the font of the _screen to match the font of the incoming object. This code changed with the final release of Visual FoxPro. Originally, an offscreen Form was created with the correct font properties, but this stopped working and it would perform reliably only with the _screen font. As a result, the code creates a dummy object that has font properties, for example a CommandButton. It then calls another font method, CopyFont(), to save the current _screen font and then change it as shown:

```
* public method Font.CopyFont

* Copy the font from one object to another

* CopyFont Method  06-Jul-95

* DOC
*    Procedure: CopyFont
*   Parameters: roObject1 - an destination object that will have its font changed
*               roObject2 - an source object that will have its font copied
*       Return: .f. if the two objects do not have font properties
* Description: This routine copies the font of Object2 to Object1
*     Revision: 06-Jul-95 Initial Release

lparameters roObject1, roObject2

if ( ( type( "roObject1.FontName" ) == 'U' ) or ;
     ( type( "roObject2.FontName" ) == 'U' ) )
   * didn't get objects with font properties
   return .f.
endif

roObject1.FontName        = roObject2.FontName
roObject1.FontSize        = roObject2.FontSize
roObject1.FontBold        = roObject2.FontBold
roObject1.FontItalic      = roObject2.FontItalic
roObject1.FontOutline     = roObject2.FontOutline
roObject1.FontShadow      = roObject2.FontShadow
roObject1.FontStrikethru  = roObject2.FontStrikethru
roObject1.FontUnderline   = roObject2.FontUnderline
```

CopyFont() first checks to see that both objects have font properties, then it sets the font properties of the first object to those of the second.

The SetFont() method activates the screen and starts the GetFont() dialog box. When the GetFont() function terminates, it checks to see if a font was selected. Then the _screen font can be restored. If a font is selected, the GetFont() return value will be parsed and the values will be assigned to the object.

The Font.EqualFont() method does a property-by-property comparison to determine if two objects have the same font. The FontMetric() method is a wrapper for the FONTMETRIC() function that handles objects:

```
* public method Font.FontMetric

* Object FontMetric Wrapper

lparameters pnAttribute, roObject

if ( type( "roObject.FontName" ) == 'U' )
   * didn't pass an object with font properties
   return 0
endif

local luRetVal, lcFontStyle

lcFontStyle = this.Style( roObject )

luRetVal = fontmetric( pnAttribute, roObject.FontName,
   roObject.FontSize, lcFontStyle )

return luRetVal
```

You can use it like this in the command window:

```
set classlib to font additive
x = createobject( "font" )
? x.FontMetric( 1, _screen )
```

This procedure would print the character height (in pixels) of
the current font used by the _screen object. The FontMetric()
method uses the Style() method, which translates from an object's
font properties to the Visual FoxPro font style string. The Style()
method is shown here:

```
* public method Font.Style

* Return a string suitable for a FONT STYLE clause

* Style Method   12-May-95

* DOC
*    Procedure: Style
*   Parameters: roObject - an object
*        Return: char
* Description: This routine builds a STYLE string based on the
* object font properties.
*      Revision: 12-May-95 Initial Release

lparameter roObject

if ( type( "roObject.FontBold" ) == 'U' )
   * didn't pass an object with font properties
   return ""
endif

local lcFontStyle

lcFontStyle = ""
```

Continued on next page

```
if ( roObject.FontBold )
   lcFontStyle = lcFontStyle + "B"
endif

if ( roObject.FontItalic )
   lcFontStyle = lcFontStyle + "I"
endif

if ( roObject.FontOutline )
   lcFontStyle = lcFontStyle + "O"
endif

if ( roObject.FontShadow )
   lcFontStyle = lcFontStyle + "S"
endif

if ( roObject.FontStrikethru )
   lcFontStyle = lcFontStyle + "-"
endif

if ( roObject.FontUnderline )
   lcFontStyle = lcFontStyle + "U"
endif

return lcFontStyle
```

As an example, enter the following in the command window:

```
_screen.FontBold = .t.
_screen.FontItalic = .t.
? x.Style( _screen )
```

This would print "BI".

But enough of fonts, it's time to get back to Inspect and
see how you can get the context menu to work. The EditBox in
Inspect is a ContextMenuResizeableEditBox. Its class tree is shown
in Figure 4-10.

Figure 4-10.

*ContextMenu
Resizeable EditBox
class tree*

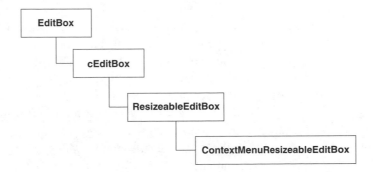

The class tree contains this RightClick() method:

```
* ContextMenuResizeableEditBox.RightClick

set classlib to cntxtmnu additive
thisform.AddObject( "moContextMenuEditBox", "ContextMenu", "EditBoxPopup", mrow(),
  mcol(), .t. )
if ( this.mlErrorFlag )
  return
endif

thisform.moContextMenuEditBox.AddItem( "\<Font...", "SetFont" )
thisform.moContextMenuEditBox.AddItem( "\<Text Color...", "SetForeColor" )
thisform.moContextMenuEditBox.AddItem( "\<Background Color...", "SetBackColor" )
thisform.moContextMenuEditBox.Activate()

thisform.RemoveObject( "moContextMenuEditBox" )
```

This method uses a dynamic ContextMenu object like dynamic persistent objects do, so it adds the CNTXTMNU class library to the environment. It then adds a ContextMenu object to the Form. It verifies that the moContextMenuEditBox object was added to the Form by checking a flag that may have been set in the Error() method. Then it uses the ContextMenu AddItem() method to add the menu prompt and the name of the routine that should be called if that menu item is selected. Next, it activates the pop-up list. When the pop-up list terminates, the moContextMenuEditBox object is removed from the Form.

This example points out another advantage to using dynamic objects instead of static objects: dynamic objects exist only while they are needed. They don't take up memory while they're not in use, and they don't have to be instantiated until they are needed. If you bundled a ResizeableEditBox and a ContextMenu into another container object, the ContextMenu object would be instantiated when the Form was instantiated. This causes the Form take longer to appear and to take up more memory. Also, because the items being set by the context menu have been made persistent, the menu might not be used more than once. This affects the user's perception of Form speed. Rather than taking the few milliseconds it takes to instantiate the ContextMenu every time the Form is instantiated, you take the delay only when the user requests it. If they never need it, they never see the delay.

Now take a look at the methods of the ContextMenuResizeableEditBox before reviewing at the internals of the ContextMenu. The method that changes the font, SetFont(), is shown here:

```
* public method ContextMenuResizeableEditBox.SetFont

* Sets the font of the control

set classlib to font additive
thisform.AddObject( "moContextMenuEditBoxFont", "Font" )

thisform.moContextMenuEditBoxFont.SetFont( this )

thisform.RemoveObject( "moContextMenuEditBoxFont" )
```

This adds a Font object to the Form and calls that object's SetFont() method with a reference to itself. When the Font.SetFont() method is done, the Font object is removed from the Form.

The SetForeColor() and SetBackColor() methods are very similar, so only SetForeColor() will be shown here:

```
* public method ContextMenuResizeableEditBox.SetForecolor

* Set the forecolor

this.ForeColor = this.SetColor( this.ForeColor )
```

Now look at how SetForeColor() sends the current color of the object to the SetColor() method:

```
* public method ContextMenuResizeableEditBox.SetColor

* Set the color of the control

lparameter pnColor

local lnColor

lnColor = GetColor( pnColor )
if ( lnColor != -1 )
  return( lnColor )
else
  return( pnColor )
endif
```

This code issues the call to the GetColor() dialog box.

Now that you've seen the methods that will do the work, take a look at the ContextMenu handler object:

```
        Name: ContextMenu of cntxtmnu.vcx
  ParentClass: cCustom of ccontrol.vcx
    BaseClass: Custom

Custom Properties and Methods:

  Public      Method      Activate            This method activates the popup
  Public      Method      AddItem             This method adds an item to the menu
  Public      Property    FontName            Menu Font
  Public      Property    FontSize            Menu FontSize
  Public      Property    FontStyle           Menu FontStyle in POPUP style format
  Public      Method      OnSelection         This method dispatches the selected
  option to the handler provided by the calling object
  Public      Property    maPopupHandler[1,0]  Array of method names to handle each menu
  item during OnSelection
  Public      Property    mcPopupName         Name of the popup
  Public      Property    mlUseControlMethod  use a control method instead of a form
  method
  Public      Property    mnItems             number of items in the menu

Property Values:

  Height = 22
  Width = 27
  FontName = Arial
  FontSize = 10
  FontStyle = B
  mnItems = 0
  mcPopupName = DefaultPopup
  mlUseControlMethod = .T.
  Name = "contextmenu"

* ContextMenu.Init

lparameters pcPopupName, pnRow, pnCol, plUseControlMethod

local lnParms

lnParms = parameters()

if ( lnParms >= 3 )
   dimension this.maPopupHandler[1]

   if ( ! empty( pcPopupName ) )
      this.mcPopupName = pcPopupName
   endif

   set classlib to font additive
   this.AddObject( "moFont", "Font" )

   if ( ! this.moFont.EqualFont( _screen, thisform ) )
      pnRow = pnRow * ( this.moFont.FontMetric( 1, thisform ) +
   this.moFont.FontMetric( 5, thisform ) ) / ;
                     ( this.moFont.FontMetric( 1, _screen ) +
   this.moFont.FontMetric( 5, _screen ) )
      pnCol = pnCol * this.moFont.FontMetric( 6, thisform ) / ;
   this.moFont.FontMetric( 6, _screen )
```

Continued on next page

```
   endif

   define popup (this.mcPopupName) ;
      from pnRow, pnCol ;
      margin ;
      font this.FontName, this.FontSize style this.FontStyle

   this.RemoveObject( "moFont" )

   if ( m.lnParms = 4 )
      this.mlUseControlMethod = m.plUseControlMethod
   endif
endif
```

The ContextMenu can be used in one of two ways: it can be statically added to a Form at design time; or it can be dynamically added at runtime using the AddObject() method. The Init() method tests the number of parameters received to determine how it is being used. If no parameters are received, it has been statically placed on a Form. In this case the ContextMenu Init() method will be explicitly called with parameters when the menu is to be activated. If the ContextMenu is being dynamically added, the additional arguments are passed in from the AddObject() call.

If the menu is being created, the array is cleared by dimensioning it. The pop-up name is changed if a new name is provided.

Next, a Font object is created so that the pop-up list will appear precisely where the mouse was clicked. Here the code has to consider the differences between the font metrics of the Form font and the _screen font. The POPUP is defined and the Font object is removed. The last IF sets a flag that controls whether a Control method or a Form method is called when the menu item is selected. Next, look at the AddItem() method:

```
* public method ContextMenu.AddItem

* This method adds an item to the menu

lparameters pcItem, pcHandler

this.mnItems = this.mnItems + 1

DEFINE BAR this.mnItems OF (this.mcPopupName) PROMPT (m.pcItem)

dimension this.maPopupHandler[this.mnItems]
this.maPopupHandler[this.mnItems] = m.pcHandler
```

This method simply adds each item to the end of the menu. Notice that it uses a polymorphic (AddItem) name to match the Visual FoxPro ListBox and ComboBox objects. Next, take a look at the Activate() method:

```
* public method ContextMenu.Activate

* This method activates the popup

local lcFormObjectName

lcFormObjectName = "_screen.ActiveForm." + this.Name + ".OnSelection( bar() )"

on selection popup (this.mcPopupName) &lcFormObjectName
activate popup (this.mcPopupName)

* this won't execute until after the deactivate sends us back to this routine

release popups (this.mcPopupName)
```

Gotcha!

Object properties cannot be used for & macro expansion.
This is because the "." that separates the object components
conflicts with the "." used to terminate the macro variable's name.
The properties must either be put into the local memory variable
lcFormObjectName, which can be & macro expanded, or they
must be used in parentheses "()" if the command will support
them. The DEFINE BAR command listed in the AddItem() method
that was just presented supports () expressions.

The Activate() method is called when you want the menu
to appear and take control. You should give the method the
same name as the ACTIVATE POPUP command for consistency.
The lcFormObjectName memory variable is used because you
need to create a name that will be valid after this method
turns control over to the menu. It will build something like
_screen.ActiveForm.moContextMenuEditBox.OnSelection(bar()),
which is the method that calls the menu item handlers. Next, look
at the OnSelection() method:

```
* public method ContextMenu.OnSelection

* This method dispatches the selected option to the handler provided by the calling
* object

lparameters pnBar

if ( this.mlUseControlMethod )
   = evaluate( "_screen.ActiveForm.ActiveControl." + this.maPopupHandler[pnBar] + "()" )
else
   = evaluate( "_screen.ActiveForm." + this.maPopupHandler[pnBar] + "()" )
endif

deactivate popup (this.mcPopupName)
```

The OnSelection() method is responsible for sending the message to the appropriate method of either the Control or the Form that is using the context menu object. So, for example, when you select the Fonts... menu item, the method does this:

```
= evaluate( _screen.ActiveForm.ActiveControl.SetFont() )
```

But the edtmValue object behaves differently depending on whether or not text has been selected:

```
* edtmValue.RightClick

if ( ! empty( this.SelText ) or ( thisform.SelLength > 0 ) )

   * text is selected so use RightClick as a shortcut for
   * pressing the page appropriate key

   select (thisform.mcCursorName)
   do case
      case ( cType $ 'PEM' )
         this.Keypress( EQUALS_KEY, 0 )

      casc ( cType == 'O' )
         this.KeyPress( V_KEY, 0 )

      otherwise
         this.KeyPress( F1_KEY, 0 )
   endcase
else
   ContextMenuResizeableEditBox::RightClick()
endif
```

If text is already selected, the method uses RightClick as a shortcut so it can perform the same actions as the Form buttons. It does this by sending the proper KeyPress message to the EditBox. If no text is selected, the message is passed on to the ParentClass.

The Inspect Form also has a context menu that is used to control three options. When you use the right mouse button to click the Inspect Form, you'll see the menu shown in Figure 4-11.

Figure 4-11.

Form level context menu

The Form basically uses the same technique to run the menu. Here is the Form RightClick() method:

```
* frmInspect.RightClick

cForm::RightClick()

* form context menu

set classlib to cntxtmnu additive
this.AddObject( "moContextMenuForm", "ContextMenu", "FormPopup", mrow(), mcol(), .f. )
if ( this.mlErrorFlag )
  return
endif

this.moContextMenuForm.AddItem( "\<Auto Font Resize", "ToggleAutoFontResize" )
set mark of bar 1 of FormPopup to this.mlAutoFontResize

this.moContextMenuForm.AddItem( "\<In Place Object", "ToggleInPlaceObject" )
set mark of bar 2 of FormPopup to this.mlInPlaceObject

this.moContextMenuForm.AddItem( "All \<Objects", "ToggleAllObjects" )
set mark of bar 3 of FormPopup to this.mlAllObjects

this.moContextMenuForm.Activate()

this.RemoveObject( "moContextMenuForm" )
```

This adds a ContextMenu object to the Form and uses AddItem() to create the three menu items. Because these are On and Off options, it also uses SET MARK OF BAR to turn the check mark on based on the three Form properties (mlAutoFontResize, mlInPlaceObject, and mlAllObjects). The three Form Toggle... methods simply invert the current state of the Form property:

```
* public method frmInspect.ToggleAutoFontResize

this.mlAutoFontResize = ! this.mlAutoFontResize
```

If you look at the RightClick() methods of other Form objects (except edtmValue), you'll see that they all simply route the message on to the Form RightClick. This is done to provide more places to activate the menu because there is so little of the Form exposed. This process is shown:

```
* Clabel1.RightClick

cLabel::RightClick()
```

```
* pass this on to the Form to activate the Form context menu
thisform.RightClick()
```

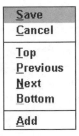

Figure 4-12.

A typical Form context menu

One exercise for you to undertake on your own is to create a Form context menu that looks like Figure 4-12.

Such a context menu could easily replace navigation buttons that are taking up space on the Form or in a separate toolbar. The menu would also be more accessible to the user because it would require much less mouse motion.

Miscellany

You've already read about the In Place Object causing the current Inspect Form to be reused when inspecting contained objects, but what about the Auto Font Resize item? Make sure it's checked, then vertically resize the Inspect Form a couple of times. As the Form gets shorter, the font height gets smaller. This was done initially to maximize the information content of the window. I almost removed this from the final version because I don't like the way it "overrides" the selected font, even during a horizontal resize. In my opinion, the effort required to maintain the relative font size is not worth it. However, by popular demand it stayed, warts and all. If you choose, you can turn the resizing off by using the Inspect menu. The font resize is handled as shown:

```
* frmInspect.Resize

cForm::Resize()

this.LockScreen = .t.

this.pgfMain.Resize()
this.edtmValue.Resize()

if ( this.mlAutoFontResize )
  * adjust font size
  this.edtmValue.FontSize = min( max( int( this.edtmValue.Height / 34 ), 7 ), 11 )
endif

this.LockScreen = .f.
```

When the Form is resized, it first calls its ParentClass. Then the Form LockScreen is turned on so the user doesn't see each object resize. The PageFrame is sent a resize message, then the EditBox is told to resize. Next, if font resizing is turned on, the EditBox FontSize is adjusted to a proportionate value between 7 and 11 points. Finally, the Form LockScreen is turned off.

The PageFrame and EditBox resize are handled in exactly the same way as the resizeable ListBox from the PREVIEW example. These classes add two properties that allow a minimum height and width to prevent the objects from getting negative size values when the container Form is resized to a size that's too small.

The code for the ResizeableEditBox.Resize() method is shown:

```
* public method ResizeableEditBox.Resize

* Method to resize the editbox

this.Height = max( ( thisform.Height - this.mnHeightDIfference ), this.mnMinHeight, 0 )
this.Width = max( ( thisform.Width - this.mnWidthDifference ), this.mnMinWidth, 0 )
```

Although you've seen this code, the cPageFrame class on which ResizeablePageFrame is based needs some special handling. Enter the following in the command window:

```
create class JunkPageFrame of xpage as PageFrame
```

This will create a new PageFrame subclass with two pages. The JunkPageFrame class can be put on a Form, but a problem arises when you try to name the pages on the Form. If you change the number of pages from two to five, you can name pages three through five anything you like. However, the Name property of the first two pages are read-only. Visual FoxPro works this way because the subclass may have code that is dependent on the two pages, and renaming them would break the subclass code. This page name problem can be avoided by saving the subclass with no pages (PageCount = 0). This is shown in the next code listing. This same problem can occur with any container class such as OptionGroup or CommandGroup.

```
       Name: cPageFrame of ccontrol.vcx
ParentClass: PageFrame
  BaseClass: PageFrame

Property Values:

   ErasePage = .T.
   PageCount = 0
   Width = 241
   Height = 169
   Name = "cpageframe"
```

When you use a cPageFrame on a Form, you simply need to set the PageCount to the number of tabs you want and they can all be named. It's a *really* good idea to name your pages because it's easy to get out of sync between the PageOrder and the Name. For example, the page named Page5 could have a PageOrder of 3. A page named pagObject won't have the same confusion. Naming pages also makes it easier to select pages on the property sheet.

This is what Inspect does when you change pages:

```
* pgfMain.pagProperty.Activate

= seek( 'P' )
thisform.cmdSetValue.Enabled = ( len( mValue ) > 0 )
thisform.edtmValue.Refresh()
```

This code seeks the proper record in the cursor, enables buttons as appropriate, then refreshes the EditBox.

When the page deactivates, the following code applies:

```
* pgfMain.pagProperty.Deactivate

thisform.cmdSetValue.Enabled = .f.
```

This simply disables the button.

> ## Gotcha!
>
> *Forms with external object references can't be closed.*
>
> ```
> close all forms and windows
> do form clastre1
> =inspect( clastre1 )
> go to the Objects page and launch another inspector on cmdOk
> double click the clastre1 command menu
> ```
>
> Notice that the CLASTRE1 Form does not close. If you click the control menu again, the Close option will no longer be present. But the Form can't close because the second inspector has an object reference to a contained object of the Form. If you find that your Forms are not closing when you think they should, it could be because someone has a reference to one of the Form's objects. The Form will finally disappear after you close the cmdOk inspector.

Click the Refresh button on the remaining Inspect Form. This gets you the dialog box in Figure 4-13.

Figure 4-13.

Trying to view a released object

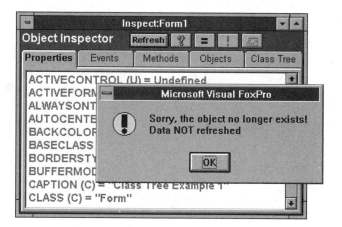

This occurs because the clastre1 object reference still exists, but it now has a value of .NULL. instead of pointing to a Form object. Notice, though, that the Inspect window still has the last contents because they are stored in the cursor.

One handy way of using Inspect can be done at a method breakpoint in a trace window. When program's execution has been suspended while a method is running and control returns to the command window, you can use "this" and "thisform" in the command window. As a result, you can put = inspect(this).

(If the debugging session is not going well, you can use a verbal emphasis on the *this* when you talk to your computer.)

You can even use Inspect on design surface objects. Begin by entering this command:

```
modify form clastre1
```

Select one of the buttons, then enter this in the command window:

```
= aselobj( laObj )
= inspect( laObj[1] )
```

If you open a property change dialog box and change one of the properties, you will see the button on the design surface change.

That's all there is to Inspect. The source code is yours to play with. If you have any enhancements, I'd like to hear about them.

5 | Advanced Topics

Abstract Data Types

In this section you'll look in more detail at two examples of abstract data types: complex numbers and binary trees.

Complex Numbers

The first example will use the mathematical abstraction of complex numbers to illustrate abstract data types. Complex numbers are comprised of (contain) a real number and an imaginary number $\sqrt{-1}$. Abstract data types allow you to bundle these two parts together in one new data type. Here are four code samples showing how complex numbers might be implemented:

In C/C++:

```
struct ComplexNumber
   {
   float mfRealPart;
   float mfImaginaryPart;
   };

ComplexNumber x;

x.mfRealPart = 7.23;
x.mfImaginaryPart = 9.84;
```

In Pascal:

```
type
   ComplexNumber = record
      mfRealPart : real;
      mfImaginaryPart : real;
   end;

var x : ComplexNumber;

x.mfRealPart := 7.23;
x.mfImaginaryPart := 9.84;
```

In FoxPro 2.x:

```
#define REALPART 1
#define IMAGINARYPART 2

dimension x[2]

x[REALPART] = 7.23
x[IMAGINARYPART] = 9.84
```

In Visual FoxPro that code is as shown:

```
* Cmplx1.PRG  23-Mar-94

define class ComplexNumber as Custom

* Public Data Members

mfRealPart      = 0.0
mfImaginaryPart = 0.0

protected procedure Init( pfReal, pfImaginary )
this.mfRealPart      = pfReal
this.mfImaginaryPart = pfImaginary
endproc

procedure Show
? this.mfRealPart, "+", this.mfImaginaryPart, "i"
endproc

enddefine
```

To use the ComplexNumber class, you'd do this:

```
x = createobject( "ComplexNumber", 7.23, 9.84 )
x.Show()
```

This would print:

7.23 + 9.84i

The ComplexNumber class will be discussed more at the end of this section.

Binary Trees

With the release of Visual FoxPro, FoxPro is finally a "real" programming language with pointers. An object reference is essentially a pointer to an object, as you saw in the part on object references. Before Visual FoxPro, the most complex data structure you could use was an array. Most complex data structures rely on being able to represent logical and physical relations between two items. It is now possible to create data structures such as linked lists, trees, graphs, and heaps. A binary tree is a data structure in which data is stored in a node. Each node also has two pointers to two other nodes. This tree is represented in Figure 5-1.

Figure 5-1.

A binary tree

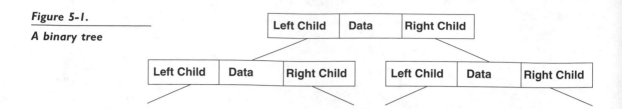

The nodes down the left child tree have key values that are less than the node, while nodes down the right child tree have key values greater than the node. Binary trees can be searched very quickly [O($\log_2$ n)]. Visual FoxPro uses a special type of binary tree called a B+ Tree to store the table indexes. Binary trees are also used to parse expressions such as 7 + 3 * 4 - 2 / 6. Most other data structures texts can provide you with a more detailed explanation of trees and ways of implementing them.

Here's a simple binary tree class for Visual FoxPro. It doesn't implement any balancing technique, so it works best with keys inserted in random order.

```
* tree3f.prg

* Fastest by assigning Name as the default value

define class BinaryTree as custom

moLeftChild  = .null.
moRightChild = .null.
muData       = .null.
Name         = "BinaryTree"

protected procedure Init( puData )
this.muData = puData
endproc

procedure Insert( puData )

if ( puData < this.muData )
   if ( IsNull( this.moLeftChild ) )
     this.moLeftChild = createobject( "BinaryTree", puData )
   else
     this.moLeftChild.Insert( puData )
   endif
else
   if( IsNull( this.moRightChild ) )
     this.moRightChild = createobject( "BinaryTree", puData )
   else
     this.moRightChild.Insert( puData )
   endif
endif

endproc
```

Continued on next page

```
procedure InorderTraverse()

if ( ! IsNull( this.moLeftChild ) )
   this.moLeftChild.InorderTraverse()
endif

?? this.muData, " "

if ( ! IsNull( this.moRightChild ) )
   this.moRightChild.InorderTraverse()
endif

endproc


procedure Destroy()

* postorder traverse to clean up tree

this.moLeftChild = .null.
this.moRightChild = .null.
this.muData = .null.
endproc

enddefine
```

After this code executes:

```
t1 = createobject( "BinaryTree", 55 )
t1.Insert( 89 )
t1.Insert( 37 )
t1.Insert( 46 )
t1.Insert( 72 )
t1.Insert( 16 )
```

The binary tree would look like (Φ = .NULL.):

Figure 5-2.

A binary tree with data

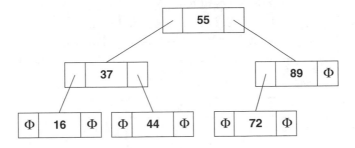

```
t1.InorderTraverse() prints this:
```

16 37 44 55 72 89

> ## Gotcha!
>
> ### Name your objects!
> During Visual FoxPro's beta testing, the binary tree class showed very poor performance [O(n²)] while inserting nodes. When more than 100 nodes were created, the class became useless because of the node creation delay. The Microsoft performance crew discovered that this occurred when a Name was not provided for the object in the class definition. If you don't supply a Name property value, Visual FoxPro will build one for you by taking the class name and concatenating a sequential number. As a result, for every object created, Visual FoxPro was performing a linear search through all the existing objects for the next sequential number to use. To create the 100th object, it had to search 99 other objects. Needless to say, this was a lot of unnecessary work.

The solution to the Gotcha! problem is for you to give the object a Name when it is created. In the tree, you never need a unique name for each object because all access is done via the root node following the child node pointers. The binary class tree code provided earlier in the section gives the fastest performance by setting the Name in the default value section. These values are loaded directly into the object from a cached definition of the class. You can also set the Name in the Init() method. The Init() method turns out to be a little slower because the code 'this.Name = "BinaryTree"' is interpreted for each object created. The test driver program tt3() can illustrate the difference in performance. The first parameter tells it how many nodes to create and the second parameter defines which way the node should be assigned its Name property. To test the difference, use the second parameter to specify which version of class to use: "0 - slow" (sequential generated name), "1 - fast" (Name set in Init), or "2 - fastest" (Name set as default value). Table 5-1 shows timing results for a Pentium 66 to demonstrate the dramatic difference this makes. All times are in seconds:

Table 5-1

Effect of unnamed objects on instantiation time

	100 nodes	200 nodes	400 nodes	800 nodes
0 - slow	3.706	26.17	205.8	You don't have this much time!
1 - fast	0.453	1.257	3.380	11.61
2 - fastest	0.298	0.758	1.941	5.623

You can see that putting the code in the Init() method takes about twice as long as assigning the value with a default. Another way to avoid this problem is to always use a .VCX to store the class definition instead of a .PRG file. This way the Class Designer will set the Name as a default value for you.

Gotcha!

Be consistent when you name your objects in .PRG classes!
Make sure that you give the class the same name you used in the DEFINE CLASS so that you don't confuse yourself:

```
* badname.prg

public o1
o1 = createobject( "MyOtherClass" )
disp objects like o*
o1.Method1()

define class MyClass as Custom
   Name = "SomeOtherName"
   procedure Method1()
      ? "MyClass.Method1()"
   endproc
enddefine

define class MyOtherClass as MyClass
   Name = "YetAnotherName"
   procedure Init()
      this.Name = "NowGuessWhatMyNameIs"
   endproc
   procedure Method1()
      ? "MyOtherClass.Method1()"
      MyClass::Method1()
   endproc
enddefine
```

The MyOtherClass.Method1() will fail with the error shown in Figure 5-3.

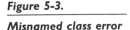

Figure 5-3.

Misnamed class error

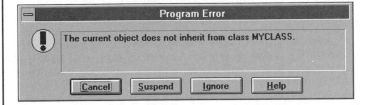

You'll save yourself a lot of grief by simply using the name supplied in the DEFINE CLASS command as the Name of the class.

Debugging Your Classes

Debugging the code in methods presents a whole new challenge to developers. You no longer have large text files of code that you can open up in the trace window and assign breakpoints where needed. The methods of classes are not available until one of the objects has been instantiated. At that point you need some way of interrupting the process, especially if you are trying to debug a Load() or Init() method.

You can open the Debug window and put a breakpoint on something like '"INIT" $ program()', but that really hits performance because the breakpoint refires each time the test value changes state. This technique will work, but it gets in the way.

One trick you can use is to put a line of code that will compile, but will fail at runtime in the method you want to trace. You can use something like "q = q + 1", which pops up the error dialog box and lets you choose Suspend. You can open the trace window, set any real breakpoints you want, and resume. Then you can choose Ignore and continue the debug session. However this method also gets cumbersome after a while.

Keep in mind that you can save yourself some time by remembering if you've put a SUSPEND in a method. If you don't happen to have the Trace window open, it can take a while to figure out why your Form suddenly stopped working.

You can stick a call to the following routine into a method and have it optionally launch one or two inspectors so you can evaluate what is going on within the objects:

```
* debug.prg   13-Jun-95

* invoke with: = debug( [this [,thisform]] )

lparameter roObject, roForm

activate window trace
activate window debug

if ( type( "m.roForm" ) == 'O' )
   = inspect( roForm )
endif

if ( type( "m.roObject" ) == 'O' )
   = inspect( roObject )
endif

suspend
return
```

This code automatically opens the Trace and Debug windows. It looks at the two optional arguments and sends arguments that are type Object to the object inspector. While you're developing a class or Form, you could put an "= debug(this)" line in the method that's giving you problems. This automatically starts all of the tools you need to debug. When this code runs in the Trace window, you can select any of the other methods for the object and set breakpoints as you need them.

You can also use the Program menu and select a Suspend to interrupt a modal Form and switch back to other non-modal Forms or the command window to do things. When you issue a Resume from the Program menu the modal Form will start running again.

The Error() Method Versus ON ERROR

The default behavior of the BaseClasses Error() method is for it to do nothing. If an error occurs while a method is running, the error is handled by the ON ERROR handler. If there is no ON ERROR handler setup, then the Visual FoxPro Program Error dialog box shown in Figure 5-4 is launched.

Figure 5-4.

Visual FoxPro's default error handler dialog box

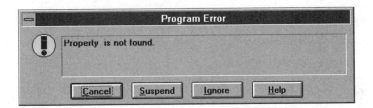

If a derived class has an overridden Error() method, then *all* errors that occur while one of the object's methods is executing the error will be routed to the object's Error() method. This means that your class could wind up handling errors that it is not responsible for and that were not expected to occur.

The sample program ERRTEST.PRG generates several intentional errors to see how they are handled. It uses objects from the hierarchy shown in Figure 5-5.

Figure 5-5.

An error handling class tree

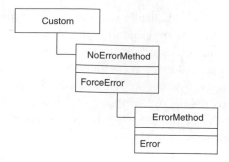

This is the method that causes the errors to occur:

```
* public method NoErrorMethod.ForceError
* This routine forces errors to occur
lparameter pnWhich
? "Object.ForceError( ", alltrim( str( m.pnWhich ) ), ")"
do case
   case m.pnWhich = 0
      ? "force error 12"
      q = q + 1

   case m.pnWhich = 1
      ? "force error 1734"
      local i
      i = this.mnPropertyThatDoesNotExist

   case m.pnWhich = 2
      ? "force error in procedural code"
      = UDFError()

endcase
```

This is the Error() method for the object:

```
* ErrorMethod.Error
LPARAMETERS nError, cMethod, nLine
? "Object.Error() Handler", nError
do case
   case nError = 12
      * variable not found error ok
      return

   otherwise
      * this will pass the error on to the Cancel/Suspend/Ignore
   error handler
      error nError
endcase
```

The next code sample is the driver program that causes some regular code errors and creates three objects, only one of which has an Error() method.

```
set development off    && prevent trace window from launching

on error do GlobalErrorHandler with error(), program(), lineno()

? "Normal code error"
z = z + 1

= UDFError()

set classlib to errtest

x = createobject( "NoErrorMethod" )
= ObjectError( x )

y = createobject( "ErrorMethod" )
= ObjectError( y )

? "Testing Custom::Error()"
z = createobject( "Custom" )
z.Error( 1 )            && this does nothing

on error
set development on
return


procedure ObjectError( roObject )
local i

for i = 0 to 2
   roObject.ForceError( i )
endfor
return


procedure UDFError
? "UDFError"
error 1
return


procedure GlobalErrorHandler( pnError,  pcProgram, pnLineNo )
? "GlobalErrorHandler:", pnError, pcProgram, pnLineNo
return
```

This is the output generated by the DO ERRTEST command:

```
Normal code error
GlobalErrorHandler:              12 ERRTEST              6
UDFError
GlobalErrorHandler:               1 UDFERROR            38

Object.Name      noerrormethod
Object.ForceError(   0 )
force error 12
GlobalErrorHandler:              12 NOERRORMETHOD.FORCEERROR
   8
Object.ForceError(   1 )
force error 1734
GlobalErrorHandler:            1734 NOERRORMETHOD.FORCEERROR
  13
Object.ForceError(   2 )
force error in procedural code
UDFError
GlobalErrorHandler:               1 UDFERROR            38

Object.Name      errormethod
Object.ForceError(   0 )
force error 12
Object.Error() Handler          12
Object.ForceError(   1 )
force error 1734
Object.Error() Handler        1734
Object.ForceError(   2 )
force error in procedural code
UDFError
Object.Error() Handler           1
Testing Custom::Error()
```

The output file shows that errors that occur in the NoErrorMethod object are sent to the ON ERROR handler. Errors that occur during the ErrorMethod object are sent to the Object.Error() method. Notice that this includes the error that occurs when the object calls the UDF that generates an error. If the current thread of execution causes an error, it will be handled by the most recent object in the thread that has an overridden Error() method. For example the code for DO ERRTEST2 is as follows:

```
* errtest2.prg  13-Aug-95

* This program illustrates how an unrelated class
* can wind up handling the errors of another class!

o1 = createobject( "ClassOne" )
o1.DoIt()

define class ClassOne as custom

procedure DoIt
```

Continued on next page

```
      this.AddObject( "o2", "ClassTwo" )
      this.o2.DoIt()
   endproc

   procedure Error( pnError, pcMethod, pnLineNo )
      ? "Error of:", this.Name, "Called", pnError, pcMethod, pnLineNo
   endproc

enddefine


define class ClassTwo as custom

procedure DoIt
   this.AddObject( "o3", "ClassThree" )
   this.o3.DoIt()
endproc

enddefine


define class ClassThree as custom

procedure DoIt
  q = q + 1      && cause an error
endproc

enddefine
```

When this runs, it prints out the following message:

Error of: Classone1 called   12 doit   1

This shows that the error is handled by the ClassOne object even though the error occurred in the ClassThree object. To avoid this situation, make sure that each class has an overridden Error() method somewhere along its branch. If each of the classes shown had been derived from cCustom and cCustom provided an overridden Error() method, the error wouldn't have made it back to an unrelated class.

If you derive each of the classes from cCustom, they will each inherit the Error() method. Here's another test driver:

```
* errtest3.prg  13-Aug-95

* This program solves the problem of errtest2 by deriving
* each class from cCustom which has an Error() method

o1 = createobject( "ClassOne" )
o1.DoIt()


define class cCustom as custom

procedure Error( pnError, pcMethod, pnLineNo )
   ? "Error of:", this.Name, "Called", pnError, pcMethod, pnLineNo
```

Continued on next page

Continued from previous page

```
   endproc

   enddefine

   define class ClassOne as cCustom
   procedure DoIt
      this.AddObject( "o2", "ClassTwo" )
      this.o2.DoIt()
   endproc

   enddefine

   define class ClassTwo as cCustom

   procedure DoIt
      this.AddObject( "o3", "ClassThree" )
      this.o3.DoIt()
   endproc

   enddefine

   define class ClassThree as cCustom

   procedure DoIt
     q = q + 1    && cause an error
   endproc

   enddefine
```

When this runs, it prints out a message that's much more appropriate than the last one:

Error of: O3   Called   12 doit   1

This phenomenon is another reason to develop your own set of custom "BaseClasses" instead of using the Visual FoxPro BaseClasses. In my ccontrol.vcx class library each of my 'c' classes has an Error method that looks like this:

```
* cCommandButton.Error

LPARAMETERS nError, cMethod, nLine
= ObjError( this, nError, cMethod, nLine )
```

You've probably noticed that it doesn't look very object oriented to send the error on to a UDF. That's exactly right, but it was done to avoid having a lot of code duplicated in each class. This is a personal preference. Many programmers hate duplicated code, and want to keep it to an absolute minimum when they are forced to use it. In fact, this is one place where multiple inheritance would allow you to create an Error class to use when deriving classes, which would allow you to override the Error() method in all of your

CCONTROL.VCX classes without using duplicated code. However, multiple inheritance is not available, so you have to use other solutions. This solution might not be "proper" object-oriented programming, but it represents "practical" object-oriented programming, which may be a more important concern.

The ObjError program is shown here. (Note that the name fits 8.3 filename conventions so you don't have to ensure there is a SET PROCEDURE TO in effect for the object error handler to be found by Visual FoxPro.)

```
lparameters roObject, pnError, pcMethod, pnLine

#include foxpro.h

local lcObject, lnResult, lcMessage1

lcMessage1 = "Error:" + padl( pnError, 6 ) + " " + message() + chr(13) + chr(13)

lcObject = "Object: " + fullname( roObject ) + "  Method: " + pcMethod + ;
           " Line:" + padl( pnLine, 6 ) + chr(13) + chr(13)

lnResult = MessageBox( lcMessage1 + lcObject + "Suspend?", MB_YESNOCANCEL +
  MB_ICONSTOP )

do case
   case lnResult = IDYES
      activate window trace
      suspend
   case lnResult = IDCANCEL
      cancel
endcase
return
```

This is a simple development type of error handler; it is not intended to be the kind of error handler that logs user errors. You can plug whatever type of error handler you prefer in its place. This routine could even pass the error on to a global error handler object that might be attached to your oApplication object. However, before it does that, it should check to verify that the handler object does indeed exist. If it doesn't exist, the error handler object could be created and then given the error. All of this verification code can be contained in *one* place, ObjError.PRG. It doesn't have to be duplicated in the Error() method of each of your custom BaseClasses.

Because you'll still have some procedural code around, you can do an ON ERROR DO OBJERROR WITH .NULL., ERROR(), PROGRAM(), AND LINENO() just as you've done all along in your FoxPro 2.x code.

SET CLASSLIB and SET PROCEDURE TO ... ADDITIVE

This is a tremendous new capability. With it, you no longer need to rely on huge monolithic procedure libraries. However, combining ADDITIVE with modeless and asynchronous actions has the potential to introduce a new problem: multiple class library references. If you have two or more objects that are dependent on the same class library, you can't easily do a RELEASE CLASSLIB from either object. Here is an illustration of the problem.

Suppose that Object A needs to have the class library Font available. It checks and finds that the Font class library is not yet loaded, so it sets a flag to indicate that it needs to SET and RELEASE the class library. It does a SET CLASSLIB TO FONT ADDITIVE, and it will use a Font object sometime later. When Object A goes out of scope, it does a RELEASE CLASSLIB FONT because it put class library Font into the environment. But now assume that at some point before Object A is released, Object B is instantiated. Object B also needs to have a Font object, so it checks and sees that the Font class library has already been loaded. It then sets a flag to indicate that it doesn't need to SET or RELEASE the class library. Before Object B uses the Font object, Object A goes out of scope and releases the class library. Object B tries to create the Font object, but it gets an error because the class library has been released out from under it!

The simple solution is to never release the class libraries. This is not such a bad solution. A more complicated choice would be to create a class library manager class that would keep a reference counter for each class library. Every time the manager's Set() method was called, it would increment the reference counter by one. Every call to the Release() would decrement the reference counter by one. When the reference counter reached zero, the class could safely be released. However this solution requires that every SET CLASSLIB and RELEASE CLASSLIB command use the manager class, which may not be possible.

> ## Gotcha!
>
> *AddObject() needs an explicit SET CLASSLIB/PROCEDURE.*
> At one point during the development of the object inspector, the
> ContextMenu class was in the CCONTROL.VCX. Because that
> classlib was used for all the controls of the inspect form, it seemed
> that the system would be doing an "implicit" SET CLASSLIB. It
> doesn't. Each object on the Form has a ClassLibrary property and
> that is used when the object is instantiated. Objects are added at
> runtime with a line of code like this:
>
> ```
> thisform.AddObject( "moContextMenu", "ContextMenu" )
> ```
>
> When this happens, the system needs to have an explicit SET
> CLASSLIB <classlib name> in place to find the definition of the
> class that is being added.

.PRG-Based Classes

Several of the Visual FoxPro BaseClasses cannot be subclassed
using the Class Designer; they can be subclassed in a .PRG. These
BaseClasses are Column, Cursor, DataEnvironment, Header, Page,
and Relation. Hopefully these classes will be added to the Class
Designer in a later release of Visual FoxPro. If you create subclasses,
you can only use them programatically in the Form Designer, and
you will not be able to see them on the design surface at design
time. The project PRGCLASS shows how you can create your own
Page classes. You can use DO FORM PRGCLASS, which launches the
Form in Figure 5-6.

Figure 5-6.

A page class

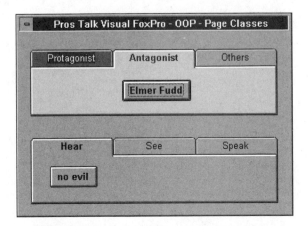

This shows how to implement a PageFrame that lets the user know which pages they've already seen by changing the BackColor of the Page in the Deactivate() method. The Page class code looks like this:

```
* prgclass.prg   02-Aug-95

define class cPage as Page
Name = "cPage"

procedure Init
this.Caption = this.Name
endproc

procedure Activate()
this.BackColor = rgb( 255, 255, 0 )
this.ForeColor = rgb( 255, 0, 0 )
endproc

procedure Deactivate()
this.BackColor = rgb( 64, 128, 128 )
this.ForeColor = rgb( 255, 255, 255 )
endproc

procedure Error( nError, cMethod, nLine )
= ObjError( this, nError, cMethod, nLine )
endproc

enddefine
```

This effect could have also been achieved by creating some custom PageFrame methods calls and having each page use them, but to do this you would have to copy the necessary method into the methods of each page on your Form. However, this alternate technique would allow you to work fully with the visual designers for the small cost of copy and paste code in the page methods.

There are several drawbacks to creating .PRG-based classes, the biggest of which is that you can't visually design with them. However, if you need some type of functionality it may be worth the effort. You can try creating the visual equivalent and using a builder to handle the issues of translation between the original BaseClass classes and your .PRG-based classes. You need to weigh the tradeoffs to see if it is worth the effort.

Data Classes

The old reliable SCATTER and GATHER commands have probably gone largely unnoticed since Visual FoxPro added private datasessions, data buffering, and transactions. Well, even the old reliables have become object-oriented with the addition of the NAME clause. This clause allows a record to be scattered to an object. This object will have one property for each column of the table. This allows you to create things such as Customer objects that can be passed around your application. You can also derive a data class from the Custom class and give it properties, but this requires additional maintenance if the underlying table definition should change. With SCATTER NAME the object properties adjust themselves. A DATA.VCX class library is included here as a starting point. It provides methods that mimic the various SCATTER and GATHER commands:

```
 Name: DataClass of data.vcx
ParentClass: Custom
  BaseClass: Custom

Custom Properties and Methods:

    Public     Method         Gather          Gather the current row
    Public     Method         GatherMemo      Gather this row with memo fields
    Public     Method         Scatter         Scatter the current row
    Public     Method         ScatterBlank    Scatter a blank row
    Public     Method         ScatterMemo     Scatter the current row with memo fields
    Public     Property mcAlias         Alias of table
    Public     Property moRow                  Row of table

Property Values:

    moRow = .NULL.
    mcAlias = ""
    Name = "dataclass"
```

You can use the class like this:

```
define class Customer as DataClass
   procedure Init()
      use customer in 0
      DataClass::Init()
      this.Scatter()
   endproc
   procedure CreditOk
      return( this.moRow.nCurrentBalance < 10000 )
   endproc
enddefine
```

The object created by SCATTER NAME uses an undocumented BaseClass named Empty. You can derive classes from Empty, but it doesn't support any built-in events such as Init() or Destroy(). And, like all undocumented features, you are at some level of risk that it may not be supported in future releases or that its interface could change.

Class Library Granularity

At some point you need to contend with the issue of class library granularity. This issue hit home while I was developing a very small Form sample. The Form was based on a cForm class that was stored in the CFORM.VCX class library. The classlib also contained four other Form classes that were derived from cForm. The .APP was huge relative to the size of the form's .SCX file. When I probed around in the .APP file with a hexadecimal file viewer, I saw that the other four Form classes were embedded in the file. This happened because the whole .VCX file was put into the .APP.

In my case, I decided to split the class library into two parts. The two most commonly used Form classes remained in CFORM.VCX. The others were moved to a second class library file BACKFORM.VCX. Two files are more work to keep up with, but the Project Manager does most of that automatically so it's easier to keep track of more files than to have needlessly bloated applications. The same holds true for any class library. As soon as you use one class from the library the whole thing will be stuck into the .APP, so it's easier to keep only functionally similar classes in a class library. For example, all of the Resizeable classes can be kept in RESIZE.VCX. There is no dependency link between the ResizeableEditBox, ResizeableListBox, or ResizeablePageFrame, but they have enough similarities to warrant keeping them together. It is also likely that an application that needs one of these classes will need them all.

Gotcha!

If two different class libraries have a class with the same name, an object will be instantiated from the first class library in memory.

This is a problem only with objects that you create using CreateObject or AddObject. If two classes that have the same name but come from two class libraries are added to a Form in the Form Designer, they will both correctly instantiate. The project SAMENAME.PJX shows this. The Form SAMENAM1.SCX works correctly where the SAMENAM1.PRG does not.

When Does a Method End?

When an object is instantiated, parameters can be sent to the Init() method. When the Init() method ends, the object will no longer have access to the parameters. This is vastly different than when a FoxPro for Windows 2.x screen is run because the .SPR is in the call stack. The parameters are available to all the procedures within the screen. In Visual FoxPro, you need to save these parameters to properties of the object if you will need them later.

When Object A sends a message to Object B and Object B sends a message to Object C, a thread of execution is established. The same thing happens if the object calls one of its own methods, which in turn calls another method which then calls a third method. This is the same as procedural code in which program A1 calls program B1, which in turn calls program C1. The methods of A and B remain in the call stack until the method in C finishes. Then, when the method in B finishes, control returns to the method in A. The messages are not dispatched asynchronously. This means that you need to be even more careful when you are using memory variables inside methods. You should *always* declare the method memory variables using the LOCAL scope specifier because you never know who will be sending the method a message.

Gotcha!

Don't forget to make all memory variables LOCAL in created methods.

In the previous example, if a method in Object A has a variable i that it has not declared LOCAL and it calls another method that also has a variable i that has not been declared LOCAL, it will trash the first method's memory variable. This code illustrates the problem of undeclared memory variables:

```
define class BadPrivate as Custom

procedure Method1
   for i = 1 to 10
      ? i
      this.Method2()
   endfor
endproc

procedure Method2
   for i = 1 to 20
      ?? i
   endfor
endproc

x = createobject( "BadPrivate" )
x.Method1()
```

As you can see, Method2 will corrupt the value of Method1's memory variable i.

Note that this can also occur between methods of different class objects if they are sending messages to one another.

If a method such as the Click() method of a CommandButton launches a non-modal Form, control returns to the Click() method immediately after the Form Activate() method is executed.

Gotcha!

Removing a method really removes it.

```
create class testzapclass of testzap as custom
```

Now create a method named ThisWillGetZapped, and put this code into the method:

```
WAIT WINDOW "This method will self destruct in 5 seconds!"
```

Close the class designer and create a subclass of testzap:

```
create class testzapsubclass of testzap as testzapclass from
testzap
```

Now you realize that the method belongs in the subclass instead of the ParentClass.

```
modify class testzapclass of testzap
```

Open the code window, and copy the method code to the clipboard. Close the class designer.

```
modify class testzapsubclass of testzap
```

Open the code window and paste the code into the subclass method. Close the class designer.
Now remove the method from the original class:

```
modify class testzapclass of testzap
```

Use the class menu item Edit Method... and click the Remove button and confirm the removal of the method. Now go back to edit the method in the subclass:

```
modify class testzapsubclass of testzap
```

The ThisWillGetZapped method of the subclass is gone! The moral of this story is to save the method code to some safe place, delete the method from the ParentClass, re-add the method to the subclass, and move the code from the safe place.

Object-Oriented Programming Features Missing from Visual FoxPro 3.0

Operator Overloading

Operator overloading is polymorphism for operators. Operators are a language's tokens, such as +, -, and =. Most languages implement a low level of operator overloading. For example:

```
nI = 2
nJ = 3
nK = nI * nJ

fRadius = 1.2345
fPI = 3.1415
fCircumference = 2 * fRadius * fPI
? nk, fCircumference
```

In both of these cases, the language knows how to apply the operator *, which tells Visual FoxPro to multiply the operands together to produce a result. This is called *overloading*. In the first case, two integer values are the operands while in the second two floating point values are the operands. Integers and floating point numbers are stored internally in memory using very different bit representations. However, the compiler generates the proper machine instruction (IMUL versus FMUL in x86 microprocessors) and you get the correct answer stored in nK and fCircumference. If the compiler mistakenly used IMUL for the floating operands, the result would be completely meaningless.

Because Xbase is a weakly typed language, some of the operands are more overloaded. The + operator can be used with date, character string, and currency operands. There's also the issue of operand type conversion when different types of operands occur. For example:

```
{10/4/57} + 30    && add 30 days to a date
7.3425 + 3        && promotes the 3 to a float first then adds
```

But what about the new kinds of abstract data types that you can create? In the complex number example, there is a well-defined behavior (method) to add two complex numbers together. In C++, you can tell the compiler to use a particular method when the + operator has two ComplexNumber class operands. However, Visual FoxPro has no such facility. You would get a runtime error if you attempted to simply put a + between two ComplexNumber objects, so you need to resort to an explicit Add() method for the ComplexNumber class.

```
* Cmplx1A.PRG  23-Mar-94

define class ComplexNumber as Custom

* Public Data Members

mfRealPart      = 0.0
mfImaginaryPart     = 0.0

protected procedure Init( pfReal, pfImaginary )
this.mfRealPart                 = pfReal
this.mfImaginaryPart = pfImaginary
endproc

procedure Show
? this.mfRealPart, "+", this.mfImaginaryPart, "i"
endproc

procedure Add( oOperand2 )
this.mfRealPart       = this.mfRealPart          + oOperand2.mfRealPart
this.mfImaginaryPart  = this.mfImaginaryPart     + oOperand2.mfImaginaryPart
endproc

enddefine
```

Now you can add two complex numbers:

```
set procedure to cmplx1a.prg additive
oX = CreateObject( "ComplexNumber", 5.23, -2.34 )
oY = CreateObject( "ComplexNumber", 1.44, 7.95 )

oX.Add( oY )
oX.Show()                              prints: 6.67 + 5.61i
```

In C++, this would look more like a natural algebraic expression because you can overload the + and = operators yourself:

```
#include <cmplx1.h>
ComplexNumber oX( 5.23, -2.34 );
ComplexNumber oY( 1.44, 7.95 );

oX = oX + oY;
cout << oX;
```

The Visual FoxPro code is a little more cumbersome to use, but it still accomplishes what you need.

Static Properties

C++ allows an object's properties to be scoped static. A static property is shared by all instances of a class. For the DDE class I developed in C++, all of the DDE conversations with a particular server shared a single static handle. Static properties are also useful if you need instances of a class to communicate with one another. In

Visual FoxPro, the only alternative would be to use a global memory variable or to use a property scoped to an application-wide object.

Private Properties

C++ also allows properties and methods to be scoped private to the class. Private goes beyond the hiding provided by a protected property; it prevents even a derived class from having access to the class's properties and methods. There are two ways to implement a private property: use a Control class, or use a programming convention that would restrict subclasses from using properties and methods with a specific scope designation.

Multiple Inheritance

The Visual FoxPro object model implements single inheritance. This means that each class can be derived from only one other class. Some object-oriented languages such as C++ allow classes to be derived from multiple super classes. Multiple inheritance can be very useful in some situations, but it requires a very careful design. It is also very easy to misuse multiple inheritance to overcome a poor class design.

In most places, the need for multiple inheritance can be replaced with delegation and aggregation. Delegation means that one object uses the capabilities of another server object. Aggregation involves bundling the different classes into a container and delegating the tasks to the appropriate object.

Multiple inheritance is also very hard to implement in Visual FoxPro because you can only derive a class from one of the BaseClasses. Because there is a defined set of properties and methods in each BaseClass, you would always have a name collision problem. (All ParentClasses would have an Init() method, so which one(s) should be used?)

Copy Constructors and Object Copy

In other object-oriented languages it is possible to make an exact copy of an object, but Visual FoxPro has no built-in facility to copy an object at runtime. Some of the BaseClasses have a CloneObject() method, but it's available only at design time because it is primarily used by builders on design surface objects.

You can create a close approximation to a copy constructor with the following code. However it cannot copy custom properties added to Forms, and it cannot copy DataEnvironment properties of Forms.

```
* objcopy.prg   27-Jul-95

* This routine copies objects.

* Limitations:
*    It cannot copy custom properties of Forms
*    It cannot copy the DataEnvironment of a Form
*    It may not properly work for objects that need parameters sent to
*       their Init() method

procedure ObjCopy( roDestination, roSource )

* setup to handle the errors that will occur during the copy
local lcOnError
lcOnError = on( "error" )
on error do ObjCopyError with error()

if ( ! empty( roSource.ClassLIbrary ) )
   * add classlib if necessary
   set classlib to (roSource.ClassLibrary) additive
endif

* create the new object
roDestination = createobject( roSource.Class )

* use recursive routine to copy the properties and contained objects
= ObjectCopy( roDestination, roSource )

on error &lcOnError
return

procedure ObjectCopy( roDestination, roSource )
local lnMember, laMember[1], lcSource, lcDestination, i

* find all the properties and contained objects
lnMember = amembers( laMember, roSource, 1 )
for i = 1 to lnMember
   lcSource = "roSource." + laMember[i,1]
   lcDestination = "roDestination." + laMember[i,1]
   do case
      case ( laMember[i,2] == "Property" )
         * copy valid properties
         if ( type( lcSource ) != "U" )
            if ( type( lcDestination ) != "U" )
               store evaluate( lcSource ) to &lcDestination
            else
               * this is a custom property and there's no way to create it
               wait window "Can't copy:" + lcSource
            endif
         endif

      case ( laMember[i,2] == "Object" )
         * copy contained object
         local loContainedObject
         loContainedObject = &lcSource

         if ( ! empty( loContainedObject.ClassLibrary ) )
```

Continued on next page

```
            set classlib to (loContainedObject.ClassLibrary) additive
        endif

        * add the contained object
        roDestination.AddObject( laMember[i,1], loContainedObject.Class )

        * recursively copy it
        = ObjectCopy( &lcDestination, &lcSource )
    endcase
endfor

return

procedure ObjCopyError( lnError )
if ( lnError = 1743 )
   * readonly property
   return
endif

if ( lnError = 9 )
   * data type mismatch
   return
endif

if ( lnError = 1744 )
   * can't add objects like DataEnvironment
   return
endif

if ( lnError = 1734 )
   * property not found like DataEnvironment
   return
endif

wait window message()
return
```

You use the routine like this:

```
do form sample              && create a Form object to copy
oFormCopy = .f.             && create a memvar to hold the copy
= objcopy( &oFormCopy, sample )    && copy it
```

This will copy the Form object, but it won't be fully functional because of the lack of custom Form properties and methods. You can test this by dragging the copy off the top of the original and clicking the buttons and Labels. Notice that they do not work like the originals. The Click Me! button depresses, but it doesn't do anything else. However this shouldn't be much of a problem as you'll rarely need to copy a whole object.

6 | Conclusion

Well, you finally made it all the way to the end of the report. I hope you didn't skip to the end just to see which object committed the crime. I hope you've found some useful information along the way. If some areas of object-orientation are not clear, give it some time to sink in. I can't stress enough the need for further study in object-orientation; other authors will use different examples that may better fit the way you approach programming problems.

Make use of the FoxPro Forums on CompuServe GO VFOX, GO FOXFORUM and GO FOXUSER. There are many extremely helpful people providing information and solutions to all sorts of problems. It's a resource that I don't think you can afford to ignore. If you have any questions or comments about this book you can direct them to me at 72147,2635 on the FOXUSER forum in the Publications section.

In the end, I think this report can be best summarized by the following eight key points:

Dave's Rules of Object-Oriented Programming:

1. If the class doesn't work like you want, subclass it; but if the class is broke, fix it.
2. Always pass the message to the ParentClass and never higher up the tree, unless ParentClass == BaseClass, which Visual FoxPro will pass automatically.

3. If any rule doesn't work, break it, but know why you are breaking it.
4. Always use the Visual Class Designer.
5. Don't forget the this.
6. Be lazy, the best code is no code, the best class is an existing class.
7. Remember you don't want to remember to do things.
8. Don't be afraid to throw away stupid designs.

7 CD Contents

```
Directory of OOP

3D         PJT       1,023 08-05-95    4:57p
3D         PJX       1,605 08-05-95    4:57p
3D         VCT       3,160 08-07-95    4:00p
3D         VCX       1,468 08-07-95    3:58p
3DLABEL    SCT       6,303 08-05-95    5:00p
3DLABEL    SCX       2,995 08-05-95    5:00p
BACKFORM   VCT      27,206 08-11-95    2:51a
BACKFORM   VCX       3,976 08-11-95    2:51a
BADNAME    PRG         486 10-08-95    3:54p
BROWMOD    PRG       1,269 10-07-95    1:24a
CATCH22    PRG         882 09-11-95   11:27a
CATCH22    SCT       3,648 09-11-95    7:36p
CATCH22    SCX       2,123 09-11-95    7:36p
CCONTROL   VCT      14,099 08-30-95    4:02p
CCONTROL   VCX       3,322 08-30-95    4:02p
CFORM      VCT       2,065 09-21-95    8:34p
CFORM      VCX       1,686 09-21-95    8:34p
CIRCLE     PRG         415 07-20-95    2:17a
CLASTRE1   PJT       1,056 06-29-95    8:15p
CLASTRE1   PJX       1,486 06-29-95    8:15p
CLASTRE1   PRG         627 05-17-95    1:53p
CLASTRE1   SCT       6,559 06-25-95    3:13p
CLASTRE1   SCX       3,540 06-25-95    3:13p
CLASTRE1   VCT       5,036 09-07-95   12:21p
CLASTRE1   VCX       3,321 06-25-95    3:17p
CMPLX1     PRG         356 10-01-95   12:23p
```

```
CMPLX1A   PRG         537 10-01-95   12:23p
CSET      PRG       4,396 09-30-95    1:05p
CSET      VCT       6,098 09-30-95    1:05p
CSET      VCX       1,359 09-30-95    1:05p
CSET3     PRG       1,757 09-30-95   12:45p
CSET3     TXT         659 06-25-95    6:09p
DATA      VCT       1,846 10-08-95    4:03a
DATA      VCX       1,359 10-08-95    3:37a
DEBUG     PRG         308 07-27-95   12:35p
ERRTEST   PJT       1,056 08-12-95    1:26a
ERRTEST   PJX       1,486 08-12-95    1:26a
ERRTEST   PRG         773 08-12-95   12:37a
ERRTEST   TXT         887 08-12-95    1:21a
ERRTEST   VCT       2,628 08-13-95    1:49p
ERRTEST   VCX       1,577 08-12-95   12:37a
ERRTEST2  PRG         691 08-13-95    2:10p
ERRTEST3  PRG         753 08-18-95    2:49p
FULLNAME  PRG         361 12-03-95    4:52p
FUNFORMS  PJT       1,155 08-10-95    7:21p
FUNFORMS  PJX       1,843 08-10-95    7:21p
GREENBAR  SCT       1,817 08-10-95    6:47p
GREENBAR  SCX       2,123 08-10-95    6:47p
HAL9000   PRG         992 08-08-95    1:38a
HAL9000   TXT       2,563 08-08-95    1:41a
HALTEST   PRG         385 08-09-95   12:33a
HALTEST2  PRG         323 09-02-95   11:00a
LIFE1     PRG         245 06-12-95    6:40p
LIFE2     PRG         249 06-12-95    6:41p
LIFE3     PRG         605 06-12-95    6:41p
LIFE3     TXT         505 06-12-95    7:14p
LIFE4     PRG         675 06-25-95    5:12p
LIFE4     TXT         938 06-25-95    5:13p
LIFETIME  PRG         371 06-14-95    5:18p
LOCK      PRG       2,120 10-01-95   11:45p
NOTHIS    PRG         265 08-13-95    3:22p
OBJCOPY   PRG       2,482 08-05-95    2:15p
OBJERROR  PRG         570 06-16-95    1:29p
OBJREF    PJT         990 08-04-95    9:25p
OBJREF    PJX       1,486 08-04-95    9:25p
OBJREF    PRG         651 08-14-95   12:05a
OBJREF    SCT       7,592 08-09-95    8:30p
OBJREF    SCX       2,886 08-09-95    8:30p
OBJREF    TXT         104 08-14-95   12:27a
OBJREF    VCT       9,062 08-09-95    9:23p
OBJREF    VCX       5,066 08-09-95    9:23p
OVERRIDE  PRG         705 09-10-95    5:01p
PRGCLASS  PJT       1,122 08-18-95    2:53p
PRGCLASS  PJX       1,724 08-18-95    2:53p
PRGCLASS  PRG         454 08-18-95    5:46p
PRGCLASS  SCT       4,582 08-18-95    4:58p
PRGCLASS  SCX       2,014 08-18-95    4:58p
PRGCLASS  VCT       1,679 08-18-95    2:53p
PRGCLASS  VCX       1,796 08-18-95    2:53p
```

```
RECT        PRG            516 07-20-95      2:29a
RECT1       PRG            715 07-20-95      2:30a
RECT2       PRG            643 07-20-95      2:30a
SAMENAM1    PRG            168 08-14-95      2:41a
SAMENAM1    VCT            801 08-14-95      2:19a
SAMENAM1    VCX          1,359 08-14-95      2:19a
SAMENAM2    VCT            801 08-14-95      2:20a
SAMENAM2    VCX          1,359 08-14-95      2:20a
SAMENAME    PJT          1,122 08-14-95      2:41a
SAMENAME    PJX          1,724 08-14-95      2:41a
SAMENAME    PRG            125 08-05-95      3:11p
SAMENAME    SCT          1,148 08-14-95      2:21a
SAMENAME    SCX          1,687 08-14-95      2:21a
TGRAPH      PRG            695 07-20-95      2:37a
TLOCK       PRG            350 03-08-96      1:17p
TREE        VCT          2,583 08-09-95      1:07a
TREE        VCX          1,359 06-20-95      5:21p
TREE3       PRG          1,123 09-30-95      3:16p
TREE3F      PRG          1,087 09-30-95      3:13p
TREE3M      PRG          1,083 09-30-95      3:14p
TT3         PRG            621 07-17-95      1:45a
VIEW        BMP            238 06-21-95     12:00a
XY          PRG            355 07-20-95      2:17a
YELLOWPD    SCT          3,853 08-10-95      7:43p
YELLOWPD    SCX          2,995 08-10-95      7:43p

Directory of OOP\FPW26

CALLSTCK    PJX          2,386 03-14-95     11:49p
CALLSTCK    PJT          7,293 03-14-95     11:49p
TOSTR       PRG            408 08-02-95      8:16p

Directory of OOP\FPW26\PRG

CALLSTCK    PRG            113 03-14-95     11:57p
SET         PRG            170 09-30-95     12:39p

Directory of OOP\FPW26\SCR

SCREEN1     SCX          6,665 03-14-95     11:15p
SCREEN1     SCT          1,498 03-14-95     11:15p
SCREEN1     PRG            432 03-14-95     11:48p
SCREEN1     SPR          3,710 03-14-95     11:42p
SCREEN1     SPX          1,650 03-14-95     11:42p
SCREEN1A    SCX          5,919 03-14-95     11:34p
SCREEN1A    SCT          1,366 03-14-95     11:34p
SCREEN1A    SPR          3,545 03-14-95     11:42p
SCREEN1A    SPX          1,527 03-14-95     11:43p
SCREEN1A    PRG            689 03-14-95     11:48p

Directory of OOP\INSPECT

CCONTROL    VCT          4,063 02-20-96      9:14p
CCONTROL    VCX          2,450 02-20-96      9:14p
```

```
CFORM      VCT       2,130 02-20-96    9:14p
CFORM      VCX       1,687 02-20-96    9:14p
CNTXTMNU   VCT       8,271 02-20-96    9:14p
CNTXTMNU   VCX       1,578 02-20-96    9:14p
DEBUG      PRG         308 07-27-95   12:35p
FONT       VCT       9,174 02-20-96    9:14p
FONT       VCX       1,360 02-20-96    9:14p
FULLNAME   PRG         361 12-03-95    4:52p
GETMETH    SCT       4,541 11-28-95    1:00p
GETMETH    SCX       2,123 11-28-95    1:00p
GETVALUE   SCT       8,277 11-28-95    1:00p
GETVALUE   SCX       2,232 11-28-95    1:00p
HELP       BMP         246 02-16-95   12:00a
INFO       ICO       1,846 05-24-95   12:00a
INSPECT    FXP         587 11-27-95    5:52p
INSPECT    H           118 05-12-95    4:34p
INSPECT    PJT       9,042 02-20-96    9:15p
INSPECT    PJX       4,699 02-20-96    9:15p
INSPECT    PRG         699 11-27-95    5:37p
INSPECT    SCT      39,247 02-20-96    9:14p
INSPECT    SCX       2,341 02-20-96    9:14p
INSPECT    TXT       5,067 11-28-95   12:41p
INSPECT    APP     110,991 02-20-96    9:15p
MISC02     ICO         766 05-24-95   12:00a
MISC22     ICO         766 05-24-95   12:00a
OBJERROR   PRG         570 06-16-95    1:29p
OVERWHO    PRG          92 11-29-95   10:59a
PERSIST    VCT       3,960 02-20-96    9:14p
PERSIST    VCX       1,360 02-20-96    9:14p
RESIZE     VCT       3,583 02-20-96    9:14p
RESIZE     VCX       1,578 02-20-96    9:14p
VIEW       BMP         238 05-24-95   12:00a


Directory of OOP\PREVIEW

CCONTROL   VCT       2,295 07-04-95    6:49p
CCONTROL   VCX       2,449 07-04-95   12:01p
CFORM      VCT         996 07-04-95    6:48p
CFORM      VCX       1,359 06-27-95    3:45p
DEBUG      PRG         308 07-27-95   12:35p
PREVIEW    PJT       1,881 06-30-95    5:00p
PREVIEW    PJX       2,081 06-30-95    5:00p
PREVIEW    PRG         170 06-29-95   12:14a
PREVIEW    SCT       7,664 06-30-95    5:00p
PREVIEW    SCX       2,232 06-30-95    5:00p
PREVIEW    VCT       7,398 06-28-95    2:12p
PREVIEW    VCX       2,123 06-28-95    2:12p
RESIZE     VCT       1,575 06-30-95    1:24p
RESIZE     VCX       1,359 06-30-95    1:13p


Directory of OOP\VISIO

DIVIDED    VSS       9,728 07-26-95   11:59a
```

8 Class Related Commands

Here is a list of all the object-oriented commands and functions in Visual FoxPro:

:: scope resolution operator
ACLASS( )
ADD CLASS
AINSTANCE( )
AMEMBERS( )
ASELOBJ( )
CLEAR CLASS
CLEAR CLASSLIB
CLOSE PROCEDURE
COMPOBJ( )
CREATE CLASS
CREATE CLASSLIB
CREATEOBJECT( )
DEFINE CLASS
DISPLAY MEMORY
DISPLAY OBJECTS
DO FORM
EXTERNAL CLASS
EXTERNAL PROCEDURE
GETOBJECT( )
LIST MEMORY

LIST OBJECTS
MODIFY CLASS
MODIFY FORM
OBJTOCLIENT()
RELEASE
RELEASE CLASSLIB
RELEASE PROCEDURE
REMOVE CLASS

> **Warning:** this command deletes a class, it will invalidate other class libraries, forms or programs that use the class being removed.

RENAME CLASS

> **Warning:** this command renames a class, it will invalidate other class libraries, forms or programs that use the class being renamed.

SCATTER NAME
SET CLASSLIB
SET PROCEDURE
WITH..ENDWITH

Index

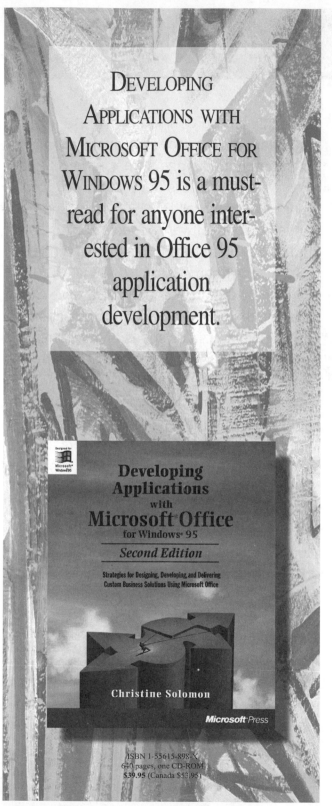

Register Today!

Return this
The Pros Talk Microsoft® Visual FoxPro™ 3
registration card for a Microsoft Press® catalog

U.S. and Canada addresses only. Fill in information below and mail postage-free. Please mail only the bottom half of this page.

1-57231-233-5A

**THE PROS TALK MICROSOFT®
VISUAL FOXPRO™ 3**

Owner Registration Card

_____

NAME

_____

INSTITUTION OR COMPANY NAME

_____

ADDRESS

_____

CITY   STATE   ZIP

Microsoft®*Press*
Quality Computer Books

**For a free catalog of
Microsoft Press® products, call
1-800-MSPRESS**